BASIC TEXAS BOOKS

BASIC
TEXAS BOOKS

An Annotated Bibliography of Selected
Works for a Research Library

By JOHN H. JENKINS

Revised Edition

TEXAS STATE HISTORICAL ASSOCIATION
Austin

Library of Congress Cataloging-in-Publication Data

Jenkins, John Holmes.
Basic Texas books: an annotated bibliography of selected works for a research
library / by John Jenkins.—Rev. ed.
p.   cm.
Includes index.
ISBN 0-87611-086-3 : $29.95
1. Texas—History—Bibliography.   2. Texas—Bibliography.
3. Bibliography—Bibliography—Texas.   I. Title.
Z1339.J39 1987
[F386]
016.9764—dc19

87-22899
CIP

TEXAS STATE HISTORICAL ASSOCIATION
*2/306 Sid Richardson Hall   University Station
Austin, Texas 78712*

FOR MY WIFE MAUREEN

CONTENTS

PREFACE

These are in my opinion the fundamental Texas books, the works every general Texana library should include. No two people, no matter how similar their interests or tastes, would choose the same 224 books out of the hundred thousand or more that have been published about Texas. Any other compiler would, without doubt, exclude some of my selections and include some I have omitted. Suffice it to say that anyone who has read all of the works encompassed in my selections is a person knowledgeable in Texas history and culture, and any library that contains all 224 of these works has a solid basis upon which to build.

The plan of this guide is to give bibliographical details on every known printing and variant of each of the works included, followed by a critical discussion encompassing: (1) what others have said about the book; (2) what I think about the book; (3) what I have been able to find out about the writing of the book; (4) the background of the author; (5) the strengths and weaknesses of each text; (6) occasional representative quotations from the text; and (7) citations to other bibliographical references.

The bibliographical arrangement I have chosen as best suited for this guide is to describe the first regular trade edition in the main entry, followed by a listing (under the general heading of "Other issues") of all special and limited editions, variant issues and states, and subsequent printings and editions, including extracts, in chronological sequence. I am an expert neither in cartographic nor illustration bibliography, and have therefore only mentioned the presence and number of maps and illustrations in each book rather than making what would be an inept attempt to provide detailed bibliographical descriptions of maps and plates.

In addition to the 224 main entries, I have within the text discussed about a thousand additional Texas books that would be valuable additions to a basic Texas research library. An appendix at the end lists 219 bibliographies on specialized areas of Texas history and culture, with my comments on the relative usefulness of each.

I have taken Mr. Dobie at his word, and made full use of his *Guide to Life and Literature of the Southwest*. I should point out, however, that most of his comments I have quoted come from his book reviews and

articles rather than from the *Guide*. Other quotations about the books
are from the bibliographies cited for each entry or from book reviews.
Since my purpose in quoting from these reviewers was merely to show
what other writers had said about the books, I have omitted citing the
exact source of each. The Barker Library of the University of Texas
maintains permanent and extensive files of reviews of books by Texas
authors. Anyone desiring a detailed reference to any review I have
quoted may easily obtain it from that library. Quotations from obscure
sources are cited within my text.

This is a guide for a research library, not a guide to good reading.
I have arbitrarily excluded all works of fiction and creative writing.
Fortunately, A. C. Greene has recently issued a checklist of "the fifty
best Texas books," which consists of his choices of the best works of
Texas literature. Greene is a competent judge of creative writing (which
I am not) and I believe that his list, though eccentric, is a good selection
of the best examples of *belles lettres* produced by Texans.

This guide also excludes works having a scope which is larger than
Texas proper, except for a few where Texas comprises either the majority
of the text or the main thrust of the thesis. To do otherwise would
necessitate the inclusion of so many works that the purpose of this guide
would be defeated. Also excluded are works that relate to Texas after
1940.

Because of their multiplicity and generally poor quality, all histories
of religious denominations have been omitted, as have histories of
counties, towns, schools, and institutions, except for a few containing
content of a more general nature. I have also excluded most fine press
books, since this bibliography is a guide to research content rather than
external design. The publications of the Book Club of Texas, for
example, are beautiful books, but erratic in content. Al Lowman's
Printing Arts in Texas is an excellent study of Texas fine printing and
serves quite adequately as a guide in that respect.

Excluded, too, are all periodicals, although no Texas research
library would be complete without a file of *Southwestern Historical Quarterly*
and of *Southwest Review*. There are other valuable Texas periodicals, of
course, especially *Texana Magazine, Military History of Texas and the Southwest, Texas Quarterly,* and *Frontier Times*, as well as the journals of the
various historical and special interest associations throughout the state.

The criteria for inclusion, therefore, are those works about Texas
which I believe are fundamental for use in general research, arbitrarily
excluding (1) works of fiction; (2) works whose scope is larger than

Texas; (3) works relating to the period after 1940; (4) histories of religious denominations; (5) county, town, and school histories; (6) fine press books; (7) periodicals; and (8) pamphlets; with a few exceptions.

Many Texas books familiar to Texas scholars and collectors are not present in my guide. Their absence in every instance is intentional. One of the books I most regret having had to reject is John Graves' *Goodbye to a River*. Yet it is admittedly a combination of fact and fiction: "Though this is not a book of fiction, it has some fictionalizing in it. . . . I have not scrupled to dramatize . . . or occasionally to change living names and transpose existing places and garble contemporary incidents." My own decision, after careful study of this great book, is that it belongs more to the realm of literature and the creative arts than to non-fiction, so I have reluctantly left it out. Certainly, every Texas library should contain a copy of this book.

Another specific title I regret feeling obliged to omit is Walter Prescott Webb's *The Great Plains*. Not only is it probably the most significant book ever written in Texas, it is also essential to any understanding of Texas. Nevertheless, its scope is far too broad for inclusion in a bibliography of books specifically on Texas. The same is true regarding William Goetzmann's two superb classics, *Exploration and Empire* and *Army Exploration in the American West*.

I began preparing this guide fourteen years ago. In 1970, I wrote to 52 Texas scholars, historians, librarians, and collectors seeking their recommendations; of these, only J. Evetts Haley failed to respond. Through the years, I have received literally hundreds of letters sending suggestions, bibliographical details, and anecdotes relating to Texas books. To all those who have been so kind, I offer my sincere appreciation. I am especially indebted to J. P. Bryan, Seymour Connor, Charles Downing, Llerena Friend, Terry Halladay, Archibald Hanna, Dan Kilgore, Al Lowman, Malcolm McLean, Michael Parrish, Ben Pingenot, William Reese, Marilyn Sibley, Dorothy Sloan, and Ray Walton, each of whom read the entire final draft of the manuscript and made valuable suggestions. I also wish to thank Sherri Tomasulo, who typed the manuscript several times, and Pat Pond, who not only set the type but proofread the final text several times. Finally, I wish to thank my wife Maureen for her patience and encouragement, as well as her willingness to overlook my bibliophilic eccentricities.

A disastrous fire in December of 1985 destroyed a large number of copies of the first edition of this work. The negatives, however, were saved. It was therefore a great relief and pleasure to me when Ron Tyler,

Director of the Texas State Historical Association, offered to issue under their imprint this new revised edition. It not only enabled me to make a number of needed revisions and alterations to the text, but also to incorporate additional printings of the main entries published since the first edition.

John H. Jenkins
Austin, Texas
August, 1987

BASIC TEXAS BOOKS

BASIC
TEXAS BOOKS

1   Alessio Robles, Vito (1879-1957)

COAHUILA Y TEXAS EN LA EPOCA COLONIAL.

Mexico: Editorial Cvltvra, 1938.
xii,751,[2]pp. 8 maps (7 folding). 9 plates (3 in color). 24cm.
Heavy paper wrappers.
1000 copies printed.

Other issues:
(A).   Same, limited edition, on heavier paper. 100 copies printed.
(B).   Second edition. Mexico: Editorial Porrua, 1978. 3000 copies printed.

[also]

COAHUILA Y TEXAS DESDE LA CONSUMACION DE LA INDE-
PENDENCIA HASTA EL TRATADO DE PAZ DE GUADALUPE
HIDALGO.

Mexico: [Talleres Grafico de la Nacion], 1945-1946.
Two volumes: xv,542;540,[1]pp. 8 maps (7 folding). 7 plates (1 in color) 24cm.
Heavy paper wrappers.
2000 copies printed on special paper and numbered.

Other issues:
(A).   Same, limited edition, on heavier paper. 100 copies printed.
(B).   Second edition. Mexico: Editorial Porrua, 1979. 3000 sets printed.

This work presents the history of Texas as a Spanish province and state from the Mexican viewpoint. F. B. Steck called it "a magnificent study, heavily documented and enriched with valuable illustrations and charts." Ohland Morton deemed it "the first comprehensive study of any section of northern Mexico," one that would "enrich the already well-cultivated fields of Texas history." According to Charles

C. Griffin, it "provides a rich, solid history. . . . This is a major work and will long be considered a standard work of reference."

During much of Texas history the area of Coahuila in northern Mexico was joined politically and economically with Texas. From 1824 to 1836, Coahuila y Texas functioned as a single state in the Mexican republic. This in itself was one of the chief grievances of the Anglo-Americans in Texas, who had to travel to the provincial capital at Saltillo to conduct state business. After the Texas Revolution, Mexico maintained the fiction of a single Coahuila y Texas until the end of the Mexican War.

Utilizing many virginal sources, Alessio Robles presents the history of the area from Spanish colonial times through 1848. Ohland Morton pointed out that "the history of Coahuila has been touched upon from time to time by various writers who had neither the time nor inclination to check their sources, and the result was a considerable number of inaccuracies. Robles set himself to correcting these, thus adding to the interest and value of his work. On the other hand there are abundant and excellent monographs on the history of Texas. The author skillfully weaves these and his investigations concerning Coahuila into a single fabric, beautiful and complete. . . . Not many regions of similar size have undergone the changes, suffered so much from indifference, or experienced the political upheavals that Coahuila and Texas have."

The volumes are enriched by the numerous folding maps, plates, portraits, facsimiles, and textual charts. Several chapters are devoted exclusively to the geography, geology, and ethnology of the area. Sections of the text devoted to economic and social conditions shed much light on Mexican attitudes, opinions, and actions concerning Texas. There are, nevertheless, factual errors in the text; the reader must be careful of minor errors in specifics. Some of the material is almost a direct translation from the works of Hubert H. Bancroft.

Of special interest are the 57 pages of bibliography, which reveal that the author did research in Coahuila, Nuevo Leon, Chihuahua, Durango, Guadalajara, and Mexico City, as well as in Texas and in Spain. Many of these sources had never been utilized fully before, nor have been since. Both works have excellent indexes, totalling 94 pages. It is interesting to note that Alessio Robles pays special thanks to the "maestro," Carlos E. Castaneda, and refers several times to his works in the text, while Castaneda in his monumental work makes no mention whatsoever of Alessio Robles, and does not list a single article or monograph of Alessio Robles in his bibliography.

None of the volumes has been published in English, but two theses translate portions. Laron Donald Jorda translated the chapters covering the early 1830's as a master's thesis at Southern Methodist University in 1950, and David Glenn Hunt translated the chapters from 1835 through the fall of the Alamo as a 1950 master's thesis at the same school. Both include critical annotations discussing Alessio Robles's facts and conclusions.

Vito Alessio Robles grew up in Saltillo, and became an army engineer and a professor of military history. He fought in the Mexican Revolution under Carranza and Pancho Villa, serving briefly as Minister of War. Later, he became a newspaper editor, educator, and historian. The author of numerous works on the early history of Texas and Mexico, he was a pioneer in bibliographical studies of Texas and the northern Mexican states.

Griffin 2458 and 4903. Howes R382.

2 Almonte, Juan Nepomuceno (1803-1869)

NOTICIA ESTADISTICA SOBRE TEJAS.

Mexico: Impreso por Ignacio Cumplido, Calle de los Rebeldes n.2, 1835.
96,[4]pp. Three folding tables. 15cm.
Printed wrappers. Also marbled boards with calf spine.

Other issues:
(A). Reprinted, in slightly different arrangement, in Vicente Filisola, *Memorias para la Historia de la Guerra de Tejas*, Mexico, Rafael, 1848-49, Vol. II, pp. 535-615.
(B). English translation by Carlos E. Castaneda, *Southwestern Historical Quarterly*, XXVIII, 177-222, January, 1925.

One of the most valuable descriptions of Texas on the eve of revolution, this volume was written by an agent for the Mexican government. Acting under special instructions of the Gomez Farias administration, Almonte was in a unique position to observe and describe Texas at the time. He was educated in the United States, served as Mexican envoy to London in 1825, became a newspaper editor, and with the exception of Stephen F. Austin (who was in prison in Mexico at the time) was possibly the most literate and sophisticated man to set foot in Texas up to that point.

Almonte sailed to New Orleans in early 1834 and entered Texas via Nacogdoches, spending May and June there. Beginning in mid-July, he spent a month in San Felipe, then visited Brazoria, Velasco, Matagorda, and Harrisburg. By September he had arrived at Monclova.

Almonte's instructions from Vice President Valentin Gomez Farias, in three different drafts, still exist in the Mexican National Archives. E. C. Barker summarized them as follows: "He was to explain that the confusion arising from plague and civil war had prevented attention to the needs of the colonists; that the government was now firmly established, however; and that he was to hear their complaints and transmit them for consideration. He was to try to reconcile the colonists to a territorial government; and if questioned about Austin was to say that he was accused of attempting to incite revolution but that he would no doubt soon be released and return to Texas a peaceful citizen. Almonte's private instructions were more enlightening. He was to observe the number and distribution of the colonists, with their arms and resources for defense; cultivate loyal leaders and consult with them . . . and do everything possible to paralyze menacing preparations of the colonists in order to gain time for the government. . . . In some prudent way he was to get information to the negroes that the laws of Mexico made them free . . . It was evident that Farias believed that Texas was on the verge of revolt and that he impressed his belief on Almonte."

In short, he was to placate the colonists and spy out their weaknesses and strengths. That he did so is evidenced by a letter from William H. Jack written in July: "Col. Almonte is here; he is intelligent and agreeable and apparently candid. He says that Austin will be released soon. That the govt. has been grossly [misinformed] in relation to Texas . . . and that his representations will be of the most favorable character." By the end of his visit, Almonte was half convinced in favor of the colonists. On the one hand, he recommended relief from their grievances; on the other, he urged the immediate dispatch of an army to be stationed in Texas near the Louisiana border. On the whole, it seems that the Texans were convinced of his friendship, and he was convinced that they should be helped by the government.

Almonte made his report to Gomez Farias and then compiled the non-political elements into his *Noticia Estadistica sobre Tejas*, which was released in February, 1835. It includes descriptions of towns, roads, ports, and people, as well as a detailed description of the physical terrain. There are sections on the Indian tribes and on wildlife, flora, and fauna. Almonte also urges colonization of Texas by Mexicans and states that he expects to return soon to Texas as Commissioner of Colonization. When he did return, it was as military aide on the staff of Santa Anna's invading army.

Almonte was captured at San Jacinto and helped draw up the Treaties of Velasco. He later served Mexico as minister to Belgium, France, England, and the United States. He was one of the guiding spirits in bringing Maximilian to Mexico, and served in 1862 as President of Mexico.

Clark III-5. Howes A186. Rader 125. Raines, p.8. Streeter 816.

3 Atwood, Elmer Bagby (1906-)

THE REGIONAL VOCABULARY OF TEXAS.

Austin: University of Texas Press, [1962].
xiii,237pp. 125 maps and tables. 24cm.
Cloth, dustjacket.

Other issues:
(A). Same except verso of title: "Second Printing, 1969."
(B). Paperback edition. 23cm. Verso of title: "First paperback edition, 1975."

This is the most important work on Texas linguistics. In some ways, Texas may be considered almost as distinct from the United States as is the United States from England; not least among these differences is in its forms of English dialect. Atwood's study of Texas dialect is a scholarly, yet utterly fascinating, explanation of the origin and usage of the words and phrases that grew out of the state's rich cultural heritage.

Professor Atwood studied the vocabulary of native Texans for many years, culminating his investigations with an IBM computer study that was one of the pioneer efforts at using computers in the field of linguistics. This was especially fortuitous because in the late 1950's the distinctive rural areas of Texas were on the verge of yielding to the homogenizing influence of city living and television. Thus, he was able to study word origins in Texas from people who were likely to remember or understand their deriviations, and at the same time take advantage of the new computer technologies to interpret the data gleaned.

Texan dialect was derived and in many cases blended from the state's unique mixture of racial and cultural influences—Indian, Negro, Spanish, Mexican, French, Cajun, German, and Anglo-American, especially Southern. It also grew out of the rigors imposed by geography, and from vocations such as the cattle, oil, and lumbering industries. From these influences came *Maverick, bronc, pinto, dogie, tow sack, norther, gully washer, cedar chopper, hoosegow, water tank, light bread, hackamore, cinch, hidy, mustang, cowpoke, bluejeans, yonder, scrub oak, corral, chaps, pully bone, tuckered out,* and *horny toad.* Many of these words came to Texas from other regions but evolved special meanings in Texas.

Most interesting are the histories behind the words and the explanations of their special meanings. Thus, older Texans have breakfast, dinner, and supper rather than breakfast, lunch, and dinner. *You all* is an actual improvement on the English language, being used only as the plural of you and never as a substitute for the singular. Any southerner or Texan can recognize an outsider by his misuse of *you all.* Rural Texans in Atwood's time knew the difference between *nicker* and *whinny*; almost none used *neigh.* Throughout Texas, a long way was a *far* (or *fur*) *piece.*

Of especial interest and value are the 125 full-page geographical occurrence maps that chart the frequency of use of terms of different parts of the state. A cloudburst in the city is a gully washer in the country. One gets red bugs in East Texas and chiggers in West Texas. It is bayou in the east, branch in the west.

"The most interesting and important words," states Atwood, are "those which first gained currency within Texas. Many of these have spread for considerable distances . . . I have no hesitation in classing virtually all of Texas and an indeterminate portion of the surrounding states as a major branch of General Southern, which I will label

Southwestern,'' containing a vast quantity of words and phrases which "clearly distinguishes the vocabulary of Texas from that of the South Midland, or any other area that has been demarcated in the East," and which also "sets it off from other portions of the West which may share the Southwestern usages, either as borrowings from Texas or as independent acquisitions from Spanish-speaking settlers . . . It is rare to find, within a widely spoken language, a single feature in a given area that is unique and that appears in no other dialect . . . In this sense the vocabulary of the Southwest has a character that sets it apart from all others."

In 1930, a project known as the Linguistic Atlas of the United States and Canada was begun, the first segment—for New England—being completed in 1943. Atwood's work, comprising Texas and those surrounding states which derive portions of their culture from it, takes its place as part of these studies. As Dr. D. M. McKeithan said, "*The Regional Vocabulary of Texas* is a major contribution to the Linguistic Atlas of the United States."

Some related works are Gilberto Cerda, et al., *Vocabulario Espanol de Texas* (Austin: University of Texas Press, 1953, 347pp.); Glenn G. Gilbert, *Linguistic Atlas of Texas German* (Austin, 1972, 148pp.); Fred A. Tarpley, *From Blinky to Blue John: A Word Atlas of Northeast Texas* (Wolfe City, 1970, 338pp.); and L. K. and M. E. Vasquez, *Regional Dictionary of Chicano Slang* (Austin: Jenkins Publishing Company, 1975, 111pp.).

4 Austin, Stephen F. (1793-1836)

THE AUSTIN PAPERS

Washington and Austin: 1924-1928.
Compiled and edited by Eugene C. Barker.
Four volumes, as follows:

(1). *Annual Report of the American Historical Association for the Year* 1919. Vol. II, Part 1. Washington: Government Printing Office, 1924. vii,1008pp. 24cm. Cloth.

(2). *Annual Report of the American Historical Association for the Year* 1919. Vol. II, Part 2. Washington: Government Printing Office, 1924. [2], 1009-1824pp. 24cm. Cloth.

(3). *Annual Report of the American Historical Association for the Year* 1922, in Two Volumes and A Supplemental Volume. Vol. II, Vol. II. Washington: United States Government Printing Office, 1928. vii,1184pp. 25cm. Cloth.

(4). *The Austin Papers: October, 1834-January, 1837.* Volume III. Austin: Published by the University of Texas, [1927]. xxxv,494pp. 25cm. Cloth.

Austin's papers are an essential source on the beginning of Anglo-American Texas. J. Frank Dobie wrote in *The Alcalde* when the final volume appeared: "The *Papers* comprise letters to and from Austin, political documents, contracts, hotel bills, all sorts of communications relating to Texans that came into Austin's hands—in short, all sorts of contemporary evidence revealing the manners and motives of Austin and other Texans . . . *The Austin Papers* furnish the most significant contribution ever made to the social history of the men and women who wrested Texas from the wilderness." L. W. Payne called them "the richest primary source of information we have about the colonization and early history of Texas."

The papers, in spite of their confusing appearance in the American Historical Association series, follow a chronological sequence. The first volume (*A.H.A.* 1919, Vol. II, pt. 1) contains a preface by Barker, a genealogical record of the Austin family (written in three hands: Moses Austin, Stephen F. Austin, and Mrs. James F. Perry), and correspondence dated 1789-1824. The second volume (*A.H.A.* 1919, Vol. II, pt. 2) contains correspondence dated 1825-1827, a calendar of the papers through 1827, and an index. The third volume (*A.H.A.* 1922, Vol. II, Vol. II) contains a preface by Barker, correspondence dated 1828-September, 1834, a calendar of the papers from 1828 to 1837, and an index. The fourth volume (Univ. of Texas, "Vol. III") contains a preface by Barker, a calendar from October, 1834 through 1837, correspondence from October, 1834 through 1837, and an index. Unfortunately, there is no cumulative index.

Barker states that "*The Austin Papers* are the collection of materials accumulated by Moses and Stephen F. Austin in the progress of their busy enterprises from Virginia through Missouri and Arkansas to Texas. They consist of business memoranda, physiological observations, petitions and memorials to local and superior governments, political addresses and proclamations, and much personal and official correspondence. Moses Austin illustrated in his own career the typical aspects of the business man in the Westward Movement; and Stephen F. Austin was, to a degree not approached by any other colonial proprietor in our history, the founder and indispensable guardian and director during its early vicissitudes of a great American Common-wealth . . . In their entirety *The Austin Papers* are an absorbing human document, reflecting the life of the Austin family . . . and illuminating the social and economic history—and to some extent the political history—of the American frontier from 1789 to 1836.''

The Austin family papers, with a few exceptions, were given to the University of Texas in 1901 by the literary executors of Austin's nephew, Guy M. Bryan. *The Austin Papers* include the bulk of these as well as scattered material from the Bexar Archives, the Nacogdoches Archives, the Mexican National Archives, the Texas State Archives, and other places.

A large number of Austin papers, however, have never been published. In the preface to the third volume, Barker states that ''exigencies of space have made it necesssary to omit a considerable number of documents which the collection contains. Some are listed in place in the text of the four volumes, some are listed in the calendars, and some are not listed at all. These papers, together with the published papers, comprise collection #73 in the University of Texas Archives in the Eugene C. Barker Texas History Center, taking up nine and a half shelf feet of space. An Austin family heir, James Perry Bryan, Sr., planned the publication of the unpublished papers but died before the project came to fruition. It is hoped that these will be published in the future. Moreover, many of the published papers are in Spanish and have never been translated into English—another project worth the effort and expense.

5 Baker, DeWitt Clinton (1832-1881)

A TEXAS SCRAP-BOOK, MADE UP OF THE HISTORY, BIOG-RAPHY, AND MISCELLANY OF TEXAS AND ITS PEOPLE.

New York, Chicago, and New Orleans: A. S. Barnes & Company, [1875].
[7],vi-xii,[4],[17]-657pp. 33 plates. 22cm.
Pictorial cloth.
Preface dated Austin, December, 1874.
A publisher's dummy of 20pp. bound in cloth was also issued.

Other issues:

(A). Same, reprinted N.Y., 1887.
(B). Facsimile reprint: Austin: The Steck Company, 1935. 22cm. Cloth. 2000 copies printed.

This scissors-and-paste compilation is still a highly useful resource on early Texas. C. W. Raines called it "an invaluable book of references as to information about Texas." Baker, aware of the haphazard disorder of his volume, admits that "this book is not offered to the world as a model of literary excellence, but as an urn in which to gather the ashes of days gone by." It contains no less than 315 separate essays, biographies, memoirs, and articles on almost every aspect of early Texas history, with lists of the Old Three Hundred, San Jacinto participants, Fannin's men, veterans, etc., down to lists of district attorneys and house clerks. In his task Baker was assisted by such prominent Texans as F. W. Johnson, E. M. Pease, Swante Palm, and others.

Baker first saw Texas as a teenager in the 1840's when he travelled to Texas from his native Maine with a group of surveyors on a sailboat, the *Billow*. In 1850 he settled in Austin and became the founder and father of its first public library. He was instrumental in the founding of its public school system, keeper of the first official weather records in Texas, collector for the internal revenue, Bible society activist, essayist, and poet. From his earliest days in Texas, however, his avocation was the gathering of vanishing historical records.

"As year by year has passed away," he writes, "and one after another of the active participators . . . has been gathered to his fathers, source after source of information has been taken away from us. Many incidents of surpassing interest have never been written down, and much that would be prized by our posterity can never be given to them. With these thoughts the writer has for years been collecting whatever of interest he could find relating to the history, biography, and miscellany of Texas and its people."

The volume emphasizes the history of the Texas Revolution and Republic, but there is material on the Spanish period, the Civil War, Indian fights, explorations, botany, ornithology, geography, geology, and other subjects. There are 112 separate biographies, many of which contain our only information on early Texas leaders; a 47-page section listing biographical information on hundreds of veterans of the Texas

Revolution and Indian battles; and a "list of old Texans who have died and been killed by Mexicans and Indians from 1828 to 1874." Unfortunately, no edition thus far contains an index.

In addition there are essays written by early Texans, such as Col. F. W. Johnson on the Anahuac Campaign of 1832, John Henry Brown on the Convention of 1836, Swante Palm on the Texas Navy, William J. Russell's eyewitness account of the 1835 reconciliation of Stephen F. Austin and William H. Wharton, J. C. Robinson on the Dawson Massacre, George H. Gray on the Archive War, J. H. Kuykendall on the Karankawa Indians, Moses Austin Bryan on the Texas Revolution, W. D. C. Hall on the Gutierrez-Magee Expedition, A. R. Roessler on Texas mineralogy, H. Wickeland on the Texas Panhandle, George J. Durham on the wild game in Texas, and S. B. Buckley on Texas geology ("various sections of the State . . . promise large yields of petroleum").

These eyewitness and expert accounts are a goldmine of information and fascinating anecdotes. Lt. M. Muzquiz, in his diary of the capture of Philip Nolan, for example, relates: "At daybreak Nolan and his men commenced firing. The fight lasted until nine o'clock a.m., when, Nolan being killed by a cannon-ball, his men surrendered. They were out of ammunition. . . . His men had long beards. Nolan's negroes asked permission to bury their master, which I granted, after causing his ears to be cut off, in order to send them to the Governor of Texas."

As in all such early compilations, there are errors of fact and prejudice. Mexicans and Indians are treated as the enemy, and this is patently the white man's side of the story throughout. But it is, as C. W. Raines states, "an invaluable book of reference" and provides, as Sister Agatha says, "a sincere and intelligent attempt to preserve the records of Texas." We would know much less about early Texas without it.

Charles DeMorse's section (pp.204-218) states: "We shall find no more Austins, Milams, Travises; no more Rusks, Houstons, nor Sidney Johnstons; no more Tom McKinneys; no more Deaf Smiths. We may find others as intelligent, as brave, as honest, but not of that type of manhood. The men were suited to their era. Their character grew out of the surroundings."

Agatha, pp.50-51. Campbell, p.171. Dobie, p.61. Howes B47. Rader 235. Raines, p.18.

6 Bancroft, Hubert Howe (1832-1918)

HISTORY OF THE NORTH MEXICAN STATES AND TEXAS, 1531-1889.

San Francisco: A. L. Bancroft and Company, 1883; and San Francisco, The History Company, 1889.
Two volumes: xlviii,751; xvi,888pp. 2 folding maps. Illus. 23cm.
Comprises volumes XV and XVI of *The Works of H. H. Bancroft.*
Cloth. Also calf, sheep, and morocco.

Other issues:
> [The works of Bancroft were reissued from the same plates several times. The most recent is a facsimile reprint: New York, etc.: An Arno Press book published in cooperation with McGraw Hill Book Company, ca. 1967.]

A century after it was written, this remains one of the best single histories of Texas. In 1895, C. W. Raines stated: "Were I restricted to a single book on Texas, I would, without hesitation, take Bancroft's History; for in that I would learn something of most other writers on Texas, as well as the facts of our history." Eugene C. Barker said that it was "written with critical objectivity and a wealth of bibliographical equipment, and is the most satisfactory comprehensive history of Texas available." Seymour V. Connor said its "scholarship is valid, the footnotes extensive, and the treatment objective."

The Bancroft Building in San Francisco, erected in 1869, became known as "Bancroft's history-factory." With a massive collection of documents and books and with some six hundred employees, Hubert H. Bancroft directed the writing of 39 thick volumes of histories of Western states, Mexico, and Central America. The mammoth project took sixteen years, from 1874 to 1890. It was one of the largest history writing projects ever attempted, and the results are of inestimable value.

Bancroft did not, of course, write all the text himself, and he has been criticized by some for not giving more credit to his hundreds of history gophers. He did, however, frequently state his debt to these workers, and it is clear that the genius as well as much of the actual text were his. Bancroft later said: "The work of my assistants besides saving me an immense amount of drudgery and manual labor, left my mind always fresh, and open to receive and retain the subject as a whole." According to W. A. Morris in *Quarterly of the Oregon Historical Society,* IV, pp.287-364, Bancroft's main assistants on *North Mexican States* were Henry L. Oak, Joseph J. Peatfield, and William Nemos.

Most of the first volume is devoted to the Spanish Southwest in general, with emphasis on Texas. The list of "Authorities Quoted" contains over 1200 printed works, not including manuscripts. The second volume covers the history of Texas in the 19th century up to 1888, with additional chapters on education, industry, commerce, and railroads. Eleven final chapters deal with the Mexican border states, all containing information of Texas interest. In volume II there are some map errors of which the user should be aware. The map of the troop movements on page 252 is repeated on page 362, at which place there should be a map of the battle of Mier. This Mier map appears on page 256, at which place there should be a map of the battle of San Jacinto. The map of the battle of San Jacinto is nowhere to be found.

The Texas volumes are so valuable and useful today because of the literally thousands of footnotes and bibliographical citations. The sheer quantity is overwhelming, but the serious student of any aspect of Texas history will soon discover them to be accurate and reliable. Moreover, the Bancroft Library, now a part of the University of California, still maintains the extensive collection of books, pamphlets, broadsides, documents, and interviews on which the Texas volumes are based. Many of these were collected for Bancroft by a remarkable Frenchman, Alphonse L. Pinart, who travelled the Southwest and Mexico for over a decade gathering materials. A catalogue of the Bancroft manuscript research files for the Texas volumes was published in 1963, *A Guide to the Manuscript Collections of the Bancroft Library,* edited by Dale L. Morgan and George P. Hammond, the Texas material appearing on pages 267-302.

Agatha, p.xix. Cowan, p.ii. Graff 155. Griffin 994. Howes B91. Raines, pp.20-21.

7 Barker, Eugene Campbell (1874-1956)

THE LIFE OF STEPHEN F. AUSTIN, FOUNDER OF TEXAS, 1793-1836: A CHAPTER IN THE WESTWARD MOVEMENT OF THE ANGLO-AMERICAN PEOPLE.

Nashville [and] Dallas: Cokesbury Press, Importers, Publisher, 1925.
[Verso of title:] Copyright, 1925, by Lamar & Burton.
xv,551pp. Folding map. Double-page map. 7 plates, 25cm.
Dark red cloth, embossed on front cover with gilt bust of Austin, spine gilt, bottom and outer edges untrimmed, dustjacket.

Other issues:
(A). Same as first edition, bound in dark blue cloth. Sequence of red and blue bindings unknown. One encounters autographed copies of this book almost as frequently as in *Recollections of Early Texas*.
(B). Limited edition. Same collation except for added limitation notice reading: "This deluxe edition . . . is limited to two hundred and fifty numbered copies signed by the author. . . ." Boards, morocco label.
(C). Same as first edition, dated 1926 on title page and copyright page. Printed on very thick paper. 23cm. Brown buckram.
(D). *The Father of Texas*. Indianapolis [and] New York: The Bobbs-Merrill Company, Publisher, [1935]. viii,[8],11-248pp. Five illus. by W. R. Lohse. Cloth. Dustjacket, with subtitle reading: "A Life of Stephen F. Austin for Young People." Juvenile version.
(E). Same as (D), but with slip pasted over the publisher's imprint on title page reading: "The Steck Company, Austin," and with "Steck" at the bottom of the spine on the binding. Nevertheless, the dustjacket retains the Bobbs-Merrill imprint.
(F). New edition. Austin: The Texas State Historical Association, 1949. xvii,477pp. 25cm. Cloth. Dustjacket. "Preface: Second Edition" by Barker dated January 15, 1949.
(G). Facsimile reprint of (A). New York: DaCapo Press, 1968. ix,xv,551pp. 24cm. Cloth. New introduction by Seymour V. Connor.
(H). Same as (F). Paperback edition, [1969]. 22cm. Texas History Paperback Series TH-1.
(I). Facsimile reprint of (A). New York: AMS Press, [1970]. 23cm. Cloth.

This is the most-praised of all Texas biographies. L. W. Payne called it "the best biography that has ever been written in Texas." Sister Agatha called it "by far the best biography yet written of a Texas leader." H. Bailey Carroll pronounced it "the finest biography in Texas literature." Joe B. Frantz said it "has been called the finest

single piece of historical writing yet done in Texas." J. Evetts Haley pronounced it "the finest biography in Texas literature." Herbert E. Bolton said that in Barker, Austin had his Boswell, and Ray Allen Billington called it "essential to the story of American settlement; not only a biography but a history of the era."

There is no question that Barker's biography of Austin is the finest yet written. It is one of the greatest contributions to our understanding of Texas. No one has known more about Austin; no one has understood the Austin era as well as Barker. Yet Stephen F. Austin deserves more than Barker's biography. Even at the time, Walter Prescott Webb recognized the essential flaw in the book, and briefly touches on it in an otherwise effusive review. The problem is one of objectivity. Sometimes Barker fails to be objective in his support of Austin; at other times, he tries so hard to be objective that he fails to give Austin his due. Moreover, much of the volume is history rather than biography, and many interesting and essential details about Austin and his career are touched only briefly. Barker varies between giving us deep and mature insights, and presenting conclusions that are at best arguable. For example, Barker at his best:

"Austin's success was due, in fact, to his complete and whole-hearted adoption of the obligation of a Mexican citizen. He strove honestly to make Texas a model state in the Mexican system—a Utopian dream, as he came to realize, but how reluctantly and for what reasons he abandoned it we have seen."

On the other hand, here is Barker at his weakest: "Undoubtedly Mexico would have adopted an immigration policy sooner or later; but it seems pretty evident that nothing but Austin's unremitting pressure caused the passage of the impaired colonization law. Without that law, even upon the unlikely assumption that everything else might have happened as and when it did, Austin's original contract would not have been confirmed . . . there would have been no settlement of Texas, no revolution, no annexation, no Mexican War; and the Louisiana Purchase, in all probability, would still define the Western boundary of the United States."

Samuel Asbury summarized the problem best in a respectful but critical review of Barker's biography, pointing out the complexities of understanding Stephen F. Austin: "There was the lower Austin, the

Austin of sharp practice and ready bootlegging subterfuges to avoid the Mexican slavery laws; the grasping Austin of the Robertson Colony Controversy; the subtle Austin attempting to bribe Teran; the tortuous Austin in Mexico City. . . . But there was the higher Austin, the Austin who stayed on when his hope of splendid fortune disappeared with Saucedo's annulment of the land fees; and the Austin who . . . came to look with horror at the possibilities to Texas from his own previous activity in making his colonies slave territory; and the Austin of ready service in any capacity his countrymen chose for him: the last journey to Mexico, the mission to the United States, and his death-service as Secretary of State of the infant republic.''

The printing history of the book is interesting. Charles Scribner's Sons offered on May 20, 1925, to publish Barker's biography of Austin in 2000 copies, and Century Company was also interested. Barker agreed on May 25 to allow Scribner's to publish it, but objected to it being in their school book format, which he said ''seems to me to be about as cheap a book in its make-up as a respectable publisher could get his consent to issue.'' Scribner's agreed to issue a higher quality volume, and in June sent a contract to Barker. Meanwhile, Cokesbury offered to publish 2000 copies in a handsome format, which Barker accepted. As late as January 13, 1926, he had not notified Scribner's that they were not to be the publisher.

Barker's decision not to use Scribner's was a mistake, as the sales by Cokesbury were relatively poor. A year after publication, historian Charles A. Beard wrote Barker: ''I have tried out on two publishers the proposition looking toward a wider circulation of your most excellent book, but in vain I am sorry to report. They say that your publisher has already skimmed the cream off the sales and the publicity. . . . This is a matter of great regret to me because I think the book ought to reach more people.'' In 1929, Guy M. Bryan bought 500 unsold copies and sent them out as gifts to public libraries throughout the country. ''The plates,'' says Sister Agatha, ''were later purchased by the author and turned over to Southwest Press, Dallas, for reissue and distribution.''

In 1935, Bobbs-Merrill issued a young people's edition, following closely the original edition in spite of Barker's statement in his preface: ''Since the book is intended primarily for younger readers, I have exercised the liberty now and then of simplifying the vocabulary of the quotations from Austin's letters. The book is not a condensation of *The Life of Stephen F. Austin,* but a complete rewriting from the sources.''

In 1949, a new edition was finally issued, in which Barker wrote: ''This second edition . . . is identical in text, except for a few technical differences here and there to adjust space. New make-up has reduced the number of pages . . . but the Index is revised to fit the new paging.''

There have been dozens of biographies and analyses of the other major Texan, Sam Houston, but only Barker (except for a few puerile attempts) has written on Austin. Marquis James' biography of Houston led to other fine studies of Houston the man, the Senator, the commander. Barker's biography of Austin has not led to further studies. Perhaps this is because no one has ever felt he could get to know Austin as well as Barker did. Charles W. Ramsdell wrote when the Barker biography appeared: ''This life of Austin is definitive. It will never need to be done over. There is no need for another.'' That is poppycock. Austin has not in fact had his Boswell in Barker, nor has he had his Sandburg, his Freeman, his Commager, nor his Brodie. Barker gave us a genuinely great first biography, but more intensive studies are needed before we will be able to fully understand Stephen F. Austin and his place in history.

Agatha, p.79. Campbell, p.32. Dobie, p.84. Howes B137.

8   Barker, Eugene Campbell (1874-1956)

MEXICO AND TEXAS, 1821-1835: UNIVERSITY OF TEXAS RESEARCH LECTURES ON THE CAUSES OF THE TEXAS REVOLUTION.

Dallas: P. L. Turner Company, Publishers, 1928.
vii,[1],167pp. 21cm.
Cloth, blue dustjacket printed in red.
Note: On the contents page, the word ''Appreciations'' is altered by hand to ''Apprehensions.'' Also other errors in text corrected by hand.

Other issues:

University of Texas Research Lectures on the Causes of the Texas Revolution

Mexico and Texas
1821 - 1835

By
EUGENE C. BARKER
Professor of American History
in the University of Texas

CONTENTS

"The Texan revolution was neither the culmination of a deep-laid program of chicanery and greed, nor the glorious response of outraged freemen to calculated oppression of tyrants."—*The Author.*

(A). Apparently the same printing, but with a variant dustjacket, green paper printed in purple. Errors uncorrected, but with printed errata slip.

(B). Facsimile reprint. New York: Russell & Russell, 1965. Same collation. 23cm. Cloth.

This seminal series of studies analyzes the break between Texas and Mexico. J. Fred Rippy said it "presents in an admirably clear and concise form the author's conclusions regarding the causes of the Texas revolution. It is the result of years of patient investigation." Ray Allen Billington deemed it "the best description of the governmental system" of the period. William C. Pool called it "a concise narrative which represents a condensation of Barker's immense storehouse of knowledge on the complex causes of the Texas revolution. . . . True to his basic philosophy, Barker approached his investigations without prejudice; he collected all the evidence available; and he formed his deductions and conclusions with a critical mind. He tried to be impartial and objective in learning the truth as nearly as it could be learned and in relating this small segment of truth to the whole fabric of American history. . . . He was intellectually honest and tolerant on matters and concerns where Texans often find objectivity rather difficult."

Barker was one of the first Texas historians to try to rise above the provincial attitude that the troubles between Texas and Mexico were all the fault of the latter. Beginning with a series of articles published in 1911 in the *Annual Report of the American Historical Association,* *The Quarterly of the Texas State Historical Association,* and *The University of Texas Record,* he gradually came to the conclusion that there was a dual responsibility for the revolution, and that attempts to place the blame on any one issue, movement, or series of events were fallacious. In the main, his conclusions in *Mexico and Texas* have stood the test of time, with the exception of those which he expressed as follows:

"The Texas revolution," states Barker, "was neither the culmination of a deep-laid program of chicanery and greed, nor the glorious response of outraged freemen to calculated oppression of tyrants." He describes the two cultures: "On the one side was the Anglo-American immigrant, blunt, independent, efficient, a rebel against authority, a supreme individualist. On the other side was the Latin American master of the soil, sensitive, secretive, subtle and indirect in his ways, by training and temperament a worshipper of tradition and a creature of authority. With the political ascendancy of the two elements reversed, the situation would have held no threatening aspects, but with the Mexicans in the political saddle conflict was certain." Barker later regretted this analysis, and rejected this theme. For a more objective viewpoint, see David J. Weber's *The Mexican Frontier,* entered here separately. Barker is on more solid ground with his statement that the causes of the revolution "are more than a study in local history. Misapprehensions concerning them and of the consequences to which the Revolution led lie at the bottom of much of the suspicion and distrust which have animated Latin-American relations with the United States for nearly a hundred years."

The volume consists of five papers: "The Radical and Political Background," "Mexican Apprehensions and Defensive Precautions," "Colonial Grievances," "The Development of the Revolution," and "Public Opinion in Texas Preceding the Revolution." The first four were delivered as lectures at the University of Texas in 1928, the last as an address before the American Historical Association. An outgrowth of this study was William C. Binkley's own series of lectures at Louisiana State University in 1950, published as *The Texas Revolution* (Baton Rouge: Louisiana State University Press, 1952, 132pp.). Binkley's study is very similar to Barker's, except that he continues the analysis through the revolution and a short time thereafter.

Barker's writings on Texas history extend over a period of more than fifty years. His first book length work is found in *The Quarterly of the Texas State Historical Association* for April, 1901 (vol. IV, no.4), the entire issue of which is devoted to his "The San Jacinto Campaign." He also edited *Readings in Texas History* (Dallas: Southwest Press, 1929, 653pp.), which includes much on the Texas-Mexican question, as does his *Speeches, Responses, and Essays, Critical and Historical* (Austin: E. C. Barker History Center, 1954, 307pp.). There is an interesting biography of Dr. Barker by William C. Pool, *Eugene C. Barker, Historian* (Austin: Texas State Historical Association, 1971, 228pp.).

9 Barker, Nancy Nichols (1925-   ) [comp.]

THE FRENCH LEGATION IN TEXAS.

The French Legation
in Texas

Translated and Edited with an Introduction by
Nancy Nichols Barker

The diplomatic correspondence of the French chargés d'affaires to the Republic of Texas. Hundreds of on-the-scene reports by French agents, instructions from Paris, and related documents, affording both a vast store of Texana and an essential tool for research. Beginning with consideration of recognition of the new republic, they continue almost without interruption until the annexation of Texas to the United States.

An introduction for each volume, by Dr. Barker, places the correspondence in historical perspective.

Winner of the Gilbert Chinard Prize, awarded by the Institut Français de Washington and the Society for French Historical Studies, for the most distinguished scholarly work in the field of Franco-American relations.

Winner of the Summerfield G. Roberts Award given by The Sons of the Republic of Texas for the work best portraying "the spirit, character, strength and deeds" of the men of the Republic of Texas.

Winner of an Award of Merit given by the American Association for State and Local History for outstanding achievement in the field of state and local history.

Winner of an Award of Excellence at the 23rd Texas Writers Roundup.

Volume I. *Recognition, Rupture and Reconciliation.*
                                    ISBN 0-87611-026-X $12.00*

Volume II. *Mission Miscarried.*   ISBN 0-87611-030-8 $12.00*

Texas State Historical Association
2/306 Richardson Hall   University Station
Austin, Texas 78712

*Texas residents add 5% sales tax.

Austin: Texas State Historical Association, [1971-1973].
Designed by William R. Holman. Foreword by John Connally.
Two volumes: 357,[1];[10],369-710,[1]pp. Illus. 26cm.
Cloth, dustjackets. The first volume was originally issued in an imprinted clear
plastic dust wrapper.

This work is a compilation of original reports on Texas confidentially
prepared for the government of France. Joseph Milton Nance said that
"these documents contain valuable information about the Republic of
Texas, its government, politics, personalities, economy, geography,
and climate," and Seymour V. Connor said the work "represents the
highest degree of excellence in American scholarship." The volumes
comprise one of the basic archives of contemporary reports on Texas,
particularly valuable since they were written not for publication but
for the eyes of the French minister of foreign affairs, and through him
the king. They sparkle with gossip and intrigue as well as with factual
information.

The work consists of 313 reports from Texas between 1838 and 1846,
covering every imaginable aspect of Texas affairs, mostly written by
the French charge d'affaires to the Republic of Texas, Alphonse Dubois
de Saligny, and by a special agent, Viscount Jules de Cramayel. The
correspondence was found in the archives of the French Foreign
Ministry in Paris, bound in ten manuscript volumes. A microfilm set
of the complete file has been deposited in the Austin Public Library
in Texas. From this microfilm, Nancy Barker toiled over the near-
illegible handwriting to produce these superb translations. Her understanding of the nuances of the French language of the period and of
the personal and political idiocyncrasies of the erratic Frenchmen
involved make her translations and annotations all the more useful.
She also includes in her introduction the best biography yet done of
that eccentric individual, Dubois de Saligny. Perhaps unfortunately
for the scholar, Barker excluded what she considered unimportant
papers, as well as those papers which had already appeared in George
P. Garrison's *Diplomatic Correspondence of the Republic of Texas.*

Saligny was sent to make an inspection tour of Texas in 1838. Upon
his return to France, Texas was recognized as an independent nation
and Saligny was sent back to Texas as charge d'affaires. From 1840 to
1846, he sent reports on Texas to France. A pompous, self-serving

misfit, he antagonized the Texans and lied to his government with abandon. The documents in this work, therefore, must be used only with the greatest of caution. Saligny's subaltern, Viscount Jules de Cramayel, was more honest but less fulsome in his descriptions than Saligny. On the whole, however, the correspondence of the French legation provides a significant addition to the fund of information available on this era in Texas history. While it would be a mistake for the student of the period to rely on the accuracy of the reports, it would be even more of a mistake to ignore them.

Perhaps the most valuable contributions in these documents are the purportedly verbatim conversations with leading Texans such as Lamar, Houston, and Jones. A considerable amount of light is shed on the personalities and objectives (often more readable between the lines than literally) of these men, all of whom were capable of running intellectual circles around Saligny. These two volumes will provide more grist for study than many reviewers have thus far acknowledged.

10   Barr, Alwyn (1938-   )

BLACK TEXANS: A HISTORY OF NEGROES IN TEXAS, 1528-1971.

Austin: Jenkins Publishing Company, The Pemberton Press, 1973.
Designed by Larry Smitherman.
xi,[1],259,[16]pp. Illus. 22cm.
Cloth, dustjacket.
Other issues:
(A). Reprint, 1982.

The best summation of Texas black history, this remains the only published work covering the whole of the black experience in Texas. James Smallwood said: "A brilliant study by a leading authority, *Black Texans* will long remain an outstanding contribution to Texas, Black, and Southern history." John W. Graves called it "a lean, lucid, tightly organized synthesis of a wealth of information." The *Journal of American History* review deemed it "a very fine contribution to the field of Negro history." Ron Tyler described it as "a solid document that will provide much of the leavening necessary to see the conflict of cultures that is Texas." Joe B. Frantz said: "Barr, who probably has the broadest knowledge of Texas black history of anyone in the state, shows it here. . . . In a way, the book is a sort of historical resurrection morning for blacks in Texas. *Black Texans* will likely be the orientation book of persons writing on [blacks in] Texas for years to come."

Barr writes that "black people have lived in Texas, though not continuously, for over four hundred years—longer than any other section of the United States—considerably longer than the dominant Anglo-population of the state, as long as the Spanish ancestors of its Mexican-Americans, and preceded only by the forebears of its few remaining Indian citizens." The 182,566 blacks in Texas in 1860 represented the peak percentage—about thirty percent—of the total population of Texas. Even at present, with over a million blacks, Texas has the largest black population of any state in the Union except New York.

It is remarkable, therefore, that so little has been written on black history in Texas. What little there was prior to Barr's volume was mostly paternalistic, racist, or Uncle Tom. Most modern writings have been unpublished theses or journal articles. The only prior book of any length was J. Mason Brewer, *Negro Legislators of Texas* (Dallas, 1935; reprint Austin: Pemberton Press, 1970), although there have been a number of works on Negro folklore of Texas. Roger A. Griffin wrote that Barr "recounts the discrimination, violence, and economic and political exploitation, which black Texans have suffered at the hands of the white majority throughout the history of the state. His account should be required reading for all of us who are a part of that majority." Barr also records the achievements of black Texans in many fields despite of the obstacles with which they had to contend.

Barr's volume is a general, episodic summary of the black role in Texas history, and a starting base for more specific studies. The first section relates to blacks during the periods of exploration and colonization, the second to slavery in Texas, the third to blacks in Reconstruction, the fourth to the struggle to retain the freedoms gained, the fifth to the 20th century black, and the sixth to the modern civil rights movement in Texas. Barr also discusses notable blacks in Texas history, from Cabeza de Vaca's Estevanico through legislator Norris Wright Cuney and boxer Jack Johnson to Barbara Jordan, and describes the areas of Texas history in which blacks were influential. He points out, for example, that about one in five of the cowboys on the Texas cattle drives was black. Almost every paragraph relates to a subject worthy of a separate and more detailed study, and some of these areas have been recently covered. Ron C. Tyler and Lawrence R. Murphy edited a useful book in this respect, *The Slave Narratives of Texas* (Austin: The Encino Press, 1974, 143pp.), which includes 308 short autobiographies of former Texas slaves recorded during the 1930's and an excellent essay on slavery in Texas by Tyler. Lawrence D. Rice wrote another good book, *The Negro in Texas, 1874-1900* (Baton Rouge: LSU Press, 1971, 309pp.); and Charles C. Alexander's *The Ku Klux Klan in the Southwest* (Lexington: University of Kentucky Press, 1966, 288pp.) has much on Texas, but little on blacks. Alexander's *Crusade for Conformity: The Ku Klux Klan in Texas, 1920-1930* (Houston: Texas Gulf Coast Historical Association, 1962) deals with the fundamentalist religious motivation of the later Klan activities.

The last section of the Barr book is an excellent narrative bibliography. As Karl E. Snyder wrote, one of the best features "of the book for the student is the bibliographical essay which concludes the book. Here on 30 pages is gathered a long list of background works with some explanation of where they fit into a development of the story of the Negro in Texas." Barr also wrote a fine related study, *Reconstruction to Reform: Texas Politics, 1876-1906* (Austin: University of Texas Press, 1971, 315pp.), which is considered by many as an even more significant contribution than *Black Texans*.

11 Barry, James Buckner (1821-1906)

A TEXAS RANGER AND FRONTIERSMAN: THE DAYS OF BUCK BARRY IN TEXAS, 1845-1906.

Dallas: The Southwest Press, 1932.
Edited by James K. Greer.
xi,[1],254pp. 6 plates. 24cm.
Cloth, dustjacket.

Other issues:
(A). Facsimile reprint. Waco: Friends of the Moody Texas Ranger Library, 1978. 24cm. Cloth, dustjacket. Limited to 1000 numbered copies, signed by Greer. Contains a few insignificant additions, including a new preface quoting newspaper reviews of the first edition.
(B). Facsimile reprint of (A). Lincoln and London: University of Nebraska Press, [1984]. Paperback.

This is the best memoir of a Texas Ranger during the mid-19th century. Walter P. Webb called it an "excellent account" that "should rank with Samuel C. Reid's and J. B. Gillett's accounts." The editor, James K. Greer, wrote: "No writer of western stories has created better . . . adventure than this quiet, unassuming, early settler lived, although he does not meticulously detail it. But, perhaps, by its very simplicity—this commendable restraint—his story gains in force."

Greer, the first person to receive a doctorate in history from the University of Texas, edited the memoirs, which were incomplete at Barry's death. They are based on his manuscript reminiscences, his diaries, and his correspondence. In general, the reminiscences cover the period up to 1855, the diary from 1855 to 1862, and the correspondence from 1862 to 1867. Greer cast the whole into a single first-person narrative, "weaving them together so that they complete the tale . . . in keeping with Barry's method." This sometimes proves an irritant to the scholar, but I have used the original manuscripts (now in the University of Texas Archives), and have found the Greer version to be generally faithful to the Barry original.

Barry's memoirs cover his early life in North Carolina as hunter and schoolteacher, his trip at the age of 23 through Texas in the last year of the republic, his service in the Mexican War under Jack Hays, and his life as a pioneer on what was then the farthest frontier of Texas. The most extensive part of the memoir, however, is devoted to his services as sheriff, Indian fighter, and Texas Ranger in the period 1847-1867.

As a colonel of the Rangers during the Civil War, he commanded a force that protected virtually all of the western border of settled Texas from Indian incursions. It is this part of his memoirs which is the richest in detail. "We were perhaps in more fights than any other Confederate regiment," Barry writes, although "I served all during the war and never saw a Yankee soldier" except for some prisoners. The fights were against Plains Indians, who raided unmercifully during the war. C. M. Cureton, later Chief Justice of the Texas Supreme Court, said: "He was one of the most successful Indian fighters I ever knew. Some men, probably the McCullochs and Jack Hays, had a reputation before his day, but whether they were any better Indian fighters, I have my doubts."

Barry's contemporaries thought him the epitome of the Indian-fighting ranger. Charles Goodnight, who served under him, said:

"When he gave an order we knew he meant it. He was a man of very quick and accurate decision; his coolness in engagements was remarkable." R. W. Aycock said: "He was one of the best men that ever lived, when he was treated right, but if a man didn't want to do the right thing, or wanted a scrap, he could get it out of Buck any time." When Barry ran for a state office in 1898, his neighbors issued a signed statement reading in part: "He has been in more fights and killed more Indians . . . than any other officer that was ever on the frontier. . . . We believe the people of Texas owe him more than any other man now living." W. M. Bridges wrote: "Colonel Barry had a horror of outlaws and thieves and did much to put law on top. He was kind, jovial, a lover of horses and of Indian fights." Nevertheless, he killed Indians only when necessary. A number of incidents in the memoirs show him letting Indians go when they were found innocent of hostility, and perhaps no other frontiersman made better use of friendship with such peaceful Indians as the Tonkawas.

Barry's recollections prior to his Indian-fighting days offer interesting sidelights on men and events of the time. He was in Austin in 1845 when the Convention of 1845 met to declare for statehood: "The members were camping out, sleeping on their blankets. There was a company of Rangers there to keep the Indians from scalping the delegates . . . although each member was heavily armed and a first-class Ranger himself." He also gives us a vivid Mexican War account of Jack Hays during the attack on Monterrey:

"[Early one morning] day revealed to us a regiment of lancers approaching us [and we knew] they were after our blood. Our colonel, seeing our situation, with some of the boys barely yet awake, tried to gain a little time to better prepare us to receive the charge. He rode out front with his saber in his hand and challenged the colonel of the lancers to meet him halfway between the lines to fight a saber fight. . . . Hays knew no more about saber fighting than I did, but his object was [to gain a little time]. So, as soon as the Mexican colonel could divest himself of all encumbrances, he advanced waving his saber, while his horse seemed to dance rather than prance. Within a few feet of the Mexican, Hays pulled a pistol and shot him dead from his horse."

Barry says that "this relieved all suspense and anxiety; they charged as like mad hornets . . . they fought through our lines, formed in our rear and charged through the line again, formed in our front and charged through our line a third time." Barry was wounded, and states: "I have never called a Mexican a coward since."

One of Barry's most valuable contributions is his account of the daily life of the pioneer on the edge of civilization. Back east he had bought a watch for four dollars; in Texas he "traded it for the land on the forks of the Bosque where my farm is now located." Times were hard almost beyond belief. One winter was so cold, he came upon a wandering horse "and found his rider frozen to death. . . . A party of men started out to bring the man in. When they found him, the horse had frozen also." He lost many loved ones to the vicissitudes of the frontier: "I returned home one day in February, after an Indian hunt, in time to be present at the burial of our baby, Cora. Six months later we laid our little girl, Mary, by her. But . . . there was work that had to be done. So despite the loneliness we had to go ahead. . . ." Yet he says that "behind this story of toil there was the background of much life in the open and some greater recompense. A realization was prevalent that the soil and the grazing, the fruits and the nuts . . . would some day inaugurate a development which would yield returns surprising to the nation."

His hunting tales are sheer delight, and it is regrettable that Greer deleted a number of these because he felt they were "of no permanent historical value." Barry nevertheless revels in the hunt. "I killed fourteen panthers one fall," he says, and even tells of chasing one panther up a tree armed only with a Bowie knife. The panther welcomed the charge with a growl: "I knew he was telling me the truth, so I climbed back down." He and his friends wrestled alligators, and killed bear, deer, turkeys, and buffalo. Ammunition was so scarce and valuable (nearest store 200 miles away) that he killed two panthers and one buck with the same bullet, retrieving it each time from the carcass. He killed for food; frequently he makes statements such as: "One [buffalo] was more meat than we wanted so I ran the others off."

Dobie, p.60. Howes G398. Rader 1682.

12   Bartlett, John Russell (1805-1886)

PERSONAL NARRATIVE OF EXPLORATIONS AND INCI-
DENTS IN TEXAS, NEW MEXICO, CALIFORNIA, SONORA,
AND CHIHUAHUA, CONNECTED WITH THE UNITED STATES
AND MEXICAN BOUNDARY COMMISSION, DURING THE
YEARS 1850, '51, '52, and '53.

New York: D. Appleton & Company, 346 & 348 Broadway, [1854].
Two volumes: xxii,506,[6]; xviii,624pp. 23cm. 16 lithographs. (The "Tucson, Sonora"
plate on p.292, vol. II, is not listed and there is only one geyser plate instead of two
as listed.) 94 other illustrations. Folding map: "General Map Showing the Countries
Explored & Surveyed . . ."
Cloth.

Other issues:
(A). London, 1854. Same collation.
(B). One volume edition, New York and London, 1856. Same collation except for
     omission of Tucson view, resulting in only 15 lithographs.
(C). Facsimile reprint: Chicago: Rio Grande Press, 1965. Cloth. Includes a new
     introduction by Odie Faulk and an additional map of the disputed border area.

Bartlett's *Narrative* is the most scholarly and scientific description of
Southwest Texas of its era. Thomas W. Streeter called it "the first
thoroughly scholarly description of the Southwest" and F. S. Dellen-
baugh labeled it "a valuable addition to the literature of the Southwest."

President Zachary Taylor appointed Bartlett commissioner to run
the boundary line between the United States and Mexico. Bartlett, a
bibliographer and antiquary, was an odd choice for this mammoth
task. He managed to get himself into numerous petty squabbles with
such officers as J. D. Graham and certainly proved himself to be as
contentious as the average antiquarian bookseller. Yet he served for
three years, travelled thousands of miles, and produced one of the
best American travel books ever written.

Although he was unsuccessful as a leader, he turned out to be
superb as a scientist. Not only did he tackle the task of defining the
border, but he also made a valuable contribution toward determining
the route for the immensely important southern transcontinental
railroad, studied the suitability of camels for use in the West, and kept

a detailed diary of his travels. As he said in his preface, "I have endeavored to make it particular and accurate, in order that my book may become a useful guide to emigrants and other travelers."

Bartlett arrived at Indianola, Texas, in August, 1850, with 105 scientists, artists, teamsters, and surveyors, escorted by 85 soldiers. His *Narrative* gives a day-by-day account of their movements to San Antonio, Fredericksburg, El Paso, thence to San Diego and back to El Paso, down into Mexico, back up to Ringgold Barracks, and finally to Corpus Christi on New Year's Day, 1853.

Bartlett's expedition was valuable for contributions regarding mines, minerals, and geology in general, and vastly advanced knowledge of the natural history, ethnology, meteorology, and topography of the areas traversed. Bartlett states that "no exertions were spared, and no suitable opportunities omitted, to do all in my power to advance the cause of science." While his goal of defending his command decisions mars some of the work ("A number of incidents described by Bartlett have been differently interpreted by his associates"—Everett D. Graff), his scholarship has been universally praised ("His ability in careful observation and his literary style all contribute to the excellence of this work"—Thomas Clark).

In addition to the 45 chapters of chronological narrative, Bartlett includes four chapters giving a general summary of the activities of the commission, the results of his natural history investigations, on the best railway route, and on the use of camels for transportation. Appendices quote some of the official documents of the commission, although the bulk of these appear in various official U.S. government document publications. Bartlett states that Sam Houston tried to get the government to publish the Bartlett report, but "the efforts of the learned Senator however were unsuccessful, and the resolution was laid on the table." Thus Bartlett arranged for publication himself with Appleton. Bartlett's manuscripts and correspondence are at the John Carter Brown Library.

Bartlett's contribution has been aptly summarized by Chester V. Kielman: "Bartlett's failure as boundary commissioner and the frequently *opera bouffe* character of his career in the Southwest do not require restatement. His striking inadequacies on the one hand were balanced by equally affirmative qualities on the other, and for these, which produced the *Narrative,* several generations of researchers have incurred a debt of monumental proportions." And F. W. Hodge states: "Bartlett produced a work of lasting importance to science and history. His narrative possesses high literary merit, is exact almost beyond criticism, and altogether is one of the best works devoted to the southwest that has ever appeared." A good analysis of Bartlett and the boundary survey may be found in Odie B. Faulk, *Too Far North . . . Too Far South* (Los Angeles: Westernlore Press, 1968).

Agatha, p.40. Clark III-272. Cowan, p.36. Dobie, p.86. Graff 198. Howes B201. Larned 2019. Powell, *Southwestern Century* 9. Rader 287. Raines, p.22. Sabin 3746. Wagner-Camp 234.

13   Bedichek, Roy (1878-1959)

ADVENTURES WITH A TEXAS NATURALIST.

Garden City, N.Y.: Doubleday & Co., Inc., 1947.
Illustrations by Ward Lockwood.
xx,293pp. 21cm.
Cloth, dustjacket.
[Verso of title:] Printed in the United States at The Country Life Press, Garden City, N.Y. First edition.

Other issues:
(A). Same as above, but without the words "First Edition" on verso of title page.
(B). Same as (A), with a printed label on fly-leaf: "Distributed by the Texas Folklore Society in Lieu of an Annual Publication for 1947."
(C). *Adventures with a Naturalist.* London: V. Gollancz, 1948. 258pp. 23cm. Cloth, dustjacket. First English edition.
(D). Garden City: The Natural History Library, Anchor Books, [1961]. xxv,[3],330,[2]pp. 22cm. Paperback. New foreword by Dean Amadon.
(E). Revised edition. Austin: University of Texas Press, [1961]. 330pp. 22cm. Cloth, dustjacket. "New (Revised) Edition." Of this edition, Lon Tinkle wrote: "A handsome edition, with . . . two important new features. One of these is a brilliant preface, written in flawless prose, by a longtime Bedichek friend and admirer, H. Mewhinney of the *Houston Post.* The other is an appendix of Bedi's list of emendations from Bedicheck's marginal comments . . . on a copy of the original text. The latter . . . reveal Bedicheck's unfailing dedication to precision and his near absolute good taste in matters of style."
(F). Paperback edition of (E). 22cm. Cover drawing by Ed Lindhof.
(G). Same as (E). Austin: University of Texas Press, [1966].
(H). Same as (E). Austin: University of Texas Press, [1980].

This book is for Texas what *Walden* is for New England. Frank Dobie called it possibly "the wisest book in the realm of natural history produced in America since Thoreau," written by a man whom Dobie later called "the wisest and justest and best man that I have ever known." Lon Tinkle said: "His prose is modest and seemingly without art. And then you discover that this man who paid profound attention to everything writes like an angel." William A. Owens thought the book "as pleasant as a stroll through a Texas countryside, and twice as informative."

In a very real sense, the book is the result of the efforts of Frank Dobie and Walter Webb. Bedichek was approaching his seventies, and his two friends knew he had at least one masterpiece in him if they could get him to produce it. Dobie initiated a movement to get a year's paid leave of absence for Bedichek from the University of Texas, and Webb assisted in that effort, and badgered Bedichek to accept. Bedichek later said that Webb "encouraged me to the point where I really got to work and wrote a book." Webb also provided his Friday Mountain Ranch, ten miles south of Austin on the Edwards Plateau, on which Bedichek lived alone for a year. Bedichek called it "my year of stocktaking." He wrote his book at a large oak poker table confiscated in a gambling raid by Texas Ranger Captain Frank Hamer and liberated for the famous Hamer-Webb weekly poker games.

Bedichek worked on the book for a year, but it is a distillation of seven decades of study and experience. Bedichek graduated from the University of Texas in 1903. Ronnie Dugger writes: "For fifteen years after college he bummed around the country and the world. He picked cotton in the South, peeled potatoes on a river boat, gathered berries in New Jersey, washed dishes in a Chinese cafe in New York City, tramped over the English, French, and German countrysides, assisted a fake divine in Boston, dug coal and explored rivers in West Virginia, cut off hogs' heads in a Chicago slaughterhouse, and homesteaded a dugout in Oklahoma." He then returned to Texas and spent most of his active career as head of the University Interscholastic League.

The book contains twenty-two chapters of essays on various subjects related to natural history. The longest section is three chapters on the mockingbird, of which Dobie said: "His treatment of the mockingbird is beyond all doubt the richest, fullest, and most interesting that has ever been published." There are sections on the swallow, the primrose, the Inca dove, and the golden eagle, and on fences (Bedichek is a fencecutter at heart), denatured chickens versus the farmyard variety, nature folklore, and the other subjects. In most cases, the overt subject of his essays is used as a means for informal reflections on philosophy, life, and nature. But this is deceptive, for Bedichek is a consummate scientist. Mary Adkins pointed out that "the book has a large and solid core of fact, arrived at by the arduous, painstaking methods of a scientist. No other book I know suggests more convincingly the stubborn zeal, but the controlled and objective zeal, of the scientific spirit. . . . The weighing of evidence in the moot questions of the mockingbird as a mocker and the manner of the wood ducklings' initial descent from their nest are two examples of objectivity, as are the attempts to disentangle folklore from fact: the investigation of whether a praying mantis can catch, hold, and eat a hummingbird, and an examination of the malign influence of the owl."

Bedichek's love of nature, as well as his delicious sense of humor, are revealed by his comments on camping: "A stationary camp is quickly cluttered up. Stay too long or return to the same camping place too often, and the inevitable encrustation appears. You fix up a cupboard, install a bench between two trees. These and other little conveniences may be nothing more than a few pimples, but they indicate that the disease of civilization is setting in. You had better be on your way again; otherwise, you may build a camp house, then a summer home, then neighbors, and eventually find yourself right back where you started."

Walter Webb sums up the effect Bedichek's book has had on readers through the years, although he said it immediately after publication and before any reviews had appeared: "This book marks a departure in Texas literature. There has been nothing like it come out of Texas before. . . . Here is a book you will read and caress and read again. You will place it on a shelf where you can see it often and be reminded of the delightful things within."

14   Berlandier, Jean Louis (ca. 1805-1851), and Rafael Chovel

DIARIO DE VIAGE DE LA COMISION DE LIMITES QUE PUSO EL GOVIERNO DE LA REPUBLICA, BAJA LA DIRECCION DEL EXMO. SR. D. MANUEL DE MIER Y TERAN.

Mexico: Tipografia de Juan R. Navarro, Calle de Chiquis Numero 6, 1850. 298,[1]pp. 23cm. A few copies are known with a frontispiece. Howes and Raines call for two maps, but no known copy has any and I doubt there ever were any. Half morocco.

Other issues:
(A). *Viage a Texas en el Ano* 1828. Mexico: Vargas Rea, 1948. 77pp. 21cm. Printed wrappers. 100 copies printed.
(B). *The Indians of Texas in* 1830. Washington: Smithsonian Institution Press, 1969. xi,[1],209pp. 39 illus. and 20 plates. 26cm. Cloth, dustjacket. Edited with introduction by John C. Ewers. Translated by Patricia Reading Leclercq.
(C). *Journey to Mexico during the Years* 1826 *to* 1834. Austin: The Texas State Historical Association in Cooperation with the Center for Studies in Texas History, University of Texas, [1980]. Two volumes: xxxvi,[2],287; vii,[5],[289]-672,[1]pp. 34 color plates. Map. 27cm. Cloth. Boxed. Translated by Sheila M. Ohlendorf, Josette M. Bigelow, and Mary M. Standifer. Introduction by C. H. Muller. Botanical notes by C. H. Muller and Katherine K. Muller.
(D). Special edition of (C), limited to 150 numbered sets, signed by the contributors, boxed, with two additional color plates.

This is the best scientific study of Texas during the colonial period. Berlandier came to Mexico to collect botanical specimens for a group of Swiss naturalists, and to accompany Gen. Manuel de Mier y Teran on his scientific expedition to Texas in 1828. Afterward, Berlandier settled in Matamoros and made several more explorations in Texas. During the period from his coming to Mexico in 1826 up through 1834, Berlandier kept diaries, wrote reports, collected specimens and artifacts, and drew pictures of what he saw. He was observant, careful, and intelligent, and he left us a record that is unmatched for his era in Texas.

C. H. Muller states: "The thoughtful student of vegetation can find invaluable historical information in Berlandier's journal. His descriptions . . . are, in many instances, the only records ever made in some areas now vastly changed." John C. Ewers called Berlandier's accounts "the nearest approach to a well-rounded ethnography of the Comanche Indians written by an observer of that tribe during the days before the buffalo were exterminated. . . . The coverage is both broad and remarkably detailed. . . ." Samuel W. Geiser said Berlandier "did monumental work for botany in early Texas and in Mexico." Not until the Bartlett-Salazar boundary survey would there be a study of the area superior in scope to those conducted by Berlandier for Mier y Teran. My copy of the Berlandier-Chovel volume, by the way, is a presentation copy from Jose Salazar to John R. Bartlett, dated El Paso, October, 1852.

Berlandier's reports on the Texas settlers and their towns, farms, and ranches, and on the Indian tribes, are especially interesting due to their objectivity. Berlandier had no axe to grind on the political scene; as a trained scientific observer, he viewed the people and their towns and improvements much in the same way he would have viewed an ant colony. He is virtually unique in that regard among early visitors to Texas. He visited the Indians not as a missionary nor soldier nor trader nor bureaucrat nor land grabber, but simply as a curious visitor—he was therefore received openly by them, even by the Comanches. Ewers states: "In addition this Frenchman wrote simply and clearly and with a considerable charm—attributes not commonly found in the writings of men of science. He recognized the Comanches and their Indian neighbors not as wild, untameable creatures of nature, but as human beings, men of considerable intelligence . . . I believe that in the future Berlandier will be remembered as one of the most enlightened and one of the best amateur ethnographers of the American West during the frontier period."

Berlandier's description of the Anglo-American colonies, especially in the 1980 edition, is one of the most reliable extant. In a lengthy six-page description of San Felipe de Austin, for example, he writes: "The dwellings are scattered about after the manner of new Anglo-American towns. One finds at the most forty to fifty families, for most of the colonists live amid their fields. The streets are laid out with a measuring tape, and, although edged with several plants of *Melia* azedarach [chinaberry trees], improperly called Louisiana lilacs, they still have a wild look. The town is formed of about two hundred to three hundred persons, among whom are found the families of the most comfortably off colonists, who enjoy a house in town and another on their lands. San Felipe de Austin is the seat of the municipality and the home of some loafers who are most often drunk." Compare this with the description in Noah Smithwick's *Evolution of a State*.

After his sudden death from drowning while crossing the Rio Grande in 1851, Berlandier's manuscripts and specimen collections were sold by his widow in 1853 to Lt. Darius Nash Crouch, a West Point graduate on leave to conduct explorations for Joseph Henry. Crouch shipped 39 boxes to the Smithsonian from Brownsville. The Smithsonian purchased a portion from Crouch, who then distributed and sold the remainder in America and Europe. Some of these are now in the Library of Congress, Yale, the Gray Herbarium at Harvard, and the Gilcrease Institute. All published versions are from different manuscripts.

The 1850 edition, although it also carries the name of Chovel as co-author, actually was almost entirely from Berlandier's journals. The Chovel (or Chovell, as signed in the preface) diary is now at Tulane. This 1850 edition also includes Berlandier's diary of his expedition and visit to the Comanche Indians, which had been first printed in *El Museo Mexicano* (Mexico, 1844, vol. 3, pp. 177-187) under the title "Caza del Osa y Cibola, en el Nor-oueste de Tejas." Berlandier had also published a pamphlet in 1832 entitled *Memorias de la Comision de Limites*, which is the first printed botanical description of Texas.

The Vargas Rea edition of 1948 is from a manuscript sent by Berlandier to General Mier y Teran; it is now in the Mexican National Archives. The Ewers edition of 1969 is from the manuscript at the Gilcrease Institute. This edition contains an excellent introduction and notes by Ewers, as well as his description of the Lino Sanchez y Tapia watercolors from the expedition and a description of the artifacts collected by Berlandier.

The edition of 1980 is from the manuscript at the Library of Congress, with illustrations from specimens at the Gray Herbarium. It is the most complete version published to date. A biography of Berlandier is long overdue. As T. N. Campbell wrote in January, 1983, "it is evident that Berlandier studies are just beginning."

Graff 278. Howes B379. Raines, p.24. Wagner-Camp 178a.

15 Biesele, Rudolph Leopold (1886-1960)

THE HISTORY OF THE GERMAN SETTLEMENTS IN TEXAS, 1831-1861.

Austin: Press of Von Boeckmann-Jones Co., [1930].
xi,259pp. 9 maps, some folding. 22 plates. 24cm.
Cloth.

Other issues:
(A). Facsimile reprint. [Austin, 1964]. Same collation. 24cm. Cloth. No publisher
     identified.

This monograph remains one of the best scholarly studies of the
German migration into Texas. Eugene C. Barker said of it: "In its
broader aspects this study is a contribution to the history of the
German element in the United States. From a narrower, but in some
sense a more important, point of view it is a valuable chapter in the
social and economic history of Texas." Marcus L. Hansen in *American
Historical Review* wrote: "Dr. Biesele has shown what ingenuity and
persistence can do with a theme which has already had several
historians. Not content with using material readily available, he has
secured access to private papers, paged through county histories, local
newspapers, and obscure yearbooks, corresponded with German archi-
vists and editors, and ransacked the records of land offices. The result
is a clear presentation of a movement which involves confusing
matters." Biesele, himself the son of German immigrants to Texas,
grew up and taught school in the region of thickest German settlement
and knew many of the early settlers, although he bemoans not having
begun his study earlier, "while many of the old German settlers were
still living."

Biesele's study began as a 1928 doctoral dissertation for the University
of Texas, and the text as published remains substantially unchanged
except for a slightly different arrangement and the addition of some
maps and illustrations. Some portions of the book and expansion of
special themes appeared as articles in the *Southwestern Historical Quarterly*.
It is interesting to note how much the Texas historians of this period
assisted one another on their projects of producing the first scholarly
secondary studies of aspects of Texas history. There apparently was a
much closer comradeship than today, and certainly far less backbiting
and jealousy. Biesele, for example, expressly thanks for specific
assistance Eugene C. Barker, E. W. Winkler, Charles Ramsdell, Winnie
Allen, Mattie Austin Hatcher, and Harriet Smither. Biesele later
became a professor of history at the university and is said to have

supervised more Texas history theses and dissertations than any other person except possibly Barker himself. He also served as an editor of the *Southwestern Historical Quarterly,* the *Journal of Southern History,* and the *Southwestern Social Science Quarterly.* The original manuscript and Biesele's notes for his book are now in the University of Texas Archives.

Biesele's work, he states, is a study of "how the dissatisfaction with the prevailing social, economic, and political conditions in Germany during the first half of the nineteenth century caused German emigrants to direct their footsteps toward Texas after that distant, promising land became known to them. Various plans were submitted to the Spanish and Mexican governments in the interests of German colonization in Texas, but these, as well as the proposals made later to the republic of Texas, proved unproductive." A trickle of Germans began to settle, however, in the early days of Anglo-American colonization, and began to write back home about Texas.

In 1831, what he calls "a matter of great significance for the history of the German settlements in Texas" took place. Friedrich Ernst, who had planned to found a settlement in Missouri, changed his mind when he learned Stephen F. Austin was attempting to entice German and Swiss settlers to his colonies. Ernst settled in Texas and wrote a widely circulated letter praising Texas, leading to a significant increase in German interest. Biesele presents the results of his extensive study of contemporary German newspapers and archival collections to show how Germans, particularly in the Nassau and Hesse areas, became eager to emigrate from Germany into Texas.

This led to what Biesele calls "the second significant event in the history of German settlements in Texas," the formation of the Verein zum Schutze Deutscher Einwanderer in Texas, better known as the Adelsverein. This Society for the Protection of German Immigrants to Texas, especially under Prince Carl of Solms-Braunfels and Baron von Meusebach, organized and published an announcement in 1844, which Biesele translates in full (and transcribes in the original German in an appendix); it contains the prophetic statement:

"The Society wishes neither to encourage nor to excuse emigration. The desire exists, a fact which can not be denied . . . Many causes are working together to increase emigration: the displacement of manual labor by machinery, the great periodic depressions which affect commerce, the increasing poverty, caused by overpopulation . . . After a long and careful examination the Society has decided that Texas is the land which will best suit the emigrant.''

This led to the immigration of thousands of middle-class Germans into Texas. By 1860, there were over 20,000 in Texas, representing about three and one half percent of the population. Biesele points out that, from the very beginning, they became patriotic Texans—even sending a full company to fight in the Mexican War under Albert Sidney Johnston. Biesele devotes two chapters to a study of how the German settlers entered into the Texas political, social, and economic stream. He points out, as well, how the Germans were generally better educated and more inclined towards music and the arts than the average Anglo-American Texan of the time.

There is an extensive bibliography, as well as considerable commentary within the text and annotations on German source materials. In this regard, the past two decades have led to the discovery of several enormous archives of materials relating to German immigration into Texas; for this reason, there should be far more studies of this massive migration in the future than there have been in the past.

Three other secondary accounts on German Texans are Moritz Tiling, *History of the German Element in Texas from 1820-1850* (Houston, 1913); Gilbert G. Benjamin, *The Germans in Texas: A Study in Immigration* (Philadelphia: University of Pennsylvania, 1910); and Terry G. Jordon, *German Seed in Texas Soil: Immigrant Farmers in 19th-Century Texas* (Austin: University of Texas Press, 1976).

16 Binkley, William Campbell (1889-1970)

THE EXPANSIONIST MOVEMENT IN TEXAS, 1836-1850.

Berkeley: University of California Press, 1925.
x,253pp. 8 maps. 25cm.
Printed wrappers.
University of California Publications in History, Volume XIII.

Other issues:
(A). Facsimile reprint. New York: DaCapo Press, 1970. 24cm.

The most comprehensive account of Republic of Texas imperialism and the eventual setting of the western borders of the state, this work was undertaken at the suggestion of Herbert E. Bolton. It is one of those rare works in Texas historiography that perfectly blends extensive research into hitherto untapped sources, clear and smooth narrative style, and intelligent, fresh conclusions. A. K. Christian in 1925 called it "a real contribution to the increasing literature of Southwestern history," and it has remained useful to the present time, as attested by Ray Allen Billington.

Binkley's account fulfills his stated purpose "to give for the first time, and in some portions from a new point of view, a consecutive narrative of the efforts of Texas both as an independent republic and as a state, to extend its territorial jurisdiction; to show what factors exerted an influence in guiding the Texan desire for expansion; and to fit the movement into the larger field of the westward extension of the United States."

Immediately after winning independence in 1836, many of the Texan leaders began a concerted and overt movement for the expansion of the boundaries of the new republic. The first efforts were to assert control southward beyond the Nueces to the Rio Grande. Binkley explains and analyzes the attempts to secure California for Texas, the efforts of President Lamar to negotiate a treaty for a boundary extending to the Pacific, and the expeditions to conquer and occupy New Mexico. He also recounts the fascinating story of how these boundary claims were taken up and settled after annexation by the Texan leaders in Congress, notably Sam Houston and Thomas J. Rusk. The boundary was finally settled as part of the Compromise of 1850.

Of special interest is his treatment of the expeditions of Jacob Snively and Charles Warfield. He states that "Warfield has hitherto been considered as a private raider, while Snively has fared but little better. The evidence indicates, however, that the work of both of these men, no matter how detached it may seem, was a part of the general program of Texas to bring New Mexico under the jurisdiction of its government."

17 [Blessington, Joseph Palmer (1841-1898)]

THE CAMPAIGNS OF WALKER'S TEXAS DIVISION, BY A PRIVATE SOLDIER.

New York: Published for the Author by Lange, Little & Co., Printers, 108 to 114 Wooster Street, 1875.

314pp. 23cm.

Cloth.

Other issues:

(A). Facsimile reprint. Austin: The Pemberton Press, 1968. [10],314pp. Cloth. 23cm. Introduction by Alwyn Barr.

(B). Facsimile reprint. [Pine Bluff, Ark.: B.R. Scallion, 1983]. Cloth.

This is the only complete history of the largest single unit of Texas troops in the Civil War, the only division in the Confederate army composed of troops from a single state. Raines called it "one of the best war histories written, as to the Texas troops." Written by a corporal on the staff of General Richard Scurry, it was derived from his own diaries, "jotted down on the long and weary march, in the quiet camp, before and after the fierce conflict of deadly strife."

Walker's Texas Division, also known as the "Greyhound Division," was organized by Gen. Henry E. McCulloch in 1862, commanded from January 1863, to June, 1864, by Major General John G. Walker, and from then until May, 1865, by Gen. John H. Forney. At one time or another during the war it included the 3rd, 10th, 11th, 12th, 14th, 16th, 17th, 18th, 19th, and 22nd Texas Infantry; the 13th, 15th, 16th, 18th, 25th, 28th, 29th, and 34th Texas Cavalry; as well as Edgar's Texas Battery, Haldeman's Texas Battery, Gould's Texas Cavalry Battalion, Daniel's Texas Battery, and the Texas Partisan Rangers.

The unit served primarily in Texas, Arkansas, and Louisiana, and was the backbone of the Confederate forces of the Trans-Mississippi West. Its major contributions were in opposition to Gen. N. P. Banks' invasion of Louisiana, especially at Mansfield, Pleasant Hill, Jenkins' Ferry, and Milliken's Bend. Other general officers serving in the division included W. R. Scurry, T. N. Waul, James M. Hawes, W. H. King, Horace Randal, R. P. Maclay, Richard Waterhouse, and James Deshler. Three governors of Texas were in the division: Edward Clark, O. M. Roberts, and R. B. Hubbard.

Blessington was only a corporal on Gen. Scurry's staff; this, he states, "precluded a knowledge of the strategic reasons for the marches and battles which he merely chronicles." He nevertheless faithfully maintained his diaries, consulted official records, and interviewed many other surviving members. He remained in 1875 an unreconstructed Rebel, stating that the war was one wherein "Southerners endeavored, by force of arms, to establish their independence, and preserve untarnished the principle of constitutional liberty bequeathed to them by their ancestors, and baptized and consecrated with their best blood, from the despotic domination of Radicalism." Blessington made extensive use—even verging on plagiarism—of Col. T. R. Bonner's "Sketches of the Campaign of 1864," which appeared in the October and November, 1868, issues of *The Land We Love*. Another well-edited account of the activities of this unit is in Norman D. Brown [ed.], *Journey to Pleasant Hill: The Civil War Letters of Captain Elijah P. Petty, Walker's Texas Division* (San Antonio: Institute of Texan Cultures, 1982, 471pp.).

The narrative is in some places turgid, in many spellbinding. Even occasional lapses between first and third person fail to lessen the impact of some of his descriptions: " 'McCulloch's Brigade, advance!' is heard . . . They are greeted by a murderous fire of minie balls. Gaps are opened in the ranks, but they are closed again and move still onward . . . It was impossible for our troops to keep in line of battle, owing to the many hedges we had to encounter . . . so we had to get the best way we could . . . The battle became general. The enemy opened a terrible fire of musketry. We were ordered to charge them with the bayonet. Without stopping to reload, the troops . . . rushed upon the enemy. The enemy gave way and stampeded pell-mell over the levee, in great terror and confusion. Our troops followed after them, bayoneting them by hundreds . . . General McCulloch exclaimed 'Bravo, bravo!' in ecstasy of admiration and delight . . . Dead bodies were found lying in every direction. Let us take a look along the shattered ranks. An awful sight! See that number of brave fellows now stretched in their gore, who but an hour ago . . . had marched with stout hearts to the fray—a march only from earth to eternity."

After one battle, Blessington came upon a makeshift hospital in some shanties: "If one wishes to view the havoc of war, next to the battlefield this is the place to witness it; so fearful, so horrible are the scenes, that, long after you leave the place, perhaps haunting you to the verge of life, the screams of the wounded, the groans of the dying will ring in your ears . . ." The war Blessington presents is not by any means pleasant, but it is war from the front lines, and as he says in his preface, "this book is a chapter from its bloodiest record."

Howes B533. Nevins I-61. Raines, p.27.

18 Bollaert, William (1807-1876)

WILLIAM BOLLAERT'S TEXAS.

Norman: Published in Co-Operation with the Newberry Library, Chicago, by the University of Oklahoma Press, [1956]. Edited by W. Eugene Hollon and Ruth Lapham Butler.
The American Exploration & Travel Series Number 21.
xxiii,423,[1]pp. Map. Illus. 23cm.
Cloth, dustjacket.
[Verso of title:] First edition.

The most entertaining book on the Republic of Texas, this is also one of the most perceptive. Robert S. Maxwell called it "a delightful addition to the literature of this region . . . informative, amusing and provocative." Stanley Pargellis said it presents "as good a picture of social life in Texas on the eve of annexation as any record that has survived . . . [It] stands as one of the most interesting, most unprejudiced, and most sympathetic that has come down to us." Herbert Gambrell said "his record is valuable because it is accurate, firsthand data. It is delightful because it is multifaceted, touching matters that other travelers overlooked; and it is absorbing reading because the unique personality of this minor genius shines through it."

William Bollaert was uniquely qualified to produce a discerning account of his tours through Texas. As a young man he was a chemical assistant to Sir Humphry Davy and Michael Faraday, later doing his own studies in the fields of chemistry, geography, geology, and ethnology. He had travelled in Peru, worked in its silver mines, and was one of the first men to cross and explore the desert of Atacama. He had served as a soldier in Portugal, writing a book on his war experiences, and in Spain as a diplomatic courier for the pretender to the Spanish throne.

Bollaert became interested in Texas after reading William Kennedy's *Texas*. He was chosen as agent of the British admiralty to gather materials for a map of Texas, and by Kennedy and others to negotiate for the acquisition of some four million acres south of San Antonio that had been promised to Kennedy by Sam Houston. His diaries, notes, and essays on Texas were never published, although a few essays were printed in newspapers and journals of the time. Bernard Quaritch of London obtained Bollaert's papers after his death, and Edward Ayer acquired some 1274 pages of his manuscript material on Texas from Quaritch in 1902, donating them to the Newberry Library in Chicago in 1911. For nearly a half century more they remained unpublished, and it came to be said that all Texas historians could be divided into two types, those who had examined the Bollaert papers and those who had not. When the papers were finally edited and published in 1956, this invaluable resource on early Texas was presented in a capable, well-annotated, reliable edition. A sampling of Bollaert's original drawings were reproduced as well, although all of them deserve a separate, fuller publication.

When Bollaert landed in Texas in early 1842, nine-tenths of its 75,000 population lived within a hundred miles of Galveston. By July of 1844, when he sailed for England, Bollaert had thoroughly traversed virtually all of populated Texas, and had become well acquainted with most of the prominent citizens. While he was in Texas, San Antonio was twice captured by invading Mexican armies and Texas learned the fate of its Santa Fe Expedition of the previous year. During this same period, the Mier Expedition occurred, and Jack Hays and other Texas Rangers set out on numerous Indian campaigns. It was a time of excitement, worry, and near bankruptcy for Texas, and Bollaert observed it all with an honest eye. He tells for example, of President Sam Houston arriving at Washington-on-the-Brazos with his wife and some cabinet members: "On searching for quarters, the President was informed that it was requested to pay the week's board in advance— his melliferous accents had no effect here—and it is said he had ultimately to return to the plantation of a friend with his wife and government."

Joe B. Frantz summed up the value of Bollaert's work: "William Bollaert was that rarity in early Texas—a trained observer, a man who had seen a good bit of the world in a number of professional capacities and who, thank the Lord, knew how to write to be read . . . Every page is quotable, while the choice of subjects ranges as widely as Texans themselves. There are observations on music and dances, on Indians and Negroes, on agriculture and commerce, on the Alamo, and on a nation's Capitol overrun with 'bats, lizards, and stray cattle,' not to mention passages on horse racing, land speculation, and gratuitous titles. On the whole Bollaert was a bull on Texas—but a generally realistic bull. . . . Although it has become commonplace to say that a book is a 'must,' nonetheless it is merely truthtelling when I suggest that this book becomes a standard reference immediately on its appearance.''

"Very little escaped Bollaert's notice," wrote Otis Singletary. "He was introduced to such dignitaries as Houston, Lamar, and Burnet, attended the partisan political rallies which marked the Houston-Lamar struggle, and kept himself informed on the political intrigues of the annexationists. He rapidly adopted the Texan's attitude toward Mexico, joined the Texas Navy, and sailed for a short cruise aboard a privateer. He not only remarked about those two topics which invariably interested all visitors to Texas—rattlesnakes and northers—but also investigated the procedures for growing, ginning, and marketing cotton and made a revealing survey of the myths and realities of the 'peculiar institution' as it operated in Texas. He associated freely with the people; attended their parties, hunting trips, camp meetings, weddings, and horse races; contracted their diseases and swallowed their remedies; ate their food, smoked and chewed their tobacco, and drank their whiskey, egg nog, and persimmon beer. And he wrote about it all.''

19   Bolton, Herbert Eugene (1870-1953) [ed.]

SPANISH EXPLORATION IN THE SOUTHWEST, 1542-1706.

New York: Charles Scribner's Sons, [1916].
Original Narratives of Early American History: Reproduced under the Auspices of the American Historical Association. General Editor: J. Franklin Jameson.
xii,[2],487pp. 22cm. Three folding maps.
Cloth.

Other issues:

✓ (A). New York: Charles Scribner's Sons, 1925. Same collation.
(B). New York: Barnes & Noble, [1959]. x,486pp. 22cm. Cloth. Curiously, this
edition shows the original copyright as 1908.

This volume contains the best English translation of six major
narratives of explorations into Texas, as well as others into New
Mexico, Arizona, and California. Most of the accounts appear here
either for the first time in print or the first time in English. W. S.
Campbell deemed the work "Bolton at his unexcelled best on Spanish-
American history." Lawrence Clark Powell called it "the best source
in English translation of Southwestern beginnings. To read these
original narratives . . . is to leave the muddy present and ascend the
stream of history to its crystalline headwaters."

Bolton states that this volume "is logically the successor in the series
of original narratives to the one edited by [F.W.] Hodge and [T.H.]
Lewis under the title of *Spanish Explorers in the Southern United States,
1528-1543.* In one important respect the present volume differs from the
series in general. The other volumes consist mainly of reproductions
of documents which have hitherto appeared in English; but of this
volume approximately only one-third of the documents have hitherto
been published in English; about one-third have been published in
Spanish only; while nearly one-third have never been published
hitherto in any language. Of the five documents in the collection
which formerly have been published in English, three have been
retranslated for this work." The Massanet "Carta" was translated by
Lilia M. Casis, the De Leon "Itinerary" by Elizabeth West, and the
remainder by Bolton.

The text includes the Texas exploration diary of Fernando del
Bosque of 1675; the journal of Juan Dominguez de Mendoza of 1684;
the account of Father Damian Massanet of 1690; the accounts of
Alonso de Leon of 1689 and 1690; and records of the Espejo and Onate
expeditions into New Mexico, both of which passed through Texas.
The Bosque account is from a manuscript in the Coahuila Archives,
published in part in Spanish in Esteban L. Portillo, *Apuntes para la
Historia Antigua de Coahuila y Texas* (Saltillo, 1886). The Mendoza
material is from a manuscript in the National Archives of Mexico,
hitherto unpublished. Seymour V. Connor states that he compared the
Mendoza translation with the original and considered it "not a very

good one. Some material is deleted. I suspect some graduate student of Bolton was assigned the job." The Massanet account is from a manuscript at Texas A & M, revised from a translation printed in 1899 in the *Quarterly of the Texas State Historical Association* (vol. II, pp. 253-312). The records of the De Leon expeditions appeared in Spanish in Genaro Garcia's *Historia de Nuevo Leon con Noticias sobre Coahuila, Tejas y Nuevo Mexico por el Capitan Alonso de Leon* (Mexico, 1909).

Each diary, journal, itinerary, and report is prefaced by an introductory account by Bolton summarizing the expedition and giving bibliographical details of all surviving related manuscripts. Each account contains annotations giving variant readings, historical commentary, and explanations of geographical locations. Of the latter, Father Stanley said that Bolton "not only traced the documents, but retraced the routes" as well. J. Franklin Jameson, general editor of the series in which the volume appeared, praised the special value of the works in the series: "No subsequent sources can have quite the intellectual interest, none quite the sentimental value, which attaches to these early narratives, springing direct from the brains and hearts of the nation's founders."

A valuable modern study of this period may be found in Elizabeth A. H. John, *Storms Brewed in Other Men's Worlds: The Confrontation of Indians, Spanish, and French in the Southwest,* 1540-1795 (College Station: Texas A & M University Press, 1975, 805pp.).

Basler 3203. Campbell, p.54. Dobie, p.38. Howes B588. Powell, *Southwestern Century* 46. Rader 398.

20 Bolton, Herbert Eugene (1870-1953)

TEXAS IN THE MIDDLE EIGHTEENTH CENTURY: STUDIES IN SPANISH COLONIAL HISTORY AND ADMINISTRATION.

Berkeley: University of California Press, 1915.
University of California Publications in History, Volume III. H. Morse Stephens and Herbert E. Bolton, Editors.
x,[2],501pp. 13 maps and illus. (3 folding). 25cm.
Printed wrappers; also cloth.

Other issues:

(A). New York: Russell & Russell, Publishers, 1962. 501pp. Illus. 23cm. Cloth. 400 copies printed.

(B). Austin & London: University of Texas Press, Published in cooperation with the Texas State Historical Association, 1970. [x],[2],501pp. Two maps, one folding. 22cm. Cloth. Dustjacket.

(C). Paperback edition of (B). Texas History Paperbacks, TH-8. 22cm.

(D). Fascimile of first edition. Millwood, New York: Kraus Reprint Co., 1974. 13 illus. and maps. 24cm. Cloth Verso of title: "Printed in Germany."

This is the best work of scholarship on 18th century Texas. J. Lloyd Mecham called it "the outstanding work on Texas during the entire Spanish period," but Castaneda's seven-volume work must surely be more deserving of that statement. W. E. Dunn more accurately said that it gives "for the first time an authoritative and connected account of the chief events in the history of Texas during the years from 1730 to 1789." It is one of the first works in which Bolton develops his theme of the interrelationship between international influences and local history.

This volume was the outgrowth of four monographs published in the *Southwestern Historical Quarterly,* greatly revised and with much new material. Bolton explained: "In the middle eighteenth century Texas occupied an important position in the northeastern frontier of New Spain . . . In spite of its importance, the history of [Spanish] Texas after 1731 has been little known, and has been regarded as more or less barren. As a matter of fact, the province in that period experienced much activity, and its history offers many and varied interests . . . The present volume is not a history; it is, rather, a collection of special studies, closely related in time and subject-matter, and designed to throw light upon a neglected period in the history of one of the most important of Spain's northern provinces."

The most valuable section of the book is the introductory survey (pp. 1-133), which summarizes the nature of Texas as a buffer province between New Spain and French Louisiana. This is followed by four special studies: "The San Xavier Missions (1745-1768)," "The Reorganization of the Lower Gulf Coast (1746-1768)," "Spanish Activities on the Lower Trinity River (1746-1771)," and "The Removal from the Reoccupation of Eastern Texas (1773-1779)." These are followed by 54 pages of bibliography and index.

The special studies are of interest not only from the standpoint of history, but to the students of ethnology, of economics, and of government as well. Bolton states: "The special studies here presented are based almost exclusively upon manuscript sources, chiefly in the archives of Mexico, Spain, and Texas, and for the most part hitherto unknown and unused. The assembling of these materials, during a period of thirteen years, has been the greater part of my task. My quest has been as romantic as the search for the Golden Fleece. I have burrowed in the dust of the archives of Church and State in Mexico City, in a dozen Mexican state capitals, in Natchitoches, Louisiana, and in numerous places in Texas. The distance travelled in my pursuit of documents would carry me around the globe. I have lived with the *padres* in ruinous old monasteries in out of way villages in the mountains of Mexico . . . I have ridden by team long distances over the Old San Antonio Road, and on horseback in mud fetlock deep."

These travels by Bolton unearthed some of the greatest archival treasures ever found relating to Texas and the Spanish Borderlands. In 1902 George P. Garrison reported that the Mexican archives "constitute, I think it would be safe to say, an almost unexplored wilderness for investigators in the United States." Bolton's mammoth *Guide to Materials for the History of the United States in the Principal Archives of Mexico* (Washington, 1913) provided historians for the first time with a guide to using these new materials for study. In this respect, Bolton's own works must today be studied with care, because so much more new unpublished and unstudied material has become available that much revision is needed in all previous analyses of Spanish Texas. As J. Frank Dobie perceptively wrote: "To some minds Dr. Bolton's habitual justification of Spanish acts and policies will not always seem warranted. . . . He is not a master of English prose, but as a pioneering master of a vast field of history his name will certainly live."

Howes B589. Rader 399. Rittenhouse 70.

21 Bracht, Viktor Friederich (1819-1886)

TEXAS IM JAHRE 1848, NACH MEHRJAHRIGEN BEOBACH-TUNGEN DARGESTELLT.

Elberfeld and Iserlohn: Julius Baedeker, 1849.
xii,[2],322pp. 18cm.
Cloth. Folding map (in some copies).

Other issues:
(A). *Texas in 1848*. San Antonio: Naylor Printing Co., [1931]. xxiv,[2],223pp. 23cm.
Cloth. 2 illus. Contains an additional preface, a chapter entitled "Biographical
Sketches of Viktor Bracht and Dr. Felix Bracht" by translator Charles Frank
Schmidt, an obituary notice of Viktor Bracht, translator's footnotes, and a
page of bibliography.

One of the best Texas immigration guides, this book is also a
valuable contribution to our knowledge of early Texas. Bracht is one
of the few early writers on Texas who based his report almost entirely
on his personal observations. Few men have loved Texas more than
Bracht, whose enthusiasm for his adopted land was based on a careful
study of the country, its flora and fauna, and its people. Yet his book
is one of the few guides to contain criticism as well as praise, and
forthright warnings to prospective immigrants. Terry G. Jordan called
Bracht's work "notoriously unreliable," but I disagree; compared to
most similar Texas books of the period, Bracht's ranks among the
most dependable.

Bracht was born in Duesseldorf, Germany, on September 17, 1819.
He came to Texas in behalf of the German government to assist
colonization activities, landing at Galveston about June 19, 1845. *The
Handbook of Texas* (I,202) is in error when it states that he "proceeded
to New Braunfels, where he lived for a year. He was back in Germany
in 1846-1847 but returned to Texas in 1848." In fact, Bracht stayed in
Texas continuously throughout 1846 and 1847, sailed back to Germany
in 1848, and returned to Texas early in 1849. He traveled throughout
the state and made extensive explorations along the Medina, Guadalupe, San Antonio, Pedernales, Llano, upper Colorado, and San Saba
rivers.

In 1848 Bracht married Sebilla Shaefer in Indianola, then returned
to Germany. There he wrote and published his book, sometime after
November 11, 1848, the date of the Preface contributed by his brother,
Dr. Felix Bracht. The two Brachts then left Germany for good, Viktor
settling in New Braunfels and his brother in northern Bexar County.
In 1855 Viktor moved to San Antonio, running a wholesale grocery

business there until 1860, when he sold out and went to New York. Later in 1860 he settled in Mexico as agent for a railroad company. In 1867 he returned to New York, and in 1869 came back to Texas, settling in Rockport, where he died in 1886.

Part One of the book offers "Contributions . . . Pertaining to Topography, Statistics, and Natural History." Bracht was an astute observer and an accomplished naturalist. In his enthusiasm for his new land he states that "few parts of the earth may be compared to it in productiveness," and that "Texas abounds in game animals beyond any other country in the world." Yet he remarks critically that "One might pronounce the location of Texas especially favorable to world commerce, if the advantages of an extensive and comparatively safe coast line were not greatly lessened by lack of good harbors for large vessels."

On Texas farmers, he comments: "Not even on the oldest plantations in Texas has fertilizer been used. The most that has been done was to let the less fertile sandy lands lie fallow for a year . . . The American, who readily submits to the most arduous labor, shows little taste for the culture of flowers and vegetables. This is due mainly to his practical bent of mind and to his frugality. He appears to be content when he has milk and coffee, corn bread and bacon, chewing tobacco and whiskey."

On Texas culture, Bracht is effusive: "Perhaps no other country in the world with as small a population as that of Texas can boast of so large a percentage of thoroughly, scientifically and liberally educated men of the upper and middle classes as can Texas."

Part Two relates to "Reports about European Colonies in Texas, opinions about Emigration . . . Information for German Emigrants to Texas." Bracht discusses the various German, French, Norwegian, and Irish colonies, describing the towns and countryside of each. He has the highest praise for the lands held by the Germans and French in West Texas, stating that "the Guadalupe River . . . is perhaps more beautiful than any other river in the world." He offers advice and warning to prospective colonists in considerable detail, outlining locations, methods and routes of travel, costs, equipment needed, first crops, building materials required, land values, and how to avoid being cheated or swindled upon arrival.

Part Three contains excerpts from letters written by him from Texas between June, 1845, and November, 1847. These letters, written during his travels in Texas form such places as New Braunfels, Austin, Galveston, Fredericksburg, and Castroville, constitute a valuable addition to the book. They offer on-the-spot reports and impressions of the people and countryside. Various charts follow the letters, and the book ends with a "Final Word to the Readers," a philosophical discussion of why disenchanted Europeans, particularly Germans, can find a new and fruitful life in that "splendid country," Texas.

Agatha, p.7. Clark III-278. Dobie, p.50. Howes B682. Raines, p.29. Sabin 7161.

22 Brown, John Henry (1820-1895)

HISTORY OF TEXAS, FROM 1685 TO 1892.

St. Louis: L. E. Daniell, Publisher, Printed by Becktold & Co., [1892-1893].
Two volumes: 631;591pp. 25 illus. 2 maps. 24cm.
Issued in gray cloth and in full calf, gilt. The work is sometimes found with an 8-page pamphlet index to vol. I and a 7-page pamphlet index to vol. II loosely inserted. A quarto broadside advertisement in my collection advertises the set at $10.00 in cloth, $12.00 in leather, issued by Thos. B. Mitchell, Agent, 241 Live Oak St., Dallas, Texas, and includes complimentary testimonials by Rufus C. Burleson, A. T. Watts, and Seth Shepard. A publisher's dummy in 49pp. bound in cloth was also issued.

Other issues:
(A). Facsimile reprint: Austin and New York: Jenkins Publishing Company, The Pemberton Press, 1970. 2 vols. Cloth. Index added. 600 sets printed.

This is the earliest comprehensive history of Texas written by an active participant. Brown arrived in Texas in November, 1839, on board the steamship *Columbia,* served as an Indian fighter in a Texas Ranger company under John C. Hays, was wounded in the Battle of Salado during the Woll Invasion of 1842, served as a colonel in the Texas militia in the Mexican War, and was at various times a printer and newspaper publisher throughout his career. He composed the "Declaration of Causes which Impel the State of Texas to Secede from the Federal Union" in 1861, was a leader in the Texas Secession Convention, and was Adjutant General of H. E. McCulloch's brigade

HISTORY OF TEXAS.

IN TWO VOLUMES.

By JOHN HENRY BROWN.

REFERRING to the testimonials herewith, from President Rufus C. Burleson, of Baylor University; Judge A. T. Watts, formerly of the Commission of Appeals, and Hon. Seth Shepard, of the Court of Appeals, Washington, D. C., I beg to announce that the above work, handsomely bound, 1220 pages of reading matter, illustrated, will be promptly sent to any part of the state, post paid, on receipt of the price. Cloth edition per set, $10.00, full leather, $12.00. Address, *Mrs Mary M. Brown—184 N. Pearl St Dallas Texas.*

~~THOS. B. MITCHEL,~~ Agent,

241 Live Oak St., Dallas, Texas.

Waco, Texas, June 16.

All lovers of history will rejoice to learn that Col. John Henry Brown, the venerable old Texian, has written a history of Texas, a task for which he is eminently fitted. Few things are so little understood as the real life history of Texas. Several men have written of Texas history with great ability, but few of them were eye-witnesses of what they wrote or have taken the pains to inform themselves impartially of the early history of Texas

I have known Col. John Henry Brown for forty-five years and have always found him honorable and careful in his statement of facts and thoroughly devoted to the honor of Texas. To assume that he or any other man has made no mistakes would be folly. But I think the careful reader of Col. Brown's history will find that he has made as few mistakes as any historian of ancient or modern times.

Rufus C. Burleson, President Baylor University.

Dallas, Texas, September 7th, 1893.

Mr. T. B. Mitchel, Dallas, Texas.

Dear Sir:—After a careful examination of the History of Texas, by Major John Henry Brown, it affords me pleasure to state that I regard this the most thorough, impartial and accurate history of Texas ever published. It is truly a history, prepared by a historian, who, although a participant in very many of the most important events described, impartially treats the whole subject matter of the work. Besides the author, by patient and laborious researches, has been enabled to give many important documents, facts and incidents, heretofore unknown to the public.

I cheerfully venture the prediction, that this will ever remain the standard history of the particular period and subject matter to which it relates. Yours truly,

A. T. Watts.

Washington, D. C., September 5th, 1893.

Thos. B Mitchel, Esq., Dallas, Texas.

Dear Sir:—The two volumes of Texas History are at hand and I am well pleased with my examination of them. The book fills a long-felt want and I trust will have a wide circulation, not only in but out of Texas. Please remember me kindly to Major Brown. Truly yours,

Seth Shepard.

during the Civil War. After the war he was mayor of Dallas and a leader in drafting the 1876 Texas Constitution, which still governs the state. Brown's massive personal correspondence and research files, which occupy 33 shelf-feet in the University of Texas Archives, are among the most useful collections for Texas historical research.

Brown collected materials for fifty years, then devoted four entire years, from 1889 through 1893, to writing his history of Texas, spending the last year in St. Louis to be near the publisher and help the work through the printing process. Rufus C. Burleson, President of Baylor University, wrote at the time of its appearance: "Several men have written of Texas history with great ability, but few of them were eye-witnesses of what they wrote [as was this] venerable old Texian." A. T. Watts wrote that it was "the most thorough, impartial and accurate history of Texas ever published." On the other hand, Eugene C. Barker wrote that it "is bitterly hostile to [Stephen F.] Austin, is uncritical, and is not always honest, but the book contains many documents and is useful when used with care."

Another reviewer stated that Brown's work could "be scrutinized in vain to find a deliberate utterance antagonistic to public or private virtue or unfaithful to the glory of Texas"—which is the work's primary shortcoming. Less than a hundred pages are devoted to the period before Anglo-American colonization. The Anglo-Texans are presented uniformly in a complimentary light; the Mexicans are always villains. As may be expected, the period of the Confederacy is treated in less than an objective manner.

His description of John S. "Rip" Ford, for example, during one of the last Civil War battles, fought in South Texas, states: "He addressed his small force, while Springfield rifle balls were whistling around him, about as follows: 'Men, we have whipped the enemy in all our previous fights! We can do it again.' The men shouted hurrah for Old Rip. As the hurrahs ceased, he cried with a fierce stentorian voice, *forward! charge!* The response was a Texian yell, and a charge which no infantry line ever formed on the Rio Grande could withstand. I have often been asked why no negroes were captured in the last fight of the war. In response, I have generally said, 'they outran our cavalry horses.' "

Nevertheless, Brown's history is replete with historical facts presented for the first time, and with incidents that would not have been remembered without Brown's work. His descriptions of events in which he participated are vivid and memorable. The set is still useful today, and forms one of the basic research sources for 19th century Texas.

Howes B856. Rader 513. Raines, p.32.

23   **Brown, John Henry (1820-1895)**

INDIAN WARS AND PIONEERS OF TEXAS.

Austin: L.E. Daniell, Publisher, [1896].
[Verso of title:] Press of Nixon-Jones Printing Company, St. Louis, Mo., Becktold Printing and Book Mfg. Co., St. Louis, Mo., Binders.
762pp., in double columns. 124 plates. 30cm.
Full morocco.
There are two issues, priority unknown, one with better impressions of the plates and a slightly different setting of the title page. In my copy of the book is a loosely-inserted advertisement card from the Delbridge Co., St. Louis, offering the book at $5.00, stating this is cheap because of it being "2 inches thick and weighing seven pounds" and because it "will be held and handed down from generation to generation as a priceless heirloom . . . will soon pass 'out of print' and in a few years, or generations, will be sold for large sums."

Other issues:
(A). Facsimile reprint: Easley, South Carolina: Southern Historical Press, 1978. 762pp. plus index. 30cm.

This is Brown's most important book and one of the best works on Texas Indian fighters and early pioneers. The information was gathered over his entire fifty years in Texas, and the text was completed shortly before his death. Although he felt his *History of Texas* was his major contribution, that work pales beside *Indian Wars and Pioneers of Texas* for interest, information, and reliability.

The large volume contains hundreds of biographical sketches of early Texans of the 19th century, with an immense amount of material that appears nowhere else. Most valuable of all are the accounts of the numerous fights and skirmishes between early Texans and Indians.

Only in the works of J. W. Wilbarger and A. J. Sowell does one find a comparable amount of historical data on this facet of Texas history.

Brown was himself a participant in some of the bloodiest battles. Regarding the Battle of Plum Creek in 1840, he states: "The writer, then a boy of nineteen, was the youngest of the party . . . The Indians, as we neared them, took position in a point of oaks . . . Bands of warriors then began encircling us . . . In one of the isolated combats it fell my lot to dismount a warrior wearing a buffalo skin cap surmounted with horns. He was dead when I dismounted to secure the prize, which was [later sent] to the Cincinnati museum, and was still there in 1870."

Brown worked sporadically on this project throughout his career, contributing sections of it to periodicals such as *DeBow's Review* and *Texas Farm and Ranch Magazine*. There is an interesting letter from another Texas historian, James T. DeShields, in Brown's archives, dated 1887, complaining that Brown was stealing his idea: "Long before I knew of you or had even corresponded with you, I was scribbling on 'Indian Wars' in Texas [but since Brown announced his work] I did not continue my efforts in that direction but at once commenced to collect & compile sketches of noted Texians, as I thought this would not conflict with your work. Recently I see you are including sketches of famous Texians, etc. I shall now leave the field open to you, by giving up my last cherished idea." Nevertheless, DeShields continued to compile his own work, *Border Wars of Texas;* it was published in 1912 and is distinctly inferior.

Without question, Brown used all the sources he could find, sometimes stepping none-too-lightly on the toes of other writers. My own family, for example, never forgave him for quoting large sections verbatim from the newspaper articles of my forebear, John Holland Jenkins, without getting permission or giving any credit. The result for Brown, however, was a book with few peers in the historiography of Texas Indian fighting. Mrs. Henry Joseph Morris issued *Everyname Index of 7,000 Entries Extracted from The Indian Wars of Texas by John Henry Brown* (Dallas: Texas State Genealogical Society, 1976, 12pp.).

Howes B857. Rader 514.

24 Cabeza de Vaca, Alvar Nunez (ca.1490-1555)

LA RELACION QUE DIO ALVAR NUNEZ CABECA DE VACA DE LO ACAESCIDO ENLAS INDIAS ENLA ARMADA DONDE YUA POR GOUERNADOR PAPHILO DE NARBAEZ DESDE EL ANO DE VEYNTE Y SIETE HASTA EL ANO D'TREYNTA Y SEYS QUE BOLUIO A SEVILLA CON TRES DE SU COMPANIA.

Zamora: Por los honrrados varones Augustin de paz y Juan Picardo companeros impressores de libros vezinos dela dicha cuidad, a costa y espensas del virtuoso varon Juan pedro musetti mercader de libros vezino de Medina del campo, [1542]. [134]pp. [Title and 66 leaves: Sig: A-H, eight leaves in each; I, which has three leaves].

Other issues:

(A). *La relacion y comentarios del gouernador Alvar Nunez Cabeca de Vaca, de lo acaescido en las dos jornadas que hizo a las Indias.* Valladolid: por Francisco Fernandez de Cordoua, [1555]. [292]pp. [Title; numbered leaves ii-lvi, second title leaf and one unnumbered leaf; numbered leaves lvii-clxiiii. Sig.: A-S, eight leaves each, with two unnumbered leaves between Sig. G. and H. Folios xv, lxxxv, and cxliv misnumbered xxv, lxxxiii, and clxiiii respectively.]

(B). Ramusio, Gian Battista [ed.]. *Delle Navigatione e Viaggi.* Venice: Heredi di Luc' Antonio Giunti, 1556. Volume IV of a series. Includes a translation into Italian of the 1542 edition of Cabeza de Vaca. The Ramusio collection has been reprinted many times. First edition in Italian.

(C). Purchas, Samuel. *Purchas: His Pilgrimage* . . . London, 1625. Includes in vol. IV, book 8, an extract translated into English. The Purchas set has been reprinted many times. First English edition of any part of Cabeza de Vaca's narrative.

(D). Gonzalez Barcia, Andres, [ed.]. *Historiadores Primitivos de las Indias Occidentales* . . . Madrid, 1749. 3 volumes. Includes the text of Cabeza de Vaca in the second volume, as well as Antonio Ardoino's *Examen Apologetico de la Historica Narracion de los Naufragios* . . . *de Alvar Nunez Cabeca de Vaca,* originally printed in Madrid in 1736.

(E). *Voyages, Relations et Memoires Originaux* . . . *Relation et Naufrages d'Alvar Nunez Cabeca de Vaca.* Paris: Arthus Bertrand, 1837. [4],302pp. Also another volume containing the Commentaries. Paris: Arthus Bertrand, 1837. [4],507pp. First edition in French.

(F). *Amerika, Seine Entdeckung und Seine Vorzeit.* Meissen: F. W. Goedsche, 1839. 2 volumes. Includes a translation of Cabeza de Vaca from the 1837 French edition into German by L. von Alvensleben. First edition in German.

(G). *The Narrative of Alvar Nunez Cabeca de Vaca.* Washington: [George W. Riggs], 1851. 138pp. Maps. Translation of the 1555 edition by Buckingham Smith. 110 copies printed, 10 on large paper. First American edition, and first true translation in English.

(H). Vedia, Enrique de [ed.]. *Historiadores Primitivos de Indias* . . . Madrid, 1852. Includes a reprint of the 1555 edition in vol. xxii of the series entitled *Biblioteca de Autores Espanoles*.

(I). Davis, W. H. H. *Spanish Conquest of New Mexico*. Doylestown, Pa., 1869. Includes a paraphrase of (G).

(J). Kingsley, Henry. *Tales of Old Travels*. London, 1869. Includes a paraphrase of (G).

(K). *Relation of Alvar Nunez Cabeca de Vaca*. Albany: Printed by J. Munsell for H. C. Murphy, 1871. 300pp. Illus. Revision of the Buckingham Smith translation by John Gilmary Shea, with added material. 100 copies printed.

(L). Reprint of (H). Madrid, 1877.

(M). *The Journey of Alvar Nunez Cabeza de Vaca* . . . New York: A. S. Barnes, 1905. xxii, [2], 231pp. Map. Cloth. Edited by Ad. F. Bandelier and translated by Fanny Bandelier. Best English translation.

(N). *Relacion de los Naufragios y Comentarios* . . . Madrid: V. Suarez, 1906. Two volumes. Best edition in Spanish, with lengthy introduction.

(O). Hodge, F. W. [ed.]. *Spanish Explorers in the Southern United States, 1528-1543*. New York: C. Scribner's Sons, 1907. xv, 411pp. Illus. Includes a translation of Cabeza de Vaca by Hodge, and other narratives, with excellent introduction.

(P). Same as (N). Madrid, 1917.

(Q). *Naufragios y Comentarios* . . . Madrid: Calpe, [1922]. xiv, 468pp. Maps.

(R). Same as (M). New York: Allerton Book Co., 1922. Same collation.

(S). *Schiffbuchs die Ungluecksfahrt der Narvaez-Expedition nach der Suedkueste von Nordamerika* . . . Stuttgart: Strecker und Schroeder, 1925.

(T). Same as (N). Madrid, 1927.

(U). *Naufragios y Relacion de la Journada que Hizo a la Florida* . . . Madrid: Cia. Ibero Americana Publicaciones, [1928]. viii, 194pp.

(V). *Relation That Alvar Nunez Cabeca de Vaca Gave of What Befel* . . . San Francisco: Grabhorn Press, 1929. [10],122,[2]pp. Illus. Reissue of the 1871 Buckingham Smith translation. 300 copies printed.

(W). Same as (Q). Madrid: Espasa-Calpe, 1932. xiv, 355pp.

(X). Same as (W), 1934.

(Y). Same as (V), 1936.

(Z). Long, Haniel. *Interlinear to Cabeza de Vaca: His Relation of the Journey* . . . Santa Fe: Writer's Editions Inc., [1936]. An edited paraphrase.

(AA). Reprint of (Z), [1939].

(BB). Hallenbeck, Cleve. *Alvar Nunez Cabeza de Vaca: The Journey and Route* . . . Glendale, Calif.: The Arthur H. Clark Company, 1940. 326pp. Includes a paraphrase translation by Hallenbeck.

(CC). *Naufragios y Comentarios*. Buenos Aires: Cia. General Fabril Financiera, 1942. 262pp. Map.

(DD). *Naufragios y Comentarios, con Dos Cartas*. Buenos Aires: Espasa-Calpe Argentina, 1943.

(EE).   *Naufragios de Alvar Nunez Cabeza de Vaca* . . . Mexico, 1944. 3 vols. With other material.

(FF).   Same as (W), 1944.

(GG).   Reprint of (Z) under a new title: *The Power Within Us: Cabeza de Vaca's Relation of His Journey* . . . New York: Duell, Sloan and Pearce, [1944]. 37pp.

(HH).   *Naufragios* . . . Madrid: Aguilar, Imp. Engenio Sanchez Leal, [1945]. 463pp. Illus.

(II).   Same as (DD), second edition, 1946.

(JJ).   Same as (H). Madrid, 1946.

(KK).   Same as (GG). London: Drummond, 1946. Foreword by Henry Miller.

(LL).   Same as (DD), third edition, 1947.

(MM).   Facsimile reprint of (O). New York: Barnes & Noble, Inc., [1953].

(NN).   *Cabeza de Vaca's Adventures in the Unknown Interior of America.* New York: Collier Books, [1961]. 152pp. Translated and edited by Cyclone Covey.

(OO).   *Schiffbrueche Bericht uber die Ungluecksfahrt der Narvaez-Expedition nach der Suedkueste Nordamerikas* . . . Munich: K. Renner, [1963]. 181pp. Translated by Franz Termer.

(PP).   Facsimile reprint of (M). Chicago: Rio Grande Press, [1964]. xxxvi,[2],231pp. New introduction by Donald C. Cutter.

(QQ).   *Relacion of Nunez Cabeza de Vaca.* Ann Arbor, Mich.: University Microfilms, [1966]. Facsimile of the 1871 Buckingham Smith edition.

(RR).   Reprint of (Z). [Pittsburgh:] Frontier Press, [1969].

(SS).   Reprint of (O). New York: Barnes & Noble, [1971]. xiii, 413pp.

(TT).   *The Narrative of Alvar Nunez Cabeza de Vaca.* Barre, Mass.: Printed for the Imprint Society, 1972. 271pp. Reprint of the Bandelier translation, with some new material. Introduction by John Francis Bannon.

(UU).   Facsimile reprint of (R). New York: AMS Press, 1973.

(VV).   Reprint of (O). New York: Barnes & Noble, [1977].

This is the first book relating to Texas. F. W. Hodge called Cabeza de Vaca's journey "the most remarkable in the record of American exploration, and as a narrative of suffering and privation the relation . . . perhaps has no equal in the annals of the northern continent." Donald C. Cutter said that "of all the strange and wonderful stories that the discovery and exploration of the New World produced, there is none for sheer courage and struggle for survival against long odds that can compare with the tale of Alvar Nunez Cabeza de Vaca. His account . . . is the prototype and masterpiece of this genre of true adventure." Rosenbach called it "the cornerstone of the history of the Spanish Southwest."

Cabeza de Vaca, also known as Nunez Cabeza de Vaca or simply as Nunez, joined the expedition of Panfilo de Narvaez to conquer and colonize the northern coast of the Gulf of Mexico. With 600 colonists and soldiers, Narvaez set out in 1527, landing near Tampa Bay, Florida, in 1527, after losing some of his ships and many men. With only 300 men left, Narvaez sent his ships off to skirt the coast and then led the settlers inland on foot, planning to meet the fleet at a pre-arranged point. After many hardships, Narvaez arrived but found no fleet. In desperation, the remaining group built rafts and launched into the Gulf—directly into a storm. About eighty men were washed ashore somewhere in Texas, probably near High Island on the Boliver Peninsula. Others believe they landed on Galveston Island.

By the spring of 1529, there were only fifteen survivors, among whom was Cabeza de Vaca. A band of Indians captured them, and they were worked as slaves for several years. Gaining a reputation as a medicine man and trader, Cabeza de Vaca with three others gradually made his way towards Mexico. He finally arrived on the western coast of northern Mexico in 1536. The hardships of the group were virtually unparalleled. Cabeza de Vaca was sent back to Spain to report on his adventures to the king. He gave the first reports of the buffalo, and the first reports of the mythical cities of gold. One of the men with Cabeza de Vaca was Estevanico the Black (or the Moor), who later accompanied Fray Marcos de Niza on his explorations.

Cabeza de Vaca was appointed captain general of Rio de la Plata in Paraguay in 1540, and after adventures there returned to Spain in 1545. In 1542, his *Relacion* of his Texas adventures was published. Only one perfect copy (New York Public Library) and two incomplete copies (John Carter Brown Library and British Museum) of this edition are known. In 1555, a revised edition, including his *Comentarios* on South America, was issued at Valladolid. About fifteen copies of this edition are known to exist, of which only two are in Texas.

The best bibliographical study of the Cabeza de Vaca narrative is in Henry R. Wagner's *The Spanish Southwest*. Wagner offers evidence to indicate that there may have been an earlier edition, possibly in 1537. No one has successfully identified all the printings of the work, and the 49 listed above represent only a beginning at a complete listing. Nor has anyone succeeded in tracing Cabeza de Vaca's exact route of travel, although many have tried. Cleve Hallenbeck, *Alvar*

Nunez Cabeza de Vaca (Glendale: Clark, 1940), makes a detailed attempt in this regard.

Agatha, p.1. Church 100. Clark I-4. Field 230. *Fifty Texas Rarities* #1. Harrisse 239. Leclerc 2487. Palau 197101. Raines, p.38. Sabin 9768. Streeter *Americana Beginnings* 8. Vail 2. Wagner *Spanish Southwest* #1.

25 Carter, Robert Goldthwait (1845-1936)

ON THE BORDER WITH MACKENZIE; OR, WINNING WEST TEXAS FROM THE COMANCHES.

Washington, D.C.: Eynon Printing Company, Inc., Publishers. 812 15th St., N.W., [1935].
[2],xviii,418,[2],419-542pp. 3 plates. 23cm.
Cloth.

Other issues:
(A). New York: Antiquarian Press, 1961. 580pp. Illus. 23cm. Cloth. Foreword by Jeff Dykes. Includes reprints of six additional pamphlets by Carter.

This is one of the best sources on the Federal cavalry campaigns against the Indians in the 1870's. Jeff Dykes described it as "the most complete account of the Indian wars of the Texas frontier in the Seventies." John M. Carroll wrote that "Carter's enormously important writings on frontier military history will be recognized as source material for all future historians." L. F. Sheffy called it "a splendid contribution to the early frontier history of West Texas. . . . It is a story filled with humor and pathos, tragedies and triumphs, hunger and thirst, war and adventure."

Robert G. Carter participated in 21 major engagements in the Union army in the Civil War, then entered West Point and graduated in 1870. Three months later he married a New England socialite and left for the Texas frontier eight days after his wedding. He begins his narrative with an account of his "wedding trip" through the Indian-infested countryside to a wedding bower in a tent at Fort Concho. For five years thereafter, Carter crisscrossed West Texas with the Fourth U.S. Cavalry chasing hostile Indians. His young wife, who nearly died several times and who bore him two children while following the cavalry camp, became almost as famous as Elizabeth Custer. Gen.

Charles King wrote to Carter: "The history of your own career . . . is almost without parallel but, to my knowledge and belief, hers stands unrivaled."

John Warren Hunter said of Carter: "He became familiar with every trail made by the savages and outlaws; mastered every phase of Indian ruse, signs, signals and strategy, and in the course of time, he became a terror, not only to the Comanches, but to evil doers of every description." Frank Tankersley, an old pioneer, once said of Carter: "He'll follow their trail to the jumpin' off place, and when he comes up with 'em and gets through with 'em, the ground will be tore up, the bushes bit off, an' blood, hair, livers, and lights will be scattered all round."

For his bravery in one battle, Carter was awarded the Medal of Honor. His immediate commander was another legendary figure, Ranald S. Mackenzie, who had graduated at the top of his West Point class, been breveted major general in the Civil War, and received four battle wounds before coming to Texas—where Carter watched him calmly continue to command in a skirmish while having an arrow pulled out of his thigh. Indian warfare was new to both men. Carter writes: "It differed so greatly from what we old Civil War veterans had seen, and so little was known of it that it proved to be an absolutely new kind of warfare, and the experience we had to gain, and that quickly . . . was of a kind we had never seen or encountered." Their cannons were so useless that they lay neglected; when Gen. William T. Sherman arrived to tour their outpost, they could find no one among them who even knew how to fire them as a welcome salute. But Mackenzie's men did learn to use Colt revolvers and repeating rifles, and to laugh at the little Smith and Wesson pocket pistols "which would not bruise a man at fifteen feet."

Carter's narrative is poorly written, his ego is a bit trying at times, and he almost bursts with what we now call prejudice. On the other hand, he pulls no punches in this outspoken narrative, and the reader always knows where he stands. This is best exemplified in his vilification of his old enemy, Quanah Parker, especially when Quanah was called a hero for bringing in his band to make peace—only after, in Carter's view, there was no hope of survival otherwise. Carter was particularly galled when he saw Quanah at "Theodore Roosevelt's second inauguration . . . ride up Pennsylvania Avenue in the inaugural column with other 'good Indians,' most of whom had dipped their hands in many a white settler's blood on the once far off borderland of the West.'' It must be remembered that Carter wrote this volume over a twenty-year period between the ages of 70 and 90, and had watched his old fellow Indian Campaign officers struggle in vain to get pensions, while the Indians they had fought were given land and aid.

Some chapters of the book appeared in magazines as early as 1886, and some were printed as separate pamphlets in 1919-1920, each limited to 100 copies for private distribution to friends. Jeff Dykes says that ''the text of this book was ready for the printer many years before it was finally issued. It was offered to at least a dozen publishers—it was praised by some but they did not buy it. . . . One publisher thought that he might be interested provided the captain would convert the book to a novel with an Indian heroine. Another suggested that the captain secure the services of a professional writer to 'whip the manuscript into shape'. . . . Carter indignantly rejected both suggestions.'' It is a shame he did not accept the latter advice.

Nevertheless, Carter's work is of great value and interest not only for his special, if prejudiced, point of view, but also for the intimate view it gives us of the Federal cavalry on the western Texas frontier. Carter states: ''So far little attention has been paid to the facts having to do with the history of West Texas, while every phase of the history of the older portions of the State have been dealt with. This section has a history all its own just as fascinating and colorful as any other part of Texas; probably more so.'' Two modern accounts of the Mackenzie years that are excellent studies are Ernest Wallace, *Ranald S. Mackenzie on the Texas Frontier* (Lubbock: West Texas Museum Assn., 1964, 214pp.) and Ernest Wallace [ed.], *Ranald S. Mackenzie's Official Correspondence Relating to Texas, 1873-1879* (Lubbock: West Texas Museum Assn., 1868, 241pp.).

Campbell, p.177. Howes C195. Rader 611.

26   Casdorph, Paul Douglas (1932-   )

A HISTORY OF THE REPUBLICAN PARTY IN TEXAS, 1865-1965.

Austin: The Pemberton Press, 1965.
Introduction by Dwight D. Eisenhower.
[14],315pp. Illus. Jacket design by William D. Wittliff. 24cm.
Cloth, dustjacket.

Other issues:
(A). Special edition, bound in calf, signed by the author, and limited to 250
    numbered copies. Four of these copies were also signed by Eisenhower.

To date this is the only monograph on the history of the Republican
Party in Texas. O. Douglas Weeks, in *American Historical Review*, stated:
"With the emergence of the Republican party to new prominence in
Texas beginning with the first Eisenhower victory in 1952, there has
been a need for a published history of the party and its activities in
the state. This has been filled to a considerable extent by the present
volume, which covers a century of history from the birth of the party
during Reconstruction to the defeat of Goldwater in 1964." Allen
Maxwell said Casdorph "has filled a real need by writing a factual,
nonpartisan history." E. W. Benton called it "an interesting, objective,
readable, and fact-filled book," and Dayton Kelley deemed it an
"excellently-written and scholarly-researched narrative." Dudley Sharp
said it is "a most revealing history which should be important reading
to all interested in government," and Harold Simpson called it "a
definitive and much needed contribution to the political history of the
Lone Star State."

Professor Weeks outlined the contents as follows: "This chronological
account carries us through the ups and downs of the Republican
organization from its brief dominance in the later 1860's and early
1870's through the various phases of its role as a small minority party
during the late nineteenth and much of the twentieth centuries. The
period of Negro leadership under Cuney from 1883 to 1898 and the
succeeding struggle between the 'Black and Tan' and the 'Lily White'
elements for the control of the party machinery are the subjects of
two chapters. Meanwhile, during the last quarter of the nineteenth
century, the Republicans played politics with the Greenback party and
its successor, the Populist party, a part of the story to which the
author might have given more attention. Three chapters cover the
first half of the twentieth century and deal with the Bull Moosers, the
rivalry of Wurzbach and Creager for control of the party, and the

long regime of Creager . . . '' The remainder of the work deals with
the party after World War II.

Ironically, there is no comparable history of the Democratic Party
in Texas, although the Democrats have dominated most of Texas
history since statehood. Vincent P. DeSantis, in *Journal of American
History,* wrote of the Casdorph book: "Both major parties in the
United States are venerable institutions, and both have been closely
associated with some of the most important events and developments
over the last hundred years or so. Like other important, useful
institutions, they deserve written histories. But there are few books
dealing with the history of either one of the two major parties,
especially on the state level. Thus Paul Casdorph's book is a welcome
addition to the literature on the Republican party. . . . The book
makes a contribution in several ways. It is the first systematic account
of the Republican Party in Texas and thus will be useful to those
interested in both national and state party history. Second, it will
serve as a reference for students of Texas history. There are statistics
and information about conventions and personalities, as well as
biographical sketches of Republican candidates, officers, and convention delegates. In the appendix there is a complete roster, over three
thousand names, of every Texas delegate and alternate to the Republican national conventions from 1868 through 1964.''

Casdorph's book has two flaws, one on the part of the author and
one on my part as publisher. Casdorph fails to give any critical analysis
whatsoever. He states that it is his deliberate intention that "no great
attempt has been made to explain or analyze party platforms and
organization or voting patterns across the state." The book would be
much better and more useful if he had interpreted the motives of the
party and the influences leading to party support, or lack of it, in the
various sections of the state. These analyses have yet to be done in
any systematic manner in any Texas book. Casdorph's work consists
primarily of the events occurring during fifty-three elections depicted
seriatim. It nevertheless contains such a wealth of data and statistics
unavailable elsewhere, that I believe it worthy of inclusion in a
collection of basic Texas books. One excellent new book that provides
interpretation of a key era is Carl H. Moneyhon, *Republicanism in
Reconstruction Texas.* (Austin: University of Texas Press, 1980. 319pp.).

The other fault of the book is the plethora of typographical errors, as well as some minor factual errors, that could have been corrected had I taken the time or gone to the expense of providing adequate proofreading. Joe B. Frantz in 1975 wrote that Jenkins publications "invariably show certain signs of haste. Proofreading is erratic, and not infrequently the book itself has a slapdash quality about its makeup." This criticism can be justly laid against a number of Pemberton Press publications between 1963 and 1975, during which period I left all proofreading entirely in the hands of the author and neglected to provide the editorial guidance incumbent upon a publisher.

27 Castaneda, Carlos Eduardo (1896-1958)

OUR CATHOLIC HERITAGE IN TEXAS, 1519-1936.

Austin: Von Boeckmann-Jones Company, 1936-1958.
Edited by Paul J. Foik. Prepared under the auspices of the Knights of Columbus of Texas.

Seven volumes, as below:
I.   THE MISSION ERA: THE FINDING OF TEXAS, 1519-1693. (Austin, 1936) [xxii],444pp. Fld. map., 7 illus. 26 cm.
II. THE MISSION ERA: THE WINNING OF TEXAS, (1692-1731. Austin, 1936) [xv],390pp. Fld. map, 7 illus. 26cm.
III. THE MISSION ERA: THE MISSION AT WORK, 1731-1761. (Austin, 1938) [xv], 474pp. Fld. map, 6 illus. 26cm.
IV. THE MISSION ERA: THE PASSING OF THE MISSIONS, 1762-1782. (Austin, 1939) [xv],409pp. Fld. map., 7 illus. 26 cm.
V.   THE MISSION ERA: THE END OF THE SPANISH REGIME, 1780-1810. (Austin, 1942) [xv],514pp. Fld. map, 8 illus. 26cm.
VI. TRANSITION PERIOD: THE FIGHT FOR FREEDOM, 1810-1836. (Austin, 1950) [xvii],384pp. Fld. map, 7 illus. 26cm.
VII. THE CHURCH IN TEXAS SINCE INDEPENDENCE, 1836-1950. (Austin, 1958) [xx],561pp. Fld. map, 9 illus. 26cm.
Cloth.
Other issues:
(A). Facsimile reprint. New York: Arno Press, 1976. 7 volumes. 23cm. Cloth. The Chicano Heritage Series. Carlos E. Cortes, Advisory Editor.

The best history of the three centuries of Spanish and Mexican Texas, this became for the author a lifetime project. Eugene C. Barker

Does your library contain this set of

BOOKS

Our Catholic Heritage In Texas

BY CARLOS E. CASTAÑEDA

IN SEVEN VOLUMES

THE MOST COMPLETE HISTORY OF TEXAS AND THE SOUTHWEST WRITTEN IN A CONTINUOUS NARRATIVE — EXCITING AS A NOVEL — MORE THRILLING THAN A MYSTERY — THIS IS ONE SET OF BOOKS THAT EVERY LIBRARY SHOULD HAVE

PUBLISHED BY

VON BOECKMANN-JONES COMPANY

110 EAST NINTH ST. — AUSTIN, TEXAS

said of it: "The important contribution of the author is the smoothly organized, unified, authoritative and readable narrative. As a history of Texas for the period [it] leaves nothing to be desired." George P. Hammond called it a "splendid contribution to southwestern history. . . . The author has pioneered new ground." As William R. Hogan pointed out, "the choice of the title was unfortunate" because it does not indicate the full scope of the subject matter, which is comprehensive and includes every aspect of Texas history.

Castaneda gives us the first detailed account of literally dozens of expeditions and settlements in Texas. "The traditional eight or ten expeditions into Texas up to 1731," he states, "have been enlarged to ninety-two, and the list of missions expanded from an equal number to more than fifty." The story of Cabeza de Vaca, for example, is well known, but Castaneda discovered an account of a band of Spaniards shipwrecked in Texas in 1553, all but two killed by Indians. "Nowhere in the annals of American history," he says, "is a more impressive episode to be found." He opens a world of entirely new history for the Big Bend region and for South Texas, and provides by far the most complete account of the missions in the San Antonio-Goliad region and in East Texas. For a period of history in Texas once thought to have been virtually barren except for scattered desultory expeditions, Castaneda shows us a Texas "throbbing with activity."

Castaneda was aided by Paul J. Foik, who served as general editor of the first four volumes, but died during preparation of the fifth. The two men performed the most extensive research study ever conducted, before or since, into the virtually untapped manuscript collections in Mexican and Spanish archives. Literally tens of thousands of documents, journals, diaries, and letters relating to Texas were examined which had never before been read by a historian. For example, in the third volume there are thirty pages of bibliography, only three of which are devoted to printed works. In all there are 150 pages of bibliography and superb indices in each volume totaling 248 pages. Numerous original maps and paintings are reproduced for the first time in this work. On the other hand, Castaneda is not always dependable in his analyses of the events he describes, and his work is best utilized as a guide to the original sources.

The coverage of the latter part of the period 1800-1836 is weakest, emphasizing the Mexican viewpoint but doing so fairly and with many hitherto unused sources. But the coverage of the early years of the 19th century is extraordinary, and remains by far the best source at the present time. "Few Texan or Mexican historians," Castaneda writes, "have realized that the 1811 revolution of Casas in San Antonio proved a powerful incentive to the leaders of the movement for independence in Mexico and induced Hidalgo and his companions to wind their way to the north, and that the counterrevolution of Zambrano not only ended the first Texan revolt but also lead to the ultimate capture of the leaders of Mexican independence, an incident which changed the whole course of events and delayed the consummation of independence for a decade. Likewise, it has never before been brought out that the declaration of independence drawn . . . in San Antonio in 1813 is the first of its kind in Spanish North America."

The last volume, unlike the others, is devoted strictly to a history of the activities of the Catholic Church in Texas from 1836 to 1950. Ironically, this proved to be the most difficult volume to write. Castaneda states: "Record keeping by the Spaniards was a conscientious task meticulously observed and in spite of the ravages of time, weather, and political strife in Mexico, abundant and complete records were found that made the reconstruction of the past much easier than that of more recent times." This volume concluded the project, of which Castaneda remarks: "Planned as a cooperative enterprise under a general editor originally, each volume was to have been written by a different author in order to distribute the burden. But after [the first two] the author was prevailed upon to write one more volume in the series while other authors could be found. . . . But as years passed the historical commission . . . argued that the writer continue with the remaining volumes to give the series uniformity of style and presentation. Reluctantly the author agreed to write each succeeding volume, prolonging a labor of love. . . . The author is greatly relieved to bring to a conclusion at last a task undertaken almost a quarter of a century ago."

28 Castaneda, Pedro de (ca. 1515-ca. 1554)

. . . RELACION DU VOYAGE DE CIBOLA, ENTERPRIS EN 1540.

Paris: Arthus Bertrand, 1838.
Volume IX of Voyages, *Relations et Memoires Originaux pour Servir a l'Histoire de la Decouverte de l'Amerique,* edited by H. Ternaux-Compans.
[4],xvi,392pp. 22cm.
Wrappers.

Other issues:

(A). "Account of the Expedition to Cibola Which Took Place in the Year 1540, in Which All Those Settlements, Their Ceremonies and Customes are Described" and "Relacion de la Journada de Cibola . . . " In: *Fourteenth Annual Report of the Bureau of Ethnology to the Secretary of the Smithsonian Institution,* Part I. Washington: Government Printing Office, 1896. [1],lxi,[1],637pp. Illus. Maps. Accompanying papers, "The Coronado Expedition," by George Parker Winship, pp. 339-613. The Spanish text is on pages 414-469 and the English translation by Winship is on pages 470-546. First edition in English, and first edition in the original Spanish.

(B). Winship, George Parker [ed.]. *The Journey of Coronado, 1540-1542 . . . As Told by Himself and Others.* New York: A. S. Barnes & Company, 1904. xxxiv,251pp. First separate edition in English, taken from the Winship translation of 1896. Winship states: "In the present book many passages . . . have been revised and corrected."

(C). *The Narrative of the Expedition of Coronado, by Pedro de Castaneda.* In Frederick W. Hodge, *Spanish Explorers in the Southern United States,* 1528-1543. New York: Charles Scribner's Sons, [1907]. xv,411pp. The Winship translation of Castaneda is on pages 273-387.

(D). Reprint of (B). New York: Allerton Book Co., 1922.

(E). *The Journey of Francisco Vazquez de Coronado, 1540-1542, as Told by Pedro de Castaneda, Francisco Vazquez de Coronado, and Others.* San Francisco: The Grabhorn Press, 1933. xxvii, [3],134,[12]pp. The Winship translation with notes by F. W. Hodge. 550 copies printed.

(F). Hammond, George P., and Agapito Rey [eds.], *Narratives of the Coronado Expedition,* 1540-1542. Albuquerque: University of New Mexico Press, 1940. [12],413pp.

(G). Reprint of (C). New York: Barnes & Noble, Inc., [1953].

(H). Facsimile reprint of (A). Chicago: The Rio Grande Press, [1964]. xv[1],403pp. New introduction by Donald C. Cutter. The publisher, incredibly, extracted only the Coronado section from the Ethnology report and renumbered the pages; consequently, all the many page references in the footnotes and index are rendered unusable.

(I). Meredith, Robert K. *Riding with Coronado, from Pedro de Castaneda's Eyewitness Account* . . . Boston: Little, Brown, [1964]. xiv, 107pp. Paraphrase of the Winship translation.

(J). Reprint of (B). New York: Greenwood Press, [1969;].

(K). Reprint of (C). New York: Barnes & Noble, [1971].
(L). Reprint of (D). New York: AMS Press, [1972].
(M). Reprint of (C). New York: Barnes & Noble, [1977].

This is the best account of Coronado's famous expedition in search of the seven cities of gold, much of which occurred in Texas. Thomas D. Clark called it "of monumental importance in the history of the American Southwest." George Parker Winship said it tells "the story of one of the most remarkable explorations recorded in the annals of American history . . . [Coronado] had failed to find any of the things for which he went in search. But he had added to the world as known to Europeans an [enormous] extent of country." F.W. Hodge said Castaneda's account "bears every evidence of honesty and a sincere desire to tell all he knew of the most remarkable expedition that ever traversed American soil. . . . Castaneda's narration is by far the most important of the several documents bearing on the expedition, and in some respects is one of the most noteworthy contributions to early American history."

When Cabeza de Vaca returned from his amazing cross-continent journey in 1536, he reported that the natives had told him of the seven rich cities of the north. Viceroy Antonio de Mendoza sent Fray Marcos de Niza with Estevanico northward in 1539 to verify Cabeza de Vaca's report. Estevanico was killed on this journey, but Fray Marcos returned and told the viceroy the stories were true. Immediately, Francisco Vasquez de Coronado, governor of Nueva Galicia, was appointed to lead an expedition to find the cities. Coronado and about a thousand men set out in the spring of 1540, traveling into New Mexico, Texas, and other areas in search of the cities of gold. From Palo Duro Canyon, Coronado led a group northward, probably through the Texas Panhandle and possibly as far north as Kansas. Failing to find the object of their quest, the expedition returned to Mexico early in 1542.

The reports of Coronado and his officers were not published contemporaneously, except for a letter of Coronado and some material in Ramusio's *Navigationi et Viaggi* of 1556 and an account of the trip in Lopez de Gomara. The original Castaneda manuscript was never published and has long been lost, but a manuscript copy made in 1596 survived and is now in the Lenox Collection of the New York Public Library. In 1838 the Lenox copy was translated into French and published by Ternaux-Compans. In 1896 the same manuscript was published by George Parker Winship for the first time in the original Spanish and for the first time in English. Winship states that in the French edition "the style and language . . . were much more characteristic of the French translator than of the Spanish conquistadores . . . Ternaux not only rendered the language of the original . . . with great freedom, but in several cases he entirely failed to understand what the original writer endeavored to relate." The French edition, then, is more of a paraphrase than an exact translation, making the 1896 edition not only the first in the original language and the first in English, but in one sense the first complete edition in any language.

The Winship translation has stood the test of time. All of the subsequent editions that I have been able to locate are from his translation. Herbert E. Bolton rated Winship's edition, with its additional documentary material, "a monumental source book containing most of the essential documents at that time known." Donald C. Cutter said in 1964 that "the Winship work has remained as an outstanding translation" and that "new material has disclosed relatively few major errors in the Winship work." F. B. Steck said Winship's "pioneer work . . . will always remain the standard work on the Coronado enterprise." This is all the more remarkable because the translation was done at the age of 21 by Winship as a Harvard undergraduate. It was Winship's major contribution to history during a long career; he was still writing for publication at the time of his death in 1952.

Many historians, including Adolph Bandelier, F. W. Hodge, and others, have sought to identify the exact route of Coronado. The best account of the expedition is Herbert E. Bolton's *Coronado: Knight of Pueblos and Plains,* (Albuquerque: Whittlesey House, 1949, 491pp.), and the best sources for bibliographical and documentary details are in the 1933 Grabhorn Press edition of Castaneda, in the 1940 Hammond and Rey edition of Castaneda, and in Wagner's *Spanish Southwest.*

Clark I-5. Graff 626. Howes C224a and W571. Palau 47521. Rader 624. Raines, p.44. Rittenhouse 653. Sabin 11379. Wagner *Spanish Southwest.* 5n.

29 Celiz, Francisco

DIARY OF THE ALARCON EXPEDITION INTO TEXAS, 1718-1719.

Los Angeles: The Quivira Society, 1935.
Translated by Fritz Leo Hoffmann.
[12],124pp. 8 illus. 2 maps. 25cm. Boards, cloth spine.
[Verso of title:] Lancaster Press, Inc., Lancaster, Pa.
Quivira Society Publications Volume V.
Colophon on page [vi] reads: "Six hundred copies printed for the Quivira Society, of
which this is No. _____"

Other issues:
(A). Special edition, with an inset between pages 110 and 111 consisting of a title
      page and 52 numbered pages of facsimile of the diary. Printed on special Rives
      Paper. Colophon reads: "One hundred copies of the facsimile edition printed for
      the Quivira Society, of which this is No. _____" Each copy signed by Hoffmann.
(B). Reprint edition, without the diary facsimile. New York: Arno Press, 1967. 24cm.
      Cloth.

The Celiz diary records of the founding of the town of San Antonio
and the mission of the Alamo, known then as Bejar and San Antonio
de Valero. It also reports on the expedition through the interior of
Texas to the missions in deep eastern Texas. Lost for two centuries, it
was found in January, 1933, by accident in the Mexican National
Archives in Mexico City. The two scholars who found it, Luis Ceballos
and Maria Viamonte, showed it to Vito Alessio Robles, who immediately recognized its significance and arranged for its transcription,
translation, and publication. At the same time, he published the diary
in the original Spanish in *La Universidad de Mexico* (volume V, numbers
25-28), early in 1933.

Previous to the discovery of the diary, most information on this key
expedition came from reports and letters of Father Antonio Olivares,
an enemy and detractor of Alarcon. Hoffmann states: "With the
finding of the diary . . . it is easier to obtain a more unbiased estimate
of Alarcon's role in the early history of Texas. Probably owing to the
fact that the evaluation of the work has heretofore been based almost
wholly on letters written by Father Olivares, the habitual complainer
. . . his efforts have been minimized. . . . This estimate can now be
changed to well-deserved praise."

The manuscript is the diary of a priest from Coahuila who states at
the end: "All that is contained in this diary I certify to and as is
contained therein. As an eye-witness [and] because of having been
chaplain of this entire undertaking, and because therefore it is the
truth, I signed it" at San Antonio de Bejar, February 10, 1719. The
diary begins on April 9, 1718, the day the expedition crossed the Rio
Grande into Texas.

The expedition was under the command of General Martin de Alarcon, Governor of the State of Coahuila and the Province of Texas. Alarcon's instructions were to found a town and a mission in the area of the San Antonio River and to strengthen the tiny settlements in East Texas, which "because of their location . . . would ultimately become the defense of all New Spain." The expedition included 72 soldiers, priests, and settlers, 548 horses, numerous sheep, cattle, and farm animals, and a cargo of supplies.

On May 1, 1718, Celiz reports on Alarcon's official founding of San Antonio, "with the requisite solemnity," and the mission of San Antonio de Valero "established by the said governor about three-fourths of a league down the creek." The expedition then explored in several directions, including the area of Matagorda Bay, and moved on to East Texas and back. The diary is valuable for its description of the country explored and especially of the Indians encountered, almost all of whom were friendly. Celiz reports a few instances of the contrary, such as on June 17, 1718: "The governor, finding himself unable to proceed with his trip, since he had not a single Indian, owing to the fact that the devil had them perverted and rebelling against God and against the King," was delayed in his plans.

The publication consists of a fine preface and introduction by Hoffmann, the text of the diary, annotations, and an index. The 83 footnotes to the introduction and the 243 footnotes to the diary are especially valuable. Another manuscript diary of the expedition was later found in the Franciscan archives in Queretaro. It was translated by Hoffmann and published in the *Southwestern Historical Quarterly* (Volume 41, pp. 312-323) in April, 1938. Written by Father Pedro Perez de Mezquia, it is far inferior to the Celiz version and stops at June 22, 1718, but is useful in confirming the accuracy of Celiz.

Clark I-13. Howes C254.

30 Clark, James Anthony (1907-), and Michel Thomas Halbouty (1909-)

SPINDLETOP.

New York: Random House,[1952].
xvi,306pp. 7 diagrams. 16pp. of illus. Map endpapers. 24cm.

Cloth, dustjacket.

[Verso of title:] First Printing . . . Designer: Ernes Reichl.

On page [3] of the earliest issue is a four-paragraph statement headed "Beaumont Edition" stating: "The book is one of a limited printing . . . "

Other issues:

(A). Same as above, with page [3] blank. First trade edition.

(B). Special edition for Helmerich & Payne International Drilling Co., with "Special Edition" on copyright page.

(C). Second printing, so stated on verso of title.

(D). Third printing, so stated on verso of title.

(E). Facsimile reprint. Houston: Gulf Publishing Company, [1980]. Pictorial cloth.

This is the best account of the great discovery of oil near Beaumont on Spindletop Mound, "where oil became an industry." John S. Ezell called the book "an interesting account of the adolescence of a great American industry." Dan Ferguson said that "this book is no extravagant bit of braggadocio but . . . a sound piece of accurate reporting carefully checked by an experienced geologist and oil operator. A lively, animated and absorbing narrative . . . probably the best coverage now extant of this event of such unusual historic importance." J. Frank Dobie said: "This book, while it presumes to record what Pat Higgins was thinking as he sat in front of a country store, seems to me to be the 'true story.' The bare facts in it make drama."

It is possible that the authors may indeed have known what Pattillo Higgins was thinking, since he was still alive and assisted the authors in their research on the book. Fortunately, many of the men who were there in 1901 and two decades later for the second boom were still alive to recount their versions, such as Al Hamill, Will Orgain, Marrs McLean, Ed Prather, and Anthony F. Lucas.

For half a century oil had been becoming a valuable resource, and about 175,000 barrels a year were being removed from scattered oil wells. The Lucas Gusher of 1901 changed the history of the world, for the Spindletop wells brought in over twenty million barrels in their first two years of operation and over forty million by 1911. The second strike brought in twenty-seven million barrels in one year. Everett DeGolyer said: "Dramatic, spectacular, exciting, it was more than the lucky discovery of a new oil field or region: it was the beginning of the modern petroleum industry." In a very real sense, it made the great technology of the 20th century possible; it ended the steam age and began the age of the combustion engine.

James Clark worked in oil fields as a young man and became an associate of Glenn McCarthy. For many years he was oil editor of the Houston *Press*. Michel T. Halbouty is an "eminent geologist and petroleum engineer who is also recognized as an outstanding authority on Salt Domes, [and] has been instrumental in the discoveries and operational development of many Gulf Coast oil fields." Halbouty and Clark also collaborated on *The Last Boom* (New York: Random House, 1972, 305pp.), a superb book about the discovery of the East Texas oil field by Dad Joiner and others. In 1979, Halbouty's major work, *Salt Domes of the Gulf Region* (Houston: Gulf Publishing Company, 1979, 584pp.) was reprinted in a revised edition, and in the same year a biography of Halbouty was issued by Jack Donohue, *Wildcatter: The Story of Michel T. Halbouty and the Search for Oil* (New York: McGraw-Hill, 1979, 268pp.).

The story of Spindletop is as exciting as it is important, and the authors have told the story with forgiveable journalistic enthusiasm. The book is delightful to read: "Deals involving millions of dollars were as common as popcorn sales at a fair. . . . The Crosby House became a center for this madness. . . . The bar and cafe became twenty-four hour operations along with the remainder of the hotel. It was here that most of the traders chose to assemble. They would stand on tables and chairs and offer to buy or sell leases. One night a man stood on a chair in the center of the lobby waving a hundred $1,000 bills, which he was offering for a single acre of proven territory. The crowd laughed. That was the price a twenty-foot lot would bring next to an oil well."

The book has its faults. Dobie is correct regarding there being too much of putting thoughts in people's minds and quoting conversations without citation of authority. There are unquestionably cases where fictionalized dialogue is incorporated. The authors rationalize the rampant dishonesties and crooked deals as an endemic part of the oil business, but history has shown that this is probably true. There are some repetitions and a few discrepancies. Yet such an exciting story deserves an exciting telling. Carl Coke Rister and C. A. Warner have written the basic dry facts; Clark and Halbouty give us the spirit.

31 Coleman, Robert M. (c.1799-1837)

HOUSTON DISPLAYED; OR, WHO WON THE BATTLE OF SAN JACINTO? BY A FARMER IN THE ARMY.

Velasco: 1837.
38pp. 21cm.
Sewn. Printed by the Velasco *Herald*.

Other issues:
(A). *Houston Displayed; Or, Who Won The Battle Of San Jacinto? By A Farmer In The Army, Reprinted From The Velasco Edition of 1837.* [Houston: Printed at the Telegraph Office, 1841]. [2],ii,[5]-38pp. 24cm. Sewn. Contains a new unsigned introductory note dated Bastrop, March, 1841.
(B). *Houston Displayed; Or, Who Won The Battle Of San Jacinto? By A Farmer In The Army, Reproduced From The Original.* Austin: The Brick Row Book Shop, 1964. [4],xvii,[1],44,[5]pp. 18cm. Cloth. Edited with an introduction by John H. Jenkins. Verso of title: "Limited to 500 copies." This little reprint, although ugly in format, contains data on Coleman and on the history of the pamphlet, footnotes on the text, and an index.

The first detailed account of the San Jacinto campaign, other than Houston's battlefield report, this is also the first account written by a veteran of the campaign. Consequently, it has been drawn upon by most subsequent writers to a much greater degree than is generally realized. Although no name is given as author, the pamphlet has always been known as "Coleman's Pamphlet." Robert M. Coleman was sufficiently well-educated to have written it entirely by himself, but it has frequently been claimed that it was ghostwritten by various others, such as A. P. Thompson, John A. Wharton, or even David G. Burnet. Nevertheless, as early as 1840 it was tagged by the *Telegraph and Texas Register* as "Coleman's Pamphlet," and thus it was accepted by those in a position to know. On July 17, 1841, for example, Adolphus Sterne wrote in his diary: "An old Publication against Sam Houston by Col. Coleman is republished."

Coleman participated in the Battle of Gonzales and in the Siege of Bexar. In the San Jacinto campaign he was aide-de-camp to Houston, with the rank of major. A lawyer, he was first mayor of Bastrop and a member of the Consultation of 1835. As a delegate to the Convention of 1836, he signed the Texas Declaration of Independence and participated in the debates leading to the Constitution of 1836. After the

Revolution he was colonel of a Texas Ranger force, but was arrested on possibly trumped-up charges by Houston shortly after the publication of the book. Coleman drowned on May 12, 1837, a few days after being released from custody by Chief Justice James Collinsworth. His wife and son were killed by Indians two years later. His place in Texas history has been generally overlooked; in all the early histories of Texas, the only sketch of him is in John Henry Brown's *History of Texas* (II, 129), reading in full: "A gallant soldier, but an impetuous man, governed too much by passion. That this allusion is void of prejudice or unkindness is evidenced by the fact that he who pens this note, more than twenty years after his death, named the county of Coleman in his honor."

The volume was issued, without doubt, as a political maneuver, but it must be remembered that Sam Houston himself seldom wrote a word that was not. Scurrilous and biased as it is, there is truth to at least some of the accusations, and it was undoubtedly believed to be literal truth by scores of veterans of the campaign. Many of its accusations were substantiated by some of Texas' most highly revered heroes of that era. One finds, in fact, that a considerable majority of the officers in Houston's army were severely critical of Houston's actions in the campaign. These men sincerely felt that his laurels were too easily won and too lightly granted by the thousands of post-revolution immigrants who, fed by a pro-Houston press in the United States, came to Texas thinking of Houston as Texas' saviour. General Edward Burleson, second in command, despised Houston till the day he died because of the campaign, as did Col. Sidney Sherman, third in command. David G. Burnet, President of Texas, was even more fanatical than Coleman in his denunciation of Houston's part. Gen. Thomas J. Rusk, Adj. Gen. John A. Wharton, Lt. Col. J. C. Neill, Lt. Col. Mirabeau B. Lamar, Lt. Col. John Forbes, Maj. J. H. Perry, Maj. James Collinsworth, Maj. Lysander Wells, Captains Turner, Moreland, Billingsley, Baker, Calder, Heard, Kuykendall, Ben Smith, Karnes, Fisher, Gillespie, and Surgeons Anson Jones and William Labadie all criticized some of Houston's actions in the campaign. Only three officers—Henry Millard, Alexander Somervell, and J. L. Bennett—appear to have unceasingly supported Houston.

All three Presidents of Texas besides Houston upheld Coleman. Lamar and David G. Burnet in 1855 signed a joint statement that "we believe the facts he sets forth, revolting as some of them are, to be mainly true." Anson Jones wrote that same year: "My own recollection now is, though the narrative was couched in terms of much severity and censure, that most of its facts and details are substantially true. I was as you know intimately acquainted with Col. Coleman . . . and can vouch for his unsullied reputation for truth, integrity, and honor. . . . I do not wish to be understood as denying to Genl. Houston, merit on some subsequent occasions."

The work was reprinted in 1841 during the Presidential campaign between Sam Houston and David G. Burnet. This edition contains an unsigned introductory note dated Bastrop, March, 1841, stating that the original printing "was found to contain so many TRUTHS relative to the conduct of Gen. Sam Houston" that it had been suppressed to the extent that "although it had been circulated widely through the Republic, in three months after its publication, scarcely a copy could be found."

The Texas public was divided in its reception of the pamphlet. The *Weekly Houstonian,* July 29, 1841, refers to it as the "vilest production which has ever disgraced the Texian press . . . [It was] such a tissue of falsehoods and misrepresentations that it had no influence whatever upon the public mind." The Austin *Texas Centinel,* August 5, 1841, however, states that "such were its blighting expositions, and withering truths, that Gen. Houston betook himself to bed, and drowned his reflections in the bottle."

David G. Burnet, Sidney Sherman, and others planned in 1855 to republish the volume, but if it were done no copies now exist. Gen. Hugh McLeod wrote to Mirabeau B. Lamar on September 15, 1855, that Burnet was "busy arranging for the pamphlet, which by being ready for the next Congress, will rile Houton dead." Houston was not riled dead by any means, but he did lose the race for governor of Texas in 1857, the only time he was ever defeated.

Again in 1859 a reprint was planned but abandoned. Sherman wrote to Amasa Turner on July 15, 1859: "It was our intention at first to publish Colemans Pamphlet . . . but we found it would take too long a time, and cost too much."

The bitterness of the work is its basic flaw. Coleman was as vehement about Houston as J. Evetts Haley was about Lyndon Johnson in *A Texan Looks At Lyndon*. The careers of both Houston and Johnson contain ample grounds for honest criticism without any need for exaggeration or slander. The two works are parallel in a number of respects; had either author presented his case objectively and calmly, the results would have been infinitely more significant. My inclusion of the Coleman work in this bibliography is because it initiated a controversy that lasted throughout Houston's career and has not yet ended. The Coleman pamphlet is the initial anti-Houston casebook and is therefore important despite its lies and slanders.

Coleman, for example, is at his weakest when he accuses Houston of being a coward. The Coleman pamplet is also the original printed source of the accusations regarding Houston's drunkenness. When Houston prepared to leave Washington-on-the-Brazos to join the Texas Army, Coleman says, "he mounted in front of Mrs. Mann's boarding house, where he had the unblushing impudence to acknowledge, to the bystanders, that he did not recollect to have set out from any place sober or free from intoxication, during the last five years; but on that occasion he considered himself sober."

The pamphlet put Houston on the defensive for the remainder of his career. His own version is excellently presented in his official account, which appeared as a pamphlet and was reprinted hundreds of times in subsequent publications. The important pro-Houston accounts of the San Jacinto campaign by other participants are included in this bibliography. The other anti-Houston accounts may be found in volume four of the *Quarterly of the Texas State Historical Association* and in the David G. Burnet, Amasa Turner, Jesse Billingsley, Guy M. Bryan, and Moseley Baker papers in the University of Texas Archives.

The San Jacinto controversy was a major issue in every Texas presidential election and in all of Houston's campaigns for office after statehood. Seldom a year and never a decade has passed since 1836 but that some article, pamphlet, or book has been issued condemning or lauding Houston for his actions in the spring of 1836. This little volume is the granddaddy of them all.

Howes C571. Streeter 190 and 440.

32   Connor, Seymour Vaughan (1923-)

THE PETERS COLONY OF TEXAS: A HISTORY AND BIO-
GRAPHICAL SKETCHES OF THE EARLY SETTLERS.

Austin: The Texas State Historical Association, 1959.
[Verso of title:] Printed . . . by Von Boeckmann-Jones Company, Austin, Texas.
Illustrated by Frances Pearce.
[16],473pp. Illus. Maps. Charts. 24cm.
Cloth, dustjacket. Map endpapers.

This is the best study of one of the largest land grants in Texas
history, totalling 16,000 square miles of North Texas, an area now
including some 26 counties and one-fourth of the Texas population.
The volume is a masterpiece of weaving together the threads of an
extremely difficult historical puzzle with only the meagerest of source
materials. Herbert Gambrell called it a "fine example of the use of
research tools" and Ray Allen Billington said it "not only tells the
story of a principal colonizing venture, but uses mass data to reveal
the nature of the typical Texan pioneer" in the colony.

"In size, in number of persons involved, in the length of time it
played an active role on the Texas scene," Connor states, "the Peters
Colony was the largest *empresario* enterprise in Texas under the Republic
[of Texas] or Mexico. Nevertheless it has been relegated to a minor
position; barely mentioned or often forgotten in textbooks and general
narratives of Texas history; the story of the Peters Colony, consequently, has almost sunk into oblivion."

This is because from the original 1841 grant as the Peters Colony
through 25 years of changes and additions as the Mercer Colony and
the Texas Emigration and Land Company, the story of the colonization
of the northern Texas plains was one of the most confusing puzzles of
Texas history. Connor states: "The sources from which this study of
the Peters Colony should have been made were the records and
correspondence of the [colonizers], which unfortunately have not been
located. It seems probable that they were brought from Louisville,
Kentucky, to Texas . . . and destroyed by fire. As a consequence the
story . . . has been pieced together from the scattered information
available." Whereas other colonizing ventures, such as Austin's colonies, left enormous archives of documents and letters intact for the

THE PETERS COLONY
OF TEXAS

by Seymour V. Connor

An account of the largest *empresario* grant made by the
Republic of Texas.

Contains a graphic description of:

Texas in 1841
The Four contracts
Reorganization as Texas
Emigration and Land Company
Peters Colony Controversy and
Hedgcoxe War
Principal areas of settlement
Biographical sketches of colonists

Publication date
November 15, 1959

$7.50

TEXAS STATE HISTORICAL ASSOCIATION
Box 8011, University Station
Austin 12, Texas

historian, and others left behind enough materials for multiple-volume resource publications, such as the work of the McLeans on Robertson's Colony, the Peters Colony ventures left behind nothing but a dribble of disconnected records.

Connor, working out the complicated sequence of events, admits freely that "inference, interpretation, and sheer guess work have played far too large a role in this history." Yet Connor's study succeeds beyond all expectation in answering most of the questions about the history of the colony, and all of Connor's inferences and guesswork are clearly labelled as such. Herbert Gambrell wrote that "questions remain unanswered ever after the appearance of Connor's careful study. The fault is not Connor's. He . . . set out hopefully to find and record the facts, only to discover that the facts are nowhere to be found. He is unique . . . for his persistence. He has pursued every clue and followed up every hunch, like the first-class detective he is; and it seems likely that he has found everything that can be found, [and] has pieced together the fragments and published the only detailed account . . . that has been or probably shall be made available to the public. . . . If more historians would publish results of research that falls short of completeness because of unavailability of materials, as Connor has done, fewer novices would travel down blind alleys and dead-end streets that have already been explored. A man naturally wants to say the final, definitive word. But if that word can't be said, he has a sort of obligation to let others know it, if the topic is important."

Connor begins his narrative with a discussion of the history of land grants and land development in the Republic of Texas, and does so with more clarity than any other Texas historian. He then describes how in 1841 a group of unknown musicians and piano makers in Kentucky, joined by some mysterious American and English business-men, petitioned for a colony land grant in Texas and, in spite of numerous more worthy applicants, was given a huge land concession. Even Connor is astounded: "That the type of people whose names are on the petition could be capable of instigating the colonization venture and could have the initiative to draw up the petition is hard to believe."

The Peters Colony grant totalled millions of acres in the region where Dallas is now located. The colonizers were to bring in settlers who would receive clear title to 640 acres each, provided they "shall have built a good Comfortable Cabin upon it" and fenced in at least fifteen acres under cultivation. Sam Houston later approved additional grants to the colonizers and agreed that they should receive up to half the land for themselves "at a little less than two cents an acre." The grant ultimately involved more land and more people than any other colonizing venture in Texas, including Stephen F. Austin's.

Peters himself apparently never came to Texas. The Englishmen sold their interest to other Englishmen, and the grantees fought among themselves over ownership for decades. Even the old scoundrel, Samuel Swartwout, played a role. Nevertheless, colonists began to arrive into what a contemporary Texas newspaper called "the garden spot of Texas, being in the vicinity of that Eldorado, the Three Forks of the Trinity." By 1844, an observer reported counting 225 wagons of immigrants enroute to the colony, and 75 returning who had seen the elephant. Gradually, the area filled up, with many conflicting titles. The Texas legislature slowly resolved the issue with nearly a dozen acts, one of which was the first Homestead Pre-emption Law in the United States.

Connor concludes his narrative with a series of sociological studies on the settlers drawn from census records and other sources, the result of an early use of computers in Texas historiography. In these studies he concludes that the colony resulted in "a trend of migration to North Texas from the Ohio River Valley. . . . These people were farmers, small land owners, merchants and artisans, and in small ways were different in character from earlier migrants to other parts of Texas. Commercially the Peters Colony region developed more rapidly than the rest of the state, despite being in a less advantageous geographical position. Union sentiment was quite strong . . . "

The final 271 pages of the volume are devoted to some two thousand biographical sketches of the colonists, a prodigious feat in itself and obviously of considerable value for any future study of the colony. There is a bibliography that shows just how sparse the available records are, and a competent index.

Connor's book came into existence by the traditional scholarly route. He began the project as a history student under Walter Prescott Webb in 1950 with the aid of a Clara Driscoll Scholarship. He completed it as his 1952 doctoral dissertation at the University of Texas under the title of "The Peters Colony in North Texas, 1841-1854." A version was then published under the title, "Kentucky Colonization in Texas: A History of the Peters Colony," in eight consecutive issues of *Register of the Kentucky Historical Society* (Vols. LI-LII, January, 1953, through October, 1954). A research grant from Texas Technological College enabled Connor to prepare his final revision, which was published in 1959 by the Texas Historical Association. Connor has authored a number of important works on Texas history, including one of the best general textbooks, *Texas, a History* (New York: Thomas Y. Crowell, 1971). He also edited the valuable six-volume series, *The Saga of Texas, 1519-1965* (Austin: Steck-Vaughn Co., 1965).

33 Considerant, Victor Prosper (1808-1893)

AU TEXAS.

Paris: La Librairie Phalansterienne, 1854.
[2],190,[2],[191]-194pp. Two folding maps. 22cm.
Cloth; wrappers.

Other issues:
(A).   *Au Texas. Quatrieme Partie . . . Bases et Statuts de la Societe de Colonisation Europee-Americane au Texas.* Brussels: Au Siege de la Societe; Paris: Librairie Phalansterienne, 1854. [2],113pp. Table. 22cm. Supplement, occasionally found bound with the first edition.
(B).   *Au Texas. Appendice. Chapitre Final.* [Brussels: Impr. de J. H. Briard, 1855?]. 23,[1]pp. Folding table. 23cm.
(C).   Second edition, enlarged. Brussels: Au Siege de la Society de Colonisation; Paris: A la Librairie Phalansterienne, 1855. [4],334pp. Folding map. Two folding tables. 19cm.
(D).   *Auswanderung Nach Hoch-Texas.* Zurich: Orell, Fuessli, 1855. 3 volumes in 1: 50;32;52pp. 19cm. First German edition.
(E).   *Au Texas; With The Addition Of The Great West, And European Colonization In Texas.* Philadelphia: Porcupine Press, 1975. 324,60,38pp. Two leaves of plates. 23cm. Introduction by Rondel V. Davidson. The American Utopian Adventure Series No. 2. Facsimile reprint of (C), with two pamphlets in English and an excellent historical introduction.

This is an eminent philosopher's account of Texas and his audacious plans for a socialist colony there, the direct result of which was the establishment of La Reunion Colony near Dallas. Eberstadt said it contains "a wealth of optimistic observations on the country, based on personal travels through Texas," and Marilyn Sibley refers to "Considerant's glowing descriptions of the country," although she mistakenly calls *The Great West* an English translation. Actually, the volume has never been translated into English. Thomas D. Clark states: "Considerant proved to be a good observer. More than three-fourths of the book is devoted to Texas. Not only does he give a careful and full description of that state, but . . . this is a useful travel account and is an unusually full one to have come from a Latin visitor. It does not have the sting that many of the hypercritical accounts of this period contained."

In 1853 Victor Considerant and Albert Brisbane journeyed by horseback through Texas, and Considerant returned to Europe full of plans for creating a utopian socialist colony there. He raised over a million francs and purchased 47,000 acres in Texas. In 1855 he returned with colonists and established the settlement of La Reunion near Dallas. Subsequently, close to 500 colonists settled there. These included writers, musicians, artists, artisans, and free spirits, but only two farmers. As might be expected, a couple of years of utopian bickering and successive Texas droughts brought the experiment to a speedy collapse. The colony was abandoned, and Considerant moved to San Antonio, where he lived until 1869, when he returned to France.

Many of the colonists at La Reunion were well-educated, and Julie Considerant organized a salon in a cedar brake along the banks of the Trinity, where the colonists met to discuss the ideas of Fourier, Proudhon, Cabet, Sue, Hugo, and other writers and philosophers. Some colonists brought with them extensive libraries, several of which have found their way intact into university libraries in Texas.

Au Texas includes Considerant's journal of his tour of Texas with Brisbane from December, 1852, to May, 1853, and a rather full description of Texas. These glowing accounts should be compared with those of Savardin and Olmsted to see just how differently honest men can view the same subject. The work also includes an elaborate and pragmatic plan for colonizing Texas. Rondel Davidson states: "In fact, nowhere in the planning of the other European communal endeavors in the United States can one find a more practical and possibly workable blueprint for immigration procedures, housing accommodations, employment, agricultural, industrial, and commercial subsistence, cultural and educational development, and financial solvency. Considerant even went so far as to itemize a budget for the first two years. If the elaborate instructions . . . had been adhered to and the necessary financial backing had been attained, it is probable that some type of permanent and self-sufficient community would have been established in Texas." Considerant seems to have correctly analyzed everything except human foibles and Texas weather.

The book created a sensation in socialist circles in Europe; as a propaganda tool, it appears to have succeeded perhaps too well, since so many colonists subscribed so quickly. This is perhaps because of Considerant's high standing among the Fourier socialists of the era. Not a posturing dandy like Alphonse de Saligny, Considerant was a brilliant theorist and the acknowledged leader and exponent of Fourier socialism. His relationship to Karl Marx has been the subject of much analysis. In 1843 Considerant had produced "Manifeste de la Democratie Pacifique," which many scholars have called a forerunner of the *Communist Manifesto*. Some have even accused Marx of plagiarizing from Considerant. The Texas colony was to have proved the workability of communism.

Considerant's works on Texas have caused some bibliographical confusion. *Au Texas* appeared in Paris in 1854 and was followed in the same year with *Au Texas: Quatrieme Partie,* a supplement printed in Brussels containing the regulations for the colony. This supplement is frequently found bound with the original volume. Some time later *Au Texas: Appendice, Chapitre Final* appeared, it being a final supplement also printed in Brussels, usually found bound with the second edition, which was printed in Brussels in 1855, greatly enlarged; it is the best edition in French.

In 1856 Considerant issued a pamphlet about his colony entitled *Au Texas!!!Ou Expose Fidele* (Paris: Joubert, 1856, 35pp.). Considerant's *Du Texas* was published in 1857 in Paris; it announces the failure of the La Reunion colony. Two related works by Considerant were published in English in New York, but neither is a translation of any of the French works. The first of these was *The Great West: A New Social and Industrial*

Life in Its Fertile Regions (New York: Dewitt & Davenport, 1854, 60pp.). It contains much material on Considerant's colonization plans in Texas that also appears in *Au Texas*, but it is in no way a translation. The second was *European Colonization in Texas: An Address to the American People* (New York: Baker, Godwin & Co., 1855, 38pp.), with a folding map of Texas by Colton and a folding weather chart; it was issued to counter the Know-Nothing anti-socialist nativism then rampant.

Clark III-292. Howes C697. Rader 901. Raines, p.53. Sabin 15925.

34 Cox, James (1851-1901)

HISTORICAL AND BIOGRAPHICAL RECORD OF THE CAT-
TLE INDUSTRY AND THE CATTLEMEN OF TEXAS AND
ADJACENT TERRITORY.

St. Louis: Published by Woodward & Tierman Printing Co., 1895.
743pp. 32cm. Color frontis. by Gean Smith. 272 Illus.
Full morocco, gilt.

Other issues:
(A). Facsimile reprint. New York: The Antiquarian Press, Ltd., 1959. With a new
6-page introduction by J. Frank Dobie. Two volumes. Half calf. Boxed.
Limited to 550 numbered sets.

This compendium on Texas cattle and cattlemen is also one of the rarest Texas books. J. Frank Dobie once said: "In 1928 I traded a pair of store-bought boots to my uncle Neville Dobie for his copy of this book. A man would have to throw in a young Santa Gertrudis bull now to get a copy." Conceived as a mug book to be sold primarily to the people whose biographies appeared in it, the final published book contained so much of value on the cattle industry that it has become a classic in its field.

Nearly 400 pages are devoted to biographies of some 449 Texas cattlemen, and these sketches are a goldmine for research into the cowboy and cattle industry. The compiler of this portion of the work was Sylvester D. Barnes, editor of *Outdoor Sports and American Angler* in St. Louis. It is through these pages, and those of only a few other contemporary works, that we obtain much of our knowledge of the

ANTIQUARIAN
PRESS, LTD.

Announces the republication of the extremely rare and important...

early Texas cattlemen. Jeff Dykes has called it "an unequaled source of information and pictures of pioneer cattlemen."

The biographical section includes such notables as Charles Goodnight, Oliver Loving, Shanghai Pierce, J. M. Mathis, Tom Coleman, Sam Burk Burnett, John Chisum, J. M. Dobie, Richard King, J. A. McFaddin, D. M. and T. M. O'Connor, C. C. Slaughter, Dan Waggoner, and others. Many of the biographies contain meaty historical data on earlier Texas history.

The other half of the volume, written by Cox, provides one of the two or three best contemporary accounts of the history of the Texas cattle trade. Thirteen chapters are devoted to the subject, and include sections on barbed wire, mavericks, cattle drives, economics of the industry, improving the longhorn breed, and Indian depredations on the cattle range. One of the best sections is entitled "The Cowboy, as He Was, and Is, and is Supposed to Have Been." Dobie found that chapter more valuable than the works of Emerson Hough and Philip Ashton Rollins.

The Cox volume, being sent primarily to biographees, never entered the mainstream of the bookstore market—although it is said the work sold at $25.00 per copy. In addition, the spine of the book was unequal to the task of holding together 743 folio pages and many copies literally fell apart. Furthermore, the publisher's remaining stock was destroyed, either by accidental fire or by simply being dumped on the trash heap. Thus are rarities created in the world of books.

Adams Herd 493. Dobie, p.100. Graff 891. Howes C820. Merrill *Aristocrat*. Rader 1891. Reese *Six Score* 24. Saunders 2846.

35 Cranfill, James Britton Buchanan Boone (1858-1942)

DR. J. B. CRANFILL'S CHRONICLE: A STORY OF LIFE IN TEXAS WRITTEN BY HIMSELF ABOUT HIMSELF.

New York, etc.: Fleming H. Revell Company, [1916].
xi,[3],496pp. Illus. 21cm.
Cloth.

This is the hearty autobiography of a Texas trail driver, editor, doctor, preacher, and prohibitionist. J. Frank Dobie called it "down-

right and concrete," and said Cranfill "was a lot of things besides a
Baptist preacher—trail driver, fiddler, publisher, always an observer."

Cranfill was born in Parker County, reared in Bastrop County,
taught school in McLennan County, and practiced medicine in Coryell
County. He spent time in several western Texas areas, as a newspaper
editor. He became a leader in the prohibitionist movement and was
the Prohibitionist candidate for Vice President of the United States in
1892. By the turn of the century he had become a Baptist preacher in
Waco, continuing to be an editor and author until his death in 1942.

Of his *Chronicle,* he writes: "When I announced to my good friend
Cullen Thomas that I was writing an autobiography, he said, 'I should
think it would be very interesting—*to you!*' It *has* been interesting to
me, so I spared him, and it may be, kind reader, that before this
recital is done you will wish that I had spared you. Until I wrote this
book I had never talked about myself as much as I wanted to. Every
time I have sat down with a friend to talk to him six or seven hours
about *myself,* he has butted in to talk about *himself,* with the result that
I have never until now been allowed to finish the story. Here it is,
however, in all its gorgeous fulness."

Full it is, too, of the activities of this remarkable man. There is
much on growing up in pioneer Texas, more detailed by far than most
pioneer memoirs. There are good sections on cattle raising, as well as
on murders and outlawry on the frontier. Cranfill tells us about
vigilante actions and about his drawing his six-shooter against a close
friend. From him we learn much about country newspaper editing
and country doctoring. Even the material on his preacher days and
anti-liquor campaigns are interesting, especially his rousing defeat of
Roger Q. Mills in a debate. Throughout, he sparkles with wit and
honesty, relating his life in such a forthright manner that the most
mundane events are infused with interest. His is the most revealing of
all Texas preacher memoirs.

Adams Herd 603. Dobie, pp.65 and 109. Howes C864a. Rader 955.

36 Davenport, Jewette Harbert (1882-1957)

THE HISTORY OF THE SUPREME COURT OF THE STATE OF
TEXAS, WITH BIOGRAPHIES OF THE CHIEF AND ASSOCI-
ATE JUSTICES.

Austin: Published by Southern Law Book Publishers, [1917].
[6],434pp. 24cm.
Cloth, leather label.

This is still the most comprehensive study of the Texas judiciary. Curiously, no comparable work has been written on the Texas Supreme Court since the publication of this volume in 1917, leaving a void in Texas studies in that area. The Davenport work is quite rare, only three copies having been offered for sale in the past thirty years.

Despite the rather misleading title, Davenport includes in his book a history of the higher courts in Texas during the period of the Republic of Texas, including biographical sketches of the judges and interpretive commentary on some of the important cases discussed. The most useful work on case law during the Texas republic is in James Wilmer Dallam's *A Digest of the Laws of Texas: Containing a Full and Complete Compilation of the Land Laws; Together with the Opinions of the Supreme Court* (Baltimore: John D. Toy, 1845, 632pp.). Nearly half of this often-reprinted book is devoted to the Supreme Court opinions in cases decided between 1840 and 1844.

The main text of Davenport's work is devoted to a history of the activities of the state supreme court during the 19th century, with extensive biographical sketches of the justices. Of special value are Davenport's concise and clear summaries of significant cases brought before the court. The volume concludes with a chapter on "Proposed Reforms in Supreme Court Procedure," which includes proposals for increasing the number of justices and other significant alterations. An appendix gives the text of the then-current "Rules for the Courts of Texas."

One earlier book is still of value regarding courts in Texas: James D. Lynch, *The Bench and Bar of Texas* (St. Louis: Nixon-Jones Printing Co., 1885, 610pp.), which includes a treatise on the nature of Texas law and biographical sketches of numerous early Texas judges.

37 Davis, Rev. Nicholas A. (1824-1894)

THE CAMPAIGN FROM TEXAS TO MARYLAND.

Richmond: Printed at the Office of the Presbyterian Committee of Publication of the Confederate States, 1863.

[165],[1]pp. 2 illus. 20cm. A printing error resulted in the final three leaves being numbered as follows: 161, 164, 163, 162, 167, and index.
Printed wrappers. The wrapper title adds the words "with the Battle of Fredericksburg."

Other issues:
(A). Same, with pagination corrected, last page numbered 168.
(B). *The Campaign from Texas to Maryland.* Houston: Telegraph Book and Job Establishment, 1863. 87pp. 21cm. Printed wrappers. Contains textual revisions. Known only in the University of Texas and Yale copies.
(C). Facsimile reprint of the Richmond edition. Austin: The Steck Company, 1961. Printed wrappers.
(D). *Chaplain Davis and Hood's Texas Brigade, Being An Expanded Edition of the Reverend Nicholas A Davis' The Campaign from Texas to Maryland, with the Battle of Sharpsburg.* San Antonio: Principia Press of Trinity University, 1962. xiii, [3],234pp. 23cm. Cloth. Edited and with an Introduction by Donald E. Everett. The best edition, expanded from contemporary sources.

One of the best books on Hood's Texas Brigade, this is also one of the best American war travel books. Davis presents a straightforward and altogether memorable account of the eventful march of the Hood unit from its rendezvous at Buffalo Bayou near Houston to Richmond, culminating in the Battle of Sharpsburg in Maryland. As Richard Harwell says, "Davis was a good historian and his work has stood up well."

The Davis diary follows Hood's Brigade, particularly the Fourth Texas Regiment of which he was chaplain, from Houston by rail to Beaumont, by boat to Sabine, on foot and by train to New Orleans, and thence across the South to Richmond. From there the unit quickly became one of the most famous in the Confederate Army, especially in the fighting at Gaines' Mill, Malvern Hill, Seven Pines, Second Manassas, and Sharpsburg. Davis's account includes much on camp life and battle scenes, as well as on the hardships of wartime travel.

Davis is best at describing battle scenes; for example, of the Battle of Eltham's Landing, he writes: "The [Yankee] regiment now advancing, 1st California, evidently *intended* to fight well, and . . . attempted to charge . . . A whole-souled hearty *yell* now went up from the Texans, such as only Southerners can give, and they in turn charged . . . and the enemy broke and fled. . . . After the rout of this regiment, the enemy did not attack us, but contented themselves with shelling us . . . while this was going on, the boys had a hearty laugh at the conduct of an INDIAN WARRIOR, who was attached to the 1st Texas

Regiment. During the entire battle, with musketry, he had conducted himself in a most gallant manner, and had even succeeded in capturing a Yankee, whom he turned over to the proper officer, with the brief announcement 'Major, Yank yours; gun mine,' and again participated in the struggle. When the first shell came tearing through the tree-tops . . . he uttered a significant 'ugh!' and . . . sprang to his feet, exclaiming, 'no good for Indian,' and made for the rear with the agility of an antelope. The boys did not, however, reproach him, because it has long been understood that Indians won't be shot at by wagons . . . ''

The Appendix gives a detailed list of casualties of the 18th Georgia, First Texas, and Fifth Texas Regiments, and a muster roll of the Fourth Texas Regiment. The Houston reprint, Davis wrote at the time, "is considerably amended by the author, and many new biographies introduced," but this version omitted the appendices. The excellent 1962 expanded edition, edited by Donald E. Everitt, contains extensive added material, such as 149 footnotes and an index. It also includes material from the original manuscript Davis diaries, which were still in the hands of descendants, with microfilm copies deposited in the Trinity University Library, San Antonio.

The Reverend Davis, at the end of the Houston edition, explains why he published the diary in the midst of the war: "I should not have put the work to press so early and in such an imperfect form, but from the fact that the press in Richmond had not given Texas the credit due her gallant sons, consequently I determined to publish it . . . and let the world know who had done their duty in this struggle."

Coulter 116. Crandall 2621 and 2622. Dornbush 1079. *Fifty Texas Rarities* 42. Harwell, *Confederate Hundred* 27. Harwell, *In Tall Cotton* 35. Howes D127. Nevins I-79. Raines, p.64. Winkler-Friend 917 (Houston edition).

38   DeCordova, Jacob (1880-1868)

TEXAS: HER RESOURCES AND HER PUBLIC MEN: A COMPANION FOR J. DECORDOVA'S NEW AND CORRECT MAP OF THE STATE OF TEXAS.

When "Texas: Her Resources and Her Public Men" was published in 1858, the author, Jacob de Cordova, had purchased or otherwise accumulated scrip on a million acres of Texas land and doubtless knew Texas better than any other man. His book was the culmination of more than twenty years devoted to stimulating an interest in Texas and in promoting immigration into the state.

In 1849, de Cordova became part owner of the Waco Village tract of land on the Brazos River and was authorized to lay out the town which became the present Waco. He and his brother Phineas began publication of "De Cordova's Herald and Immigrant's Guide," a monthly newspaper devoted mostly to advertisements of land offered for sale by Jacob de Cordova. In that year, also, he published his first major effort to attract settlers to Texas. This was his "New Map of the State of Texas," of which there were to be nine different editions in the following few years. Rights to the map, one of the first of its kind to be published, were acquired in 1855 by the J. H. Colton Company of New York which published five of the editions.

"Texas: Her Resources and Her Public Men," first printed in 1858 by Ernest Crozet in Philadelphia and reprinted later the same year by J. B. Lippincott and Company. "Texas: Her Resources and Her Public Men," probably grew out of de Cordova's two earlier publications, "The State of Texas; Her Capabilities and Her Resources" and "The Texas Immigrant and Traveller's Guide Book." Both of these contained a great amount of information about all of Texas and the last was hardly off the press before de Cordova was planning an enlarged and better edition. To accomplish this he seized upon the idea of including biographical sketches of the leading men of Texas and began to write to many of them to ask that they supply what would surely be the most accurate accounts of their lives. In addition, he wrote to newspaper editors all over Texas and placed advertisements with them requesting information about their newspapers. County clerks were asked to supply other information about their municipalities, and specialized articles were solicited from experts in various fields of endeavor such as farming, sheep raising, railroads, etc.

When all the material was gathered, compiled and printed in a single volume, Jacob de Cordova had what Texas State Librarian E. W. Winkler later described as "A fine Texas encyclopedia at the time." In addition to the biographical material on some of Texas' greatest men and the specialized materials solicited by de Cordova, he also provided information on Texas land laws and listed in advertisements some of the thousands of acres of land he had available for purchase in dozens of Texas counties.

The reader of "Texas: Her Resources and Her Public Men" will be surprised that the book has this long escaped the eye of the reprint publishers who abound in the land today, and will be pleased that the Lippincott edition was selected over the Crozet edition for publication because of the valuable index the former contains. Also, according to a comparison of the two editions made by Winkler in 1943, the Lippincott edition seems to be the more complete.

Partial list of contents:
- Population of Texas
- Advice to Immigrants
- Farming in Texas
- Texas Schools and Churches
- List of Texas Counties, with Descriptions
- Texas Rivers
- Stagecoach Routes
- Biographies of Famous Texans
- Postage Rates
- Advertisements

Also included in the book is a reprint of "Lecture on Texas," delivered by Mr. J. de Cordova April 15, 1858.

- Cloth Bound
- 430 Pages
- Indexed

Published by

TEXIAN PRESS

TEXAS
HER RESOURCES AND HER PUBLIC MEN

by
Jacob de Cordova

Philadelphia: Printed by E. Crozet, Cor. Thirteenth & Market, 1858.
371,[1]pp. 20cm.
Printed wrappers. Also cloth.

Other issues:

(A). Same as above, with index added: Philadelphia: J. B. Lippincott & Co., 1858.
375pp. Contains the words "First Edition" on title page.

(B). Facsimile reprint of (A). [Waco: Texian Press, 1969]. vii, [1],375,32pp. 19cm.
Cloth. Best edition. This volume has the distinction of being covered in one of
the only nice-looking bindings ever done in Waco. New introduction by Dayton
Kelley; also contains a facsimile of DeCordova's *Lecture on Texas* (Philadelphia:
E. Crozet, 1858).

The first attempt at an encyclopedia of Texas, this work contains a
wealth of still-useful material. Dayton Kelley states that at the time of
its publication, DeCordova "had purchased or otherwise accumulated
scrip on a million acres of Texas land and doubtless knew Texas better
than any other man. His book was the culmination of more than
twenty years devoted to stimulating an interest in Texas and in
promoting immigration into the state." He has been called "a walking
encyclopedia of knowledge" about Texas, and "a visionary Texan,
only slightly ahead of his time."

DeCordova, a native of Jamaica, was one of the earliest Jewish
settlers in Texas. He supplied goods for the Texas Revolution from
New Orleans and settled in Galveston in 1837. The *Jamaican Gleaner,*
which he founded, is still published by his descendants. He was fluent
in English, German, French, Spanish, Hebrew, and several Indian
languages. He became one of the leading land merchants in Texas,
and worked for thirty years promoting immigration into the state.

In 1849 he published the first edition of his masterpiece, *Map of the
State of Texas,* which he and Robert Creuzbaur compiled and upon
which almost all future Texas cartography was based. Sam Houston
delivered a speech praising the map on the floor of the U.S. Senate
and obtained a government purchase of 500 copies. In an argument
with Jefferson Davis during the debate, Houston stated: "Years have
been employed in the compilation of the map, and for that reason on
account of the character of the individual who has been engaged in
preparing it," he could assert that it was "the most correct and
authentic map of Texas" ever compiled.

Texas: Her Resources and Her Public Men was issued concurrently with a revised edition of his Texas map, publication of which had been taken over by the J. H. Colton Company. DeCordova did some of the first genuine scholarly research ever done in Texas while compiling the book, interviewing leading men, researching newspaper files, searching county court records, and striving for pinpoint accuracy.

The volume includes biographies, land laws, climatology, statistics, and a substantial amount of land promotion material. There are articles on railroads, the cotton industry, sheep raising, "Information for Housewives," geology, taxes, schools, farming, slavery, churches, cattle, the lumber industry, gambling, and other subjects. There are articles on each Texas county and lists of every post office and fort in the state.

DeCordova also issued an array of pamphlets with similar titles during the 1850's: *The Texas Immigrant and Traveller's Guide Book* (Austin: 1856, 103pp.); *The State of Texas: Her Capabilities* (Galveston, ca.1858, 68pp.); *Texas: Her Capabilities* (Manchester, 1858, 114pp.); *Lecture on Texas* (Phila., 1858, 32pp.); *Lectures on Texas and Cotton Cultivation* (London, 1858, 58pp.). There is a good biography of DeCordova by James M. Day, *Jacob DeCordova: Land Merchant of Texas* (Waco: Texian Press, 1962, 189pp.).

Howes D201. Raines, p.68.

39 De la Pena, Jose Enrique (1807-1842)

LA REBELION DE TEXAS; MANUSCRITO INEDITO DE 1836, POR UN OFICIAL DE SANTA ANNA.

Mexico City: Edicion, Estudio, y Notas de J. Sanchez Garza, 1955.
[2],321pp. Illus. Map. Thirty appendices. 23cm.
[Verso of title:] Segunda Edicion, Junio 20 de 1955.
Cloth; also printed wrappers.

Other issues:
(A). Special edition, limited to 250 copies, printed on special paper, bound in vellum.

(B). *With Santa Anna In Texas: A Personal Narrative of The Revolution*. College Station: Texas A & M University Press, [1975]. Translated and edited by Carmen Perry. Introduction by Llerena Friend.

xxix, [3],3-302pp. 24cm. Cloth. Dustjacket. First edition in English. Omits the thirty appendices. Index, which does not encompass the excellent preface and introduction.

(C). Same as (B). Second printing. Same date and collation.

Written by an intelligent and perceptive Mexican staff officer, this is one of the most important eye-witness records of the Texas Revolution, and especially of the Siege of the Alamo. Llerena Friend called it "the detailed story by a participant observer who had military training and who also was well read, observant of the natural scene and of human character, and passionately devoted to his country. It should help dispel some of the myths or answer some of the questions that challenge the research historian." Carmen Perry called it "significant because he was an active participant, an eyewitness and a trained officer, who had advantages in observation and evaluation coupled with an honest objectivity. His rank of lieutenant colonel did not require that he send reports or issue orders during the campaign that later had to be explained or justified, although he frequently was present at closed meetings of his superior officers where important decisions were made."

A version of the narrative must first have appeared in September, 1836, probably in a Matamoros newspaper, but no copy of any contemporary printing can now be located. Jose Urrea in his diary which was published in 1838 quotes from "Diary of an Unknown Officer," which De la Pena asserts was his own diary. De la Pena's narrative was finally published in full in 1955 by Jose Sanchez Garza with thirty appendices that De la Pena collected to support his own narrative, but Sanchez Garza's editorial deletions and emendations make his version untrustworthy. He called his publication "Segunda Edicion," and began the diary with a purported reprint of a title page reading *Resena y Diario de la Campana de Texas* Matamoros, Tamps., Septiembre 15 de 1836, but it is likely that the Garza edition is the actual first separate printing of the complete narrative. The best edition of the narrative, and its first printing in English, is the Texas A & M Press edition of 1975. It is carefully and accurately translated by Carmen Perry. Unfortunately, the appendices of the Sanchez Garza edition are not included, although they are cited in footnotes. Some of Perry's annotations are misleading and unclear.

De la Pena's narrative covers the march of Santa Anna's army into Texas, the siege and storming of the Alamo, and the retreat back to Mexico. He did not participate in the San Jacinto campaign, but gives us one of the best accounts of the activities of the retiring Mexican army through June, 1836. His account of the storming of the Alamo is a masterpiece of narration, and gives us perhaps the most detailed and accurate account of that event.

It is from De la Pena that we get the most-likely-true version of the death of David Crockett. De la Pena's version, which caused considerable public uproar when the 1975 edition was released, states:

"Some men had survived the general carnage and, under the protection of General Castrillon, they were brought before Santa Anna. Among them was . . . David Crockett . . . Santa Anna answered Castrillon's intervention in Crockett's behalf with a gesture of indignation and, addressing himself to the sappers, the troops closest to him, ordered his execution. The commanders and officers were outraged at this action and did not support the order . . . but several officers who were around the president . . . thrust themselves forward, in order to flatter their commander, and with swords in hand, fell upon these unfortunate, defenseless men just as a tiger leaps upon his prey. Though tortured before they were killed, these unfortunates died without complaining and without humiliating themselves before their torturers. . . . I turned away horrified in order not to witness such a barbarous scene."

This paragraph in De la Pena's account led to the publication of a fine monograph by Dan Kilgore, *How Did Davy Die?* (College Station: Texas A & M University Press, 1978). Kilgore compares the various accounts and points out that six other surviving accounts by Mexicans present support, in the main, De la Pena's version. Kilgore also edited a supporting narrative, Francisco Becerra's *A Mexican Sergeant's Recollections of the Alamo & San Jacinto* (Austin: Jenkins Publishing Company, 1980).

The original manuscript diary of De la Pena was owned for many years by the Sanchez Garza family until it was purchased in 1974 by

John Peace, from whence it found its permanent home in the John Peace Memorial Library of the University of Texas at San Antonio. Also included with the diary were De la Pena's personal papers, articles, and military records.

40 De la Pena, Juan Antonio

DERROTERO DE LA EXPEDICION EN LA PROVINCIA DE LOS TEXAS, NUEVO REYNO DE PHILAPINAS, QUE DE ORDEN DEL EXCMO. SENOR MARQUES DE VALERO, VI-REY, Y CAPITAN GENERAL DE ESTA NUEVA-ESPANA PASSA A EXE-CUTAR EL MUY ILLUSTRE SENOR D. JOSEPH DE AZLOR, CAVALLERO MESNADERO DEL REYNO DE ARAGO. MAR-QUES DE S. MIGUEL DE AGUAYO, GOVERNADOR, Y CAPI-TAN GENERAL DE DICHAS PROVINCIAS DE TEXAS, NUEVAS PHILIPINAS, Y DE ESTA DE COAGHUILA, NUEVO REYNO DE ESTREMADURA.

Mexico: En La Imprenta Nueva Plantiniana de Juan Francisco de Ortega Bonilla, en la Calle de Tacuba, 1722.
[60]pp.: title, 29 numbered leaves. Maps on leaves 21, 24, and 27, and another map inserted between leaves 22 and 23.

Other issues:
(A). *Pena's Diary of the Aguayo Expedition.* Austin: Preliminary Studies of the Texas Catholic Historical Society, Volume II, Number 7, January, 1935. [2], 68pp. Printed wrappers. Translated by Rev. Peter P. Forrestal. Reprint from Records and Studies of the United States Catholic Historical Society, Volume XXIV, October 1934. First edition in English, but an inadequate translation.
(B). *Documentos para la Historia Eclesiastica y Civil de la Provincia de Texas, o Nuevas Philipinas,* 1720-1779. Madrid: Ediciones J. Porrua Turanzas, 1961. xi,463pp. Illus. 26cm. Edited by Jose Porrua Turanzas. Coleccion Chimalistac de Libros y Documentos Acerca de la Nueva Espana, 12. Limited to 225 copies, the first 25 lettered A to X.
(C). *Aguayo Expedition into Texas, 1721: An Annotated Translation of the Five Versions of the Diary Kept by Br. Juan Antonio de la Pena.* Austin: Jenkins Publishing Co., 1981. [16],17-133pp. 16 maps. 27cm. Cloth. Designed by Larry Smitherman. Edited by Richard G. Santos. Best edition, and first full edition in English, with 374 footnotes.

This is the first book devoted solely to Texas. Henry R. Wagner called it "one of the chief sources of Texas history" and Thomas D. Clark said that it "is an important document in the literature of the founding of Texas." The Pena Diary is the official report of one of the most significant events in Spanish Texas history, which Charles W. Hackett said "established so definite a Spanish claim to Texas that it was never again disputed by France."

The Aguayo Expedition, 1721-1722, led by the Marques de San Miguel de Aguayo of Coahuila, was designed to thwart French encroachments into Texas. When Aguayo entered Texas, following the pell-mell withdrawal of the Spanish from East Texas in 1719, there were no Spanish forts or missions in operation in Texas except at San Antonio; when he left, there were ten missions, four forts, and over 300 permanent settlers in Texas.

The expedition of five hundred men and four thousand horses and livestock reached San Antonio on April 4, 1721. From there, accompanied by Father Margil de Jesus and Father Isidro Felix de Espinosa, the expedition moved into East Texas. Negotiations with St. Denis, the French Commander in East Texas, led to the French agreeing to withdraw permanently east of the Sabine, which henceforth was at least the *de facto* border between Louisiana and New Spain. The missions were rebuilt in East Texas by Aguayo. Also, another mission and presidio was set up at La Bahia and later moved to Goliad.

Juan Antonio de la Pena was official chaplain of the expedition. As soon as the expedition returned to Monclova in May, 1722, Pena began editing his journal, completing the task on June 21. Two days later Dr. Joseph Codallos y Rabal, who had also been on the expedition, signed the manuscript to attest to its accuracy. It was quickly forwarded to Mexico City and printed. There are nine known surviving copies of the book, two of which have an additional manuscript map inserted of Bahia del Espiritu Santo. Richard Santos discovered that there are four additional versions of the diary that have survived in manuscript, three in the Mexican National Archives and one in Spain. All are slightly different from one another.

The Santos edition is a variorum edition which makes tentative identifications of the specific locations and provides 16 excellent maps of the Texas presidios.

Clark I-22. *Fifty Texas Rarities* 4. Howes P195. Raines, p.163. Wagner, *Spanish Southwest* 83.

41 DeMezieres, Athanase (ca. 1700-1779)

ATHANASE DE MEZIERES AND THE LOUSIANA-TEXAS
FRONTIER, 1768-1780: DOCUMENTS PUBLISHED FOR THE
FIRST TIME, FROM THE ORIGINAL SPANISH AND FRENCH
MANUSCRIPTS, CHIEFLY IN THE ARCHIVES OF MEXICO
AND SPAIN.

Cleveland: The Arthur H. Clark Company, 1914.
Edited and Annotated by Herbert Eugene Bolton.
Two volumes: 351;392pp. Folding map. 2 illus. 6 facsimiles. 24cm.
Cloth.

Other issues:
(A). Facsimile reprint in one volume. New York: Kraus Reprint Company, 1979.

This work provides the best insight into the Indians of Texas during
the period, and into the Spanish and French activities among them.
Bolton summarized the value of the DeMezieres materials as follows:
"DeMezieres was so versatile that he could write an official report in
French, berate a presumptuous Texas governor in Spanish, or indite
a friendly missive to a Franciscan padre in Latin. The history of the
French and Spanish regimes in Louisiana and Texas is to a great
extent the story of an Indian policy in its various aspects; and for the
light they throw on Indian affairs in the north and east Texas area for
the period between 1768 and 1779 there is no single group of documents
so important as the reports of DeMezieres. They became a sort of
statesman's manual for the region."

The volume consists of 252 documents written by or to DeMezieres,
an educated Parisian who came to Louisiana in 1733, married the
daughter of St. Denis, and spent fifty years in Natchitoches as a
soldier, trader, and planter. After the cession of Louisiana to Spain,
he was chosen to lead the efforts to win the allegiance of the Texas
Indians. Bolton says he was "for years the foremost Indian agent and
diplomat of the Louisiana-Texas frontier." The papers in this work
relate to those efforts. Eugene C. Barker said of the DeMezieres
material that "the activity and the comprehensiveness of the administration will be a surprise to those who are accustomed to the common
estimate of Spain's 'stupid and slothful' colonial system . . .
DeMezieres's letters are well written, and aside from their historical

and ethnological interest, unfold an attractive and forceful personality which would repay the study of an ambitious historical novelist.''

The documents are published here for the first time in any language, having been discovered in the Mexican National Archives by Bolton, who also added others found in the Bancroft Library, the Bexar Archives, the British Museum, the Archives du Ministere des Colonies in Paris, and the Archivo General de Indias in Seville. Bolton's original manuscript was once in my collection, but is now in the Price Daniel Library in Liberty, Texas.

Bolton's own contribution as editor included the gathering, translating, and editing of the documents, as well as a book-length introduction of 122 pages, of which J. Lloyd Mecham said: ''Dr. Bolton has not only made available valuable documents in this carefully edited work, but he has also made a notable contribution to the literature of the field in his introduction to the documents. His most helpful service has been in the classification and location of the Indian tribes of Texas and vicinity.''

Howes B584. Rittenhouse 66.

42   Dienst, Alex (1870-1938)

THE NAVY OF THE REPUBLIC OF TEXAS, 1835-1845.

Temple, [1909].
[12],150,[9]pp. [Blank leaf between pages 38 and 39]. Illus. 24cm.
Calf. Also cloth.

Other issues:
(A). Facsimile reprint. [Ft. Collins, Colo.:] The Old Army Press, [1987].xvi,167pp. New index. Cloth. Limited to 150 copies.

This is the first, and still best, history of the Texas Navy in the revolution and republic. Eugene C. Barker called it ''a comprehensive, useful, and authoritative study of the subject,'' and Jim Dan Hill said it ''has long stood as the most scholarly effort'' on the Texas Navy. It initially appeared in the *Southwestern Historical Quarterly* (vols. XII-XIII) from January through October, 1909. It is by this journal appearance that it is generally known; the book edition is one of the great Texana rarities. It contains a six-page preface and an index not in the journal edition.

In my copy Dienst has written: "Privately Printed . . . This has been a private publication—only intended for members of my family, intimate friends and presentation to Texas Universities. No copies for sale. 1st Edition 20 copies . . ." The volume contains no copyright but mine has a carbon of Dienst's letter submitting it for copyright. A few other copies were apparently released later, however, as some copies are known with a double sheet tipped in containing an "Appreciation" of Dienst by Eugene C. Barker. This appreciation, which is almost identical to Barker's sketch of Dienst in the *Handbook of Texas*, mentions Dienst's "death in 1938." I estimate about fifty copies were actually issued in all: twenty numbered copies in presentation morocco, and about thirty bound in cloth, circa 1940.

In his preface Dienst states: "My attention was attracted to this field of labor many years ago, by the numerous references I found to the Texas Navy in the files of New Orleans newspapers of 1835-45. As early as 1897 I was concentrating my efforts in securing Texas historical material bearing upon the navy. In October, 1900, in an article . . . I made the statement that I would write a history of the navy of the Revolution. Upon further reflection I concluded to write the history of the navy throughout its existence, and this, necessitating much more research and labor, has occupied all my spare moments for the past few years. Had I written this preface before I finished the work, I should no doubt have remarked that is was a 'labor of love'—writing the preface at the close of nine years of unremitting labor, irksome, tedious . . . and so forth, the expression would be anything but truthful; only those who have labored similarly can appreciate fully what toil and self-denial are required . . . for such a work as this . . . As to my qualifications for the work I have here undertaken, I have none to boast of, save a deep love for . . . Texas."

The text of the book is divided into eighteen chapters divided into two general parts—the navy of 1835-1839 and the navy of 1839-1846. Dienst was aided by his own collection, which included the valuable papers of Texas naval officer William A. Tennison and the Bryan-Hall-Christy Papers. These and other of Dienst's remarkable collections are now in the University of Texas Archives, while many of the books from his library are now in circulation. These, the bane of Texas collectors, are easily identifiable by the atrocious purple ink with which he scribbled in every book he ever owned.

Regarding earlier accounts of the Texas Navy, Dienst states: "Yoakum, who had very excellent opportunities, gives about seven pages to the navy; his statements contain several errors. Thrall gives about four pages, containing some good matter, but also a number of errors. Bancroft gives the same space as Yoakum, with very little new material. Brown . . . makes gross errors in the four pages he devotes to the Navy; Morphis has some four pages, copied from the other histories; he presents no new matter. [In] Pennybacker . . . less than one page is devoted to the first navy, and not one word is said in regard to Commodore Moore and the second navy."

Since Dienst's book, other books on the Texas Navy have been written. Jim Dan Hill's *The Texas Navy in Forgotten Battles and Shirtsleeve Diplomacy* (Chicago: Univ. of Chicago Press, 1937, 224pp.) builds on Dienst's volume but is unscholarly and overreaching in its conclusions. Hill's admirable goal of integrating "the maritime activities and naval operations with the complexities of the foreign and domestic affairs of the turbulent Mexican and Texan Republics" is not achieved in his text. C. L. Douglas's *Thunder on the Gulf; or, the Story of the Texas Navy* (Dallas: Turner Company, 1936, 128pp.) does little except add imaginary and improbable dialogue to Dienst's work. Tom Henderson Well's *Commodore Moore and the Texas Navy* (Austin: University of Texas Press, 1960, 218pp.) is scholarly and reliable regarding the second navy of the Texas republic.

Surprisingly, there is still another choice source for the Texas Navy that has never been utilized by any Texas naval historian at all: S. W. Cushing's *Wild Oats Sowings; or, the Autobiography of an Adventurer* (New York: Daniel Fanshaw, 1857, 483pp.). This work contains no less than ten chapters on Cushing's service in the Texas Navy during 1836, and is apparently authentic—Cushing did at least receive land grants for his service in the navy (Miller, *Bounty and Donation Land Grants of Texas*, p.206). Cushing has not been cited in any article or Texas book of which I am aware. His book is extremely rare, and this may explain why it has been so totally neglected.

Howes D339.

43 Dixon, Sam Houston (1855-1941), and Louis Wiltz Kemp (1881-1956)

THE HEROES OF SAN JACINTO

Announcement—

TO THE TRADE

This Book will be distributed by The Texas News Co.
Dallas, Texas, at the usual
discounts. It will be ready
November 1st.

THE HEROES OF SAN JACINTO

APRIL 21, 1836

By

SAM HOUSTON DIXON

and

LOUIS WILTZ KEMP

Illustrated
Centennial Edition

THE
ANSON JONES
HOUSTON PRESS TEXAS
1932

The Greatest Texas Book of Our Generation!

Houston: The Anson Jones Press, [1932].

xv,462pp. 8 plates. 25cm.

Blue cloth. Also red cloth. Every copy I have examined has the words "Centennial Edition" on the spine. Each copy also has a limitation notice signed by both authors reading: "This edition, each copy of which is autographed, is limited to one thousand and thirty-three copies for subscribers only." I have seen copies with the letters "G" and "Q" instead of numbers. Moreover, a four-page leaflet issued by the publisher, announcing the book will be published August, 1932, states that three editions will be issued: (1) "Descendants Edition," numbered 1 to 100 and interleaved with blanks; (2) "Centennial Edition," numbered 101 to 1033; (3) "Regular Trade Edition will be issued in the autumn." Actual copies I have seen bear no resemblance to this statement.

This is the best book to start any research on what has been called the sixteenth decisive battle in the history of the world. J. Frank Dobie said "it is likely to be turned to as long as people have any interest in Texas History." Clarence Wharton said that "this work is invaluable to students of Texas history [regarding the battle that] decided the fate of an empire." Herbert Gambrell said it succeeded in putting us in possession of most of the essential facts of the battle, which will always remain one of the most fateful on record, [one which] created the Republic of Texas and changed the course of American, and to a certain extent world history."

The work records the known facts about each of the 911 Texan participants in the battle, and includes an excellent 34-page historical summary of the battle itself. The data came primarily from muster rolls, bounty and donation certificates, comptroller's military service records, headright certificates, and pension records in the Texas State Archives and the General Land Office, as well as from the usual sources. Gambrell points out that "only those who have had first-hand experience with the materials on which this volume is based can have an adequate appreciation of the difficulties of the researcher and the patience and judgment necessary for the completion of the undertaking." Eugene C. Barker said of it that "the amount of work involved in the study can only be appreciated by one who knows the nature of the records."

The only drawback to use of the volume is the failure to cite exact references to the source of the data. Kemp fought to include this, but the publisher refused because of the cost involved. Kemp records that "in 1930 all material gathered up to that time relative to San Jacinto veterans was published in daily installments in the Houston *Chronicle* and Houston *Post-Dispatch*. This brought a deluge of letters from descendants of veterans and much supplemental information."

In addition to bare biographical and statistical details, the work includes many contemporary letters, diary excerpts, etc. One finds from it that nearly half of the participants had been in Texas less than six months at the time of the battle. One discovers that while the companies of Sherman, Turner, and Roman had virtually all come to Texas just to join the fight, Billingsley's Bastrop company was entirely old settlers and Seguin's company was mostly native Mexicans born in Texas. It is interesting, too, to see the backgrounds of this motley group of fighters. Willard Chamberlain came to Texas only because his girl turned down his marriage proposal (after the battle she relented and married the gallant hero). Reason Banks was cited for desertion and theft of a gun in Fannin's command but fought bravely (with the stolen gun) at San Jacinto. Joseph Ehlinger was an Alsatian who had fought in the Russian campaign under Napoleon.

The volume is almost entirely the work of Lou Kemp; although Dixon actually had known many of the participants and attended every meeting of the Texas Veterans Association from its first reunion onwards, he was 77 years old at the time of publication and did little of the actual writing of the book. Kemp had spent many years developing files (now at the University of Texas) indexing data on some 30,000 Texans of the 19th century, served as president of the Texas State Historical Association and of the San Jacinto Museum, and was chairman of the historical advisory board of the Texas Centennial. No man of his era, including Barker, Webb, and Streeter, knew more about individual Texans of the revolution and republic. Virginia Taylor wrote: "In his thorough and painstaking way Mr. Kemp gathered and assembled information, not section by section, but piece by piece, until he brought together a complete and accurate picture. He looked for facts, not legend, and he continued the quest until his death [contending] that the truth of Texas history was more colorful and dramatic than any of its tall tales or myths."

There is as yet no good general history of the Texas Revolution. There are three popular books that have some merit: Frank X.

Tolbert, *The Day of San Jacinto* (New York: McGraw-Hill, 1959, 261pp.); Lon Tinkle, 13 *Days to Glory: The Siege of the Alamo* (New York: McGraw-Hill, 1958, 255pp.); and Walter Lord, *A Time to Stand: The Epic of the Alamo* (New York: Harper, 1961, 255pp.). William C. Binkley wrote a short but perceptive overview of the war: *The Texas Revolution* (Baton Rouge: Louisiana State University Press, 1952, 132pp.).

Agatha, p.73. Howes D366.

44   Dobie, James Frank (1888-1964)

A VAQUERO OF THE BRUSH COUNTRY . . . PARTLY FROM THE REMINISCENCES OF JOHN YOUNG.

Dallas: The Southwest Press, 1929.
Illustrated by Justin C. Gruelle.
xv,314pp. 6 plates. Map end papers. 24cm.
Cloth-backed boards, dustjacket. 2000 copies printed.

Other issues:
- (A). Same as above. Verso of title: "Second edition."
- (B). Same as above. Verso of title: "Third edition."
- (C). Same as first edition, but on the endpaper maps the words "Rio Grande River" are changed to "Rio Grande."
- (D). New York: Grosset & Dunlap, Publishers, [1936]. xvi,302pp. Frontispiece, but without the other plates. Cloth. 22cm.
- (E). Boston: Little Brown and Company, 1943. Printed from the plates of (D), with new imprint. 21cm. Cloth. Five unidentified printings were issued.
- (F). Same as (E). Verso of title: "Sixth Printing." New 3-page preface by Lawrence Clark Powell entitled "The Time, the Place, and the Book." Cloth. 22cm. Issued in 1959.
- (G). London: Hammond, Hammond & Co., Ltd., 87 Gower Street, W.C. 1, [1949]. 274[3]. Cloth. 22cm.
- (H). New York: Pennant Books, [1954]. [8],184pp. 18cm. Paperback. Verso of Title: "Pennant Books are published by Bantam Books, Inc." Condensation of (E).
- (I). Reprint of (F). Austin: University of Texas Press, [1981]. Paperback.

This is Dobie's first complete book, published when he was 41; it is a lasting contribution to the literature of the Texas range. It presents the memoirs of John Duncan Young, a South Texas cattleman, as interpreted by Dobie. "The method of the book," wrote E. C. Barker, "is to weave into the reminiscences of John Duncan Young a compre-

(ORDER FORM)

THE SOUTHWEST PRESS,
P. O. Box 746, 2007 Bryan,
Dallas, Texas.

Gentlemen:

     my
You may enter our order for_____ cop_____ of
  "A VAQUERO OF THE BRUSH COUNTRY"
    Octavo. Price, $3.50.

*Name*_____

*Address*_____

*City*_____

☐ *Charge to my account.*
☐ *Send C. O. D.*
☐ *Remittance enclosed.*

 (*Check here and mail to your own bookseller*)
   or the publisher)

An Epic of the Southwest

→ *Third Large Printing* ←

J. Frank Dobie's
A Vaquero of the
Brush Country

Illustrated by Justin C. Gruelle

A Contribution to American Literature

Octavo—Bound in Imitation
Rattlesnake Skin . . Price **$3.50**

Biography, swift and strange—History for the first time opening a vista into the brush country, where the cattle industry of America began. Here Cortina rode, and the "vaquero"—cowboy—had a technique as individual as that of Hudson's gauchos.

A thousand fresh observations of nature—a Western book compounded of experience and perspective, achieving flavor—style.

hensive study of many phases of the cattle business.'' Henry Nash Smith called it a ''history which is at the same time a personal expression and a prose poem . . . What fund of erudition and what countless strokes of art have gone into this easy-going, even homely narrative.'' It caused a sensation when it appeared, began Dobie's national reputation, and paved the way for his more famous book, *Coronado's Children,* on which Dobie was already at work when *Vaquero* appeared in print.

Dobie had met the legendary John Young while teaching at Alpine High School. Young wanted to write an autobiography and suggested a collaboration. Lon Tinkle said that ''the association did not 'fully satisfy' Mr. Young, either financially . . . or personally or professionally, since Dobie emphasized the 'sociology' of ranching far more than Mr. Young's individual experiences.'' Dobie, on the other hand, says that he and Young ''made medicine, and John Young began firing in certain episodes of his career. But the book that has resulted can hardly be considered as the biography of a single man.'' Thus a book was created that to some readers is a perfect blend, and to others a confusing mixture of an old cowman and a college professor. Dobie allows the narrative to flow in the first person as though by Young, but the wording and indeed many whole sections are entirely from the mind of Frank Dobie.

The result is frequently confusing, and, to me, not always successful. I want to know what John Young thought and said, in his own words, and I also want to know what Frank Dobie had to say about them, with all his amplifications—but in this book Dobie's own genius runs roughshod over all else. It is Dobie's book, and Dobie's point of view, in spite of the technique of letting the old cowman appear to do the talking.

For example, in one of the most memorable sections, Dobie has Young tell about one of the earliest roundups of wild, unbranded range steers. It is a portrayal that will live in the mind of the reader forever, but the wording (''oftener than otherwise,'' etc.) is pure Dobie; I would also have liked to hear it in Young's own words. Part of it reads: ''After a hard day's hunt we headed toward camp with around a hundred head of the wildest and shaggiest bunch of scalawag steers than I have ever seen together. They ran and fought all the way, and out of the hundred we corralled only thirty-seven head. A good portion of these had to be roped and led in. When one of these old steers headed out of the herd for the brush he was ready to hook the liver out of anything that got in front of him. The horns were not for ornament. Oftener than otherwise it did no good to rope such a steer, as he would start fighting as soon as he felt the rope tighten. Then if he was thrown down he was likely to sulk and refuse to get up. A vaquero might kick and spur the hide off his backbone, might rub sand in his eyes, and still the steer would refuse to budge. Finally if he did get up, he would be so 'on the prod' that nothing could come close enough to touch him with a forty-foot pole. While a hand was fooling with one such steer, a dozen others would get away. . . . And thus the cow hunt went on. Horses were crippled or gored daily. By something like a miracle none of us was even badly hurt. After working a few weeks we had 1200 head of steers gathered. We delivered them at the McDaniel pens. The buyer, so we heard, scattered them all the way to Kansas. I doubt if half of them ever crossed Red River. On the cow hunt next spring we found several of them back on the coast making trouble.''

The problem for the scholar is that Dobie the historian frequently conflicts with Dobie the storyteller. In one of the books in my collection, Dobie has written: ''Sometimes I make a misquotation on purpose, and sometimes I make it in ignorance . . . I used to be more conscientious about correctness of quotations than I am now. I guess Hazlitt had a bad effect on me in that respect.''

The text includes, in addition to Young's life as a pioneer cowman and outlaw chases, sections on roundups and cattle drives, on the hide and tallow business in Texas, on Billy the Kid and the Mexican outlaw Cortina, on life in the South Texas brush country, on Mexican and Indian warfare along the border after the Civil War, and on the folk ways of the Texas cattle industry.

The book was published by P. L. Turner's recently established Southwest Press, an attempt to establish a self-supporting, commercially viable Texas publishing house. Dobie was a minor stockholder. The depression brought a close to this worthy project in 1935, and Dobie never got all the royalties due him, although he was able to regain the copyright. In Dobie's own copy of the book, he wrote a note dated December 22, 1955: "To reprint this book, Grosset and Dunlap had to reset the type, the original plates having been destroyed—though I had a chance to buy them from P. L. Turner (Southwest Press). The edition did not sell well—10,000 or more copies, some of which were remaindered. I bought the plates from Grosset and Dunlap and for several years Little, Brown & Co. has used them, keeping them in print."

Adams Herd 702. Adams Guns 606. Dobie, p.102. Howes D376. McVicker A1. Reese *Six Score* 34.

45 Dobie, James Frank (1888-1964)

CORONADO'S CHILDREN: TALES OF LOST MINES AND BUR-IED TREASURES OF THE SOUTHWEST.

Dallas: The Southwest Press, [1930].
xv,[1],367pp. Illus. by Ben Carlton Mead. 24cm.
Cloth, dustjacket. Map endpapers.
In the first printing, the end of the dedication reads "a cowman of the Texas soil."

Other issues:
(A). Second state of the first edition. Dedication ending reads: "A clean cowman of the Texas soil."
(B). New York: The Literary Guild of America, 1931.
(C). Garden City, New York: Garden City Publishing Company, Inc., [1934]. Same collation, except text on page xv deleted.
(D). New York: Grosset & Dunlap, [1939]. Printed from the first edition plates. There were eleven printings, as follows: 1st, April, 1939; 2nd, October, 1939; 3rd, October, 1941; 4th, August, 1943; 5th, January, 1944; 6th, December, 1945; 7th, September, 1946; 8th, May, 1948; 9th, October, 1949; 10th, February, 1951; 11th, April, 1952.
(E). Same as (D), circa 1943, with notice on title page concerning printing "under wartime conditions."
(F). Braille edition. Louisville, Ky.: American Printing House for the Blind, 1949. Embossed in fine volumes.
(G). Paperback edition. New York: Bantam Books, [1953]. [12],371pp. 16cm.
(H). *Lost Mines of the Old West: Coronado's Children.* London: Hammond, Hammond and Company, [1960]. [16],367pp. 22cm. Cloth, dustjacket. First English edition.
(I). Austin and London: University of Texas Press, [1978]. xxii,329pp. Illus. by Charles Shaw. 23cm. Foreword by Frank Wardlaw. Barker Texas History Center Series No. 3. Cloth, dustjacket. Verso of title: "First University of Texas Press Edition."

(J).   Special edition of (I). Printed notice on page [331] stating that 300 numbered
       copies were issued, signed by Wardlaw and Shaw. Slipcased.
(K).   Special edition. Dallas: Nieman-Marcus, 1980. xiv,270,[1]pp. 33cm. Folding map
       and eleven maps and diagrams, some in color. A sumptuous edition, bound in
       half goatskin and slipcased. Colophon: "This book was designed and printed
       by the Arion Press of San Francisco in an edition limited to 300 copies . . .
       Andrew Hoyem, director. . . . "
(L).   Paperback edition of (I), [1981].

This is the best work ever written on hidden treasure, and one of
the most fascinating books on any subject to come out of Texas. About
eighty percent of the text relates to Texas. It was an outgrowth of
Dobie's *Legends of Texas,* issued in 1924 as volume III of the Publications
of the Texas Folklore Society. A mimeographed statement in Dobie's
papers dated November 22, 1930, apparently written when *Coronado's
Children* was under consideration by the Literary Guild, states: "The
history of Legends of Texas is not without significance. . . . We issued
1500 copies first. I had to take the financial risk for paying the
printer—and my wife and friends thought I'd have to pay the debt.
Within six months we made a second printing of 1250 copies."

After the success of *Legends of Texas,* in which Dobie, Webb, and
many others had recounted various Texas legends on treasure, ghosts,
and other subjects, Dobie began gathering treasure tales in earnest.
He used some of his tales for articles in *American Mercury, Yale Review,
Southwest Review,* and other magazines, then compiled them into the
book to be called *Coronado's Children.* Meanwhile, *A Vaquero of the Brush
Country* was issued by Southwest Press, in which Dobie had an interest,
and Dobie contracted to have the treasure book printed there as well.

When Dobie shipped the final manuscript to the publisher on June
19, 1930, he wrote that he was in a daze "now that I am parting with
'Coronado's Children.' For ten years I have been writing it. I doubt
if I shall ever produce anything else that will have so much of *me* in
it. These stories and the people in them are far more real to me than
any stories I ever read or the people with whom I associate daily. I
know that I should feel elated at ridding myself of them, but I don't."

In Dobie's copy of the first issue of the book, now in the Dobie
Collection at the University of Texas, he wrote: "John William Rogers,
a prig then and a rich, pudgy, selfish toad now, was right bower to P.
L. Turner, owner of the S.W. Press, when this book was printed in
1930, though it was not published until March 1931, a Literary Guild

Selection. I had read proof and when I saw this dedication page in the book, I saw I had been betrayed . . . Somebody ignorant of cow country language and possessed of an unclean mind, some oily literalist—and it could only have been Rogers—had deleted 'clean.'" In my own copy of the book, Dobie has written: "Some damned fool connected with the Southwest Press thought that *clean* was indecent and cut it out. In the second and other printings the dedication is printed as I wrote it."

Dobie wrote other books with stories of lost mines, the best of which is *Apache Gold & Yaqui Silver* (Boston: Little, Brown and Company, 1939, 366pp.), which tells of the Lost Tayopa Mine, the Lost Adams Diggings, and others. My copy is inscribed from Dobie to the man who first told him of the Tayopa legend; I also have the original of one of Tom Lea's exquisite illustrations for the book.

Dobie states that the book consists of "tales that are just tales. As tales I have listened to them in camps under stars and on ranch galleries out in the brush. As tales, without any ethnological palaver, I have tried to set them down." Frank Wardlaw's introduction to the fine University of Texas Press edition says that "in essence, but not in detail, these tales of treasure hunters are preserved just as Frank Dobie heard them. He never claimed to be a folklorist in the professional sense. He admitted that he had 'a constructive memory' and that 'after I have heard a tale I do all I can to improve it.'" Dobie also said of himself that he was "too fond of facts for a fictionlist and too fond of stories for a historian."

In this regard *Coronado's Children,* like so many of Dobie's other works, is not straight history. It is Dobie's version of other people's stories, and there is a great deal of Dobie in each of them. This makes good reading but frustrating history, although Dobie carefully annotates all his sources and includes a useful glossary of local terminology used in the text. Larry McMurtry said that the observant reader "will discover midway through *Coronado's Children* that he was . . . a hasty and impatient writer," but this is not true. Any perusal of Dobie's manuscripts, with their multiple drafts and extensive revisions, shows that Dobie was a very careful writer who took enormous pains to say what he had to say with precision. With Dobie, one must be satisfied to receive the presentation in Dobie's own chosen manner, the manner of the storyteller.

Adams Guns 600. Agatha, p.69. Howes D374. McVicker A2.

46 Dresel, Gustav (1818-1848)

GUSTAV DRESEL'S HOUSTON JOURNAL: ADVENTURES IN NORTH AMERICA AND TEXAS, 1837-1841.

Austin: University of Texas Press, 1954. Co-published with Thomas Nelson and Sons, Ltd. (Edinburgh, London, Melbourne, Cape Town, Toronto, and Paris).
Translated from a German Manuscript and Edited by Max Freund.
xxx,168pp. 9 illus. 24cm.
Cloth, dustjacket.

Other issues:
(A). Paperback edition, same date and collation. 21cm.

One of the most revealing accounts of Texas written by a German, this is also the best translation from German of any Texas text. A garbled edition from an inferior text had been published in German in 1920-21 in the yearbook of the German-American Historical Society of Illinois, but until this 1954 edition none of it had appeared in English.

Editor-translator Max Freund of Rice University worked from a 355-page manuscript acquired by the Library of Congress in 1931. He states that his translation "was practically ready for printing in 1939. Publication was postponed owing to the ensuing outbreak of war and attendant circumstances." With the assistance of E. W. Winkler, R. L. Biesele, Herbert Fletcher, Andrew Muir, and others he completed the final text in January, 1954. Walter Posey said that "probably no one was better prepared to translate the journal than Dr. Freund, a native of Saxony, a distinguished professor emeritus of German at Rice Institute, and a long-time student of the Germanic element in Texas." Freund provides a substantial introduction, giving biographical data and background as well as 25 pages of footnotes to the text.

The Dresel journal, written in the third person, covers the years 1837 to 1841, with a postscript written in 1847. Since the title of the original manuscript was "Erlebnisse in Nordamerika und Texas, 1837-

41," calling it *Houston Journal* is an unjustified and misleading narrowing of the true scope of the narrative. It is of much broader interest than the village of Houston. Dresel comments on a wide variety of subjects, such as the militia, slavery, Indians, the "sensuous ecstasy" of Methodist revivals, economics, epidemics, travel conditions, and German immigration. It is an altogether personal view of Texas in the eyes of a young man between the ages of 19 and 23.

"There can be no doubt," writes Freund, "that Dresel's account constitutes an important source for that period of the history of civilization in that part of the world. In its final form, which alone is extant, Dresel's so-called 'journal' is not a real journal or diary in the strict and original meaning of these terms. That is to say, it is not, and perhaps it never was, a day-by-day record of events. His narrative is based, however, on what must have been fairly copious notes. . . . Unpretentious as is Dresel's account with regard to form, it is not without interest for the historian of literature. . . . It is true that Dresel never breaks into verse like Heine. But there are purple patches of eloquent or humorous prose in his account, as in Heine."

Dresel's humor pops out frequently in the journal. While visiting an Alabama-Coushatta Indian village in East Texas, he watched the near-naked squaws suckling their children, and commented on their breasts: "It is striking in what unnatural manner the protusion of the upper part of the female body changes as soon as the women have children. The shapes of the girls are regular and beautiful. But those of the married women undergo so great a change that I began to believe . . . that the Indian women give their breasts to their babies even while the infants remain tied to their backs."

Dresel's youthful enthusiasm for Texas enabled him to absorb much of what was happening around him. He writes: "There was lively and varied activity going on in Houston at the time. Steamboats from Galveston tied up daily. The owners of land certificates who had selected the finest free land, and tradesmen of all sorts arrived on horseback from the interior of the country, among them many a Mexican smuggler. They brought news from the frontier, pointed out the beauty of newly discovered regions, and described their adventures with the Indians and wild beasts. In short, time passed quickly; being kept in a state of excitement, people forgot all their privations."

In 1841 Dresel returned to Germany and was soon at work for the Society for the Protection of German Immigrants in Texas, led by Prince Carl of Solms-Braunfels. He returned to Texas in 1847, with an appointment as Consul of the Duchy of Nassau for the State of Texas, as well as colonial agent for the German immigration society. He died in 1848, at the age of 30, of yellow fever, shortly after completing the 1847 addendum to his journal. An introduction to the journal by the poet Hoffmann von Fallersleben, is known to have been written, but it has never come to light.

The volume is well-indexed and contains useful illustrations, including a contemporary portrait of young Dresel smoking a cigar. Some of the annotations are ponderous and some a bit simplistic, but in the main they add greatly to understanding the text.

47 Duganne, Augustine Joseph Hickey (1823-1884)

CAMPS AND PRISONS: TWENTY MONTHS IN THE DEPARTMENT OF THE GULF.

New York: J. P. Robens, Publisher, 1865.
424pp. Illus. 19cm. Cloth. "Subscriber's Edition."

Other issues:
(A). "Second edition" [i.e., second printing]. Same date and collation.
(B). "Third edition" [i.e., third printing]. Same date and collation.
(C). *Beadle's Monthly*, N.Y., 1866, vol. I, contains in the January and February issues (pp. 38-45 and 144-148) two extracts from Duganne's book.

The best account of prison life in Texas during the Civil War, this is also one of the few good contemporary accounts of the impact of the war on Texas. Allan Nevins called it "unimpassioned and well written," and E. Merton Coulter said it is an "observant account of conditions in the Federal Army, in Confederate prisons, and the countryside of Louisiana and Texas . . . a first-rate travel account." George H. Genzmer called it "honest, vivid, and packed with detail. Its account of life in Texas during the war is of historical value."

Duganne prior to the war was the author of numerous books of poetry, philosophy, economics, and government, including fiction ranging from Beadle novels to dramatic tragedy. Virtually all of his books, before and after the war, were markedly bad. His one work of personal narrative, however, is of lasting interest and importance, telling of his adventures as a prisoner of war in Texas. Duganne entered the Civil War in the autumn of 1862 as lieutenant colonel of the 176th New York Volunteers, who were sent by ship to Louisiana in early 1863. In June through no fault of his own but partly through the lack of spirit of his men, Duganne was forced to surrender his entire command as well as Brashear City to Texas-Confederate forces. He and his men were marched through Louisiana to the Sabine, sent by steamboat to Beaumont and by rail to Houston. They were imprisoned in Houston for a time, then sent to Camp Groce at Hempstead and finally on to Camp Ford at Tyler. In July of 1864 Duganne was exchanged at the mouth of the Red River and mustered out for disability in September. He was thus enabled to immediately set to work writing *Camps and Prisons,* the result, he says, "of a promise made by the Author to his comrades in exile as prisoners-of-war. . . . Personal statements and actual observations have alone furnished material for the book."

The narrative is somewhat overwritten, changes without notice from the past to present tense and from third to first person, and yet manages to be fresh and charming. It abounds in overblown phrases such as "the pirate Semmes and his ubiquitous Alabama" and valiant Farragut who "gave back our starry flag to the arms of the Father of Waters." Whenever Duganne forgets his pose as literary artist, however, he gives us a vivid picture of his experiences. Throughout most of the narrative, he simply tells us what happened and what he saw and heard. His is the earliest and still most complete account of the part of the war he experienced. A former correspondent of Sam Houston and acquaintance of some of his Texas captors (including E. H. Cushing, who sent him free copies of the Houston *Telegraph* while he was in the prison stockades), Duganne was enabled to hear reports of both sides of the war in the Gulf and in the western arenas.

Duganne leaves us by far the best account of the Confederate prison at Camp Ford; during most of his time there he was senior officer of the prisoners. He was one of the editors of "The Old Flag," a handwritten prison camp newspaper that has since become famous. He describes the Yankee ingenuity and passion for activity that so impressed his languid Texas guards. "I venture to affirm that it would not surprise our rebel guards if we built paper mills and steam-presses, and set up a daily paper in our corral. They tell us . . . with open mouths, that our Yankee armies have 'right smart o' soldiers that kin get up sich tricks.' " His account of his relatively light treatment has frequently been compared with that at other Confederate hell holes like Andersonville. Another account that is similar to Duganne's, but less well-written, was published the same year by Duganne's junior officer, Charles Cooper Nott, who was captured, imprisoned, and released at the same time as Duganne. Nott's book is *Sketches in Prison Camps* (New York: A. D. F. Randolph, 1865, 204pp.). A modern account may be found in F. Lee Lawrence and R. W. Glover, *Camp Ford C.S.A: The Story of Union Prisoners in Texas* (Austin, 1964, 99pp.).

Duganne is surprisingly frank in his denunciation of Union activities in Texas. He describes in detail the capture and loss of Galveston, the action at Sabine Pass, and the actions against the Texas forces in Louisiana, recorded from conversations with fellow captives who were present. At the end of the chapter on the Galveson fiasco, he writes, "Thus we lost Galveston. . . . Thus Burrell and his officers were consigned to nineteen months' captivity in dungeons and corrals. And, above all, thus the entire Texas coast was lost, the rebel cause inspired and strengthened, and a rebel army organized at once from crowds of volunteers. Thus old Tom Green, Sibley, Pyron, Scurry, Majors, Leon Smith, Magruder, Baylor, and a dozen other leaders were enabled to inflate the Texas mind with overweening pride of state and personal superiority." He calls the Union commander's actions at Galveston "the most disgraceful and cowardly action upon record."

His conclusions regarding Union actions in Texas during the war: "Texas indeed was the gate and outer wall of the Confederacy. It was a prize worthy of our best steel. But what is the history of our campaigns against Texas? We captured Galveston, the key city, and lost it disgracefully. We menaced Sabine City, with a fleet and army, and were repulsed by two score militia men. We . . . penetrated the Calcasieu with gun-boats, only to withdraw irresolutely from both. We . . . pawed at the edge of the Nueces wilderness . . . then returned, without accomplishing anything. . . . So much for our invasions of Texas. I shall not discuss the 'Generalship' which directed them.''

Coulter 136. Nevins II-190.

48 Dunt, Detlef

REISE NACH TEXAS, NEBST NACHRICHTEN VON DIESEM LANDE: FUER DEUTSCHE, WELCHE NACH AMERIKA ZU GEHEN BEABSICHTIGEN.

Bremen: Gedruckt bei Carl Wilh. Wiehe, 1834.
viii,158,[4]pp. 18cm.
Boards.

This is the first book by a German devoted exclusively to Texas. The only book in German to precede it is J. Valentin Hecke's *Reise durch die Vereinigten Staaten von Nord-Amerika in den Jahren 1818 und 1819* (Berlin: H.Ph. Petri, 1820-1821), which includes two chapters on Texas. Almost nothing is known of Detlef Dunt either before or after his trip to Texas, but his *Reise nach Texas* has often been credited with starting the major flow of German immigration into Texas. This important but little-known volume has never been translated into English nor reprinted, and there are only three known copies of the original.

Dunt came to Texas after reading the famous essay-letter of Friedrich Ernst written from Mill Creek, Texas, Austin' Colony, February 1, 1832. This letter, which Dunt prints in full, contains a wealth of details on life in Texas, on the virtually free lands available to colonists, and on Ernst's happy experiences living in Austin's Colony. The Ernst letter is translated into English in Gilbert G. Benjamin's *The Germans in Texas: A Study in Immigration* (Philadelphia: University of Pennsylvania, 1910), although it is mistakenly signed Fritz Dirks instead of Friedrich Ernst. Dunt says of Ernst's letter: ''In Oldenburg, a country in which the people are generally poor, this letter could not fail to create a sensation, especially since the emigration fever had recently seized hold of the people.''

Ernst is quoted by Dunt as saying that in Texas there is ''no need for money, free exercise of religion, and the best markets for all products at the Mexican harbors. . . . We men satisfy outselves with

hunting and horse-races. . . . For my acquaintances and former countrymen I have on my estate a stopping place until they have selected
a league of land.''

Dunt decided to visit Ernst's settlement, and his book records his
five-month trip from Oldenburg to Texas via New York, New Orleans,
and Velasco, his inspection of Texas from April, 1833, to the fall of
that year, and his visit with Ernst. Dunt's preface is dated ''Plantation
of Friedr. Ernst on Mill Creek . . . in September, 1833.''

He praises Texas highly, although he was annoyed by the delays
experienced by German colonists at the land offices. He compares the
countryside to that of southern Italy and says the prairies abound in
wild flowers and that the climate is salubrious. The combination of
the Ernst letter and Dunt's confirmation induced large numbers of
Germans to desire to go to Texas. Among these were such later
important citizens as F. W. Grassmeyer and Robert Kleberg. The
Ernst community became known as Industry.

Howes D580. Sabin 21342. Streeter 1144.

49   Durham, George (ca. 1857-1940), as Told to Clyde Wantland

TAMING THE NUECES STRIP: THE STORY OF MCNELLY'S
RANGERS.

Austin: University of Texas Press, [1962].
Foreword by Walter Prescott Webb.
xx,178pp. Illus. 22cm.
Cloth, dustjacket.

Other issues:
(A). Second printing, 1969.
(B). Third printing, 1975.

This is one of the few accounts of the McNelly Rangers, told by a
member of the force. A. Ray Stephens called it ''a delightful addition
to the Southwestern literature . . . written in a clear, easy to read—
almost folksy-style with details drawn so sharply that the reader seems
to smell the acrid gunsmoke and to hear the creak of saddle leather.''
Margaret Hartley said ''Wantland has been careful to preserve all the
feeling of Durham's memoirs, and the result is good, exciting reading.''
Henderson Shuffler called it a ''gem of Texana, genuine, readable,
informative.''

George Durham was the last surviving member of McNelly's Rangers. By the time Clyde Wantland finally got him to open up and tell his story, sometime in the late 1930's, "he had become more than an institution; he was a legend, especially in law-enforcement circles. At that time he had been a resident of Texas for nearly sixty years. . . . He had been a peace officer the entire time—either a Texas Ranger or a deputy sheriff. Veteran officers estimated that Durham had 'handled' more than nine hundred outlaws and wanted men."

The narrative covers only two years of the sixty Durham spent as a lawman. It comprises his service in 1875-1876 as a member of Leander H. McNelly's Texas Rangers, during the period the rangers pacified the outrageously lawless area of South Texas between the Nueces and the Rio Grande. In his foreword, Webb states: "It was in the period between 1874 and 1880 that the Texas Rangers did their greatest work. They had then their finest opportunity, because the state was full of things requiring their attention. The Comanche Indians were still raiding in the western half of the state. The interior was plagued with lawless men, often organized into mobs, engaged in feuds which terrorized whole counties. . . . Horse thieves and train and stage robbers were numerous and elusive. The Nueces Strip stood out as something special in the way of brigandage, murder, and theft. It had more than its share. . . ."

Durham was the youngest member of the small McNelly force of about thirty rangers sent to pacify the strip. His account, although dictated from memory years after, bears all the marks of a truthful narrative. Webb says that Durham was one of the most reliable of all his sources on the Texas Rangers. After leaving the rangers, Durham was hired by Richard King as foreman of one of the divisions of the King Ranch, a post he held for many decades. During this period, Durham wrote down his recollections and stored the pages in a trunk at his home on the ranch. When he began to talk to Wantland, a free-lance reporter, he had these pages to assist him.

He recounts vividly the legendary exploits of the rangers on the border—of recovering stolen herds of cattle, stopping banditry, and the many fights against Cortina. They even crossed over the border and raided the Mexican bandit camps. When the U.S. Army commander complained to McNelly that this was illegal and ordered him to return, McNelly sent him the following message: "I shall remain in Mexico with my Rangers and cross back at my discretion. Give my compliments to the secretary of war and tell him his United States soldiers can go to hell."

Durham was, naturally, a strong admirer of Captain McNelly. The border people were not uniform in this regard, by any means, and even today McNelly's tactics are subject to criticism—not the least on account of his torturing and hanging prisoners. Durham's justification of all the much-criticized deeds of McNelly is therefore especially important, as it gives us a very clear view of how that magnetic and forceful leader was able to engender total compliance from his young rangers. Durham's awe and respect never waned. He told Wantland: "I've been a McNelly all my life. I expect to die a McNelly. And when I get Over Yonder, I want to go back to work for the Captain if he's still running an outfit."

Adams Guns 652.

50 Duval, John Crittenden (1816-1897)

THE ADVENTURES OF BIG-FOOT WALLACE, THE TEXAS RANGER AND HUNTER.

Philadelphia: Claxton, Remsen & Haffelfinger, 819 & 821 Market Street; Macon, Ga.. J. W. Burke & Co., 1871.
xii,[13],291pp. Frontis. portrait of Wallace by J. W. Orr and 7 illlus. by H. Faber. 19cm.
Cloth. Verso of title: Stereotyped by J. Fagan & Son. Printed by Moore Brothers.
The first issue has no footnote on page 173, and Derringer spelled "Deringers" on line 7, page 153. That it was actually issued in late 1870 is indicated by the fact that a copy was deposited in the Library of Congress on October 21, 1870. Also, several known copies are inscribed and dated in December, 1870.

Other issues:
(A). Same imprint and collation, with "Second Edition" and 1872 on title page. A footnote is added to page 173, Derringer is spelled "Derringers" on page 153, and other corrections are made within the text.
(B). Same imprint and collation, with "Second Edition" and 1873 on title page. The address of the Philadelphia firm is changed to 624, 626, & 628 Market St. The 1st issue, (A), and (B) each have a different style of monogrammed CRH on the spine. Printed on inferior paper.

AUSTIN   TEXAS

BIG FOOT WALLACE

by JOHN C. DUVAL

☆   ☆   ☆

THE FLAVOR and the spirit of early Texas have been captured for countless readers by John C. Duval's *Big Foot Wallace*. This riotous narrative of the adventures of one of the saltiest and most individualistic pioneer Indian fighters that the state ever produced is told in a leisurely, satirical fashion that reflects a way of life long since lost.

Duval's chronicle of one of Texas' greatest adventurers is filled with Wallace's humor and colorful speech. Wallace emerges from the book in all his vigor and robustness, and the reader is transported to a rugged, uncultivated frontier where a few men who were rough enough were carving out a new frontier.

According to reliable authorities, the first edition of *Big Foot Wallace* is the edition bearing on its title page the date 1871. It is from this edition that the new Steck facsimile reprint has been made. Both the binding and the end sheets have been carefully copied from the the original edition. *309 pages; illustrated.* $2.50

☆   ☆   ☆

WRITE FOR COMPLETE CATALOG OF TEXANA

(C). Same title and collation, except issued solely by J. W. Burke and Company, with "Third Edition" and the date 1885 printed on the title page. The title page and copyright page are reset, and the text is printed from the original plates, with the footnote "His horse" deleted from page 151. There are only five plates in addition to the frontispiece.

(D). Fourth edition. Same title, with The J. W. Burke Company, 1921, on title page. Printed from new type in a different font. xv,309pp. Frontis. and 5 plates.

(E). Same title, with faked title page. The so-called "Gammel Edition," this issue consists of the sheets of issue (D) and an altered title page. Gammel's Book Store bought 837 copies of this 1921 edition, mostly still in sheets, and had a title page substituted that deleted the "Fourth Edition," changed the publisher's name on the title page to J. W. Burke and Company (but left the newer name of The J. W. Burke Co. on the back panel) and added the fake date of 1870. [4],vii-xv,309pp. 20cm.

(F). Same title and imprint as issue (E), a facsimile of the Gammel Edition, innocently including the fabricated title page, adding The Steck Company, Austin, 1935.

(G). Same title. Dallas, Tardy Publishing Company, 1936. xxxv, 353pp. 20cm. In a new format, with notes and introduction by Mabel Major and Rebecca W. Smith. Best edition.

(H). Same title and collation as the first issue, except containing only 5 plates and frontis., the words "Facsimile by The Steck Company, Austin, Texas," at bottom of title page, and on verso of title: "1947 Facsimile Reproduction of the First Edition, The Steck Company, Austin, Texas." Having discovered the error committed in (F), Steck reprinted the true first edition from this date onward. This Steck edition was kept in print for many years through several unidentified printings.

(I). Reprint of (G). Lincoln: University of Nebraska Press, [1966]. Same collation. Bison Book 343.

(J). Paperback edition of (I). Same collation.

This is a well-written account of a fascinating Texas Ranger and hero. J. Frank Dobie called it "the rollickiest and the most flavorsome that any American frontiersman has yet inspired. The tiresome thumping on the hero theme present in many biographies of frontiersmen is entirely absent." T. M. Pearce said the portion about the Mier Expedition "stands as the most valuable account of that tragic episode of Texas history." Sister Agatha called the book "one of the best ranger stories on record, and the style in which it is told is most attractive." Mabel Major said "no book of early Texas seems likelier to become classic than this one."

Throughout most of their lives Duval and Wallace were the closest of friends. Both lost brothers in the Fannin Massacre in the Texas Revolution. Both served under Jack Hays in the Texas Rangers. They hunted together for nearly fifty years. They were the same age. Duval states that in 1867, while he was recovering from an illness in San Antonio, he decided to pay Wallace a visit. A visit in Texas at that time was no overnight affair; Duval stayed two weeks, hunting, fishing, riding, and "entertained each night with 'yarns' of his numerous 'scrapes.'" Duval convinced Wallace to allow his story to be told, and the two collaborated.

The work divides naturally into three parts: Wallace as hunter and Indian fighter; Wallace on the Mier Expedition; and Wallace's trip home to Virginia. The first part (28 chapters) contains Wallace's first-person narrative of all his adventures in the wilds of unsettled Texas, with dozens of hunting tales and even more Indian fights. The second part (11 chapters) is the nearly exact history of Wallace's service in the Mier Expedition, his capture, the drawing for the black beans, and his term in Perote Prison. The last part (7 chapters) is an hilarious first-hand account of his trip via New Orleans to Virginia.

The work certainly contains dramatizations and some downright fiction. Dobie said: "Always free and at home with himself, Bigfoot opened up to his old friend Duval with gusto, and Duval helped him stretch the blanket." Wallace himself considered it a story mainly for children, and an exaggerated portrait. After Duval's death, Wallace retold his life story to Andrew J. Sowell, who published it as *Life of "Big Foot" Wallace . . . the Only Reliable History of the Famous Frontiersman* (Devine, Texas?, 1899, 123pp.). This was in turn reprinted by J. Marvin Hunter in 1927; Hunter said: "Wallace told a number of people it [the Sowell book] was the only authentic and correct history of his life ever written." So one can choose between two Bigfoot Wallace lives, both having had Wallace's aid and blessing: one full of spark and favored by the literary-minded, and one dry and factual, favored by the literalists.

I would say that the hunting adventures in Duval are stretched for effect, that the Mier account is almost straight history, and that the trip to Virginia is more fiction than fact. Wallace's story of his stay in a New Orleans hotel and visits to a theater and dance are too akin to the Davy Crockett tradition to be anything close to the literal truth—even though they make entertaining, if a bit insipid, reading.

Stanley Vestal (W. S. Campbell) wrote *Bigfoot Wallace, a Biography* (Boston: Houston Mifflin, 1942, 299pp.), but there is still no really good modern scholarly biography of Wallace. Vestal states in his preface, without giving his source: "*The Adventures of Bigfoot Wallace* by John C. Duval did not satisfy Wallace: for some time he refused Duval's request to write him up, and on giving his consent begged Duval not to caricature him; it seems likely that Bigfoot gave the true story to Sowell because of his dissatisfaction with Duval's book. Duval was a competent writer, knew Wallace well, and might easily have produced a sound biography had he taken the same pains with Bigfoot's life-story that he devoted to the recounting of his own adventures. As it was, he turned out a pretty juvenile, fatuously supposing that he could invent a better man than Bigfoot. Duval created a very readable yarn, but no portrait; the genteel tradition vitiated his work."

Agatha, p.51. Clark, *New South* I-65. Dobie, p.55. Graff 1187. Howes D602. Rader 1247. Raines, p.73.

51   Duval, John Crittenden (1816-1897)

EARLY TIMES IN TEXAS.

Austin: H. P. N. Gammel & Co., Publishers, 1892.
135,[1],1-253pp. 20cm.
Cloth.

Other issues:
(A). Same as above, deleting the section "The Young Explorers." Austin: H. P. N. Gammel & Co., Publishers, 1892. 135,[4],244-253pp. 18cm. Printed wrappers, with notice on front that the two works have been separated and issued "separately in paper cover and sold at 25 cents each, postage prepaid. Address, Jno. W. Maddox, Austin, Texas."
(B). Same as (A), in printed wrappers bearing only the title and author, with "Austin, Texas. Gammel's Book Store" at bottom on front cover. 19cm.
(C). *The Story of an Escape from the Massacre at Goliad.* Houston: The Union National Bank, [1927]. [2],2-5,[2],7-91pp. 23cm. Printed wrappers. Consists of a complete reprint of *Early Times in Texas.*

(D). Facsimile reprint of the entire first edition. Austin: The Steck Company, 1935. 21cm. Cloth.

(E). Barrington, George W. *Back from Goliad.* Dallas: Southwest Press, [1935]. [4],152pp. 20cm. Cloth. "A retelling of *Early Times in Texas* in feeble and thin novel form."—J. Frank Dobie.

(F). Reprint of (C), 1936. 64pp. Type reset. Printed wrappers.

(G). *Early Times in Texas, or the Adventures of Jack Dobell.* Dallas: Tardy Publishing Company, 1936. [2],v-xxiv,[4],284pp. 20cm. Cloth. Edited by Mabel Major and Rebecca W. Smith. Illustrated by Jerry Bywaters. Best edition, with excellent introduction and annotations.

(H). Facsimile reprint of (D). Austin: Steck-Vaughn Co., [1967]. 238pp. 22cm. Cloth. Introduction by John Q. Anderson.

This is the most literate of all 19th century Texas memoirs. Unlike the author's other writings, it is authentic history, with only a little exaggeration thrown in here and there. Mabel Major said it has "been generally accepted as a trustworthy record of Duval's experiences. . . . The story would be exciting even if it were not true. [It] is one of the classics of pioneer literature." J. Frank Dobie said "the historical accuracy of Duval's *Early Times in Texas* has been noted by all scholars who have collated it with the accounts of other escapes. . . . Emphatically Duval was truthful." Dobie also called it "a Texas classic. Of all personal adventures of old-time Texans it is perhaps the best written and the most interesting."

Duval in this book gives a vivid account of his capture and miraculous escape from the massacre of Fannin's command at Goliad in 1836. Duval's brother, Burr H. Duval, had brought a company of volunteers from Kentucky to Texas in 1835. Early in 1836, the company joined James W. Fannin's army at Goliad. After Fannin's surrender, almost the entire command was executed by Santa Anna's order on March 27, 1836. John C. Duval escaped and after many vicissitudes he reached the Texans on May 2. He then returned to the United States. He studied engineering at the University of Virginia and in 1840 returned to Texas, where he became a noted land surveyor and Texas Ranger under John C. Hays.

Some time later, Duval prepared a journal of his escape. This journal was seen by various Texas historians of the period (such as D. W. C. Baker, who quotes from the journal itself in his *Texas Scrap-Book,* pp. 368-373) and fragments of it exist in the John C. Duval papers in the University of Texas Archives. J. W. Burke states that Duval wrote the journal in Georgia in 1864 while he was on sick leave from the Confederate army. Burke made a copy and published it serially in his children's magazine, *Burke's Weekly,* in Macon, Georgia, under the title "Jack Dobell; or, A Boy's Adventures in Texas," it ran in the issues from August 10, 1867, through March 7, 1868. He also wrote a fictitious sequel under the title "The Young Explorers," for the same magazine.

In 1892, H. P. N. Gammel talked Duval into allowing him to do a book edition. Gammel printed both of the *Burke's Weekly* stories in the same volume in a confusing manner. The title page has John C. Duval as author and makes no mention of the second text. The "Early Times in Texas" narrative runs through page 135, with running heads reading "Early Times in Texas" on the left and "Adventures of Jack Dobell" on the right. On the leaf following page 135, a new pagination begins, with the caption title "The Young Explorers; or, Continuation of the Adventures of Jack Dobell," with running heads reading "The Young Explorers." This ends on page 238, followed by a blank leaf and then an Appendix: "List of Men under the Command of Col. J. W. Fannin in 1835-36," which runs from page [241] through page 253. The whole is printed on the cheapest possible paper. Later, Gammel reprinted the two texts separately, adding the appendix to the *Early Times in Texas* text, but never removing the "Adventures of Jack Dobell" running heads. He also reissued the second half under the title, *Young Explorers, or, Adventures of Jack Dobell in Texas.* All these various printings have led to much confusion among later bibliographers.

Shortly after Duval's death on January 15, 1897 (the *Handbook of Texas* article on Duval incorrectly dates his death as 1891), the first issue of the new *Quarterly of the Texas State Historical Association* (later *Southwestern Historical Quarterly*) was issued. It contains a fine article on Duval by William Corner, carefully authenticating Duval's narrative of his escape, and including an excellent two-color map of the route taken by Duval. In 1939, J. Frank Dobie wrote *John C. Duval: First Texas Man of Letters,* a fine study of Duval that includes biography, bibliography, criticism, and ten previously unpublished writings of Duval. Dobie reckons Duval the best Texas writer of the 19th century, a claim supported by most other critics. Of these, Mabel Major and Rebecca Smith Lee state that Duval's adventures after his escape from Goliad made Duval seem the Robinson Crusoe of Texas, and John Chapman says the narrative is "an epic—for it is easily comparable with the stories of Beowulf or Roland or the Cid."

There are other important accounts of the Fannin episode, one of the best and earliest of which is a 36-page pamphlet by Joseph E. Field, *Three Years in Texas* (Greenfield, Mass.: Justin Jones, 1836). Field, a surgeon, was released by the Mexicans. Another account by a doctor who was released is Hobart Huson [ed.], *Dr. J. H. Barnard's Journal* (Goliad, 1949).

Agatha, p.51. Dobie, p.55. Graff 1188. Howes D603. Rader 1248. Raines p.74.

52   Eby, Frederick (1874-   )

THE DEVELOPMENT OF EDUCATION IN TEXAS.

New York: The Macmillan Company, 1925.
[Verso of title:] Published March, 1925. Norwood Press. J. S. Cushing Co.—Berwick & Smith Co. Norwood, Mass., U.S.A.
xv,[1],354pp. 20cm.
Introduction by William Seneca Sutton (dated July 16, 1924).
Cloth.

This is still the best history of education in Texas. H. L. Mencken in 1926 wrote: "How far will this debauching of education go? Will the universities sink eventually to the level of the schools of such barbarous states as Texas?" The ninth edition of *Encyclopedia Britannica* contains the statement that "Texas occupies the anomalous position of having the best school fund and the poorest school system in the United States." Eby's goal in writing this book was to explain the reasons for that anomaly, through an examination of the history and cultural background of education in Texas. Dean W. S. Sutton wrote of Eby's work: "He has set forth in a plain and illuminating manner the development of our schools from the earliest period of our history and has shown the influences which operated effectively during the days of Spanish control and Mexican sovereignty, as well as during the independence of Texas as a republic, and during her career as a state up to the present day. It is an extraordinarily interesting and profitable treatise.''

Eby explains the special nature of the education problem in Texas: ''The history of Texas education has a peculiar importance for the scholar who is investigating the development of American social life. In no other state has the struggle of such diverse traditions and ideals been so prolonged and bitter. Many have wondered at the slow and fitful development of education in a state so large and wealthy . . . this peculiarity can only be understood when a clear analysis has been made of the cultural background and traditions and the economic history of the Texas people.''

The volume includes a chapter on the European roots of Texas education, and a chapter each on education during the Spanish, Mexican, Republic of Texas, ante-bellum, and Civil War periods. There is an intriguing section on education during the Radical Republican era of the 1870's, and three chapters bringing the subject up to the 1920's. There are separate sections on high schools, on institutions of higher learning, and on Negro education. One of the best sections is the last chapter, which deals with the projected future for education in Texas, with Eby's astute recommendations—many of which have since been put into effect.

The book was the outgrowth of another fine volume compiled by Eby, *Education in Texas: Source Materials* (Austin: The University of Texas, University Bulletin 1824,1918,963pp. This massive volume contains the largest amount of basic source data for education in Texas ever compiled, and is the primary starting point for any research on the subject. Dr. Sutton states that this work ''set a standard for such work in America.''

Conrad 5.

53 Edward, David Barnett (1790-1870)

THE HISTORY OF TEXAS; OR, THE EMIGRANT'S, FARMER'S, AND POLITICIAN'S GUIDE TO THE CHARACTER, CLIMATE, SOIL AND PRODUCTIONS OF THAT COUNTRY; GEOGRAPHICALLY ARRANGED FROM PERSONAL OBSERVATION AND EXPERIENCE.

Cincinnati: Stereotyped and Published by J. A. James & Co., 1836.
[Verso of title:] Printed by James & Gazlay, No. 1, Baker Street, Cincinnati, O. 336pp. Folding map. 18cm. Some copies have a leaf of adv. inserted. Cloth with printed paper label.

Other editions:
(A). Austin: The Pemberton Press, 1967. [xi],336,[6]pp., plus 8pp. adv. Folding map. 22cm. Facsimile reprint with new introduction by John H. Jenkins and new index. Issued as Volume V in the Brasada Reprint Series.

One of the best accounts of Texas on the eve of the revolution, this also includes the early actions in the revolt through 1835. C. W. Raines accurately termed it "one of the few choice early histories of Texas, though the author was rather Mexican in his politics." The book attempts to be unprejudiced, but the author was clearly anti-Texan at heart.

In addition to giving what was to that date the most accurate description of the land, settlements, and economy of Texas, Edward devotes considerable space to colonization regulations and activities. He quotes the full texts or important extracts (mostly translated for the first and only time into English) from Mexican regulations concerning colonization, the system of justice, and trade. Especially useful are the sections giving the 1829 Decree #39 on the regulation of justice, which is not in Kimball or Gammel, and the Law of April 17, 1834, on administration of the courts, given only incompletely in Kimball and Gammel. He includes the full text of the proposed Constitution of 1833, known otherwise only in the extremely rare New Orleans original printing. He gives official documents on both sides during the period 1832-1835, up to the departure of Austin for the United States. An appendix translates the Mexican Constitution of 1824 in full. The map, which must have been printed no earlier than January, 1836, includes a note about the death of Ben Milam on December 10, 1835.

David B. Edward was born in Scotland, lived in the West Indies and Columbia, and settled in Louisiana in 1819. He moved to Texas in 1830 and became principal of one of the earliest schools in Texas, in Gonzales. It was in this town, center of Mexican, Irish, and Anglo-American activities, that he prepared his book, although he obviously did some of the research in New Orleans. He applied for a copyright in 1834 for a book entitled *Observations on Texas, Embracing the Past, the Present, and the Future,* claimed to have been published by Smith & McCoy in Alexandria, Louisiana. No copy exists and it is probable that it was never actually published.

Because of what his contemporaries considered his pro-Mexican leanings, he came under severe attack. John T. Mason, whom Stephen F. Austin thought had written the book, wrote to Austin on July 5, 1836, that Edward was the author and that the book was "a slander on the people of Texas." Mason then made comments preliminary to challenging Austin to a a duel over the matter, but Branch T. Archer calmed him down in a letter dated July 23, 1836. E. M. Pease wrote to his father at the time: "Be cautious of using Edward's History of Texas. There is little in his work that can be relied on except what is stolen from Mrs. Holley." Indeed, Edward copped entire sentences verbatim from the 1833 book by Mary Austin Holley, and made use of every available source without giving credit. Edward himself found it necessary to leave Texas for good; he died in Ohio in 1870.

Edward was particularly disliked for remarks such as: "The inhabitants in general are . . . composed of a class who had been unfortunate in life; as it could hardly be supposed that the *fortunate* . . . would voluntarily make a choice of [Texas] . . ." He rails against the "shouting and howling" of the Texas Methodists, devoting a dozen pages to discrediting their activities. On the other hand, he says of the Spanish church that "Nuns are diminishing; very few have become so of late years, no young ones; only a few old women tired of the world—or rather dissipation."

It is interesting to note that in late 1835 he was referring to the people of Texas as "Texicans" and as "Texasians." George P. Garrison summed up the book by stating: "The style of the book is bad, and the narrative often difficult to follow. Its chief value lies in the insight it gives to the 'Tory' view of the Revolution and in its reprinting entire several rare and important documents."

Bradford 1511. Clark III-35. Graff 1208. Howes E48. Larned 2030. Rader 1279. Raines, p.74. Sabin 21886. Streeter 1199.

54   Ehrenberg, Hermann (ca. 1818-1866)

TEXAS UND SEINE REVOLUTION.

Leipzig: Otto Wigand, 1843.
iv,258,[2]pp. 22cm.
Printed wrappers.

Other editions:
(A). *Der Freiheitskampf in Texas im Jahre* 1836. Leipzig: Verlag von Otto Wigand, 1844. [2],iv,293,[3]pp. 13cm. Printed wrappers. This issue contains a foreword by the publisher not in any other edition, dated Leipzig, February 1, 1844.
(B). *Fahrten und Schicksale Eines Deutschen in Texas.* Leipzig: Verlag von Otto Wigand, 1845. iv,258,[2]pp. 23cm. Cloth.
(C). *With Milam and Fannin: Adventures of a German Boy in Texas' Revolution.* Dallas: Tardy Publishing Company, Inc., [1935]. xv, 224pp. 21cm. Cloth. Translated by Charlotte Churchill. Edited by Henry Smith. Typography by Mariana Roach. Foreword by Herbert Gambrell. Illustrated by Jerry Bywaters. A portion of this translation appeared in advance of the book's publication in the July, 1935, *Southwest Review.*
(D). Same as (C). Austin: The Pemberton Press, 1968. xv,224,[3]pp. 21cm. Cloth, d.j. This issue has an index added.

One of the earliest German accounts of Texas, this is also an important source work on the events of the Texas Revolution. Ehrenberg, born in Thuringia, Germany, migrated to New Orleans via Canada, and joined the New Orleans Greys in 1835 to go to the aid of Texas. He participated in the siege and capture of Bexar in December, 1835, and was in the battle of Coleto in 1836. Ehrenberg was with Fannin at Goliad but escaped the massacre, losing his precious diary during his escape. Thus he wrote his memoir from memory.

Ehrenberg was the youngest member of the famous New Orleans Greys, who formed about the only uniformed company in the Texas Revolution. He describes their march into Texas through San Augustine, Nacogdoches, Washington, Bastrop, and San Antonio, and provides a graphic if somewhat uncomplimentary account of the storming of Bexar under Ben Milam: "Cannon-balls and bullets whizzed and crashed above our heads, leaving us frightened and bewildered. . . . A bullet struck another very tall fellow, tore off part of his forehead, and dashed its fragments on the flagstone and on those of us who stood around him. [It soon became evident] that it was our own men who were firing from the building, and several of us immediately went to Colonel Milam . . . but not before another man had fallen a victim to this blunder."

After many adventures, Ehrenberg was captured with James W. Fannin after the battle of Coleto on March 19, 1836. Miraculously, he escaped the massacre of 342 of his fellow prisoners on Palm Sunday, March 27, 1836. Ehrenberg and the Greys were placed in line in front of a firing squad, but the first volley missed Ehrenberg, who at the last moment had been warned by a fellow captive to drop to the ground: "A fearful crash interrupted him, then all was quiet; thick clouds of smoke rolled slowly towards the river. . . . Around me the last convulsions of agony shook the bodies of my friends. Close to me Martin and Curtman were struggling with death. I saw no more; quickly making up my mind, I sprang up and took advantage of the thick smoke which hid me to rush along the hedge and make for the river. A heavy blow on the head from a sword made me reel; the small form of a Mexican lieutenant emerged from the smoke in front of me and a second thrust of his sword hit my left arm, with which I tried to parry it. . . . Shouting 'The Republic of Texas forever!' I jumped into the waters of the stream."

Ehrenberg returned safely to the Texan camp, and on June 2, 1836, at Velasco, Mirabeau B. Lamar, then Secretary of War, wrote that "in consideration of the many hardships endured by the bearer Herman Ehrenberg as a private in Captn. Brice's Company of New Orleans Greys in the service of Texas, he is this day honorably discharged from the Army of this Republic with the approbation of this Department for his fidelity and valor."

At this point Herman Ehrenberg dropped from sight in Texas. The Lamar discharge was apparently filed away and forgotten because in 1859 his "heirs" applied for, and in 1880 were granted, 960 acres of land in Liberty County, "320 acres for service and 640 acres in consideration of said Ehrenberg having fallen with Fannin in 1836." Actually, Ehrenberg had gone home to Europe, published three issues of his memoirs, taught English at Halle University, and returned to America. In 1840 he travelled overland from St. Louis to Oregon, voyaged several years in the Pacific, amassed a fortune in California during the gold rush years, made the first map of the Gadsden Purchase for the U.S. Government, built the noted Ehrenberg Road from Mexico to Arizona, served as Indian Agent for the Mohaves, and was killed by Indians in October, 1866, near his home in the town of Ehrenberg, Arizona, which he had founded. Ehrenberg's memoirs have never been published in full in English, the Churchill translation being severely abridged. A full translation, however, was made by Edgar William Bartholomae for his M.A. Thesis at the University of Texas in 1925. As Herbert Gambrell writes, Ehrenberg's "story of his experiences in Texas reveals him as a man of education, judgment, lively imagination, and generous impulse. He came to Texas from a radically different environment, and recorded what he saw and felt in more graphic and detached fashion, perhaps, than a citizen of the United States could have done."

Fifty Texas Rarities #25. Clark III-36. Graff 1226-1228. Howes E83. Jones 1069. Rader 1285-1286. Raines, p. 75. Sabin 22071 and 22072. Streeter 1454.

55 Emmett, Chris (1886-1971)

TEXAS CAMEL TALES; INCIDENTS GROWING UP AROUND AN ATTEMPT BY THE WAR DEPARTMENT OF THE UNITED STATES TO FOSTER AN UNINTERRUPTED FLOW OF COMMERCE THROUGH TEXAS BY THE USE OF CAMELS.

San Antonio: Naylor Printing Co., 1932.
xv,275pp. 32 illus. 23cm.
Cloth.
Verso of title: "Of the 300 individually numbered copies of the restricted first edition this is copy number _____." All copies seen of this issue are autographed.

Other issues:
(A). Same as above, first trade edition. Verso of Title: "July, 1932."
(B). Variant of (A), without "July, 1932" on verso of title.
(C). Second printing. Verso of title: "August, 1932."
(D). Third printing. Verso of title: "June, 1933."
(E). Austin: A Steck-Vaughn Reprint, Steck-Vaughn Company, [1969]. xx,234pp. 40 illus. 23cm. Cloth. Dustjacket. New introduction by James M. Day. An edited reprint: "Obvious typographical errors in the first printing have been corrected in this issue and on occasion, where the story strayed from the camels, parts of the copy were cut. When this occurred, a footnote has been added to summarize the material omitted."—pp.x-xi.

The best account of the famous camel experiment in Texas, this volume is also a successful blend of the numerous official records of the experiment with the memoirs and anecdotes of the people involved.

When Caravans of Camels Trekked the Texas Prairies

NOVEL EXPERIMENTS INTERSPERSED WITH THE HIS-
TORICAL HIGHLIGHTS OF THE ERA OF THE FIF-
TIES ARE INTERESTINGLY AND VIVIDLY TOLD IN

TEXAS CAMEL TALES

BY

CHRIS EMMETT

*Incidents growing up around an attempt by the War Dept. of the United States
to foster an uninterrupted flow of commerce through Texas by the use of Camels*

". . . . relative to "Texas Camel Tales," by Chris Emmett, permit me to
say I have read the book with much pleasure.

The author has skillfully interwoven with the camel tales a mass of
most interesting historic events of the heroic era of Texas as with majes-
tic sweep he extends the view from the Alamo and Goliad to the days of
Reconstruction. His style is clear and pleasing. There is not a dull page
in the book, and I heartily congratulate the author on his achievement.

From the material point of view, I wish to congratulate the publisher
also, as the book is a fine example of the printer's art.

Very truly yours,

417 Burr Road,   B. B. BUCK,
San Antonio, Texas,   Major General, Retired.
September 23, 1932.

FEW readers are familiar with the famous camel experiment of the U. S. Army during the
administration of President Franklin Pierce when Secretary of War Jefferson Davis, appre-
ciating the obstacles confronting the transportation service of the cavalry units then stationed
in Texas, adopted the idea advanced by Major Crosman, of the practicability of camels as the best
means of transportation in moving the supplies of the army and in expeditions against the
unfriendly Indians.

Some of the most glamorous pages of Texas history, prior to, and following the ad-
vent of the camels, gathered by the author from original sources, heretofore unpublished, and
the compilation of many interesting bits of history unknown to the present generation makes this
by far one of the greatest historical contributions any Texas author has offered in many years.

Albert Sidney Johnston, who afterwards won immortal fame as a Confederate General during the War Between the States, was then in command of the Department of Texas, U. S.
Army; Robert E. Lee, then a colonel of cavalry and destined to become the world's greatest
military chieftain, was stationed in San Antonio and serving under Johnson.

J. Frank Dobie stated in a review that "Emmett gives a full account of the [official experiment and] he tells the strange stories that cluster about the subsequent career of the camels, some of which lingered on in the Southwest until near the end of the last century." J. Evetts Haley said that "Emmett has successfully searched out the camel tales and contributed his share of adventurous incident to the annals of Texas." Wayne Gard said of it: "The sprightly Emmett account shows again that history can be intensely interesting."

Chris Emmett studied history in Austin under Bolton and Barker, then attended law school. He served briefly as a county judge and with the 90th Infantry Division in France in World War I. Thereafter, for the rest of his career he worked for the Southern Pacific Railroad. On a hunting trip in 1929, he happened to sleep at Camp Verde in the room once used by Robert E. Lee during the decade of the camel experiment. Emmett later said that "my curiosity quickened into a consuming fire," catching him up in the project of writing a book on camels in Texas. He avidly interviewed survivors of the period, listening to the "romance-stories-facts, mumbled by aged men, both white and black, who resurrected" the tales. Emmett's papers, including the manuscript and research material for the book, are now in the Barker Center of the University of Texas Library.

As early as 1836, recommendations were made to the U.S. government to introduce camels into the country. Finally, at the urging of Secretary of War Jefferson Davis, Congress approved an experiment in 1855. The *U.S.S. Supply,* under David D. Porter, sailed to Africa and landed thirty-odd camels, three Arabs, and two Turks at Indianaola on the Texas coast in the spring of 1856. The camels were taken to Camp Verde and experiments were made in using them. The next year forty-one more were shipped in. During the next few years, successful explorations and caravans were undertaken, involving such men as Robert E. Lee, Albert Sidney Johnston, and Edward F. Beale. The Civil War intervened, and the camels came under Confederate control, one being used throughout the war to carry baggage for Sen. Sterling Price. Although the experiments proved their usefulness, the coming of the railroads after the Civil War marked their doom. Some of the camels were sold, some turned loose and scattered. Some survived until at least as late as 1905 in parts of West Texas.

Emmett traces the full history of the camels in Texas, and includes numerous interviews with people who handled them. These memoirs are what give the volume its special and lasting appeal, such as the remarkable incident of the old camel, stationed in Arizona in 1885, that broke loose and made its way hundreds of miles back towards Texas. It walked calmly into the military post and scarred the wits out of the young son of the post commander, forming ever after one of his "clearest recollections." The boy was Douglas MacArthur.

There are several other valuable works on the camel experiment, notably Lewis B. Lesley's *Uncle Sam's Camels,* published by Harvard University Press in 1929, and Jefferson Davis' *Report of the Secretary of War Communicating. . . . Information Respecting the Purchase of Camels for the Purposes of Military Transportation* (Wash., S.E.D. 62, 1857). These works, however, relate to the experiment as a whole rather than Texas in particular, and include little anecdote. Emmett's work, in the words of James M. Day, "is filled with desert dust and camel musk and still reeks with the flavor of Hi-Jolly and his fellow Arabs and the others who sought to fit the camels to the prairies and plains of Texas."

Agatha, p.65. Campbell, p.172.

56   Emmett, Chris (1886-1971)

SHANGHAI PIERCE, A FAIR LIKENESS

Norman: University of Oklahoma Press, [1953].
xiii,326pp. Illus. by Nick Eggenhofer. Plates. Maps. 24cm.
Cloth, dustjacket.

Other issues:
(A). Norman: University of Oklahoma Press, 1974. xii, 334pp. 21cm. Cloth, dustjacket.

This is one of the best biographies of a Texas cattleman. Ramon Adams called it "an interesting book about one of Texas' most colorful cattlemen." A. B. Guthrie said: "You can't go far in cattle-country reading without cutting the trail of that flamboyant and engaging personality, Shanghai Pierce. Part rascal, part gentleman, part poseur, part just himself, he was all color. Strangely enough, no full-length treatment of him has been done until now. But now it has been done, and done faithfully, painstakingly, with attention to a great number and variety of clues to character. It is a welcome addition to the literature of Texas and the range."

Abel Head Pierce (1834-1900), better known as Shanghai, stowed away on a schooner in 1853 (not 1854, as stated in *The Handbook of Texas*) and landed at Indianola, Texas. Moving to Port Lavaca, he went to work on the Richard Grimes cattle ranch. After serving in the Confederate cavalry, he began to round up wild cattle on the open range and build a herd of his own. He and his brother established the Rancho Grande, near the present town of Pierce (named for him), in 1871. After he "helped with the hanging of five cow thieves in Texas," he spent eighteen months in Kansas, then returned to Texas and began to build a 250,000 acre ranch empire known as Pierce-Sullivan Pasture Company. His company sent untold thousands of cattle up the northern trails from Texas. Pierce and D. M. O'Connor were also responsible for the eventual importation of Brahman cattle to Texas, although none arrived until after Pierce's death.

In the words of Jeff Dykes, Pierce "was a booming-voiced blustering braggart and inclined to sharp dealing. Emmett does not try to make him anything else." Dan Ferguson said that "Shanghai, the would-be colossus of all cowmen, has lived on in the realm of legend, myth, and tall tale. . . . Pierce was a typical product of his era, part rascal, part gentlemen; in his acquisitiveness he was at times ruthless, resorting to bluffing, chicanery, and fencing without consent. 'Reward your friends and punish your enemies' was his own terse statement of his basic philosophy. . . . Although he was never convicted on any indictments, his activities were the subject matter of many civil lawsuits throughout the coastal area."

Emmett states that "Pierce was one of the most prodigious of letter-writers even though he had no formal education." Fortunately, J. Evetts Haley was able to get hold of Pierce's correspondence and have it deposited in the University of Texas Archives. Letters to Pierce and letter-copy books of his own letters provided the basis of Emmett's research. Emmett's book suffers from a confusing chronology and is full of undated quotations, but the letters give the flavor of the range. John McCroskey, for example, wrote to Shanghai Pierce while on a cattle drive:

"We are holding on the Little Washita and are getting along very well, but I am satisfied that Forsythe's men beat me out of eleven head. He gathered them right where I had a stampede. . . . Our horses are very poor and sick. We had ten stolen a week ago. Everybody is down on a Texas herd and are strictly on the steal. If our horses dont die or some rascal dont steal them we can hold the cattle until about the middle of July, but I will ceep coming up the trail untill I am Stop."

Emmett gives us Shanghai Pierce with the warts and all. His volume makes both good reading and competent biography. There are some apparently imaginary conversations and a few errors of fact, especially in relation to the outlaws and lawmen who crossed his path. These included men such as John Wesley Hardin, Ben Thompson, Charlie Siringo, Leander H. McNelly, and Wild Bill Hickok. There is material as well on cattlemen such as Ab Blocker and Ike Pryor. Unfortunately, for a book so full of good stories about so many men, the index is so atrociously incomplete that it is worse than none at all.

The book won the Summerfield G. Roberts Award in 1953. Emmett's manuscript, research material, and notes are now at the University of Texas Archives.

Adams Guns 678. Adams Herd 764. Dobie-Dykes 56. Reese, *Six Score* 38.

57 Emory, William Hemsley (1811-1887)

REPORT ON THE UNITED STATES AND MEXICAN BOUND-ARY SURVEY, MADE UNDER THE DIRECTIONS OF THE SECRETARY OF THE INTERIOR, BY WILLIAM H. EMORY, MAJOR FIRST CAVALRY AND UNITED STATES COMMIS-SIONER.

Washington: A. O. P. Nicholson, Printer, 1857-1859.
34th Congress, 1st Session, Senate Executive Document 108.
Serial 832-834.
Two volumes bound in three: (vol. I:) xvi,258,viii,174pp. (vol. II, part I:) 270,78pp. (vol. II, part II:) 62,[33],35,85,[3]pp.
Two maps, one folding. Folding chart. Folding profile. 346 plates. 29cm.
Cloth; also calf.

Other issues:

(A). House edition. Washington: Cornelius Wendell, Printer, 1857-[1859]. 34th Congress, 1st Session, House Executive Document 135. Serial 861-863. Same collation.

(B). Variant. Title of volume I reads: *United States and Mexican Boundary Survey. Report of William H. Emory, Major First Cavalry and U.S. Commissioner.* Washington: Cornelius Wendell, Printer, 1857. Same collation.

This is one of the most significant of all government reports on western and southern Texas. According to J. Frank Dobie, "Emory's great two-volume report is, aside from descriptions of borderlands and their inhabitants, a veritable encyclopedia, wonderfully illustrated, on western flora and fauna." William Goetzmann said: "Emory, bluff, blunt picturesque cavalry man though he appeared to be, was actually the perfect man for the task. He was a Maryland aristocrat and friend of Jefferson Davis; the army was his career; but he was particularly interested in the scientific aspects of military life. . . . Emory embodied the outdoorsman and military man of action as Western savant. He was another Fremont, ready to use his explorer's skill to help shape the national destiny." Goetzmann said also that "in organization and style of writing, Emory's *Report* was much inferior to that of Fremont. . . . The scientific content of the *Report,* however, was of the greatest significance, and it equalled the findings of Fremont."

Emory graduated from West Point a year ahead of Henderson Yoakum, and began to rise through regular army ranks as a topographical engineer. In the Mexican War, he was decorated for battle heroism. After the war he was assigned as chief astronomer for the laying out of the official American-Mexican boundary line, "in which he served under the difficulties of a civilian-controlled, politically conscious, sectionally oriented organization." In 1848 he published *Notes of A Military Reconnoissance from Fort Leavenworth, in Missouri, to San Diego . . .* (Wash., Sen. Doc. 7, 1848, 416pp.), in which he provided some of the first scientific information on the new territories gained from Mexico. In 1854 he was appointed United States Boundary Commissioner to replace the civilian, John R. Bartlett, and served until the completion of the boundary survey in 1857.

The cause of Emory's appointment was the Gadsden Purchase. The surveys made under Bartlett had been controversial, and many of the military engineers refused to accept Bartlett's proposed boundary line, as it left to Mexico the only known area capable of supporting a southern transcontinental railroad. The Gadsden Purchase settled the question politically, and the task was given to Emory of actually performing the surveys. Emory was accompanied by a varied group of scientists and explorers, who examined the unknown parts of western Texas. His orders directed him to perform "an examination of the country contiguous to the [boundary] line to ascertain its practicability for a railway route to the Pacific; and also information to be collected in reference to the agricultural and mineral resources, and such other subjects as would give a correct knowledge of the physical character of the country and its present occupants."

The Emory report consists of his own narrative, marred by his castigation of Bartlett, followed by Lt. Nathaniel Michler's report of the topography of the San Antonio-El Paso region and other reports on far western areas. Much of the contents of the set are scientific reports, and many of the exquisite plates were prepared in support of these reports. Emory points out that if the Atlantic and Pacific "were to rise 4000 feet above" present level, almost the whole area would be covered, and one would find that "at El Paso, he would be within gun-shot of both shores." Arthur Schott, Dr. C. C. Parry, and James Hall made geological studies, and Parry introduced his notable theory of mountain-making and continental uplift. John Torrey sent assistants who made studies from which he made a report on the botany of the area. Spencer F. Baird made a similar report on the natural history of the region. Emory himself worked on the cartography, which Carl I. Wheat said were the "best specific cartographic reports" of the area.

The report was published in two volumes bound as three large quarto volumes. Ten thousand copies were printed of the first volume, ordered to be printed on August 15, 1856, but not completed until 1857. Congress was upset by the enormous cost of the first volume, and printed only three thousand of the remaining two volumes, at a later date. Consequently, the set is only rarely found complete. Emory's extensive manuscript papers (about 4000 documents) relating to the boundary commission, which contain valuable unpublished material on Texas and the West, are at Yale University.

Emory was not the first to describe West Texas, but his report, because of his reputation and that of his staff, was given particular attention and its impact on congressional and presidential planning was substantial. For example, Emory wrote: "Whatever may be said to the contrary, these plains west of the 100th meridian are wholly unsusceptible of sustaining an agricultural population, until you reach sufficiently far south to encounter the rains from the tropics. . . . The whole legislation of Congress directed heretofore so successfully towards the settlement of lands east of the 100th meridian must be remodeled and reorganized to suit the new phase which life must assume under conditions so different from those to which we are accustomed." Emory was almost the only man until Walter Prescott Webb to understand the implications of the change of terrain at the 100th and 101st meridian.

Bob Becker summarized the contribution of Emory when he said that "as explorer, observer, and reporter of the virtually unknown, newly-won territory of the Southwest, he performed an outstanding service for his country. He was truly the right man in the right place at the right time."

There are numerous other published government documents relating to the Mexican Boundary Survey and the controversies among the men involved. One of the most detailed is J. D. Graham, . . . *Report on the Subject of the Boundary Line between the United States and Mexico* (Wash., 32nd Cong., 1st Sess., Sen. Exec. Doc. 121, 1853, 250pp.). I have Graham's own copy, bound in cloth for public distribution, with his handwritten corrections to the text.

Field 500. Howes E146. Raines, p.76. Wagner-Camp 291.

58 Erath, George Bernard (1813-1891)

MEMOIRS OF MAJOR GEORGE BERNARD ERATH.

Austin: Texas State Historical Association, 1923.
Dictated to and Arranged by Lucy A. Erath. Edited by E. W. Winkler.
[4],105pp. Index. 23cm.
Printed wrappers.
About 100 copies printed.

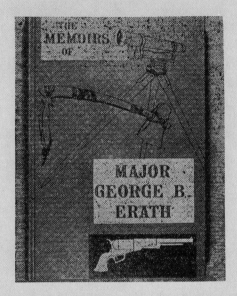

Other issues:

(A). *The Memoirs of Major George B. Erath*, 1813-1891. [Waco: Bulletin Number Three
      of the Heritage Society of Waco, 1956]. viii,[4],105pp. Illus. 23cm. Cloth. New
      foreword by Roger N. Conger.

Erath's memoirs provide one of the most important sources on the
Texas Revolution and on pioneer days in the 1830's and 1840's. Erath,
an Austrian who was educated at the Vienna Polytechnic Institute,
came to America in 1832 and to Texas in 1833. He found work as a
surveyor in Robertson's Colony and soon became an Indian fighter
in John H. Moore's ranger company. He served in Jesse Billingsley's
company in the Texas Revolution and later became captain of a ranger
company in Milam County. He served as a representative from that
county in the congress of the Republic of Texas and in the state
legisature after annexation. As a surveyor, he laid out the towns of
Caldwell, Stephenville, and Waco. Settling permanently in Waco, he
served in the state senate and as a major in the Confederacy. Erath
County was named in his honor.

In 1876, when John Sleeper and Jere C. Hutchins began compiling
the first Waco city directory, they approached Erath to contribute his
recollections. He complied with "a good size roll of brown paper" full
of his memoirs. Only a small portion was used in the directory, and
Roger Conger states that "John Sleeper reminisced many years later
that this brown paper manuscript was stored away in a metal trunk,
which was itself stored in a damp basement. When the trunk was
moved out, its entire bottom fell away, revealing that the contents had
been destroyed by dampness and termites." J. W. Wilbarger, John
Henry Brown, James T. DeShields, and others urged Erath frequently
to write his memoirs again, but he gradually declined in health.
Fortunately, in 1886 his daughter convinced the old man to dictate his
recollections to her. "At the time these pages were written," she states,
"my father was seventy-three years of age, in very poor health and
blind. Mentally, his vigor was the same as it had always been."

Lucy Erath retained her notes until 1916, when she says she "put
the manuscript in shape for publication." It was given to Ernest W.
Winkler, who made "slight changes" and added some footnotes to
those of Lucy Erath. Winkler published the memoirs in the *Southwestern
Historical Quarterly* (volumes 26 and 27) between January and October,

1923. About a hundred copies were printed separately for Lucy Erath, none offered for sale. In twenty years of bookselling in Erath's home town of Waco, W. M. Morrison only handled two copies, and I have acquired only one since 1963, and it is in my personal collection.

Erath's autobiography is arranged into self-explanatory sections as follows: Youth in Austria; Journey to America, 1832; Getting Settled, 1832-1834; Surveyor and Indian Fighter, 1834; At San Jacinto, 1836; Aftermath of San Jacinto; Little River Fort Established and Elm Creek Fight, 1836-1837; The Somervell Expedition and Battle of Mier, 1842; Congressman and Legislator, 1843-1846; Activity as a Surveyor from 1846 to 1857; Protecting the Frontier, 1858-1865; and Aftermath of the Civil War.

Erath's memoirs are outspoken in regard to the San Jacinto campaign and the Somervell Expedition, particularly in his hostility to Sam Houston. There are a number of discrepancies from other accounts, and the text should be treated for just what it is, remembered events by an active partisan dictated late in life. The memoirs also differ somewhat from the version published in the Waco city directory. Nevertheless, his recollections provide many insights into important aspects of pioneer Texas.

59   Espinosa, Isidro Felix de (1679-1755)

EL PEREGRINO SEPTENTRIONAL ATLANTE: DELINEADO EN LA EXEMPLARISSIMA VIDA DEL VENERABLE PADRE F. ANTONIO MARGIL DE JESUS, FRUTO DE LA FLORIDISSIMA CIUDAD DE VALENCIA, HIJO DE SU SERAPHICA OBSER-VANTE PROVINCIA, PREDICADOR MISSIONERO, NOTARIO APOSTOLICO, COMISSARIO DEL STO. OFFICIO, FUNDADOR Y EX GUARDIAN DE TRES COLEGIOS, PREFECTO DE LAS MISSIONES DE PROPAGANDA FIDE EN TODAS LAS INDIAS OCCIDENTALES, Y ACLAMADO DE LA PIEDAD POR NUEVO APOSTOL DE GUATEMALA: DEDICASE AL ATLANTE DE MEJOR CIELO SAN ANTONIO DE PADUA: A EXPENSAS DE LOS AMARTELADOS DEL V. PADRE.

Mexico: Impressa con Licencia . . . por Joseph Bernardo de Hogal, Ministro, e Impressor del Real, y Apostolico Tribunal de la Santa Cruzada en todo este Reyno, 1737.

[38],456,[4]pp. Copper plate engraving. Title in red and black. 21cm. Limp vellum.

Other issues:

(A). Variant issue. In the 10th line of the title the reading is *Santo Officio* instead of *Sto. Officio,* and the 5th line up from the bottom reads "Con Licencia" instead of "Impresso con Licencia." Also a different arrangement of the words following the author's name.

(B). Same title. Valencia: Por Joseph Thomas Lucas Impressor del Ilustrissimo Senor Obispo de Teruel, 1742. [10],411,[4]pp. 21 cm. Plate. Limp vellum.

(C). *Nuevas Empressas del Peregrino Americano Septentrional Atlante, Descubiertas en lo Que Hizo Quando Vivia, y Aun Despues de su Muerte ha Manifestado el V. P. F. Antonio Margil de Jesus.* Mexico: En la Imprenta Real del Superior Gobierno, y del Rezado, de Dona Maria de Rivera, 1747. [24],46pp. 15cm. Limp vellum. This supplemental work adds additional material on the life of Margil, including duly authenticated miracles.

This is the life of the man known as "the Apostle of Texas," written by a friend who accompanied him in his travels. Lathrop Harper called this volume "one of the most important books ever issued for the study of Southwestern history." Father Margil and Espinosa were involved in the founding of several missions in Texas in the early 18th century, and Margil is credited with the conversion of Texas Indians and many acts of heroism in Texas.

Margil was born in Spain in 1657, entering the Franciscan order in 1673. For the next 53 years he served as a missionary in Yucatan, Costa Rica, Guatemala, and Texas. In 1716 he and Espinosa accompanied the Domingo Ramon expedition into Texas and founded the missions of Nuestra Senora de los Dolores de los Ais, San Miguel de Linares de los Adaes, and Nuestra Senora de Guadalupe de los Nacogdoches. Margil stayed in Texas for several years, also founding the mission of San Jose in San Antonio. He is still under consideration by the Vatican for sainthood, and both this volume and the 1747 supplement include many miraculous acts allegedly performed by Margil.

Espinosa clearly considered him a saint, and his touching account of Father Margil in Texas is particularly loving. Margil retired from Texas in 1722 to become guardian of the College of Zacatecas, where he died in 1726. Father Hermenegildo Vilaplana wrote a biography of Margil entitled *Vida Portentosa del Americano Septentrional Apostol el V.P.*

Fr. Antonio Margil de Jesus, published in Mexico City in 1763 and reprinted in Madrid in 1775. Herbert E. Bolton located in Zacatecas an unpublished 300-page manuscript biography of Margil. There are also collections of manuscripts and letters of Margil in the University of Texas Archives and in the San Jacinto Museum of History.

Beristain I-418. *Fifty Texas Rarities* 5. Graff 1260. Howes E184. Jones 444. Leclerc 1129. Medina 3461. Palau 82703. Raines p.78. Sabin 22898. Wagner *Spanish Southwest* 102.

60   Espinosa, Isidro Felix de (1679-1755)

CHRONICA APOSTOLICA, Y SERAPHICA DE TODOS LOS COLEGIOS DE PROPAGANDA FIDE DE ESTA NUEVA-ESPANA, DE MISSIONEROS FRANCISCANOS OBSERVANTES: ERIGIDOS CON AUTORIDAD PONTIFICIA, Y REGIA, PARA LA REFORMACION DE LOS FIELES, Y CONVERSION DE LOS GENTILES. CONSAGRADA A LA MILAGROSA CRUZ DE PIEDRA, QUE COMO TITULAR SE VENERA EN SU PRIMER COLEGIO DE PROPAGANDA FIDE DE LA MUY ILUSTRE CIUDAD DE SAN-TIAGO DE QUERETARO, SITA EN EL ARZOBISPADO DE MEXICO.

Mexico: Por la Viuda de D. Joseph Bernardo de Hogal, Impressora del Real, y Apostolico Tribunal de la Santa Cruzada en todo este Reyno, 1746.
[100],590,[24]pp. 30cm.
Vellum.

Other issues:
(A). Supplemental volume: Arricivita, Juan Domingo. *Cronica Serafica y Apostolica del Colegio de Propaganda Fide de la Santa Cruz de Queretaro en la Nueva Espana.* Mexico: Por Don Felipe de Zuniga y Ontiveros, 1792. [20],605,[16]pp. [Numerous mistakes in internal pagination]. 30cm. Considered by many to be Part II of the above.
(B). Reprint: Canedo, Lino G. [ed.]. *Cronica de los Colegios de Propaganda Fide de la Nueva Espana.* Washington: Academy of American Franciscan History, 1964. cii,972,[1]pp. 29 illus. New introduction, notes, biblography, index.

This work and its 1792 supplement comprise the most important contemporary account of the activities of the Franciscans in Texas. J. Lloyd Mecham said of it: "Much of his history is based on personal experience. This is the standard history of the colleges of Propaganda

Fide of the Franciscans in New Spain. It constitutes the best printed account of the missionary work in the northern provinces, and especially in Texas down to 1746." Lathrop Harper claimed that Espinosa "is our chief source for the missionary activities of that great organization."

Beristain de Souza called Espinosa "the Julius Caesar of the Faith in New Spain because he fought battles in the day and wrote all night." Espinosa, a native of Queretaro, became a Franciscan in 1696 at the age of sixteen. He participated in numerous *entradas* into Texas and assisted in the founding of a number of missions including Concepcion, which "with his own hands he aided in the work of constructing temporary structures of puncheons with thatched roofs to serve as a church and dwelling." He taught himself the dialect of the Tejas Indians. He accompanied the Domingo Ramon expedition in 1716, the Martin de Alarcon expedition of 1718, and the Aguayo expedition of 1721.

His *Chronica Apostolica* includes his account of Father Massanet's activities and the expeditions of Alonso de Leon, as well as those in which he participated himself. He writes much on Father Margil de Jesus, with whom he worked closely. He was an intelligent observer and careful historian, working with documents no longer extant. His style is pleasing, logical, and uniquely free of the digressions so common to works of that era.

In 1792, Juan Domingo Arricivita published what is frequently called the second volume of Espinosa's *Chronica Apostolica*. This work includes a biography of Father Margil, further accounts of the Texas missions, and an account of the journeys of Father Francisco Garces in Texas.

Beristain I-418. Clark I-79. Howes E182. Medina 3769. Palau 82707. Raines pp.77-78. Sabin 22896. Wagner *Spanish Southwest* 117.

61 Filisola, Vicente (1785-1850)

REPRESENTACION DIRIGIDA AL SUPREMO GOBIERNO . . . EN DEFENSA DE SU HONOR Y ACLARACION DE SUS OPERACIONES COMO GENERAL EN GEFE DEL EJERCITO SOBRE TEJAS.

Mexico: Impreso por Ignacio Cumplido, calle de los Rebeldes, casa N.2, 1836.
82pp. 23cm.
Printed wrappers.

Other issues:
(A).   *Evacuation of Texas: Translation of the Representation Addressed to the Supreme Government
by Gen. Vicente Filisola, in Defence of His Honor, and Explanation of His Operations
as Commander-in-Chief of the Army Against Texas.* Columbia, Texas: Printed by G.
& T. H. Borden, Public Printers, 1837. [6],[3]-68pp. 21cm. Printed wrappers.
First edition in English. 300 copies were printed.
(B).   Castaneda, Carlos E. *The Mexican Side of the Texas Revolution, by the Chief Mexican
Participants* . . . Dallas: P. L. Turner Company, Publishers, [1928]. vii,391pp.
24cm. Cloth. Contains a translation by Castaneda of *Representacion* on pages
[160]-203, but does not include the fifteen appended documents.
(C).   *Boletin del Archivo General de la Nacion,* Volume X. Mexico: D.A.P.P., 1939. 24cm.
Printed wrappers. Includes the full text of *Representacion* and all its appendices
except the first, on pages 146-180 and 349-379.
(D).   Facsimile reprint of (B). Dallas: P. L. Turner Company, Publishers, [1956].
Same collation. 23cm. Cloth.
(E).   Facsimile reprint of (A). [Waco:] Texian Press, 1965. xii,iv,68pp. 22cm. Cloth.
Contains a new introduction by James M. Day, and an unsatisfactory index.
(F).   New edition of (B). Austin and Dallas: Graphic Ideas Incorporated, Publishers,
1970. xi,402pp. 22cm. Pictorial cloth. "This edition changes the original only
by minor corrections, a new index, and the addition of new illustrations." The
Filisola text is on pages [164]-209.

The best contemporary account of the Mexican retreat from Texas
after the defeat of Santa Anna, this was written by Santa Anna's
second in command shortly after his return to Mexico. It is called by
Streeter "the classic account of the retreat of the Mexicans through
Texas after the battle of San Jacinto and a masterly defense of Filisola
of his acts in ordering and conducting the retreat." The English
edition is especially important because it is, other than legal publications, the first book printed in Texas.

In November, 1836, a copy of the first edition was sent to Stephen
F. Austin, then serving as Secretary of State of the new Republic of
Texas. Austin recommended that it be translated into English, stating
that it was of "importance to the public interests" because it gave
"the history of the military movements and views of the enemy during
the invasion . . . last spring." President Sam Houston agreed, and
urged the Texas Congress to republish it at public expense. On

November 24, 1836, Congress voted to have 500 copies printed. George Louis Hammeken, a good friend of Stephen F. Austin, made the translation. During this period Hammeken was in close attendance upon the dying Austin, who actualy died in Hammeken's arms on December 27.

The book was printed by Gail Borden and his brother and released for sale in February, 1837. The Bordens billed the government for 300, not 500, copies. J. P. Bryan, Jr., owns a copy of the book that contains a manuscript certificate, dated January 8, [1837], signed by Secretary of State Barnard E. Bee, stating that "the work here annexed . . . was published by order of the House of Representatives of the First Congress at Columbia," making it in effect the copyright copy of the first book printed in the Republic of Texas.

In his translation, Hammeken includes an interesting preface dated Brazoria, January, 1837, presenting the Texan view of the account, as well as some comments on how the Texans would defeat any future Mexican invasion. He also remarks that "General Filisola viewed Texas with the eyes of a soldier, and a farmer must not be guided by his account of the country. He calls the largest portion of it mud." Hammeken, patriotic to the new republic and worried about the effect of this statement on immigration, quickly points out that "this mud, so fatal to him and to his troops, is a rich mould . . . which will compare in fertility to the best soil of the United States."

Filisola's *Representacion* gives a fascinating account of the Mexican viewpoint of the Texas campaign. Shortly after Santa Anna's capture and the utter defeat of his contingent of the Mexican army in April, 1836, he commanded Filisola to round up the bulk of the Mexican forces and to retreat immediately back across the Rio Grande. Filisola did so, encountering numerous difficulties. Since these Mexican forces numbered over 4000, and outnumbered the Texas forces four to one, Filisola immediately stripped of his command and ordered to stand trial for treason when the news reached Mexico City. Filisola's subordinate, Gen. Joe Urrea, issued a blistering attack on Filisola and managed to gain command in his place. By mid-summer, however, Filisola seems to have convinced the Mexican authorities that his actions were justified; he wrote this defence to exonerate himself to the public at large. Although he was not officially cleared until early in 1837, he was ordered by the acting Mexican president to plan and prepare for a new invasion of Texas on August 23, 1836. Interestingly, Filisola's defence is dated August 19, so he probably was aware at the time of writing it that he would not be convicted.

Filisola's narrative is followed by an appendix containing fifteen highly important documents written in Texas during the campaign, dated between April 28 and June 10, 1836, all of which shed much light on Mexican operations. Filisola and Urrea never forgave each other and remained bitter enemies for the rest of their lives. Urrea published his own diary of the Texas campaign in 1838, claiming that Filisola had insulted, abused, satirized, and belittled him, all of which was true, and all of which could be said of Urrea's treatment of Filisola as well.

Other Mexican officials entered the fray and issued their own accounts, notably Juan Jose Andrade, Agustin Alcerreca, Ramon Martinez Caro, Jose Maria Tornel, and Santa Anna himself. Those of Filisola, Santa Anna, Martinez Caro, Urrea, and Tornel were translated into English and published in 1928 by Carlos E. Castaneda under the title, *The Mexican Side of the Texan Revolution*. The Filisola portion omits the documents in the appendix. The Castaneda translation is better and more reliable than that of Hammeken in the 1837 English edition.

Fifty Texas Rarities #17. Graff 1321. Howes F127. Rader 1379. Raines, p. 82. Sabin 24326 and 24323. Streeter 853 and 191.

62   Filisola, Vicente (1785-1850)

MEMORIAS PARA LA HISTORIA DE LA GUERRA DE TEJAS.

Mexico: Tipografia de R. Rafael, 1848-1849.
Two volumes in one: 602, errata leaf; 615pp. 19cm.
Calf.

[Also:]

MEMORIAS PARA LA HISTORIA DE LA GUERRA DE TEJAS.

Mexico: Imprenta de Ignacio Cumplido, 1849.
Two volumes: 512,[3];267pp. 23cm.
Calf.

Other issues:

(A). Another issue of the Rafael edition in two volumes of 587 and 625 pages.

(B). Facsimile reprint of the Rafael edition. Mexico: Editorial Nacional, 1957. 4 volumes. Paperback.

(C). Reprint of (B). Mexico: Editorial Nacional, 1968. 2 vols. Paperback.

(D). *Memoirs for the History of the War in Texas*. Austin: Eakin Press, 1985-1987. Two volumes. Cloth. English translation by Wallace Woolsey of the Rafael edition, with some material omitted and some material from the Cumplido edition added.

This is the best account by a Mexican contemporary of the American conquest of Texas. Eugene C. Barker called it "the only comprehensive history of the colonization of Texas and the Texas Revolution from the Mexican point of view." As yet untranslated into English, it is one of the most important sources on Texas from the 1820's through 1837.

This work—or works—is bibliographically confusing. It is actually composed of two different works of two volumes each, both with the same title. The Rafael edition contains affairs in Texas up to 1833 in the first volume and from 1834 through April, 1836, in the second volume. The Cumplido edition repeats some material from the Rafael edition, but is basically an entirely new work, relating primarily to the period from March, 1836, through July, 1837. The Cumplido edition, therefore, is neither a reprint of the Rafael nor a continuation. Moreover, the Rafael edition itself appears in two issues, each with differing pagination and with pagination errors. The Rafael and Cumplido editions each stand on their own as separate works but complement each other so much that both are necessary to have the complete account.

Filisola had been working on his memoirs for a number of years, interrupted by his service in 1847 as commander of one of the three Mexican divisions in the Mexican War. In 1848 he was made president of the Supreme Tribunal of War and Marine, with little to do after the Mexican surrender. He began sending sections of his memoirs to the Mexican periodical, *El Universal,* which published them in installments. Their popularity created a demand for a book edition. The first volume of the Rafael edition contains a prologue by the *Universal* editors dated November 16, 1848, "offering our countrymen the lessons of experience in the following Memoirs." I suspect that by the time the second volume of the Rafael edition appeared in 1849, Filisola had become disenchanted with the Rafael bungling of the printing and transferred mid-stream to Cumplido, the firm which had originally printed his *Representacion* in 1836.

Filisola was a native of Italy who joined the Spanish army at an early age, participating in over twenty battles of the Napoleanic wars by the year 1808. Sent to Mexico, he served the Royalist army until 1821, when he became a key officer under Iturbide. Thereafter he rose in rank steadily, serving at times as commander-in-chief and as Secretary of War. In 1831 he received a colonization grant in Texas which he never fulfilled, and in 1833 was given specific charge of quelling the American immigration into Texas, with headquarters at Matamoros. In November, 1835, he became second in command to Santa Anna for the invasion of Texas. After Santa Anna's capture, he became commander-in-chief. No other Mexican commander had the range of experiences nor the intimate personal knowledge of Texan affairs that Filisola had. His account of the Texas Revolution, especially as given in the Cumplido edition, is particularly valuable regarding the siege of the Alamo, the invasion of the Texas interior, the retreat after San Jacinto, and the attempted reinvasion of Texas in the winter of 1836-1837. The volumes of both editions are enriched with scores of original documents and military orders unavailable elsewhere.

Howes F125 and F126. Palau 91612. Raines, p. 82. Sabin 24324.

63 Foote, Henry Stuart (1804-1880)

TEXAS AND THE TEXANS; OR, ADVANCE OF THE ANGLO-AMERICANS TO THE SOUTH-WEST; INCLUDING A HISTORY OF LEADING EVENTS IN MEXICO, FROM THE CONQUEST BY FERNANDO CORTES TO THE TERMINATION OF THE TEXAN REVOLUTION.

Philadelphia: Thomas, Cowperthwait & Co., 1841.
[Verso of title:] J. Fagan, Stereotyper. T. K. and P. G. Collins, Philadelphia.
Two voumes: viii, 13-314pp.;403pp. With either 16 or 24pp. of adv. at end of Vol. I. 19cm.
Cloth.
Note: James H. Young's *A New Map of Texas* (Phila., S. Augustus Mitchell, 1842), with the notice "Sold by Thomas, Cowperthwait & Co." is occasionally found inserted. It is probable the publisher inserted these in remaining copies of the book in 1842 when the map was issued.

Other issues:

(A). Facsimile reprint. Austin: The Steck Company, 1935. Same collation except for new preliminary title pages in each volume. One of the series by Steck entitled "Original Narratives of Texas History and Adventure." 2000 sets printed.

One of the most influential books on Texas in its time, this work is still of considerable value and interest. It suffers from the intense prejudices of the author and from his too-frequent digressions, but it nevertheless provides material on numerous aspects of Texas history not available elsewhere. As Sister Agatha points out, "as a historian, Foote lacks the first essential, a conservative conscience in evaluating action," but C. W. Raines called it nevertheless "one of the best histories of Texas for the period covered."

Volume one consists of five chapters of Mexican history, followed by chapters on the effects of the Reformation in England, Spanish-American relations, the Burr Conspiracy, and on James Long. Four chapters (among the best in the book) are devoted to the Fredonian Rebellion. Volume Two consists of a history of colonization and the Texas Revolution.

At the end of the second volume Foote includes Ashbel Smith's *A Brief Description of the Climate, Soil and Production of Texas,* which was also issued as a separate pamphlet in 1841. It may actually have been Smith who gave Foote the idea for the book, for Smith wrote to Foote from Houston on March 11, 1839, commenting that a true history of the revolution "should be submitted to the world," and that Foote should engage in the endeavor, as the "memorials of its early history are scattered and many of them are liable to perish, the actors in the struggle for freedom must by the course of nature, soon leave the scenes of their triumph!" On June 5, 1839, Memucan Hunt wrote Mirabeau B. Lamar from New Orleans: "I shall leave here in a few days for Mississippi where I expect to meet with Gen. Foote previous to his departure for Texas to compile its history."

Foote spent the summer in Texas but was back in Jackson on November 20, 1839, when he wrote to Lamar that "my History is progressing rapidly. . . . It will be more extended than I anticipated when I saw you." The work shows Lamar's influence throughout, a fact not missed by his foe Sam Houston. In a speech in November,

1841, Houston said: "I will name the book *the Foot history*. I call it the Foot history because it will be more footed than eyed."

The introduction to the work is dated Raymond, Mississippi, January 5, 1841, but it must not have been released for several months, as Foote wrote to Ashbel Smith from Philadelphia on March 11, 1841, enclosing the proof sheets for Smith's contribution to the work. Foote obviously worked from interviews with active participants in the Texas Revolution, and in fact Foote claims that he was invited to write the book "by more than twenty of the most conspicuous actors in that war." He states that a third volume would be issued in 1842, but this was never published.

Foote later led an active political career, including service as Governor of Mississippi, having defeated Jefferson Davis for that office in 1851. He and Davis were bitter enemies, and the two actually had a fist-fight in 1847 when Foote was elected to the U.S. Senate. These events are related by Foote in his *Casket of Reminiscences* (Washington: Chronicle Publishing Company, 1874).

Eugene C. Barker remarks that "one's impatience with Foote's betrayal of the historian's obligation to tell the truth as he knows it gives way to amusement at the ingenuity of his grandiose distortions." In other words, Foote wrote his work as a deliberate piece of propaganda, with the goal of encouraging annexation of Texas to the United States. This objective led Foote into some startling statements, such as his remarks against the Mexicans, "whose extermination may yet become necessary for the repose of this continent!"

The Rev. William Y. Allen wrote in the *Texas Presbyterian,* July 9, 1880, that Foote "visited Texas in 1840. He was a man of immense talking capacity. He made a very good temperance speech, in Houston, during his visit there. Temperance was a new subject in Texas then. I spent a day with him sometime afterward, at the house of General Thos. J. Green, at Velasco. Dr. Branch T. Archer was of the company. Foote and Archer did most of the talking, freely, while Foote and I played temperance. Dr. A. was the only man I ever heard undertake to justify himself in swearing in common conversation, by saying he meant to honor God by the use of such language."

Bradford 1725. Graff 1376. Howes F238. Larned 2032. Rader 1425.
Raines, p.84. Sabin 25019. Streeter 1377.

64   Ford, John Salmon (1815-1897)

RIP FORD'S TEXAS.

Austin: University of Texas Press, [1963].
Edited by Stephen B. Oates.
[2],xlviii,[2],519pp. Illus. 23cm.
Cloth, dustjacket.
Personal Narratives of the West: J. Frank Dobie, General Editor.

These are the personal memoirs of one of the most colorful Texans of his time, ably edited by a fine scholar. Frederic Remington, after an interview with Rip Ford, said that Ford could "tell you stories that will make your eyes hang out on your shirt front." Of Oates' work, Margaret Hartley said: "The job of editing that has been done here is truly a creative one. . . . The memoirs have been turned into a lively and readable book, conveying much of the exceptional vitality that characterized 'Old Rip' and gave him an obvious joy in living and fighting." W. J. Hughes commented: "For the first time there is available the body of Ford's writings in logical, coherent, chronological fashion."

The problem with John S. Ford's unpublished memoirs was that they consisted of nearly 1300 handwritten pages on hundreds of topics, without concern for arrangement or chronology, and with considerable duplication. Moreover, Ford's adopted daughter had destroyed many sections, taking scissors to portions she deemed indiscreet or indelicate. I speak from experience when I say that past historians using the Ford manuscripts found the task of penetrating them a very difficult one indeed. Stephen Oates' splendid editorial work resolved that problem. Oates explains his task: "I reorganized much of the material so that it would read as a connected narrative, integrated articles that covered the same topic, corrected quoted material against the originals, corrected grammatical errors, but did not change the actual wording unless the diction was wrong or the phraseology was hopelessly obscure. In this reorganization I followed two rules of thumb: preserve Ford's style; and, if a sentence can be understood at all on first reading, don't fuss with it. In short, no matter what overhauling I did of Ford's sentences, they are still his: they are still his words, his ideas, his style, his thoughts, his criticisms, remarks and anecdotes." No doubt

MEMOIRS OF JOHN S. FORD, FROM 1836 TO 1886.

The undersigned, with the view of assisting in the collection and preservation of data to be used in writing a correct and comprehensive history of Texas, has prepared a manuscript, at considerable labor and some cost, with the intention of publishing a work to be entitled:

" MEMOIRS OF JOHN S. FORD, AND REMINISCENCES OF TEXAS HISTORY, CIVIL, MILITARY AND PERSONAL, RANGING FROM 1836 TO 1886."

The style is unpretentious; the design being only to state facts, and to contribute to the truth of history without being biased by prejudice, malice, partisan or personal enmity. The writer has aimed to do justice to every person mentioned, to describe the situation, and let the reader draw his own conclusions, and to steer clear of unseemly egotism inducing many to write themselves down as heroes. Incidents are presented to illustrate the traits of character of distinguished persons in connection with important events.

Campaigns against Indians and Mexicans, scouts, battles, peace-talks, sketches of pioneer life, have been introduced to give an idea of the toils, privations and loss of life incurred to place Texas in the proud position she occupies now. Notices of leading Texians have been made. Political affairs have received attention, particularly the causes and action culminating in the annexation of Texas to the United States. Mexico was a valueless cipher. We feared England and France.

In short, the writer has been actuated by the laudable ambition to get up a book which every Texian can read with pleasure and profit. He has not confined himself to the insipid details of the every-day life and doings of an ordinary individual, but has left them to the "snapper-up of unconsidered trifles."

The part ready for publication comes down to the year 1860 It will make a volume of more than five hundred octavo pages, according to the calculation of printers. The purpose is to use good paper and leather binding. The price is five dollars.

The undersigned asks the indulgence and the confidence of his friends and the public in the matter of subscribing for the first volume, and paying in advance, in order to enable him to pay for printing the same. He feels sure he will give each subscriber the worth of his money.

The following gentlemen have spoken in commendation of the work:

EX-GOV. O. M. ROBERTS, Austin.
HON. THOMAS J. DEVINE, San Antonio.
COL. H. C. KING, San Antonio.
CHARLES W. OGDEN, ESQ., San Antonio.
COL. H. F. YOUNG, San Antonio.
GEN. H. P. BEE, San Antonio.

GEN. W. H. YOUNG, San Antonio.
MAJ. JOHN A. GREEN, San Antonio.
GEN. W. H. KING, Austin.
DR. R M. SWEARINGEN, Austin.
REV. DR. R. K. SMOOT, Austin.

JOHN S. FORD.

SAN ANTONIO, APRIL, 1887.

SUBSCRIPTION.

NAME	POST OFFICE	AMOUNT

Ford himself would have heartily approved of the Oates rendition of his memoirs. After all, they were only a rough draft, written over a period of a decade or more.

The volume consists of a biographical essay on Ford, followed by 34 chapters divided into six chronological sections: the Republic of Texas period, the Mexican War, the Indian campaigns, the South Texas years, the Civil War, and the post-war period. In all, the Ford memoirs cover the fifty year period from 1836 to 1886, written between 1886 and 1897. At the end are two appendices, "Shapley P. Ross and Times in Old Texas" and "Richard King and Miflin Kenedy: The Business Wizards of South Texas." Oates summarizes Ford's career after coming to Texas in 1836: "John Salmon [Ford] would not only become a moderately successful doctor, but a lawyer, a surveyor, a respectable journalist, a trail blazer, a legislator of some distinction, a leading spirit in the annexation movement [he introduced the motion in Texas to accept annexation], an adjutant in the Mexican War [to Jack Hays], a state's righter [he helped write the secession ordinance], and one of the leading military men in the state, serving off and on as a Texas Ranger captain and in the Civil War as a colonel in the Confederate cavalry. An adventurer at heart, he was also involved in . . . many of the revolutionary movements along the Rio Grande. . . . He was active in pratically every important event from 1836 until he retired in 1883 to write the memoirs."

Although John S. Ford was one of the most well-known men of his time, historians have tended to ignore him. Bancroft does not mention him at all. William Goetzmann in his *Army Exploration in the American West* (1959) confuses him with Robert S. Neighbors, making Ford an Indian agent and Neighbors a Texas Ranger. In his later *Exploration & Empire* (1966), he corrects the error but gives the name as John L. Ford.

Ford's memoirs are literally full of the anecdotes that make history come alive. He tells of Sam Houston at Nacogdoches shortly after marrying Margaret Lea: "General and Mrs. Houston were taking breakfast. Walling was at the table. He inquired: 'Mrs. Houston, have you ever been in Shelby County?' The reply was in the negative. 'You ought to go there, madam. General Houston has forty children in Shelby County.' At this announcement the lady looked rather confused.

'That is, named after him,' Walling added. 'Friend Walling,' General Houston remarked, 'you would oblige me very much by connecting your sentences more closely.' "

He tells of Mirabeau B. Lamar in Austin one day when an Indian alarm was given. Everyone rushed down to the Colorado, waving weapons "in real warhorse style." No Indians showed, and "we solaced our disappointment by telling what we would have done had they audaciously remained to be annihilated by our ruthless and irresistible onslaught." During the furor, someone turned to Lamar. "He was asked: 'General, where are your arms?' 'In my pockets,' was the prompt reply."

Ford recites many of his exploits chasing Comanches, giving fascinating details on Indian fighting: "Never ride on a [mounted] bowman's left; if you do, ten to one that he will pop an arrow through you. When mounted, an Indian cannot use his bow [effectively] against an object behind and to his right."

Ford fought the Mexican War as adjutant of the Hays Rangers, the most fearsome unit in the American army. One day an Englishman from another outfit had an argument with Michael Chevaille, one of the Texans, and in Ford's words, "a misunderstanding ensued," meaning they had a fist-fight. The Englishman complained to General Joe Lane. Ford says "the following colloquy took place: Englishman: 'General, Major Chevaille has been beating me.' General: 'Did he beat you badly?' Englishman: 'Yes, quite badly.' General: 'Keep a sharp look out or he will beat you again.' "

A year after the Oates volume was published, a fine biography of Ford appeared, written by W. J. Hughes: *Rebellious Ranger: Rip Ford and the Old Southwest* (Norman: University of Oklahoma Press, 1964, 300pp.). Ford's original manuscripts and papers are in the Texas State Archives and in the University of Texas Archives.

65   Frantz, Joe Bertram (1917-)

GAIL BORDEN, DAIRYMAN TO A NATION.

Norman: University of Oklahoma Press, [1951].
xiii,310pp. 18 illus. 24cm.
Cloth, dustjacket.

This is one of the most interesting of all Texas biographies, written about a man whose Horatio Alger success story made him so famous nationally that his large contributions to the creation and development of Texas were almost forgotten. Herbert Gambrell said "it is the kind of book that could be read for the sheer pleasure of the reading by a man who had never heard of Borden or seen a can of condensed milk or known that there once was a Republic of Texas. . . . It is a great biography by any standards."

Frantz became interested in Borden when working on his 1940 University of Texas master's thesis, "The Newspapers of the Republic of Texas." He says: "I became aware that the story of one Texas publisher, Gail Borden, carried more than ordinary interest and importance. Here was a man who had founded an industry, who had pioneered in sanitary handling of that most important of modern foods, milk, who played a large behind-the-scenes part in the birth of free Texas, who had tried a dozen things before hitting on the one thing that made his name known to almost every housewife in the nation," a man who left behind as a namesake a company that in 1951 had fifty thousand stockholders and over half a billion dollars in sales annually. Frantz selected Borden for the subject of his doctoral dissertation, approved in 1948, entitled "Infinite Pursuit: The Story of Gail Borden." Several more years of extensive research and travelling led to the published book.

Gail Borden came to Texas in 1829 and remained until 1851 when he went east to market his inventions. He returned to Texas after the war and died at Borden, Texas, in 1874. Frantz's intensive research (over ten percent of the book is bibliography, footnotes, and index) presents a Borden whose contribution to Texas history was considerably more pervasive than had previously been realized. Gail Borden and his brother Thomas became official surveyors for Stephen F. Austin's colonies almost immediately after their arrival, and Gail assumed many of Austin's duties during Austin's absences from Texas. He became a force in the activities leading towards revolution, and in 1835 began what soon became the most important Texas newspaper of its era, the *Telegraph and Texas Register.*

Borden somehow managed to keep the presses running as the Texans retreated before Santa Anna's onslaught, and his newspaper issues and broadsides were of crucial importance in rallying Texans to defeat the Mexicans. He and his brother hocked all their Texas property to help contract a loan for Texas. After the revolution Borden became one of the founders of the city of Galveston and of Baylor University. Meanwhile, he began inventing, mostly in the American tradition of try, try again. His meat biscuit, which he and Ashbel Smith tried to market worldwide, was a flop and all but bankrupted him.

Between 1853 and 1856 he developed and patented his now-famous process for condensing milk. The Civil War brought huge orders and he achieved long-sought and well-earned success. Borden, a unionist, stayed in Connecticut during the war, but had sons serving on each side during the conflict. He later pioneered the packing and other industries in Texas, and in fact he could be justly called the father of Texas industry.

Frantz's biography never lags, imbued as it is with his splendid understanding of his subject. The volume won the 1951 Texas Institute of Letters award for the best Texas book of the year.

In a fascinating article entitled "On Being Definitive" in *Southwest Review,* Winter, 1959, Frantz tells of discovering 285 pounds of additional Borden manuscript material, including over 30,000 pages of correspondence, subsequent to the publication of his biography. These manuscripts are now located in the Borden Company archives.

Frantz later became director of the Texas State Historical Association and author of many books and essays on Texas history. His intelligence, wit, and graceful style permeated the decade of his editorship of the *Southwestern Historical Quarterly.* He then made some history of his own when he headed the national Oral History Project for the Lyndon Johnson administration.

66   Friend, Llerena Beaufort (1903-)

SAM HOUSTON: THE GREAT DESIGNER.

University of Texas Press, 1954.
Austin: University of Texas Press, 1954.
xiv,394pp. 21 illus. 24cm.
Cloth, dustjacket.
The first 1000 copies were issued in red cloth.

Other issues:

(A). Same, but the remainder of the first edition was issued in blue cloth.

(B). Second printing, 1965. Same collation.

(C). Paperback edition, 1969. Same collation. Texas History Paperbacks Series TH-2.

The most scholarly biography of Sam Houston, this is also one of the most interesting. I doubt whether anyone will ever understand Sam Houston as well as Llerena Friend. H. Bailey Carroll called her book "a definitive study of fundamental importance to the history of Texas and the United States [and] an important contribution to Amercan biography." Marquis James said that "rarely does a book appear concerning a period so remote that should correct so much current error." Rupert N. Richardson called it the first biography of Houston "written with an objective approach, after exhaustive research, in keeping with the exacting standards of modern historical scholarship."

After graduating from the University of Texas, Llerena Friend taught in Wichita Falls and Vernon with summer study in Austin and at the Universities of Colorado and California. She returned to the University of Texas as a Research Assistant in Texas History to work on the *Handbook of Texas* project until she was appointed librarian of the newly-created Barker Texas History Library. A 1954 news release explains that she had continued her studies, until there "came a time when Miss Friend had done everything for a doctoral degree except writing a dissertation. She needed a subject that could be researched during lunch hours and after 5 p.m. Dr. Eugene C. Barker came up with the suggestion that she write on Houston. Miss Friend replied that Houston had been 'done'—and by experts. Dr. Barker replied that no major Houston biography had been written since Houston's writings were compiled. A new, documented biography was needed, he insisted. . . . Finally the dissertation was completed, under Dr. Barker's supervision. At the suggestion of Dr. Walter Prescott Webb, whose grader she had been as a senior in 1924, the study was submitted to the University of Texas Press for publication."

Webb suggested the title, and the press published the book. It immediately won the Summerfield G. Roberts Award for the best Texas book of the year. Rupert Richardson said: "The author states without apology that this book grew out of her doctoral dissertation.

In fact, the thesis was written under the guidance of scholars who believe that theses are written for people to read and think it no sin that one be interesting.'' Would that all books-from-dissertations were as lively and readable as Friend's.

The biography stresses Houston as statesman rather than Houston as frontier hero. She states that her goal is ''to show Houston's place in national politics, including only such local history as was necessary to delineate his position in the American scene. . . . Everybody is acquainted with the 'buckskin hero from Tennessee,' but questions concerning him tend to relate to his life with the Indians, his marital problems, and his conviviality, and to ignore his work as a practical politician and a statesman.'' To this end, Friend devotes the first 161 pages of her narrative to his career through 1845, and the remaining 192 pages to the period between 1846 and 1863. Marquis James, on the other hand, devoted 358 pages to the first period and 74 to the latter.

This shift in emphasis naturally presents Houston more in his role as an actor on the national scene. Friend has an uncanny knack of understanding Houston's motives during this period, complex as they were. As anyone knows who has tried to decipher his mystifying letters and speeches, Houston seldom said exactly what he meant and frequently made contradictory statements so outrageous that he obviously intended the contradiction. With great care and cool intelligence, Friend analyzes and clarifies. Where Marquis James makes us feel the charisma of the man, Friend reveals his profundities.

The Texas years are not neglected, in spite of the emphasis on later events. Friend is squarely a rationalist on Houston's Texas motivations: ''I have not been able, had it been my wish, to prove that Houston came to Texas as Jackson's tool to win the area for the United States or that he was involved in a capitalist conspiracy to speculate in Texas lands as a corporation lawyer. The Texas revolution was inevitable, with or without Houston.'' The revolution, she states, established Houston as a symbol around which Texas politics would polarize for the rest of his life. Friend's biography is the best analysis of those years that has yet been written.

67 Gaillardet, Theodore Frederic (1808-1882)

SKETCHES OF EARLY TEXAS AND LOUISIANA.

Austin: University of Texas Press, [1966].
Translated with an Introduction by James L. Shepherd III.
xx,[2],169pp. Illus. 22cm.
Cloth, dustjacket.

Other issues:
(A). Paperback edition, same collation, no date. Texas History Paperback TH-13.

Written by one of the most literate of all visitors to the Republic of
Texas, this work contains perceptive insights into the men and manners
of the young nation. Marilyn Sibley called it "a welcome contribution
to the travel literature of the Southwest." J. D. Bragg said that
"Gaillardet was no ordinary newspaper correspondent. He was a man
of considerable literary talent, and his sketches . . . provide delightful
reading." James L. Shepherd III, the translator, writes that "of the
considerable number of French visitors to the Republic of Texas toward
1839, Theodore-Frederic Gaillardet was the only professional writer of
note. His remarks are therefore the most interestingly written, the best
organized, the most cohesive."

Gaillardet was a friend of Pierre Soule and Victor Hugo. Soule said
in 1845 that Gaillardet was "the man who for ten years has done the
most for the glory of the French name in America and who is himself
the most illustrious representative of it." In 1832 he collaborated with
Alexander Dumas on a play which provoked a literary quarrel, six
lawsuits, and a duel between the two. In 1837 he sailed to New Orleans
to write a book to correct the false impressions of America left by
Alexis de Tocqueville, and in 1839 he accompanied Alphonse de Saligny
on a tour of Texas. From April through July of that year he travelled
in Texas, writing articles for publication in French newspapers. He
became, he wrote, a "Texian in the heart," and his articles were
influential in bringing about official French recognition of Texas as a
republic.

The Texas chapters of this book include a report urging recognition
of Texas, a report from Velasco on Anglo-American settlement of
Texas, reports from Brazoria and San Antonio recounting the Texas
Revolution, an analysis of the new republic written from San Felipe,
and a report from New York concerning French immigration to Texas.
Much of the material is plagiarized from Chester Newell's *History of
the Revolution in Texas,* but enough of it is Gaillardet's own intelligent

observations to warrant its inclusion, in my opinion, as a primary resource on the Republic of Texas.

Shepherd's translation includes Gaillardet's dispatches to Paris and his articles for the *Courrier des Etats-Unis* of New York, and for the *Journal des Debats Politique et Literaires* and *Le Constitutionel* of Paris. Unfortunately, Shepherd's introduction and annotations are poorly written and unclear regarding exact dates of publication; some dates are given and some are not. His statements regarding the historical value of the six chapters on Texas are somewhat given to hyperbole. He states that none of the material has appeared in English translation, which may be true, but I own a contemporary manuscript translation, possibly by Gaillardet himself, of the entirety of the main section on Texas, which appears as Chapter Five, dated San Felipe, June 30, 1839. On the other hand, Shepherd's translation itself is excellent. Shepherd also translated Leclerc's *Texas and Its Revolution* (entered here separately) and Eugene Maissin's *The French in Mexico and Texas* (Salado: Anson Jones Press, 1961). Maissin's journey to Texas occurred about the same time as Gaillardet's and provides an interesting alternative French view of the new republic.

68　Gambrell, Herbert Pickens (1898-1982)

ANSON JONES: THE LAST PRESIDENT OF TEXAS.

Garden City: Doubleday & Company, Inc., 1948.
viii,[2],462pp. Illus. 22cm.
Cloth, dustjacket.
[Verso of title:] First edition.

Other issues:
(A). Austin: University of Texas Press, [1964]. xiv,[2],530pp. Verso of title: "Second Edition, with Annotations and Enlarged Bibliography." Foreword by William Ransom Hogan. Best edition by far, because it includes Gambrell's extensive annotations, which had been omitted by the publisher in the first edition.

This is the best biography of a Texan, better written than Barker's *Austin* and more scholarly than James' *Raven*. Walter P. Webb called it a "portrait which no one in Texas has surpassed in biography," and J. Frank Dobie said it is "the most artfully written biography that

Texas has yet produced." William R. Hogan said it "has the most sprightly sense of humor I have ever encountered in the pages of a serious book," and Henry Nash Smith wrote that it "reminds us that the merits of a biography, like those of a novel or a painting, depend on treatment rather than subject."

Prior to this biography, Anson Jones was a virtually forgotten man, treated by historians as an insignificant, unsympathetic character. The reasons for this misunderstanding of Jones were twofold. First, Jones was elected President of Texas only because his opponent, Gen. Edward Burleson, was a semi-literate with no claims to the office other than being a frontier hero. Jones, never popular even after becoming president, further exacerbated the Texans by playing a cat-and-mouse game of international politics regarding whether Texas should be annexed or should remain independent, with English and French guaranties of support and with the collateral Texan dependence on Europe for security. Most Texans, then and afterwards, believed Jones favored Europe, and most Texans wanted statehood instead. In 1846, when Jones pulled down the Lone Star flag to officially end the republic and begin statehood (saying "the final act in this great drama is now performed: the Republic of Texas is no more"), he received no applause. He was never called upon to serve Texas again.

Second, the only significant published defence of Jones was his own *Memoranda and Official Correspondence Relating to the Republic of Texas.* Unfortunately, this ponderous 648-page tome does a poor job of presenting Jones in a favorable light. Written during the 1850's when Jones was sour and bitter over the way he had been bypassed for office in the new state, it suffers from the harshness which Jones let seep into it. Moreover, it was published after Jones committed suicide, by his wife, who issued it just as "left by him, without note or comment [as written by a man] wounded, deeply wounded."

Never has a more forgotten and misunderstood man been more effectively resurrected. Webb said the Gambrell work makes "the mediocre Mr. Jones an unforgettable character." Hogan stated in a review that prior histories had "served to stamp Anson Jones as the churlish little doctor whose brief period of glory went to his head. The reviewer himself pleads guilty. But he hereby hastens to recant." Gambrell gives us an Anson Jones who knew what he was doing for

Texas and who deserved a better fate. "With power and skill and play of wit," wrote Dobie, "Herbert Gambrell has gone down into a human soul."

Gambrell shows that Jones always worked towards statehood, playing a masterful game of baiting the United States, Mexico, England, and France with the notion that Texas might join the United States, might become a dependent of Europe, or might build an independent empire of its own. In the last stages of the movement to gain annexation, Jones—even more than Sam Houston—played the crucial and possibly deciding role in bringing about the ever-so-close favorable vote of the U.S. Congress offering statehood. In doing so, he not only outfoxed the international community but, without meaning to, deceived his own constituency so completely that they disbelieved him later when he tried to explain his motives.

As Gambrell states, Jones "was to puzzle foreign ministers and diplomatists on two continents. He was to play a hand in a game for fabulous stakes, and there would be a time when statesmen at London and Paris and Washington watched him more closely than they did each other. It was a game that determined the course of American and, to a certain extent, world history."

One of the most enjoyable features of Gambrell's biography is his insight into the Texas of that period, based on extensive research and presented with wit and careful pruning. He tells, for example, of the political rally at which one anti-annexation speaker "had steamed up too high for the occasion. Though an admirable speaker, upon taking the platform he gazed vacantly at the crowd and, in a moment more, measured his full length upon the floor. The chairman, who was an ardent annexationist and a very ready man, pointed at the prostrate man and said most emphatically, in a loud tone, 'Gentlemen, Colonel Lawrence has the floor.' This settled the question, and the gathering with much merriment left the hall."

Campbell, p.33. Dobie, p.86.

69 Gammel, Hans Peter Nielson (1854-1931) [comp.]

THE LAWS OF TEXAS, 1822-1897.

Austin: The Gammel Book Company, 1898.
Introduction by C. W. Raines.
Ten volumes. 25cm.
Calf.
Some advance copies have a "Compiler's Notice" on a leaf after the title page of
the first volume announcing the publication "will be issued at the rate of one volume
every sixty days till completed. . . ."

Other issues:
(A). Special edition, limited to ten sets only, each with a special two-color title
        page.

This is the most valuable compilation of early laws of Texas, and
still the most useful. C. W. Raines said of the set: "These are
essentially the connecting links of our legal and political history. . . .
Not a heterogeneous mass, but a related whole, this compilation is the
ethical expression of the period covered, or more plainly speaking, the
prevailing idea of right and wrong as applied to the social compact."
Gammel himself claimed that "perhaps this is the largest and costliest
work on private account ever printed in Texas." Z. T. Fulmore stated:
"It would be difficult to estimate the value of this great repository of
jurisprudence and history. . . . We have here an encyclopaedia of
Texas law and political history in convenient form, adapted to use in
private as well as public libraries." E. W. Winkler called it Gammel's
most important publication—"a monumental work."

The set includes all the laws of Texas as a republic and state, from
1836 to 1897, congress by congress and legislature by legislature. Equally
important, however, is the inclusion of related materials. These consist
of facsimile reprints of Austin's colonization laws and contracts; the
Mexican Constitution of 1824; the Mexican national colonization law
of 1824; the Coahuila y Texas colonization law of 1825; the Fredonian
Declaration of independence of 1826; the laws and decrees of Coahuila
y Texas, 1824-1835; the constitution of Coahuila y Texas of 1827; the
colonization law of Tamaulipas, 1826; the Mexican national naturali-
zation law of 1828; the proceedings of the Convention of 1832; the
Journals of the Consultation of 1835; the proceedings of the General
Council, 1835-1836; the Goliad Declaration of Independence of 1835;
the journals of the Convention of 1836; the ordinances and decrees of
the Consultation, 1835-1836; the Texas Declaration of Independence of

1836; the Constitution of 1836; proclamations and treaties of the Republic of Texas; the annexation joint resolutions of 1845; the Constitution of 1845; the ordinances of the Secession Convention of 1861; the Texas Constitution of 1861; the Confederate Constitution of 1861; the Address to the People of the Convention of 1861; the Constitution of 1866; the ordinances of the Convention of 1866; the Reconstruction Acts of 1870; the ordinances of the Convention of 1868; the Constitution of 1871; the ordinances of the Convention of 1875; the Constitution of 1876; and the resolutions and proclamations of the state legislature, 1846-1897.

The set has never been reprinted, although it is one of the half-dozen or so most important works on Texas history, government, and politics. A complete set of the original printings would be nearly impossible to assemble. Three indexes have been published, all incomplete, difficult to use, and generally unreliable—although it is even more difficult to use the set without them. They are: Cadwell W. Raines, *Analytical Index to the Laws of Texas,* 1823-1905 (Austin: Von Boeckmann-Jones Company, 1906); George P. Finlay and D. E. Simmons, *Index to Gammel's Laws of Texas,* 1822-1905 (Austin: H. P. N. Gammel, 1906); and Weaver Moore, *Index to Proper Names in Gammel's Laws of Texas,* Volumes I-VIII (No place, 1966, 418pp.).

In 1901 Gammel obtained a million dollar printing contract from the state by which he was to receive the excess accumulation of court and department reports, laws, and journals for a period of twenty years in exchange for printing a continuation of the laws of Texas and for supplying the state three sets of the *Laws of Texas.* Gammel was unable to fulfill the contract for long, and the state released him from the obligation. In later years, Gammel got in serious trouble with the state over some of the transfers of state publications, and had a number of fires and incidents that were questioned by the Texas Rangers. A recent biography of Gammel by his family ignores this part of his life and is generally worthless. Gammel also ran the largest rare book store in Texas for many years, as well as publishing other useful works of Texas history.

While Gammel's set is indispensable, it does have gaps. None of the journals of the Texas congress or legislature are included. For these one must go to the original editions, except for the journals of the 4th and 6th Congress, which were first published after the turn of the 20th century. Texian Press published some of the Texas-Confederate legislative materials which had not before been printed. The journals of the Convention of 1845 were not included in Gammel, nor the journal of the Convention of 1861, nor the journal of the Convention of 1875. These have since been reprinted: *Journal of the Convention [of] 1845* (Austin: Shoal Creek Publishers, 1974), edited by Mary Bell Hart; *Journal of the Secession Convention of Texas* (Austin: Austin Printing Company for the Texas Library and Historical Commission, 1912), edited by E. W. Winkler; *Debates in the Texas Constitutional Convention of 1875* (Austin: University of Texas, 1930), edited by Seth S. McKay. Gammel reprinted the laws of Coahuila y Texas from the John P. Kimball edition of 1839, which had gaps and sometimes poor translations, but it is still the best available. There are two excellent sources for Mexican national laws relating to Texas: Basilio Jose Arrillaga, *Recopilacion de Leyes . . . de la Republica Mexicana,* published periodically from 1834 to 1866, and Manuel Dublan and Jose M. Lozano, *Legislacion Mexicana* (Mexico, 1876) in five volumes. These two works each contain Texas material not in the other. The Sayles work mentioned below also has translations of many early laws relating to Texas.

Other useful works are David B. Gracy [ed.], *Establishing Austin's Colony: The First Book Printed in Texas, with the Laws, Orders and Contracts of Colonization* (Austin: Jenkins Publishing Company, 1970); E. W. Winkler [ed.], *Secret Journals of the Senate, Republic of Texas, 1836-1845* (Austin, 1911); Seymour V. Connor [ed.], *Texas Treasury Papers, 1836-1846* (Austin: Texas State Library, 1955, 3 vols.); T. W. Streeter, *Bibliography of Texas, 1795-1845* (Cambridge: Harvard University Press, 1955-1960, 5 vols.); E. W. Winkler and Llerena Friend, *Check List of Texas Imprints, 1846-1876* (Austin: Texas State Historical Assn., 1949-1963, 2 vols.). It is necessary to consult the latter two bibliographies to find various additional laws, decrees, journals, etc., not in Gammel.

Four times the early laws of Texas have appeared in digest form. James W. Dallam, *Digest of the Laws of Texas* (Baltimore, 1845); Oliver C. Hartley, *Digest of the Laws of Texas* (Phila., 1850); W. S. Oldham and G. W. White, *Digest of the General Statute Laws of the State of Texas* (Austin, 1859); and George W. Paschal, *A Digest of the Laws of Texas, 1754-1873* (Wash., 1874). Annotated statutes were issued by John and

Henry Sayles, *Early Laws of Texas,* 1731-1879 (St. Louis, 1888), followed by modern compilations by Vernon and by West Publishing Company. The essential guide to these various publications and their use is Marian Boner, *A Reference Guide to Texas Law & Legal History: Sources and Documentation* (Austin: University of Texas Press, 1976).

Dallam's *Digest,* mentioned above, is one of the basic Texas sources not because of its digest of laws but because it included the first publication of the "Opinions of the Supreme Court of Texas" during the republic period. Dallam has been frequently reprinted under the title *Dallam's Decisions* . . . This was followed by *Texas Reports* in 164 volumes, 1846-1963, and *South Western Reporter* in 300 volumes, 1887-1928 and second series beginning in 1928. Other court reports are described in Boner.

70   Gard, Wayne (1899-)

THE CHISHOLM TRAIL.

Norman: University of Oklahoma Press, [1954].
xi,296,[2]pp. Drawings by Nick Eggenhofer. 24cm.
Cloth, dustjacket.
[Verso of title:] First edition.

Other issues:
(A). Second printing, June, 1954.
(B). Third printing, October, 1954.
(C). Fourth printing, June, 1959.
(D). Fifth printing, September, 1965.
(E). Sixth printing, January, 1969.
(F). Seventh printing, 1976.

Entertaining and scholarly, this is the best book on the Chisholm Trail. Dan Ferguson called it "the most complete coverage extant and unlikely to be supplanted soon . . . an invaluable source book." Ross Santee called it "a magnificent piece of work," and Eugene Hollon called it "an exciting work." *Time Magazine* listed it as one of the outstanding books of 1954, "a scholarly narrative, but the material of a true saga bursts from the book's learned seams." Joseph Henry Jackson said it is the kind of book "every writer who chooses some phase of American past as his theme sets out to give, though so few of them do."

Gard writes: "For more than a dozen tempestuous years, beginning in 1867, the Chisholm Trail was the Texas cowhand's road to high adventure. It held the excitement of sudden stampedes, hazardous river crossings, and brushes with Indian marauders. . . . It carried what probably was the greatest migration of domestic animals in world history. In a period when Texas still lacked railroads for shipping its surplus cattle to northern states, the trail to Kansas served an urgent need. This pathway, which took the imprint of several million Longhorns, helped Texas dig herself out of the poverty that followed the Civil War. It also spurred railroad construction in the West and the Southwest."

Gard's research was extensive; his bibliography includes 31 manuscript collections, 65 newspaper files, and hundreds of books and articles consulted. He and his son traveled up the trail to verify the route, conducting extensive interviews. He even managed to locate and interview surviving trail drivers. Aware of the need for "a comprehensive account of this historic trail," a large number of fellow historians provided assistance, including J. Frank Dobie, Carl Coke Rister, Edward Everett Dale, Ralph Bieber, and Ramon Adams. It would be difficult to imagine a more solidly researched book.

The first book relating to the trail was by one of the men responsible for its establishment: Joseph G. McCoy, *Historic Sketches of the Cattle Trade of the West and Southwest* (Kansas City: Ramsey, Millett & Hudson, 1874). The second significant book on the trail was Sam P. Ridings, *The Chisholm Trail* (Guthrie, Okla.: Co-operative Pub. Co., 1936). McCoy's book is one of the great classics of the cattle industry, but relates to the whole of the western cattle business. Ridings' book, written by a man who had ridden the trail, is excellent but relates primarily to the Oklahoma section of the trail. Wayne Gard's work places the emphasis on the trail as a Texan's trail.

The trail, as Gard delineates it, began very near the southern tip of Texas and ran northward past or through San Antonio, Austin, Waco, and Fort Worth up through Oklahoma to Kansas. Virtually every feeder trail from other parts of Texas—and there were dozens of them—was also known to the drovers as part of the Chisholm Trail. The cattle driven northward, says Gard, "helped to relieve the beef shortage in other parts of the country. . . . Others were used to stock

new ranches and thus spread cattle raising into the northern part of
the Great Plains and the Rocky Mountain region.'' Economically, the
profits from the trail drives enabled Texans to develop better breeds
of cattle and enabled shippers to develop new processes of refrigeration.
The opening of the trail was a significant event in the history of the
United States and a major event in the history of Texas.

For the cowboys who rode the trail, it was the experience of a
lifetime. Gard concludes his book with the following tribute: ''Even
for the puncher who viewed the drive less as a business venture than
as a lark, the Chisholm Trail had lasting rewards. Every trail hand
carried memories of far horizons, winding rivers, faithful mounts, and
thundering stampedes. He had survived dangers that made the hazards
of a more settled life seem tame. . . . He would treasure to his last
moment the vision of a Longhorn herd strung out on the green prairie
or bedded down for the night under the gleaming stars.''

Adams Guns 797. Adams Herd 875. Kurtz p.43.

71   Gard, Wayne (1899-   )

SAM BASS.

Boston and New York: Houghton Mifflin Company, The Riverside Press Cambridge,
1936.
vi,[4], 262pp. Illus. 21cm.
Cloth, dustjacket.

Other issues:
(A). Paperback edition. Lincoln: University of Nebraska Press, [1969]. Same colla-
tion. Bison Book 391.
(B). Reprint of (A), circa 1976. Bears the 1969 date on verso of title, and indication
of second printing.
(C). Cloth edition of (B).

One of the most authentic of all outlaw biographies, this is by far
the best account of any Texas badman. Walter Prescott Webb said it
is ''a biography that bears the stamp of authenticity in every sentence
. . . the whole story of Bass is told here for the first time, told so
accurately, so dispassionately, and with such wealth of detail—names,
dates, and specific events—that the job of telling the truth about Sam

Bass is now completed." Ramon Adams stated: "I believe that I have read every book written about Sam Bass, and all of those containing any information on him, and I can safely say that Mr. Gard's book" is the best ever written on him, and that "it is accurate and dependable in every detail."

In late 1935, when Gard was about half through with his manuscript, Professor John McGinnis of Southern Methodist University introduced the editors of Houghton Mifflin Company to Gard, and a deal was struck. In my copy of the book, Gard has written that it was "published July 21, 1936, on the anniversary of the death of Sam Bass. No later printings were made by Houghton Mifflin. Film rights were sold to Republic Productions in 1944. The book went out of print about July, 1944. Republished by the University of Nebraska Press in its Bison Books paperbacks series in 1969; the Bison edition went out of print in 1972."

Shortly after this, Gard approached me about reprinting the book, but I delayed making a decision. In May of 1975 he wrote to me that "a few weeks ago, I received an unexpected phone call from David H. Gilbert, new director of the University of Nebraska Press, saying that he wanted to put *Sam Bass* back into print. I agreed. Since then I have signed a contract to that effect, for both hard cover and paperback editions." Thus I lost the opportunity to do an edition of this classic Texas book.

Ramon Adams states in *The Adams* 150: "My first book, *Cowboy Lingo,* and Gard's book were published simultaneously by Houghton Mifflin and I met Gard in 1936 at a book store where we were autographing books, and we have been friends for the past forty years."

There were four contemporary books written about Sam Bass, all more or less inaccurate but providing much information on his career: (1). [Thomas E. Hogg], *Authentic History of Sam Bass and His Gang, by a Citizen of Denton County, Texas.* (Denton: Monitor Job Office, 1878, 143pp.). This was written by Gov. James Hogg's brother; since he was a member of the posse which chased Bass, some of his account is firsthand. (2). Alfred Sorenson, *"Hands Up!" or, the History of a Crime: The Great Union Pacific Express Robbery* (Omaha: Barkalow Brothers, 1877, 139pp.). This includes the best account of this particular robbery.

(3). *Life and Adventures of Sam Bass* . . . (Dallas: Commercial Steam Print, 1878, 110pp.). The name of the author of this volume has never been discovered. (4). [Charles L. Martin], *A Sketch of Sam Bass, the Bandit* (Dallas: Herald Steam Printing House, 1880, 153pp.). Written by a lawyer and editor, this is the most extensive contemporary treatment of Bass and his gang. Many other books contain information about Bass; Adams estimated he had nearly two hundred books in his library that devote space to him.

Gard's research unearthed a great deal of previously unknown material on Sam Bass. In Indiana he found documents on his family history, as well as surviving relatives who were induced to talk. In Denton County he located the Bass hideouts and talked with many people who knew him and a few who had ridden with him. In Round Rock he found the bullet holes from a Bass street battle and talked to a woman who witnessed it. He interviewed Texas Ranger June Peak, who had chased Bass. He found court and archival records that filled out the story.

Gard's book sticks to the unvarnished facts, a feature uncommon in books about outlaws. Only in the final chapter, "Texas Robin Hood," does he recount the legends. Sam Bass was "not much of an outlaw as outlaws go," wrote Ramon Adams. "He was no gunman, nor was he a killer." It is strange, therefore, how he became so notorious. In the chapter on the Bass legends, Gard delves into this, remarking that the famous song sung by the cowboys may have enhanced his reputation. "Many of the legends that took root in cattle camps and hearthsides," writes Gard, "magnified Sam's crimes as well as the size of his loot. . . . As long as they persist, no Texan can be sure he will not wake some morning to find a ton of earth removed from his front yard by some romanticist who has just come into possession of the one authentic map."

Adams Guns 803. Adams One-Fifty 60.

72 Garrett, Julia Kathryn

GREEN FLAG OVER TEXAS: A STORY OF THE LAST YEARS OF SPAIN IN TEXAS.

New York and Dallas: The Cordova Press, Inc., 1939.
xv,275pp. 23cm. Illus. Maps by Creola Searcy.
Cloth, dustjacket. Foreword by Herbert E. Bolton.

Other issues:
(A). Same as above. Austin and New York: Jenkins Publishing Company, The
Pemberton Press, [1969]. xv,275pp. 24cm. Cloth. Dustjacket. Texas Heritage
Series. The word "Foreword" is incorrectly spelled "Foreward" on the title
page.

This is the best account of the abortive Texas Revolution of 1811-1813, the Gutierrez-Magee Expedition, and the Green Flag Republic. It is also one of the best accounts in English of that neglected period of Texas history during the decline of Spanish rule in the New World. Garrett was teaching high school in Ft. Worth when she undertook writing this book at the suggestion of Herbert E. Bolton, who said of the finished work: "Dr. Garrett has turned a veritable flood of new light on a dramatic episode in Southwest history. . . . She has made vivid the details . . . She has brought out of the fog of obscurity a hitherto little-known emblem, the 'Green Flag over Texas.'" J. V. Haggard wrote that the book, "like a candle in an attic crowded with treasured heirlooms, casts a flood of light into a hitherto seldom explored recess of Texas history."

The volume is based on thorough research. Dr. Garrett studied records available in Washington, Mexico City, Texas, California, and elsewhere. Much of the material she unearthed had never been utilized before; one suspects much of it has not been utilized since. Harbert Davenport stated: "Almost alone among Texas historians, Dr. Garrett's work is based on researches that have been equally adequate in the archives of the American government and in those of Texas, Mexico, and Spain. Her handling of this material is admirably proportioned. . . . The Gutierrez episode is given, once and for all, its true international perspective."

Ironically, this superb use of documentary resources is not complemented by sufficient research into previously published materials. The volume derives almost totally from archival records. The personal memoirs of survivors and the analyses of contemporary writers are neglected, giving the book a lack of balance and perspective. For example, Garrett makes no use of the painstaking interviews by

Mirabeau B. Lamar of nearly every survivor of the Gutierrez-Magee Expedition and those who fought against it, all of which had been published in the 1920's. Her book thus suffers for its want of personal, rather than official, points of view. Nevertheless, her outstanding discoveries of new materials deserve great praise, from her unearthing of the cache of letters of Dr. John Sibley to her exciting discovery of the hitherto unknown first Texas newspaper, the *Gaceta de Texas* of 1813.

73 Garrison, George Pierce (1853-1910) [ed.]

DIPLOMATIC CORRESPONDENCE OF THE REPUBLIC OF TEXAS.

Washington: Government Printing Office, 1908, 1911.
Three Volumes: 646;807; v,808-1617pp. 24cm.
Cloth.
Part I issued as Vol. II of *Annual Report of the American Historical Association for the Year* 1907; Parts II and III issued as Vol. II (1) and Vol. II (2) of *Annual Report of the American Historical Association for the Year* 1908.

This is the basic source work for official diplomatic papers of the Republic of Texas. It is indispensable for any study of this period of Texas history. Garrison states of this era: "Except for the years in which the United States has been actually at war, there is no decade of our history more abundantly filled with intense and instructive national experiences than that during which Texas was an independent republic." Garrison, whom Eugene C. Barker called "an important figure in the building of the University of Texas," was educated at the University of Edinburgh and University of Chicago, settling in Texas in 1874, where he soon joined the staff of the new university. His proteges included Barker, Binkley, Webb, Winkler, and Bugbee. It was through his influence that the Bexar Archives and Stephen F. Austin Papers were rescued and placed at the university, and he was a founder of the Texas State Historical Association and editor of its quarterly.

Issued as the Eighth Report of the Historical Manuscripts Commission of the American Historical Association, the work was prepared under the direction of a committee consisting of J. Franklin Jameson, Edward G. Bourne, Worthington C. Ford, Frederick W. Moore,

Thomas M. Owen, and James A. Woodburn, although the compilation was entirely prepared by George P. Garrison. The calendar was prepared by E. W. Winkler, who also helped in the editorial work. There are two valuable introductions by Garrison, and these should be consulted before using the text. Part II contains a note referring to Garrison's unfortunate death in July, 1910, "before reading a single page of the proof" of Parts II and III. Eugene C. Barker directed the completion of the project.

Sources are primarily the official records in the Texas State Archives and the Texas Department of State, with some from private collections such as the Stephen F. Austin Papers of the University of Texas. None of the correspondence in federal archives was included, but this was later published in William R. Manning's *Diplomatic Correpondence of the United States* (Volume VIII, Wash., 1937). Garrison states: "The books of the [Texas] legation at Washington seem to have been brought to Texas, but only one of them is now in the archives of the State. . . . An inscription in the volume indicates that it was taken from the convicts in the state penitentiary at Huntsville in 1868 by one of the officials [who] states that he found a box of books in possession of the convicts and that he rescued this one. The statement does not show what the other books were, nor is there anything in it to assist an inference as to how the lot happened to be in Huntsville."

Part I consists of "Texan Diplomatic Correspondence with the United States," between December 7, 1835, and December 30, 1842, comprising 647 official letters, documents, memoranda, certificates, and receipts. Garrison states: "The efforts of Texas to establish diplomatic relations with the United States began with the appointment by the Consultation, on November 12, 1835, of three commissioners to that country." Hence the section includes the correspondence of commissioners Stephen F. Austin, William H. Wharton, and Branch T. Archer with officials of the United States and with members of the General Council in Texas prior to the formal declaring of independence in Texas on March 2, 1836.

Part II continues the correpondence with the United States from January 11, 1843, through March 25, 1846, comprising 245 entries, 44 of which are items between 1836 and 1842 found since publication of Part I. The remainder of Part II consists of 220 entries under the heading "Correspondence with Mexico," and 13 entries under the heading "Correspondence with Yucatan." These cover the period May 17, 1836, through March 18, 1845.

Part III comprises "Correspondence with European States," consisting of 290 entries for Great Britain, 122 for France, five for Spain, three for Prussia, six for Belgium, ten for The Netherlands, and 21 for the Hanse Towns. At the end of the volume are two excellent indices, one listing each item of correspondence alphabetically by writer and the other a detailed general index.

Unfortunately, the work does not include letters and documents previously published. These are, however, listed in place in the text with references to the original publication. The work would have been greatly enhanced if these had been printed in full, because many of the most important letters may even now only be found in such places as the U.S. serial volumes and contemporary newspapers.

74 Geiser, Samuel Wood (1890-   )

NATURALISTS OF THE FRONTIER.

[Dallas:] Southern Methodist University, 1937.
Foreword by Herbert Spencer Jennings.
341pp. Frontis. Maps. 24cm.
Cloth, dustjacket.

Other issues:
(A). Revised edition. [Dallas:] Southern Methodist University, 1948. 296,[1]pp. Illus. 24cm. Cloth, dustjacket. Designed by Merle Armitage. Best edition, with considerable additional material, although printed in smaller type.

This is the best introduction to the history of natural science in Texas. R. L. Biesele called it "a valuable and scholarly contribution to Texana and to biographical writing and is a very agreeable blend of science, genealogy, and history." William R. Hogan said "Geiser made his subjects literally come alive as he sent [them] stalking their prey. Some of the writing reaches a sufficient intensity of performance to glow with its own heat." Rogers McVaugh called it "a valuable scientific document," but said its "primary appeal may well be, however, to those who like a good story for its own sake."

The volume is an early example of fine printing and design by a Texas publisher. It was, in fact, the first book published by Southern Methodist University Press; the text itself first appeared in serialized form in *Southwest Review* between 1929 and 1937 (volumes XIV-XXII). Starting with an interest in Jacob Boll, Geiser found himself enmeshed in a decade-long study before finally publishing his work, only to find himself so enthralled with the subject that it became the dominant theme of his scholarly career. The second edition contains a lengthy bibliography of Geiser's writings in the field.

The volume contains accounts of Jacob Boll, the Swiss naturalist whose studies in Texas included geology, zoology, entomology, botany, and paleontology; Jean Louis Berlandier, who made several early expeditions into Texas and left precious manuscripts, drawings, and watercolors; Thomas Drummond, an English botanist who toured Texas in the early 1830's and named many Texas flowers; Louis C. Ervenberg, the German minister who made studies of Texas trees and plants; Ferdinand Jacob Lindheimer, the German who became a Texas editor and botanist; Ferdinand Roemer, the father of Texas geology; Charles Wright, the Englishman who discovered so many new plants in Texas; Gideon Lincecum, the Georgian entomologist and paleontologist; Julien Reverchon, the Frenchman who collected 2600 plant species in Texas; and Gustaf Belfrage, the Swedish nobleman and "most exotic figure of all," who collected and described Texas ants, beetles, and butterflies.

There is also an introductory chapter on natural historians of the Southwest and an appendix, "A Partial List of Naturalists and Collectors in Texas, 1820-1880," which includes brief biographies of about 150 naturalists. This section was later expanded into a volume by Geiser entitled *Scientific Study and Exploration in Early Texas,* (Dallas, 1939), increasing the biographical sketches to 340, and further expanded in a series of articles in *Field & Laboratory,* 1958-1959, issued in a bound volume with a separately printed title page in 1959 as *Men of Science in Texas,* 1820-1880. Geiser also wrote a related work of considerable value, *Horticulture and Horticulturalists in Early Texas.* (Dallas, 1945).

Geiser's purpose is not only to present the biographies of these important but little-known men in Texas, but to pose the question, "what, in general, is the effect of exploration—contact with raw frontier life, contact with the riches of unexplored land—on the man of science?'' Geiser answers: ''The frontier has broken scientists as well as made them.'' Nevertheless, Geiser found an astonishing number of hitherto neglected scientific studies undertaken in early Texas. His research was complicated by the fact that so many of the genuine scientists were Europeans, who sent their reports back to obscure European journals. Geiser's search for Texas naturalists took him to such places as Scotland, Sweden, and ''a thousand obscure publications.'' No Texas historian ever studied his field more exhaustively in the face of more discouraging obstacles.

Campbell, p.46. Lowman, *Printing Arts,* p.29.

75 Giles, Leonidas Banton (1841-1922)

TERRY'S TEXAS RANGERS.

[Austin: Von Boeckmann-Jones Co., Printers, 1911].
105pp. 18cm.
Cloth.

Other issues:

(A). Facsimile reprint. Austin: The Pemberton Press, 1967. [11], 105,[14]pp. Portrait. 22cm. Cloth, dustjacket. New introduction by John H. Jenkins. Brasada Reprint Series III.

Giles' short narrative is one of the best memoirs of the famous 8th Texas Cavalry Regiment, better known as Terry's Texas Rangers. The unit entered the war 1200 strong, fought and claimed victory in over 200 battles, and wound up with scarcely enough men to form a single company. H. Bailey Carroll called it ''one of the great recollections of that sterling group of Terry's Texans in the Civil War, and incidentally, has come to be one of the rarest pieces of Texana.'' Dr. S. O. Young said it ''is so intensely interesting and so charmingly written that I defy anyone to take it up and lay it aside.''

Giles, a native of the Republic of Texas, was attending Baylor University when the Civil War began. He joined the Terry regiment and served throughout the war, suffering a battle wound in Kentucky on December 17, 1861. The regiment was formed by Benjamin F. Terry,

a member of the Texas Secession Convention; he was killed in the
same battle in which Giles was wounded. Gen. Joseph Wheeler called
the unit "matchlessly brave and daring" and Gen. John B. Hood said
there was, "in my opinion, no body of cavalry superior to that" of
Terry's Texas Rangers. Gen. Thomas Jordan said of the unit: "The
privates included a large number of the wealthiest and best educated
young men of Texas, who, with many others specially trained in the
business of stock raising on the vast prairies of that state, had acquired
a marvelous skill in horsemanship. The career of this regiment has
been one of the most brilliant in the annals of war."

Written fifty years after the war began, the Giles volume contains
some errors of fact due to the author's faulty memory. Giles himself
writes: "It is now perhaps too late to attempt anything like a complete
history of the regiment, as the necessary data can hardly be procured.
. . . I wish with all my heart I could make my story as complete as
it ought to be, for I firmly believe that a well written narrative of the
regiment's wonderful career would be the most entertaining book in
the literature of war." Giles was assisted by two other former rangers,
D. S. Combs and A. B. Briscoe, the latter of whom "placed at my
service a large lot of ms. of his personal memoirs."

There are several other memoirs of members of the unit, mostly
with the same type of inaccuracies as the Giles volume, all produced
in small quantities and now quite rare: William A. Fletcher, *Rebel
Private, Front and Rear* (Beaumont: Greer Print, 1908, 193pp.); H. W.
Graber, *The Life Record of H. W. Graber, a Terry Texas Ranger* (No place;
1916, 442pp.); James K. P. Blackburn, *Reminiscences of the Terry Rangers*
(Austin: University of Texas, 1919. 79pp.).

Coulter 184. Howes G168. Nevins I-93.

76   Gillett, James Buchanan (1856-1937)

SIX YEARS WITH THE TEXAS RANGERS, 1875 TO 1881.

Austin: Von Boeckmann-Jones Co., Publishers, [1921].
332pp. 8 illus. 19cm.
Cloth. Dustjacket.

Other issues:

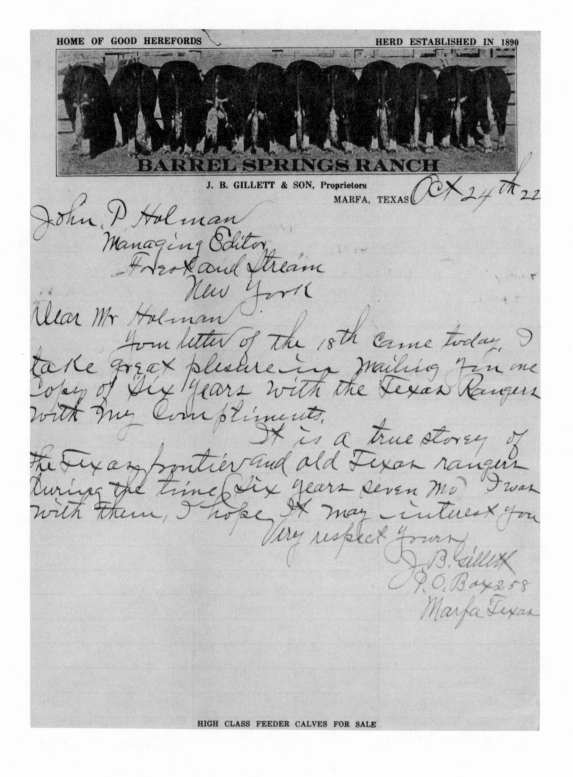

HOME OF GOOD HEREFORDS — HERD ESTABLISHED IN 1890

BARREL SPRINGS RANCH

J. B. GILLETT & SON, Proprietors

MARFA, TEXAS Oct 24th 22

John. P Holman
Managing Editor
Frost and Stream
New York

Dear Mr Holman.

Your letter of the 18th came today, I take great pleasure in mailing you one copy of Six Years with the Texas Rangers with my compliments. It is a true storey of the Texas frontier and old Texas rangers during the time Six years seven mo I was with them, I hope It may interest you

Very respect yours

J B. Gillett
P. O. Box 258
Marfa Texas

HIGH CLASS FEEDER CALVES FOR SALE

(A). New edition, edited with an introduction by Milo M. Quaife. New Haven: Yale University Press; London: Humphrey Milford, Oxford University Press, 1925. xvi,259pp. Illus. 24cm. Cloth, dustjacket.

(B). *The Texas Ranger, A Story of the Southwestern Frontier*. Yonkers-on-Hudson, N.Y., and Chicago: World Book Company, 1927. xiii,[1],218pp. Illus. Map. 20cm. Cloth. Pioneer Life Series. "By James B. Gillett, in collaboration with Howard R. Driggs." Illustrated by Herbert M. Stoops. With a new introduction by Driggs. "Delightfully illustrated, and the illustrations are true to life."—J. Frank Dobie. Driggs apparently added nothing to the volume but his name.

(C). Reprint of (A). Chicago: The Lakeside Press, R. R. Donnelley & Sons Co., 1943. xxxii,264pp. Illus. Folding map. 17cm. Cloth. The Lakeside Classics No. 41.

(D). Reprint of (A), incorrectly labeled "Second printing." New Haven and London: Yale University Press, [1963]. xxxvi,259,[4]pp. Illus. 21cm. Cloth, dustjacket. New foreword by Oliver Knight.

(E). Paperback edition of (D). Yale Western Americana Paperbounds Series. 21cm.

(F). Facsimile edition of (D). Lincoln: University of Nebraska Press, [1967]. Same collation. 20cm. Cloth.

(G). Paperback edition of (F). First Bison Book Printing, 1976. Same collation.

This is one of the finest personal memoirs of Texas Ranger service. Peter Decker called it "perhaps the best account of the rangers ever published," and Stanley Vestal called it "the best of ranger autobiographies." Jeff Dykes said: "I heard Capt. Gillett tell this story and it reads like he talked—you simply live those six years with him." J. Frank Dobie, who did more than anyone else to promote the book, said: "I regard Gillett as the strongest and straightest of all ranger narrators. He combined in his nature wild restlessness and loyal gentleness. He wrote in sunlight."

Jim Gillett's father was 46 when Jim was born. He had himself led an interesting life, having journeyed to Santa Fe about 1830, been captured by Indians, served in the Mexican War, settled in Paris, Texas, served in the Texas Legislature, was Adjutant General of Texas, was quartermaster of a Texas Ranger battalion on the eve of the Civil War, and at the age of 54 served as a private in the Confederacy. From his father's stories, Gillett says, "I early conceived a passionate desire to become a frontiersman and live a life of adventure. . . . When school closed in the early summer of 1868 I went fishing, and never attended school an hour thereafter." Gillett helped his father, who had become one of the early Texas cattle drivers at the age when most men retired.

Gillett struck out on his own as a cowboy, and relates his first encounter with Indians, around a campfire late one night when he was 16: "When the Indians began shooting and yelling I sat up. . . . As I did so an Indian, mounted on his pony, almost ran over me. . . . I was wide-awake by this time and ran for a thicket barefooted and in my undergarments."

In 1874 John Holland Jenkins resigned as Captain of Company D, Texas Rangers, and Lt. Dan W. Roberts assumed the command. The next spring Jim Gillett enlisted in the company, at the age of 17. He served in the Rangers from 1875 to 1881, mostly with the rank of sergeant. Most of his book is devoted to those years, although a portion relates to his later service as Marshal of El Paso in the days of John Wesley Hardin and Dallas Stoudenmire. Thereafter Gillett became a successful rancher, ultimately running a 30,000-acre spread near Marfa.

His memoirs were written with the aid of an unknown editor, privately printed, and sold by Gillett himself. The Yale edition was further revised and has become the standard edition. J. Frank Dobie, in a review written in 1927, stated: "Three years ago I read [Gillett's book] for the first time. I thought it then one of the most engaging and enlightening chronicles that I had ever read. . . . I will not say it is as great a book as *Robinson Crusoe,* but I will say that I had as lief read it as *Robinson Crusoe*—and I am very fond of Defoe's narrative. Once you start reading Captain Gillett's story of the dog that guarded the Indian-besieged camp in Crow Flat; of the chase of old Victorio, Apache, into Mexico; of the round-up of outlaws in the Junction country; of the desperate ride after Sam Bass; of the Peg Leg robber gang on the San Saba; of the long ride with General Baylor from San Antonio to El Paso, you can not stop until you have finished the story, and then you want to begin the next."

Gillett wrote from memory 45 years after he joined the rangers, and his narrative is not entirely trustworthy in detail. His account of the Sam Bass gang is faulty, as Ramon Adams has pointed out in *Burs Under the Saddle,* and some of his dates are quite naturally inaccurate. Gillett himself stated: "I am not an historian . . . I cannot at this late date recount in detail . . . I have told my story just as I remember it, to the best of my ability and without any effort to embroider it with imagination . . . My ranger days and ranger service [are] but a memory, albeit the happiest one of my life.''

Adams Guns 829. Adams Burs 148. Adams One-Fifty 62. Campbell, p.78. Clark I-83. Dobie, p. 59. Graff 1553. Howes G177. Rader 1591.

77 Gouge, William M. (1796-1863)

THE FISCAL HISTORY OF TEXAS, EMBRACING AN ACCOUNT OF ITS REVENUES, DEBTS, AND CURRENCY, FROM THE COMMENCEMENT OF THE REVOLUTION IN 1834 TO 1851-52, WITH REMARKS ON AMERICAN DEBTS.

Philadelphia: Lippincott, Grambo, and Co., 1852.
xx,[17]-327,16pp. 24cm. Cloth.
[Verso of title:] Philadelphia: T. K. and P. G. Collins, Printers. Some copies have a slip pasted over "ex-" in the bottom line of page [iii].

Other issues:
(A). Same as above, but 32pp. of advertisements at the end instead of 16. These are numbered 1-20, 23-34.
(B). Facsimile reprint. New York: A. M. Kelly, 1968. xx,327pp. Reprints of Economic Classics Series.
(C). Facsimile reprint. New York: Burt Franklin, [1969]. xx,327pp. The Burt Franklin Research & Source Works Series 353.

The standard account of the financial history of the Texas Revolution and of the Republic of Texas, this book is much more interesting reading than the title suggests, mixing humor, anecdotes, and historical sidelights with statistics, finance, and fiscal theory.

The preface, in which Gouge acknowledges the aid of Peter H. Bell, James B. Shaw, John M. Swisher, James H. Raymond, Washington D. Miller, Thomas Duval, Jacob DeCordova, and others, is dated November, 1852. Chapter I deals with the Consultation of 1835; Chapters II-VI with the Provisional and Ad Interim Governments of 1835-1836 and with the Texas Revolution; Chapters VII-XXII with the Republic, 1836-1845; Chapters XXIII-XXXIV with general views, comparisons, and recommendations. The appendices, A to W, contain some excellent statistical material, including data on revenues, imports, exports, customs, agriculture, and bounties.

Gouge begins by stating that Texas financial history is of interest because of the example it presents in miniature: "Texas, though it, from 1835 to 1845, formed no part of the American Union, was yet an American State. It was a State *without* the Union. The people were Americans by birth, thought, habits, feeling. . . . All the fiscal faults which the great nations of Europe and America have committed on large scale, the Texans have committed on a small."

Gouge, a native Philadelphian, was editor of the Philadelphia *Gazette,* editor of *The Journal of Banking,* and author of several other books on finance. *Dictionary of American Biography* (IV, Pt. I, 444) comments laconically that Gouge was "an uncompromising opponent of banks, paper money, and corporations." His anti-currency theory is one of the two central themes of the book. Texans, says Gouge, "had within them the disease which taints all American blood, the paper-money disease, inherited from their ancestors." Texas paper money, which fell to one-twentieth of par at times, was a source of great mischief in the Republic of Texas. The Constitution of 1845, written when Texas entered the Union, expressly provided (Article VII, Section 8) that "in no case shall the legislature have the power to issue treasury warrants, treasury notes, or paper of any description intended to circulate as money."

The other theme is the public debt created by Texas. The debt should be paid, in full and at par, and not scaled or depreciated: "No matter how unwise it may have been expended . . . it ought to be paid." Gouge states that Texas, regrettably, "maintains, through her authorities, that a State, in the times of her prosperity, is not bound to fulfill the engagements she entered into in the times of her adversity, but is at liberty to modify them to such extent as to herself may seem equitable." C. W. Raines said of Gouge's text: "If it had been written at the instance of the creditors of Texas, and to prevent a scaling of our debt, it could not better have served their purpose. However, in spite of Gouge, the debt was scaled to its proper equitable amount and paid."

Although the Texans did not understand currency and bond trading, Gouge remarks, they were masters at land trading. They financed their revolution and populated their republic with land. They offered large numbers of acres to soldiers for agreeing to serve a few months

in the army, and to settlers simply for coming: "This seemed very
liberal; but the cash value of the article bestowed was very small.
Land, to him who has neither capital to stock it nor skill to cultivate
it, is worth only what others are willing to pay for it. . . . The offer,
however, drew volunteers from the United States, as they were more
or less governed in estimating the value of the bounty by the price
which land bore in their own neighborhoods. . . . For a time, indeed,
after the battle of San Jacinto . . . land-claims occasionally sold as
high as $200 or $300. . . . But they subsequently sold . . . at a fraction
more than one cent and a half an acre."

Gouge's work has been severely criticized for his bizarre fiscal views.
Sam Houston exclaimed on the floor of the U.S. Senate: "Who is the
gentleman who has written the book? . . . G-O-U-G-E—nothing less
than Gouge. . . . I have no time to do Mr. Gouge justice. I could
comment on the accuracy of his style, the precision of his calculations,
his statesmanlike reflections, and a great many good things could be
said about him, but I will leave him to somebody else. . . . But I
assure him that I hope he will have no influence to 'gouge' Texas."

George P. Garrison states that the book "is pervaded by a tone of
rasping criticism. . . . It should not . . . be regarded as a fair historical
presentation of the subject." I disagree. I find it no more biased than
any of the other early volumes on Texas, and a lot more interesting
and informative than many of the more famous works.

My favorite part of the book is where Gouge recounts the controversy
between the French Charge-d'Affaires to Texas, Count Alphonse de
Saligny, and Richard Bullock, Texas tavern keeper. They quarrelled
over Bullock's pigs, with the result that the irate Saligny prevented
Gen. James Hamilton, Texas Minister to France, from succeeding in
his attempt to obtain a large loan for Texas. Gouge states: "Mr.
Bullock's pigs were the aggressors. The Texan editors, with an amiable
partiality for everything belonging to their own country, conceal the
fact; but we have been on the spot, and inquired into the particulars.
M. de Saligny had a number of horses which were fed with corn. Mr.
Bullock's pigs intruded into the stables to pick up the corn the horses
suffered to fall to the ground. One of M. de Saligny's servants killed
some of the pigs. Mr. Bullock whipped the servant. This enraged M.

de Saligny; he influenced his brother-in-law, M. Humann, the Minister of Finance at Paris, and Gen. Hamilton's loan was defeated.

"We have had occasion to observe before that, however, the Texans might quarrel among themselves, they would always unite against the common enemy, the Mexicans. So it was on this occasion . . . All Texas stood by Mr. Bullock and his pigs. Houstonites and Anti-Houstonites were of one accord. Nor will it be too much to say that, as Rome was saved by the cackling of geese, so Texas was saved by the squeaking of pigs. If the loan had been obtained, it would have been that the debt of Texas, instead of being twelve millions, would have been twenty-five, thirty, perhaps forty millions. The most intelligent Texans agree in opinion that this would have been the result. All honor, then, to Mr. Bullock and his pigs; and this heretofore much despised animal must be regarded hereafter as possessed of classic interest. If his figure, carved in marble, should be placed over the entrance of the treasury of Texas, it would serve as a memento to future ages of his having been the salvation of the Republic, and teach Mr. Branch Tanner Archer's 'thousands and millions, born and unborn,' that the humblest of agents may be instrumental in producing consequences of the utmost importance."

Larned 2858. Rader 1634. Raines, p.96. Sabin 28071.

78   Gould, Lewis Ludlow (1939-)

PROGRESSIVES AND PROHIBITIONISTS: TEXAS DEMO-CRATS IN THE WILSON ERA.

Austin & London: University of Texas Press, [1973].
xvi,339pp. 12 plates; 8 illus. in text. Folding map.
Cloth, dustjacket.

Other issues:
(A). Paperback edition, [1976].

This is the best single book on any aspect of Texas during the early part of the 20th century. Robert C. McMath called it a "well written and thoroughly researched monograph" that "provides a sturdy framework within which . . . questions about the social dimensions of

Texas politics can be explored.'' Arthur S. Link said it ''recounts in fascinating detail the crusades, Democratic primary contests, and legislative battles, including the impeachment and removal from office of Governor James E. Ferguson in 1917, that convulsed Texas politics from 1910 to 1920.'' The book won the Texas Institute of Letters award for the best Texas book of the year 1973.

Gould casts his subject as a study of progressivism, particularly in regard to the prohibition issue, during the second decade of this century. It is, however, an excellent introduction to Texas politics and society in the first fourth of the century. In it we find the best analysis yet written of the careers of Joe Bailey, Jim Ferguson, and E. M. House, as well as a study of the influence of Texas on the Woodrow Wilson years and the impact of Wilson on Texas.

Gould states: ''Modern historians may shrink from an endorsement of the aims and goals of dry, fundamentalist America between 1910 and 1930, but the movement deserves at least sustained examination. . . . Few states in the South offer a better opportunity for an examination of the progressive-prohibitionist wing of the Democrats than Texas. . . . After 1910 the progressive movement in Texas identified liquor as a major area in need of change and concentrated its energies on this cultural reform. . . . A heritage of evangelistic religion imparted decisive weight to the temperance messages of clergymen and church journals. At the same time, the growth of cities, and the role of Mexican Americans, Negroes, and Germans sparked apprehensions among the white, old-stock, rural majority. . . . Focusing on the prohibition issue as the major divisive element in state politics, this study also explores the relationship between the national party under Wilson and the activities of local Democrats.''

The stage was set in the 1912 race for the Democratic nomination for the presidency. At the convention, the Texas delegation held out as a unit steadily for Wilson for 46 ballots, even when they were told that Texan Charles A. Culberson could get the nomination if they broke. After Wilson was nominated, Mrs. Wilson declared, ''But for Texas we would not be here today.'' I have always felt that this was the watershed in Texan politics of the 20th century. Political alliances were made based on that event, and politicians were thrust forward, that retained residual power bases through the Depression and the second world war to the present time. Because of the Texas stand, Texans provided the Wilson years with three cabinet officers and his most influential advisor.

In 1911, Governor Colquitt said, "We have only one political party in Texas, but there are enough political fights in that one for half a dozen." The major issue was prohibition, and because the forces for and against were so equally divided, Texas became a battleground on the issue. It was the leading goal of the progressives and the anathema of the conservatives, who detested the extension of government over private life. Gould uses the issue to explore and explain the enormous social changes that occurred in Texas during the period, and it is in this that his book has its lasting value.

Although I believe one finds the most perceptive understanding of the Texas leaders of the period in Gould, there are a number of other important sources. For Joseph W. Bailey, there is the prejudiced but massive William A. Cocke, *The Bailey Controversy in Texas* (San Antonio, 1908, 2 vols.) and a fine biography by Sam Hanna Acheson, *Joe Bailey: The Last Democrat* (New York: Macmillan, 1932). For Texas governors of the period, there are James W. Madden's idolatory *Charles Allen Culberson: His Life, Character and Public Service* (Austin: Gammel, 1929), James A. Clark and Weldon Hart's *The Tactful Texan: A Biography of Governor Will Hobby* (New York: Random House, 1958), and Fred Gantt's *The Chief Executive in Texas* (Austin: University of Texas Press, 1964). There is no biography of value of James E. Ferguson, but there is the useful compilation by Will C. Hogg, *Record of Investigation . . . of Charges Filed against Gov. Jas. E. Ferguson* (Austin: A. C. Baldwin, 1917). Another very valuable work is Seth S. McKay, *Texas Politics, 1906-1944* (Lubbock: Texas Tech Press, 1952), as is Ralph W. Steen, *Twentieth Century Texas: An Economic and Social History* (Austin: Steck, 1942). For Texans in the Wilson administration, there is A. L. and J. L. George, *Woodrow Wilson and Colonel House: A Personality Study* (New York: John Day Co., 1956), Charles Seymour [ed.], *The Intimate Papers of Colonel House* (Boston, Houghton Mifflin, 1926-1928, 4 vols.), and the delightful *Washington Wife: Journal of Ellen Maury Slayden from 1897 to 1919* (New York: Harper & Row, 1962), edited by Walter P. and Terrell Webb. Another fine book is Mary Lasswell's *John Henry Kirby, Prince of the Pines* Austin: Encino Press, 1967), as is James R. Green's *Grass-*

Roots Socialism: Radical Movements in the Southwest, 1895-1943 (Baton Rouge: Louisiana State University Press, 1978).

79   Gray, William Fairfax (1787-1841)

FROM VIRGINIA TO TEXAS, 1835: DIARY OF COL. WM. F. GRAY, GIVING DETAILS OF HIS JOURNEY TO TEXAS AND RETURN IN 1835-36 AND SECOND JOURNEY TO TEXAS IN 1837.

Houston: Gray, Dillaye & Co., Printers, 1909.
Preface by Allen Charles Gray.
viii,230pp. 23cm.
Wrappers.

Other issues:
(A). Facsimile reprint. Houston: Reprinted by The Fletcher Young Publishing Co., 7731 Wynlea, 1965. [6],viii,230pp. 26cm. Buckram. New prologue by Karen Sagstetter, containing numerous inaccuracies. New preliminary note by Fletcher C. Young. New portraits of Gray and his wife.

Gray left us the best account of events in Texas during the revolution written as they occurred. His is the only extensive diary written by an outsider to have survived. Historian Andrew Forest Muir, not given on any occasion to effusive praise, called Gray's diary "a faithful record of the proceedings [of the convention declaring Texan Independence], in some cases more complete than the official journal." It remains one of the best and most unbiased records of the turmoil in Texas during its most important winter and spring.

Gray was a man of culture and education. He had been a captain in the War of 1812 and a colonel of the Virginia militia. In 1824, he was the official host in Fredericksburg to Gen. LaFayette on his tour of the United States. He was a lawyer of note and relatively prosperous, although hurt substantially by the panic of 1833, when the national bank controversy reached its height. Gray came to Texas at the instigation of Tom Green and Albert T. Burnley of Washington, both of whom, according to Gray's son, "had been bitten by the stegomia which inoculates the land speculation virus." They desired to buy lands in Texas, and induced Gray to visit that province in their behalf.

His instructions by Green were: "Get all the information about Texas lands. . . . Do not be in too great a hurry, but examine well, and be very particular. . . . Keep a diary."

His diary begins in Virginia on October 7, 1835, and continues unabated until his return on June 26, 1836. A supplemental diary of another trip to Texas covers the period between January 17, 1837, and April 8, 1837. Gray stayed with Stephen F. Austin in New Orleans, arranged to buy lands to finance the revolution, crossed the Sabine at Gaines' Ferry on January 28, 1836, and traveled to Nacogdoches where he voted as a Texas citizen in the election for delegates to the Convention of 1836. It was Gray who carried and personally delivered the fateful letters from Stephen F. Austin to Sam Houston and Thomas J. Rusk telling of the approach of Santa Anna's army, ending: "This, of course, leaves us no remedy but one, which is an immediate declaration of independence."

He then continued to Washington-on-the-Brazos, where he stayed throughout the Convention, recording in great detail his observations on the activities surrounding the writing and signing of the Texas Declaration of Independence. He then retreated in company with President Burnet and Vice President Zavala (who "rode a little mule") on their retreat before the advance of the Mexican army.

He records the earliest written account in any detail of the fall of the Alamo, written out immediately after he received it from the lips of Travis' slave Joe. He stayed on Zavala's plantation awhile, witnessing and recording some of the activities of the fledgling Texas Navy, and returned to New Orleans, all the while recording the events of the Runaway Scrape. From New Orleans, Gray wrote to Burnet on May 10: "We are all on the housetops here, with the news of the glorious victory of the 21st. . . . All is joy and hope among the friends of Texas."

Gray is at his best in his character analyses of the leading Texans. Stephen F. Austin "appears to be a sensible and unpretending businessman." Branch T. Archer is "particularly excited and vehement. He talks too much and too loud." George A. Nixon "professes great disinterestedness and candor. I rather suspect he has neither." Governor Henry Smith, who told him Austin should be hanged for his Mexican "principles and policy," did not fool Gray: "My impression of Governor Smith is, that he is a strongly prejudiced party man. Too illiterate, too little informed, and not of the right *calibre* for the station he has been placed in.'' He declined to be out-horse-traded by Robert M. Williamson—quite a feat in itself. Zavala was ''the most interesting man in Texas'' but possessed of ''inordinate ambition.'' Sam Houston, who told him the General Council had been ''bribed'' into its fight against Governor Smith, is described as ''evidently the people's man, and seems to take pains to ingratiate himself with everybody. He is much broken in appearance, but still has a fine person and courtly manners.''

It is these perceptive insights into character that make Gray's diary so significant. As T.R. Fehrenbach has written: ''Differences exist not only between Texan and Mexican accounts, as would be expected, but between Texan and Texan. For example, all of the principal figures at the battle of San Jacinto were at odds with each other before the battle, and most became political enemies following it. [Most accounts] tend to be self-serving and must be suspect. But Gray wrote spontaneously about people with whom he had had no previous contact, and his impressions, although acquired on short acquaintance, add greatly to our understanding of the key men in the great drama unfolding around him.''

Of Texans in general, Gray had mixed emotions. When the convention met on Sunday he was aghast: ''They are a most ungodly people.'' On the other hand, he clearly fell in love with the land and with the spirit of the pioneer families. In Nacogdoches, where Anna Raguet translated Spanish for him, he wrote: ''I was really surprised that so shabby a looking place could assemble so many good looking, well dressed and well behaved women.'' On his return to Texas in 1837, he wrote: ''Rude hospitality and unaffected kindness are the characteristics of the *old settlers* that I met with. . . . The new race are adventurers, sharpers, and many of them blacklegs. The observing of the old settlers are sensible of this, and . . . say they had no occasion for locks in Texas until within the last two years, and now no property is safe. None of the offices of the new Republic are filled by the old settlers. . . . The old men see and feel this with deep but smothered indignation.''

Gray nevertheless believed Texas to be the land of the future, and moved his family there in 1837. He settled in Houston, held several public offices, and practised law until his death in 1841. One of his two sons, Peter W. Gray, founded the famed Baker, Botts law firm in Houston, and the other founded a publishing company that operated from 1865 to 1959. This latter son, A. C. Gray, printed the Gray diary at the age of eighty.

Clark III-171. Howes G341.

80   Green, Thomas Jefferson (1802-1863)

JOURNAL OF THE TEXIAN EXPEDITION AGAINST MIER; SUBSEQUENT IMPRISONMENT OF THE AUTHOR, HIS SUFFERINGS, AND FINAL ESCAPE FROM THE CASTLE OF PEROTE, WITH REFLECTIONS UPON THE PRESENT POLITICAL AND PROBABLE FUTURE RELATIONS OF TEXAS, MEXICO, AND THE UNITED STATES.

New York: Harper & Brother, Publishers, 82 Cliff Street, 1845.
xiv,[2],[17]-487pp. 24cm. Two maps. Eleven engraved plates: "Illustrated by drawings taken from life by Charles M'Laughlin, a fellow prisoner." The plate entitled "Shooting Capt. Cameron" is listed as appearing on page 285, but in all known copies it is used as the frontispiece. Cloth.

Other issues:
(A). Facsimile reprint. Austin: The Steck Company, 1935. [2],[xvi],[17]-487pp. 23cm. A total of 2500 copies were printed.
(B). Facsimile reprint. New York: Arno Press, 1973. 487pp. Cloth.

The most important account of the tragic Texan expedition against Mier and the drawing of the black beans, this is also one of the most vitriolic Texas books. In the words of Ray Allen Billington, it is "not only most readable but also transmits the feeling of the Texans during the period of the Texas Republic." Everett D. Graff called it "one of the most exciting accounts . . . a vivid and terrifying tale."

The book recounts the abortive expedition in 1842 under William S. Fisher and Thomas J. Green into Mexico after the withdrawal of the Somervell Expedition. The small group of Texans raided and plundered the area, and attacked a large Mexican force in the town of Mier on

December 25, 1842. Although the Texans inflicted heavy losses on the Mexicans, they were tricked—according to Green—into surrendering. Because President Sam Houston had ordered the Texans not to cross the Rio Grande, the captured Texans were considered filibusters and the entire force was ordered to be executed as outlaws. This was later partly rescinded, and one in ten were ordered to be shot by Santa Anna. In what became known as the Black Bean Episode, the Texans were forced to draw beans from a jar, and those drawing black beans were executed. The remainder were imprisoned in Perote Prison near Vera Cruz.

General Green and some others eventually managed to escape, and the remainder were finally released in late 1844 under intense pressure from the U.S. government. Green never forgave Sam Houston, whom he blamed for their not being treated as prisoners of war. His book was issued with the deliberate goal of proving Houston's villainy. As Mier Expedition scholar James Day has said, "on its pages Houston found his name recorded no fewer than 117 times, and not once was the reference favorable." Despite Houston's opposition, Green and all the Mier force were later paid salaries for their services in the expedition, Green receiving $3,044.00.

Rough drafts of portions of the book were first printed in the Houston *Morning Star* in December, 1843, and in the Clarksville *Northern Standard* in March, 1844. The published volume consists of an introductory chapter lambasting Sam Houston, seven chapters regarding the expedition and battle, and twelve chapters concerning their imprisonment and the executions, escapes, and release. A supplemental chapter gives Green's predictions and advice on the future of Texas, including the recommendation that Mexico be conquered and annexed to Texas. He also makes the bizarre recommendation that when slavery is "inevitably abolished" in the United States, a portion of Mexico should be given to the blacks as a separate nation. Nine appendices give very valuable lists of participants and official correspondence, much from Green's own personal files.

Green's vilification of Sam Houston so incensed Houston that he made a lengthy speech refuting it on the floor of the U.S. Senate, August 1, 1854, stating that the copy in the Library of Congress should be "expelled therefrom, and given to some of the sewers of the city," and calling Green a loafer, a pirate, a robber, a fugitive, a felon, a slanderer, a swindler, a reckless villain, and a dastardly coward. Houston maintained that the Mier Expedition under Green was "without authority," made in order to "filibuster, rob, steal, and pilfer." Green in turn published a pamphlet containing further gasconades denouncing Houston entitled *Reply of Gen. Thomas J. Green to the Speech of General Sam Houston.* (Wash., 1855?).

The Green account, states C. W. Raines, is "one of the best war histories of that period, and as fascinating as a romance." J. Frank Dobie wrote that the book "will always be one of the most vivid and vigorous personal narratives associated with Texas history"; this was because, Dobie wrote in another essay, Green "lived in wrath and wrote with fire." The other basic accounts of the Mier Expedition, in addition to William P. Stapp's *Prisoners of Perote* entered here separately, are Thomas W. Bell, *A Narrative of the Capture and Subsequent Sufferings of the Mier Prisoners in Mexico* (De Soto Co., Miss.: R. Morris, 1845); Frederick C. Chabot [ed.], *The Perote Prisoners, Being the Diary of James L. Truehart* (San Antonio: The Naylor Company, 1934) as it relates to Perote Prison; Marilyn M. Sibley [ed.], *Samuel H. Walker's Account of the Mier Expedition* (Austin: Texas State Historical Association, 1978); and Joseph D. McCutchen, *Mier Expedition Diary* (Austin: University of Texas Press, 1978). The best analysis of these accounts and others is in James M. Day, *Black Beans and Goose Quills: Literature of the Texas Mier Expedition* (Waco: Texian Press, 1970).

Bradford 1984. Campbell, p.65. Dobie, p.55. Graff 1643. Howes G371. Jones 1104. Rader 1670. Raines, p.98. Sabin 28562. Streeter 1581.

81   Haley, James Evetts (1901-   )

CHARLES GOODNIGHT, COWMAN & PLAINSMAN.

Boston and New York: Houghton Mifflin Company, The Riverside Press Cambridge, 1936.
xiii,[3],485pp. Illus. by Harold Bugbee. Map by Thomas L. Jones. 22cm.
Cloth, dustjacket.
5000 copies printed.

Other issues:

(A). New edition. Norman: University of Oklahoma Press, [1949]. xiii,[3],485pp.
Illus. Map. 24cm. Cloth, dustjacket. The preface, dated Canyon, March 2,
1949, is slightly enlarged and includes the statement: "The text has been
occasionally slightly revised in order to bring it up to date or to include more
recently discovered facts." The Western Frontier Library Number 34.

(B). Second printing of (A). 1951.

(C). Third printing of (A), 1958.

(D). Fourth printing of (A), 1962.

(E). Fifth printing of (A), 1966.

(F). Sixth printing of (A), 1970.

(G). Seventh printing of (A), 1977.

(H). Eighth printing of (A), 1979.

This is a superb biography of one of the greatest Texans. William
Reese called it "the best biography of a cowman ever written. . . .
Haley's beautifully written biography . . . is an ample vehicle for a
mighty figure, and is a classic of American biography." L. F. Sheffy
called it "one of the most valuable and distinctive books of its kind."
Dean Krakel deemed it "solid, careful, historically true, and well
written." To E. C. Barker it was a "classic in the literature of the
range industry, [about] the greatest cattle man in western history . . .
not a factual statistical record of a man's doings, but a vivid, breathing
image of the man himself and of the world in which he lived."

Haley grew up in the shadow of Goodnight. For ten years after
leaving college, he prepared for writing about the man, and was
fortunate both in being allowed to interview him extensively (Goodnight had refused most others) but also in that even in his nineties
Goodnight's mind was still fresh as ever. Goodnight was born in 1836,
three days after Texas declared its independence and the day before
the final attack on the Alamo. Haley writes: "He rode bareback from
Illinois to Texas when he was nine years old. He was hunting with
the Caddo Indians beyond the frontier at thirteen, launching into the
cattle business at twenty, guiding Texas Rangers at twenty-four, blazing
cattle trails two thousand miles in length at thirty, establishing a ranch
three hundred miles beyond the frontier at forty, and at forty-five
dominating nearly twenty million acres of range country in the interests
of order. At sixty he was recognized as possibly the greatest scientific
breeder of range cattle in the West, and at ninety he was an active
international authority on the economics of the range industry . . .

thus, he lived, intensely and amply. Nor is it too much to say that whenever his vibrant personality touched the life of the short-grass country, it blazed great trails, plain, straight, and long. One of these led through my boyhood range.

"Ten years ago [1926] I left the home ranch beside the Goodnight Trail to follow Goodnight's Trail through history. It has been an extended pursuit. I have cut for sign from the mouth of the Rio Grande to his old range in the Rockies. I have tracked his associates from the West Coast to the Gulf; from the deep South into Mexico. I have confirmed my statements of fact through conventional sources in public libraries, though most of my material has been of a fresher if more difficult sort. I have back-tracked tens of thousands of miles in the open country, listening to tales of Western men who knew Goodnight and his time." He interviewed Andy Adams, Jim East, Charlie Siringo, John Rumans, and Walter Cochran. "But still the story is incomplete. Certain experiences in life seem to evade the written word. The faint tremors of the High Plains mirages do not dance upon my page; the 'feed' of sourdough in a dishpan has to be felt; and the sudden loss of a horse from under the rider is not an imaginative experience. Hence I regret not the thousands of pages of unused notes in my files, and the reams of rejected though relevant material in public libraries and archives. These are tangible and still available, while the missing qualities of rugged and vibrant personality that I cannot picture in my pages have passed with the dusts of the Goodnight Trail."

Haley's son, Evetts, Jr., himself a fine writer, described his father's writing style: "On the subject of language and verbs, he has frequently told me, 'write like you talk, and talk like a cowpuncher walks by using short choppy sentences and vigorous, active verbs. When editing copy written by others, he makes his blue pencil most destructive of useless adjectives and prepositional phrases. . . . Even though many of his sentences are long and involved, they do seem to flow, and unlike many writers with less talent and discipline, he is capable of logically defending his use of every word. . . . Most any reader of the Goodnight book will understand the following premise. The proof of the style of J. Evetts Haley is that his books are read over and over by people who are not at all interested in the minute factual detail of an episode in history.''

J. Frank Dobie rejoiced over Haley's style: "The naturalness, flavor, and vigor of his language are marked. It is the language of the range, of the soil, and the biographer himself uses it as readily as Goodnight. 'Davidson fogged into camp ahead of a cloud of dust.' 'Old Millsap's appetite for lead had entirely soaked up.' 'The blue horse fell in two and chinned for the moon.' 'As tough as bull-neck rawhide, as independent as a hog on ice, and as reckless as any drunk Indian, John Rumans was born to be a cowboy' . . . 'The mule went by like a bat out of a brush pile'; 'as much show as a stump-tailed bull in fly time' . . . Goodnight was a subject worthy of any biographer, and the biographer has proved himself worthy of his subject.''

Adams Guns 890. Adams Herd 960. Dobie, p.104. Howes H36. Merrill *Aristocrat*. Reese *Six Score* 53. Robinson 8.

82   Haley, James Evetts (1901-   )

THE XIT RANCH OF TEXAS, AND THE EARLY DAYS OF THE LLANO ESTACADO.

Chicago: The Lakeside Press, 1929.
Introduction by John V. Farwell.
xvi,261,[2]pp. Illus. Maps. 23cm.
Cloth.
1380 copies printed; withdrawn from circulation.

Other issues:
(A). New and revised edition. Norman: University of Oklahoma Press, 1953. xiv,258pp. Illus. Maps. 24cm. Cloth, dustjacket. Deletes about six pages of text, the introduction by Farwell, and half the pictures.
(B). Reprint of (A). Norman: University of Oklahoma Press, 1967. Same collation. 20cm. Western Frontier Library 34.
(C). Same as (B), "Second Printing" on the front flap of dust jacket.
(D). Same as (B), third printing, [1977].
(E). Paperback edition of (D).

Haley's first book, this is nevertheless one of the best examples of his scholarship. John L. McCarty called it "a monumental work" and

Chandler Robinson termed it "an epic account of the largest and most famous ranching operation of the early West. It is one of the most highly regarded landmarks in the literature of the cattle country." E. C. Barker praised Haley's "unmatched and phenomenal ability to weave fascinating personalities and innately interesting events into vivid narrative."

Haley describes the topic of his book: "During the middle eighties the XIT Ranch was established. It was the largest ranch in the cow country of the Old West, and probably the largest fenced range in the world. Its barbed wire enclosed over 3,050,000 acres of land [about 5000 square miles] in the Panhandle of Texas, patented by the state to a Chicago firm in exchange for the capitol at Austin. From 100 to 150 cowboys, with combined remudas of more than 1000 cow ponies, 'rode herd' upon approximately 150,000 cattle that wore the XIT brand. This story is concerned with the development of this pastoral enterprise and its relations to the history of Texas." The XIT brand, according to cowhand legend, stands for "Ten [counties] in Texas," relating to the number of counties encompassed by the ranch. Haley doubts this, believing the brand was devised simply as an expedient format that was difficult for rustlers to alter.

By 1900, the ranch had over 1500 miles of fencing, dividing it into 94 pastures. Afterwards, the ranch was gradually sold off in parcels. George W. Littlefield bought 225,858 acres to be resold in small tracts to farmers. This venture is recounted in David B. Gracy's excellent and highly readable *Littlefield Lands: Colonization on the Texas Plains, 1912-1920* (Austin: University of Texas Press, 1968, 161pp.). By 1950 only 20,000 acres remained, although the owners retained the extremely valuable mineral rights to much of the original property. The extensive manuscript records of the ranch are now in the archives of the Panhandle-Plains Historical Society.

Written for the owners of the ranch, Haley's book naturally presents their viewpoint. Shortly after publication, Haley and the owners were sued for libel by members of the Spikes family, about whom defamatory statements were made in the chapter entitled "A Long Fight for Law." The book was withdrawn from circulation and lawsuits ensued, until Haley was able to prove in court that his accusations were true. Eventually what Wayne Gard called "deaths and cooled tempers" made it possible for an expurgated edition, deleting about six pages of the outlaw section, to be published in 1953. About 1957, copies of the original edition began mysteriously to crop up in the market, although the first edition remains a rarity. The full story of the lawsuit is told in J. Evetts Haley and William Curry Holden, *The Flamboyant Judge James D. Hamlin* (Canyon: Palo Duro Press, 1972), pp. 235-256.

The volume is well-written, if a bit florid in places. Some of the writings of both Haley and Dobie from this early period wax sentimental about the range in a way that seems cloying nowadays. The 28-year-old Haley dedicates the book "to my cowhorses . . . that have faithfully shared my roughest trails, longest hours, and hardest ranges with unflagging love . . ." There are also a few errors that should have been caught during the various printings, but "desiccated" remains misspelled even in the latest printing. On the whole, however, the book will last because it contains such a vivid picture of every aspect of life on a big ranch, expertly told by Haley.

An old cowhand told Haley that his book viewed the XIT through the eyes of its owners, and that Lewis Nordyke's *Cattle Empire* (N.Y.: Morrow, 1949, 273pp.) viewed it through the eyes of the managers and foremen. This left the story from the viewpoint of the cowhand still to be told. This gap was amply filled in Cordia Sloan Duke and Joe B. Frantz, 6,000 *Miles of Fence: Life on the XIT Ranch of Texas* (Austin: University of Texas Press, 1961, 231pp.), which combines the recollections of some eighty XIT cowhands in order "to let the XIT cowboy tell the story of his workaday world as he saw it, stripped of the false heroics . . ."

Adams Herd 969. Adams Guns 894. Dobie, p.104. Graff 1718. Howes H39. Merrill *Aristocrat*. Rader 1731. Reese *Six Score* 54. Robinson 3.

83 Haley, James Evetts (1901-   )

FORT CONCHO AND THE TEXAS FRONTIER.

San Angelo: San Angelo Standard-Times, 1952.
[12],382,[2]pp. Illus. by H. D. Bugbee. Maps by Jose Cisneros. 24cm.
Cloth, dustjacket.
[Verso of title:] Designed and Produced by Carl Hertzog, El Paso, Texas. Copyright 1952 by Houston Harte.

ANNOUNCING . . . . THE FIRST
DEFINITIVE HISTORY OF WEST TEXAS

Fort Concho
and the
Texas Frontier

By J. EVETTS HALEY

Illustrations by H. D. BUGBEE

*Published November 7th
—85th Anniversary of the
Founding of Fort Concho*

Designed and Produced by CARL HERTZOG *at El Paso Texas*
Published by SAN ANGELO STANDARD-TIMES, *San Angelo Texas*

ORDER FROM

H. C. REVERCOMB — *Americana*

1830 Walker Avenue

Kansas City 2, Kansas

Other issues:

(A). "San Angelo Edition." Limited to 185 numbered, autographed copies, slipcased, with special bookmark laid in.

This is one of the best books about any of the vital string of federal forts established in West Texas to tame the frontier. According to Eugene C. Barker, "this book began as a history of San Angelo and the adjacent region drained by the Concho rivers. It grew, in writing, into a history of West Texas. It embodies Evetts Haley's unequaled knowledge of the country from the Rio Grande to the Canadian, from San Antonio to Austin to the border of New Mexico. . . . It is no less than a history of West Texas in its heroic age." J. Frank Dobie said that "not even Lawrence of Arabia knew the sun-blasted land that gave him fame more intimately than Evetts Haley knows the Staked Plains and the territory fringing them; nor did he put more geography into *The Seven Pillars of Wisdom* than Haley has put into *Fort Concho and the Texas Frontier.*"

H. Bailey Carroll wrote that "Evetts Haley with the co-operation of three other staunch West Texans—Houston Harte as promoter and publisher, Harold Bugbee as illustrator, and Carl Hertzog as designer and producer—has in *Fort Concho and the Texas Frontier* set a new standard of excellence in the writing and publication of local history. Originally projected as an early history of Tom Green County, the work grew to cover [much of West Texas]. . . . The subject matter is almost universally appealing and is in many ways typical of the opening of any frontier area except, perhaps, that in the Concho country it was even more so."

Haley says: "Fort Concho was not only the center of significant events; it was the geographic and strategic hinge upon which history swung. From this vital pivot swung the great campaigns that swept the Comanches off the southern plains, that blocked at last the renegade Apaches along the Mexican border, and that extended a generally protective shield across the heart of Texas . . . By the very magnitude of its stage and the vital movements of its time, it was destined to occupy a place in history."

The volume began as a twenty-year project of Houston Harte in gathering historical data regarding Tom Green County, which originally included much of West Texas and ultimately became thirteen separate counties. In 1945, Haley was hired to write the book, with Hertzog as overseer of the physical production. Al Lowman quotes a conversation between Haley and Hertzog during the publishing process, in which Hertzog got Haley to agree to hyphenate a number of two-word terms, using the dictionary as his authority: "Haley conceded most of these points. Until they got to 'six-shooter,' which Haley had written 'sixshooter.' 'It should be hyphenated,' Hertzog told the author. Haley looked in the dictionary, then at Hertzog. Finally he said: 'As a writer, I agree with you. But as a cowman, I refuse to do it. I want my sixshooter in one piece.'" Lowman said the finished product, "in my own estimation, is their greatest [joint] venture. . . . The finest talent of three notable West Texans is assembled in perfect register between its covers."

Unfortunately, Haley laced his text with homiletical conclusions that have no place in a volume of this sort. He says that the post library had "many standard works, but no modern liberal literature befouled the place." Regarding the separate post schools for blacks and whites, he writes: "Obviously, the jurisdiction of the authoritarian-minded Supreme Court did not reach the Conchos. . . . Nobody dreamed it was discriminating, and in their ignorance all were proud and happy." Also, Haley overlooked a number of interesting facts about Fort Concho, being unaware, apparently, that Col. Abner Doubleday of baseball fame was there in 1871 as president of the court martial of Lt. Charles Snow, charged with having "criminal intercourse with the wife" of a fellow officer. These shortcomings mar the otherwise fluid narrative and lessen the impact of an otherwise important and significant work.

Lowman 79. Robinson 23.

84 Hardin, John Wesley (1853-1895)

THE LIFE OF JOHN WESLEY HARDIN, FROM THE ORIGINAL MANUSCRIPT, AS WRITTEN BY HIMSELF.

Seguin: Published by Smith & Moore, 1896.
144pp. Illus. by R. J. Onderdonk. 19cm.
Printed wrappers.

Other issues:

(A). Same printing as above, with a full-page portrait of Hardin inserted. The small inset portrait on page [3], labeled "John Wesley Hardin," was found upon publication to be a picture of his brother instead.

(B). *Life of John Wesley Hardin, Written by Himself, and Published from Original Manuscript in 1896 by Smith & Moore.* Bandera: Republished with Additions by Frontier Times, 1925. 62pp. 28cm. Printed wrappers. Includes a new unsigned introduction by J. Marvin Hunter and four pages of articles from the Galveston *News,* 1877, about Hardin.

(C). *The Life of John Wesley Hardin, as Written by Himself.* Norman: University of Oklahoma Press, [1961]. xxi,[1],152,[1]pp. Illus. 19cm. Boards. New introduction by Robert G. McCubbin. The Western Frontier Library 16.

(D). Second printing of (C), 1966.

(E). Third printing of (C), 1972.

(F). Fourth printing of (C), 1977.

(G). Fifth printing of (C), 1980. Paperback.

This is the autobiography of one of the most ferocious of all Texas killers. Robert G. McCubbin says in his introduction to the latest edition that "Hardin has become somewhat of a legend in Texas. He ranks head and shoulders above other notorious desperadoes of that state, which certainly had no scarcity of the breed. . . . [His] book is an accurate and amazing account of one of the West's most notorious badmen and gunslingers." C. L. Sonnichsen wrote that "Hardin was an unusual type killer, a handsome, gentlemanly man who considered himself a pillar of society, always maintaining that he never killed anyone who did not need killing and that he always shot to save his own life. Many persons who knew him or his family regarded him as a man more sinned against than sinning. The fact that he had over thirty notches on his gun is evidence that no more dangerous gunman ever operated in Texas."

Son of a preacher-lawyer, Hardin grew up in Polk and Trinity counties and killed his first man at the age of fifteen. The man being a Negro soldier and the year being 1868, Hardin fled rather than stand trial. By the time he was seventeen, he had killed an additional half dozen men. In 1871 he went up the Chisholm Trail as a cowboy, killing six men enroute and another three in Kansas. He returned to Texas, married, and settled down in Gonzales County. He soon killed another four men, was put in jail, escaped, and became a participant in the Taylor-Sutton feud. In 1874 he killed a deputy sheriff in

Comanche, Texas. Fleeing into Alabama and Florida, he added at least six more victims to his list before being captured in Pensacola. Tried and convicted in 1878, he served in Rusk Prison until he was pardoned in 1894. While in prison he studied law, taught Sunday school, and made repeated attempts to escape.

In 1895 Hardin went to El Paso to act as attorney for a relative, Jim Miller, thought by many to have been the real murderer of Pat Garrett. On August 19, he was shot in the back of the head by Constable John Selman, himself a notorious character. A short time later, Selman was killed by George Scarborough, who was himself later killed.

The manuscript of Hardin's autobiography was found in his trunk. A lawsuit over the ownership of the trunk ensued. Hardin's son won control, and the book was published in 1896. Hardin's daughters objected, and the book was withdrawn from circulation a few days after publication and stored in a San Antonio warehouse. The warehouse burned and destroyed all of the edition except for 400 copies sold surreptitiously to a local bookseller. These were later sold off a few at a time. The edition has now become rare.

The Hardin text ends abruptly with the year 1889, and is supplemented by some newspaper accounts of his death. Some historians, including Burton Rascoe, have maintained that Hardin did not write the book. It seems quite clear now, however, that he did. His surviving letters indicate that he was capable of writing in the literate style of the book, and mention that he planned to write it. J. Marvin Hunter in 1951 wrote: "I met John Wesley Hardin at Mason, Texas, in the early part of the year 1895, when he came into the Mason *Herald* office to get an estimate of the cost of printing a small book, the story of his turbulent life. At this time Hardin was forty-two years old, about five feet ten inches in height, weighed about 160 pounds, and wore a heavy mustache." A clipping in the University of Texas library from the 1950's states that the original manuscript was then in the hands of "E. D. Spellman, prominent Texas ranchman," but no information as to its present whereabouts is known. There is an accurate biography of Hardin by Lewis Nordyke, *John Wesley Hardin, Texas Gunman* (New York: Morrow, 1957, 298pp.).

Adams Guns 919. Adams One-Fifty 66. Agatha, p.84. Graff 1780. Howes H188. Rader 1773.

85   Hartmann, L. and Millard, —.

LE TEXAS, OU NOTICE HISTORIQUE SUR LE CHAMP D'ASILE, COMPRENANT TOUT CE QUI S'EST PASSE DEPUIS LA FORMATION JUSQU'A LA DISSOLUTION DE CETTE COLONIE, LES CAUSES QUI L'ONT AMENEE, ET LA LISTE DE TOUS LES COLONS FRANCAIS, AVEC DES RENSEIGNE-MENS UTILES A LEURS FAMILLES, ET LE PLAN DU CAMP.

Paris: Chez Beguin, editeur, rue Jean-Pain-Mollet, no. 10; Bechet aine, libraire de la Renommee, quai des Augustins, n. 57; Delaunay, libraire, Galerie de Bois, Palais-Royal. Et a Gand, chez Houdin, Imprimeur-Librarie, de l'Université, Juin, 1819. [10],135pp. Folding plan as frontispiece. 22cm.
Plain wrappers. Some copies have statements attesting to the authenticity of the edition signed in ink by the publisher and/or authors on the verso of the half title.

Other issues:
(A). *The Story of Champ D'Asile as Told by Two of the Colonists.* Dallas: The Book Club of Texas, 1620-26 Main Street, [1937]. 180,[3]pp. 3 plates, in color. 25cm. Cloth. Slipcased. "Translated from the French by Donald Joseph and Edited with an Introduction by Fannie E. Ratchford." First edition in English of the Hartmann and Millard; also contains a translation of *L'Heroine du Texas* by "G.F." The colophon at the end reads: "Three hundred copies of this book have been printed for members of the Book Club of Texas by Rydal Press, Santa Fe, New Mexico . . ."
(B). Facsimile reproduction of (A). Austin: Steck-Vaughn Company, [1969]. xiv,180,[2]pp. Cloth. Slipcased. 24cm. Contains a new introduction by Wilson M. Hudson. Steck-Vaughn Life and Adventure Series.

This is the best contemporary account of the ill-fated colony of Napoleonic refugees in Texas. Of the four accounts by contemporaries, Thomas W. Streeter calls this one "an indispensable source and by far the best of the group." Besides giving an eyewitness account of one of the most fascinating events in Texas history, it includes much valuable information on Texas during a period that still remains historically clouded.

The text consists of two diaries, the first by Hartmann and the second by Millard. The Hartmann section includes a list of the colonists and the text of Gen. C. F. A. Lallemand's Proclamation from Galveston, beginning: "Brought together by a series of misfortunes which exiled us from our homes [in France] and scattered us abroad in various countries, we are resolved to seek an asylum. . . . We are attacking no one, and we have no hostile intentions [but if we are attacked] we have arms. . . ."

Lallemand, in founding Champ d'Asile near present-day Liberty, intended to start a massive French colony which might ultimately begin a movement to win the throne of Mexico for Joseph Bonaparte. The group of about 150 colonists landed at Galveston on January 14, 1818, and sailed up the Trinity River on March 20 to build their colony. Attempts were made to make peace with Jean Laffite, whose pirate band was then operating out of Galveston. When the Spanish governor of Texas sent a force against the colonists, they abandoned the settlement in late July and retreated to Galveston. They were saved from starvation by Laffite, who helped them get to New Orleans. Although attempts were made to renew the colony, the project languished.

The handsome Book Club of Texas translation has a number of shortcomings, such as the failure to recognize among the Indian tribes mentioned that Chactas are Choctaws, Panis are Pawnees, Dankhaves are Tonkawas, Koasati are Coushattas, etc. One section on women (on page 78 of the original) is left out entirely. Nacogdoches is spelled three different ways by the translator and Vasquez appears both correctly and as Waskes for the same family. The editors nowhere mention the date of the original publication. There are too many typographical errors for a work intended as fine printing. Moreover, as Lon Tinkle wrote, "the table of contents is printed on page 23, after the frontispiece, the title page, the preface, and the introduction, which may be a convention in 'fine editions' but is puzzling and awkward none the less, since the first impression is that it has been forgotten, and when it is at last found, that it might just as well have been forgotten." On the other hand, the Book Club translation was made from a copy of the book which had emendations in a contemporary hand, and these have been included.

Fifty Texas Rarities #6. Howes H270. Monaghan 792. Rader 1807. Raines, p.109. Sabin 30706. Streeter 1069.

86 Hastings, Frank Stewart (1860-1922)

A RANCHMAN'S RECOLLECTIONS: AN AUTOBIOGRAPHY IN WHICH UNFAMILIAR FACTS BEARING UPON THE ORIGIN OF THE CATTLE INDUSTRY IN THE SOUTHWEST AND OF THE AMERICAN PACKING BUSINESS ARE STATED, AND CHARACTERISTIC INCIDENTS RECORDED.

Chicago: Published by the Breeder's Gazette, 542 South Dearborn St., 1921.
Preface by Alvin H. Sanders.
xiii,[1],235pp. 14plates, including frontispiece by Frank Tenney Johnson. 20cm.
Pictorial cloth.
[Verso of title:] The Lakeside Press, R. R. Donnelly & Sons Company, Chicago.

More than a history of the SMS Ranches, this is one of the best books on the Texas cattle industry. Walter Prescott Webb said of it: "There are in the book many things of peculiar interest to Texas people. . . . There is hardly a cattleman or a man connected with the beef industry that Mr. Hastings did not know personally."

The book first appeared as a series of sketches in *The Breeder's Gazette* of Chicago during the summer and fall of 1920. Hastings, in his preface dated Stamford, June 1, 1921, credits Alvin H. Sanders and DeWitt C. Wing of that journal for helping edit the sketches into a book, while Sanders in a publisher's preface gives full credit to Hastings himself: "We thought we knew him well, but we now find that he has gifts not hitherto suspected. . . . We count ourselves fortunate in having the privilege of giving his work this permanent form."

Frank Hastings was a remarkable man. Born in Kansas, he studied at Notre Dame and at the University of Michigan. He went to work for Armour Packing Company in 1889 and became an expert on cattle and cattle breeding. He was hired as manager of the huge SMS Ranch in 1902. Mary Whatley Clarke, in *The Swenson Saga and the SMS Ranches* (Austin: Jenkins Publishing Co., 1976), wrote: "He was a dynamic, smallish man, a natural born leader with plenty of know-how where ranches and stock were concerned. A renaissance took place on the ranches under his leadership and is still felt today. . . . Hastings' friendly personality and 'down-to-earth' manner endeared him to the cowboys. The least educated cowboy on the ranches felt at ease and talked freely with him when the opportunity came along. Because of his receptiveness, Hastings became a storehouse for stories of early-day cowboys which he recounts in his book. . . . Frank Hastings died June 12, 1922. That was half a century ago but his name is still an affectionate by-word on the ranches.''

The volume contains a great deal on the SMS Ranches and their history, but also contains much on the packing industry, cattle breeding, famous cattlemen, and cattle drives. The stories told to Hastings by the cowboys themselves, however, are what make the book so valuable to those interested in the Texas cattle era. J. Frank Dobie said of one chapter: '' 'Old Granpa,' one of the best horse stories of America, entitles the book to enter any select list.'' One cowboy told him of stopping by the Spur Ranch late one night, about ten o'clock, and staying over. At three o'clock the next morning the ranch bell woke everyone up for an early breakfast. As the cowboy rode off he quipped, ''A man can sure stay all night quick at this ranch.''

Walter Webb reviewed the Hastings book in 1927; he too, was especially enamored of the cowboy tales: ''Mr. Hastings has placed us all in his debt by saving some of the ranch stories. As storytellers the western pioneers have never been surpassed. They had the knack of giving to a story an elemental dramatic force that ordinarily is exercised by those highly talented. Most of the stories are those told by Mage, one of the SMS men. . . . I think they are the best stories I have ever read, even if they were told by Mage, the cowboy on the SMS Ranch.'' One paragraph from a Mage story, for example, describes a storm: ''We hadn't much more'n got to the herd when the air freshened an' things was gettin' right. Then it got cold an' we could hear it comin'. Thunder and lightnin' seemed to spring out of the mesquites. The foreman passed the word: 'Hold 'em till they git wet,' an' we began to circle. The cattle was on their feet in a second, with the first cold air; but we got the mill started by the time the storm hit. I've seen lightnin', an' this little show tonight was a purty good imitation, but thet was lightnin' right. As far as thet's consarn', I've seen balls o' fire on the end of a steer's horn many a time, but there was a ball o' fire on the end of both horns of every one of them thousin' steers, an' the light in the balls of their eyes looked like two thousin' more. Talk about a monkey wrench fallin' from a windmill an' givin' you a sight o' the stars, or one of them Andy Jackson fireworks clubs puttin' off Roman candles at a Fort Worth parade! They're just sensations; this here show I'm tellin' you about was a real experience. We seen things.''

Adams Herd 1009. Campbell, p.83. Dobie, p.105. Dobie-Dykes 5. Graff 1814. Howes H287. Merrill *Aristocrat*. Rader 1819. Reese *Six Score* 56.

87 Hatcher, Mattie Austin

THE OPENING OF TEXAS TO FOREIGN SETTLEMENT, 1801-1821.

Austin: Published by the University of Texas, 1927.
University of Texas Bulletin No. 2714.
368pp. 2 folding charts. 5 maps (4 folding). 22cm.
Printed wrappers.

A seminal study of the beginning of foreign immigration into Spanish Texas, this monograph covers the period prior to the colony of Stephen F. Austin, during which a surprising amount of immigration and settlement in Texas occurred. Hatcher gives what is still one of the best explanations and analyses of the political and cultural activities of this period within Spain, Mexico, and Texas—activities that led slowly but inexorably to the opening of Texas to Anglo-American colonization. I doubt that it is possible for anyone to fully understand the Anglo-American takeover of Texas without reading this book.

Hatcher states that during the first twenty years of the 19th century "Texas—at first absolutely closed to foreigners—was considered the most vital point in the Spanish Dominions of America; that by 1820 all royalists who understood the situation had come to believe that colonization was that one thing needed to make the much coveted provinces safe against attack; and that by 1821 the liberals were prepared to welcome foreigners, even the Anglo-Saxons . . . if by this means Texas could be developed.''

On the other hand, she says that "historians have assigned but little importance to the story of the frontier province of Texas for the first quarter of the nineteenth century. In the main, they have neglected

its economic and diplomatic history and have confined their attention
to the military defenses undertaken by the Spaniards against certain
relatively unimportant 'filibusters' and against the possibility of aggression from the United States government—intent upon securing Texas
as a part of the Louisiana Purchase." As a result, she maintains, little
has been written of Spanish diplomatic efforts and the many activities
related to securing Texas from Indians, the French, and the overflow
from Louisiana. "Colonizing activities of the period," she states,
"were vastly more than the feeble reaction against foreign aggression
of the periods more familiar to the student of Texas history. In fact
the records show that, although the Spaniards were unable to induce
any considerable number of native immigrants to settle in the wilds of
Texas . . . there was a splendid effort towards developing the country
by the settlement of vassals from Louisiana and Mexico [and] that a
very creditable beginning was made. . . . The way was at last prepared
for its development by the North Americans."

88 Hayes, Charles Waldo (-1905)

GALVESTON: HISTORY OF THE ISLAND AND THE CITY.

Austin: Jenkins Garrett Press, 1974.
Preface by Larry J. Wygant. Publisher's Notes by Jenkins Garrett, Jr.
Design by Larry Smitherman.
Two volumes: [10],xiii,[1],548;[6],549-1044pp. Illus. 24cm.
Cloth, boxed.

This is one of the most comprehensive histories of any area of
Texas, written and set in type in the 1870's but never published. The
author had access to documents now lost, as well as to early settlers
and pioneers of Galveston Island. The work contains much primary
and secondary historical information on Texas unavailable elsewhere,
and reaches far beyond the Galveston region.

Larry Wygant, archivist of the Rosenberg Library in Galveston,
states that Hayes was born in Pennsylvania, served in an Illinois
company in the Civil War, was captured and imprisoned in Alabama,
and became a railroad man and journalist in Galveston during
Reconstruction. His book "represents five years of work by Mr.

Hayes. Upon its completion, in 1879, it was sent to Cincinnati and set in type, however the printing plant burned down destroying the plates. A single copy of the revised proofs had been sent to the publisher and this proof became the only existing copy of the most complete history ever written of Galveston. This proof copy passed through the hands of several dealers,'' and became part of the fabled Jenkins Garrett Collection, now in the Jenkins Garrett Library at the University of Texas at Arlington. Garrett and his son published the work as the initial volume of their Basic Texiana Series, making the text available to scholars for the first time.

The original title page read: *History of the Island and City of Galveston, from the Discovery of the Island in 1526, from the Founding of the City in 1837, Down to the Year 1879*, by Charles W. Hayes, Cincinnati, 1879. Jenkins Garrett, Jr., points out that editorial markings in pencil on the page proofs failed to reproduce in the printed edition, and that no text appeared on pages 174, 181, 182, 883-886, and 982. Garrett added an excellent index.

In 1957, Walter Prescott Webb wrote: "Texans have written much about the land, the Indians, the cowboys, the oil fields, but we have written practically nothing about the 750 mile salt water edge of Texas. We have ignored the Gulf, the Golden Crescent, and the strange life of those who live on the edge of the Texas sea. There is as yet no literature about it, and scarcely any history." Because of the development of shipping along the Texas coast, the Gulf of Mexico could without too much exaggeration be called the Gulf of Texas, but few sea traditions exist in Texan culture. With a sea coast longer than that of New England and most other maritime cultures, it is surprising that Texas should have produced so totally land-based traditions. Yet the Gulf has always been a vital part of the history and development of Texas, and the Hayes volume provides an excellent and comprehensive study of its early history.

The volume is divided into 25 chapters of chronological history, followed by a statistical section and 173 pages of biographies, including sketches of Gail Borden, X. B. DeBray, Ben C. Franklin, Levi Jones, N. D. Labadie, James Love, Francis R. Lubbock, Thomas F. McKinney, M. B. Menard, Sidney Sherman, and Samuel May Williams, almost all written with the aid of persons and materials now unavailable. Wygant points out that "Hayes consulted persons actually involved with the making of the city and he had access to newspapers, documents, and records which were destroyed long ago." The narrative itself encompasses the recollections of many early Texans, such as Amasa Turner, Robert J. Calder, and others, and includes much on Jean Lafitte, Samuel Bangs, the Texas Revolution, the Texas Navy, the invasions of 1842, and the Civil War.

An excellent modern treatment of the Galveston area in the 1850's is Earl Wesley Fornell, *The Galveston Era: the Texas Crescent on the Eve of Secession* (Austin: University of Texas Press, 1961, 355pp.). By far the best book on the devastating Galveston Storm of 1900 is John Edward Weems, *A Weekend in September* (New York: Henry Holt and Company, 1957, 180pp.).

89 Heartsill, William Williston (1839-1916)

FOURTEEN HUNDRED AND 91 DAYS IN THE CONFEDERATE ARMY: A JOURNAL KEPT . . . FOR FOUR YEARS, ONE MONTH, AND ONE DAY: OR, CAMP LIFE, DAY-BY-DAY OF THE W.P. LANE RANGERS, FROM APRIL 19TH, 1861, TO MAY 20TH, 1865.

[Marshall, Texas: 1874-76].
[8],264,[1]pp. 19 plates containing 61 pasted-down photographs. 20cm.
Cloth.

Other issues:
(A). Facsimile reprint. Jackson, Tenn.: McCowat-Mercer Press, 1954. xxiv,[8],264, [1],[267]-332pp. Illus. 23cm. Cloth. Edited by Bell I. Wiley. Best edition, with a superb introduction by Wiley, the extended manuscript journal by Heartsill of the Chickamauga Campaign, additional illustrations, index, and other valuable material.
(B). Jenkins, John H. *The Most Remarkable Texas Book: An Essay on W. W. Heartsill's Fourteen Hundred and 91 Days in the Confederate Army, with a Leaf from the Original Printing.* Austin: The Pemberton Press, 1980. [15]pp. Illus. 30cm. Half morocco. Limited to 64 numbered copies, each containing a leaf from the original printing, taken from a fragment of the first edition discovered in May, 1941, by Charles F. Heartman, who gave it to E. W. Winkler, from whose estate it was purchased by Franklin Gilliam and sold to Jenkins in 1975.
(C). Facsimile reprint of (A). [Little Rock, 1983].

W. W. Heartsill's *Fourteeen Hundred and 91 Days in the Confederate Army* is the rarest and most coveted book on the American Civil War. Only one hundred copies were printed, of which merely a handful have survived. Dr. Llerena Friend said of it: "This book deserves its description as 'probably the most unique book in the entire field of soldier narratives.' " Dr. Bell I. Wiley wrote: " 'Unique' is a much abused adjective, but it can be safely applied to the Confederate journal of William Williston Heartsill. The title is strikingly unique; so is the method by which the diary becomes a book. Heartsill printed the journal himself, one page at a time, on an 'Octavo Novelty Press,' a crude machine which cost about ten dollars. The press was kept at Heartsill's store, and the printing done at odd times when business was slack. Sometimes the completion of a single page required several days; and the printing of the whole book extended over the period December 9, 1874-July 1, 1876."

Moreover, Heartsill included in each copy sixty-one different original photographs. During the lengthy printing of the book, Heartsill encouraged his former comrades-in-arms to send him photographs of themselves. Sixty-one complied, and Heartsill—lacking any better method—had a hundred prints of each photograph made and pasted them down, four to a page, with the name of each man printed underneath his portrait.

The journal itself is historically important. Heartsill wrote it on the scene in small notebooks that he kept in his pocket. These were sent back from the front to Texas, one by one, as they filled up. This four-year record is one of the most vivid and intimate accounts of Civil War battle-life that has survived. Heartsill himself writes in the Preface: "You will find this journal 'chock full' of three things, First, doings of the W. P. Lane Rangers; second, bad orthography; and thirdly, a great deal of shocking grammar."

There are two surviving drafts of the manuscript in Heartsill's hand (one in the University of Texas Archives, and the other at Rice University) which show that he endeavored to correct his misspellings and grammatical defects. Nevertheless, the book retains the flavor and drama that could only come from an eyewitness report.

Heartsill was twenty-one when the war began. He was among the first to enlist, joining what became one of the most famous units of the war: Walter P. Lane's Texas Rangers. He signed up on April 19, 1861, in Capt. Sam J. Richardson's company. On May 23, this unit of mounted Rangers officially became Company F, 2nd Regiment, Texas Cavalry, under command of another famous Texan, Col. John S. "Rip" Ford.

The unit spent the first year of the war in Texas fighting Indians and protecting the western frontier at such places as Fort Clark, Fort Inge, and Camp Wood. Heartsill's account adds substantially to our very sketchy knowledge of Texas at this time, containing information on ranching activities, Indian and Mexican affairs, and natural history.

In 1862 the unit moved into Arkansas as a cavalry unit, operating out of Arkansas Post. Only a few weeks after Heartsill's arrival, the whole post was overwhelmed by a large Federal force and the Confederate troops captured. The captives were sent to Camp Butler, a prisoner-of-war camp near Springfield, Illinois.

In April, 1863, the captives were shipped by train to Baltimore, and by boat to City Point, Virginia, where they were released in exchange for Federal troops captured by the Confederacy. Heartsill and most of the unit were then assigned to General Braxton Bragg's army in Tennessee. Heartsill gives an unforgettable account of the bloody battle of Chickamauga, which occurred shortly thereafter.

The Texans found service under Bragg distasteful in the extreme, because they were split up among various units under officers they did not care for, and especially because they were dismounted— something no Texas Ranger could ever tolerate for long. So in November, 1863, most of the unit began, a few at a time, to simply disappear and move westward to rendezvous at Marshall, Texas.

Heartsill and three other Rangers walked 730 miles in 47 days. At the Mississippi, they broke up the flooring from a cabin, caulked it with cotton, cut oars with pocket knives, and created what they called the "Lady King" to journey down the river. They made it all the way back to rejoin and reorganize their unit of Texas Cavalry.

For a time the unit was placed in charge of the famous prison for captured Federal troops, Camp Ford, at Tyler, Texas. Then, in July of 1864, the unit joined General E. Kirby Smith in Louisiana, and spent the remainder of the war there and in Arkansas. The unit was disbanded on May 20, 1865. Heartsill had kept up his diaries during the entirety of this period, keeping track of all the members of the unit. He includes in his book an appendix comprising a complete unit roster, with biographical and service records of all 206 members.

After the war, Heartsill entered business in Marshall, Texas, selling groceries and saddles. He was active in local civic affairs until he moved to Waco, where he died in 1916. He began production of his famous book on December 9, 1874, little knowing what he was getting himself into.

Al Lowman, in *Printing Arts in Texas,* comments on how difficult Heartsill's project actually was: "It was printed page-at-a-time on an Octavo Novelty Press, and each time, the machinery was brought to a full stop for re-inking with a hand roller. The type had to be distributed after each press run in order to set the next page. The task consumed a year and a half. It is hardly surprising that Heartsill produced only one hundred copies. . . . No two are alike. Bindings are not uniform in color or size. Page margins vary greatly in width, and some of the books lack all the pictures."

Heartsill himself relates that "in cold weather the ink was too thick, in summer I would sometimes get too much on the roller, and thus I worked, and have succeeded in turning out a very poor work mechanically, and I might truthfully say, altogether." When he finished, he wrote: "Sacred history records one event that will never occur again—the flood—and as sure, a 'second edition' of this journal will never be printed by [me] on an 'Octavo Novelty Press.'"

Coulter 224, Harwell, *In Tall Cotton* #86. Howes H380. Nevins I, 102. Raines, p. III. Winkler-Friend 3778.

90 Helm, Mary (Sherwood) (1807-1886)

SCRAPS OF EARLY TEXAS HISTORY, BY MRS. MARY S. HELM, WHO, WITH HER FIRST HUSBAND, ELIAS R. WIGHTMAN, FOUNDED THE CITY OF MATAGORDA, IN 1828-9.

Austin: Printed for the Author at the Office of B. R. Warmer & Co., 1884.
[2],iv,198,[1]pp. 22cm.
Cloth.

Other issues:
(A). Reprint. Austin: W. M. Morrison Books, 1985. 123pp. New introduction by Richard Morrison and new index.
(B). Reprint. Austin: Eakin Press, 1987. xxxix,120pp. Cloth. New preface, annotations, and index by Lorrain Jeter.

This valuable book contains not only the personal recollections of Mrs. Helm in Texas, but also a lengthy description of Texas written in the 1820's by her first husband, Elias R. Wightman. One of Stephen F. Austin's Old Three Hundred, Wightman came to Texas in 1824 as a surveyor for the new colony. According to Mrs. Helm, he wrote the first description of the colony and "compiled the first map of Texas in 1828, from which all subsequent maps obtain their basis."

The volume begins with an extraordinary account of the Texas Revolution from a woman's viewpoint, including one of the best descriptions extant of the Runaway Scrape. Mrs. Helm had visited New York in 1835 and returned by sea via New Orleans in February, 1836, and made an exciting landing at Matagorda in the midst of the Revolution. During her subsequent retreat she was accompanied by the wife and children of James W. Fannin, of whom she writes: "Mrs. Col. Fannin and children were [with us]. I was pleased with her deportment, knowing that she was probably a widow. . . . I pitied more than blamed, also, some other ladies whom I had known years before and at whose homes I had received hospitality . . . but *now* I was ignored. . . . Multitudes upon multitudes continued to make their appearance, most of whom had left their homes, no doubt, before we had. Despair was on their faces. There were very few white men; negroes seemed to be the protectors of most of the families. . . . Children were born on the route. I saw one babe that had got separated from its mother in the crowd, by taking different routes, but they got together at this great rendezvous. . . . All sorts of false reports of dangers continued to come in, and no news of any kind from the army." Finally, learning of the Battle of San Jacinto, she recalls that "then we all turned shouting Methodists. Some danced; some laughed; some clapped their hands."

In the second section, in twelve chapters, Mrs. Helm relates her adventures in Texas between 1828 and 1835, including the initial colonization of the Matagorda Bay area. This section is distinctive in presenting pioneer life from the viewpoint of a woman. These memoirs are followed by a section on religion, "Scraps of Theology Found on the Texas Coast," which contains little of interest.

The remaining fifty-nine pages consist of Elias Wightman's very valuable description of Texas written while he was surveyor for Stephen F. Austin. He discusses the twelve colony contracts in Texas, the Fredonian rebellion, Indians, etc. Wightman's description of the physical characteristics of Texas is the best by far up to that time. He even mentions the silver mines in Texas, concluding that the cost of mining and extracting ore are so high that they would probably "run the impresario ashore before anything be realized."

Clark III-53. Graff 1847. Howes H399. Rader 1846.

91 Hogan, William Ransom (1908-1971)

THE TEXAS REPUBLIC: A SOCIAL AND ECONOMIC HISTORY.

Norman: University of Oklahoma Press, [1946].
[Verso of title:] Composed and Printed by the University of Oklahoma Press at Norman, Oklahoma, U.S.A. First Edition.
xiii, [1],338pp.
Cloth, dustjacket. 24 illus. 22cm.

Other issues:
(A). Same as above. [Verso of title:] Second Printing, October, 1947.
(B). Same as above. [Verso of title:] Third Printing, March, 1969. xiv,338pp. 20cm. This edition contains a new foreword,"Afterthoughts, 1946-1969," and deletes the original preface.
(C). Paperback edition. Austin and London: University of Texas Press, [1969]. xiv,338pp. 20cm.
(D). Same as (C). Second paperback printing, 1975.
(E). Same as (C). Third paperback printing, 1980.

This is the best social history of the Republic of Texas. It is a mature and penetrating analysis of the forces which blended together to give the Republic of Texas its peculiar national character and to create the image of Texan nature which persists to the present day. Hogan writes in a sophisticated and lively style, judiciously extracting from a vast mass of documentary and printed sources some of the most acute insights and enlightening anecdotes to be found in any volume ever written on Texas. Herbert Gambrell said it has "a vividness, a humor, and a sureness rare in historical writing and seldom encountered in sociological analyses." Frank Wardlaw wrote that it "remains and will, I believe, continue to remain, one of the finest books ever written about Texas."

A FRONTIER SOCIETY

... and a hardy tradition

THE

TEXAS

REPUBLIC

A SOCIAL AND ECONOMIC HISTORY

BY

WILLIAM RANSOM HOGAN

A UNIVERSITY OF OKLAHOMA PRESS BOOK

Illustrated. Published in November, 1946. $3.00

Books on early Texas generally place great emphasis on the cultural and racial clash of the Anglo-Americans with the Mexicans, detailing the struggle through the Battle of San Jacinto. Thereafter the story of Texas is usually presented either as a part of the westward movement, manifest destiny, the slavery question, the diplomacy of annexation, or as the preliminaries to the Mexican War. Few studies have been devoted to the internal workings of the Republic itself and the characteristics of the people who created it. Hogan's book more than adequately fills this void.

Many outsiders consider Texans a breed apart, supposedly possessing a character all their own, wild-eyed devil-may-care individualists, delightful in their robust self-confidence and appalling in their absurd exaggerations and naivete. Texans themselves seem to feel they have a special "national character." Illusory though it actually may be, this image is believed by so many people that a search for its roots is a worthwhile endeavor. Hogan offers his study of life during Texas' period of national independence as a partial answer to the question of whether the Texan's reputation has a genuine historical basis.

The most interesting part of the book is the chapter entitled "Rampant Individualism," in which Hogan describes the antics of such characters as Strap Buckner, Bigfoot Wallace, Branch T. Archer, the Whartons, and Presidents Burnet, Houston, and Lamar. Some incredible-but-true Texas-style duels and challenges are described, such as nearsighted William H. Jack's challenge to Ira Lewis of shotguns across a table, and fearless Strap Buckner's proposal of rifles at ten paces. Hogan, however, fails to mention the challenge once issued by Thomas J. Rusk of howitzers across the Rio Grande. He does record Gen. Zachary Taylor's unforgettable comment that Texans were neither cowards nor gentlemen.

The other eleven chapters of the book inspect such fields as transportation methods and problems, frontier architecture, food and clothing, drinking and temperance, land speculation, banks and banking, amusements, religious activities, education and schools, sickness and medicine, Texas' legal system and its peculiarities, gambling, and crime. Of great value are the 27-page small-font bibliography, the 373 footnotes, and the excellent index. Hogan draws his conclusions in a final summary chapter, which ends: "So there arose a Texan way of life that still exists, even in the face of all the mass promotion and standardization of machine civilization. Stamina, individualism, "go-ahead" initiative, pride in everything Texas—these were and still are, in varying degrees, among the ingredients of the Texas spirit. Bitter courage, wry or raucous laughter, and kindliness stood out amidst the drabness and coarseness of frontier life. An astonishing number of urbane and intelligent men found a satisfying freedom from compulsion. Indeed, the Republic of Texas worked a curious alchemy with its citizenry, educated and untutored alike. It took the sons and daughters of Tennessee, the Carolinas, Georgia, Mississippi, New York, France, and Germany and set its own ineffaceable stamp on their souls. The same process is still working in Texas today.''

The 1969 edition contains a new preface entitled "Afterthoughts, 1946-1969." Hogan comments: "I came to regret even using the phrase 'a Texan way of life,' but I did not have the slightest doubt that there was a Texas tradition and that many of its ingredients had been present since the days of the Republic of Texas. . . . All of these ingredients were present elsewhere in America, but here the mixture was neither Southern, Far Western, nor Middle Western—but Texan.'' In his new preface Hogan also quotes a classic example of a panning review—in this case grossly unfair—from the Wichita, Kansas, *Eagle:*

"William Ransom Hogan, B.A., M.A., Ph.D., has looked long and hard at 10 of the most fascinating years in American history and managed to kill all the romance, glamour and interest of the period. Bristling with footnotes as irritating as a peanut under a new upper denture, the style of the book is such that it will win sighs from scholars and indifference from laymen. Hogan has gone back to sources for his material. He has scanned old newspapers, letters, and court records. He has presented his findings with a dust-bowl dryness that belies the colorful figures of which he writes. It is painful to imagine the author, probably stooped over records yellow with age, as he pries into the life of the lusty young republic fathered by such men as Houston, Lamar, and Strap Buckner. It is doubtful that Hogan, the Scholar, could have lasted 20 minutes in such rugged company. Except for the value it will have for other Ph.D's this book is an enormous waste of time, both for Hogan and the reader.''

This is one of my favorite Texas books. No one can read Hogan without understanding Texas and Texans a little better. I agree wholeheartedly with Charles Ramsdell, Jr., who wrote: "Surely the book deserves a place alongside that short row of regional studies which are not only valuable contributions to our knowledge of the past but are essentially works of art."

Basler 4193. Campbell, p.172.

92 Hogg, James Stephen (1851-1906)

SPEECHES AND STATE PAPERS OF JAMES STEPHEN HOGG, EX-GOVERNOR OF TEXAS, WITH A SKETCH OF HIS LIFE.

Austin: The States Printing Company, 1905.
Edited by C. W. Raines.
453pp. Frontis. 23cm.
Cloth.

Other issues:
(A). *Addresses and State Papers of James Stephen Hogg, Centennial Edition* Austin: University of Texas Press, 1951. xi,[1],579pp. 17 illus. 24cm. Cloth, dustjacket. Edited and with a Biographical Sketch by Robert C. Cotner. Foreword by Eugene C. Barker. Best edition, enlarged and annotated.

These are the public papers of the most important Texan of his time. Eugene C. Barker said of him: "Probably only two other men have left their impression so deeply on the history of Texas as did James Stephen Hogg. Those two were Stephen F. Austin and Sam Houston; and perhaps only Houston affected popular feeling so strongly, both favorably and unfavorably." J. C. Clark said that the Cotner edition "has made available a timely book of such pertinent political significance and such obvious importance to students of the historical and political scene since the late nineteenth century and currently that it comes as a surprise that the public utterances of this militant Texan have been allowed so long to remain inaccessible."

One of the first acts of Hogg as governor was his appointment in 1891 of Cadwell Walton Raines as librarian of the Texas State Library. Raines organized the library and archives, wrote the first bibliography of Texas, was a founder of the Texas State Historical Association, edited Governor O. M. Robert's memoirs, indexed the laws of Texas, and edited Hogg's papers the year before the governor's death. The first sentence of Raines's preface to the Hogg papers reads: "It goes without saying that James Stephen Hogg is the most unique personality that ever figured in Texas politics."

Hogg presided over Texas during a period of American history which Andrew Carnegie said was ruled by "a philosophy of Grab and Hold." Of this period, J. L. Clark wrote: "The slush pools of corruption had overflowed into Texas through uncontrolled corporate greed, absentee-ownership of natural resources, 'foreign cattle barons,' and other exploiters of the people's inalienable rights. Railroad consolidations were in progress, accompanied by pools, rebates, long-and-short-haul rate differentials, watered stock, and wildcat companies. With passionate zeal . . . Hogg championed the cause of the people. From the selections in the book, two guiding principles in Hogg's career stand out clearly. He believed, with Grover Cleveland, that 'public office is a public trust,' and . . . second, to Hogg the Constitution was indeed the 'supreme law of the land.' "

Dr. Barker wrote that "nobody can read his public and private papers without being convinced of his profound honesty and sincerity. He did not hesitate [as a Democrat] to condemn a Democrat President who in his judgment misapprehended the ultimate welfare of the people or, more noteworthy, to praise a Republican President who met his standards. . . . One need not believe that he was always right, but only a convinced partisan can doubt his intellectual integrity."

The Raines edition contains no table of contents or index. It begins with a laudatory sketch of Hogg's life and jumps without fanfare into the chronological series of his addresses. In 1951, Robert C. Cotner issued a carefully revised edition of 53 speeches, messages, proclamations, debates, and interviews, followed by an appendix giving the basic state documents of Hogg's era: The Railroad Commission Law, the Alien Land Law, the Corporation Land Law, the Railroad and Stock Bond Law, and the County and Municipal Bond Law. Cotner's edition omits a few items and adds new material, thereby making both volumes necessary to the researcher, but Cotner's is in every way a superior edition, well annotated and indexed.

The editing of Hogg's papers was undertaken by Cotner concurrently with his writing of an extensive biography of Hogg. In this work, *James Stephen Hogg: A Biography* (Austin: University of Texas Press, 1959, 617pp.), Cotner not only makes full use of the official Hogg papers in the Texas State Archives but also draws on the wealth of private letters and papers of Hogg now preserved in the University of Texas Archives. Of this biography, Herbert Gambrell wrote: "Like its subject, the biography is sometimes heavy and slow-moving but never dull. . . . It is more than good biography. It is the best account of Texas politics from Reconstruction to the turn of the century."

93 Holley, Mary Austin (1784-1846)

TEXAS: OBSERVATIONS HISTORICAL, GEOGRAPHICAL AND DESCRIPTIVE, IN A SERIES OF LETTERS, WRITTEN DURING A VISIT TO AUSTIN'S COLONY, WITH A VIEW TO A PERMANENT SETTLEMENT IN THAT COUNTRY IN THE AUTUMN OF 1831.

Baltimore: Armstrong & Plaskitt, 1833.
[Verso of title:] Printed by J. W. Woods, 1, N. Calvert Street [No copyright notice.].
167pp. Folding map by W. Hooker. 19cm.
Cloth.

Other issues:
(A). Same, verso of title has pasted-in slip with copyright notice of Armstrong & Plaskitt, 1833.
(B). Same, verso of title has printed copyright notice.
(C). Hatcher, Mattie Austin. *Letters of an Early American Traveller: Mary Austin Holley, Her Life and Her Works,* 1784-1846. Dallas: Southwest Press, [1933]. xi,216pp. 24cm. Folding map. Gray cloth imprinted in black, dustjacket. Contains a complete reprint on pages [95]-210 of Holley's *Texas,* lacking only the dedication notice. Also contains over a hundred letters by Holley.
(D). Same as (C), but bound in brown cloth stamped in silver.
(E). Facsimile reprint of (B). New York: Arno Press, a New York Times Company, 1973. 22cm. Cloth. The Far Western Frontier Series, Ray A. Billington, Advisory Editor.

(F).   Facsimile reprint of (B). Salem, N.H.: Ayer Publishing Co., 1979. 22cm. Cloth.
(G).   New edition. Austin: The Overland Press, 1981. xii,[2],92,[3]pp. 34cm. Folding
       map. Foreword by Ron Tyler. Limited to 340 copies, 325 of which are
       numbered and signed by Tyler. Designed by Thomas Whitridge. The first 15
       copies are bound in full leather, slipcased, and numbered A through O. The
       foreword by Tyler is excellent.

The first book on Texas by an Anglo-American, this was written by
Stephen F. Austin's cousin with his personal assistance. Thomas W.
Streeter called it "the first book in English entirely on Texas" and
"one of my favorite books on life and travel in Texas." Rupert N.
Richardson said it is "the best descriptive book of Texas written by a
contemporary." Marilyn Sibley said that "Holley opened the great
era of travel literature in Texas," and Fannie Ratchford called it
"valuable to students and delightful to casual readers."

Mrs. Holley's book is actually more of a description of Austin's
Colony than of Texas as a whole, although she does describe briefly
the other sections. She admits this freely, stating that her 1831 visit to
Texas "was to Austin's Colony alone," and adds that she delayed
publication for a month in hopes of obtaining material on the other
colonies "promised by a gentleman every way qualified to prepare it.
A pressure of important business, alone, prevented him" from sending
her anything for her book. The volume itself consists of twelve chapters,
or letters, from Texas in 1831, and two appendices. The first appendix
answers "Questions relative to Texas [propounded] by the London
Geographical Society" regarding immigration, and the second is an
excellent group of documents relating to the disturbances against
Bradburn and Ugartechea in 1832.

She calls Texas "a tract of surpassing beauty, exceeding even our
best western lands in productiveness, with a climate perfectly salubrious, and of a temperature, at all times of the year, most delightful
. . . a *splendid* country—an enchanting spot." This statement alone,
following her promise of absolute objectivity, must have been a key
force in inducing subsequent immigration to Texas. Explaining that
the old Spanish regime had vehemently objected to Anglo-American
settlement, she quotes Nemesio Salcedo saying "that he would stop
the birds from flying over the boundary line between Texas and the
United States, if it were in his power." This former hostility being

removed, Texas was now ripe for settlement. She also mollifies the fears about the hostility of the Indian tribes: "The natives do not *kill and eat people* there, nor always insult and rob them." In fact, her only absolute complaint is that "it is the common practice with settlers here, to cut away every tree of a clearing . . . a very mistaken policy, as well as most wretched taste."

Stephen F. Austin and Mary Holley had something of a romance during her stay in Texas, and it is plain from their correspondence that marriage was considered. For reasons no one has been absolutely able to discover, they parted deep friends but unbetrothed. Nevertheless, Austin guided her in every aspect of the writing of her book, which she dedicated to him. His map of Texas, the best by far up to that time, was reprinted in a smaller format for use in the book with corrections given by Austin to Holley. Both appendices came from Austin, as well as most of the statistics in the text. Mrs. Holley's brothers Henry and John Austin and her brother-in-law, Orville Holley, all helped with publication details. The printing bill, according to Ron Tyler, "came to something over $300. Since Mrs. Holley estimated that she would make $400 to $500 after paying all the bills, and since the book retailed at $1 to $1.50, it can be estimated that fewer than 1000 copies were printed, perhaps as few as 400." Since there are three states of the book (one without copyright notice; one with pasted-down copyright; one with printed copyright), it is possible that another printing was done. This is unlikely, however, since the extensive Holley papers still extant mention only a single edition.

By the time the book was published and distributed, Stephen F. Austin was a prisoner in a dungeon in Mexico City, arrested by order of Santa Anna. In her 1836 book, Mrs. Holley adds this note (p.297): "While in prison in Mexico the little volume . . . written, they said, by his sister, was shown to General Austin (he had not before seen it) *translated for the President* [Santa Anna]—who obtained from it nearly all he knew of the country." Mrs. Holley compliments Santa Anna in the text, but makes remarks that undoubtedly reinforced Santa Anna's opposition to the Anglo-Americans. She says: "Their numbers are rapidly increasing, and there cannot be a doubt, that, in a few years, Texas will become one of the most thriving, if not the most populous, of the Mexican States." She urges separate statehood for Texas, which

Santa Anna opposed. She states that Texas' "civil and political condition is of course altogether prospective and uncertain" and worries what will happen "if it should hereafter become the victim of foreign domination, or the theatre of domestic oppression." Perhaps the statement most alarming to the Mexicans, coming as it does from Austin's cousin, is: "It is very possible, however, that an unwise course of administration, on the part of the general government [Santa Anna's], might provoke a separation. What might be the ultimate result of such a separation, I shall not attempt to conjecture."

Bradford 2348. Clark III-56. Dobie, p. 51. Graff 1935. Howes H593. Rader 1912. Raines, p.116. Sabin 32528. Streeter 1135.

94   Holley, Mary Austin (1784-1846)

TEXAS.

Lexington, Ky.: J. Clarke & Co., 1836.
[2],viii,410pp. Folding map by W. Hooker. 18cm.
Cloth.

Other issues:
(A). Facsimile reprint. Austin: The Steck Company, 1935. 21cm. Folding map. Cloth.
      Original Narratives of Texas History and Adventure Series. 2000 copies printed.

An entirely different book from Mrs. Holley's 1833 volume, this contains a great deal more information on Texas history, geography, and society. Bancroft praised it for its "very correct description of the physical features of Texas." The Louisville *Journal* shortly after publication wrote: "Mrs. Holley's pen has lost none of its sprightliness and grace. She is an agreeable writer, adorning every subject and adding an interest to the dryest details." Thomas W. Streeter felt, on the other hand, that the volume was merely a "conventional account [that] entirely lacks the charm of Mrs. Holley's earlier book."

When Stephen F. Austin returned from prison in 1835, he was a revolutionary. Convinced finally that Texas had no hope under Santa Anna, he became a leader in the revolutionary movement. In late 1835, he began a tour of the United States to urge support for the Texas cause. Mary Austin Holley had been working for some time on a new book about Texas. On November 8, 1835, John P. Austin wrote to Stephen F. Austin that Mary "has made arrangements for publishing in Lexington an other Texas—to be out in about six weeks, with a request that I send her 200 Copies of the Map. . . . She was not then aware of your troubles, which when she hears it may delay her book." Stephen F. Austin came to Lexington and stayed in her home, giving her advice on her manuscript.

Julius Clarke, her publisher, probably aided a great deal in an editorial capacity as well; the book shows more order in arrangement than any of her other writings, and in her preface, she thanks the "distinguished young gentlemen who assisted in compilation and arrangement." In order to get to press, she omitted sections on geology and botany she had hoped to include, as well as a revised map of Texas, using instead the map from the 1833 volume. On June 1, 1836, she wrote to Austin: "Am closing the last chapter—terrible struggle to get the book out. We have a grand close—with Houston's proclamation." Just before publication, news had come of the victory at San Jacinto, and she was able to include Sam Houston's official report and details of the battle—their first appearance in a book. The book appeared in early July, selling for $1.50 per copy and had sales probably better than double that of her 1833 book.

In spite of Streeter's belief that it is a conventional account, the 1836 volume is a much more important book, and had considerably more influence than her earlier work. In addition to the San Jacinto reports, it includes the first book printing of the Texas Declaration of Independence, of the Republic of Texas Constitution, of Travis' famous letter from the Alamo, of Austin's Louisville Address of 1836, and other key documents of the revolution. It includes the full text of the Mexican Constitution of 1824 and translations of the colonization laws, as well as chapters on money and banking, the mails, trade, natural history, society and manners, religion, and Indians. It includes the best physical description of Texas up to that time, and a clear and concise analysis of the colonization and land grant system and of Austin's colonization activities.

That she was able to achieve all of this for an early July publication date, along with the hundreds of hours she devoted to raising funds and support for the Texas cause, is little short of phenomenal. In her preface she confesses that the text is only "the best the circumstances

permit," and remarks how events have moved like "a flitting shadow
. . . treading on each other's heels with the swiftness of the phantas-
magoria." She notes how her earlier work had been plagiarized by
David B. Edward and other writers, and how she had made a further
trip to Texas to gain new materials. This, together with her extensive
correspondence with Austin and other prominent Texans, put her in
a unique position that made her feel it imperative that she issue her
new book at a time when accurate, up-to-date information was essential
to an understanding of the events taking place in Texas.

There is an excellent biography of Mrs. Holley: Rebecca Smith
Lee, *Mary Austin Holley, a Biography* (Austin: University of Texas Press,
1962, 447pp.). Mattie Austin Hatcher published Holley's correspondence in *Letters of an Early American Traveller: Mary Austin Holley, Her Life
and Her Works,* 1784-1846 (Dallas: Southwest Press, 1933, 216pp.). Her
diary of her later trips to Texas, edited by J. P. Bryan, Sr., was
published as *Mary Austin Holley: The Texas Diary* 1835-1838 (Austin:
Humanities Research Center, 1965). Her original manuscripts are
partly in private hands, partly in the University of Texas Archives.
My own copy of her 1836 book belonged to Moses Austin Bryan,
Stephen F. Austin's nephew and Mary Austin Holley's cousin, with
corrections and additions in his hand.

Graff 1935. Howes H593. Rader 1911. Raines, p.116. Sabin 32528. Streeter 1207.

95 Horgan, Paul (1903-)

GREAT RIVER: THE RIO GRANDE IN NORTH AMERICAN
HISTORY.

New York and Toronto: Rinehart & Company, Inc., 1954.
Two volumes: xviii,447; ix,[5],443-1020pp. 4 maps. 24cm.
Cloth, boxed.
The first issue is indicated by the presence of the publisher's monogram on the
verso of the title.

Other issues:

(A). Limited edition. Same collation, except for tipped-in leaf before half-title: "This limited edition of one thousand copies, of which nine hundred and fifty are for sale, has been especially illustrated and signed by the author." Also contains 16 added color plates.

꙳ (B). Later printing of first edition, without publisher's monogram on verso of title.

(C). Single volume edition. New York, Chicago, San Francisco: Holt, Rinehart and Winston, [1968].

This is the most thorough and most civilized account of the vast region draining into the river that forms 900 miles of Texas border. Oliver La Farge called it a "splendid account . . . a work that comes close to being monumental, and that leaves [Horgan] with definite standing as a historian. The writing is extraordinarily well sustained." The London *Times* called it "one of the most fascinating books in recent American historiography." Carl Carmen said it is "one of the major masterpieces in American historical writing. It deserves to stand with the works of Motley, Prescott, Bancroft." The Manchester *Guardian* deemed it "as eloquent as Macaulay," and Allan Nevins said that "this is assuredly one of the best pieces of regional history yet written in the United States. . . . It is, in the best sense of the word—literature."

A much more balanced view of its value as research history was given by James M. Day, who wrote: "It is his most ambitious endeavor in the field of history, and he worked on it for fourteen years. The product is not a monument of original research, but it is the finest example of the application of Horgan's literary craft to history . . . The reactions to this work have been extreme in either direction. On the one hand, it earned for Horgan the Bancroft Prize . . . and it received the Pulitzer Prize. On the other hand, it has been accused of 'lofty pretentiousness,' 'too much literary license,' weakness in bibliography, and errors of fact. The work has also been charged with carelessness of description and questionable statements of historical interpretation, but these may be mitigated to some extent by the observation that description is not properly a subject for criticism on historical grounds, and that historical interpretation is always open to question."

The work is arranged into four sections, chronologically, representing the four cultures that were imposed upon the river valley—Indian,

Spanish, Mexican, and American. Each section is subdivided into chapters representing a broad range of related subjects. There are a few footnotes at the end of each section—in all a total of 108 footnotes for a 1020-page narrative, or less than one annotation per ten pages of text. This, together with a rather cavalier attitude towards compiling the general bibliography, have annoyed historians and readers alike. Walter Prescott Webb said of Horgan's free-style disdain: "When the artist turns historian, he would do well to concede something to the customs of the house."

The result is that the work should be used with care. Horgan's goal is to interpret and he does so with considerable license—but since he is a genius of Southwestern creative literature, we are fortunate indeed to have his interpretation. He himself states: "Without, I hope, departing from the inflexible limits of respectful [sic] scholarship, I took every opportunity to stage a scene. . . . For I agree with Professor Nevins that the writing of history, in addition to being a technical craft, is also an art. Its proper aim is to produce, in literary form . . . a work of art. To realize this purpose may require the historian to invoke certain flexibilities of method." William Goetzmann said it "is highly imaginative and thus not always admissible as 'scientific' history." Horgan devoted fourteen years to the preparation of these two volumes, and anyone who reads them will forever view the Rio Grande region with enhanced vision. It is perhaps instructive, or perhaps only accidental, that this great work was reviewed throughout the English-speaking world, but was never reviewed in the two publications from which Horgan derived so much of his material: the *Southwest Review* and the *Southwestern Historical Quarterly*. Were they overlooked, or merely ignored, by the publisher when review copies were dispensed?

Horgan succeeds in penetrating as did no one before him into the substance of the various cultures that ruled, or contended to rule, the Rio Grande Valley. In addition to history, Horgan develops at great length such areas as "The Stuff of Life" in the Indian section and "Hacienda and Village" in the Spanish section. Areas such as folklore, language, arts, and crafts are presented with skill, and are obviously the result of vast research and study. The concluding chapter, "Utility and Vision," is an essay of exceptional brilliance.

Adams Herd 1065. Basler 4197. Kurtz, p.22.

96   Houston, Sam (1793-1863)

THE WRITINGS OF SAM HOUSTON, 1813-1863.

Austin: The University of Texas Press, 1938-1943.
Edited by Amelia Williams and Eugene C. Barker.
8 volumes. 23cm.
Cloth. 500 sets printed.

Other issues:
(A). Austin and New York: Pemberton Press, Jenkins Publishing Company, 1970. 8
     volumes. 24cm. Cloth.

This compilation is the basic source for the writings of the most famous Texan. It contains all the letters, addresses, messages, speeches, and other writings of Houston from all sources, public and private, available to the editors at the time. Herbert Gambrell wrote that "they cover a wide geographical sweep and touch more aspects of American and state political history than do the papers of [any] of Houston's great Texan contemporaries and in consequence will be of value to a greater company of students," and called the set "an indispensable reference tool for the study of Southwestern and United States history."

The set covers Houston's entire career: service in the U.S. Army and as Indian agent, as Congressman, as Governor of Tennessee, in the Texas Revolution, in the Texas Republic, as U.S. Senator, and as Governor of Texas. Even a cursory glance through his writings shows the breadth of this great American's activities and contributions to the era in which he lived. No research into any facet of Texas history between 1830 and 1860 would be complete without utilization of this work.

The work contains over 2,500 entries and about 10,000 footnotes. Barker, who wrote a preface for each volume, explains that Williams prepared the footnotes. "I have assisted Miss Williams," he said, "as an occasional consultant and have read critically the text and her editorial notes. My chief contribution has been made in the relatively

SAM HOUSTON

The University of Texas
Announces the Publication, Under the
Auspices of the Bureau of Research
in the Social Sciences, of

The Writings of Sam Houston

Volume I, 1813–1836

Edited by

AMELIA W. WILLIAMS
and
EUGENE C. BARKER

Cloth $3.25 Postpaid

Liberal discount to libraries and
advance paid subscriptions

unimportant matter of editorial technique.'' The annotations are an outstanding contribution to the usefulness of the work, and include hundreds of biographical sketches, many of which were inexplicably not included in the subsequent *Handbook of Texas.* For this reason, the set is useful in searching for information on early Texans not found in the *Handbook,* although there are a number of factual errors in the annotations. Unfortunately, the index at the end of the set is not by any means complete. Both annotations and index must be used with caution.

The papers appear chronologically, but since acquisition and editing of the papers was spread over a period of six years, many new Houston items were found as work progressed. These newly found materials were inserted at the beginning of each subsequent volume, rather than being saved for a single addenda section at the end. Moreover, no cumulative calendar was issued at the end. Consequently, the user cannot be sure of the chronology without checking each volume—an infuriating process. For example, volume I consists of letters from the period 1813-1836, but additional letters from this period appear in every other volume as well. Letters from 1832 appear in four different volumes.

Naturally, many new Sam Houston letters and documents have come to light since publication, and a supplement is badly needed. When the *Writings of Sam Houston* first appeared, William C. Binkley remarked that it was ''unfortunate that members of his family still withhold some of his personal papers from publication or examination.'' These were the papers of Andrew Jackson Houston, which have since been given to the Texas State Archives. They include several hundred important Sam Houston letters which have never been published. A large number of subsequently released Houston letters from the period 1835-1836 appear in Jenkins (ed.), *Papers of the Texas Revolution.* Still more appear in the excellent *Ever Thine Truly: Love Letters from Sam Houston to Anna Raguet* (Austin: Jenkins Garrett Press, 1975).

97 Houstoun, Matilda Charlotte (Jesse) Fraser (1815?-1892)

TEXAS AND THE GULF OF MEXICO; OR, YACHTING IN THE NEW WORLD.

London: John Murray, Albemarle Street, 1844.

[Versos of titles:] Printed by W. Nicol, 60, Pall Mall.

Two volumes: viii,314;viii,360pp. 10 plates. 20cm.

Cloth.

Some copies have 16pp. of adv. at end of vol. II; some have 4pp. of adv.

Other issues:

(A). Same title. Philadelphia: G. B. Zieber & Co., 1845. Verso of title: "C. Sherman, Printer." 288pp. One plate. 16cm. Printed wrappers. The Home & Travellers Library Semi-Monthly I. First American edition.

(B). Same as (A). Cloth, gilt.

(C). Facsimile reprint of (A). [Austin: Steck-Warlick Company, 1968]. [8],288pp. 15cm. Printed boards. Introduction by Dorman H. Winfrey. Acknowledgment by Jack C. Vaughn.

This sprightly account was written by a wealthy English lady who visited Texas in 1842 in her husband's private yacht. Her view of the Texans is surprisingly free of snobbery, although she viewed them with the same paternalism that the English of her day viewed all non-Englishmen. Moreover, she had that rare gift of intellect and character that enabled her to perceive the idiosyncrasies of the Texans without the bitterness and mockery of Dickens or Mrs. Trollope. Her narrative is so light and breezy that it is easy to shrug it off as superficial; in fact, she gives us some exceptional insights into Texas of the 1840's.

She was the daughter of Edward Jesse, a writer on natural history and friend of King William IV, and the wife of Captain William Houstoun of the 10th Hussars. Captain and Mrs. Houstoun sailed from England on their 200-ton yacht *Dolphin* in September, 1842, stopping at various islands and landing in New Orleans in early December. On December 18, 1842, they anchored at Galveston. For some reason, Mrs. Houstoun says all this happened in September-December, 1843, and Streeter, Clark, Sibley, and other writers follow her incorrect statement. Actually, William Bollaert saw them dock at Galveston and recorded the event in his diary on December 18, 1842, and several Texas newspapers of late 1842 have articles on Capt. Houstoun and his visit (see Houston *Telegraph,* Dec. 21, 1842, and Galveston *Civilian,* same date). From December, 1842, through March, 1843, they lived on board the *Dolphin* in Galveston Bay and made brief but frequent inland journeys.

After returning to England, Matilda Houstoun began writing her book on Texas, which had charmed her beyond any of the other places she had visited. William Falconer, released from captivity and returned to England, provided assistance. Part of the narrative appeared in the London *News*; when the book edition appeared, the London *Times* gave it a good review. In America, *Smith's Weekly* ran it serially in vol. I, nos. 7-9 (Feb. 12-26, 1845).

Ferdinand Roemer, in a conversation with Mrs. Houstoun on her second trip to Texas, says she told him her first trip "had afforded her a great deal more pleasure, since they had come over in their own private yacht, commanded by her husband. Such a trip across the ocean in a ship equipped with all necessities for comfort and luxury, carrying a complement of more than twenty men, six cannons for defense, and a physician, furnished an example to what extent and on what a grand scale the rich of England seek some of their pleasure."

Mrs. Houstoun's wealth did not prevent her from being an intelligent observer. She met Commodore Moore and speaks highly of the little Texas Navy, but when her own yacht was mistaken in New Orleans for a Texas privateer, she says frankly: "Truly, though I wish them every success, I hope I may never hear the voices of our six-pounders in their behalf." Of Galveston, she says: "The only bricks I saw in Galveston were those forming one solitary chimney. The houses are all raised a foot or two from the ground. . . . This is ingenious; it raises the house out of the road, and in the summer keeps out the snakes, to say nothing of the pigs. . . . The city contains about three hundred covered buildings, which a bold person would, or might, call houses."

Matilda Houstoun had much to say about social life of the Texans, sometimes with humor, sometimes seriously: "Were I asked what is the national religion of the Texan people, I should answer none." She called Texans "an impatient people; they drive to, and at their end, with greater velocity than any individuals I ever saw or heard of. Nothing stops them in their go-ahead career. To 'go-ahead' is essentially the motto of the Texan people; and let them once get well on their legs, and no other people are better calculated to do it faster." She predicted a future intra-coastal canal and railroads. She saw through the pro-England sham of the Houston-Jones group and foresaw annexation. She feared a possible Civil War over slavery. She writes:

"On some future day the flourishing city of Galveston may be swept away by the overwhelming incursions of the sea."

Clark III-182. Howes H693. Raines, p.120. Sabin 33202. Streeter 1506.

98   Hughes, Thomas (1822-1896) [ed.]

G.T.T. GONE TO TEXAS: LETTERS FROM OUR BOYS.

London: Macmillan and Co., 1884.
[On last page:] Oxford: Printed by E. Pickard Hall, M.A., and Horace Hart, Printers to the University.
xiii,[2],228pp. 19cm.
Cloth.

Other issues:
(A). Same as above. New York: Macmillan and Co., 1884. This edition was printed at Oxford, England, simultaneously with the version bearing the London imprint. It contains the same printers' notice on the last page.
(B). Variant of (A). No printer's imprint on last page.
(C). Variant. Verso of title: "Oxford: printed by Horace Hart . . ."

A valuable and entertaining account of three young English immigrants to Texas, this was edited by the author of *Tom Brown's School Days*. The book consists of letters written home between 1878 and 1883 from three of his sons and other family members, describing their ranching activities. Thomas Clark said it ia "a capital book and gives an excellent account of cattle- and sheep-ranching in Texas," and called it "one of the best accounts of Texas immigrants and ranch life."

In 1870, Thomas Hughes visited America for the first time, to see his friend James Russell Lowell and to invest in American lands. When he and his brother lost heavily, their teenage children were faced with making their own way in life. Eighteen-year-old William decided to G.T.T. He sailed to New York, from which he wrote the first letter in the book on September 15, 1878. Less than two weeks later, he had arrived by train in San Antonio. Known to the family as Willy, he hired out as sheep herder near San Antonio and began saving his money. He travelled as drover through Beeville, Roma, Rio Grande City, Laredo, and into Mexico, gaining experience and writing letters home, one being headed "Guinagato Ranche, 20 miles from anywhere, Texas."

He wrote: "I shall know pretty well about all south-western Texas by the time we finish this trip. All the cattle-men one comes across are the very essence of good-humour and open-handedness; the great failing with them is that they can't keep out of the bar-rooms, and this is the reason why one hears such an account of the dangers about here. If they went about their business in a sober way, and didn't get into rows in gambling-hells and bar-rooms, they wouldn't be always getting killed."

Willy induced his brothers Harry and Chico to join him, and his cousin Timothy in 1879 brought some Oxforshire rams and ewes to Texas via Galveston. After travelling by train to join Willy at San Antonio, Timothy wrote home: "Freight trains on these lines are about the slowest things in creation. I frequently used to jump off and cut cactus leaves for my [sheep while the train was moving] and catch her up again before she'd gone a hundred yards. In fact, I was cautioned about walking too fast in front in case I lost sight of her altogether."

The boys bought 800 acres near Boerne, surrounded by state-owned vacant sections, and began a ranch of their own; by 1883, they had a successful cattle, sheep, and horse ranch. In 1882 their sister Madge paid an extended visit, and wrote a narrative of her Texas trip. The last letter in the book is dated Boerne, November 12, 1883. Thomas Hughes had carefully saved all the letters with the idea of publishing them as a reliable guide to future immigrants. "Every year," he says, "it becomes more clear that the openings in England for young men in the upper and middle classes are quite insufficient." For those willing to work as hard and as cheerfully as the young Hughes boys, Texas offered a viable future.

Adams Herd 1091. Clark, *New South* 108. Rader 1974. Raines, p.121.

99   Hunter, John Marvin (1880-1957) [ed.]

THE TRAIL DRIVERS OF TEXAS: INTERESTING SKETCHES OF EARLY COWBOYS AND THEIR EXPERIENCES ON THE RANGE AND ON THE TRAIL DURING THE DAYS THAT TRIED MEN'S SOULS—TRUE NARRATIVES RELATED BY

REAL COWPUNCHERS AND MEN WHO FATHERED THE CAT-
TLE INDUSTRY IN TEXAS.

[San Antonio: Jackson Printing Co.], Published under the direction of George W.
Saunders, President of the Old Trail Drivers Association, [1920-1923].
Two volumes: 498,[1];[4],3-496,[1]pp. Illus. 23cm.
Cloth. 1500 copies printed.

Other issues:
(A). "Revised Volume I . . . Second Edition." [San Antonio: Globe Printing Co.,
1924]. [4],7-494,[1]pp. 23cm. Cloth. This edition has new stories on pages 272,
276, 470, 482, 485, and 487. Those on pages 470 and 487 appear in no other
edition. Also adds eight new photographs. 1800 copies printed.
(B). Variant of (A). Due to misprinting, the pagination beginning with page 425
runs 425, 430, 431, 428, 429, 426, 427, 432, 433, 438, 439, 436, 437, 434, 435,
440, and thence correctly.
(C). "Second Edition Revised (Two volumes in One)." Nashville, Tenn.: Cokesbury
Press, 1925. xvi,1044pp. Illus. 23cm. Dark blue cloth, dustjacket. This edition
has new stories on pages 289, 387, 454, 623, 721, 843, 949, 1009, and 1017.
(D). Special edition of (C). On page [1]: "Deluxe Edition, Limited to One Hundred
Copies . . ." Numbered and signed by J. Marvin Hunter and George W.
Saunders. 25cm. Gray and blue cloth. Printed on heavier stock.
(E). Facsimile reprint of the first edition of 1920-1923. New York: Argosy Antiquarian,
1963. Two volumes: xxviii,1070pp. Illus. 24cm. New introduction by Harry
Sinclair Drago. Cloth, slipcased. Limited to 750 copies.
(F). Reprint of (C). Austin: University of Texas Press, 1985. 1136pp. 247 illus. New
introduction by B. Byron Price. New index. Cloth.

This compilation is the essential starting point for any study of
Texas trail driving days. Walter Prescott Webb called it "Absolutely
the best source there is on the cattle trail," and Ramon Adams
deemed it "perhaps the most important single contribution to the
history of cattle driving on the western trails."

In 1915, George W. Saunders, J. R. Blocker, Luther A. Lawhon,
and Col. R. B. Pumphrey organized the Old Trail Drivers' Association. The first convention was held jointly with the Texas Cattle
Raisers Association meeting in Houston in 1916, with membership
available to all "who went up the Trail with cattle or horses during
the years from 1865 to 1896." The officers and board included George
West, Ike Pryor, George W. Littlefield, and Charles Schreiner. Luther
Lawhon reported that Saunders had written letters to all known trail
drivers "asking that the parties addressed would write their reminiscences, incidents and adventures of the Trail for the benefit of the

Assocation," and stated that from the 375 members a number of sketches had been received. By the 1917 meeting in San Antonio, the paid membership had grown to 488. One of those present was J. Marvin Hunter, who later wrote in his *Peregrinations of a Pioneer Printer* (Grand Prairie: Frontier Times, 1954):

"In 1917 I attended the meeting of the Old Time Trail Drivers Association in San Antonio. Some 700 or 800 of the old cowboys of the early days were in attendance at the meeting, and when the president, George W. Saunders, announced that it was planned to publish a 500-page book containing the experiences of the men who went up the trail to Kansas with herds of cattle, I was at once convinced that it would be a wonderful book. All of the members there were asked to write their own sketches, and several hundred in the audience held up their hands when asked if they would furnish their own sketches. When the convention adjourned for the day, I went to Mr. Saunders and asked to be given the work of compiling that book, but as he said it would probably be edited and compiled by Mr. Williams of Fort Worth, I did not press my request. I learned a short time afterward that the sketches had been turned in, and that a San Antonio printing concern had been given the contract to print the Trail Drivers' book, with Mr. Ford, who edited 'Cattle Clatter' in the *San Antonio Express* as the editor and compiler.

"In 1920, while I was working on the *San Antonio Light,* I received a phone call from Mr. Saunders, who informed me that the Trail Drivers' book had not been published, and he wanted me to do the work for the association. This was on April 21, 1920. I went out to the stockyards that afternoon to talk to Mr. Saunders and learn just what had to be done. He informed me that all of the sketches which had been turned in by the old cowboys had been given to the publishing concern which was to print the book, and the concern had failed in business and its owners had left the city and that all the sketches had been lost. Mr. Ford, who was to edit the work, had suffered a nervous break-down and eventually died. Many of the trail drivers had paid in five dollars each for a copy of the book, and he, Mr. Saunders, had promised to have the books ready for delivery for a meeting which was to be held in August, 1920. He said he had turned to me for help because he knew that I could get that book ready by then. I was amazed! To edit a 500-page volume, and get it printed in ninety days, was a tremendous undertaking. I asked him what material he had in hand to start the work, and he rummaged around through his office desk and brought forth some thirty-five sketches which had not been turned in to the defunct printing concern. I checked these sketches and found they would barely fill 100 pages in the book. Mr. Saunders said: 'That's all right. I will start a round-up, and have all those old boys to send in their experiences again, and if we don't get enough to fill up the 500 pages, you have a lot of Indian stories and frontier material which can be used, and we'll give 'em a book they'll be proud of. But it must be ready in ninety days.'. . .

"I was holding a steady situation in the *Light* composing room, and my day off was Wednesday. And as the next day was my day off duty I visited several print shops and secured estimates on the cost of printing and binding a 500-page book. The best bid I could get was from the Jackson Printing Co., which agreed to print 1500 copies for $2250. Mr. Saunders said this was all right . . . I backed my ears and tackled the compiling job—and it was some task, to say the least. By the time I had worked over the sketches Mr. Saunders furnished me with at the start, he had received other sketches. The Jackson Printing Company put on a night linotype operator, and worked a day and night shift on the book. When I would leave the *Light* office at 3:30 in the afternoon I would go by the Jackson Printing Company's shop, pick up a string of proofs and read them at home that night, besides getting out sufficient copy to keep the linotype operators busy the next day, and as I came down to work at 8 o'clock each morning I brought the copy for the printers with me. I managed to get in three or four hours' sleep each night. . . .

"Two years after I came to Bandera, and had installed a linotype in my print shop, Mr. Saunders insisted that I edit a second volume of *The Trail Drivers of Texas,* and print it in my little shop. I printed this second volume, but it was a piece of printing I was always ashamed of, and was glad when Mr. Saunders arranged with the Cokesbury Press in Tennessee, to bring out a big edition of the book. The two volumes were combined, and the book of 1,044 pages was nicely printed."

The success of the project was due to the ability of Saunders to talk the old trail drivers into actually writing their recollections and to the ability of Hunter to compile and edit them into publishable form. The second volume of the first edition was not only printed by Hunter himself, but was bound by hammering nails through the sheets and cutting the edges off with wire clippers. By the time it was printed, volume I was out of print and so a revised volume I was printed, containing a number of new contributions and illustrations. As soon as it was printed, more contributions were sent in. Therefore, the 1925 edition was issued to combine all the sketches into a single volume. Unfortunately, not all of the earlier contributions were included: consequently, in order to have all the material, it is necessary to have all three earlier editions as well as the 1925 edition. Moreover, Hunter apparently exercised an all-too-free editorial hand in some of the entries. J. Frank Dobie wrote that Hunter "told me he expanded some postcard relations into pages and reduced other pages to sentences and paragraphs." T. U. Taylor's *The Chisholm Trail* (San Antonio: Printed for Frontier Times by the Naylor Company, 1936) contains a proper-name index to the 1925 edition, but it is not complete. W. M. Von-Maszewski has recently compiled a more detailed index.

Adams Herd 1103. Adams Guns 1084. Dobie, p.108. Graff 2020. Howes H816. Merrill *Aristocrat*. Rader 1988. Reese *Six-Score* 61.

100   Hunter, Robert Hancock (1813-1902)

NARRATIVE OF ROBERT HANCOCK HUNTER, 1813-1902, FROM HIS ARRIVAL IN TEXAS, 1822, THROUGH THE BATTLE OF SAN JACINTO, 1836.

[Austin: Cook Printing Co., 1936].
Edited by Beulah Gayle Green.
[2],41pp. 23cm.
Printed wrappers.

Other issues:
(A). *The Narrative of Robert Hancock Hunter* . . . Austin: The Encino Press, 1966. vii,[1],27,[2]pp. 25cm. Pictorial cloth-backed boards. Limited to 640 numbered copies. Beautifully designed and edited by William D. Wittliff.

This is the most vivid of all recollections of the Texas Revolution. Carlos E. Castaneda called it "the best account of the San Jacinto

campaign left by a veteran . . . an indispensable source." J. Frank
Dobie called it "as human a document as ever I read . . . compacted
with earthy humor and graphic details. . . . Hunter has left some of
the most revealing and lifelike word pictures of the revolution to be
found in all Texas literature." William D. Wittliff said: "In my mind,
the *Narrative* . . . is one of the great classics of what J. Frank Dobie
called 'the stuff of literature.' . . . His *Narrative* is straightforward—
without embarrassment or embellishment—and it reveals vividly the
frontier mind and tongue. There is much of the understatement in
it—usually the mark of the authentic in the personal narrative of early
days. With the exception of J. E. McCauley's *A Stove-Up Cowboy's
Story,* I can think of no other personal narrative so delightful to read."

Hunter says he came to Texas in 1822, landing at the mouth of
"what is How cald Taylors Bayou . . . We had nothing to eat. Jack
kild an aligator, & rosted the tale, & we eat it." His father being one
of Stephen F. Austin's Old Three Hundred, he received title to land
in present Harris County and the family became the first settlers
there. In 1829 they moved to Fort Bend County, where Robert grew
to manhood. When the Texas Revolution broke out, Hunter says, "in
October 1835, I volenterd to go to San Antonio to fight General Coss.
We whipt him out, & I was dischard & came home." When Travis'
call for aid from the Alamo reached the Hunter place, Hunter and
some friends were "on top of the ginn house nailing on shingles.
Father said Well Boys who of you is going to Travis. I said, I am one,
& the balance all said I with you . . . We left next morning with 65
men for the Alamo."

They received news enroute that the Alamo had fallen, and the
Hunter group joined Houston's army on its retreat. Hunter then gives
an unforgettable account of San Jacinto, including the rallying cry:
"Take them with the but of your guns, club guns, & remember the
Alamo & remember Laberde, & club guns, right & left, & nock there
brains out. The Mexicans would fall down on there knees, & say me
no Alamo me no Laberde." After the battle, a widow on whose
property the battle was fought "came to camp to see General Houston.
She wanted to know if he was going to take them ded Mexicans
[away]. They hant me the longes day I live. Houston told her no, he
wanted Sant Anna to bury them, & he would not. Sant Anna said

that it was not a Battle, that he cald it a massacre. Plage on him. What did he call the Alamo & Laberde?''

Hunter wrote the account about 1860, from notes made in his diary. He was a long-time member of the Texas Veterans Association, and my copy has his original membership certificate tipped in, signed by Gen. Walter P. Lane; I also have Beulah Green's original manuscript for her edition. Hunter's narrative, with all its flavor, remains not only an important account of the revolution, but a delight to read because, in his words, ''it is most all persnell, of myself.''

101   Huson, Hobart (1893-   )

REFUGIO: A COMPREHENSIVE HISTORY OF REFUGIO COUNTY FROM ABORIGINAL TIMES TO 1953.

Woodsboro, Texas: The Rooke Foundation, Inc., 1953-1955.
[On copyright page:] Printed . . . by the Guardsman Publishing Co., Houston, Texas.
Two volumes: [6],xvi,[2],596,[19];[14],xiii,[3],633,[1]pp. Illus. 24cm.
Cloth.

Without doubt, this is the most comprehensive compilation on the history of any Texas county; it is included here because its scope reaches far beyond Refugio County. Ohland Morton stated that it ''is more than a county or local history, since its stage is a sector of the Texas coast extending from the Lavaca River to the Rio Grande.'' It was the result of fifteen years of research, the typing of the initial draft having been completed in 1944. Unable to obtain local financial support, Huson had to wait nearly a decade longer until the Rooke Foundation provided the necessary assistance.

Huson wrote to me regarding the publication of the work: ''A thousand copies of Vol. I were printed, but only 500 originally were bound as the history received little support in Refugio County. Only 560 copies of Vol. II were printed and bound, some two years later. General Rooke and myself at first decided to have the unbound Vol. I copies destroyed; but on reflection had them cheaply bound and distributed to the schools of Texas.''

The first volume covers the history of the era up to the beginning of the Civil War, and is especially meaty for information on local

Announcing Publication About January 1, 1944

of

"REFUGIO"

A Comprehensive History of Refugio County, Texas

By HOBART HUSON, LL. B., etc.

THE HISTORY will contain from 650 to 1000 pages of printed matter, and may have to be produced in two volumes. The basic territory includes the ten littoral leagues of the Texas coast between the Nueces and Coleto-Guadalupe, and the Islands of Matagorda, St. Joseph, Mustang, etc., during the times any portion thereof was a political integer of Refugio County. The period covered by the history extends from the aborigines to World War II, concluding with the Twenty-First Battalion, Texas Defense Guard.

The subject matter is rich in events, places, and personalities. Refugio County may be ranked as one of the five most historically interesting counties of Texas.

It was the locale of Karankawas, Lipans, Cabeza de Vaca, Early Explorers, José de Escandon's Labors, Pirates and Filibusters, Refugio Mission, Power and Hewetson's Irish Colony, Entry Port for many other colonies, the beginning of Texas War for Independence and many of its battlegrounds and concentration depots, Phillip Dimmitt's Garrison, Goliad Declaration of Independence, Johnson and Grant Expedition, Organization of Fannin's Regiment, the Bloody Nueces Border, Cowboys, Desperadoes, Soldiers of Fortune, Center of Intrigue in Federalist Wars of Northern Mexico, Mexican Invasions, Indian Fights and Depredations, the Landing of Taylor's Army, the Organization of Hobby's Eighth Texas Infantry, C. S. A., Battlegrounds of the Civil War, Hide and Tallow Factories, the "Brush Country," Cattle Industry, Old Trail Drivers, Bad Men, Gamblers and Vigilantes, Irish Horse Races and Tournaments, Oil and Gas Industry, Royal Irish Regiment and Twenty-First Battalion, Texas Defense Guard, the Old Towns of Refugio, Aransas City, Aransas, Lamar, Port Preston, St. Mary's, Saluria, Rockport, Fulton, etc.

THE HISTORY gives broad coverage to Fannin's and Dimmitt's commands, and is probably the most comprehensive history of those units so far written.

This territory was the home of such glamorous personalities as Martin de Leon, Colonel James Power, John White Bower, Captain Ira Westover, Walter Lambert, Thomas O'Connor, Captain James C. Allen, Victor Loupe, Captain Don Carlos de la Garza, Captain Ewen Cameron, Colonel Richard Roman, Colonel Henry L. Kinney, Colonel Samuel Plummer, Governor Henry Smith, Governor James W. Robinson, Daniel O'Driscoll, Captain John Reagan Baker, Captain Phillip Dimmitt, Colonel Neill Carnes, Captain James W. Byrne, Mrs. Sabina Brown, Captain James B. Wells, Nicholas Fagan, Mrs. Rebecca J. Fisher, Colonel Alfred M. Hobby, Judge E. E. Hobby, Willard Richardson (of Galveston News), Major John H. Wood, Judge Milford P. Norton, Judge Benjamin F. Neal, Colonel George W. Fulton, Captain Dan C. Doughty, Thomas Marshall Duke, Major Lieuen M. Rogers, the two Sea-Captains Johnson, Moses Simpson, Captain Henry Scott, Captain Edward Fennessy, Mrs. Clara Driscoll, and scores of other men and women of purpose. General Houston was Refugio's delegate to the Convention of March 1, 1836.

Distinguished personages galore, such as General Mirabeau B. Lamar, Samuel Colt, General Randolph B. Marcy, Henry Stuart Foote, Henderson Yoakum, John C. Duval, and Colonel Pryor Lea, had a part in our history, as well as such interesting characters as Ben and Bill Thompson, John Wesley Hardin, Sallie Scull, and others.

THIS is one local history which ought to be <u>interesting reading</u> to lovers of Texas history generally. It will be well indexed.

Price, per copy, $15.00

Carriage prepaid if cash accompanies orders. All advance payments will be deposited in a general trust fund in one of our county banks, pending publication. In this connection, enough local support has been given to practically assure publication, irrespective of subscriptions solicited by this prospectus.

HOBART HUSON, Refugio, Texas

PRINTED BY REFUGIO TIMELY REMARKS

Indian tribes, the Spanish period, the Power and Hewetson Irish colony, Fannin and Dimmitt in the Texas Revolution, Mexicans in the Republic of Texas, the invasions of 1842, and border settlement relations during early statehood. The second volume provides a comprehensive account of the Civil War along the lower Texas coast and in the western part of settled Texas, John S. Ford's campaigns, and county history through World War II. Thirteen appendices include Civil War and other rosters, oil statistics, and county data. The bibliography and index comprise 132 pages, and there are about 5000 footnotes.

Huson's work is not easy to read, and contains peculiarities of style and presentation, but it is unquestionably a fundamental resource for any study of Texas history in which men of Refugio had any part.

Adams Herd 1108. Adams Guns 1091.

102 Huson, Hobart (1893-)

CAPTAIN PHILLIP DIMMITT'S COMMANDANCY OF GOLIAD, 1835-1836: AN EPISODE OF THE MEXICAN FEDERALIST WAR IN TEXAS, USUALLY REFERRED TO AS THE TEXIAN REVOLUTION.

Austin: Von Boeckmann-Jones Co., 1974.
xxix,[1],299,[2]pp. Illus. Maps. 23cm.
Cloth.

This is this is the most comprehensive study of the Dimmitt command during the Texas Revolution. Bill Winsor called it "exhaustively researched, replete with documentation and footnotes, and prepared in a style that gracefully conveys the reader over the complexities of our histories. . . . The author's style and authoritative command of the English language, coupled with sound and unimpeachable research, warrant respect. As a research tool, this work provides an invaluable wealth of primary information." Dan Kilgore said of it: "Those seeking light reading must look elsewhere; this is a book of substance. It is bedrock history, exhaustively researched, with reprints of many documents and lengthy lists of names. Like the author's history of Refugio County, it is primarily a reference work, basic to an understanding of events in Texas in the fall and early winter of 1835."

In April, 1974, Huson wrote to me that his Dimmitt book "is probably off press by now. I expect it will meet with similar fate here in Refugio [as the county history], but should be absorbed within a year or so elsewhere. The edition is of 1000 copies, plus 300 which I am having run off for reviews and for those who have contributed to its production." In June, it was still not printed and he wrote to me: "It is being printed in Kingsport, Tenn. Its publication is sponsored by a friend with my freedom of choice of manufacturer. I nominated Von Boeckman-Jones as the publisher, not knowing that it had been taken over and gutted by a conglomerate. . . . I never was supplied with definitely paginated page proofs from which a proper index might be compiled. . . . Now as to your inquiry as regards the different spellings of the name Dimmitt: Casual research reveals that he himself subscribed his name as 'Demit,' 'Dimitt,' 'Demmit,' etc."

The volume thus has no index, and Huson was forced to postpone preparing one for use in a proposed—and as yet unissued—supplemental volume which would also include a comprehensive selection of maps and a large group of biographical sketches. The text as published is nevertheless a goldmine for scholars. In addition to the Dimmitt activities, it includes extensive sections on Mexican Federalist operations in Texas, the Lipantitlan Expedition, the Siege of Bexar, the Goliad declaration of independence and the Johnson and Grant Expedition. There are appendices that include a full roster of Dimmitt's command and important related documents. The volume suffers from a lack of proofreading and from certain eccentricities of presentation.

Dan Kilgore, upon the publication of this book in 1974, wrote a beautiful tribute to the unique and worthy author: "It is impossible to assess impartially the work of a man long known and admired. The author, a courtly gentleman and savant, writes from an extended life time devoted to law, philosophy, and history. Yet in a day when youth is king, one can only envy a man of his scholarly achievements, who at eighty can smile at the ladies and have them return the favor."

In my most recent letter from him, he said that he is hard at work on "several literary projects, including the definitive, exhaustive biography of Pythogoras—a trilogy—of which the first containing some 1700 typewritten pages in its 8th revision has been completed."

103 James, Marquis (1891-1955)

THE RAVEN: A BIOGRAPHY OF SAM HOUSTON.

Indianapolis: The Bobbs-Merrill Company, Publishers, [1929].
[14],3-489pp. Illus. 23cm.
Cloth, dustjacket.
[Verso of title:] First edition.

Other issues:

(A). Variant state. This state has the portrait "Sam Houston at Thirty-Three" as the frontispiece instead of the 1856 photograph by Frederick. In the "List of Illustrations" there is no mention of the 1856 photograph and it does not appear at all in this preliminary issue, of which I have been able to locate only two known copies.

(B1). Same as first edition, except without the words "First edition" on verso of title.

(B). Limited edition. Same collation except no "First edition" on copyright page. Tipped in leaf in front reading: "The Raven. Limited edition, Autographed by the author. This is copy Number ____." Signed by James. Issued after the book won the Pulitzer Prize.

(C). First English edition. London: Hutchinson & Co. (Publishers) Ltd., 34-36 Paternoster Row, E.C. 4, [1929]. Same collation; printed from the same plates as the first edition on slightly larger paper. 24cm. Cloth.

(D). James, Bessie Rowland, and Marquis James. *Six Feet Six: The Heroic Story of Sam Houston.* Indianapolis: The Bobbs-Merrill Company, [1931]. [12],11-251pp. Woodcuts by Lowell Balcom. 21cm. Cloth, dustjacket. First juvenile edition. Of this edition, J. Frank Dobie said: "I do not see how any healthy boy who takes it up can fail to be enthralled by the narrative."

(E). New York: Blue Ribbon Books, Inc., [1932]. Dated 1929 on copyright page but has notice on dustjacket: "This dollar edition is reprinted absolutely unabridged from the plates of the original edition, published over two years ago." 22cm. Blue cloth, dustjacket printed in red, white, and black.

(F). Same as (E), without reprint notice on dustjacket. Red cloth.

(G). Same as (F), "Texas Centennial Edition" on title page. Map endpapers added.

(H). Same as (F), dustjacket printed in red, black, and orange.

(I). Garden City, New York: Halcyon House, [1949]. 21cm. Cloth, dustjacket.

(J). Facsimile reprint of first edition, circa 1957. Contains a new two-page introduction by Henry Steele Commager. 24cm. Cloth, dustjacket.

(K). Paperback edition. New York: Paperback Library, Inc., [1962]. 384pp. No illus. 18cm. Verso of title: "Paperback Library Edition. First Printing: May, 1962."

(L). Dunwoody, Georgia: Norman S. Berg, Publisher, [1969]. Poor facsimile of the first edition.

(M). Indianapolis: The Bobbs-Merrill Company, Inc., [1975]. 23cm. New title page, otherwise a facsimile of the first edition. Cloth, dustjacket.

(N). Paperback edition. New York: Ballantine Books, [1975]. 384pp. No illus. 18cm. Verso of title: "First Printing: March, 1975."

(O). Same as (N). Verso of title: "Second Printing: February, 1977."

One of the great biographies in American historical literature, this remains one of the most readable Texas books. Winner of the Pulitzer Prize, it has stood the test of time. Sister Agatha said "James shows honest research, wide sympathy, and competent scholarship. The work is dramatic, but so was the life it paints." Peter Molyneaux wrote of the book in 1929: "No Texan can pretend to know what he should know about [Houston] until he has read it. . . It will always occupy a permanent place in the literature of the subject."

In an article in *Texas Monthly* (July, 1930), James tells about writing the book: "In June, I think it was, of 1925, I went to Dayton, Tennessee, to cover the monkey trial, or Scopes anti-evolution case, for the flip and saucy *New Yorker*. Down there I picked up a copy of Houston's virtual autobiography, *Sam Houston and His Republic*, which I had previously read. I used it now to put myself to sleep in the noisy little hotel. By some impulse still unexplained, when I returned home I dropped all my work . . . and informed my friends that I would come out of my shell a year from date with a red hot life of Sam Houston."

James wrote a biography, then read what he had written: "Sparkling sentences still emitted a glow of a sort. Pert paragraphs still stood up." The end result was nevertheless superficial, and he burned his first manuscript entirely. "I wrote bum chapters after that but didn't burn them. I put them by and eventually salvaged what seemed to be admissible. I began to see my man as you find in The Raven. *Began* to see him. What I first saw was that nobody really had got more than one or two quick looks at the real Houston."

This led James to get down to the business of actual research. He spent weeks in Washington in the Indian Bureau doing research in historically virgin archives. Somehow he managed to gain access to the extensive Sam Houston papers owned by Houston's children and grandchildren, which no historian except Lester and Yoakum had ever laid eyes upon—and which few have done since. He appears to have been the only man ever to be allowed to read William A. Philpott's collection of some two hundred Houston letters. Having known Temple

Houston as a child, James had heard the story of San Jacinto from the lips of Houston's son. He met other still-living people who had known Houston, and gathered verbal recollections. When his manuscript was completed, it was checked by E. W. Winkler, Harriet Smither, Mattie Austin Hatcher, and others.

The book is not without its faults. James fails to comprehend the significance of Anson Jones and the role he played in the annexation issue. He seems never to have understood the complexities of the Texas diplomacy with Europe and the interplay of the powerful forces and more powerful minds in Texas, England, and the United States in that battle. He overemphasizes the part played by Andrew Jackson. His understanding of Houston's dual role after annexation as Texan and American is weak. Along with all other Houston biographers, he overrates Houston's significance in the Texas Revolution.

On the other hand, James adds immeasurably to our understanding of Houston as Houston saw himself, without swallowing it but without letting it detract from his appreciation of Houston's genius. James emphasizes the significance of Houston's Cherokee years on his character and personality, and this emphasis is not misplaced. One reviewer said that James' "descriptions of environment reacting on character are not surpassed by Carl Sandburg's study of Lincoln's prairie years." James seems more than any other writer to have understood Houston's place in American history. He is the only biographer of Houston who has managed to catch the spirit of this romantic figure without succumbing to the temptation to romanticize the facts, for the bare facts are romantic enough.

As Henry Steele Commager states, Houston's life "is the stuff of which legend is made. . . In a sense he serves the history of Texas in the same way Charlemagne and Alfred and Barbarossa and Valdemar Sejr serve the histories of the nations they helped to make. In a sense Houston is too good to be true, this man who wrought such mighty deeds . . . in a sense if he had not existed we should have had to create him. And what better testimony is there to the romantic quality of our history than that our most legendary characters are authentic, and our most sober history wildly improbable . . . [Houston] never found a more faithful or more talented portraitist than Marquis James. When Mr. James paints the Raven, he paints not only the lineaments of this nation builder, but the lineaments of the young Republic: of romanticism, of democracy, of the frontier, of expansion, of nationalism. The Raven himself was an authentic expression of the American spirit; it is clear that this portrait of the Raven is an expression of that spirit in history and in literature.''

As Father Stanley said of James' book, ''Houston is brought out of Texas mythology into the light of common day, yet without loss of stature.'' Sam Houston, his granddaughter once said, was ''just another man, with the faults common to men and the strengths we wish were common to mankind.''

104   James, Will S. (1856-   )

27 YEARS A MAVRICK; OR, LIFE ON A TEXAS RANGE.

Chicago: Donahue & Henneberry, Publishers, Printers, and Binders, [1893]. Introduction by I. F. Mather.
[2],6,9-213pp. Illus., including two photos of the author. 19cm. Printed wrappers; also cloth.

Other issues:
(A). *Cow-Boy Life in Texas; or, 27 Years a Mavrick: A Realistic and True Recital of Wild Life on the Boundless Plains of Texas, Being the Actual Experiences of Twenty-Seven Years in the Exciting Life of a Genuine Cow-Boy among the Roughs and Toughs of Texas.*
    Chicago: Donohue, Henneberry & Co., Publishers, [1893]. [2],9-213pp. Illus. 20cm. Printed wrappers; also pictorial cloth. Some assert that this is the first printing, but I believe it to be the second.
(B). Same as (A). Chicago: M. A. Donohue & Co., [1893]. Actually printed in 1898. Printed wrappers; also cloth. Verso of page 213 is an advertisement for ''Flashlight Detective Series.'' The edition in wrappers has ''Cow Boy Life in Texas'' on the spine. No preface or introduction.
(C). Variant of (B). The edition in wrappers has ''No. 92 Cow-Boy Life in Texas'' on the spine.
(D). Variant of (B). Dated 1898 on title page.
(E). Variant of (B). Shows a copyright date of 1898.
(F). Variant of (B). Shows a copyright date of 1899.
(G). Facsimile reprint of the first edition. Austin: Steck-Vaughn Company, Publishers, [1968]. [8],[2],6,9-213pp. 20cm. Cloth, dustjacket. ''Publisher's Preface'' by R. H. Porter, and additional illustrations.

Written by a cowboy turned preacher, this is a valuable account of the life of the Texas cowhand. James was born on his father's ranch in Tarrant County near Fort Worth. "When I was one year old my father moved his cattle to a western country. This was in the fall of '57, only a short time before the last great outbreak of hostilities on the part of the Indians." He worked as a cowhand from childhood until 1885 when he was converted, after which, he says, "I went out among the cattlemen and worked as a missionary." Frank Dobie said James was "a genuine cowboy who became a genuine preacher and wrote a book of vitality. This is the best of several books of reminiscences by cowboy preachers."

James states that "everything I have yet seen in print concerning the class of men known as 'Cow Boys' has been of a character to, in a large measure, mislead the public. . . . I have tried to portray his character as I know him, leaving out much of the sensational. . . . Some of the stories here related are merely given as they came to me through others, but the greater part of them are actual occurrences coming under my personal observation, many of them personal experiences. In the recital I have withheld, or substituted names.

"The title '27 Years a Mavrick' has a special significance and refers to the age of the author when caught with the Gospel Lariette. Some one might ask, why the name Mavrick is not spelled like the name from which the term originated, which has an e, making, Maverick; the reason is that I prefer to spell it as designated in the title and if that is not sufficient, I am at a loss how to apologize . . ." For the same reason, apparently, he uses cayote and kernel.

The narrative is unusual because of James' deliberate avoidance of the sensational, which he so abhorred in pulp fiction. He gives straightforward descriptions of the cowboy and of ranch life. One of the most interesting chapters is entitled "Style on the Ranch," in which he traces with truth and humor the fashions among the cowboys: "He has his flights of fancy as clearly defined as the most fashionable French belle." In 1867 he wore homespun, boots with sharp thin spurs, and a homemade hat of rye straw. "Sometimes a fellow would get hold of a Mexican hat, and then he was sailing. . . . By 1872 most everything on the ranch had undergone a change," with the style being wool hat, leather leggings, high-heeled boots, and spurs with long shanks and bells. "In this age of the cowman, they wore buckskin gloves with long gauntlets. . . . The style changed again by '77," he says, and men wore the new "Stetson hat with a deeper crown and not so broad a rim, and the ten-ounce hat took the cake. . . . Cowmen in many places adopted the box-toed boot with sensible heels."

James also gives us many anecdotes of range life, such as: "I shall never forget the first wire fence I ever saw. I took a trip to Fannin County with my grandfather to buy some cow horses. While passing through Tarrant County we . . . saw a horse that had been cut across the knee, and we were told that the wire fence we had just passed was the cause. When I saw a barbed-wire machine at work . . . I went home and told the boys they might just as well put up their cutters and quit splitting rails. . . . I was as confident then as I am today that wire would win and just as confident when we landed the first train-load of cattle at Fort Worth, that between wire and railroads the cow-boy's days were numbered, as I am that he is now almost a thing of the past."

R. H. Porter, in the Steck reprint edition, examined dozens of copies of the variants of this book. He reports: "No edition examined had a page 7 or 8. In all editions the chapter numbers jump from Chapter XIII to Chapter XVI without a break in pagination. In all the reprints . . . the Introduction by I. F. Mather and the Preface by the author are omitted. Also omitted is the frontispiece photograph of the author as a cowboy and the photograph of him as a preacher." None of the editions had 50 illustrations as called for on the reprint title pages, and many of the illustrations used bear no relation to the text.

Adams Herd 1159. Agatha, p.60. Dobie, p.108. Graff 2194. Howes J51. Merrill *Aristocrat*. Raines, p.125.

105 Jenkins, John Holland (1822-1890)

RECOLLECTIONS OF EARLY TEXAS: THE MEMOIRS OF JOHN HOLLAND JENKINS.

Austin: University of Texas Press, [1958].
Edited by John Holmes Jenkins III.
Foreword by J. Frank Dobie.
xxvi,307pp. Illus. Maps. 22cm.
Cloth, dustjacket.

"Recollections of Early Texas"

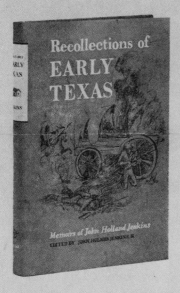

Other issues:

(A). Second printing, 1964.

(B). Third printing, 1973.

(C). Fourth printing, 1975.

(D). Dobie, J. Frank. *Prefaces*. Boston: Little, Brown, and Company, [1975]. Reprints Dobie's foreword.

(E). Fifth printing, 1987.

This is one of the better pioneer memoirs of early Texas. Lewis Nordyke said the author "wrote vividly of his experiences. . . . The story is a fascinating one—clear, frank, terse." Dan Ferguson called it "a great classic and an enduring and endearing piece of Texiana." Kay Farquhar said the memoirs "are bright with detail . . . recalled in a forthright and honest manner . . . a valuable contribution to our knowledge of early Texas." Ray Allen Billington called it "readable and interesting . . . edited with careful scholarship." *The New Yorker*, of all places, called the book "an artlessly effective work, a splendid job of editing a splendid piece of Americana." Lon Tinkle, on the other hand, called the book "of marginal value. . . . Little that is new is to be found here."

Jenkins wrote his memoirs in the 1870's and 1880's, contributing some to the Bastrop *Advertiser* and many to historians John Henry Brown and John W. Wilbarger, who used his material without giving credit. Jenkins came to Texas with his family in 1828, settling in the farthest western reaches of Austin's Little Colony. When he was eleven, his father was killed by Indians, and he became the head of the family until his mother's remarriage to a Methodist preacher just before the revolution. During this time, young Jenkins defended their home from the numerous Indian incursions, and even ate some bits of dead Comanche at a Tonkawa war party celebration. When his stepfather was killed in the Alamo, Jenkins, then thirteen, became the youngest man in Sam Houston's army during the San Jacinto campaign. Shortly before the San Jacinto battle, Houston detailed him to deliver a warning to the western settlements of the approach of Sesma's division. He therefore missed the battle but provides one of the best accounts of the Runaway Scrape. General Edward Burleson became his guardian. In subsequent years, Jenkins fought as a Texas Ranger, participated in the Battle of Plum Creek and the campaigns of 1842, fought in the last battle of the Civil War at Palmetto Ranch, and ended his career as a Ranger captain in 1874 in John B. Jones' Frontier Battalion. For a while on the last campaign, Dan W. Roberts was one of his lieutenants.

In 1890, Jenkins was killed in a gunfight in Bastrop in the act of saving the life of his son, who was sheriff, from an ambusher. His memoirs in manuscript and the surviving clippings of his articles were forgotten. When I was fourteen, in 1954, I found the memoirs and began to edit them into a connected narrative, worked on editing the manuscript for about a year, then added footnotes and a section of 75 biographies for an appendix. I kept the work a secret from my parents and friends, doing most of the work at my grandmother's house.

In the summer of 1955 I took the manuscript to J. Frank Dobie, who agreed to read it. A short time later, I received a telephone call from Frank Wardlaw at the University of Texas Press, saying they would like to publish it. At this point, I told my parents what I had been doing and they drove to Austin and signed a contract, by which the royalties were to be held for me in a scholarship fund until I came of age. I later learned that not only had Dobie recommended it, but Llerena Friend as well. I received the first copy of the book on the day I graduated from high school; the next year, I was surprised to have it assigned to me as a collateral text in a history course after I entered the University of Texas.

Those were heady years. Dobie wrote in the foreword: "My people never did believe that in voting for a Confederate veteran for public office solely because he was one-armed, one-eyed, half-witted, or possessed of some other defect calculated to influence the majority of voters. When I became acquainted with Johnny Jenkins, he was just past fifteen and was doing the research and editorial work that now add much to [the book]. I do not vote for Johnny Jenkins because he became an editor so young but because he has edited so ably. Many a Ph.D. thesis shows less scholarship and less intelligence than Johnny's editorial work and is not nearly so interesting. . . . Johnny Jenkins seems to consider it his duty to put down the truth whether it is complimentary or not."

Almost everything I have done since that time is an outgrowth of the inspiration I received as a teenager from Frank Dobie and Frank Wardlaw. A few days before I left high school, Dobie wrote to me:

"Without your having said so, I judge that you are going to be a historian. To me that means that you will cultivate lucidity and a way of making the past vivid as well as you'll cultivate knowledge. It also means that you will cultivate a liberated mind, free from prejudices and superstitions." Mostly, he said, I would have to read, read, read. This bibliography is one direct result of that advice.

106 Jenkins, John Holmes III (1940-) [ed.]

THE PAPERS OF THE TEXAS REVOLUTION, 1835-1836.

Austin, Presidial Press, Brig. Gen. Jay A. Matthews Publisher, 1973.
Publisher's Foreword by Jay A. Matthews.
Ten Volumes. 22cm.
Cloth.

The most extensive collection of primary resources relating to the Texas Revolution, this set is also the largest single compilation of original source materials on any Texas subject. Archie P. McDonald called it "the most important publication on Texas history of its kind in years." *Southwest Review* said "this outstanding work promises to become a landmark in Texas history." Allan C. Ashcraft said "it will stand as the major source for future research on the subject." Joe B. Frantz wrote that "these *Papers* will invariably be the starting place for studies of these two momentous years." Ben Procter called the work "a valuable contribution to the scholarship of the period" that will "facilitate and augment research and further study." The work won the Summerfield G. Roberts Award for the best Texas book of 1973.

The introduction states: "This work should be useful for the following reasons: (1) it prints several thousand important letters and documents on the Texas Revolution never published before in any form; (2) it prints hundreds of letters and documents that were printed during the revolutionary era, but which have hitherto been virtually lost for historical purposes because of the rarity of the original printing or the obsurity of its location; and (3) it includes all material within its scope from all sources including modern works, thus presenting for the first time the full primary source material on the Texas Revolution,

Announcing the publication of

PAPERS OF THE TEXAS REVOLUTION

1835-1836

John H. Jenkins, General Editor

For the first time, all of the known letters, papers, and documents of the Texas Revolution have been published in one work. Over four thousand individual items, most of which have never before been published, are collected here in ten large volumes totalling some five thousand pages. Included are the official documents and reports, as well as numerous private papers which have remained in private hands for over 175 years. The work includes hundreds of previously unpublished letters from the private papers of Sam Houston, Thomas J. Rusk, Thomas J. Green, and many others, as well as numerous unpublished letters of William B. Travis, James W. Fannin, Stephen F. Austin, Ben Milam, David Crockett, and James B. Bonham. There are also over a thousand Mexican documents detailing all phases of the Mexican campaigns, including previously unknown letters of Santa Anna, Filisola, Cos, Urrea, and Tornel.

Under the editorship of John H. Jenkins, each entry has been carefully annotated with historical references, notes, and citations to over three hundred different sources. Completely and thoroughly indexed to insure easy use by the general reader and the scholarly researcher, these papers represent the largest single compilation of original source materials ever published on Texas.

10 volumes. Annotation. Index.   115.00

PRESIDIAL PRESS
Gen. Jay A. Matthews, Publisher
Box 1763, Austin, Texas 78767

in chronological sequence. The plan of the work is to include all letters and documents relating to the Texas Revolution written between January 1, 1835, and the inauguration of Sam Houston as President of the Republic of Texas on October 22, 1836. All material known to the editor has been included, with the exception of letters and documents of a personal or business nature not related to the Revolution." The materials include all known writings from both Mexican and Texan sources, as well as correspondence from the United States and Europe relating to the revolt.

The collection consists of 4366 letters and documents from over 300 sources, each with a footnote citing the source and some with commentary or clarification. The last five items entered are complete facsimile reprints of Dr. Joseph E. Field, *Three Years in Texas, Including a View of the Texas Revolution* (Greenfield, Mass.: Justin Jones, 1836); William H. Wharton, *Texas, A Brief Account . . . Together with an Exposition of the Causes Which have Induced the Existing War with Mexico* (Nashville: S. Nye, 1836); *Journals of the Consultation Held at San Felipe de Austin, October* 16, 1835, (Houston, 1838); *The [Journals of the] General Convention at Washington, March* 1-17, 1836 (Houston, 1838); and *Ordinances and Decrees of the Consultation, Provisional Government of Texas and the Convention which Assembled at Washington March* 1, 1836 (Houston, 1838). In all, the set includes over three hundred primary documents each on the Siege of Bexar, Fannin Massacre, Alamo siege, and San Jacinto campaign, and over a hundred letters each from Sam Houston, Stephen F. Austin, David G. Burnet, Thomas J. Rusk, Santa Anna, Filisola, and others.

The project was initiated in the 1960's while Jay Matthews and I were serving in the intelligence branch of the Texas National Guard. We enlisted the assistance of an editorial advisory board consisting of Gen. Thomas S. Bishop, Charles Corkran, Robert Cotner, James M. Day, John Kinney, Malcolm D. McLean, Richard Santos, Robert Weddle, and Dorman H. Winfrey. The National Guard Association of Texas provided financial aid. Further assistance was provided by Harry Ransom, Hobart Huson, Hal Simpson, Edward Clark, Robert E. Davis, Chester Kielman, and Price Daniel, Sr.

The material included is either printed in full, in part, or summarized. The material printed in part is from instances where "the bulk of the letter was non-related or, more often because we were forced to quote from a secondary source'' when the original had not survived. The summaries are of letters known to have been written but not located or, as in the case of the Bexar Archives, known to exist but unavailable for publication: ''Most of the Bexar Archives were undergoing microfilming during our compilation period and we were forced to use card files and copies in many instances.'' The Bexar Archives microfilm project has now been completed, and sets are available from the University of Texas Archives.

The contents include letters from a number of previously unpublished collections, including the Thomas J. Rusk Papers from the University of Texas Archives and the Thomas J. Green Papers from the University of North Carolina Archives. ''By far the most significant group of papers published here,'' I state in the introduction, ''is the Andrew Jackson Houston Collection. During the six years of gathering materials for this work I had known of the existence of this collection, but had no idea what it contained. As we neared press time in early 1973, I was graciously granted permission by the family to examine and make use of these papers. It turned out that the collection consisted of the personal correspondence files of Sam Houston during almost his entire career, never before examined by any historians except W. C. Crane, Andrew J. Houston himself, and perhaps Henderson Yoakum. The nearly five hundred entries in our work that come from this collection, because of their particular significance and because of being hitherto virtually unknown, should be of immense interest to students of every facet of the Texas Revolution.''

As editor, I acknowledged the previous work done by William C. Binkley, compiler of *Official Correspondence of the Texan Revolution 1835-1836* (New York: D. Appleton-Century, 1936, 2 vols.) Binkley's work contains only about a fourth of the materials in the later compilation, but contains very valuable annotations by that learned scholar that are still quite useful. Many of the original documents have been dispersed or disappeared since the Binkley work, and in many cases the documents have been moved to different locations or collections. Both the University of Texas Archives and the Texas State Archives have rearranged some of their major collections since 1973, making it now difficult to locate some of the originals through the citations in either compilation.

I have continued to gather additional primary source materials for a supplemental volume. A reissue would also benefit from better proofreading and from the substitution of a more detailed subject index for the present inadequate proper name index.

107 Jennings, Napoleon Augustus (1856-1919)

A TEXAS RANGER.

New York: Charles Scribners Sons, 1899.
x,[2],321pp. 19cm.
Pictorial cloth.

Other editions:
(A). Dallas: Southwest Press, [1930]. xv,[1],287pp. 24cm. Cloth, dustjacket. Contains a 6-page foreword by J. Frank Dobie, dated Austin, Texas, San Jacinto Day, 1930. Best edition, although poorly proofread.
(B). Same as (A), but with "Revised Edition, Third Printing" on verso of title, and "Revised March 16, 1936," on p.viii at the conclusion of Dobie's Foreword.
(C). Austin: The Steck Company, 1959. Facsimile of the first edition. Pictorial cloth. Slipcased.
(D). Frontier Book Co., Ruidoso, New Mexico, 1960. Cloth.
(E). Same as (A), but with imprint: Dallas: Turner Company, [1965]. x,158pp. "Revised edition, third printing."
(F). Reissue of (B). Austin-Dallas: Graphic Ideas, Incorporated, publishers, [1972]. 196,[1]pp. Paperback. 22 illustrations by Charles Shaw have been added.

Written by a young reporter who served under L. H. McNelly, this is one of the most interesting accounts of the life of the Texas Rangers in the late 1870's. Stanley Babb called it "more interesting, as a panorama of life in Texas in the old days, than a dozen of the formal academic histories put together." J. Frank Dobie wrote that "if any time of the past was ever vivid and vital enough to live on through mere reporting—reporting without adornment or other adventitious trappings—it was the time when McNelly's rangers rode the bloody border of Texas. Hence it is exceedingly fortunate that a man who was to become a skilled reporter rode with them and later saw reason for putting down some of the things he had been a part of."

A TEXAS RANGER

BY N. A. JENNINGS

Eighteen-year-old Napoleon Augustus Jennings came to Texas in 1874 and joined a special force of Texas Rangers that was doing border patrol work. He served with it until 1878, when he returned East on account of the death of his father. He soon returned to the West, however, where he remained until 1884. Then he went to Philadelphia and began his work as a newspaper reporter. While serving as a newspaperman, he gave to the world the first personal account of the Texas Rangers in his little book A TEXAS RANGER, published in 1899 by Charles Scribner's Sons in New York.

Walter Prescott Webb, the historian, says in his book TEXAS RANGERS, "Jennings' book a TEXAS RANGER abounds in errors and misrepresentations."

J. Frank Dobie, the storyteller, says in his introduction to a second edition of A TEXAS RANGER in 1936, "Why the book has been allowed to run out of print is a puzzle; but why during recent years copies when available have brought twenty-five to thirty dollars is not hard to explain. I defy anyone to read it without being engaged by its brightness and ranger-swift directness. The swing of young men in the saddle runs through its pages."

Ramon F. Adams, the bibliographer, in his SIX GUNS AND SADDLE LEATHER says, "The first edition is exceedingly scarce and contains much material on Texas gunmen, such as John Wesley Hardin and King Fisher, and on the Taylor-Sutton feud and other border troubles."

We think you will like Jennings' account of his experiences with an early border patrol of Texas Rangers—whether you read it as a historian, as one who enjoys a good story, or as one who likes to read an early book about Texas Rangers and Texas badmen that is a bit hard to come by.

The illustrations in this facsimile edition have been added to the original by Elizabeth Rice (Mrs. Emmett Bauknight) of New Braunfels, Texas, who is well known for her book illustrations. She has given the book added appeal with her colorful and accurate original water color drawings. The cover is an offset facsimile of the original five-color stamped cover.

FACSIMILE 321 pp. $7.50

THE STECK COMPANY AUSTIN TEXAS

Jennings left school in New Hampshire in 1874 to visit Texas. He was eighteen, and states that "my mind was inflamed by the highly colored accounts of life in the Lone Star State. I read every word in the papers, and believed all I read." He joined Leander H. McNelly's Texas Ranger Company, serving from May 26, 1874 to February 1, 1877, and then returned to the East to become a well-known journalist. In 1899 he wrote and published his account of serving in Texas. It is from all evidence a truthful account except in one respect. Shortly after publication, Jennings wrote McNelly's widow: "In the book I made myself a member of the company a year before I actually joined. I did this to add interest to the recital and to avoid too much of a hear-say character. Told in the first person adventures hold the attention of the reader. . . ." Thus he was not present during McNelly's earliest adventures but, as Dobie states: "If his own eyes did not see every act he has described, we may yet be sure that the stuff of his book, which is only incidentally autobiography, came to him from eye witnesses."

Not everyone agreed about the veracity of the book. George Durham, author of *Taming the Nueces Strip*, wrote: "This Jennings was taken on at Laredo as a field clerk to do the writing. Later on he sure wrote. He sold stories on McNelly to a big magazine, and he put it in a book. The boy took it mostly out of his head, and it is pretty awful."

Jennings served at a time when South Texas was almost totally lawless. Some three thousand Mexican guerillas under Cortina and others raided on both sides of the Rio Grande almost at will, and hundreds of outlaws and riffraff from the United States sought refuge in the area as well. McNelly's small ranger company was given the task of bringing law and order to the region. L. H. McNelly and Lee Hall led the company on many exciting forays, and Jennings gives a lively account of their activities.

The Texas Rangers were nearly all young men, some still teenagers, and they loved their life in the saddle. Jennings tells of the famous Texas yell that made such an impression on outsiders: "Of a sudden they stopped and gave a series of wild, bloodcurdling yells. . . . The men on the great silent plains feel sometimes that they must let out their voices with all their power, just to break the monotony of a seemingly limitless prairie. . . . We had a fashion . . . of yelling like wild Indians at times, for nothing at all except to give vent to our exuberant spirits, born of the free, big life of the prairies."

McNelly sent his men into the heart of the lawless area. "We went there," Jennings states, "for two reasons: to have fun, and to carry out a set policy of terrorizing the Mexicans at every opportunity. Captain McNelly assumed that the more we were feared, the easier would be our work of subduing the Mexican raiders; so it was tacitly understood that we were to gain a reputation as fire-eating, quarrelsome daredevils as quickly as possible. . . . Perhaps everyone has more or less of the bully inherent in his make-up, for certain it is that we enjoyed this work hugely. 'Each Ranger was a little standing army in himself,' was the way Lieutenant Wright put it to me, speaking . . . of those experiences. The Mexicans were afraid of us, collectively and individually, and added to the fear was a bitter hatred."

Within a short period the Rangers arrested over eleven hundred men, and reputedly killed many more. Jennings gives interesting accounts of such noted badmen as King Fisher and John Wesley Hardin, but most of his account relates to the fights with Mexicans. The Rangers, he comments, "were nearly all remarkably fine shots, both with their carbines and six-shooters. . . . We also spent much time in practicing the gentle Texas art of 'drawing a gun' quickly from its holster. It isn't the best shot who comes out ahead always in an impromptu frontier duel; it is the man who gets his six-shooter out and in action first."

Naturally, Jennings did not think much of Mexican marksmanship, claiming that they "could shoot oftener in a given space of time without hitting anything than seem credible. They may have been able to do some fair shooting at a target, but when it came to fighting, their marksmanship was ludicrous. Their one idea seemed to be to pull the trigger as often as possible and trust to luck. I never saw one take aim in a fight."

Jennings had one fight with a fellow Ranger: "I had some words with Rector, and we both pulled our six-shooters and were about to fire, when Armstrong and one or two got between us and we were disarmed. . . . We decided to fight a duel at daylight." Somewhat miraculously, both men came down with measles during the night and by the time they had recovered "we made up our quarrel and shook hands. The reader may be curious to know why we were going to fight and what caused our quarrel. Strange as it may seem, I cannot remember . . . I only know that we had words about something at camp, but what the something was I do not remember. It is only another illustration of the reckless kind of fellows we were in those good old days of Ranger life. . . ."

The publication of the Dobie edition in 1930 precipitated a row between Dobie and W. P. Webb that nearly cost their friendship. Webb had been working for a decade on his book, *The Texas Rangers*, when Dobie's edition of *A Texas Ranger* appeared, Webb was stunned and angry. E. C. Barker stepped in, writing Webb that "I know nothing, not even time, can ever quite remove your feeling of injury [but feel sure] Dobie did not realize the implications and consequences." Webb, in addition being hurt by his friend having published a work without his knowing about it on the subject he had spent years researching, felt the Jennings book "was of doubtful authenticity" and said so in a review. "His adventures," wrote Webb, "as told by himself would make the exploits of Jack Hays and Ben McCulloch for the same length of time pale and insipid." He also said the book "abounds in errors and in misrepresentations." Webb and Dobie, of course, patched up their quarrel and became the closest of friends again.

Adams Burs 218. Adams Guns 1173. Adams One-Fifty 85. Campbell, p.78. *Fifty Texas Rarities* 50. Dobie, p.60. Graff 2208. Howes J100. Rader 2086.

108 Johnson, Adam Rankin (1834-1922)

THE PARTISAN RANGERS OF THE CONFEDERATE STATES ARMY.

Louisville, Ky.: Geo. G. Fetter Company, 1904.
xii,[2],476pp. 23cm. 65 full-page photographic illustrations.
Edited by William J. Davis. Cloth.

Other issues:
(A). Facsimile reprint. Hartford, Ky.: McDowell Publications, 1979. Cloth. Adds pages 477-516 and index.

This is one of the most interesting first-hand narratives of Texas Indian fighting, stagecoaching, and Confederate cavalry operations. Johnson fought Indians in Texas in the 1850's, was a driver for the Butterfield Overland Stage in Texas, and surveyed a vast amount of virgin territory in West Texas. In the Civil War his famed Texas Partisan Rangers cavalry unit fought under Nathan Bedford Forrest and John Hunt Morgan. Wounded and blinded, he was imprisoned in

Fort Warren. After the war, in spite of his blindness, he was so active in pioneering business ventures in West Texas that his home of Marble Falls became known as "the blind man's town."

In 1854, at the age of 20, Johnson moved to Burnet County, Texas, and for the next six years was active in Indian fighting, surveying, and overland mail operations. Four chapters of his memoirs are devoted to this period, and include material on Nacona, Cynthia Ann Parker, and Placido of the Tonkawas.

The bulk of the narrative, however, deals with Johnson's Civil War experiences, encompassing nineteen chapters of his memoirs. Johnson ultimately reached the rank of brigadier general and his Partisan Rangers operated for the most part independently, in Kentucky and Tennessee. Although the memoirs of this period are vivid and full of anecdotes, it must be remembered that they were dictated forty years later and contain numerous errors of detail.

The last three chapters contain a further record of Indian fighting in Texas after the war, as well as some of Johnson's business activities. Part II of the book, comprising virtually half the text, consists of very valuable first-hand narratives by members of the Partisan Rangers and other Texas-Confederate veterans. These include chapters on "Morgan and His Men" by Gen. Basil W. Duke, "Escape from Camp Morton" by F. A. Owen, "Prison Life at Camp Douglas" by T. B. Clore, and a tribute to Johnson by Gov. F. R. Lubbock. There are also rosters and biographies of members of the Partisan Rangers.

Thomas S. Miller in the last narrative of the volume, says of Johnson: "Paladin of old was not more daring and heroic than this Southern knight on the field of battle. . . . No man in the Southern army, no matter how high his rank, displayed more military skill. . . . He was literally the 'Swamp Fox' of Kentucky. [In spite of his blindness] perhaps no man has led a more cheerful and happy life."

Coulter 257. Graff 2213. Howes J122. Nevins I-113.

109 Johnson, Francis White (1799-1884)

A HISTORY OF TEXAS AND TEXANS, BY . . . A LEADER IN THE TEXAS REVOLUTION.

Chicago and New York: The American Historical Society, 1914.
Edited and Brought to Date by Eugene C. Barker . . . With the Assistance of Ernest William Winkler.
5 volumes. Illus. 27cm.
Cloth.

Other issues:
(A). Reprint of above, 1916, with some additional biographies.

This work combines the memoirs of an early Texas leader with the scholarship of two of Texas' ablest historians. In addition, it includes several hundred biographies of early and prominent Texans which are of value to the historian and genealogist. It is a work that was literally fifty years in the making.

Col. Frank W. Johnson came to Texas in 1826 to recover from malaria. He became one of the first surveyors in Texas, plotting much of the Ayish District in the late 1820's. In 1831 he became alcalde, or mayor, of San Felipe de Austin, and subsequently a leader in the movements that led to the Texas Revolution. He was a captain in the Anahuac disturbances of 1832 and a close associate of Travis and Bowie. He was Inspector General during the Texas Revolution and in actual command of the Siege of Bexar after the death of Milam. He commanded the Matamoros Expedition in 1836 and narrowly escaped capture and execution. For over thirty years thereafter he gathered materials for this history of Texas, and served seven consecutive terms as president of the Texas Veterans Association. He died while doing research for his book in Mexico in 1884.

Johnson's manuscripts were left to literary executors, chief among whom was Judge A. W. Terrell, who intermittently pursued the project of publication. "In August of 1912," writes Eugene C. Barker, "the American Historical Society of Chicago asked me to write for them a history of Texas. I was unable to undertake the task and suggested that they publish Johnson's manuscript with editorial additions which would bring it down to date and give the results of research since Johnson's time. They accepted the suggestion and Judge Terrell welcomed the opportunity to publish the book and consented to write a sketch of Johnson as an introduction. His sudden death two months later prevented his carrying out this intention."

Barker edited Johnson's manuscript into twenty-four chapters, to which he added documentary material and annotations. He then enlisted the assistance of E. W. Winkler, who wrote fourteen additional chapters on the history of Texas since annexation. This comprises the first volume (610pp.) of the work. The second volume (446pp.) is devoted to "an addendum of economic and local data covering all the county divisions of the state," and comprises the first serious attempt at a history of each Texas county. The remaining three volumes (1609pp.) are mug books, devoted to biographies of early pioneers and prominent Texans. Because they fell under the careful scrutiny of Barker and Winkler, these sketches are considerably more valuable and reliable than those of the ordinary biographical encyclopedia. They are also considerably more lengthy and detailed than those in the *Handbook of Texas* and elsewhere, and include many important Texans of the 19th and early 20th centuries. My own set of this work once belonged to Thomas W. Streeter, who wrote in 1928 inside the first volume: "Vols. 3,4,5 contain only biographical sketches and have been thrown away." Since my set contains the last three volumes, with a slightly different shade of binding, I deduce that Mr. Streeter relented in later years and found the need to re-complete his set.

An index to all five volumes is hidden away on pages xi-xliv of the first volume, which to my chagrin I discovered only after using the set in my researches for nearly ten years.

The most valuable portion of the work, without doubt, is that written by Colonel Johnson and containing his personal observations on events in Texas in the 1820's and 1830's. The user must be careful to determine whether Johnson or Barker is speaking. Some of Johnson's material is in first person and some in third, and occasionally one finds Barker speaking not only in the footnotes but in the main text as well. Both Johnson and Barker frequently inserted lengthy letters and documents, which are useful but which make the narrative tedious to follow. Most of Johnson's original manuscripts are now in the University of Texas Archives; however, I have owned several original historical manuscripts written by Johnson, some of considerable length, which have never been published.

Rader 2094.

110   Johnson, Sidney Smith (1840-   )

TEXANS WHO WORE THE GRAY.

[Tyler, Texas, 1907].
[16],5-407pp. Illus. 23cm.
Cloth, stamped "Volume One," although no other volumes were published.

This is one of the most useful biographical compilations relating to Texans who served in the Confederacy. Johnson's friend Ed W. Smith said of the work: "He has one characteristic in a pre-eminent degree, in these self-seeking times, and that is a disposition to rescue and save from oblivion the records which the worthy men and women of his section have made . . . and to give them enduring form in the literature of his county and state." Johnson himself states: "It has been said that the history of any country resolves itself into the biographies of its representative citizens. This modest volume then we hope will not only preserve biography . . . but will also record history that might not be preserved in any other way."

The discursive volume includes biographies of 384 participants in the Civil War, as well as 66 personal anecdotes of war service. Charles W. Ramsdell, Sr., said that it relates to "Texas soldiers, officers for the greater part, in the Civil War, interspersed here and there with anecdotes of the camp and field. While it leaves something to be desired in selection and proportion, the material is to the point and will prove of value to the student of Texas history. The book would be more serviceable if the matter were arranged in some regular order, either by suitable grouping or alphabetically, but this defect is remedied somewhat by a good index."

Johnson was born in Choctaw County, Mississippi, and moved to Texas with his family at the age of nine, settling finally in Tyler in 1854. He served as a Texas Ranger under John S. Ford on the Mexican border in the late 1850's. He joined Capt. D. Y. Gaines's company, Third Texas Cavalry, in 1861 and was elevated to the rank of captain within a year. He served under Gen. Ben McCulloch in the Western campaigns and then as captain of cavalry in Ross's Brigade, Jackson's Division, being wounded several times. He finished the war as a cavalry captain under Nathan Bedford Forrest. After the war he was an attorney and newspaper editor in Tyler. In 1900 he edited and published *Some Biographies of Old Settlers: Historical, Personal, and Reminiscent* about pioneers of the Tyler region.

Interspersed through the volume are personal remiscences of Texas-Confederate officers that provide interesting insights into the life and attitudes of the common soldier. Lt. I. E. Kellie, color-bearer of Whitefield's Legion, for example, writes about being lost in battle behind Federal lines: "I was slipping along through the thick woods, when I spied a Federal soldier, and, getting the drop on him, made him throw down his gun and pistol, dismount, and walk off. I got on his horse, and left him to find his way out—if he could. I went first one way and then another until I came to a field where I saw a command in line of battle. I soon found out they were Confederates and the Legion was among them. The boys were delighted to see the flag (they did not express any joy over me), as the Legion had never lost its flag, and they thought it was gone. . . . The horse I rode the balance of the war. Well, I have the old Legion's flag yet. When the war ended I took it off of the staff, wrapped it around my body under my clothes, and brought it safely home."

Howes J152. Nevins II-225.

111   Johnston, Joseph Eggleston (1807-1891), et al.

REPORTS OF THE SECRETARY OF WAR, WITH RECONNAISSANCES OF ROUTES FROM SAN ANTONIO TO EL PASO, BY BREVET LT. COL. J. E. JOHNSTON; LIEUTENANT W. F. SMITH; LIEUTENANT F. T. BRYAN; LIEUTENANT N. H. MICHLER; AND CAPTAIN S. G. FRENCH, OF Q'RMASTERS DEP'T; ALSO, THE REPORT OF CAPT. R. B. MARCY'S ROUTE FROM FORT SMITH TO SANTA FE; AND THE REPORT OF LIEUT. J. H. SIMPSON OF AN EXPEDITION INTO THE NAVAJO COUNTRY AND THE REPORT OF LIEUTENANT W. H. C. WHITING'S RECONNAISSANCES OF THE WESTERN FRONTIER OF TEXAS.

Washington: Printed at the Union Office, 1850.
31st Congress, 1st Session, Senate Executive Document 64. Serial 562. [On first page:] July 24, 1850. Ordered to be printed and that 3,000 additional copies be printed, 300 of which are for the Topographical Bureau.

250pp. Two folding maps. 72 plates (Nos. 2, 21, 39 not published; No. 49 in duplicate). 23cm. Plates 65, 66, and 67 were printed by Ackerman & Co., N.Y.; the balance of the plates and the maps were printed by P. S. Duval, Philadelphia. In a few copies, plates 1, 3, and 4 are listed as engraved by E. Weber; in others, by Duval. Some of the plates are in color; all of them relate to the Simpson report. Full calf. Also cloth.

This is a valuable compendium of reports of government explorations that led to the opening of West Texas to travel and settlement. William Goetzmann stated that, by these explorations, Johnston had been able "to survey what was to be the most important supply route for the outer chain of defense posts, and he had also been able to gain some idea of the suitability of the terrain for a [southern transcontinental] railroad. . . . [The surveys] provided official confirmation of a route across West Texas. These routes remained for years the main lines of communication for soldier, settler, and gold seeker alike. When the railroads were built through Texas, the Texas Pacific followed generally along Bryan's trail and the Southern Pacific followed part way along the lower road."

The reconnaissances were instigated by Col. J. J. Abert of the United States Corps of Topographical Engineers, and were under the direction of Col. Joseph E. Johnston, who commanded the Topographical Engineers stationed in Texas, with headquarters at San Antonio. The volume includes a statement from Capt. S. G. French, written from San Antonio at the end of 1849, which summarized the value of these explorations: "The valley of the Rio Grande, in proper hands, is capable of supporting a large population . . . on the American side. El Paso, from its geographical position, presents itself as a resting-place on one of the great overland routes between the seaports of the Atlantic on one side and those of the Pacific on the other. . . . Should the route from El Paso to the seaboard on the West present no more difficulties than that from [San Antonio], there can easily be established between the Atlantic States and those that have so suddenly sprung into existense in the West—and which are destined to change, perhaps, the political institutions and commercial relations of half the world—a connexion that will strengthen the bonds of union by free and constant intercourse. The government has been a pioneer in the enterprise, and the little labor bestowed may not be lost to the public weal."

This same Captain French reported on arriving at El Paso that "the grape is extensively cultivated on the irrigable lands. . . . Some of the old wine is *said* to possess a fine flavor." The italics are his; after all, it was an official government report.

The volume, which has neither a table of contents nor an index, consists of the following: Lt. William F. Smith's reconnaissance from San Antonio to El Paso, February-May, 1849, pp.4-7; Lt. Nathaniel H. Michler's expedition from Corpus Christi to the Leona, 1849 (reporting numerous wild cattle), pp.7-13; a report from Las Crucitas on the Rio Grande of Lt. Smith's reconnaissance in September, 1849, of the Sacramento mountains, pp.13-14; Lt. Francis T. Bryan's journal of his expedition from San Antonio to El Paso via Fredericksburg, June-July, 1849, pp.14-26; a report from Col. Joseph E. Johnston describing the area between San Antonio and El Paso, dated Dec. 28, 1849, and analyzing the effectiveness of the Colt revolver, pp.26-29; Lt. Micheler's journal of his exploration from the south branch of the Red River to the Pecos River, November 9, 1849-January 24, 1850 (covering 1300 miles), pp.29-39; J. E. Johnston's report on the navigability of the Colorado River, April 16, 1850, pp.39-40; Capt. S. G. French's report of the journey of a government wagon train from San Antonio to El Paso in 1849, pp.49-54; James H. Simpson's report on his Navajo country expedition of 1849, pp.[56]-168; Capt. Randolph B. Marcy's expedition from Fort Smith, Arkansas, to Santa Fe across the Llano Estacado and back, April-November, 1849, pp.169-233; and Lt. W. H. C. Whiting's "Reconnaissance of the Western Frontier of Texas," 1849-1850, pp.[235]-250.

The Michler report of 1849-1850 is also printed as *Routes from the Western Boundary of Arkansas to Santa Fe and the Valley of the Rio Grande* (Wash., 31st Con., 1st Sess., House Doc. 67, 1850, Serial 577). Simpson's report of the Navajo Country was reprinted privately as *Journal of a Military Reconnaissance from Santa Fe, New Mexico, to the Navajo Country* (Phila., 1852). Most of the original journals and correspondence for the expeditions are in National Archives in Washington. Simpson's papers are at the Huntington Library.

Many of the routes taken by these military explorers are traced in great detail by J. W. Williams in *Old Texas Trails* (Burnet: Eakin Press, 1979). This book, although poorly written, contains a wealth of information on trails, roadways, and routes of early travellers in Texas between 1716 and 1886.

Bradford 2724. Field 1289. Graff 2228. Howes J170. Leclerc 995. Raines, p.128. Sabin 36377. Wagner-Camp 184.

112 Johnston, William Preston (1831-1899)

THE LIFE OF GEN. ALBERT SIDNEY JOHNSTON, EMBRACING HIS SERVICES IN THE ARMIES OF THE UNITED STATES, THE REPUBLIC OF TEXAS, AND THE CONFEDERATE STATES.

New York: D. Appleton & Company, 549 and 551 Broadway, 1878.
xviii,755pp., plus 4pp. adv. 9 plates. Maps in text. 24cm.
Cloth. Also offered in sheep and half turkey.

Other issues:
(A). Same, dated 1879 at bottom of title page.
(B). Same, dated 1880 at bottom of title page.

 This is an important book on early Texas as well as on Albert Sidney Johnston. Douglas Southall Freeman said of it: "Better perhaps than any Confederate biography of so early a date, it retains historical authenticity." Gen. Joseph Hooker said it was "the best book, by all odds, published by either side." There is an excellent modern biography of Johnston by Charles P. Roland, *Albert Sidney Johnston, Soldier of Three Republics* (Austin: University of Texas Press, 1964. 384pp.), but it lacks the detail and the power of William Preston Johnston's account.

 William Preston Johnston's own career was overshadowed by that of his father, but was in itself so remarkable that it is a shame he never wrote his own autobiography. He graduated with high honors from Yale in 1852 at the age of 21 and received a law degree from the University of Louisville less than a year later. Early in the Civil War, he rose to the rank of lieutenant-colonel, but illness forced him to leave a promising command. He became a colonel and aide-de-camp to Jefferson Davis. He was Davis' most trusted staff officer, responsible for direct communication between the president and commanders in the field; as such, he was present at more major battles than perhaps any other man. He was captured with Davis and imprisoned with him after the war, then spent a year in exile in Canada. Robert E. Lee coaxed him into becoming head of the history and literature department at Washington and Lee University, of which Lee was president.

It was during his ten years in this position that he wrote the biography of his father. He later served as president of Louisiana State University, and was a founder and first president of Tulane University. His writings include works on Shakespeare and his own sonnets.

His biography of his father gives an intimate portrayal of that remarkable man's impact on Texas. Albert Sidney Johnston graduated from West Point in 1826. His brother, a U.S. Senator, urged him for a position on the staff of Winfield Scott. Although it incurred Scott's enmity, Johnston refused in order to take a field position in the Black Hawk War. Soon after, Johnston's young wife died tragically, and he despaired. He happened to hear Stephen F. Austin deliver his famous 1836 Louisville address imploring aid for Texas, and he determined to join the Texas army. He arrived soon after the Battle of San Jacinto, and joined up as a private. Soon discovered in the ranks, he was immediately made adjutant-general, and a few months later offered full field command of the Texas Army, which was then expecting a further invasion by Mexico. He became Secretary of War under Mirabeau B. Lamar and led the 1st Texas Rifle Regiment in the Mexican War. He then became a regular officer in the U.S. Army— one of the few Texas military men who was permitted to do so—and performed brilliantly as brigadier general in campaigns in Texas and the Far West.

When the Civil War broke out, Johnston was offered a position second in rank only to the aging Winfield Scott, whose early retirement would have made Johnston head of the Union armies. Upon the secession of Texas, however, Johnston resigned and became commander of the Western Department of the Confederacy, briefly outranking Lee. He was killed at Shiloh in 1862, a loss which Jefferson Davis called "irreparable."

In writing the biography, the son is keenly aware of the potential charge of white-wash. Johnston was involved in many controversial events, and his son admittedly defends his actions. The younger Johnston states that he "has felt keenly the restrictions and obligations imposed by the filial relation. Hostile criticism can always begin its argument with the charge that it is impossible for a son to be fair; and the writer's heart teaches him how difficult it is to be fair and just. . . . But it is not necessary to be impartial, in order to be truthful." Moreover, he says, his own "lines of life and habits of thought have been widely remote from his father's." With these dilemmas well in mind, the son manages relatively well to present a whole picture of the character of a difficult, generally taciturn man, and to defend his actions in a balanced, scholarly manner.

His method is as much as possible to let his father and his father's associates do the speaking on controversial subjects. This was made easier because, he states, his father's "own papers have been preserved almost entire since 1836; and these, including his Confederate archives, complete, have supplied ampler and more perfect materials than most biographers enjoy." These papers are now housed in the Tulane University Archives. The son was also aided by the active assistance of Jefferson Davis, Braxton Bragg, Don Carlos Buell, Fitz-John Porter, and many others on both sides of the Civil War and on all sides of the Texas issues.

The son, on the other hand, was able to provide many anecdotes that only a son could know. When Johnston arrived in 1837 to take command of the Texas army, Felix Huston refused to yield the post, and the two fought a duel. Perhaps no duel has ever been described more fully than this one. Johnston was wounded severely but gained his command and the respect of the troops, "I remember," the son writes, "when I was a little boy, asking my father 'if he did not hate Felix Huston.' He replied, 'No,' and then I asked him what he would do if he were to meet him then. He laughed, and answered, amusedly, 'As he would be a stranger here, I would ask him to dinner.' I thought a good deal about this. . . ."

When Johnston received his command in 1855 of a cavalry regiment to be sent to fight Indians on the Texas frontier (his junior officers including Robert E. Lee, E. Kirby Smith, John B. Hood, and Earl Van Dorn), the son writes: "It was a happy day for General Johnston when, mounting his splendid gray charger, he led a regiment of U.S. regular cavalry, nearly 800 strong, on the road toward Texas. As Texas was to be their home for some years . . . Johnston's wife [he had remarried] and family were packed into an ambulance-wagon, and occupied a tent ten feet square during the halts. . . . At Fort Mason, General Johnston reserved only one small room for his family."

The significance of the book for Texas, however, extends beyond the biographical material. The work is the best early defence of the administration of President Lamar. Johnston quickly fell under the jealousy of Sam Houston; the two were about as far apart in temperament as two natural leaders of men could be. Most 19th century works either take the side of Houston or are so violently anti-Houston as to be ineffective. This book, on the other hand, presents a sound case for the policies and themes of Lamar, particularly in regard to military and Indian affairs. As Johnston was repeatedly urged to run for president himself, the extensive quotations from his private papers shed much light on the political scene as well.

The book was published in July, 1878, after being submitted to Jefferson Davis, who read the manuscript and made suggestions. By 1880, the publisher reported some 4000 copies had been sold, but the author claimed Appleton "never sold any books in N.C., S.C., Geo., Ala., Mo., or Ark., or offered them for sale. . . . Little or nothing has been done in Texas." Appleton offered to sell Johnston the plates for $600.00 for him to do a reprint, but this was never done.

The son falters in his attempt to be objective in three areas. First he is too fervent in his attachment to Jefferson Davis' theories of Southern rights, but this is only to be expected. Second, he fails to be objective about his father's role as a Confederate commander in the events leading up to Shiloh, but no contemporary writer was objective in that regard. Third, he drops all hint of objectivity regarding the events surrounding the removal of his father's remains to Texas after the war in 1867. In this last, I do not blame him at all.

When General Johnston's remains arrived at the docks in Galveston, enroute to the state cemetery in Austin, General Griffin refused to permit its unloading until the mayor pledged not to permit public mourning. The mayor appealed to Gen. Sheridan, who replied: "I have too much regard for the memory of the brave men who died to preserve our Government, to authorize . . . demonstrations over the remains of any one who attempted to destroy it." Federal occupation troops prevented the planned solemnities, but virtually the entire male and female populations of Galveston, Houston, and Austin lined the road for miles, silently, in his honor and dared the troops to act. The son's account of this last trip with his father's body, a minor event in itself, is one of the most eloquent portrayals of the humiliation of defeat I have ever encountered.

Howes J175. Larned 2223. Nevins II-68. Raines, p.128.

113 Jones, Anson (1798-1858)

MEMORANDA AND OFFICIAL CORRESPONDENCE RELAT-ING TO THE REPUBLIC OF TEXAS, ITS HISTORY AND ANNEXATION. INCLUDING A BRIEF AUTOBIOGRAPHY OF THE AUTHOR.

New York: D. Appleton & Co., 346 & 358 Broadway, 1859.
[2],648,[4]pp. Portrait. 24cm.
Cloth.

(A). Facsimile reprint. Chicago: The Rio Grande Press, Inc., [1966]. 7,[1],xiii,[5],648,[3],5-30[1],705-736pp. 23cm. Folding map. Folding facsimile. Contains new material: Foreword, by John Connally, July, 1966. "About This Book and Some Acknowledgements," by John T. Strachan and Robert B. McCoy. Introduction by James M. Day. Also includes a facsimile of *Letters Relating to the History of Annexation* by Anson Jones (Galveston, 1848), the 1844 map of Texas by W. H. Emory, and Jones' manuscript of his valedictory address as president of Texas. New index. "The index is a marvel of accuracy."—Herbert Gambrell. Special edition in leather, boxed, limited to 150 numbered copies.
(B). Same as (A), bound in buckram.
(C). Facsimile reprint of the first edition. New York: Arno Press, 1973. 23cm. Cloth. The Far Western Frontier Series.

Anson Jones left us the only formal autobiography of a president of the Republic of Texas. From Bancroft to Billington, its importance has been noted: In 1889, Hubert H. Bancroft called it "especially valuable . . . on the campaign of 1836, the annexation question, and the schemes of England." In 1902, George P. Garrison praised its "special value for the light it throws on the inner history of the time— the personal relations of prominent men of the republic, and especially those between Jones and Houston." In 1966, James M. Day said that "Any history of the Republic of Texas must dwell on the name of Anson Jones; likewise, any scholarly study of that dramatic period of the Texas past must include research in Anson Jones' book." In 1982, Ray Allen Billington called it "one of the fullest accounts of the early history of Texas and an essential source of information on its republican period and annexation.''

Jones came to Texas in 1833 and became a participant in the activities leading to the revolt against Mexico, surgeon and judge advocate at the Battle of San Jacinto, Secretary of State under Houston, and last President of Texas. His activities in behalf of Texas led him to be called, quite justly, ''the Architect of Annexation.'' After Texas joined the Union, Jones was forgotten by an ungrateful public. Herbert Gambrell states: ''For twelve years Jones brooded over his neglect . . . became increasingly moody and introspective, and his dislike for Houston turned into hatred.'' When the state legislature failed to elect him U.S. Senator, he committed suicide.

Like Mirabeau B. Lamar, Anson Jones carefully collected and preserved his papers with the intention of writing a history of the Republic of Texas. During the decade of his despair, he worked regularly on the project, and deposited the manuscript with his banker a few days before taking his life. His wife Mary, aided by Ashbel Smith and Ebenezer Allen, sought to have the massive manuscript published. Smith took it to New York to Appleton, who agreed to print a thousand copies for $600.00. After many delays and the threat of a lawsuit, Appleton finally in late 1861 sent the books, along with a bill for $1,755.50. On the advice of Smith and Allen, Mrs. Jones refused to accept the books, and they were left in a warehouse in Galveston. She later wrote: ''I have learned that the boxes or some of them were broken open during the war and books taken by anyone who felt curious enough to read them.''

In 1929, Herbert Fletcher found the boxes and purchased the remaining 585 copies for less than a dollar each. With the profits he made from selling the books he was able to start his rare book business and publishing company, which he appropriately named the Anson Jones Press.

The volume consists of a short section of private memoirs, completed by Jones in 1849, which we wish had been much longer; a section of ''memoranda,'' in diary and journal form, covering the period 1838-1854; and a lengthy section of letters and correspondence, covering the period 1836-1857. He also includes a few short essays and speeches.

The whole, says Mrs. Jones, was issued exactly as "left by him, without note or comment."

Jones writes with unusual frankness, although when talking of enemies he is subject to calescent exaggeration. Nevertheless, he gives scores of insights into the men of the times. For example, writing of his arrival in San Felipe in late 1835 for the Consultation, the first formal movement towards independence, he says: "I was introduced to Bowie—he was dead drunk; to Houston—his appearance was any thing but decent or respectable, and very much like that of a broken-down sot and debauchee. The first night after my arrival, I was kept awake nearly all night by a drunken carouse in the room over that in which I 'camped.' Dr. [Branch T.] Archer and Gen. Houston appeared to be the principal persons engaged in the orgie, to judge from the noise. . . . The whole burden of the conversation, so far as it was, at times, intelligible, appeared to be abuse and denunciation of a man for whom I had the highest respect, Gen. Stephen F. Austin."

The major weakness of the *Memoranda* is the bitterness and anti-Houston sentiment that runs throughout the narrative. For a man who spent the entirety of his years of prominence as one of the most ardent supporters of Houston and his policies, this presents something of a warped and contradictory viewpoint. Jones, like so many Texas statesmen, felt betrayed by Houston in the decade of the 1850's, and this was the period in which he wrote the *Memoranda*. Much of this is corrected in Herbert Gambrell's superb biography of Jones, due to his use of the extensive unpublished diaries, manuscripts, and letters of Jones, now in the University of Texas Archives. These, in Gambrell's words, "reveal an Anson Jones more in harmony with the impressions of his contemporaries and correct some of the distortions of the *Memoranda*."

Agatha, p.46. Howes J191. Larned 2052. Raines, p.129.

114 Joutel, Henri (c. 1643-1723)

JOURNAL HISTORIQUE DE DERNIER VOYAGE QUE FEU M. DE LA SALE FIT DANS LE GOLFE DE MEXIQUE, POUR TROUVER L'EMBOUCHERE, & LE COURS DE LA RIVIERE

DE MISSICIPI, NOMMEE A PRESENT LA RIVIERE DE SAINT
LOUIS, QUI TRAVERSE LA MORT, & PLUSIERS CHOSES
CURIEUSES DU NOUVEAU MONDE, PAR MONSIEUR JOU-
TEL, L'UN DES COMPAGNONS DE CE VOYAGE, REDIGE &
MIS EN ORDRE PAR MONSIEUR DE MICHEL.

Paris: Chez Estienne Robinot, Librairie, Quay & attenant la Porte des Grands
Augustins, a l'Ange Gardien, [1713].
xxxiv,386pp. Folding map. 17cm.
Calf.

Other issues:
(A). *A Journal Of the Last Voyage Perform'd by Monsr. de la Sale, to the Gulph of Mexico,
      to Find out the Mouth of the Mississippi River; Containing, An Account of the Settlements
      He Endeavour'd to Make on the Coast of the Aforesaid Bay, His Unfortunate Death, and
      the Travels of His Companions for the Space of Eight Hundred Leagues across that Inland
      Country of America, Now Call'd Louisiana, (and Given by the King of France to M.
      Crozat,) Till They Came into Canada, Written in French by Monsieur Joutel, a
      Commander in that Expedition.* London: Printed for A. Bell, 1714. [2],xxi,[9],
      205,[5]pp. 20cm. Folding map. First edition in English.
(B). Same as (A), but dated 1715.
(C). *Mr. Joutel's Journal of His Voyage to Mexico: His Travels Eight Hundred Leagues
      Through Forty Nations of Indians in Louisiana to Canada, His Account of the Great
      River Missasipi, to Which is Added a Map of That Country, with a Description of the
      Great Water-Fall in the River Misouris.* London: Printed for Bernard Lintot, 1719.
      [2],xxi,[9],205,[5]pp. 19cm. Same printing as (A), with new title page. Some,
      but not all, copies have folding map.
(D). *Diario Historico del Ultimo Viaje que Hizo M. de la Sale para Descubrir el Desembocadero
      y Curso del Missicipi, Contiene la Historia Tragica de su Muerte y Muchas Cosas
      Curiosas del Nuevo Mundo, Escrita en Idioma Frances por M. T. Joutel, uno de los
      Companeros de M. La Sale en el Viaje.* Nueva York: Impreso . . . por Jose
      Desnoues, 1831. 156pp. 19cm. Translated by Jose Maria Tornel, Mexican Minister
      to the U.S.; includes a Preface by Tornel. First edition in Spanish.
(E). French, Benjamin F. [ed.]. *Historical Collections of Louisiana.* New York, 1846.
      Volume I contains the Joutel journal on pages 85-193.
(F). Margry, Pierre [comp.]. *Decouvertes et Etablissements des Francais dans l'Ouest et
      dans le Sud de l'Amerique Septentrionale (1614-1754): Memoires et Documents Originaux.*
      Paris, 1878. Volume III contains the original Joutel journal on pages 89-534.
      First complete edition, with much new material. This is the only printing of
      the complete Joutel journal.
(G). *Joutel's Journal of La Salle's Last Voyage* . . . Chicago: The Caxton Club, 1896.
      [8],xxi,[9],229,[2]pp. Map. Cloth. Notes by Melville B. Anderson. 203 copies
      printed on paper and 3 copies on Japanese vellum.

(H). *Joutel's Journal of La Salle's Last Voyage,* 1684-7. Albany: Joseph McDonough, 1906. [8],258pp. Folding map. Cloth-backed boards. Edited by Henry Reed Stiles. Limited to 500 numbered copies, although copies are known without numbers.

(I). *The Journeys of Rene Robert Cavelier, Sieur de La Salle* . . . New York: Allerton Book Co., 1922. Two volumes. Cloth. Includes the Joutel journal. Edited by Isaac Joslin Cox.

(J). Same as (I). London, 1922.

(K). *A Journal of La Salle's Last Voyage.* New York: Corinth Books, [1962]. [16],187,[3]pp. Cloth. The American Experience Series. Introduction by Darrett B. Rutman.

(L). Facsimile of (A). New York: Readex Microprint, [1966].

(M). Facsimile of (I). Austin: The Pemberton Press, 1968.

(N). Facsimile of (G). New York: Burt Franklin, 1968.

(O). Facsimile of (I). New York: AMS Press, 1973.

Joutel, an eyewitness, provides the best account of the activities of La Salle in Texas. Francis Parkman said "it gives the impression of sense, intelligence, and candor, throughout." Henry Reed Stiles said it "is valuable from its exactness of detail, and the fact that in many places it corrects the careless or misleading statements of others, and it is remarkably free from the egotism which disfigures or weakens the narratives of [others]." Charlevoix said Joutel was "a very upright man and the only trustworthy member of La Salle's party." Louise P. Kellogg called Joutel "simple, loyal, practical, resourceful, and prudent. For fullness of detail and exactness of statement his is the best description of La Salle's last expedition, while his journey from Texas to Quebec as an exploit has seldom been surpassed."

After seventeen years of French army service, Henri Joutel joined his neighbor La Salle in his 1684 expedition to colonize the mouth of the Mississippi. La Salle took about 300 people in four ships but missed the mouth of the great river and landed on the Texas coast early in 1685. By summer, the La Salle party had built Fort St. Louis, on a site on the Lavaca long lost but rediscovered and excavated a few years ago. La Salle then began rather extensive exploration of Texas, traveling westward to locate enemy Spanish outposts and eastward in search of the Mississippi. Meanwhile, the number of colonists began to dwindle, due to desertions and disease—and one who was eaten by an alligator. In early 1687, La Salle was ambushed and murdered by some of his own men. Some time later, Fort St.

Louis was attacked by Indians and most of the colonists were massacred.

Joutel had the advantage of being within La Salle's inner circle, and the good fortune to be absent when La Salle was murdered. He was allowed to leave Texas with a company of six men. Joutel led them overland to the Mississippi and northward back to Canada. In 1688, Joutel returned to France. Having taken notes throughout his adventure, he prepared a manuscript account soon after his return home, but did not publish it. In 1697 Henri de Tonti's *Dernieres Decouvertes . . . de M. de laSale* appeared in Paris, although Tonti disclaimed having written it. Joutel debated whether or not to publish his own account to refute the many errors in Tonti, but delayed over a decade more. Finally, in 1712 he gave the manuscript to Estienne Robinot, who gave it to Jean Michel, who "put it into a Dress fit to appear in publick" and added an introduction. Michel cut out about half of the narrative and altered the text considerably. Joutel complained bitterly that this was not authorized by him.

All subsequent editions except one have been based on the abridged Michel edition of 1713. Fortunately, a 19th century French archivist and collector named Pierre Margry unearthed Joutel's original manuscript and a wealth of other materials on La Salle and French America. Unfortunately, for twenty years or more he refused to let anyone examine them—the materials in the public archives under his charge being "unavailable." Jared Sparks, Gabriel Gravier, Henry Harrisse, and Francis Parkman were refused access. Parkman, in his *Discovery of the Great West*, sarcastically praised Margry's "indefatigable research . . . whose labors can be appreciated only by those who have seen their results," which was no one. The American historians hit upon an ingenius idea to get access. Through their combined efforts, a bill was passed by the Congress of the United States agreeing to purchase 500 copies if Margry would publish his collections of documents. Margry bit, and between 1876 and 1886 he published his *Decouvertes et Etablissements* in six volumes. The complete original narrative of Joutel appears in the third volume. Ironically, no edition in English has ever appeared, nor has the rare Margry set ever been reprinted. Parkman was forced to rewrite his *Discovery of the Great West*, which was reissued in 1879 as *La Salle and the Discovery of the Great West*, then and now one of the classics of American historiography.

In 1831, Jose Maria Tornel, the Mexican Secretary of War who was responsible for cutting off American immigration into Texas, translated the 1713 Joutel text into Spanish; a good biography in English of this remarkable Mexican is still needed. In 1909, Genaro Garcia published the Mexican side of the La Salle era in volume XXV of his *Documentos Ineditos o Muy Raros para la Historia de Mexico*. This volume, which bears the title *Historia de Nuevo Leon con Noticias sobre Coahuila, Tejas y Nuevo Mexico* (Mexico, 1909, 400pp.), includes the first printing of Alonso de Leon's account of his expedition into Texas to drive out La Salle, and his discovery of the remains of Fort Saint Louis, which he destroyed. Other related material is in Walter O'Donnell, *La Salle's Occupation of Texas* (Austin: St. Edwards Univ., 1936) and in Lino Gomez Canedo, *Primeras Exploraciones y Poblamiento de Texas*, 1686-1694 (Monterrey, Mexico: Instituto Technologico y de Estudios Superiores, 1968). There is also an excellent account by Robert S. Weddle, *Wilderness Manhunt: The Spanish Search for LaSalle* (Austin: University of Texas Press, 1973, 291pp.), which recounts the eleven Spanish sea and land expeditions sent to extirpate the French from Texas.

Agatha, p.1. Bradford 2765. Church 855. Clark I-14. Field 808. Graff 2251. Howes J266. Leclerc 925. Palau 125174. Rader 2129. Raines, p.130. Sabin 36760. Streeter 1125. Wagner, *Spanish Southwest* 79.

115   Kemp, Louis Wiltz (1881-1956)

THE SIGNERS OF THE TEXAS DECLARATION OF INDEPENDENCE.

Houston: The Anson Jones Press, 1944.
[10],xxxiv,[24],398pp. Illus. 24cm.
Cloth, dustjacket.
Twelve leaves containing a facsimile of the Texas Declaration of Independence are inserted after the preliminaries.
Verso of title: "This edition is limited to 500 copies of which this is ____." Signed by Kemp. I have seen many unnumbered copies. My collection includes the dedication copy, inscribed and signed from Kemp to William Henry Kershaw, but unnumbered.

The Anson Jones Press

announces with pride

the publication of

The Signers of the Texas Declaration of
Independence

by

Louis Wiltz Kemp

President

The Texas State Historical Association

in

a limited, autographed edition

of

five hundred copies.

Price ten dollars

405 Fannin Street
Houston 2, Texas

Other issues:

(A). Facsimile reprint. Salado, Texas: The Anson Jones Press, [1959]. Same collation, with a new Foreword by Gov. Price Daniel, dated November 1, 1958. Cloth. The printed limitation notice on the verso of the title is still present in this printing. I have seen a copy of this work with a purported signature of Kemp on the limitation, although he died three years before it was printed.

This is the best work on the Convention of 1836, which declared Texas independence and drew up its first constitution. Eugene C. Barker wrote of it: "Primarily, it is made up of authoritative encyclopaedic sketches of the fifty-nine signers of the Declaration of Independence. Incidentally, it goes much further: correcting numerous errors heretofore firmly imbedded in historical literature and tradition and adding greatly to our knowledge of significant characters who appear only casually in relation to his principal theme. . . . He combines in rare degree the interests and talents of historian, biographer, and genealogist; and in all essentials he has done a job that nobody will ever be tempted to do again. [His work] is an interesting book to read and is a permanent contribution to every library's reference list of Texana."

The volume begins with what is still the most extensive account of the Convention of 1836. The bulk of the work, however, is devoted to lengthy, well-annotated biographies of the men who actually signed the Texas Declaration of Independence. The facsimile of the document itself is the only accurate one ever produced. Of the 59 signers, Kemp points out that only two were native Texans (Navarro and Ruiz), only one was a member of Austin's Old Three Hundred original settlers, and only ten had lived in Texas for more than six years. Seventeen had been in Texas less than six months. In the election for delegates to the convention held in Velasco, 88 men voted, 47 of whom had been in Texas *less than a week*. The convention declared independence, wrote and signed a constitution, and hurriedly disbanded in the face of Santa Anna's successful assault on the Alamo.

Kemp's research is of immense value in analyzing this most important council in Texas history. One learns that delegate Richard Ellis lived on the Red River in an area claimed both by Arkansas and Texas. Arkansas had its own convention to form a constitution as an American state in early 1836. Ellis covered both possibilities and got elected to both conventions. The Texas convention elected him as its president, and Ellis was ever after an avid Texan. Others among the signers of the declaration had served in other states as governors, senators, and congressmen; a few were former bankrupts and fugitives from justice. Scholars will draw upon Kemp's work over and over again in coming to a fuller understanding of the convention and its delegates.

116   Kendall, George Wilkins (1809-1867)

NARRATIVE OF THE TEXAN SANTA FE EXPEDITION, COMPRISING A DESCRIPTION OF A TOUR THROUGH TEXAS, AND ACROSS THE GREAT SOUTHWESTERN PRAIRIES, THE CAMANCHE AND CAYGUA HUNTING-GROUNDS, WITH AN ACCOUNT OF THE SUFFERINGS FROM WANT OF FOOD, LOSSES FROM HOSTILE INDIANS, AND FINAL CAPTURE OF THE TEXANS, AND THEIR MARCH, AS PRISONERS, TO THE CITY OF MEXICO.

New York: Harper and Brothers, 82 Cliff-Street, 1844.
Two volumes: 405; xii,[11]-406pp. Folding map. 5 plates. 20cm.
Cloth, date 1844 at foot of spine.

Other issues:
(A.) Same as above, but with date 1845 at foot of spine.
(A1). Same as above, but with no date at foot of spine.
(B). Same as above, from the same sheets, but with imprint: London: Wiley & Putnam, 6, Waterloo Place, 1844.
(C). *Narrative of an Expedition Across the Great South-Western Prairies, from Texas to Santa Fe; with an Account of the Disasters which Befel the Expedition from Want of Food and the Attack of Hostile Indians; the Final Capture of the Texans and Their Sufferings on a March of Two Thousand Miles as Prisoners of War, and in the Prisons and Lazarettos of Mexico.* London: David Bogue, Fleet Street, [1845]. [Verso of title:] London: Thomas Harrild, Printer, Silver Street, Falcon Square. Two volumes: xii,[13]-432; viii,[12]-436pp. Two plates. Folding map. 17cm. Cloth.
(D). Same as first edition, but dated 1846. [2],405,[2]; xii,[11]-406pp. Adv. at end of vol. I dated January, 1847. Cloth.
(E). Bristol: Sherwood, Gilbert, and Piper, Paternoster-Row; and Hugh Cunningham, 193, Strand; and Office of the Great Western Advertiser and Chronicle, 8, Bridge Street, [1846]. iv,599pp. 16cm. Cloth.
(F). London: Henry Washbourne, New Bridge Street, Blackfriars, 1847. iv,599pp. Cloth.

(G).   Sixth edition. New York: Harper and Brothers, 82 Cliff Street, 1847. Two
       volumes. 405,[2]; xii,[11]-406pp. Map. 5 plates. 20cm. Cloth.

(H).   Same as (G), dated 1850.

(I).   Same as (G), dated 1855.

(J).   Seventh edition. New York: Harper & Brothers, Publishers, Franklin Square,
       1856. Two volumes: xviii,[13]-452; xiii,[11]-442pp. Map. 5 plates. 20cm. Cloth.
       Best and most desired edition, with the diary of Thomas Falconer (pp.437-452)
       added to volume I and with an additional chapter (pp.407-442) on the Woll
       and Snively expeditions and Mexican War added to Volume II.

(K).   *Narrative of the Texan Santa Fe Expediton*. Chicago: The Lakeside Press, R. R.
       Donnelley & Sons Co., 1929. xxxiv,585pp. Folding map. 2 illus. 17cm. Cloth.
       Greatly abridged edition, consisting of volume I and the first chapter of volume
       II only. New introduction by Milo Milton Quaife.

(L).   Facsimile reprint of the first edition. Austin: The Steck Company, 1935. Two
       volumes. 22cm. Cloth. Original Narratives of Texas History and Adventure
       Series. 2000 copies printed.

(M).   Facsimile of (C). New York: Readex Microprint, 1966.

Not only is this the best account of the Santa Fe Expedition, it is
one of the best campaign narratives ever written. Rupert Richardson
said Kendall's experiences "represent practically every element of
adventure and peril that could have befallen men on the southwestern
frontier. Through his skillful organization and superb narrative and
descriptive ability, he produced one of the classics of western Americana." Sister Agatha said it is "the best book dealing with its phase
of Southwestern life in the early 19th century." L. W. Payne said "the
story is almost epic in its proportions and in its interest. The author
had an eye for the picturesque and the romantic, and . . . he managed
to make his whole narrative engrossing and convincing."

George W. Kendall founded the New Orleans *Picayune* in 1837 and
became one of the leading trumpeters for Texas. In 1841, learning of
Texan plans to conquer Santa Fe, he set out for Texas and joined the
expedition. Travelling through a new and hostile environment, and
improperly equipped, the expedition nearly starved, surviving on
hippophagy. The members straggled almost to Santa Fe and were
gulled into surrendering without a fight. The captives were taken to
Mexico and imprisoned for nearly two years, some longer. Kendall,
although casting himself as a non-combatant member of the press,
was locked up with the others.

Considerable diplomatic pressure was mounted to obtain Kendall's release. George Fenlon wrote Sam Houston from New York on April 7, 1842 (in the A. J. Houston Papers, Texas State Archives): "It is rumored here that Mr. [Waddy] Thompson, the new U.S. Minister to Mexico, has received definite and positive instructions to make a preemptory demand for the release of Kendall, and others, and should his demand not be immediately complied with, he is to demand his passports and withdraw, in which event a blockade will ensue."

Kendall was released in May of that year and returned to New Orleans. Whenever possible, he had sent back letters describing his adventures. A total of 23 of these appeared in the New Orleans *Picayune* between June 17, 1841, and April 30, 1842. Home at last, Kendall began writing a book on the expedition. The narrative appeared serially in the *Picayune* between June 1, 1842, and the end of August, 1842, in 58 articles, followed by a series of sketches. Entitled "Mexican Sketches" and "Santa Fe Sketches," these began on November 26, 1842, and ran in 62 articles until April 1843. The letters, narratives, and sketches were reprinted in many newspapers in the United States and England, and a few appeared in Mexican journals. They form the basis of his book, but include much additional material as well.

In May, 1842, the narrative of Thomas Falconer was printed by the *Picayune* in seven articles in the issues of May 1, 3, 4, 5, 6, 7, and 8. These were reissued a few days later as a pamphlet, *Thomas Falconer's Journal of the Santa Fe Expedition* (New Orleans: Published by Lumsden, Kendall & Co., Office of the Picayune, 1842, 12pp.). A different version of the Falconer material with other material was issued in the *Journal of the Royal Geographical Society of London*, vol. XIII, Part 2, pp.199-222, 1844, and was reissued as a pamphlet the same year under the title *Notes of a Journey through Texas and New Mexico, in the Years 1841 and 1842.* (London, 1844, 28pp.). Still another version was printed in the seventh edition of Kendall in 1856, and all three were reprised in F. W. Hodge, *Letters and Notes on the Texan Santa Fe Expedition, 1841-1842* (New York, 1930). Hodge apparently made little use of two original diaries of the expedition by Falconer, now at Yale, which are as yet unpublished.

In 1843, while revising the *Picayune* articles into book form, Kendall was outraged to learn that Frederick Marryat had plagiarized Kendall's articles into a book entitled *Narrative of the Travels and Adventures of*

Monsieur Violet (London: Longman, 1843; and New York: Harper, 1843).
Marryat even went so far as to copy whole sections from Kendall's
articles verbatim. Kendall immediately issued a statement to the press,
published in December, 1843. Horace Greeley said of Marryat: "The
gross humbug, so far as it poaches upon his manor, is thus effectively
demolished by Mr. Kendall." Thomas Falconer also issued a statement
denouncing Marryat in the European press. Kendall did not sue; in
fact, he made a contract with Marryat's American publisher to issue
Kendall's own narrative. In his preface, Kendall wrote that some parts
of his text "have since been stolen . . . by Captain Marryat. . . . The
author has deemed this exposition [of Marryat's plagiarism] necessary,
lest some of his readers, unacquainted with the circumstances and
who may peruse both books, should suspect him of having poached
upon the wondrous tale of Violet. The larceny lies at the door of
either the Captain or the Monsieur."

One of the Santa Fe prisoners, Robert D. Phillips, sent Kendall
some additional information for his book in 1843; the Texas State
Archives has Kendall's reply, dated January 21, 1844, in which he
states that he did not receive the letter "until the first volume of the
book was stereotyped" and that he will use part of the information in
the second volume. "I regret that circumstances put it out of my
power to give you an agency for the sale of my narrative. The Messrs.
Harper, my publishers, have exclusive and entire control of the book,
and employ none other than book-sellers scattered through the country
in its sale. . . . The work will not appear before the middle of next
month. . . . What a pity that last Santa Fe Expedition [the Snively
Expedition] so signally failed! Hunt, Lubbock, Snively, and many of
our old comrades were along, and knew the country and had plenty
of provisions. How could they make out so badly? They might have
walked 'rough-shod' over Armijo, and taken Santa Fe with the greatest
ease had they kept ahead. There appears to be some strange fatality
in the every late undertaking of the Texans."

The Kendall narrative went through a number of contemporary
printings, and John S. Kendall later stated that 40,000 copies were
sold in eight years, a noteworthy record for a non-fiction work of
almost 900 pages. George W. Kendall later became known as the
world's first war correspondent for his on-the-spot coverage of the

Mexican War. He finally settled in Texas as a sheep rancher in the
section now named Kendall County in his honor. There is a good
biography of Kendall by Fayette Copeland, *Kendall of the Picayune, Being
His Adventures in New Orleans, on the Texan Santa Fe Expedition, in the
Mexican War, and in the Colonization of the Texas Frontier* (Norman
:University of Oklahoma Press, 194, 351pp.). An excellent study of the
route of the expedition is H. Bailey Carroll's *The Texan Santa Fe Trail*
(Canyon: Panhandle-Plains Historical Society, 1951, 201pp.)

Agatha, p.14. Bradford 2809. Dobie, p.56. Field 818. Graff 2304. Howes K75. Rader
2157. Raines, p.131. Rittenhouse 347. Streeter 1515. Wagner-Camp 110.

117 Kennedy, William (1799-1871)

TEXAS: THE RISE, PROGRESS, AND PROSPECTS OF THE
REPUBLIC OF TEXAS.

London: R. Hastings, 13, Carey Street, Lincoln's Inn, 1841.
[Verso of title:] London: Printed by William Clowes and Sons, Stamford Street.
Two volumes: lii,378pp; vi,548pp. 4 maps (2 folding). 23cm.
Cloth.

Other issues:
(A). "Second Edition." Same collation.
(B). *Texas: Its Geography, Natural History, and Topography.* New York: Benjamin and
Young, John Street; Sold by Burges, Stringer, & Co. . . ., 1844, x,118pp. 23cm.
Printed wrappers. This is a reissue of the first 201 pages of Volume I of the
original edition.
(C). Same as (B), but with the imprint: New York: William Jackson, 177 Broadway
. . . , 1844, [1],118pp. 21cm. Printed wrappers.
(D). *William Kennedy's Geographie, Naturgeschicte und Topographie von Texas.* Frankfurt
am Main: Druck und Verlag von Johann David Sauerlaender, 1845. 212pp.
22cm. Folding map. Plain boards. First edition in German, translated by Otto
von Czarnowsky.
(E). Same as (D), 1846. 180pp. Folding map. 23cm. Wrappers.
(F). Facsimile reprint of (A). Fort Worth: The Molyneaux Craftsmen, Inc., 1925.
[4],[ix]-xlviii,939pp. 3 maps (1 folding). 24cm. Fabricoid. Some copies have a
limitation leaf inserted, signed by Peter Molyneaux, indicating a limited edition
of 1250 copies.
(G). Facsimile reprint of the 1925 facsimile reprint (F). Clifton, New Jersey: A. M.
Kelley, 1974. Same collation. 23cm. Cloth. American Through Eurpoean Eyes
Series.

This is the most comprehensive account of Texas published during
its decade as an independent nation, and a work of such profound

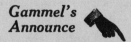

influence that it was a key factor in gaining English recognition of Texan independence. Bancroft said Kennedy "was a keen observer; and better still, his observations were conducted without prejudice, and are correct. His conclusions are just." Eugene C. Barker said Kennedy "wrote with real historical spirit, and, in some respects, his book has not been superceded." Sister Agatha said Kennedy wrote in a "dignified style that has made his work remain to this day a dependable source book for historical reference."

It is astonishing that an Irish poet and journalist, after visiting Texas only from April to June, 1839, could write such a thorough, comprehensive account of the history and geography of Texas. Homer S. Thrall stated: "It is wonderful how a stranger from across the ocean, could in so short a time, gain so completely a knowledge of the country and its institutions. His style is clear; his facts well arranged; his descriptions of the country just and striking; and his personal sketches of leading men remarkably true and life-like."

The work had enormous influence in Europe, especially in England and Germany. So powerful was its pro-Texas impact in England that N. D. P. Maillard's *History of the Republic of Texas* (London, 1842), an anti-Texas work, was written in reply to it. Ferdinand von Roemer advised Germans that Kennedy's book was "the ground work for an accurate and comprehensive knowledge about Texas," and Prince Carl of Solms-Braunfels wrote: "Mr. Kennedy is a man of genius, talent, and true honesty. He distinguishes that which he saw with his own eyes from that which was described to him by others. If there are any mistakes in his narrative, it is due to the fact that he received erroneous reports."

Kennedy himself gives a clue as to how he was able to obtain such a wealth of reliable data when he reveals that he was given access to M. B. Lamar's private papers—a collection that was then and is still now an unexcelled mine of information on Texas history and geography. Kennedy also tells us that, when he returned to England, making an "explanation of Texas affairs was no easy task; some asking if the people were Indians, others if they were Spaniards, and others apparently suspicious that I had established advantageous relations with the land pirates; and hence my zeal. A veteran member of

Parliament asked me if Texas were not a State lying contiguous to Florida.''

The book begins with a personal narrative of Kennedy's tour of Canada, the United States, and Texas in 1838-1839. This is followed with an extensive geography and natural history section, of which Raines said: "The physical description of Texas [was] the best published up to the time." The next section is a history of Texas with lucid commentary on contemporary men and events. The work ends with a lengthy section of appendices containing public documents, among which are the first printing in England of the Texas Declaration of Independence and of the Constitution of the Republic of Texas. Included also is John C. Beales' own account of his settlement of Dolores near the Rio Grande, 1833-1836.

The large map by John Arrowsmith ranks with those of Tanner and Emory as the best maps of Texas during the period of the republic. It is a monument of Texas cartography, but apparently was included in only a portion of the copies of the original edition, as only a small percentage of surviving copies contain it.

Shortly after the appearance of Kennedy's book, Arthur Ikin published one of the rarest of all Texas books, *Texas: Its History, Topography, Agriculture, Commerce, and General Statistics . . . Designed for the Use of the British Merchant, and as a Guide to Emigrants* (London: Sherwood, Gilbert, and Piper, 1841, 100pp.), in which Ikin praises and recommends Kennedy's larger work. The Ikin volume is promotional in nature but includes useful information on immigration and commerce. Ikin was at the time consul of Texas at London.

Kennedy was appointed by the Texas government to replace Ikin as Texan Consul; in 1842, Kennedy switched and became British Consul at Galveston, which position he held until annexation. William Bollaert wrote that Kennedy became ill "at Galveston (I have no doubt that he was a little dissipated in his life—Drink! Drink! Drink!!) when he took advantage of leave of absence & is now in England (Decr. 1846) searching for health." Kennedy recovered and wrote several more books before his death in 1871.

Agatha, p.30. Bradford 2814. Graff 2308. Howes K92. Larned 2053. Rader 2159. Raines, p.132. Sabin 37440. Streeter 1385.

118   Lamar, Mirabeau Buonaparte (1798-1859)

THE PAPERS OF MIRABEAU BUONAPARTE LAMAR.

Austin: A. C. Baldwin & Sons [vols. I-II]; Von Boeckmann-Jones, Inc. [vols. III-VI], 1921-1927.
Six Volumes: I:viii,496pp. [1921]. II: xi,[i],599pp. 1922. III: [4],600pp. n.d. IV, Part I: [4],300pp. 1924. IV, Part II: 241pp. 1925. V: 515pp. [1927]. VI: 543pp. n.d. All in printed wrappers. 23cm.
Charles A. Gulick and Katherine Elliott edited volumes I-III, Gulick and Winnie Allen edited volume IV, and Harriet Smither edited volumes V and VI.

Other editions:
(A).   Facsimile reprint. Austin and New York: The Pemberton Press, 1968. Issued as Number VII in the Brasada Reprint Series. 6 volumes in 7. 23cm. Cloth. Volume I has a new foreword by John H. Jenkins, a 17-page biography of Lamar by Dr. Dorman H. Winfrey, and 13 pages of illustrations. 500 sets printed.
(B).   Facsimile reprint. New York: AMS Press, 1973. 6 vols. 23cm.

The papers of President Lamar comprise one of the most valuable collections of historical data on Texas ever published. The 2814 letters, documents, and manuscripts were purchased by a special act of the Texas legislature on March 19, 1909, from Lamar's daughter, Mrs. Loretta Calder, for ten thousand dollars. They were placed in the Texas State Archives, where they still repose. In 1914 Elizabeth Howard West compiled a *Calendar of the Papers of Mirabeau Buonaparte Lamar*, 355pp., published in Austin by the Texas Library and Historical Commission. Gulick and the other editors devoted most of the 1920's to editing and publishing the bulk of the collection. In 1980, the Texas State Archives acquired a large collection of additional Lamar Papers and reprinted the 1914 calendar with corrections, an excellent new index, and a supplemental calendar bringing the total number of papers in the Lamar collection to 3366.

Lamar came to Texas in 1835 determined from the outset to write a history of Texas. Within a year he was a hero of San Jacinto and Vice President of the new Republic of Texas. From that point on he was second in importance in Texas only to Sam Houston, serving as President of Texas from 1838 to 1841. Throughout his active career, nevertheless, Lamar aggressively collected and preserved historical data, and the notes in his papers prove him an indefatigable researcher.

He never produced his projected history, but the documents and notes he collected now form one of the very best Texas research collections extant, and are as much a monument to him as are the University of Texas, the City of Austin, and the Texas Philosophical Society, all of which he founded.

The most important of the papers are the correspondence received by Lamar during the periods of the Republic of Texas and pre-Civil War statehood. Almost equally important, however, are the materials collected by Lamar. These include documents and letters relating to such events and people as early colonization activities, Jean Lafitte, the Austin family, James Long, Indians, Mexican leaders, and even a draft biography of Santa Anna. Lamar records the recollections of numerous early settlers and interviews with contemporary leaders. Nowhere else, not even the *Writings of Houston,* does one find such a wealth of primary source material on the first sixty years of the 19th century in Texas.

Mirabeau B. Lamar left an immensely important heritage to Texas culture. He was known as the "poet president" of Texas and was certainly the most important literary figure in Texas during his era. That this poetic philosopher could be elected to the chief political office of the rambunctious republic is remarkable in the extreme; that he could at the same time be an active research historian is little short of amazing. Lamar's most famous statement, which has become the motto of the University of Texas, can serve equally well as his own epitaph: "The cultivated mind is the guardian genius of democracy."

There are three significant biographies of Lamar. The first is A. K. Christian, *Mirabeau B. Lamar* (Austin: Von Boeckmann-Jones Co., 1922), and the second is Herbert P. Gambrell, *Mirabeau Buonaparte Lamar: Troubadour and Crusader* (Dallas: Southwest Press, 1934). In my collection I have a copy of Gambrell's book with extensive revisions inserted for a "revised edition, 1944," an edition that was never published. The third is Stanley Siegel, *The Poet President of Texas: The Life of Mirabeau B. Lamar, President of the Republic of Texas* (Austin: Jenkins Publishing Company, 1977).

119 Lane, Walter Paye (1817-1892)

THE ADVENTURES AND RECOLLECTIONS OF GENERAL
WALTER P. LANE, A SAN JACINTO VETERAN, CONTAINING

SKETCHES OF THE TEXIAN, MEXICAN, AND LATE WARS, WITH SEVERAL INDIAN FIGHTS THROWN IN.

Marshall, [Texas]: Tri-Weekly Herald Job Print, 1887.
vi,114pp. plus errata sheet. Frontis, 17cm.
Printed wrappers. Also limp morocco, gilt.

Other issues:
(A). Marshall, Texas: New Messenger Pub. Co., [1928]. 180pp. Two illus. 19cm. Cloth. The original text ends on page 129, the remainder being biographical and historical data on Lane prepared by his niece, Mary Jane Lane. Best edition.
(B). Reprint of (A). Austin and New York: Pemberton Press, Jenkins Publishing Company, 1970. 180pp. Frontis. 24cm. Cloth, dustjacket.

One of the best Texas military memoirs, this is also a prime source on the period from the Texas Revolution through the Civil War. No Texas military hero spent more time in the thick of the action than Lane, and his memoirs are meaty with anecdotes and incidents relating to the revolution, the Indian campaigns, the Mexican War, and the Civil War. As Colton Storm has stated, the book contains "exciting and unusual personal accounts, especially the 'Indian fights thrown in.'"

A native of County Cork, Ireland, Walter P. Lane was brought with his immigrant family to Maryland in 1821, and thence to Ohio and Texas. He served at San Jacinto with great valor, being wounded and singled out for special commendation and battlefield promotion. In 1838 he was one of four out of twenty-five to escape alive, though wounded, at the Battle Creek Indian fight. In the 1840's he served in the Texas Ranger campaigns under Jack Hays and as an officer under Hays in the Mexican War, participating in the siege of Monterrey and at Buena Vista, again receiving battlefield commissions for valor. In 1849 he went to California among the first gold rushers. In the Civil War he served in numerous battles, was wounded at Mansfield, and received numerous citations and promotions for bravery in action, ending his service in the Confederacy as a brigadier general.

Lane's narrative is salty and pure Texian. Writing of the skirmishes on the evening before the San Jacinto battle, he states: "We got in half a mile of their line, when their cavalry came out to interview us, [yelling insults and inviting attack]. We did. . . . Charge! rang out,

and we went through them like a stroke of lightning. . . . My horse—
a powerful animal—had got excited, and, having more zeal than
discretion, took the bit in his teeth and ran me headlong into the
midst of the enemy, much to my disgust. The order was given to
retreat. I was unanimously in favor of it, but my horse wanted to go
through. . . . Just then a big Mexican lancer charged me in the side,
running me through the shoulder with his lance . . . and knocked me
ten feet off my horse. I fell on my head, stunned and senseless. Gen.
[Mirabeau B.] Lamar rode up to succor me, shot the Mexican, and,
thinking I was dead, fell back on the command. My comrades had
got some forty yards, when I regained consciousness and my feet at
the same time. Twenty Mexicans were round me when I rose, but it
so surprised them to see a dead boy rise to his feet and run like a
buck, that I got ten steps before they fired at me. Capt. [Henry W.]
Karns saw me coming, and ordered his company to wheel and fire
on my pursurers, which they did, killing a few, when the balance
halted. An old man told me: 'Son, get up behind; I recon' the old
mare kin take us both out.' I did. (She was a sorrel mare and thin in
flesh; I would know her hide if it was dried on a fence even now, and
she had the sharpest backbone it has ever been my fortune to
straddle.)''

In the Mexican War, Lane led a detachment on a bold raid deep
into Mexican territory and into the middle of the enemy-held town of
Salado. Forming a cordon, he and his men surrounded the cemetery
and forced the townspeople to dig up the bones of some Texas heroes
who had been massacred earlier by the Mexicans. The remains
secured, his company rode back through Mexican lines and sent the
bones back to Texas, where they were reinterred on Monument Hill
at La Grange. It was "only fitting," thought Lane.

About a third of Lane's narrative relates to the Civil War, and this
section sparkles with similar tales of valor. These are followed by
tributes to Lane by Victor M. Rose and John Henry Brown, adding
a few more anecdotes of Lane's career. The 1928 edition contains the
statement: "General Walter Paye Lane produced his 'Adventures and
Recollections' by insistence of his niece, Miss Mary Jane Lane. When
he urged that 'he was better calculated to make history than to write

it,' she answered that she would willingly do the writing if he would furnish the data, and thus it came about that the book was written.''

It is likely, as well, that J. W. Pope, who wrote the introduction (dated Marshall, Dec. 23, 1887), had a hand in preparing the text. He states that ''these recollections might be styled semi-historical, for while the writer does not assume to write history, there is much of history in the little volume, but narrated in a manner to give it a charm superior to dry history, and it is therefore adapted to the entertainment of those minds which have neither the inclination nor time to read what a large number consider dull reading.'' How much history has been yielded up to charm will never be known (''Twenty Mexicans were round me . . .''), but the result is one of the most fascinating narratives ever produced in Texas.

Graff 2384. Howes L69. Nevins I-119. Rader 2198. Raines, p.136.

120 [Lawrence, A. B.]

TEXAS IN 1840, OR THE EMIGRANT'S GUIDE TO THE NEW REPUBLIC; BEING THE RESULT OF OBSERVATION, ENQUIRY AND TRAVEL IN THAT BEAUTIFUL COUNTRY, BY AN EMIGRANT, LATE OF THE UNITED STATES. WITH AN INTRODUCTION BY THE REV. A. B. LAWRENCE, OF NEW ORLEANS.

New York: Published by William W. Allen, and Sold by Robinson, Pratt & Co, 73 Wall Street, Collins, Keese & Co., 254 Pearl Street, and by the Booksellers Generally, 1840.
[4],vii-xxii,[23]-275pp. Frontispiece view of Austin, dated 1840 (sometimes found in color) drawn by Edward Hall. 20cm.
Cloth.

Other issues:
(A). *Texas in 1842* . . . Same printing as above, with cancel title changing both the date in the title and in the imprint to 1842.
(B). *A History of Texas, or the Emigrant's Guide to the New Republic, by a Resident Emigrant, Late from the United States.* New York: Published by Nafis & Cornish, No. 278 Pearl Street, 1844. Same collation; from the same printing as the original, with new cancel title added. Some copies have the dedication leaf and some do not. In some copies the original frontispiece is included, and in some a reprint dated 1844 is substituted.

(C). Same as (B), dated 1845. Also from the sheets of the first printing with cancel
title substituted. Some copies have the frontispiece dated 1840 and others 1844.
Some of the plates in later editions have been reworked to show more people.

(D). Facsimile reprint of original edition. New York: Arno Press, 1973 [10],vii-
xxii,[23]-274,[3]pp. 22cm. Cloth. The Far Western Frontier Series.

(E). Facsimile reprint of the original edition. Austin: W. M. Morrison Books, 1987.
275,[5]pp. Cloth. New index. Limited to 100 copies.

Although basically a scissors and paste job, this is still a valuable
work on the Republic of Texas. The book was written by a Presbyterian
preacher who visited Texas in 1839-1840, the Rev. A. B. Lawrence,
who also wrote the introduction. This attribution is verified by another
Presbyterian clergyman, William Y. Allen, who wrote a series of
reminiscences when he was an elderly man covering his days in Texas
during the period 1838 to 1842. They were published in the *Texas
Presbyterian* between 1876 and 1885. In the issue for December 20, 1878
(vol. III, no. 43), Allen made the following statement: "In 1839, while
the . . . Congress of Texas was in session in Houston, the Rev. A.
Lawrence, editor of the *New Orleans Presbyterian,* and a gentleman
named Stille, a publisher of Philadelphia, came to Houston. They
wished to get up a history of the Republic. They asked for the use of
my room, a shanty on the edge of the town, for three or four days.
Lawrence put into writing what meagre information each of them had
picked up by inquiries among the people, as they happened to meet
them. And, lo! a history of Texas! the result of four days writing, and
the authors were off, Lawrence to his tripod in New Orleans, and
Stille to publish the little work in Philadelphia. I do not think I ever
saw it after it left my room in manuscript."

It is obvious from the content that the book was not written in four
days, and I believe Lawrence, with or without Stille, probably wrote
the book in Austin before leaving Texas. The volume includes on
pages 29-80 Lawrence's diary, January 1-25, 1840, of his tour from
Galveston and Houston through Washington-on-the-Brazos, Ruters-
ville, La Grange, and Bastrop to Austin, where he made an extended
visit. The description of Austin is detailed and one of the most
extensive given in any contemporary work. The view of the new
capital is the earliest visual record of the town. While there, Lawrence
preached a sermon in the new frame capitol and baptized Vice
President David G. Burnet's son. He interviewed Burnet (to whom

the book is dedicated) and others in Austin, the most extensive interview being with Gen. Edward Burleson. Much of the material in the book relating to Indian campaigns and the outlying territories unquestionably came from Burleson.

About 200 pages of the text are devoted to chapters on the physical nature of Texas, agriculture, geology (of which Lawrence appears to have had more than a passing knowledge), flora and fauna, cattle and other livestock, ornithology and entomology, and religion. There are chapters on towns and areas not personally visited, as well as a rather perceptive but preacher-like chapter entitled "Inhabitants, Manners and Society." Lawrence, like so many others, defends Texas against all charges: "It has been objected to Texas that it was the common receptacle of thieves, murderers and criminals of every description. . . . That fugitives from justice have frequently made this country their city of refuge is undoubtedly true; but that they are numerous or possess influence here is entirely a mistake." Of the scientific sections, Sister Agatha states: "Many chapters are pithy in style and valuable. . . . The author was not ignorant of science, and from the geological, zoological, and botanical points of view the book is worthwhile as an addition to scientific materials on Texas."

Lawrence gives advice to prospective immigrants and maintains that he himself plans to settle in Texas, although he never did. Who the man Stille was is unknown, although C. J. Stille the future historian from Philadelphia had just graduated from Yale, and possibly he or one of his large family was visiting Texas at the same time as Lawrence. Raines, Sabin, and Howes assert incorrectly that G. A. Scherpf's 1841 account of Texas is little more than a translation of Lawrence. Actually, Scherpf was with Lawrence on his tour to Austin, and includes "Abbreviated Excerpts from the Diary of a Fellow Traveler of the Author in 1840 from Houston to Austin" in an appendix. This excerpt is indeed an extract from the Lawrence book, but the rest of Scherpf's volume bears little resemblance, in form or substance, to Lawrence's *Texas in 1840*.

Agatha, p. 23. Adams Herd 2276. Clark III-248. Field 895. Howes L154. Raines, p. 203. Sabin 95091. Streeter 1361.

121   Lea, Tom (1907-   )

THE KING RANCH.

Boston and Toronto: Little, Brown and Company, [1957].

Research [by] Holland McCombs. Annotations [by] Francis L. Fugate. Maps and Drawings by the Author.

Two volumes: [10],467,[2]; [10],[469]-838, [3]pp. 43 drawings. 11 facsimiles. 24cm.

Cloth, boxed. In first printing, page 507 begins "Alice . . . ." In all later printings it
᾿ begins: "For Alice . . . ."

Other issues:

(A). Limited edition. Kingsville, Texas: Printed for the King Ranch, 1957. Same collation. Colophon at end of the first volume: "This book was designed, printed and bound in Texas by the photo-offset process; plates and presswork by Guynes Printing Company . . . Typography by Carl Hertzog of El Paso, chapter titles designed by the author. Binding by Universal of San Antonio." Colophon at end of the second volume: "This book was designed, printed and bound in Texas. Three thousand copies have been produced by the photo-offset process . . . the all-rag paper was made especially for this book by the Curtis Paper Company and watermarked with the [Running W] brand. The cover is a facsimile of the saddle blankets woven and used on the King Ranch. . . ." Bound in heavy crash linen, in slipcase with leather label.

(B). Variant of (A), with Carl Hertzog's name on the title page, the same size as that of Fugate. Twelve copies were done thusly, but a controversy arose over the matter, and Hertzog removed his name.

(C). Same as first trade edition, later printings. The 2nd through 4th printings have no printing notice. From the 5th printing on, the printing is designated on the verso of the title. The colors used on the spines vary in shade.

(D). Special issue of the trade edition with special printed leaf reading "This edition is especially printed for the friends of Sami S. Svendsen, 407 South Dearborn Street, Chicago 5, U.S.A. Selling agent . . . in animal casings and glands."

This is the best account of the most famous ranch in the world. William Reese called it "perhaps the most exhaustive ranch history ever written." Frank Goodwyn said that "in addition to being an encyclopedic compedium of information on the ranch, the book is also a work of art, not only because of Lea's drawings but also because of his literary style. . . . The writing has the sweep, the rhythm, and the ferver of an epic. . . . It should be owned by all who are interested in good cattle, good horses, good range management, good art, and good writing." Wayne Gard wrote that "to his laurels as an artist and a novelist, Lea has added equally green ones as a historian."

Like Haley's *The XIT Ranch of Texas*, this book was instigated and paid for by the owners of the ranch; Lea, however, was given a free hand. The research for the book was partly done by Holland McCombs, and the sixty-six pages of footnotes were prepared by Frances L. Fugate. Lea and Carl Hertzog planned from the beginning of the project how the book would look. Hertzog later wrote: "We did not go to Kingsville to begin the project. We went to Brownsville and spent three days there." They first went out into the mouth of the Rio Grande "to see the country the way Capt. King did, in the same sequence." They went up the river to Rio Grande City and vicinity and only then made their way up to the southern tip of the ranch. "Bob Kleberg met us there at a cow camp lunch. This was no Hollywood scene. The vaqueros had greasy chaps and were unshaven. I think Tom's idea to visit the country the way Richard King did helped him to capture the feeling and the flavor of what went on a hundred years ago."

The first volume consists of a biography of Richard King, and contains the best of Lea's writing. It records the gradual development of the ranch empire from 1853 through all the troubles with the Civil War, outlaws, and cattle thieves. The second volume records the history of the ranch in the 20th century up to 1953. This part of the narrative contains a bit too much eulogizing and is painfully prosaic, but begins to flow again as Lea tells of Bob Kleberg's innovations in recent times. Some of the meatiest parts of the work are in the nineteen appendices, which include numerous original documents relating to King Ranch history and related subjects, such as game conservation, race horses, oil development, breeding techniques, and an account of the ranch's branches in Australia, Cuba, and Brazil.

Lea manages to present the ranch owners' side of the story without stretching the truth; as Wayne Gard has pointed out, he "never lapses into distortion or fiction." Nevertheless, there are certainly differing viewpoints that can be held. Richard King, arriving nearly penniless in South Texas, built the greatest ranch in history in the middle of one of the most lawless parts of the world. Walter Prescott Webb once wrote: "If the Kings and Kenedys and Armstrongs did not put their brand on other people's stock, they are about the only cow people of the age who failed to do so."

The book was intended as a 1953 tribute to the centennial of the ranch, but the research and writing took several extra years, and the book was not released until 1957, after a condensation had appeared in *Atlantic Monthly* in two installments, the first being the cover story for April, 1957, the second appearing in May, 1957. Parts of the story also appeared in *Life Magazine* for July 8 and 15 of that year. No copies of the limited edition were ever sold, most being given away by the owners of the ranch, but John O. West in 1967 reported that 30,000 copies of the trade edition were sold in the decade following publication. The work won the Summerfield G. Roberts Award for the best Texas book of the year and numerous design awards.

Few, if any, Texas books have had such a perfect blend of text, design, and illustration. Lea and Hertzog took great pains on the project, and Hertzog said that "seldom do the illustrator and typographer have a chance to work together in developing a design where the type and drawing are developed as a unit. Generally they don't even know each other (and the author would seldom get into the act). Our close cooperation was unique and paid off, too." The results are stunning. Mary Lasswell said, for example: "The heading of Chapter XII is a drawing of a mesquite twig, feathery and shadowed . . . each ferny leaf in the negative was slit by hand with a razor blade to make the paper take the ink. . . . I would rather have drawn that piece of mesquite than to have written *Death Comes for the Archbishop*."

Adams Herd 1318-19. Hinshaw 114. Lowman, Hertzog 99. Reese *Six Score* 69.

122   Leclerc, Frederic (1810-1891)

LE TEXAS ET SA REVOLUTION.

Paris: Imprimerie de H. Fournier et Ce, 14, Rue de Seine, 1840.
104pp. Folding map. 22cm.
Printed wrappers.

Other issues:
(A). *Revue des Deux Mondes*. Paris: March 1-April 15, 1840. The introduction to the Fournier edition states that the text first appeared in this journal, but I have been unable to locate a copy.
(B). "Texas and Its Revolution," *Southern Literary Messenger*, Richmond, May & June 1841 (Vol. VII, nos. V and VI), pp. 398-421. Translated "by a Gentlemen of Philadelphia." First edition in English.

(C). *Texas and Its Revolution.* Houston: The Anson Jones Press, 1950. 148,[3]pp. Folding map. Smooth cloth. Translated with an introduction by James L. Shepherd III. Contains a notice at the end stating: "Of this first English edition . . . five hundred numbered copies have been printed, of which this is _____."

(D). Same as (C), but in a pebbled binding. Apparently a remainder binding from the same sheets.

Written by a young French physician, this slight volume contains astute reflections and observations on the Republic of Texas. C. W. Raines said that "there is reflected in the work the author's scientific attainments and political sagacity." James L. Shepherd observed that the "report lacks the poetic inspiration of Chateaubriand, but is on the other hand a thoroughly straightforward and workmanlike presentation of the facts, and it reveals keen insight into the life of the frontiersman, an awareness of the essentials of practical politics, and a true appraisal of the physical potentialities of the land. . . . [The text] is also the work of a thoroughly impartial and detached observer. A foreigner with no stake in the outcome of the issues involved, yet possessing a lively curiosity in the subject, the author was particularly well suited to undertake such a book."

Leclerc studied medicine as a youth and by the time of publication of his book had become "Doctor of Medicine of the Faculty of Paris, Chief Physician of the General Hospital of Tours, Member of the Society of Natural History of France, of the Entomological Society of France, &c." It is known that Leclerc was in Cincinnati in the summer of 1837 and that he arrived in Texas, for a nine-month tour in early 1838, visiting Galveston, Houston, San Felipe, Goliad, and San Antonio. His book is dedicated to President Mirabeau B. Lamar, apparently because of his French name, since Leclerc never met Lamar personally. Leclerc was back in France by January, 1839, to take up his post at Tours, where he served with acclaim until 1872. At that time he returned to the United States, dying in Bloomfield, New Mexico, in 1891.

Leclerc's historical material is sketchy and mostly made-up from Newell and other contemporary sources, but his observations on the physical and political scene are quite useful. He makes one of the best concise analyses of the Poinsett mission to Mexico, of which he states:

"The rumor which had spread through the United States in 1829 to the effect that negotiations were under way with Mexico for the cession of Texas, was well founded. Mr. Poinsett [as] representative of his country in the Mexican Republic, perhaps hoped to succeed in this difficult negotiation, thanks to his intimate relations with Zavala, who was the backbone of President Guerrero's administration, and with the *Yorkinos* party, which the revolution of the month of December, 1828, had brought to power. Zavala had himself first obtained some enormous land grants in Texas, and in order to give them some value, he must have desired that this province be transferred to the United States. [When Guerrero abolished slavery in Mexico in 1829], the American ambassador found himself in a most difficult position in Mexico. The Scottish party would never forgive him the revolution of December preceding. . . . The Democratic party . . . menaced the United States by the implications of its abolitionist stand. In both factions public opinion was instinctively outraged by the designs of the Washington cabinet on Texas, and it is probable that English influence had something to do with this unanimous manifestation of hostility toward the United States."

Leclerc obviously did not like Sam Houston, and mentions him only a few times in the text, including this comment on him in 1838: "His differences with the Congress over the handling of public lands and over the organization of the military, his lack of taste and lack of aptitude for the affairs of state, his unsoldierly deportment, and his undignified manners made people forget his former services."

The map, entitled "Carte du Texas," is quite good and contains considerable material compiled by Leclerc himself. It was also used the next year by Leclerc's publisher, Henri J. J. Fournel, in his own book, *Coup d' Oeil Historique et Statistique sur le Texas.* Fournel's work draws on that of Leclerc, and may in fact have been written by Henri Castro, thus presenting some interesting connections among the French Texanophiles.

The 1841 English version is incomplete and an inept translation. The 1950 edition is much better; E. W. Winkler says of it: "The format is dignified: a volume beautifully printed on excellent paper." On the other hand, I very much doubt the limitation notice, and have handled many copies with the limitation number not filled in.

Clark III-193. Howes L171. Leclerc 934. Monaghan 946A. Rader 2214. Raines, p.137. Sabin 39652. Streeter 1362.

123 Lee, Nelson (1807-)

THREE YEARS AMONG THE CAMANCHES: THE NARRATIVE OF NELSON LEE, THE TEXAS RANGER, CONTAINING A DETAILED ACCOUNT OF HIS CAPTIVITY AMONG THE INDIANS, HIS SINGULAR ESCAPE THROUGH THE INSTRUMENTALITY OF HIS WATCH, AND FULLY ILLUSTRATING INDIAN LIFE AS IT IS ON THE WAR PATH AND IN THE CAMP.

Albany: Baker Taylor, 58 State St., 1859.
xii,[13]-224pp. Portrait. 19cm.
Printed wrappers; also cloth. A Prospectus was issued, 12pp., with the caption-title "Truth is stranger than fiction." Bound copies sold for 75¢, paper for 50¢.

Other issues:
(A). Troy, New York, 1871. 240pp. Cloth.
(B). Same title, except "Comanches" spelled properly. Norman: University of Oklahoma Press, [1957]. xvi,179,[1]pp. 20cm. Boards. The Western Frontier Library, No. 9. Introduction by Walter Prescott Webb. Best edition.
(C). Same as (B), "Second Printing, September, 1967."

Besides drama and hair-raising excitement, this book offers the best contemporary description of the life of the early Texas Rangers, and one of the few surviving eye-witness accounts of the life and activities of the ferocious Comanche Indians. "During my minority," Lee comments, "I was remarkable for nothing I can recall, save a most hardy constitution and athletic frame, and an intense longing to rove out into the world." Seldom have a man's desires been so abundantly fulfilled. Lee became a raftsman on the St. Lawrence and Mississippi, fought in the Black Hawk War, chased pirates between Africa and Brazil under Captain Salters, sailed with the Texas Navy to Yucatan under Commodore Moore, joined the Texas Rangers under Jack Hays, fought at Plum Creek and many other Indian fights, participated in the Battle of Salado and Mier Expedition, served with Hays under Taylor and under Scott in the Mexican War, captured and herded mustangs, was captured by the Comanches, and spent three terrifying years as their captive and slave.

The editor states that the text was recorded, "as received from his lips, from day to day, not precisely in his own words, inasmuch as he is not an educated, though an intelligent man, but his history is told substantially as he relates it." Since Lee returned from his escape to the United States on November 10, 1858, the book was prepared with surprising alacrity, and that portion of the narrative dealing with his recent captivity is particularly vivid. On numerous occasions Lee's own vernacular creeps into the narrative. He sometimes gets his "risibles" up and in a chase "distances" his pursuers. Proper name spellings come from Lee's frontier accent: Panta Clan for Lipantitlan, Beremindo for Veramendi, Sevilla for Cibolo, etc. After describing an affray in which he shot a fourteen-foot alligator, Lee comments that he felt great satisfaction in knowing that it "would frighten the wits out of a poor devil no more forever."

Of the fifteen chapters, the first brings Nelson Lee to Texas, seven contain his adventures in the Republic of Texas and Mexican War, and seven tell of his Indian captivity. The accounts of the Texas Ranger service, Mier Expedition, and Mexican War are generally accurate, always fascinating, and add considerably to our knowledge of those events. Inexplicably, his account has been overlooked by historians. Walter P. Webb in his introduction to the reprint states: "There is no better description of the life of the Texas Ranger than that by Nelson Lee." Yet in his great *The Texas Rangers*, written some twenty years earlier, he fails to mention or quote Lee at all. Joseph M. Nance, whose *Attack and Counter-Attack* is the most significant modern work on the early Ranger fights and Mexican troubles, tells several of Lee's encounters, quoting a secondary source, but misquoting Lee, giving him the name John Lee and failing even to include the work in his bibliography. Seymour V. Connor and Odie B. Faulk, in their *North America Divided: The Mexican War, 1846-1848*, offer a 766-item bibliography, but do not include Lee. This is all the more remarkable, as Lee's Mexican War activities were particularly pithy and significant. Perhaps the title of the book, and its general unavailability until 1957, contributed to this.

Lee calls the Texas Rangers "a military order as peculiar as it has become famous." He describes them picturesquely: "The qualifications necessary in a genuine Ranger were not, in many respects, such as are required in the ordinary soldier. Discipline, in the common acceptation of the term, was not regarded as absolutely essential, a power of endurance that defied fatigue, and the faculty of 'looking through the double sights of his rifle with a steady arm,'—these distinguished the Ranger, rather than any special knowledge of tactics. He was subjected to no 'regulation uniform,' though his usual habiliments were buckskin moccasins and overhauls, a roundabout and red shirt, a cap manufactured by his own hands from the skin of the coon or wildcat, two or three revolvers and a bowie knife in his belt, and a short rifle on his arm. In this guise, and well mounted, should he measure eighty miles between the rising and setting sun, and then, gathering his blanket around him, lie down to rest upon the prairie grass with his saddle for a pillow, it would not, at all, occur to him he had performed an extraordinary day's labor. The compensation received from government at that time was one dollar a day. . . ."

Nelson Lee, like so many frontiersmen, had little use for Sam Houston. After Gen. Adrian Woll invaded San Antonio in 1842, the public demand was great for an expedition to meet and defeat the Mexicans on their own soil, ultimately leading to the Mier Expedition. Lee writes: "President Houston, though apparently yielding to the popular demand, was, nevertheless, at heart, opposed to the project. I rest this statement principally on the fact that about this time I was sent by Jack Hays with dispatches to the Executive, then at Washington-on-the-Brazos, informing him of the recent movements of the Rangers, and of the general feeling of the inhabitants in the west. Houston sent me forward to Galveston with instructions to the authorities to prevent volunteers joining the expedition, and ordering them to repair the defenses in the vicinity of that city. Notwithstanding these instructions, however, when my mission was fulfilled and I departed on my return to San Antonio, twenty of the citizens of Galveston accompanied me, among them Colonel Walton, the mayor of the town."

Lee participated in the Mier Expedition,* and fought in the Battle of Mier, but was not a Mier prisoner. "At the time of the surrender," he states, "myself and ten others had become separated from the main body. . . . The firing having ceased for some time, I sallied out, and

---

*Listed as a private in Capt. P. Y. Coe's company, 1st Regt., South Western Army, mustered in October 17, 1842 by Col. James R. Cook. (Muster roll, Sam S. Smith Papers, Texas State Archives.)

looking round a corner, saw our men marching into the square without arms. Running back, I informed by comrades that the troops had surrendered, but expressed, at the same time, the determination to die rather than go to a Mexican prison. Without lingering to deliberate upon the matter, I leaped out of the back window," and managed to escape. He suffered many hardships, returning alone, the first participant to reach San Antonio.

In 1844-46 Lee was a mustanger and cattle drover, driving his herds to Ft. Jesup in Louisiana for the American army: "On one of these occasions, having arrived with a considerable drove in excellent condition, as I supposed, a portly officer met me near the fort, gruffly demanding if it was my intention to poison the army of the United States by furnishing them such carrion, and without allowing me time to reply to the imputation, continued to heap upon me the' most violent epithets the English language afforded. I was so taken by surprise, and his abuse was so unmeasured and unreasonable, that I lost my temper, and placing my hand upon my pistol, threatened, unless he 'shut up,' to shoot him. Thereupon, he turned suddenly on his heel and walked away with a grin on his face, not exactly in consonance with the terrible wrath he had just exhibited. Presently Charley May approached me, inquiring what I had been about, saying General Twiggs had just sworn that that Texan cattle drover had no more sense than to shoot a man."

Joining Captain Walker's scouts under Jack Hays in 1846, he accompanied Walker enroute to Taylor's headquarters at Fort Brown at the time the American forces were surrounded by thousands of Mexicans, riding hell-for-leather straight through the amazed Mexican forces. Lee fought at the Battle of Monterrey: "In all my experience in war, I have seen nothing that could be compared with the long and terrible battle of Monterrey. . . . The ghastly corpses that filled its streets still haunt my sight, and the groans and shrieks and agonizing cries for water and for mercy of its dying and wounded men are still ringing in my ears." After Monterrey, Lee served under Hays on the long, gruelling march to join Scott in Mexico City. "Perhaps no body of men ever presented a rougher or more ridiculous appearance than we did on that occasion," Lee recalls of their entry into Mexico City.

The latter half of the book covers the period from March, 1855, to November, 1858. Leaving Matamoros with a drove of horses and mules, Lee and some others set out for California. On April 2, 1855, they were attacked by Comanche Indians. Lee was captured and lived with the Indians for three years. Leaving a tomahawk in the back of the head of his guard, he finally escaped and travelled alone for two months until he reached the settlements near El Paso. "It is his account of life among the Indians," wrote Webb, "that makes this book of unique value. The story he tells is absorbing, but the information he conveys about how the Comanches lived before they were affected by the white man is invaluable." It is a book, Webb said, that should be "welcomed by all lovers of such characters as Cabeza de Vaca, Huckleberry Finn, and the Ancient Mariner. They all had this in common: Each made a hard journey and returned home to tell about it." I might only add that the mighty Ulysses himself would contemplate Nelson Lee's exploits with awe.

John Chapman, in *Southwest Review* (Spring, 1958), claims the latter part of the book is a fraud, and that Lee's exploits are nothing more than "a typical piece of illiterate Western fiction." Moreover, that indefatigable scholar of the Comanches, Gaines Kincaid, maintains that much of what Lee says about the Comanches is fraudulent. Exactly where the truth ends and the fiction begins in Lee's narrative will unquestionably be debated for years to come.

Ayer 182. Dobie, p.34. Field 905. Graff 2444. Howes L212. Rader 2215. Sabin 39778. Wagner-Camp 334.

124 [Lehmann, Herman (1859-1932)]
Jones, Jonathan H.

A CONDENSED HISTORY OF THE APACHE AND COMANCHE INDIAN TRIBES FOR AMUSEMENT AND GENERAL KNOWL-EDGE, PREPARED FROM THE GENERAL CONVERSATION OF HERMAN LEHMANN, WILLIE LEHMANN, MRS. MINA KEY-SER, MRS. A. J. BUCHMEYER AND OTHERS.

San Antonio: Johnson Bros. Printing Co., 1899.
235pp. Illus. 22cm.
Cloth.
[Verso of title:] Copyright 1899 by Herman Lehmann.
[Cover title:] *Indianology.*

Other issues:

(A). Lehmann, Herman. *Nine Years Among the Indians, 1870-1879 . . . the Story of the Captivity and Life of a Texan Among the Indians.* Austin: Von Boeckmann-Jones Co., Printers, [1927]. x,235pp. Cloth. Frontis. and 8 plates. 19cm. Cloth, dustjacket. Edited by J. Marvin Hunter.

(B). Second edition of (A), revised. Austin: San Felipe Press, [Printed for Maurice J. Lehmann], 1971. x,264pp. 19cm. Cloth, dustjacket.

(C). *The Last Captive: The Lives of Herman Lehmann, Who Was Taken by the Indians as a Boy From His Texas Home & Adopted by Them; His Career as an Authentic Wild Warrior With the Apache & Comanche Tribes; His Subsequent Restoration to the Bosom of His Family & the Difficulties & Confusions Faced in Adjusting His Savage Training to A Civilized Society; His Experiences Carrying Him from the Time of the Scalping Knife To the Very Threshold of Our Atomic Age; Together With Verifying Accounts by Members of His Family and Others Who Shared Some of Those Extraordinary & Historical Events.* Austin: The Encino Press, [1972]. [2],xxi,[1],161,[1]pp. Illus. 26cm. Special edition, limited to 250 copies, "signed by the author" [A. C. Greene], bound in quarter morocco and slipcased. [Edited] by A. C. Greene.

(D). Same as above, first trade edition. xxi,[1],161,[1]pp. Illus. Printed paper boards, slipcased.

One of the most remarkable accounts of life among hostile Texas Indians, this is also one of the few surviving accounts of life in 19th century Texas from the Indian point of view. A. C. Greene said that "of all the captive narratives, I believe the finest story is Herman Lehmann's."

Lehmann was the son of a German pioneer family living on the far frontier in Mason County. He could not read or write, and spoke only German. In 1870, when he was ten years old, he was captured by an Apache raiding party. For eight years he lived with the Indians, and became an Indian so completely that when he was returned to his family in 1878, it had to be done by force. He rode with the Apaches, and later with a band of Comanches, on many raids against the white men, and killed and scalped many of them. Even after he returned to civilization, married, and had a family, Lehmann maintained contact with the Apaches who had adopted him so completely.

He was considered until his death a full member of the tribe, and received his share of the government land granted to the Apaches in Oklahoma. He was the last, or almost the last, white captive who was returned and live to tell of it. His story is the most fascinating narrative, in any of its versions, ever written about Indian life in Texas.

There are three versions of Herman Lehmann's story, all in the first person as though written by Lehmann himself. Actually, Lehmann never wrote a word of his story, although he told it verbally to the first two of his editors.

The first to appear was *A Condensed History*, which carried the title *Indianology* on its front cover and spine, and by which it is generally known. Published in 1899, *Indianology* was "prepared from the general conversation of Herman Lehmann" and others by Jonathan H. Jones. Judge Jones states that he had "a long association with Herman Lehmann" and that "it is a treat to listen to Herman's descriptions, and much of the spice of his personality is gone in writing what he tells." The Jones version is too full of Jones, however, and includes preposterous Victorian religious digressions and unrelated poetry that obviously never fell from the lips of Lehmann. A. C. Greene says of the Jones volume: "There is a certain charm to the effusiveness and digressions of Judge Jones in the 1899 edition. However, one also wearies of the tiresome string of prolixity and pietism which clogs it and the ridiculous pedanticism which, for example, has a wild Apache warrior turning to Herman, on the occasion of Herman's first sight of a buffalo, and saying, 'See alaman? Bos americanus!' Spanish we can accept, but Latin . . .?"

The second version, published 28 years later, was edited by J. Marvin Hunter, who states: "I have known Herman Lehmann personally and intimately for thirty-five years. When he was brought back from his captivity my father . . . was living at Loyal Valley, the home of Lehmann's mother." Hunter acknowledges the Jones publication, but states that his own version is more nearly "a true recital of facts" which "were related to me by the ex-captive, who, at this date, May 28, 1927, is with me and telling me of his harrowing and hair-raising experiences." The Hunter version is much more down-to-earth than that of Jones, but each has valuable material not in the other.

In my copy of the Hunter version there is an inscription by J. Marvin Hunter which reads: "Written by me in 1926 for Herman Lehmann, who came and spent several weeks with me in Bandera, and gave me his experience while a captive among the Apaches and Comanches. Lehmann was illiterate, could not read or write, and in many ways expressed himself as an Indian. His nephew, Maurice J. Lehmann, financed the publishing of the book, and paid me for my work. After I delivered the completed manuscript to him and he sent it to the publisher, the title which I had given it was changed, and one paragraph (on page 93) was added, describing how flint arrowheads were made." This paragraph on arrowheads, added by Hunter, is inaccurate and unreliable.

Finally, in 1972, A. C. Greene issued a version combining the two earlier versions as well as other accounts of Lehmann into a single narrative. Greene's version is a triumph of editing and scholarship. In spite of the obvious problem of trying to present a trustworthy narrative from two versions edited by men who had let their own personalities and preconceptions intrude, Greene pulled off the seemingly impossible. In his version we clearly hear the story as Lehmann probably told it. Greene does not put words into Lehmann's mouth; he erases the extraneous inserts of the two other versions. At the end of each chapter, Greene analyzes the previous text, compares the previous versions, introduces supporting material from other sources, and offers cogent commentary.

Greene only falters when he is dealing with unfamiliar ground in Texas history, such as his description of the Tonkawa Indians, whom he says the white men despised and whose language was lost. Actually, the Tonkawas were the closest of all tribes in friendship with the Texans, were treated kindly by them, and were nearly annihilated not by the whites but by other Indian tribes who hated them for their friendship with the Texans. There is an excellent dictionary and grammar by Harry Hoijer, *Tonkawa: An Indian Language of Texas* (New York: Columbia University Press, 1933).

Greene has done a masterful job of extracting the genuine Lehmann from the two other versions, and in Greene's narrative one can sense

Lehmann's singular sense of humor. For example, speaking of his capture, Lehmann says: "Between the two Indians, I was quickly overcome. . . . They gave me a sling [over a rock fence] and my face and brest plowed up the rocks and sand on the other side." They then tied him to a wild pony: "I screamed and the pony reared. I was afraid of him and he shied from me, and by a continuity of effort we stayed apart and baffled the Indians' skill, patience and strength. The pony fought and so did I, and confusion reigned for awhile."

The major significance of the Lehmann story is that it gives us a clear and virtually unique insight into the Indian warfare in Texas as it was perceived by the Indians, and into every aspect of Plains Indian culture and daily life. Lehmann became an Indian in thought and in deed. He slept with many Indian women and tells about it—at least as frankly as possible for 1899 and 1927. Greene states: "Herman is not just another frontiersman with an adventure story, but a frank, free and naive spirit—a truly unusual personality—Herman has another virtue which is not always present in early Texas memoirists. He is honest. He is not infallible—the Indians win a suspiciously large number of times when they engage in battles with the whites—but he is not reluctant to cast himself as a murdering, scalping redskin. He does not attempt to appear heroic at any time."

Lehmann tells without embarrassment of the first time he killed a white man: "I shot him through the heart with an arrow and he fell dead instantly. . . . I took my knife, made an incision all around . . . and the scalp came off with a report like a pop-gun. Soon his bloody scalp was dangling at my belt, and I was the proud recipient of Indian flattery." Of another raid, he says that "it was but the work of a few seconds to kill and scalp the man and woman and a little baby." One night he crept into Fredericksburg and watched men drinking in a saloon, but after stealing their horses he returned to his tribe.

Lehmann completely blocked out his white past from his conscience, and could not recognize his mother or understand German when he was forced to return home. When he finally recognized his brother and sister, he says "the dark curtain of oblivion which had been drawn so long began pulling back and to me there began coming some recollection of my early childhood." The story he tells of his problems readjusting is almost as fascinating as the story of his life with the Indians. It was several years before he "began to understand that everyone was not my enemy."

The Jones and Greene versions include short narratives told by Herman's brother and mother. The mother's account is in itself a valuable document of frontier life. In one instance, she recounts with seeming nonchalance a tale about Herman when he was a small child that tells us a great deal about life on the frontier and about Herman Lehmann as well. She told him and his little sister, she says, that the rattles of a rattlesnake, when worn in a bonnet, would ward off headaches. A few days later he and his little sister presented her with an enormous set of rattles. When she asked where they had killed such a large snake, he replied that they had not been able to kill it, so he held it down while his little sister cut the rattles off.

Campbell, p.86. Dobie, p.34. Graff 2246. Howes J232. Rader 2122.

125   Lehmann, Valgene W.

FORGOTTEN LEGIONS: SHEEP IN THE RIO GRANDE PLAIN OF TEXAS.

El Paso: Texas Western Press, The University of Texas at El Paso, [1969].
Topography and design by Carl Hertzog.
xv,[3],226pp. Maps. Charts. Illus. 24cm.
Cloth, dustjacket.
2000 copies printed.

Other issues:
(A). Same, limited edition of 300 numbered copies, bound in natural hopsacking with a sheepskin spine, slipcased, signed by Lehmann and Hertzog.

This is the most thorough study of the history and development of the sheep industry in South Texas. Actually, its title is misleading, because it encompasses a detailed study of the economic history of the cattle and horse industry and an ecological study of the Rio Grande Plain as well. James T. Bratcher called it "a history of grazing on the Rio Grande Plain, discussing what kinds of animals have grazed the region, for how long, and with what effects."

Lehmann spent his entire career in wildlife management in Texas, including service with the U.S. Biological Survey and the Texas Game,

Fish, and Oyster Commission. At the time of publication, he had
served for 24 years as wildlife manager of the King Ranch. Under his
direction, the ranch soon had more native game than any comparable
area in North America. He conducted pioneer research in game
preservation. His work on *Forgotten Legions* encompassed a number of
years, as shown by the correspondence and four drafts of the original
manuscript, all of which are in my personal collection. James T.
Bratcher and Wilfred D. Webb, among others, assisted in preparing
the final draft. The book was several years just in the printing stages,
but the result was a beautiful book. When he finally finished work on
it, Carl Hertzog said, "I'd walk a mile to kick a sheep."

Lehmann pierces a number of misconceptions about cattle and sheep
in South Texas. His study includes extensive research into the Spanish
period, the 19th century cattle and sheep boom, and present-day
problems. He states that wild cattle, sheep, and horses were never as
numerous as has been heretofore assumed, not even after the Civil
War. On the other hand, he shows that extensive herds of cattle and
sheep were maintained during the Spanish period, and that more, and
longer, cattle and sheep drives occurred during that period than during
the heyday of the late 19th century.

His comparisons of the 19th century cattle and sheep businesses are
astonishing. He shows that most of the men who founded the great
cattle ranches started with sheep, that more sheep were driven north
out of South Texas than cattle, and most surprising of all, that there
were more sheep in South Texas at times than there were horses and
cattle combined. "By conservative estimate," he states, "fifteen million
sheep [were driven north] in the great sheep trail era." At the same
time, only five million cattle were driven north. Moreover, only
fourteen percent of the cattle came from south of the Nueces River
and only ten percent of the cattle drives.

The cattle business declined dramatically in the 1890's, then began
to recover. The sheep business was utterly wiped out. In 1882, there
were over two million sheep in the South Texas area; in 1900, there
were two hundred thousand. "For all practical purposes the Rio
Grande Plain contained no sheep at all in 1959. It has virtually none
today." The reasons for the decline of the sheep and cattle business
are the chief subjects of Lehmann's study, along with his recommen-

dations for the future. In this respect, his book is a landmark contribution.

The primary cause was overstocking, but Lehmann provides many new insights into the exact nature of, and reasons for, this overstocking. He shows that the region was initially better suited by nature for sheep than cattle, and that sheep were actually more profitable than cattle. Men like Mifflin Kenedy recognized this and ranched sheep extensively. Eventually, the ranchers simply created a supply of sheep far greater than the land could bear, and "left scars on the land which remain as problems for this and future generations." Cattle gradually did the same. The result was a complete "change in the economic capabilities of the Rio Grande Plain."

Lehmann brings under close scrutiny the efforts to alter the natural ecology of the region in this century. The natural grasses of the region, never as extensive as has been believed, were depleted by overgrazing, which resulted in the creation during the 19th century of the thick brushlands, the chaparral of today. These are being converted by modern methods into extensive grasslands. Lehmann maintains that this has been overdone, and that the region can never maintain the extensive cattle herds that it once did, or that ranchers in the region expect.

Throughout the book, Lehmann provides not only the requisite statistics and history, but gives a fascinating picture of life on sheep ranches in each era. When the text was nearly ready for publication, he discovered an extensive unpublished correspondence from a sheep ranch in the 1880's. These letters, from Walter W. Meek of Las Hermanitas Ranch near San Diego, Texas, were included in a lengthy appendix. Written by a literate, observant man, they present perhaps the best picture of Texas sheep ranching other than possibly George W. Kendall's *Letters from a Texas Sheep Ranch.*

Lowman 242. Reese *Six Score* 72.

126 Lester, Charles Edwards (1815-1890)

SAM HOUSTON AND HIS REPUBLIC.

New York: Burgess, Stringer & Co., 222 Broadway, Corner of Ann St., 1846. [Verso of title:] S. W. Benedict, Ster. & Print., 16 Spruce Street, N. Y.

PRICE, 50 CENTS.

HOUSTON
AND
HIS
REPUBLIC

BY C. EDWARDS LESTER.

New York:

BURGESS, STRINGER & CO.,

222 Broadway, corner of Ann Street.

1846.

208pp. 23cm. Engraved portrait.
Printed wrappers.

Other issues:

(A). *The Life of Sam Houston (The Only Authentic Memoir of Him Ever Published)*. New
     York: J. C. Derby. 119 Nassau Street; Boston: Phillips, Sampson & Co.,
     Cincinnati: H. W. Derby, 1855. xi,[1],[13]-402pp. Illus. Maps. 18cm. Cloth. First
     complete edition. No author listed.

(B). Reprint of (A). Philadelphia: G. G. Evans, 1860. Same collation. 19cm. Cloth.

(C). Reprint of (A). Philadelphia: Davis, Porter, & Coates, 1866. Same collation.
     19cm.

(D). Reprint of (A). Philadelphia: J. E. Potter & Co., 1867. Same collation. 19cm.

(E). Reprint of (D). Same imprint and collation, dated 1867 on verso of title.

(F). *Life and Achievements of Sam Houston, Hero and Statesman*. New York: Hurst and
     Company, [1883]. 242pp. Frontis. 19cm. Cloth, Stamped "Arlington Edition."
     Title page has C. Edwards Lester as author. Includes a 5-page introduction by
     Lester acknowledging the authorship of the previous editions.

(G). Reprint of (F). New York: J. B. Alden, 1883. Same collation. 15cm. On cover:
     "Elzevir Library."

(H). *The Autobiography of Sam Houston*. Norman: University of Oklahoma Press,
     [1954]. xviii,298pp. Illus. 24cm. Cloth. Edited by Donald Day and altered from
     third to first person.

(I). Facsimile of (A). Freeport, New York: Books for Libraries Press, [1972]. Same
     collation. 23cm. Cloth.

This is the first biography of Sam Houston, in large part autobio-
graphical. Controversial since the day of its issue, it is still one of the
basic sources for information on the life of Houston. As soon as
Houston arrived in Washington in 1846 as United States Senator from
Texas, speculation began that he would soon become President. Ashbel
Smith continually urged Houston to run, and beat the drums in his
behalf. Houston himself seems to have quietly begun preparations,
and Smith convinced him to hire someone to prepare a biography.
The Lester volume is the result.

The man they hired was, in the words of Marquis James, "a fluent
hack named Charles Edwards Lester, a cousin of Aaron Burr." Lester
later described what took place. "It happens as follows: I first met
Sam Houston in the winter of 1845-46 at Washington, where he had
come on from Texas after [annexation] . . . Texas came into the Union
December 21st, 1845, and General Houston and Rusk took their seats
as the first Senators from the new State. They established their

quarters at the National Hotel, having under their charge the archives of Texas. . . . It was at this time that fortune favored me with an acquaintance with General Houston, which soon ripened into an intimacy that lasted till his death. Having then but recently returned from Italy on leave of absence, after several years' consular service, and having felt a deep interest in the career of General Houston . . . I was invited to write an historical record on the subject, and every facility was offered for the preparation of such a work. The chief leader, and most of the surviving actors—soldiers and statesmen—of Texas were in Washington, ready to lend their aid, while free access was had to the official archives, which furnished complete authentication for every statement and event considered necessary or desirable. I had, besides, the constant and invaluable assistance of General Houston, in whose private room the record was prepared without the intermission of an entire day during the succeeding three months. It was published shortly afterwards, under the title of *Sam Houston and His Republic*. . . . Some years later, I continued the record of Houston's public life [in a later edition]."

In Texas, the book was a sensation. Houston's enemies howled at the title, and the Senator seems overall to have lost rather than gained support as a result. Mirabeau B. Lamar wrote: "*His* republic! That is true. . . . I can regard Texas as very little more than *Big Drunk's* big ranch." David G. Burnet began immediately to prepare a rebuttal; he wrote to a friend: "I have some idea of answering some of its misstatements and in order to do so am anxious to collect all the facts possible relating to the campaign of '36. The book is full of falsehood— every *truth* is turned upside down." He bemoaned Houston as "the prince of Humbugs," and detailed errors, exaggerations, and what he called outright lies. No one seems to have doubted that Houston had himself written the book.

In 1851, Lester, who had become a sort of unofficial press agent for Houston, wrote Houston that the 1852 nomination would be "between you and Douglas. . . . It is necesssary for you to shew youself throughout the United States." About the same time an anonymous pamphlet appeared, printed by J. T. Towers in Washington, entitled *Life of General Sam Houston,* obviously derived from the Lester volume. I reprinted this in 1964, dating it circa 1855. This was an error on my part, however, for in 1852 David G. Burnet published *Review of the Life of Gen. Sam Houston, as Recently Published in Washington City by J. T. Towers* (Galveston: News Power Press Print, 1852), in which he details his objections to both the Towers pamphlet and the Lester book, saying that every long-time Texas resident knew that "the *hero* of the tale was virtually the *author*." The Towers pamphlet, he said, is but a repetition of the same falsehoods and the same absurd distortions of character."

By 1855, Houston was a genuine contender for the presidency. Lester revised his book and issued an enlarged edition, with no author listed, under the title *The Life of Sam Houston (The Only Authentic Memoir of Him Ever Published)*. Through page 262, this edition with few exceptions is a word-for-word reprint of the 1846 volume. The remainder of the volume covers his senatorial career, ending with an address from a political committee nominating Houston for the presidency. My copy of this edition belonged to Moses Austin Bryan, with his pencilled comments on passages concerning events at which he was present, particularly during the Texas Revolution.

The 1855 text was reprinted a number of times, and in 1883 was reissued with Lester shown as author and with an introduction by him acknowledging authorship of the previous editions. In 1954, a peculiar volume was published under the title *Autobiography of Sam Houston,* edited by Donald Day and H. H. Ullom. The editors reprinted the Lester text, changing it from third to first person, and interlaced it with excerpts from the *Writings of Sam Houston.* Joe B. Frantz wrote of this travesty: "This book has little excuse for existence. . . . Why did the authors bother to do it, and more insistently, why did a press of the prestige of the University of Oklahoma ever publish it?" These questions remain unanswered.

The Lester book gives much information on Sam Houston, but is only as reliable as the average 19th century political biography, which is to say, it must be used with extreme care. In 1884, William Carey Crane wrote *Life and Select Literary Remains of Sam Houston of Texas* (Philadelphia: J. B. Lippincott, 1884, 672pp). This was admittedly written at the request of Houston's widow, with the "positive injunction" that he include "at least one chapter setting forth Gen. Houston's religious character." Except for anecdotes and information supplied by the Houston family and friends, this volume is mere idolatry. Crane says that "Mrs. Houston having informed me that Gen. H. had told her that Lester's book was the only reliable account of him then written, I have taken his statements without question, and often used his language."

In 1891, an Englishman named Henry Bruce issued another biography of Houston, stating that "no life of Houston has hitherto been published which is not either imbecile or occasionally dishonest." This book, *Life of General Houston, 1793-1863* (New York: Dodd, Mead, 1891, 232pp.), points out the prejudices of Lester's work but adds little to our knowledge of Houston.

The first attempt at an objective biography is Alfred M. Williams, *Sam Houston and the War of Independence in Texas* (Boston: Houghton, Mifflin, 1893, 405pp). Williams tries to write without prejudice, but accepts too much tradition as fact. Finally, in 1929, Marquis James published his superb biography, followed in 1954 by Llerena Friend's perceptive analysis of Houston. One other biography of value has been written about Old Sam: M. K. Wisehart's *Sam Houston, American Giant* (Washington: Robert B. Luce, 1962, 712pp.), a dry, factual account that is for the most part reliable.

Howes L271. Rader 2221. Raines, p.225. Sabin 40229.

127   Linn, John Joseph (1798-1885)

REMINISCENCES OF FIFTY YEARS IN TEXAS.

New York: Published for the Author, D. & J. Sadlier & Co., 31 Barclay Street. 1883. 369pp., plus errata slip pasted to p.369. 4 plates. The plate entitled "The Alamo" is actually a woodcut of Goliad Mission by Bross. Some copies have a slip pasted over the original cutline correcting it to read "Goliad." 18cm. Cloth.

Other editions:
(A).   Same title. Austin: The Steck Company, Original Narratives of Texas History and Adventure. 1935. [2],369pp. 22cm. Cloth. Exact facsimile except for additional title leaf. Does not correct the Alamo error.
(B).   Facsimile reprint. Austin: State House Books, 1986. Cloth. New index.

This volume of personal recollections, written by an early Texas pioneer leader, is one of the basic sources on the revolutionary period.

The book was actually ghost-written for the 85-year-old Linn by his old friend Victor M. Rose, but Linn's thoughts and frontier philosophy are predominant throughout. I think Dobie's comment that the book is written "with energy and prejudice" is misleading, as is Walter Campbell's splendid cop-out: "The author is a man of decided opinions and outspoken." I find Linn to be outspoken but not opinionated, and to be far more accurate and less prejudiced than many of the more important figures of the times—than Houston, Anson Jones, and Burnet, to name a few. Linn's appraisal of Sam Houston, for example, hits closer to the truth than most other contemporaries.

Only occasionally does the writing become ponderous, and then quaintly so. Linn remarks that the 1833 Texas statehood memorial presented by Austin to Santa Anna "met no favor at the hands of the ambitious chieftain, who caused General Austin to be arrested and thrown into prison. Here the Father of Texas languished in durance vile until September, 1835." But most of the time the book is written with considerably more frankness, more gusto, and less cant than other writers of his generation.

Victor M. Rose's contribution to the book is indicated by a letter from Rose to John Henry Brown, August 11, 1889, now in possession of Dr. and Mrs. Malcolm D. McLean of Fort Worth, Texas. Rose writes: ". . . I was intimate with him from my earliest recollection to within a year or two of his death. I wrote his 'Fifty Years In Texas,' and had in my possession for weeks all his papers. . . ."

Linn states that his reminiscences "do not purport to be a history of Texas, but rather a narrative of the events connected therewith that passed under the immediate observation of the author." These events include his early merchant activities in the Victoria region, 1831-1834, the activities of the Consultation and General Council, the San Jacinto Campaign, an important interview with Santa Anna after the battle, various Indian fights and councils, and delightful anecdotes of famous Texas personalities, including Sam Houston, Stephen F. Austin, T. J. Chambers, the Whartons, Ira Ingram, Moseley Baker, Robert Potter, and Martin Parmer. About half of the volume consists of quotations and excerpts from other early figures, including: Guy M. Bryan on Austin's Colony (pp. 67-69), John McHenry on the Long Expedition of 1818 (pp. 69-76), David G. Burnet's Memorial to the Mexican

Congress in 1833 (pp. 77-96), excerpts from Juan N. Almonte's 1834 report on Texas (pp. 97-103), Reuben Potter on the fall of the Alamo (pp. 129-141), Col. Pedro Delgado on San Jacinto (pp. 225-246), and George Lord's excellent account of the Battle of Mier (pp. 313-320).

Linn was a native of Ireland who came to Texas as a merchant in 1830, opened a warehousing and general store business in Victoria, and founded the town of Linnville. He was alcalde and mayor of Victoria, served in the Consultation, was a member of the General Council, and as a member of the Convention of 1836 would have signed the Declaration of Independence but for the rapid advance of the Mexican Army, which prevented his leaving the exposed Victoria area. He was a quartermaster during the San Jacinto campaign, a Congressman during the Republic, and a leading businessman for over fifty years.

Agatha, pp.55-56. Bradford 3019. Campbell, p.98. Clark III-63. Dobie, p.57. Graff 2503. Howes L363. Rader 2239. Raines, p.139.

128   Lockhart, John Washington (1824-1900)

SIXTY YEARS ON THE BRAZOS; THE LIFE AND LETTERS OF DR. JOHN WASHINGTON LOCKHART, 1824-1900.

Los Angeles: Privately Printed, Press of Dunn Bros., 1930.
[Edited] by Mrs. Jonnie Lockhart Wallis in association with Lawrence L. Hill.
[14],336pp. 16 plates. 24cm.
Cloth. Limited to 200 numbered copies, signed by Mrs. Wallis, "printed for the relatives, descendants and friends of Dr. John Washington Lockhart."

Other issues:
(A). Facsimile reprint. New York: Published for University Microfilms by Argonaut Press, 1962. Same collation. 24cm. Cloth.
(B). Reprint of (A), 1966.
(C). Facsimile reprint. Waco: Texian Press, 1967. Cloth. New introduction by James M. Day.

This is one of the best sources for the social history of early Texas. Thomas Lloyd Miller said it "is important for the social history it gives of early Texas and its pioneers." J. Evetts Haley said: "I doubt if any recently published memoir contains a comparable wealth of human detail pertaining to the noted characters of early Texas. The book is rich not only in biographical intimacies, but also in its reflections of pioneer social history, and in anecdotes characteristic of the men, the life, and the temper of the day.''

The volume consists of a collection of essays written by Dr. Lockhart between 1893 and 1900 for the Galveston *News*, with some letters and other materials added. It also includes a poorly written biographical introduction by Mrs. Wallis, who lists herself as author on the title page. Fortunately, she appears not to have tampered much with Lockhart's text, stating that his ''style and construction, so characteristic of his time and background, have been faithfully retained.'' Since the two hundred copies produced were given away mostly to members of the family, the work was little known to scholars for many years. The *Southwestern Historical Quarterly*, for example, neither cites nor mentions Lockhart in any of its first fifty volumes, and there is no entry on Lockhart in the *Handbook of Texas* or its supplement.

Nevertheless, Lockhart was a prominent physician in his day, and a close associate of many leading Texans. For sixty years after 1839, Lockhart practiced medicine and ran a plantation in Washington County. He was a Confederate officer in the Civil War. He tells anecdotes relating to such friends as Sam Houston, Ashbel Smith, Jack Hays, Edward Burleson, Robert M. Williamson, David G. Burnet, and many others.

The volume also contains material on daily plantation life, camp meetings, pioneer medicine, steamboating on the Brazos, frontier religion, education, postal service, railroads, and Indian campaigns. Lockhart relates much reliable hearsay relating to the Texas Revolution and many eyewitness events of the Republic of Texas. Especially valuable are his account of a trip he made at Houston's request to treat with the Comanches and his lengthy account written three days after the Battle of Galveston describing that event.

Lockhart recounts many stories relating to court trials and lawyers of early Texas. His facts are sometimes confused as to exact dates and places, but his character studies are witty and perceptive. He tells, for example, of Judge R. E. B. Baylor of the Republic of Texas, and the cases before his court: ''Judge Baylor said that John Taylor reminded him of a man who had masticated and swallowed the dictionary, and afterwards swallowed an emetic. Such a downpour of beautiful words came from his throat that they were irresistible to a common jury.''

The volume is a prime source on Sam Houston. During his second presidency, Houston lived with the Lockharts when the Texas congress met at Washington-on-the-Brazos. Mrs. Lockhart was frequently "exasperated by the habit he had of spitting upon her clean porch floor, when by exerting no undue energy, and exercising a bit of consideration, he could have expectorated over the rail. To immaculate housekeepers, these old heroes were sometimes indeed trying. And yet she was glad to provide, at the General's request, a vast spread of huge hunks of beef and corn pone and hard boiled eggs for his horde of untamed blanket Indian guests, who swarmed about her generous tables, and disregarding the knives and forks, ate from their unwashed claws." Lockhart's papers are in the Rosenberg Library, Galveston.

Dobie, p.53. Howes W59.

129   Lowman, Albert Terry (1935-   )

PRINTING ARTS IN TEXAS.

[Austin:] Roger Beacham, Publisher, [1975].
Foreword by Stanley Marcus.
107,[2]pp. Illus. by Barbara Holman. 40pp. of plates. 35cm.
Cloth.
On colophon: ". . .Design & typography by William R. Holman. 395 copies printed by David Holman."

Other issues:
(A). Same as above, with colophon: "This is one of ten copies signed and specially bound for the author and is not for sale." Signed by Al Lowman, Stanley Marcus, Barbara Holman, David Holman, William R. Holman, and the binder, Ernest Brunner. Bound in morocco-backed vellum in a cloth slipcase.
(B). Same as above, with colophon: "This is one of fifty copies of the deluxe edition which has been signed and bound with hand marbled paper." Signed by Al Lowman, Barbara Holman, David Holman, and William R. Holman, numbered, and slipcased.
(C). First trade edition. [Austin:] Jenkins Publishing Company, [1981]. 107,[2]pp. 32cm. Cloth, dustjacket.
(D). Limited edition of (C), numbered, and slipcased. On colophon: "This is one of twenty-five copies which have been specially bound in natural cloth and signed by the author & designer."

This is the best history of fine printing in Texas. Itself a winner of numerous design awards, it is in the words of Jo Alys Downs "a visual and textual joy . . . a masterpiece." Jerry Bywaters called it

ANNOUNCING

An important Christmas publication

Printing Arts in Texas

BY AL LOWMAN

With a Foreword by Stanley Marcus

&

Illustrations by Barbara Holman

"the most complete history of our fine printing yet to be found. Al Lowman provides careful description and studied analysis of most of the best books published in Texas." Lee Milazzo said: "That sometimes neglected cultural area, the world of fine books, now receives its proper recognition in this magnificent collaboration by author Al Lowman and master printer William R. Holman. . . . This is a book to cherish." Tom Lea said its "content is as interesting as its format is handsome."

The volume is the joint production of the multitalented Holman family. Although *Printing Arts in Texas* would be on anyone's list of the ten most beautiful books printed in Texas, it is entered here not because of its craftsmanship but because of its text. Lowman, well-known for his affectionate and enthusiastic sponsorship of fine printing in Texas, discusses the history and development of the Texas printing arts and of "those remarkably gifted individuals who have combined inspiration, technique, and typographical taste to form books of exceptional beauty and harmony."

Stanley Marcus, in his Foreword, states: "Of course, I suppose there are those who will regard this attention to printed appearances as effete and unnecessary. Likewise a painting by Raphael might be thought superfluous to the business of common life. But the maker of a fine book is in fact aspiring to create something quite uncommon: a work of art which, by the subtle and harmonious combination of a good text and a pleasing format, can provide hours of pleasure in the appreciation of quiet beauty. For myself, I can only wish for more."

It is not difficult to wish for more when contemplating the craftsmanship of early books printed in or about Texas. The first book about Texas, Cabeza de Vaca's *Relacion,* says Lowman, "is surprisingly well printed." The work of the first printer in Texas, Samuel Bangs, is also well done: "Bangs' pride in his work and the high standard he maintained are evident in the surviving copies of his newspapers and broadsides." But most early printing relating to Texas was purely functional in nature. The first book printed in Texas, Stephen F. Austin's *Translation of the Laws, Orders and Contracts on Colonization,* was produced by Godwin B. Cotten on a crude handpress in San Felipe in 1829. The books that followed almost all showed signs of amateur or careless craftsmanship.

On the other hand, many early Texas books had printing features that made them stand out, even if sometimes in a negative sense. W. W. Heartsill's *Fourteen Hundred and 91 Days in the Confederate Army*, printed a page at a time on a novelty press over a two year period, is "probably the most unique book in the entire field of soldier narratives." Toward the turn of the century, the art of fine printing began to have true practitioners in Texas, beginning perhaps with Edwin B. Hill. Lowman describes this gradual development and discusses the work of each printer. The extraordinary and gifted work of Carl Hertzog, William D. Wittliff, and the Holmans is discussed in detail, as well as specific publications of Ed Bateman, Stanley Marcus, Bill Chiles, Dealy and Lowe, Bernhardt Wall, Jerry Bywaters, Kim Taylor, Jo Alys Downs, and even a few of the books of Jenkins Publishing Company. A bibliographical section at the end describes those books that Lowman discusses in the text, with a supplemental list of other fine printing in Texas.

130   Lubbock, Francis Richard (1815-1905)

SIX DECADES IN TEXAS; OR, MEMOIRS OF FRANCIS RICHARD LUBBOCK, GOVERNOR OF TEXAS IN WAR TIME, 1861-63. A PERSONAL EXPERIENCE IN BUSINESS, WAR, AND POLITICS.

Austin: B. C. Jones & Co., Printers, 1900.
Edited by C. W. Raines.
xvi,685pp. Illus. by E. Ilse. 16pp. of illustrations between pp.208 and 209. 24 cm. Morocco, gilt. Deluxe edition with a gilt star on front cover. An octavo printed announcement was sent out by Lubbock with a subscription form in 1899 offering the book at $2.00 in cloth and $2.50 in morocco.

Other issues:
(A). Regular edition, cloth.
(B). Facsimile reprint, with new title: *Six Decades in Texas: The Memoirs of Francis R. Lubbock, Confederate Governor of Texas*. Austin and New York: The Pemberton Press, 1968. [4],xvi,685,[8]pp. Illus. 22cm. Cloth. New introduction by Robert J. Helberg. [Half title:] Brasada Reprint Series, General Editor: John H. Jenkins. XVI.

When this interesting autobiography was published in 1900, its author had been in Texas for sixty-four years, during sixty-three of

which he had held some form of public office in his adopted state. His memoirs, prepared with the help of historian Cadwell W. Raines, are entertaining and forthright, full of humor and entirely lacking in vanity. Written in an era known for stilted, florid, overblown prose, Lubbock's pithy memoirs are a delight. As Sister Agatha has said, "for easy reading in Texas history, no book yet has surpassed *Six Decades*. . . . The account is so simple and modest a recital of the everyday matters that went to make up the life of a typical *leader* that it is irresistible. The style is admirably adapted to the form and the content. Governor Lubbock is frankness itself."

Lubbock's career in Texas began in 1836 at the age of twenty. He settled in the new town of Houston, where he became one of its first merchants. He immediately ran for mayor, narrowly losing to my great-great grandfather, James S. Holman. Lubbock was made a clerk in the First Congress of the Republic of Texas, then was appointed Comptroller of the new nation by Sam Houston. From this post he served successively as Harris County district clerk, lieutenant governor, governor, post-war tax collector, state treasurer, and parole board commissioner.

About 1895 he set out at his wife's insistence to write his memoirs. He states in the preface: "The man who has protested, from the writing of the first page to the last, that he could not write a book, has writ a book; and if there is anything of profit or pleasure in it for the people of Texas, they must attribute it, first, to my devoted wife, and second, to my able editor. The former tolled me along as a woman knows how to toll a man until she got volumes of manuscript from my memory dotted down by my rapid pen; the latter culled it to fill one volume of medium size." I have not been able to discover what happened to the original manuscript. Some of Lubbock's original correspondence relating to writing and publishing the memoirs passed through my hands some years ago; these are now in the Univeristy of Texas Archives.

Raines states that he received the manuscript notes in the spring of 1897. He moved into Lubbock's home and set to work to produce what he accurately judged would be one of the most important memoirs ever published in Texas. The task was completed in February, 1900, Raines stating that the finished product "makes no pretensions to

graces of style; it is simply a plain, unvarnished statement of facts
. . . in sturdy English.'' That was a wise choice, because it fit
Lubbock's own style of life and certainly his intentions regarding the
memoirs. Sister Agatha states that ''the nicest thing about Lubbock is
that nowhere do we get the impression that he is aware of his graces.
[He writes] in an easy, conversational style that is far from being
merely made-to-order.''

The historian Z. T. Fulmore praised ''the great charm of his
conversational powers, his wonderful memory. . . . Its value, as a
contribution to the history of Texas, consists mainly in the elaborate
background to the bare historical picture furnished by others, yet there
is enough new historic material to make it exceedingly valuable for
that alone.''

Lubbock also gives us one of the best accounts of business life in
early Texas. He literally sold the first barrel of flour and the first sack
of coffee in Houston. The memoirs are full of anecdotes and descriptions of the business activities of the early Texas merchant. Lubbock
remembers, for example, not only who he bought the lumber from
for his first store, but the size of the pine boards, how they were
milled, and what they cost. In this important regard, *Six Decades in
Texas* has often been overlooked.

During the Civil War, Lubbock served as Governor of Texas, but
resigned to get into the action. After serving in the Louisiana campaign
under Wharton, he became aide-de-camp to Jefferson Davis. He was
captured with Davis in May, 1865, and imprisoned with him. Lubbock
served eight months in solitary confinement before being released. It
is interesting to note that five of the authors in this guide were
imprisoned either in Fort Delaware or Fort Warren after the capture
of Davis: Adam R. Johnson, Joseph E. Johnston, William Preston
Johnston, John H. Reagan, and Francis R. Lubbock. His recollections
of the war years are the most extensive in the book.

Nevertheless, the sections relating to Lubbock's part in the Republic
of Texas are the most vivid and useful. Recalling the Indian raids into
Austin during Sam Houston's second term as President, Lubbock
writes: ''At nights I felt safer at my quarters than on the streets, and
you were pretty sure to find a Congressman at his boarding house
after sundown. Whether owing to the disappearance of the Indians or

not I will not say, but it is certain that our modern legislators travel around more at night than did their honorable predecessors.''

Agatha, pp.70-71. Dobie, p.52. Howes L542. Nevins II-196. Rader 2259. Raines, p.141.

131 McConnell, H. H.

FIVE YEARS A CAVALRYMAN; OR, SKETCHES OF REGULAR ARMY LIFE ON THE TEXAS FRONTIER TWENTY ODD YEARS AGO.

Jacksboro, Texas: J. N. Rogers & Co., Printers, 1889.
viii,[11]-319pp. 19cm.
Printed on pink paper.
Cloth.

Other issues:
(A). Facsimile edition. Jacksboro: Herald Publishing Company, 1963. Same collation except for one-page Preface by Leigh McGee. 20cm. Cloth.
(B). Facsimile edition. Freeport, N.Y.: Books for Libraries Press, [1970]. Same collation. 23cm. Cloth. Incorrectly states that the book was first published in 1888, even though the author's preface is dated Sept. 1, 1889.

This is the most lively and authentic account of cavalry life in West Texas after the Civil War. Col. Harold B. Simpson states: "Seldom will one find so much information on soldiering on the frontiers as in McConnell's book. It is easy to read and hard to lay down once it is started.''

McConnell was a private in the 6th U. S. Cavalry who arrived in Galveston with the Reconstruction occupiers in November, 1866. He served at Fort Belknap and Fort Richardson on the Texas frontier until 1871, then settled at Jacksboro, where Fort Richardson was located, becoming a prominent citizen. Throughout his service, he kept a journal from which he frequently quotes veratim. During this period he also issued a post newspaper, *The Flea,* from which he also quotes liberally. Of his period of service, he states: "At the time I am writing of, the 'Reconstruction' period was at hand; chaos was prevailing after the war, and somewhere about twenty regiments of regular soldiers were camping at over one hundred and seventy-five military stations in this great state.''

McConnell gives us the best surviving account of what it was like to be an ordinary cavalryman in occupied Texas as well as of life on the frontier outposts after the war. He does not at all glorify his officers or fellow soldiers; he reports on their heavy drinking, their general disorganization, their boredom, their thievery—neither with moral judgments nor with rationalization. In Austin, at Federal headquarters, for example, he wrote: "During the Christmas holidays [1866] drunkenness was prevalent, and desertions very numerous, and I began to have an insight into the thousand and one ways and means that a soldier will indulge to get whiskey."

He reports that in his initial march through Texas many members of his company traded off their equipment and even uniforms for whiskey. On this march, he writes, "cattle abounded in untold thousands, and as long as the ranchero did not catch us we could slaughter them with impunity. If we were 'caught up with' by the owners we referred them to the Lieutenant, who satisfied them with a voucher on the authorities at San Antonio; but in several instances Ahrberg . . . personated the officer in command, and gave a 'voucher' signed with a name unknown to the Army Register. . . ."

McConnell's acute insights into human nature appear repeatedly. Regarding the renowned Indian Chief Satanta, for example, he states: "The truth is, however, that neither Satanta nor Big Tree were either exceptionally bad or unusually distinguished above their fellows; in fact, they were not very prominent as chiefs in their tribe, but as they happened to be caught in the perpetration of this crime during the opportune visit of the General of the army [William T. Sherman], and were made examples of, as was proper, it is in order to depict them in the blackest of colors, and ascribe to them all the crimes in the Indian calendar, and all the savage traits in the superlative degree. They have at any rate achieved celebrity. . . ."

Like any military man in any branch of the service, McConnell thought little of those in other branches. Of the Texas Rangers in 1874, he writes: "These Rangers were tolerable Indian fighters, but most of their time was occupied in terrorizing the citizens and 'taking the town.' Shooting scrapes and rows between citizens, soldiers and Rangers in this year" became so frequent that the citizens in one town hired a marshal to fend them off.

He also gives an excellent description of Texas cowboys on a spree in Kansas after a cattle drive. There is an appendix by "W.W.W." entitled "Cattle Thieving in Texas," and another appendix by Robert G. Carter entitled "The Cowboy's Verdict" about the trial of Satanta.

Adams Guns 1393. Adams Herd 1380. Campbell, p.66. Dobie, p.52. Graff 2579. Howes M59. Rader 2280. Raines, p.142.

132   McKay, Seth Shepard (1888-   )

TEXAS POLITICS, 1906-1944: WITH SPECIAL REFERENCE TO THE GERMAN COUNTIES.

Lubbock: Texas Tech Press, 1952.
486pp.
Cloth.

This is one of the basic studies of early 20th century Texas. Eugene C. Barker described it as "notably objective and factual, giving no indication of the personal political leanings of the author. It is authoritatively documented. . . . Indeed, it might be regarded as suggestive listing of personalities and politics of the first half of the twentieth century for more detailed treatment. The author quotes a few pithy characterizations and arguments from the speeches of the campaigns, and the number of these could have been advantageously increased to lend popular reading interest to the volume had that been the purpose of the writer—which it was not." Lew Gould deemed it "still a valuable summary of major events in state affairs for the period it covers."

McKay's study is one of the earliest analyses of political forces at work in the present century, most previous works being by protagonists in the various movements or memoirs of participants. Like most works that break new ground, it provides more questions to be considered than conclusive answers. McKay is principally concerned with political campaigns for major offices and with the issues and personalities involved. It was the seminal study that laid the groundwork for a plethora of subsequent social science monographs that trace their roots to McKay. His study began as an attempt to analyze the attitudes and influences of the German elements in Texas, but became necessarily extended statewide. The first section relates to ten German counties in Texas, while the remainder relate more generally to the political races throughout the state, showing how German-Texan political beliefs gradually became less distinct from those of the rest of the population.

The volume is divided into six sections averaging four chapters each on the Ferguson era, the Moody-Neff era, the Ross Sterling campaigns, the Allred years, the O'Daniel era, and Texas politics during World War II. It is interesting to note that his bibliography includes fifty separate newspaper files and a number of unpublished dissertations, as well as official records and interviews—but only six published secondary monographs. Two of these are his own previous books: *Seven Decades of the Texas Constitution of* 1876 (Lubbock, 1942) and *W. Lee O'Daniel and Texas Politics,* 1938-1942 (Lubbock, 1944). McKay collaborated with Odie B. Faulk in a later summary of the era, *Texas after Spindletop,* 1901-1965 (Austin, 1965), a volume in Steck's Saga of Texas Series.

The volume is not as dry as Barker implies; the personalities of Texas politics during the era are so fascinating that many sections of the book are readable and even spicy. McKay's dry wit pops up when the reader is least expecting it, usually by letting the characters themselves do the talking. For example, McKay says in 1926 "Ferguson followed a plan of belittling the Moody candidacy, charging him with lack of experience, incompetency, and unfitness for office. On several occasions he referred to Moody as 'a candidate with nothing to recommend him save a lipstick, a new wife, and a big head.' In emphasizing the youth of his opponent, Ferguson read to one audience a record of the grades young Moody had made in school, whereupon Moody retaliated in his next address as follows: 'I have held three public offices in this state, and I have never been hauled before the bar or any court of justice for misconduct in any of them. . . . It may be that I have no peculiar qualifications for the office of governor, but at least I have never been forbidden by any court of impeachment from holding any office of honor, trust, or profit in Texas." When the election results in this race were in, Moody won by a large majority. McKay then drops, without comment, a tidbit about two notorious South Texas counties: "Duval County gave Moody 25; Mrs. Ferguson

1210. Starr County, however, gave Moody 1007 and Mrs. Ferguson only 3.''

133   McLean, Malcolm Dallas (1913-   ) [comp.]

PAPERS CONCERNING ROBERTSON'S COLONY IN TEXAS.

Fort Worth: Texas Christian University Press [through volume III]; and Arlington: The UTA Press, The University of Texas at Arlington, 1974-1986.
Thirteen volumes to date. Illus. Maps. 29cm.
Cloth.

This is one of the most comprehensive compilations of primary source materials on any area of Texas history. Ray Allen Billington called it a ''monumental work of modern scholarship'' and Lon Tinkle termed it ''a major event in Texas history scholarship.'' Leonard Sanders said that ''the value of such detailed primary historical materials to historians, biographers . . . and other researchers is simply beyond measure.'' R. Paul Cross said McLean ''has in essence opened up a rich new vein of source material which can prove invaluable.'' The work has won the Summerfield G. Roberts Award, the Cora H. Tullis Award, and numerous other citations.

Robertson's Colony embraced a 20,000-square-mile tract along the Brazos River north of the San Antonio-Nacogdoches Road. Granted in 1825 to a group from Tennessee known as the Texas Association, the colony began to be settled in 1830 under the direction of Sterling C. Robertson. In the early 1830's a bitter and divisive controversy ensued between the Robertson interests and those of Stephen F. Austin and Samuel May Williams, clouded by the Mexican attempts to halt Anglo-American colonization. Prior to McLean's work, so few contemporary materials were available that only an incomplete chronicle of the settlement and controversy could be attempted.

McLean, a direct descendant of Robertson, began assembling primary materials on the subject about 1939. When another descendant presented him with ''a black enameled tin box'' stuffed with original documents on the colony, he was enabled to begin assembling in earnest. McLean gradually became convinced that *The Austin Papers* were ''incomplete because of omission of almost everything touching

Announcing Volume VIII of the

PAPERS CONCERNING **ROBERTSON'S**

COLONY

IN TEXAS

VOLUME VIII
NOVEMBER, 1833,
THROUGH SEPTEMBER, 1834
ROBERTSON'S COLONY

COMPILED AND EDITED BY MALCOLM D. McLEAN

on the Austin-Robertson controversy." Certainly the McLean set is
the epitome of responsible scholarship, as it presents all evidence,
favorable to Robertson and otherwise, even as to his 1829 indictment
for murder as a result of a duel in Nashville with Edward Randolph.
With single-minded persistence, McLean and his wife pursued documentary evidence for several decades, and began publication of the
series, as yet incomplete, in chronological order. A total of fifteen
volumes is planned.

The set begins with documents dated in the 18th century relating to
the Robertsons; the ninth volume ends with March 20, 1835. Each
volume contains a detailed calendar, lengthy introduction, extensive
annotations, bibliography, and excellent index. The introductions, if
put together, comprise both a biography of Robertson and a history
of his colony. A major portion of the original Robertson Colony
Papers, once spread among a number of descendants, was purchased
in 1976 by the University of Texas at Arlington, and other portions
were donated to the same school by the McLeans and Ella Fulmore
Harlee. The published volumes include not only these but hundreds
of other documents from numerous sources, and are so broad in scope
that they include material of value on every aspect of Texas history
during the period of Anglo-American colonization.

The materials taken as a whole present the era of Anglo-American
colonization in a new and wider dimension. David J. Weber in *Journal
of American History* said that "McLean's work may alter our understanding of the process of American colonization of Texas. . . . Scholars
working in Texas or Western history in this period, then, avoid
consulting these volumes at their peril." McLean's interpretation,
through his introductory material and copious annotations, differs
radically from that of Eugene C. Barker and others. He challenges
the apotheosis of Stephen F. Austin, in the words of Margaret S.
Henson, "as the unselfish and saccharine founder of Texas." In this,
and in his presentation of the significance of the Robertsons in Texas
colonization, McLean has balanced the tables in Texas historical
writing previously so heavily tipped in Austin's direction.

134 Maillard, Nicholas Doran P.

THE HISTORY OF THE REPUBLIC OF TEXAS, FROM THE
DISCOVERY OF THE COUNTRY TO THE PRESENT TIME;

AND THE CAUSE OF HER SEPARATION FROM THE REPUB-
LIC OF MEXICO.

London: Smith, Elder, and Co., Cornhill, 1842.
xxiv,512,[2]pp., plus 16pp. adv. Folding map. 22cm.
Cloth.
[Verso of title:] William Tyler, Printer, Bolt-Court, London. [On page 512:] W.
Tyler, Printer, Bolt-Court, Fleet Street.

This is the most vitriolic denunciation of the Republic of Texas,
written with absolutely no regard for the truth. It is included here
because it comprises a compendium of everything bad that could be
claimed about Texas and Texans of those times. As Thomas W.
Streeter said, "it should be included in Texas collections as an example
of what can be said about Texas by one who hates it." Everett D.
Graff called it "Texas cut down to size—a difficult feat even in 1842,"
and Wright Howes deemed it "an antidote to the pro-Texan history"
of William Kennedy.

Maillard arrived in Texas in November, 1839, and was admitted to
the Texas bar in April, 1840. Andrew Forest Muir said Maillard
"located in Richmond, [Texas], where he acquired a reputation as a
mixer of excellent drinks and became co-editor of the Richmond
Telescope. . . . While not busily engaged in writing, he was often in the
company of James Riddell, a gunsmith and cutler, whom he had
previously known. Riddell stated that Maillard was writing a novel,
but Maillard himself said he was making notes on the law. In May
and June he made several trips to Houston and one to Austin. In July
he stated that the death of a relative in London required his presence
there, and after a dinner given by the bar he left. Shortly afterwards
Riddell also left Richmond. Maillard arrived in England about August
15 and immediately began writing letters to the press and to British
officials condemning Texas." In early December, 1841, he finished his
book, which appeared early in 1842.

Stating that he writes as "an impartial historian," Maillard says
that "my object is to present to the public an unvarnished account of
what Texas and the Texans really are," as a counter to the prejudiced,
pro-Texas book of William Kennedy. The Texans, says Maillard, are
"a people whose existence as an independent nation is owing, first,

to their own base treason, and secondly, to a political juggle of Andrew Jackson." Texas is "a country filled with habitual liars, drunkards, blasphemers, and slanderers; sanguinary gamesters and cold-blooded assassins." It is a land "stained with the crime of Negro slavery and Indian massacre," and it is "the worst governed country in all America." Stephen F. Austin was "the prince of hypocrites," but Santa Anna became dictator "without disturbing or depriving the people of any one of the great principles of republicanism."

The book did little to dampen English interest in Texas, although it aroused the eternal ire of the Texans. Ashbel Smith said it "failed to produce the slightest effect," and Texas newspapers had a field day denouncing it. William Bollaert wrote that Maillard's derogatory comments on the ladies of Texas had to be suspect, because Maillard would "never have been admitted into the Society of Texan Ladies." Victor Bracht said that "on nearly every page is exhibited party hatred, personal prejudice, offended vanity, malicious slander, plain perversion of established facts, absurd contradictions in the author's own assertions—in short, barefaced falsehoods." C. W. Raines summed up the Texan view of Maillard's book as "a tissue of misstatements and contradictions too glaring to need correction."

Why Maillard was so vicious has never been fully established. Most Englishmen who stayed in Texas were treated with considerable kindness, and went away fervent pro-Texans. It seems probable to me that Maillard, as an admitted Mexican bondholder, went to Texas deliberately to gather detrimental material. There is little question that the Mexican bonds held by Maillard and his associates in England were severely depressed as a result of the success of the Texas Revolution. Whatever his motives, Maillard left us a tirade that has never been exceeded.

Agatha, p.31. Graff 2663. Howes M225. Rader 2333. Raines, p.144. Sabin 43886. Streeter 1422.

135　Marcy, Randolph Barnes (1812-1887)

EXPLORATION OF THE RED RIVER OF LOUISIANA, IN THE YEAR 1852 . . . WITH REPORTS ON THE NATURAL HISTORY OF THE COUNTRY, AND NUMEROUS ILLUSTRATIONS.

Washington: Robert Armstrong, Public Printer, 1853.

32nd Congress, 2nd Session. Senate Document 54. Serial 666.

Assisted by George B. McClellan, Brevet Captain, U.S. Engineers.

xv,[1],320pp. 65 plates (Geology Plate II and Botany Plate XVIII were never issued, although among the 67 listed in "Illustrations"). 2 folding maps. 22cm.

Cloth, with maps in separate cloth folder.

Other issues:

(A). Washington: Beverley Tucker, Senate Printer, 1854. xv,[1], 310pp. 65 plates. 2 folding maps. 22cm. Senate Document (unnumbered). The copy in my collection is in a contemporary full morocco presentation binding, prepared for President Franklin Pierce and signed by him.

(B). Washington: A. O. P. Nicholson, Public Printer, 1854. xv,[1],286pp. 65 plates. 2 folding maps. 22cm. 33rd Congress, 1st Session. House Executive Document (unnumbered).

(C). *Adventure on Red River: Report on the Exploration of the Headwaters of the Red River.* Norman: University of Oklahoma Press, [1937]. xxxi,[199],[1]pp. Cloth, dustjacket. Edited and annotated by Grant Foreman. Verso of title: "First edition." Actually published January, 1938. Reprints only Marcy's journal and summarizes the appendices.

(D). Second printing of (C). December, 1968. Same collation.

(E). Facsimile reprint of part of the first edition. Dallas: Highlands Historical Press, 1961. 117pp. 17 plates. No maps. New foreword by Mitch Mayborn.

Written by one of the greatest 19th century American explorers, this is one of the most interesting accounts of an original exploration of unknown parts of Texas. Eugene Hollon called it "the most important exploratory-venture of his career. . . . His chief fame as an explorer would rest upon the successful completion of a task in which so many explorers before him had failed. [It] contains one of the most accurate and lucid descriptions of a portion of the Great Plains . . . one of the best organized, best conducted, and most successful expeditions that heretofore had ventured into any section of the Great Plains. Its scientific results would prove particularly notable." Grant Foreman stated it was "not only the first adequate account of the region explored by him and the Indians he saw there, but . . . one of the most valuable and interesting descriptions of our western frontier to be found in government annals."

In March, 1852, Captain Marcy induced the government to allow him to lead an exploration to discover the true source of the Red River. His second in command was Capt. George B. McClellan, who later became his commanding general as well as son-in-law during the Civil War. No American explorer was known to have hitherto explored the headwaters of the Red River, and all known maps were inaccurate. Humboldt, Freeman and Sparks, Pike, and Long had either missed them completely or produced conflicting versions. The annexation of Texas, and the consequent necessity of establishing a verified northern border with the Indian territory, made the expedition even more significant. The two captains were joined by five Delaware guides, among them the noted John Bushman and Jim Ned, the latter of whom Marcy called "the bravest warrior and the most successful horse thief in the West." The whole party consisted of about seventy men.

Between May 2 and July 28, 1852, they explored about a thousand miles going and coming in Texas and Oklahoma, under orders to "collect and report everything that may be useful or interesting." This they did. Marcy found gold samples, a new type of copper (named Marcylite in his honor), coal, and gypsum. The last was called by Dr. Edward Hitchcock of Amherst a discovery of "utmost importance to the nation," and so it proved, for sheetrock and gypboard are still produced there today. They discovered a type of mesquite sap as a substitute for gum arabic, which the Washington *Star* called "the most important western discovery since that of gold in California," which proved untrue, as none has ever been produced. They identified twenty-five species of animals and ten species of snakes, as well as a prairie dog town which covered 400,000 acres by Marcy's estimate.

It is in geography and anthropology, however, that the most important discoveries were made. Marcy found both branches of the Red River and the source of each. He was the first Anglo-American to discover and explore Palo Duro Canyon and Tule Canyon. His discovery of two Red River branches led ultimately to the loss of Greer County to Oklahoma, when Marcy was called in to testify in 1886 as to which was the main course; finally, in 1896, the U.S. Supreme Court decided the southern branch was the proper boundary of Texas.

Marcy described in detail the little-known Wichita tribe and compiled the first Wichita dictionary. He ordered all Indians encountered to cease raids into Texas, as it would now be protected by the Great White Father in Washington. He received one of the first dependable accounts of Cynthia Ann Parker and her refusal to return to civilization. When the expedition completed its journey, Marcy learned that his whole command had been reported to have been wiped out by Comanches. The whole country thought he was dead, and Marcy said later that "I had the novel satisfaction of reading . . . obituary articles upon [my] death." He and McClellan received heroes' welcomes.

The first section of the work consists of Marcy's report in diary form to Adj. Gen. Samuel Cooper, dated New York, December 5, 1852. The appendices contain the scientific reports: Appendix "A" is on meteorology; "B" is courses and distances; "C" is mineralogy; "D" is Dr. George G. Shumard's geological journal and Edward Hitchcock's analysis of the specimens gathered; "E" is paleontology; "F" is zoology; "G" is botany; and "H" consists of Comanche and Wichita vocabularies. These are followed by the exquisite Akerman lithographs, twelve of which are views of places visited and the remainder of specimens gathered. The two large maps are usually found bound in a separate volume. Marcy considered these to be the first maps ever drawn of the sources of the Red River, but the French trader Pedro Vial drew a map in 1787 that is so accurate as to indicate he had actually traversed the region; the Vial map is in the Museum of New Mexico at Santa Fe.

Marcy first came to Texas in 1845 with Zachary Taylor and fought at Palo Alto and Resaca de la Palma. He crossed Texas numerous times in his later explorations, establishing the Marcy Trail in 1849, and leading various explorations culminating in his 1852 Red River journey. Marcy returned in 1854 for another exploration, this time of the Big Wichita and the headwaters of the Brazos, an account of which is published in Sen. Exec. Doc. 60, 34th Cong., 1st Sess., 1856. He accompanied Gen. William T. Sherman through Texas in 1871. Three of his books have material relating to his experiences in Texas: *The Prairie Traveller* (New York, 1859), *Thirty Years of Army Life on the Border* (New York, 1866), and *Border Reminiscences* (New York, 1872), all published by Harper & Brothers. There is a biography of Marcy by W. Eugene Hollon, *Beyond the Cross Timbers: The Travels of Randolph B. Marcy* (Norman: University of Oklahoma Press, 1955, 270pp.). The original manuscript reports of Marcy's 1852 expedition are in the War Records Division, National Archives; most of his private papers are in the George B. McClellan Papers, Library of Congress.

Another volume on this expedition is William B. Parker, *Notes Taken during the Expedition Commanded by Capt. R. B. Marcy, U.S.A., Through Unexplored Texas, in the Summer and Fall of* 1854 (Philadelphia: Hayes & Zell, 1856, 242pp.). This is an excellent account of the expedition by a civilian acquaintance of Marcy who went along for the adventure. It is a well-written narrative and adds flavor to Marcy's report.

Clark III-354. Field 1066. Graff 2675. Howes M276. Larned 416. Rader 2346. Raines, p.146. Sabin 44512. Wagner-Camp. 226.

136 Marshall, Thomas Maitland (1876-1936)

A HISTORY OF THE WESTERN BOUNDARY OF THE LOUISI-ANA PURCHASE, 1819-1841.

Berkeley: University of California Press, 1914.
University of California Publications in History, Volume II.
xiii,[1],266pp. 30 maps (3 folding). 24cm.
Printed wrappers; also cloth.

Other issues:
(A). Facsimile reprint. New York: Da Capo Press, 1970. 24cm. Cloth.
(B). Facsimile reprint. New York: Kraus Reprint Co., [no date]. 24cm. Cloth.

This is one of the most lucid studies of the struggle to establish the boundary line between Texas and the United States. Eugene C. Barker called it "a history of the diplomacy of the Louisiana-Texas boundary. The subject has been approached from various angles by numerous investigators, but this is the first consecutive survey covering the whole period from the emergence of the Texas question in United States history to the settlement of the boundary with the Republic of Texas in 1841. Three chapters review the boundary negotiations with Spain, closing with the Treaty of 1810. . . . [Marshall's] treatment is quite the clearest and most detailed that we have."

Marshall begins with a study of the boundary negotiation with Spain, based on his conclusions that "the conception of the size of Louisiana gradually developed in the mind of Jefferson; the conclusion which he reached became the basis of American diplomacy for half a century." Spain having developed its own concept based on Pichardo's analysis, the treaty was negotiated by John Quincy Adams and Luis de Onis. Marshall then devotes seven chapters to Texas boundary relations, providing what is still the best treatment of the efforts by Jackson and Adams to purchase Texas and Anthony Butler's bumbling activities in Mexico. Marshall gives substantial treatment to the activities of Gen. E. P. Gaines, who occupied East Texas with American troops during the Texas Revolution, and concludes with two chapters on the negotiations with the Republic of Texas for the final settlement of the boundary.

In several areas, Marshall developed original theories, some of which have been subsequently substantiated and some of which have not. He states these in his preface: ''The writer wishes to indicate some of the more important phases of the subject in which he has differed with accepted theory or in which he believes he has added somewhat to the history of the subject. He finds that Napoleon decided to sell Louisiana several months earlier than the date [previously accepted]. . . . The sale of Louisiana by France having been consummated, Spain carried out an effective plan for restricting the limits of the purchase; this has never received adequate treatment. The reason for Wilkinson's betrayal of Burr and for entering into the Neutral Ground Treaty . . . seems to lie in the fact that Wilkinson sold his services to the Spanish government while he was stationed on the western frontier. . . . Historians have usually accepted the view that the claim to Texas was given up in exchange for Florida. The writer believes that the purchase of Florida was a foregone conclusion from early in 1818, and thereafter Adams yielded the claim to Texas and advanced a claim to the Oregon country. . . . The writer disagrees fundamentally with the views of some historians regarding the purity of Andrew Jackson's motives concerning Texas.''

Marshall's study takes its place as one of that remarkable group of monographs produced primarily during the second decade of this century by Justin Smith, George Lockhart Rives, Herbert E. Bolton, William R. Manning, George P. Garrison, Robert C. Clark, Isaac Joslin Cox, E. D. Adams, and Eugene C. Barker. The impetus came from the realization that there was more to American history than that regarding what happened east of the Mississippi. With this realization came the discovery of the enormous wealth of archival materials in Mexico and Spain. Many of these seminal studies have never been supplanted and all have been the foundations upon which subsequent studies have been built.

Howes M321. Rader 2354.

137 Martin, Roscoe Coleman (1903-1972)

THE PEOPLE'S PARTY IN TEXAS: A STUDY IN THIRD PARTY POLITICS.

Austin: The University of Texas, 1933.
The University of Texas Bulletin No. 3308.
280pp. Illus. 4 folding maps. 22cm.
Printed wrappers.

Other issues:
(A). Austin & London: University of Texas Press, [1970]. Same collation, except only one folding map (others reduced). Cloth, dustjacket. Published in cooperation with the Texas State Historical Association.
(B). Same as (A), paperback edition. Texas History Paperbacks TH-7.

This monograph examines the most important political party in Texas other than the two major parties, and is still the best book on any Texas political party. R. L. Biesele said it is "very well done and merits careful reading," and John S. Spratt called it "probably the best work on the unrest of Texas farmers" during the period. Charles E. Merriman said this "study of the Populist Party in Texas is one of the indispensable contributions to the knowledge of the American party and the American political process. With great care and patience, Dr. Martin has examined the available data regarding the political operations of this organization at an interesting moment in our national life, and has pieced the materials together to make a view of this episode. His monograph not only throws much needed light on the local history of Texas, but it also helps illuminate our knowledge of the radical movement of the 1890's throughout the whole country. . . . This painstaking inquiry into the detailed operations of a special party association in a special period is a contribution to political science which no student of American politics can afford to ignore."

Martin's study of the People's Party was deliberately limited to Texas "in the belief that intensiveness is to be preferred over extensiveness. The findings will lead, it is hoped, to certain conclusions which will prove of general applicability where third parties are concerned.'' He first perused the available historical works, then studied the various government reports and statistics, and finally made personal studies in 64 different Texas counties. In the field, he studied local records and newspapers, and interviewed 250 individuals—both party leaders and individuals who had been grass-roots populists, in order ''to avoid the taint of scholasticism'' so prevalent in both previous and present studies in the social sciences.

The People's Party in Texas began in Comanche County in 1886 as a part of the general populist movement that sprang up almost simultaneously in western and southern agricultural areas of the nation. Before four years had passed, movements were under way in Erath, Lampasas, Red River, and other counties, and the People's Party of Texas was officially organized in 1891. Martin incorporates into his study the part played by the Granger movement, Greenbackism, and the Farmer's Alliance. By 1896, the People's Party was threatening the supremacy of the Democratic Party in Texas, but its power was soon dissipated by Democratic Party adoption of some of its main causes. The last populist convention in Texas was held in 1908 in Fort Worth.

Martin includes chapters on the racial complexion of the party, on newspapers that supported the movement, and on the political successes of the party. A wealth of statistical data is provided in the numerous charts, which represent the results of his extensive field research. His concluding chapter is a masterpiece of analysis and interpretation, and has remained the starting point for subsequent studies of the movement, such as Lawrence Goodwyn's classic *Democratic Promise: The Populist Moment in America* (New York: Oxford University Press, 1976, 718pp.) which contains a great deal of material on the party in Texas.

138 Martinez Caro, Ramon

VERDADERA IDEA DE LA PRIMERA CAMPANA DE TEJAS Y SUCESOS OCURRIDOS DESPUES DE LA ACCION DE SAN JACINTO.

Mexico: Imprenta de Santiago Perez a Cargo de Agustin Sojo, Calle de Tiburcio num. 14, 1837.

vii,162pp. 20cm.
Printed wrappers.

Other issues:

(A). Castaneda, Carlos E. *The Mexican Side of the Texas Revolution, by the Chief Mexican Participants* . . . Dallas: P. L. Turner Company, Publishers, [1928]. vii,391pp. 24cm. Cloth. Contains Martinez Caro's account on pages [90]-159, but omits the fourteen documents between pages 71 and 138 in the original text. Translated by Castaneda. First edition in English.

(B). Facsimile reprint of (A). Dallas: P. L. Turner Company, Publishers, [1956]. Same collation. 23cm. Cloth.

(C). New edition of (A). Austin and Dallas: Graphic Ideas Incorporated, publishers, 1970. xi,402pp. 22cm. Pictorial cloth. "This edition changes the original only by minor corrections, a new index, and the addition of new illustrations." The Martinez Caro text is on pages [92]-103.

This is an eyewitness account of the Texas Revolution written by Santa Anna's private secretary. Martinez Caro had access to orders and documents available to no one else except Santa Anna, whom the secretary charges with "evident artfulness . . . in keeping with his well-known character of duplicity." Martinez Caro also divulges the text of the secret treaty of Velasco in which Santa Anna agreed to work for Texas independence and agreed that the Texas border would be the Rio Grande.

Martinez Caro, about whom little is known before or after the Texas campaign, was captured at San Jacinto and imprisoned with Santa Anna. His book was published after both were returned to Mexico, and after Santa Anna's own defence, *Manifiesto que de Sus Operaciones,* had been published. In this work, Santa Anna calls Martinez Caro the "infamous betrayer" who released to the Mexican press the details of the secret treaty. Because of this Santa Anna, who had nearly been shot in Texas, faced almost the same situation when he returned to Mexico.

Santa Anna's work was published in Vera Cruz sometime after May 10, 1837. The first part of Martinez Caro's work is dated May 20, 1837, followed by a postscript dated at the prison at Ex-Acordada, June 20, 1837, telling of his arrest on May 21, and the confiscation of his manuscript and papers. This plot "to prevent me from publishing my account" eventually failed, and he was released and finished his text on August 31, 1837. Martinez Caro devotes much of his final text to attacking the veracity of Santa Anna's volume. Since Santa Anna's work is dated May 10, 1837, it may be that Martinez Caro delayed publication of his volume after he learned of Santa Anna's. Santa Anna's text was published in Vera Cruz and Martinez Caro's in Mexico City.

At the end of the first part of the volume, Martinez Caro appends fourteen key documents related to the Texas campaign, including the full text of both "perfidious" treaties. Many of these relate to events after San Jacinto. Throughout the text Martinez Caro gives an insider's view of the whole campaign, the capture at San Jacinto, the negotiations for the treaty, and life as a prisoner. He records the various attempts to escape, including the Bartolome Pages attempt to free Santa Anna. The volume should be compared with those of Santa Anna, Filisola, and Urrea to get an overview of the events that transpired, but one gets the feeling that Martinez Caro is telling substantially the truth even though he is betraying the trust placed in him by his employer and commander.

Clark III-206. *Fifty Texas Rarities* #15. Graff 2695. Howes C155. Rader 592. Raines, p.44. Sabin 10950. Streeter 923.

139 Matthews, Sallie Reynolds (1861-1938)

INTERWOVEN, A PIONEER CHRONICLE.

Houston: The Anson Jones Press, 1936.
Introduction by Will James.
x,[2],234pp. Photographic frontispiece. 20cm.
Cloth. Also orange suede. Dustjacket.

Other issues:
(A). Blanton, Thomas Lindsay. *Pictorial Supplement to Interwoven: The Matthews-Reynolds Families*. Albany, Texas: Not for sale, [1953]. 137pp. Illus. 26cm.
(B). Same as (A), revised printing. Albany: Not for sale, [1953]. 153pp. Illus. 26cm.
(C). New edition. El Paso: Carl Hartzog, 1958. xiv,[4],226pp. 24cm. Cloth. "1500 copies of this book have been printed at El Paso Texas by Carl Hertzog." Adds photograph of the author in 1938, drawings by E. M. Schiwetz, and an introduction by Robert Nail. Deletes the Will James introduction.
(D). *Sample Pages from New Edition of Interwoven: A Pioneer Chronicle by Sallie Reynolds Matthews*. El Paso: Carl Hertzog, [1958]. [8]pp. 24cm. Wrappers.

This First-Hand Account of

Cattlemen on the Frontier

in the 1870's and 1880's

is now offered in a NEW EDITION *of* "INTERWOVEN"

› Printed on Curtis natural laid paper in large type with 2-color titles – 256 pages including illustrations.

› Bound in specially designed cloth with title and brands gold stamped – enclosed in acetate wrapper.

› Illustrated by E. M. Schiwerz with nine drawings lithographed in sepia, and twelve pen sketches.

Gateway, Lambshead Ranch – Established 1897.

› Added features are: Index, new introduction, maps, and family chart showing how five members of the Reynolds family married five members of the Matthews family – all West Texas ranch folks.

$10

SAMPLE PAGES FROM
NEW EDITION OF

INTERWOVEN
A Pioneer Chronicle

BY

SALLIE REYNOLDS MATTHEWS

DRAWINGS BY
E. M. SCHIWETZ

TWO-COLOR TYPOGRAPHY AND MAPS BY
CARL HERTZOG 1958 EL PASO TEXAS

(E). *True Tales of the Frontier . . . Taken From Her Memoirs Interwoven and Arranged, Illustrated and Published by Her Grandson, Joseph Edwin Blanton, to Commemorate the One-Hundredth Anniversary of Her Birth.* Albany, Texas: Venture Press, 1961. xii,[4],77,[2]pp. At end: "The text of this book, taken photographically from the edition of *Interwoven* by Carl Hertzog . . . was printed by the Marvin D. Evans Company of Fort Worth. The book design is by Joseph E. Blanton." Printed in brown and black throughout. 26cm. Cloth. Dustjacket. On back of dustjacket: "True tales of the frontier for adults and older children."

(F). "Third Edition." Austin & London: University of Texas Press, [1974]. xiv,[4],226,[1]pp. Illus. 24cm. Cloth. Dustjacket. "The University of Texas Press takes pleasure in presenting this third edition, whose design is largely derived from the Hertzog edition. . . ." The M. K. Brown Range Life Series Number 13. New "Publisher's Note."

(G). "Fourth edition." College Station: Texas A & M University Press, [1982]. xiv,[4],226,[3]pp. Illus. 24cm. Cloth, dustjacket.

(H). Special edition of (G). Limited to 350 sets, specially bound, numbered, and slipcased. Issued with Frances Mayhugh Holden, *Lambshead before Interwoven: A Texas Range Chronicle*, 1848-1878.

This is the best book on Texas ranch life from a woman's perspective. J. Frank Dobie said of it: "*Interwoven,* more than any other ranch chronicle that I know, reveals the famiy life of the old-time ranchers." Robert Nail said that it "is so filled with the details of pioneer living that it creates much the same impression as a Dutch painting: it is a factual and charming view into the past. It is also—and not secondarily—a view into the person of an extraordinary woman."

When the book appeared in 1936, a review in *Time Magazine* said: "*Interwoven* bears the authentic stamp of pioneer documents, is the quaint and kindly chronicle of a lady who was born near the present site of Breckenridge in 1861, carries her story, with the stories of her famiy, to 1900. Sallie Reynolds grew up when Indians were a constant menace, when families huddled together in the uncertain protection of forts in face of raids. She saw enough of the ruthlessness of early settlers to believe in 'the inherent nobility of the Red Man.' She casually tells a story of a young gunman who killed an unoffending Indian while his whole party was in the hands of savages. The Indians demanded only his life in return, flayed him alive, while in a similar situation whites would have exterminated all the Indians in the area. Sallie Reynolds traveled to Colorado and back to Texas, married Bud Matthews, bore him eight children. Her book is filled with good plain

Texas names such as Flake Barber and Si Hough, with accounts of droughts, troubles with banks, hard winters, written without heroics.''

The volume includes eleven chapters, sensibly titled the Family, Fort Davis Days, The Stone Ranch, Fort Griffin, Parker County, Colorado, Back to Texas, California Ranch, Tecumseh Ranch, Moving, and Back to the Ranch. An appendix gives ''A journal of a Trip from the Clear Fork in Stephens County to the San Saba River,'' taken in 1864 and written by Sam P. Newcomb, Sallie's brother-in-law. Stephens County was organized and created in the Reynolds ranchhouse.

Robert Nail states in the 1958 edition: ''When she wrote *Interwoven*, Sallie Reynolds Matthews' modest intention was a family history for her children and their children. The book, however, became more than a clan chronicle. . . . It is now well established as a basic source of information for research in the history of the Texas frontier. . . . Mrs. Matthews had perceiving eyes, gentle objectivity and scrupulous regard for the truth. . . . She lay no claim to being a historian, yet, a person of sensitivity, she was often able to convey, as only the best historians can, a clear idea of how it felt to live in the period about which she wrote.''

In 1958 Carl Hertzog reissued the book in a beautiful limited edition; J. Frank Dobie called it ''another instance of the last edition being more desirable than the first'' and William S. Reese commented that it ''is now in as great demand as the first.'' Al Lowman states that it is ''perhaps the printer's favorite of his books. . . . Hertzog captured the historical flavor of this classic narrative of the West Texas frontier using dusty, rough textured paper, untrimmed. The three-piece binding consists of natural cloth covers printed with a pattern of Reynolds and Matthews monograms and cattle brands.'' The volume also contains some of E. M. Schiwetz's most accomplished drawings. In 1982 a ''companion volume'' was issued by Texas A & M Press: Frances M. Holden, *Lambshead before Interwoven: A Texas Range Chronicle, 1848-1878*, which tells ''of earlier events in the area and recounts some fascinating episodes omitted from *Interwoven.*''

Sallie Reynolds had an extraordinary sense of time and place, and an uncommon understanding of her fellow human beings. She states in her foreword: ''Perhaps never before in the history of the world

has there been such rapid and phenomenal development of a country
as that of the vast stretch of territory that lies between the Rio Grande
and the Bad Lands, a development that took place within the allotted
three score years and ten of man's lifetime. . . . I shall endeavor to
give as true a picture as I can of frontier life as we lived. it . . . This
family has not been exempt from trials and tribulations. Some seem
to have more than their share of grief in this life, and we see others
who seem to float along on flowery beds of ease, but we do not know;
they may be carrying bitter sorrow deep in their hearts."

Adams Herd 1454. Campbell, p.93. Dobie, p.62. Howes M426. Reese *Six Score* #78.

140   Maverick, Mary Ann (Adams) (1818-1898)

MEMOIRS OF MARY A. MAVERICK, ARRANGED BY MARY
A. MAVERICK AND HER SON, GEO. MADISON MAVERICK.

San Antonio: Alamo Printing Co., 1921.
Edited by Rena Maverick Green.
136pp. 23cm. Errata slip pasted on back of frontispiece.
Stiff wrappers.
Line 5 of page 63, which ends, "of the blacksmith shop," is continued on line 24 of
page 69, beginning, "in the yard."

Other issues:
(A). Same as above, but errors on page 63 and 69 corrected.
(B). Green, Rena Maverick [ed.]. *Samuel Maverick, Texan: 1803-1870, A Collection of
      Letters, Journals and Memoirs.* San Antonio: 1952. xix,430pp. 23cm. Cloth. 14 illus.
      Verso of title: "Privately Printed. Manufactured in the United States of
      America by H. Wolff, New York. Designed by Marshall Lee." This volume
      incorporates Mary Maverick's memoirs, interspersed with a wealth of extracts
      from letters, diaries, and journals of Samuel Maverick. This is by far the best
      edition.

These memoirs of the wife of Samuel Maverick comprise one of the
most interesting and important narratives of life in Texas in the 1830's
and 1840's. "My grandmother," wrote Rena Maverick Green, "kept
diaries and notes during much of her married life, certainly from 1837
to the late 1850's. These she wrote up in the form of memoirs in 1880
and 1881. . . . In the summer of 1896 . . . she and my father, George
Madison Maverick, worked together over her diary: forming chapters,

making connecting links and omitting some details, thus shaping it up for the family. They had six copies printed. . . ." To the best of my knowledge, none of these six copies has survived. Rena Maverick Green arranged the memoirs for general publication in 1921.

Mary married Samuel Maverick in Alabama in August, 1836, at which point the narrative begins, and accompanied him to Texas. She was the first woman from the United States to settle in San Antonio. She had ten children and established one of the prominent families in San Antonio. Her husband was a signer of the Texas Declaration of Independence and a leading political and business figure in Texas from 1835 to 1861.

The narrative covers life in San Antonio, which was then the extreme western frontier of the Republic of Texas, from 1838 to 1842; in central Texas near La Grange and coastal Texas near Matagorda, from 1843 to 1847; and in San Antonio from 1847 until after the Civil War. The author recounts such events as the Council House Fight, the Comanche Invasion of 1840, the Indian fighting activities of Col. Jack Hays, the Vasquez Expedition, the Woll Expedition, the Dawson Massacre, and social activities in which she took a leading part.

The memoirs are engrossing and colorful. Her vivid eye-witness account of the Council House Fight is our best source of information on the event. Her description of social life in early Texas is particularly interesting and useful, presenting everyday life of both the Anglo-Americans and the Mexicans who remained in Texas after San Jacinto. She recounts numerous Indian fights, particularly those in which her husband and Jack Hays took part.

Insights into the lives of famous Texans are numerous. For example, she tells of Mirabeau B. Lamar's visit to San Antonio in 1841: "President Lamar with a very considerable suite visited San Antonio in June. A grand ball was given him in Mrs. Yturri's long room — (all considerable houses had a long room for receptions). The room was decorated with flags and evergreens; flowers were not much cultivated then. At the ball, General Lamar and Mrs. Juan N. Seguin, wife of the Mayor, opened the ball with a waltz. Mrs. Seguin was so fat that the General had great difficulty in getting a firm hold on her waist, and they cut such a figure that we were forced to smile. The General was a poet, a polite and brave gentleman and first rate conversationalist—but he did not dance well. At the ball, [Jack] Hays, [Mike] Chevalier, and John Howard had but one dress coat between them, and they agreed to use the coat and dance in turn. The two not dancing would stand at the hall door watching the happy one who was enjoying his turn—and they reminded him when it was time for him to step out of that coat. Great fun was it watching them and listening to their wit and mischief as they made faces and shook their fists at the dancing one.''

She writes of Gen. Alexander Somervell and Prince Carl of Solms-Braunfels, who visited the Mavericks in 1844 at Matagorda: ''General Somerville was a noted laugher—he saw the Prince's two attendants dress his Highness, that is lift him into his pants, and General Somerville was so overcome by the sight that he broke out into one of his famous fits of laughter, and was heard all over the Point. The Prince and suite were all very courteous and polite to us. They wore cock feathers in their hats, and did not appear quite fitted to frontier life.''

At the end of the volume are some documents relating to the origin of the term ''mavericks'' for stray cattle, some letters relating to the Alamo buildings, and a tribute to Samuel Maverick by Dr. George Cupples.

In 1952, Rena Maverick Green published an entirely new edition, incorporating the original 1921 text and adding ''probaby all Samuel A. Maverick's letters to his wife for a period of more than thirty years, as well as many other family letters'' which she ''dovetailed chronologically with the memoirs.'' She also added Samuel Maverick's surviving journals, which include those covering the Siege of Bexar in 1835, his Perote Prison account of 1842-1843, and his log of Jack Hays' Chihuahua expedition of 1848. The Bexar journal had been edited and printed earlier by Frederick C. Chabot under the title *Maverick Notes: 1835* (San Antonio: Artes Graficas, 1942) in a limited edition.

Adams Herd 1460. Campbell, p.94. Dobie, p.57. Howes M443.

141 Meinig, Donald William (1924-)

IMPERIAL TEXAS: AN INTERPRETIVE ESSAY IN CULTURAL GEOGRAPHY.

Austin: University of Texas Press, 1969.
Introduction by Lorrin Kennamer.
145pp. Illus. 18 maps (2 folding). 25cm.
Cloth, dustjacket.

Other issues:
(A). Second printing, 1972. Same collation.
(B). Paperback edition, 1975. 24cm. Same collation.

This is a fresh and enlightening study of the question whether there are cultural patterns distinctive to Texas. That Texans consider themselves a cultural whole is apparent from this study; whether they do actually represent a cultural entity, or "empire" as the author calls it, is the subject of this scholarly analysis. William B. Conroy wrote that Meinig shows that "characteristics associated with the term empire can be found both in contemporary Texas and in its historical development. However, although the idea of empire is a recurring theme, Professor Meinig's basic purpose is to describe the development of Texas as a distinctive, yet diverse, cultural area. . . . The author concludes that Texas today is a distinct 'American region, Southern in source, Southwestern in locale, but definitely Texan in Character.' . . . Indeed, those acquainted with Texas and its history will find much stimulus for thought in the fresh perspective Professor Meinig brings to familiar facts."

Meinig, graduate of Georgetown University and the University of Washington, wrote this book while professor of geography at Syracuse University. His Texas study was an outgrowth of a broader project on historical geography of the American west, under the auspices of the Guggenheim Foundation. With this background, he was particularly well-qualified to attempt an interpretation of a subject too often tackled in the past by native Texas writers suffering from their own Texan chauvinism.

Dividing Texas history into four major periods of Spanish-Mexican, republic and ante-bellum, post-Civil War, and 20th century, Meinig examines the patterns of settlement, development, population characteristics, and cultural conflicts. These are covered under the headings of implantation, assertion, expansion, and elaboration. Meinig then differentiates Texas into nine major regions and discusses cultural features distinguishable in each. He offers conclusions supporting his thesis that there are "patterns which yet remain to distinguish Texas from [the rest of] the nation: the serious insistence by the majority of Texans on thinking of themselves as different . . . the residue of certain values which sociologists have identified as especially (though not uniquely) characteristic of the main body of the Texas population; and the particular regional patterning of peoples, a distinctive mosaic, related in its parts to, but not duplicated as a whole in, any other parts of the country.''

Meinig's study of the nine cultural regions of Texas is especially significant. Previous geographers have divided the state primarily into physically distinguishable areas, the bases of which are climate, terrain, and vegetation. These physical divisions are certainly valid, distinct, and influential upon the people living within them. Meinig's geography, however, is cultural. As Lorrin Kennamer writes in his introduction, to interpret the Texan empire one must also "study the place, the people, languages, origins, and religions; in other words, the human geography of the state. The case is made accurately and in a most interesting way that, in regards to Texas, a state of mind has risen just as much as a physical state.''

142   Merk, Frederick (1887-   )

SLAVERY AND THE ANNEXATION OF TEXAS.

New York: Alfred A. Knopf, 1972.
With the collaboration of Lois Bannister Merk
xiii,[1],290,x, [2]pp. 25cm.
Cloth, dustjacket.

While this is far from Merk's best work, it is the best exposition of the slavery thesis of annexation. Allan Ashcraft called it "a beautiful example of what can be accomplished by thoroughly intensive research. . . . One can only conclude that this will be *the* definitive book on the subject. . . . A close study of the book pays rich dividends in offering the reader a unique insight into the role of the slavery issue in the annexation of Texas." Holman Hamilton said "Merk has pointed anew to many major and some minor developments preceding the annexation of Texas." Gene M. Brack said it "revives the long-somnolent slave-conspiracy thesis, stressing the role of 'slavocracy' (a term used by Merk) in promoting and achieving annexation. [It] provides a welcome and provocative alternative to Justin Smith.''

There is a wealth of evidence to sift through that relates to the Texas annexation question—so much, in fact, that there is enough to be found to support any of the prominent theories. Merk's own conclusions are that the annexation debate was largely a debate on the slavery question, that the success of the annexationists was due to propaganda and scare tactics, that it represented the evil of Manifest Destiny at its worst, and that the British threat was concocted rather than real. Holman Hamilton states: "If Justin Smith in 1911 was a fifty-four-year-old revisionist, Mr. Merk in 1972 was an eighty-five-year-old re-revisionist—demonstrating that tendencies in those directions are not confined to youth.''

Merk contends that the idea that the Texas Revolution "was an uprising against Mexican tyranny, is unfounded.'' He quotes William Ellery Channing: "The Texans must have been insane if, on entering Mexico, they looked for an administration as faultless as that under which they had lived. They might with equal reason have planted themselves in Russia, and then unfurled the banner of independence near the throne of the Czar because denied the immunities of their native land.'' He quotes John Quincy Adams' lament that annexation was "the heaviest calamity that ever befell myself and my country,'' and ends his book with the statement that the Civil War was precipitated thereby: "The roots of that tension—and of the cataclysm itself—lay deep in the soil of Texas.''

The freshest viewpoint expressed by Merk is that regarding the use of propaganda. He states: "In the period of the two world wars the significance of propaganda inspired by government became apparent to historians. This stirred fresh interest in the propaganda spread in earlier crises and suggested applying the new insights to a study of the Texas crisis. The study here is of this nature. . . . The propaganda was a mixture of fact and fancy, of truth and falsehood, of humanitarianism and racism. The antislavery propaganda emanating from the North was nearer the truth than that flowing from the Southern circle of slavery extremists urging annexation.'' He singles out John Tyler as one of the chief Southern propagandists: "In the propaganda of the Tyler circle—secret and open—there was an exceptionally high percentage of misconception, misrepresentation, and outright falsehood."

Of special interest in the volume is the 105-page section at the end of the volume giving the text of 35 contemporary documents, essays, letters, and speeches concerning annexation. Of them, Merk states: "Evidence in this direct form is essential in a volume that challenges accepted explanations of the success of the annexation cause. It is desirable in other respects. There is a freshness as well as an authority in the thought and language of a period that cannot be recaptured in the cold analysis of a later time. Most of the documents offered here are not easily accessible. Gathered conveniently, they may interest the general reader as well as the scholar."

The value of Merk's volume is not that it is the last word on the subject or that it is a startling new synthesis, for these it certainly is not, but rather that it is the best exposition of the slavery thesis of annexation—a thesis which has been the underlying theme of literally hundreds of books relating to Texas. It is a useful counterpoint to the thesis in Justin Smith's *The Annexation of Texas*. Another recent interpretation of value is in David M. Pletcher, *The Diplomacy of Annexation: Texas, Oregon, and the Mexican War* (Columbia: University of Missouri Press, 1973, 656pp.).

143   Miller, Edmund Thornton (1878-1952)

A FINANCIAL HISTORY OF TEXAS.

Austin: Bulletin of the University of Texas No. 37, 1916.
444pp. Folding table. 23cm.
Printed wrappers.

This is still the best work on the fiscal history of Texas in the 19th century. Clarence Ayers called it "the standard work in its field by the leading authority on Texas finance," and Seymour V. Connor deemed it "a great aid to the understanding of the economy of Texas at that time." It was an outgrowth of his 1909 doctoral dissertation at Harvard University, parts of which were published in the *Southwestern Historical Quarterly* beginning in 1910. Miller taught economics at the

University of Texas for forty-eight years, and was a full professor for thirty-five years.

Miller points out that "William Gouge published in 1852 his *Fiscal History of Texas*, but outside of his book the finances of state have had no historian until the present writer undertook the task. The suggestion of the undertaking came from the Carnegie Institution." In spite of its importance, the economic history of Texas has, before and since, been neglected by historians, except in the area of public lands.

Miller points out that this project was not an easy one: "The chief difficulty met with in the work has been the complete absence of financial reports for some years and the many imperfections in the reports extant. Too often do the reports of the state's financial officials seem to have been gotten out in a perfunctory way and merely to meet the minimum requirements of the law, and the author is convinced that . . . a decided reform must occur if the reports are to fulfill their purpose of presenting to the average citizen an intelligible conception of the financial operations of state government."

The volume consists of seven chronological sections: Spanish-Mexican period and Texas Revolution; Republic of Texas; pre-Civil War; Civil War; Reconstruction; "Period of Recovery, 1874-1880"; and the period from 1881 through 1915. An appendix includes nineteen excellent tables, including "Table of Confederate Currency Values," "Public Debt, 1846-1915," "Available School Fund, 1847-1915," and several tables on the revenues, expenditures, appropriations, and pubic debt of the Republic of Texas. The brief chapter on the finances of the Texas Revolution is especially concise and instructive.

There are two other related works that are useful. Avery Luvere Carlson's *A Monetary and Banking History of Texas from the Mexican Regime to the Present Day, 1821-1929* (Fort Worth: Fort Worth National Bank, 1930, 82pp.) is still the best summary of early Texas banking history. Bob Medlar's *Texas Obsolete Notes and Scrip* (San Antonio: Society of Paper Money Collectors, [1968], 204pp.) is the best guide to the paper money issued in Texas.

144 Miller, Thomas Lloyd (1913-   )

BOUNTY AND DONATION LAND GRANTS OF TEXAS, 1835-1888.

Austin & London: University of Texas Press, [1967].
xii,894pp. 26cm.
Foreword by Ralph W. Steen.
Cloth, dustjacket.

This work is the most important published guide to early military service records in Texas. Ralph Steen writes in his foreword: "The study reveals a total of 7,469 bounty warrants for 5,354,250 acres of land. In addition, most of the men who served during the Texas Revolution were declared eligible for donations of land. Donations were made to 1,816 veterans—or their heirs—and the amount of land involved was 1,162,240 acres." Bookman Robert Wilson called the volume "a monumental job of research and organization—indispensable." Hobart Huson said it "is a basic, thorough and scholarly contribution to researchers of Texas history as well as to the legal profession—of permanent value." Ray Allen Billington called it "more factual than interpretive, but a mine of information on the land system and land grants."

Miller exhaustively searched the records of the General Land Office of Texas and Texas Court of Claims to provide material on Texas Revolution service, Republic of Texas military and volunteer service, frontier Indian service, and Civil War service. The result is this volume giving the name of each original grantee, number of acres, county where located, date, military service for each grantee, date and number of patent, and present location of each file.

Mirabeau B. Lamar told the Republic of Texas Congress in 1840 that "millions of uncultivated lands are wasting their luxuriance on the air." Texas was nearly bankrupt of every other commodity of value, so land became the general method of payment for service— and land fraud became prevalent. Miller has stated elsewhere that "the words 'land' and 'fraud' were almost synonymous in Texas, [a problem which] has continued to this day." In 1839 the Texas land commissioner, John P. Borden, wrote that "so great have been the facilities for manufacturing fraudulent claims that the individual holding less than 10 [certificates] for a league and labor each is considered a small operator in this line." Exaggerated, perhaps, but indicative of the problem faced by Miller in compiling this work.

The volume also includes an explanation of the complicated sources consulted, an authoritative treatment of the legislative history of military land grants, and a history Court of Claims. Another book by Miller, *The Public Lands of Texas,* 1519-1970 (Univ. of Oklahoma Press, 1972), extends his treatment of the subject. In that work he makes the statement: "Just why did the Americans come to Texas? The answer is found in one word—land." Reuben McKitrick's *The Public Land System of Texas,* 1823-1910 (Madison: Bulletin of the Univ. of Wisconsin 905, 1918, 172pp.) is still useful though out of date.

145   Morfi, Juan Agustin (-1783)

HISTORY OF TEXAS, 1673-1779.

Albuquerque: The Quivira Society, 1935.
Two volumes: 242;[6],243-496pp. 25cm. 4 plates. Folding map.
Cloth spine, boards.
Translated, with Biographical Introduction and Annotation, by Carlos Eduardo Castaneda. Quivera Society Publications, Volume VI. Limited to 500 numbered sets. Also a special edition on different paper, limited to 100 sets.

Other issues:
(A). *Excerpts from the Memorias for the History of the Province of Texas* . . . San Antonio: Privately Published, Printing by Naylor Printing Company, 1932. xxii,85,[2]pp. 29cm. Buckram. Translated and edited by Frederick C. Chabot, revised by Carlos E. Castaneda. Limited to 200 copies, but actually 400 printed. I have owned a copy stamped #208. Some copies have no limitation notice. Excerpts of the parts relating to Indians.
(B). Facsimile reprint of the Quivera edition. New York: Arno Press, 1967. 2 vols. 24cm. Cloth.

This is the best contemporary 18th-century history of Texas. It was discovered accidentally by another notable Texas historian, Carlos E. Castaneda, a century and a half after it was written. Castaneda writes: "By a fortunate coincidence the writer discovered the manuscript of Fray Juan Agustin Morfi's *History of Texas* in the National Library of Mexico early in January, 1931. For a long time this work of the celebrated Franciscan missionary was known by name only and its existence had come to be doubted. It is, nevertheless, the most complete and detailed account known, as it presents a connected narrative of the principal events in the history of Texas from 1673 to

1779. It is wider in scope than any work now available in English or Spanish.''

The volumes consist of a biography of Morfi, a list of his writings and extant letters, the text of his history, a bibliography, and index. Morfi was born in Spain at an unknown date and became a Franciscan friar in Mexico City in 1761. In 1777 he accompanied the Teodoro de Croix expedition as chaplain, accompanying the tour from Mexico City through Tula, Queretaro, Zacatecas, Durango, and into Texas via Coahuila, returning through Chihuahua to Mexico City in 1778. Morfi died abruptly in 1783 before being able to publish his monumental history of Texas.

Morfi states that he wrote the history primarily ''to prove, by presenting the facts, the unselfish character of the missionaries,'' who had come under fire in the 1728 report of Pedro de Rivera. Morfi is less kind to the governors and civil officials in Texas, accusing them of incompetence and degeneracy. He is also bold to state that the Spanish troops stationed at the missions were inept and of little practical help to the missionaries. Throughout the work are invaluable insights into the life in the missions, villages, and presidios, as well as on the Indian tribes. Much of what we now know of 18th century Texas comes from Morfi's account; his frankness is unusual for writings of the period.

Castaneda's bibliography of Morfi's writings indicates that ''there are [five] manuscript copies of this work, all different.'' In addition, Castaneda consulted several of Morfi's ''Informe,'' ''Memorias,'' and ''Noticias'' on related subjects. He remarks that Morfi's diary was known to exist in 1816, but incorrectly assumed that this was the same as his New Mexico diary. Three diaries by Morfi have since been discovered, purchased by The University of Texas and identified by Malcolm D. McLean as in the hand of Morfi himself. For a Spanish edition of these diaries, see Eugenio del Hoyo, Malcolm D. McLean, and Escuela de Verano [eds.], *Diario y Derrotero* (1777-1781) *por Fray Juan Agustin de Morfi* (Monterrey: Instituto Tecnologico y de Estudios Superiores de Monterrey, 1967).

Of Castaneda's editorial work, J. Haggard-Villasana has said: ''A more appropriate person than Dr. Castaneda could hardly have been found to translate and edit this book. His bilingual aptitude has enabled him to make a flawless translation. The highest tribute that can be paid him is to state that the reader is not conscious the work is a translation. In addition by masterful research Dr. Castaneda has enriched Father Morfi's work with thorough and enlightening footnotes . . . in his presentation of the Franciscan's masterpiece.''

Campbell, p.172. Howes M792.

146 Morrell, Zachariah Nehemiah (1803-1883)

FLOWERS AND FRUITS FROM THE WILDERNESS; OR, THIRTY-SIX YEARS IN TEXAS AND TWO WINTERS IN HONDURAS.

Boston: Gould and Lincoln, 59 Washington Street; Bryan, Texas: Sunday-School and Colportage Board; New York: Sheldon and Company, 1872.
xviii,[19]-386,[10]pp. 20cm.
Cloth.
Verso of title: Rockwell & Churchill, Printers and Stereotypers, 122 Washington Street, Boston.
Contains a preface dated Brenham, Texas, July 9, 1872.

Other issues:
(A).   Same title. Second Edition, Revised. Boston: Gould and Lincoln, 59 Washing-
       ton Street; Bryan, Texas: Sunday-School and Colportage Board; Chattanooga,
       Tenn.: W. T. Russell, 1873. xviii,[19]-386pp. 20cm. Cloth. Frontis. of Morrell.
       Verso of title: Rockwell & Churchill, Printers, Boston. Page [xviii] contains
       ''Preface to the Second Edition,'' dated Brenham, Texas, January 25, 1873,
       which states: ''The first edition of one thousand copies of this work was issued
       a few months since. Its rapid sale, in the course of a few weeks, exhausted the
       entire edition. A second edition, with some slight verbal corrections, mostly in
       names and dates, was put to press, but while in the process of printing, the
       plates and paper, with the office in Boston where the work was being executed,
       were destroyed in the recent extensive conflagration which visited that city.
       Notwithstanding this serious loss, encouraged by the . . . unusual sale of the
       work, it has been re-stereotyped, and a new improved edition now appears.''
(B).   *Flowers and Fruits in the Wilderness; or, Forty-Six Years in Texas and Two Winters in*
       Honduras. Third Edition, Revised. St. Louis: Commercial Printing Company,
       405 N. Third St., 1882. xviii,[19]-412pp. 20cm. Cloth. Frontis. of Morrell. Adds
       Chapter XXXIII, ''Ten Years of Rapid Progress.''

(C). Same title as (B). Fourth Edition, Revised. Dallas: W. G. Scarff & Co., Publishers, 1886. [7],x-xviii,[19]-426,[2]pp. Two blank leaves between p. 412 and p. [413]. 19cm. Cloth. No frontis., but 31 portraits tipped in throughout. Adds chapter XXXIV, "A Contrast: 1872-1882," and "In Memoriam," containing obituaries on Morrell. The best edition.

(D). Same title as (B). Irving, Texas: Griffin Graphic Arts, 2408 Roger Williams Dr., 1966. [12],[ix]-xviii,[19]-412pp. 17cm. Stiff wrappers. Facsimile of (B), with 3-page "Publisher's Foreword" by T. Edward Griffin.

(E). Facsimile reprint of first edition. Waco: Baylor Library, 1976. Adds pages 387-426 from the 1886 edition at the end. New introduction by Ray Summers.

Written by a circuit-riding Baptist preacher who also fought Indians and Mexicans, this lively though mistitled volume is rich in anecdotal history. It is, as J. Frank Dobie said, "in many ways the best circuit rider's chronicle of the Southwest that has been published." Mrs. Dobie wrote to me a short time before her death that the wife of Postmaster General Albert Sidney Burleson once gave her a copy of *Flowers and Fruits of the Wilderness* "because you love wild flowers so much."

Morrell, who had preached "on an average about one sermon a day for nine years, [which] brought on hemorrhage of the lungs," moved to Texas in December, 1835. As a fiery Baptist preacher and circuit rider, Morrell entered Texas bent on conversion of souls. He never wavered from his original feelings: "Catholicism, 'the man of sin,' I considered as a sworn enemy to me as a Baptist." Morrell says he arrived "with bleeding lungs, under special orders . . . to refrain from preaching, and yet with fire burning in my bones to declare the way of salvation to the lost." Once in Texas, he found: "Here was a semi-savage, Mexican government, administered by a tyrant, himself under the tyranny of Catholicism, demoralizing in its character, and but one step in advance of the most degrading heathenism."

When Morrell crossed the Sabine, the ferryman told him: "Only a few days before a man rode up on the Louisiana side, evidently under great excitement, and at the top of his voice ordered the ferryman to bring over the boat. Supposing there was some emergency, the boat was promptly carried to the opposite shore, and the man landed as quick as possible on the Texas side. Just as he was ashore, an officer, with a body of men in pursuit of this refugee from justice, hailed on the eastern bank. The man, recognizing his pursuers, mounted his horse, rode up the hill entirely out of reach, and very deliberately made this short and pointed speech: 'Gentlemen, I am just a little too fast for your sort. You have no authority out of the United States. I am entirely safe.' Alighting from his horse and kissing the ground, he continued: 'The Sabine River is a greater Saviour than Jesus Christ. He only saves men when they die from going to hell; but this river saves living men from prison.'"

Early in 1837 Morrell preached the first sermon ever delivered, he says, in Houston. He also preached the first sermon in Washington-on-the-Brazos, and probably dozens of other places. "No cut and dried thirty-minute sermons were expected. We met at nine in the morning, and continued until the sun was low in the west."

Morrell was a participant in the activities surrounding the Comanche invasion of 1840, being one of the first to discover the Indians' approach: "My oxen were in fine condition, and being anxious to communicate this intelligence to Colonel Ed. Burleson . . . I drove thirty miles in twelve hours." His account of the Battle of Plum Creek is one of the best extant.

The latter half of the volume is mostly history of various Baptist churches in Texas, interspersed with recollections of thirty-five years of horseback journeys, gospel preaching, revivals, and—in the words of *The Handbook of Texas*—"general movements for promoting right-eousness in the state." Morrell was assisted by elders J. W. Creath and M. A. Smith in preparing the church data. This part of the book, although dull, is worth mining; for example, a remarkable account of the Tory Hill traitors at San Jacinto appears on pages 203-204 as part of a sermon.

Ten years after first publication, the book was reissued with considerable new material added. Morrell died shortly thereafter, Governor John Ireland delivering the eulogy at his graveside.

Agatha, p.125. Campell, p.88. Dobie, pp.57,66. Graff 2894. Howes M819. Raines, p.153.

147 Morton, Ohland (1902-)

TERAN AND TEXAS: A CHAPTER IN TEXAS-MEXICAN RELATIONS.

Austin: The Texas State Historical Association, 1948.
Introduction by Eugene C. Barker.
[8],191pp. Frontis. 3 maps. 25cm.
Cloth, dustjacket.

This is a superlative study of the last few years in which it might have been possible to avert the final rupture between Mexico and Texas, and of the Mexican most closely involved. Eugene C. Barker writes in his introduction: "Dr. Morton has made a welcome and praiseworthy contribution . . . in his life of General Mier y Teran. In spite of Teran's importance in Mexican history, this is the first lengthy study of the man, either in English or in Spanish; and for the period of Teran's active connection with Texas it is probably the best that will ever be written. . . . The book is a fine example of historical investigation and narration, always clear and vivid." Thomas Cotner called the work "a significant contribution" written in "a clear, concise, and readable style."

The book came into being via the standard route of beginning as Morton's 1939 doctoral dissertation at the University of Texas, followed by publication in a series of articles in the *Southwestern Historical Quarterly* (vols. XLVI-XLVIII) between July, 1942, and April, 1945, then publication in book form in 1948. As far as I can tell, however, this is the only book ever to be reviewed twice in the *Quarterly*. It was first reviewed in January, 1949, by Retta Murphy, and then reviewed again in July, 1950, by Thomas Cotner. Presumably this was done because the Murphy review is so inept and banal.

The theme of this biography of the Mexican cabinet officer is that many Mexicans worked for peace in Texas. Barker perceptively states: "The average citizen . . . has absorbed the impression that the colonists of Texas were the victims of persecution, tyranny, and calculated barbarism directed by the Mexican government and approved by all Mexicans. The truth is quite the contrary. Every important Mexican in San Antonio was solicitous for the success and prosperity of the new settlers. . . . The same was true of most state officials who had any knowledge of Texas and of national figures connected with its administration." Manuel de Mier y Teran was one of those men.

General Mier y Teran became interested in Texas in the early 1820's as a member of the Mexican congressional committee on colonization.

In 1828 he was sent on an inspection tour of Texas in conjunction with the boundary settlement between Mexico and the United States, Jean Luis Berlandier being one of his assistants. In 1829 he was placed in command of the military department which included Texas. A remarkable and intelligent man, he foresaw the inevitable effects of American settlements in Texas, and sought to avoid a conflict by urging Mexican colonization projects in Texas as well. Becoming a close friend of Stephen F. Austin, he worked for peace even though he believed the Texas hotheads would get out of hand if left unchecked. Finally, he felt compelled to recommend that American immigration be slowed down. The result of his recommendation was the Law of April 6, 1830, which forbade all further American settlement, a step bolder than Mier y Teran desired. Austin wrote Mier y Teran that "my hopes are fixed on you to save Texas." Mier y Teran and Austin strove against long odds to achieve a genuine joining of the two cultures in Texas, but in vain.

In 1832, Mier y Teran wrote to Austin that "the affairs of Texas are understood by none but you and me, and we alone are the only ones who can regulate them; but there is time now to do no more than calm the agitations." The agitations, however, grew worse. On July 2, Teran wrote despondently to Lucas Alaman: "The revolution is about to break forth and Texas is lost. . . . What will happen to Texas? It will go as God wills." The next day he walked to church and stabbed himself to death with his sword. Within a year, Austin was thrown in prison by Santa Anna and the chance for peace was lost forever.

148   Muir, Andrew Forest (1916-1969) [ed.]

TEXAS IN 1837: AN ANONYMOUS, CONTEMPORARY NARRATIVE.

Austin: University of Texas Press, [1958].
xxi,232pp. Endpaper maps. Illus. 23cm.
Cloth, dustjacket.

Other issues:
(A). Paperback edition. Same as original. 23cm.

The unknown author of this work left us the earliest written account of Texas as a republic. Andrew Muir called it "the best description of the Republic during its first year . . . as an independent nation that has yet come to light." Marilyn Sibley said that the anonymous author "stands as one of Texas' more objective visitors." James L. Nichols called it an important book that "will entertain even the most casual reader." The editors of the original 1838 magazine printing said that it was "the most intelligent, accurate, and impartial account of Texas, which has yet been given to the people of the United States."

The author has never been identified, and if the indefatigable Muir could not find out who wrote it, it is unlikely that anyone else will do so. The work was originally published under the title "Notes on Texas" between September, 1838, and April, 1839, in eight parts (volume I, numbers 5-6; volume II, numbers 1-6) in twenty-five chapters, in *The Hesperian*, a monthly magazine which Peter G. Thomson calls "the best of all the early western periodicals." The author is identified only as "R" and as "a Citizen of Ohio." In 1926, the first eight chapters were issued as a 35-page pamphlet by the Union National Bank of Houston under the misleading title *Houston and Galveston in the Years 1837-8*.

The Muir edition is the first in book form, and it is a masterpiece of editing—one of the best-edited and best-annotated of all Texas books. Andrew Forest Muir was one of those meticulous researchers with a genius for following up clues but who unfortunately seldom publish the results of their findings. In this case, his introduction and annotations are as valuable as the text itself. To give just one example, he deduces from internal evidence that the author was a Baptist lawyer from Pulaski, Tennessee. In analyzing the author's strictures on Texas government and law, Muir reflects that "he discerned only chaos and overlooked the plausible union of the common and the civil law that was soon to produce the doctrines of community property and homestead exemption, the blending of law and equity, and the abandonment of special pleading, which have spread not only through-out the United States but, in part, to wherever the English language is spoken." Muir maintains that "the greatest contribution made by Texas—and it began at this early date—to Western culture has been in the field of jurisprudence."

The author arrived in Galveston on March 22, 1837, traveled leisurely to San Antonio via Houston and back, and sailed away in early

October of the same year. Muir, who always views his subject with strict objectivity, states of the author's narrative of his tour: "Where he discusses [events and places he did not see], he is perforce obliged to use second hand information, deficient at best and misinterpreted at worst. In describing what he saw with his own eyes, he is graphic and informative. In repeating hearsay, he becomes insipid. . . . Some of his descriptions of individuals are excellent, but his group portraits are out of focus. When he discusses groups of people he engages in what the sociologists call stereotyping."

The *Hesperian* editors, William D. Gallagher and Otaway Curry, hinted that the text would be revised, enlarged, and issued as a separate book, but this was never done. Muir faults the editors for poor proofreading, but quotes their statement that they rushed to print with "hasty first drafts from the original [manuscript] memoranda." Muir states that he has "silently" corrected errors of orthography, spelling, and grammar, and cites the author's use of "Seawillow" for "Cibolo," a common rendering of the time, comparing it with the use of "Picketwire" for a stream in Colorado obviously rendered from "Purgatoire."

The author provides us with an unparalleled description of the Texas republic in its infancy, often with keen insight and humor. He is especially vivid in describing events in the new town of Houston, the first lots of which were sold only two months before he arrived. Thus he was present during the creation of one of the great cities of the world, and gives us the best surviving account of its early days. His description of the first anniversary celebration of the Battle of San Jacinto is unforgettable. He tells us of the elaborate ball that evening: "Night came and with it . . . the President [Sam Houston] dressed in a rich silk velvet suit. . . . It ought to be added to his other merits on the occasion that, during the dance, he remained perfectly sober." Muir's footnote states: "The author appears to have selected his words very carefully at this point. As a matter of fact, it seems that Houston did get drunk *after* the dance, for Benjamin Fort Smith, at whose inn there was a midnight supper following the dance, billed Houston for liquor and broken glasses. . . ."

Graff 1872. Sabin 31615.

149 Nance, Joseph Milton (1913-)

AFTER SAN JACINTO: THE TEXAS-MEXICAN FRONTIER, 1836-1841.

Austin: University of Texas Press, [1963].
xiv,642pp. 4 folding maps.
16 Illus. 24cm.
Cloth, dustjacket.

[also:]

ATTACK AND COUNTER-ATTACK: THE TEXAS-MEXICAN FRONTIER, 1842.

Austin: University of Texas Press, [1964].
xiv,750pp. 4 folding maps.
16 Illus. 24cm.
Cloth, dustjacket.
Other issues:
(A). Second printing of the first volume, 1970.

This is the most comprehensive history of the Texas-Mexican borderlands during the period. A third volume completing the trilogy through the Mier Expedition is contemplated. Llerena Friend wrote that the work "will make possible a fresh approach to Texas history," and that it "is basic for any study of Texas history."

One of the most neglected phases of Texas history has been that dealing with the area south and west of the Nueces, particularly during the period covered by these two books. Nance's exhaustive account fills that gap; he states: "It is the story of Texas-Mexican relations along a thinly populated borderland between two contrasting civilizations—one virile, aggressive, restless and frequently lawless; the other proud, traditional, militaristic, and often corrupt. Both civilizations were projected upon a third and older culture—the Indian—which played an important role in the contest between the two stronger parties." Dr. Friend, stating her "frustration at being so ignorant of the story here related . . . checked what the casual reader of Texas history might have heretofore had to read on the subject: in a school textbook, ten lines; in a college text, one paragraph; in Yoakum, three pages; in Wortham, six pages; in Brown and Bancroft, about twelve pages each."

The first volume covers the operations of the Texas and Mexican armies during 1836, subsequent cattle raids, Indian operations, frontier

Attack and Counterattack
The Texas-Mexican Frontier, 1842

By Joseph Milton Nance

IT IS 1842—a dramatic year in the history of Texas-Mexican relations. After five years of uneasy peace, of futile negotiations, of border raids and temporary, unofficial truces, a series of military actions upsets the precarious balance between the two countries. Once more the Mexican Army marches on Texas soil; once more the frontier settlers strengthen their strongholds for defense or gather their belongings for flight. Twice San Antonio falls to Mexican generals; twice the Texans assemble armies for the invasion of Mexico. It is 1842—a year of attack and counterattack.

This is the story told by Professor Nance, head of the Department of History and Government at Texas A. and M. University, told with a definitiveness and immediacy that come from many years of meticulous research. *Attack and Counterattack* continues the account of Texas-Mexican relations begun with *After San Jacinto,* the first of this three-volume series.

Illustrated $8.50

Texas residents must add 2-per-cent sales tax to total amount of order

UNIVERSITY OF TEXAS PRESS
AUSTIN, TEXAS 78712

trade and smuggling, the Cordova-Flores affair, the Federalist Wars, the Republic of the Rio Grande, and Texas Ranger activities. The second volume brings together for the first time in comprehensive fashion the events of the remarkable year of 1842: the Vasquez Campaign, the Battle of Lipantitlan, the Woll Campaign, the Somervell Expedition, the Battle of Salado, and the Dawson Massacre.

Both volumes contain appendices of muster rolls of Texas frontier forces, the result of years of research. These include such musters as Burleson's ranger command on the Cordova Expedition, Nicholas Dawson's company in 1842, the Somervell Campaign musters, etc. The indexes to the two volumes total 124 pages, of which Friend states: "The index will always be indispensable to anyone seeking biographical material on the men of the Republic of Texas." The 54 pages of bibliography will also be of great interest, as Nance used materials in Spanish and in English never before or since published or consulted. On the other hand, his research was so extensive into unique and little-known sources that he overlooked one well-known basic work for the 1842 period: Nelson Lee's *Three Years Among the Camanches*.

150 Newcomb, William Wilmon, Jr. (1921-)

THE INDIANS OF TEXAS, FROM PREHISTORIC TO MODERN TIMES.

Austin: University of Texas Press, [1961].
xviii,404pp. 12 illus. 4 maps. 23cm.
Cloth, dustjacket.

Other issues:
(A). Second printing, 1962.
(B). Third printing, 1965.
(C). Fourth printing, 1967.
(D). Fifth printing, 1973.
(E). Sixth printing, 1978.
(F). Seventh printing, 1980.
[All printings lack a number of the plates which are cited in the text, and all printings retain the error of "Nueces" for "Neches" on the last line of p.315. Some of the printings have been issued in paperback.]

The best work on Texas Indian cultures, this volume is also an important work on Texas prior to the coming of the white man.

The Indians of Texas

FROM PREHISTORIC TO MODERN TIMES

By W. W. Newcomb, Jr.

Illustrated by HAL M. STORY

$5.75

"It is the only book now available that gives both dependable and detailed information about the specific Indians who once lived in Texas."—H. Mewhinney, *The Houston Post*

"This book is so remarkably well done that it makes one reader wish that it were a bigger book describing all American Indian tribes. It tells, with authority, what most laymen want to know about Indians, and it surpasses Clark Wissler's standard works insofar as readability and sustained interest may be concerned. . . . This book will appeal to any interested reader."—Lee Ash, Yale University Library, *Library Journal*

"Dr. Newcomb writes persuasively and with economy, and he has used his materials very well indeed. Texas, big and varied as it is, was the meeting place and the battleground of various cultures even before the white man arrived. Dr. Newcomb examines some of the reasons for this. Though specifically a study of the Indians of Texas, his book applies to much of the Southwest. Synthesis though it is, the author's viewpoint gives it significance. And his presentation makes good reading of what might have been a book only for the specialists."—*Saturday Review*

University of Texas Press, Austin

Saturday Review said that Newcomb's presentation "makes good reading of what might have been a book only for the specialists." Newcomb himself states: "Those who write of the near-extermination of American Indians generally take sides. Some tell of the brutal butchery and the economic and political exploitation of the Indian by the white man; others recall the raised tomahawk, the slain child, the scalped mother, the plundered frontier cabin. Unfortunately, but naturally, many of the histories written by Americans (and especially Texans) have obscured, twisted, or rationalized the facts in favor of the white man. Recently there has been a trend in the opposite direction, and admittedly it has been fostered by social scientists biased in favor of native peoples. The present account is not an apology or rationalization for either side; it is, rather, an attempt to provide a realistic overall view of what happened when Anglo-American civilization came into contact and inevitable conflict with the Indian cultures of Texas."

The book begins with a concise account of prehistoric man in Texas. Newcomb states that "the earliest cultural relics so far discovered in Texas—and they are among the earliest found anywhere in the Americas—have been given the name Llano complex. . . . At present the earliest published date for man in America comes from a site near Lewisville in Denton County, Texas . . . thirty-seven thousand years."

Although they became diverse culturally, the initial Texas Indians were from the same basic stock: "The Texas Indians are . . . a rather homogeneous entity. All are members of the Mongoloid race and belong to its American Indian subdivision. The physical variations of Texas Indians were minor . . . being confined to slight differences in stature and skin color. If the differences in the behavior of various peoples were rooted in their varying race or biology, we should expect all Texas Indians to have had similar, if not identical, customs and patterns of behavior. Nothing could be further from the actual case. The various tribes of Texas Indians were about as diversified in their behavior as Texans, Frenchmen, Chinese, and Bantus are in theirs."

Newcomb explains the emergence of tribes in Texas, and the immigration into Texas of tribes from all directions. He discusses the crude cultures of the Coahuilticans of southern Texas: "South Texas has the appearance of a relict region, an isolated backwash in which cultures remained virtually unchanged for long periods." These Coa-

huilticans possessed some noteworthy dining habits: "Fish were sometimes roasted without cleaning, and set aside for eight days, by which
time the larvae of flies and other insects had developed in the rotting
flesh. The larvae were then consumed as an epicure's delight, as also,
apparently, was the remaining flesh. Few living creatures were overlooked as a source of food . . . spiders, ant eggs, worms, lizards,
snakes—including rattlesnakes—earth, rotten wood, deer dung, and
some 'unmentionables' being eaten with relish."

The Karankawas and Tonkawas, most noted for their ritualistic
cannibalism but otherwise dissimilar culturally, are given separate
chapters. The origins and cultures of the plains tribes—especially the
Lipan Apaches, Comanches, Kiowas, and Kiowa Apaches—are
described in some detail.

The Comanches, the strongest Texas Indian culture if not the most
civilized, are examined closely. Coming to Texas from among the
Northern Shoshones, "by 1705 they were in New Mexico and before
the century was half over were militarily in control of much of the
southern plains. The changes in their culture were revolutionary: from
a scrounging, poor, militarily weak rabble, they became in less than a
century a mounted, well-equipped, and powerful people." From the
beginnings of "Anglo-American Texas until 1875 the Comanches were
the principal and most stubborn adversaries the Texans had. . . .
Despite crushing superiority in numbers and military might, the best
that Texas and the United States could do was to defeat the Comanches
and their allies by logistic strategy. When the Comanches' ponies and
food supply gave out, they had to give up; they were not defeated in
battle in the strict sense of the term."

The Jumanos, Wichitas, Atakapans, and Caddo Confederacies are
discussed as agrarian cultures. Upsetting our customary image of the
semi-peaceful Caddoes, Newcomb describes them as being vigorous
warriors. Describing an early attack by Spaniards on an East Texas
thatched-roof Caddo village, he states:

"During the battle one cavalier climbed to an upper room of a
building which served as a granary, and found five women huddled
in a corner. The Spanish code of honor did not permit the wanton
slaughter of women, and he made motions to this effect as best he
could. Realizing the soldier was alone, the five demoniac savages

rushed upon him, and seized him by the arms, leg, neck, and penis. In his struggles to free himself one leg crushed through the flimsy floor, reducing the soldier to helplessness. Although his life was in peril, he dared not cry out, since these were but women. At this crucial moment another soldier entered the lower room. He saw the leg dangling from above and was preparing to take a swipe at it with his sword when something prompted him to investigate. Climbing to the upper floor he immediately realized the predicament of his comrade and decided it was the better part of valor to discard his code of honor.''

The concise summary chapter analyzes the crushing of Texas Indian cultures by the onslaught of the white man, concluding: ''Perhaps nothing more should be said about the near-extermination of Texas Indians. Certainly any interpretation of the events in this history runs the risk of biased rationalization, either in defense of the savage tribes, or of their Texas-American conquerors. But even at this risk, one comment cries out to be made. It is that the actions of cultural bodies, whether savage tribes or literate, civilized states, should not, cannot, be judged in terms of individual morality. Cultures are not and never have been 'moral' in their dealings and relations with one another. Their treatment of one another is and has been ultimately determined by their relative strengths and the nature of their cultures, not by whatever their internal ethical or moral institutions happen to be. . . . To view the events of Texas history from any such moralistic, narrow standpoint, as most histories have done, is to miss the magnitude and meaning of what happened. Briefly, the obliteration of Texas Indians was but a small part, a footnote really, to the nineteenth-century development and emergence of a new, and in technological terms, a tremendously powerful nation-state. Given the accelerating industrial revolution of the United States, its spurting population growth, and the vast empty spaces of the West, inhabited mostly by a few Stone Age tribes of Indians, the inevitability of what had to happen becomes clear. The dynamism of a new America, then as now, swept up willy-nilly its inhabitants, white and Indian, as a spring torrent sweeps up leaves and twigs for a journey to an unknown fate.''

Prehistoric Texas is best represented by the works of J. E. Pearce and A. T. Jackson. Pearce wrote the fascinating and popular *Tales That*

Dead Men Tell (Austin: University of Texas Bulletin #3537, 1935) and Jackson wrote the monumental and still unsurpassed *Picture-Writing of Texas Indians* (Austin: University of Texas Publication 3809, 1938), with its 49 maps, 224 plates, and 283 figures. Edwin B. Sayles wrote *An Archaeological Survey of Texas* (Globe, Arizona: Privately Printed, 1935), followed by Dee Ann Suhm and Edward B. Jelks, *Handbook of Texas Archeology* (Austin: Texas Archeological Society and Texas Memorial Museum, 1962).

151 Newell, Chester (1803-1892)

HISTORY OF THE REVOLUTION IN TEXAS, PARTICULARLY OF THE WAR OF 1835 & 36, TOGETHER WITH THE LATEST GEOGRAPHICAL, TOPOGRAPHICAL AND STATISTICAL AC-COUNTS OF THE COUNTRY, FROM THE MOST AUTHENTIC SOURCES; ALSO, AN APPENDIX.

New York: Published by Wiley & Putnam, No. 161 Broadway (J. P. Wright, Printer, Cedar Street), 1838.
x,[2],215pp. Folding map, titled "Texas." 19cm.
Cloth. The dedication is on page [iv]; page [iii] is blank.

Other issues:
(A). Same as above, but page [iv] is blank and the dedication is on page [iii]. The map is titled: "Texas, 1838."
(B). Facsimile reprint. Austin: The Steck Company, 1935. 21cm. Cloth.
(C). Facsimile reprint. New York: Arno Press, 1973. 22cm. The Far Western Frontier Series.

This is one of the earliest books published about Texas after it became a republic. The history it presents is second-hand and sometimes perfunctory, but the quotations from participants are of considerable historical value. The descriptive portions add much to our knowledge of the early republic. Newell states in the short preface: "The following work is the result of a twelve-month's residence in Texas, whither the Author repaired early in the Spring of 1837, for the benefit of his health. Three months of the twelve he spent at the capital of the Republic, exclusively and diligently employed in acquiring the information and material necessary for his work. He obtained valuable matter from documents in the War Department, and others

to which he had access; and also, much important information from
repeated conversations with several men distinguished in the war of
'35-'36—of whom he will name His Excellency Gen. Houston, Gen.
Lamar, Gen. F. Huston, Col. Poe, Col. Ward, Col. Neil, and Capt.
Shackleford.''

In the Alex Dienst Papers in the University of Texas Archives there
is a letter from Newell to Samuel May Williams, dated Baltimore,
September 19, 1838, stating: ''. . . I should choose to return to Texas
if I had the *means* . . . having exhausted all, & more than all, my
funds in getting my work through the press, and not being able to
receive any proceeds of the sale of the same (except such as I sell
myself) for some months to come. . . . I am obliged to purchase, at
the rate of fifty cents a copy of my work . . . I sell the same for one
dollar, and thus, where I can dispose of several, realise a good profit.''
Newell mentions that he is a Protestant minister, offers to teach school
in Galveston, and states that he has a league of land on the Lavaca.
Newell, a graduate of Yale, operated a school at Velasco during the
nine months that he was not in the capital at Houston. He never
returned to Texas, serving the remainder of his career as a chaplain
in the United States Navy.

The work begins with an excellent summary of Mexican history
from 1821 to 1835, followed by a sketch of Texas history from 1832 to
1835, ending with Cos' retreat from San Antonio. The events of 1836
are described, including quotations from participating Texans and from
previously published Mexican accounts, such as Almonte's diary. The
account is pro-Texan throughout, but more objective than many other
contemporary Anglo-American versions.

An Appendix at the end of the volume offers some important
documents relating to the revolution. Of particular value are the
account of Santa Anna's capture, ''given on the authority of an officer
present at that battle,'' and a reportorial account of Santa Anna's
confrontation with Houston shortly afterwards, ''as substantially related
to the author by Gen. Houston.''

Newell was one of the first to seduce Sam Houston into giving
particulars of the campaign. A letter from Newell to Houston, April
18, 1838, shows Newell's method:

"You will recollect that I remarked to you this morning that I had been making the Revolution in Texas the principal subject of my study and investigation, and that I had my own *views*: I mean, particularly, of the part you had the distinguished honor to act:—they are briefly the following: that no other man in Texas could have taken such undisciplined troops as the Texans were in the campaign of '36 and have kept them in any sort of check; that by your forbearance, prudence and watchfulness you kept together and preserved the army; and that finally, by your skill and valor, you led them to victory. Now, Sir, what is my object in the above statement! It is not, let me say in the first place, to cause difficulty, and thereby to injure another: it is not—God forbid it should be—to raise my obscure self into notice by causing misunderstanding between those in conspicious stations. It is three fold;—first to apprise you, that, being *resolved* to publish and publish in an independent manner notwithstanding difficulties flung in my way by a certain individual, to apprise you, I say, that I shall endeavor, and that it will give me much satisfaction, to do you *justice* in what I shall publish. Secondly, to get such additional information from you as will add *value* to my publication: And, thirdly, it is to warrant me in stating, that an individual, high in office here [probably M. B. Lamar], who has long contemplated the publishing a history of Texas, has at one time promised me his notes and whatever matter he had for a history, and at another time refused the same . . . and that I *know* his publication . . . will be . . . derogatory to your Excellency."

This letter elicited an immediate response from Houston, who wrote: "I was master of my own counsels, and did command my men. There was order after I took command. . . ." Houston apparently gave Newell much of his time, as his influence is evident throughout the book.

Another particularly interesting portion of the work is the section entitled "Geography, Topography, Statistics, &c., of Texas." Newell describes the towns of the republic, offers advice to immigrants, analyzes the people of Texas, and projects the future. His predictions, some sage and some ludicrous, are remarkable. For example:

"On account of its geographical position, and the character of its soil and climate, Texas is destined to become the vineyard of North America."

"It is certain that in Texas, especially the Western part, silk may be produced to more advantage that in most, if not any part of the United States."

"Silver is to be found in many parts of Texas."

"The Peach is no where better than in Texas. . . . Oranges, it is believed, may be raised in abundance in the Southern and Western parts."

"There is nothing for which Texas affords such superlative advantages over most other countries as the raising of stock . . . There is no business so inviting as raising stock in Texas."

The Republic of Texas was not noted for piety. Newell comments that "many of the Texans value churches and ministers of religion, if not religion itself, less than otherwise they would." On the moral character of Texans, Newell offers one of my favorite quotations from all the early writings on Texas: "There is existing in the minds of the people in many places, if not generally, at the North, a strong and bitter prejudise against Texas. . . . Because it has been represented to be the resort of criminals, of insolvent and fraudulent debtors, of outlaws, and bad characters of every description. Now, it cannot be, by any reasonable man, believed that the *majority* of the people of Texas are of such a character. . . . No, it is believed only that a *large part* of the people of Texas are of the character described. Well, admitting they are, should the entire population and country be then reviled?"

Clark, III-215. Graff 3010. Howes N115. Rader 2479. Raines, p.154. Sabin 54948. Streeter 1318.

152 Nichols, James Wilson (1820-1891)

NOW YOU HEAR MY HORN: THE JOURNAL OF JAMES WILSON NICHOLS, 1820-1887.

Austin & London: University of Texas Press, [1967].
Edited by Catherine W. McDowell.
xvi,[6],212pp. Illus. by Eldridge Hardie. Map by Jose Cisneros. Design and typography by Carl Hertzog. 25cm.
Cloth, dustjacket.

Other issues:

(A). Special edition, with printed limitation notice, 250 numbered copies, signed by
the editor, and slipcased. Printed slip inserted, to which a miniature Bowie
knife is scotch-taped, for use in "slitting the folded edges" of the uncut pages
of this edition.

This most spirited and forthright of all Texas memoirs is one of the
most delightful American pioneer narratives ever written, and a
valuable contribution not only to our knowledge of events in Texas
history but to our understanding of the frontier spirit as well.
Frontiersman Nichols gives us an unvarnished account of life in
frontier Texas, with no holds barred. His narrative is humorous, bold,
gruesome, opinionated, and revealing.

The journal is well-edited by Catherine McDowell, whose annotations are very useful in comparing Nichols' account with those of
Sowell, Wilbarger, and others. The index, however, is incomplete and
unreliable. McDowell received the manuscript as a gift to the D.R.T.
Library in San Antonio from the Nichols heirs. It was missing some
parts, obviously removed by the family. McDowell states that there
was bad blood between the Sowell and Nichols families, although they
had previously been close and intermarried: "In later years animosities
and jealousies developed, and somehow the Journal became involved—
how, the missing pages of this manuscript would probably tell."

Nichols was possibly the worst speller in Texas history, and that is
a large claim. He states: "Three monts was all the scooling I ever got
but the teacher boarded with Father . . . and taken a likeing to me
and taught me at school in day time and till late at night at home. . . .
He told me I aught to keep a memorandom of all the noted incidences
. . . and I commenced to keep a journal of my life . . . and kept it
up and now I write from this." He says he kept the book from the
time he was twelve until about 1887, when he compiled his memoirs.
His main reason for writing it was to correct the errors of Sowell and
others "who have gone beyond their own abilities in the performance
even to pervert plain facts." He claims that "chin music goes a long
ways with some of the late writers." Nichols tells his side of events
without hesitation, even to calling certain men cowards even though
they were still alive at the time.

The Nichols family moved to Texas in late 1836, settling in the
Guadalupe region near San Antonio. James Nichols soon became a

regular Indian fighter and scout, serving in most of the campaigns from 1837 through 1848. His most memorable service was in the Texas Rangers under Jack Hays and Bigfoot Wallace. Nichols gives us a remarkable account of how the Hays Rangers trained in 1843: "Thos not on a scout ware every day practising horsemanship and marksmanship. We put up a post about the size of a common man, then put up another about 40 yards farther on. We would run our horses full speed and discharge our rifles at the first post, draw our pistles and fire at the second . . . We had not practised two months until thare was not many men that would not put his balls in the center of the posts. Then we drew a ring about the size of a mans head and soon every man could put both his balls in the circul. We would practics this awhile, then try rideing like the Comanche Indians. After practising for three or four months we became so purfect that we would run our horses half or full speede and pick up a hat, a coat, a blanket, or rope, or even a silver dollar, stand up in the saddle, throw ourselves on the side of our horses with only a foot and a hand to be seen, and shoot our pistols under the horses neck, rise up and reverse, etc."

Although he voted against joining the Union, Nichols says: "In 1845 the Republic of Texas died and was burried in the anexation to the United States and was riserected in the shape of the State of Texas." He tells of his service in the Mexican War under McCulloch and in many later Indian campaigns. When the Civil War began, Nichols was against secession, and was hounded unmercifully, as were many people in his region of Texas. His account of the treatment of unionists is vivid and pungent. When vigilantes came to run him off his land, he told them that "the first man that crosses that fence is my meat. Now you hear my horn." Apparently, he was never forgiven by his Confederate neighbors and he never forgave them, for his last page states that "that ring chick, paper collar, kid glove, gold stud, mooveing mass of filthy corruption still exists in Blanco with a few addisions and all git their sustainments by sucking the paps of great hydreheaded monstrossity . . . Som have gone whare . . . hope nor mercy never can reach them."

153   Nixon, Patrick Ireland (1883-1965)

THE MEDICAL STORY OF EARLY TEXAS, 1528-1853.

[Lancaster, Pa.:] Published by the Mollie Bennett Lupe Memorial Fund, 1946.
[Verso of title:] Printed in the United States of America by Lancaster Press, Inc.,
Lancaster, Penn.
xv,507pp.28 illus. 25cm.
Dark green cloth, paper labels on spine and front cover.

Other issues:
(A). Special edition, bound in white cloth and light green boards. On verso of title:
      "This Edition, limited to one hundred copies. . . ." Some copies are found
      signed, some not.

The best work on Texas medical history, this is also one of the best
state medical histories ever published. It is well-annotated, carefully
factual, and lucidly written. A graduate of Johns Hopkins in 1909, Dr.
Nixon practiced medicine in Texas for fifty-six years, and gathered
materials for his history during much of that time. His determination
to stick to the facts is evident from a paragraph in his preface:

"Every effort has been made to maintain a proper sense of values
in this story of medicine in Texas. When we view our medical
forefathers through the mists of time, there is a natural tendency to
magnify their stature. These men were human, just as we are. Some
were heroes and leaders; the great majority were average doctors and
average men of their day; a few were unworthy doctors and unworthy
men. So every endeavor has been made to eschew words of adulation
or enthusiasm which transcend the facts of history. Historic accuracy
would be violated if it were said, as Williams said of a similar group
elsewhere [S. W. Williams, *American Medical Biography,* p.xv], that the
lives of all these medical pioneers of Texas 'will ever stand as pole
stars to direct the course of the future traveller on the road to medical
honor, distinction, and usefulness.' So, without resorting to the
elaborate use of superlatives, much satisfaction has come from rescuing
the names of many a Texas doctor from what Sir Thomas Browne has
happily termed the 'iniquity of oblivion.' "

The dates covered in the book are not arbitrary. The year 1528 was
when Cabeza de Vaca, "the first man to treat the Texas Indians and
the first white doctor in the Western Hemisphere," set foot in Texas.

The year 1853 marked the founding of the Texas Medical Association. The book, nevertheless, begins with an interesting chapter on Indian medicine in Texas. There are five chapters on the Spanish period; one on French doctors in Texas; four on the early Mexican period, 1821-1836; five on the period of the Texas Revolution; eight on the period of the Republic of Texas; and two on early statehood. An appendix lists several hundred early Texas doctors and their place of residence. There are chapters on quackery, military and naval medicine, diseases peculiar to Texas, hospitals, and other related subjects.

Dr. Nixon wrote two related books that are of importance, *A Century of Medicine in San Antonio* (1936) and what amounts to a sequel of his major work, *A History of the Texas Medical Association, 1853-1953* (1953).

Dobie, p.70. Howes N161.

154 Noel, Theophilus (1850- after 1904)

A CAMPAIGN FROM SANTA FE TO THE MISSISSIPPI; BEING A HISTORY OF THE OLD SIBLEY BRIGADE FROM ITS FIRST ORGANIZATION TO THE PRESENT TIME; ITS CAMPAIGNS IN NEW MEXICO, ARIZONA, TEXAS, LOUISIANA, AND ARKANSAS, IN THE YEARS 1861-2-3-4.

Shreveport: Shreveport News Printing Establishment—John Dickinson, Proprietor, 1865.
152pp. Folding table. 22cm.

Other issues:
(A). Facsimile reprint. Raleigh: Charles R. Sanders, Jr., 1961. [26],[5]-152,[4]pp. 26cm. Verso of title: "Printed in U.S.A. Whittet & Shepperson, Richmond, Va." Introduction by Neal Austin. Limited to 500 numbered copies. Cloth-backed boards, boxed.
(B). Reprint of first edition. Houston: Stagecoach Press, 1961. xxvii,183pp. Maps. 24cm. Introduction and notes by Martin Hardwick Hall and Edwin Adams Davis. "Explanatory notes make this the best edition"—Allan Nevins.

There were three Civil War campaigns of compelling significance for Texas—the New Mexico campaign, the battle for Galveston, and the Red River campaign—and this is the story of the only brigade that participated in all three. It has the added value of being one of the few Texas-Confederate unit histories published before the war was over. Richard Harwell called it "one of the rarest and most fascinating of Confederate books," and Neal Austin called it "a remarkable book, with clarity and feeling." Martin Hall said: "Noel's account is historically valuable because, in addition to being a first-hand history of an important military unit, it reveals a common soldier's frank, unvarnished view of life in the Confederate Army . . . His opinionated and critical comments add a greater richness to the book, and give a far better picture of the author and the common Confederate soldier than do the ordinary and impersonal diaries and reminiscences of most soldiers."

Noel served with the unit throughout the war, although he missed large chunks of the unit's service due to illness and captivity. He was captured in April, 1863, and paroled in May, then recaptured enroute home, and paroled again in July. His own journal was stolen or lost at the Battle of Pleasant Hill, and he had to rely on memory, his fellow soldiers, and what official reports he was able, as a lowly sergeant, to obtain. A note by Alex Dienst in one of the few surviving copies states that during 1864, W. Randolph Howell gave Noel his own diary and a hundred dollars in gold to help underwrite the venture. Another surviving copy has a note, "bought of Howell, April 5, 1865," so the book must have been completed in late 1864 and printed in the early months of 1865.

Noel states in his preliminary comments that his book "was born in the tented field, amid the din and confusion of soldiers life. By piece-meals—a paragraph here, a sentence or more somewhere else— after stopping in the very centre of one to perform the duties incumbent upon me as a private soldier in the ranks, has my work been moulded."

The text begins with a narrative of the Sibley Campaign. It was crucial for Sibley to drill his volunteer recruits into a commandable army before setting off across the desert to New Mexico. Noel gives us the best surviving account of how the Texans balked at being trained: "We had drills, drills . . . on all occasions . . . The strictest guard that we ever had around our camp was while we were camped on the Salado, a thousand miles or more from a foe. We had a camp guard, a picket guard, and every thing was so guarded that one had to be on *guard* when he spoke. . . . [We were] left drilling, dress-parading, &c., as though the whole welfare of the country depended upon that job being perfected.'' After a hilarious and utterly disrespectful account of Sibley's inept speech to the army, ''we left San Antonio armed with squirrel-guns, bear guns, sportsman's-guns, shotguns . . . in fact, guns of all sorts.'' Throughout the narrative, Noel is sassy about officers and bigwigs.

The Sibley campaign into New Mexico had many unusual features. Sibley convinced Jefferson Davis that he could conquer the west for the South, that with 4000 men he could double the size of the Confederacy. His command was almost entirely made up of Texans, five of whom eventually became Confederate generals. His opponent in New Mexico, E. R. S. Canby, was his own brother-in-law. The expedition of the Sibley brigade westward was the largest movement of men ever yet made through that country. Noel's account of the successful victory at Valverde, the capture of Albuquerque and Santa Fe, the defeat at Glorietta Pass, and the painful retreat in disarray back through West Texas, hounded by Apaches, is skimpy in overview but vivid in detail. Only about half of the unit made it back. No other attempt was ever made to conquer the West, but neither was any western invasion of Texas ever attempted.

After recuperation in Texas, the brigade participated in the recapture of Galveston on January 1, 1863, ending the Union thrust into Texas by sea. In April, the brigade moved into Louisiana and spent the rest of the war contesting General Banks. This culminated with the Battle of Mansfield, in which the brigade lost its boldest fighter and best leader, Gen. Tom Green. Noel inserts the memorial address on Green by Gov. Murrah of Texas, as well as some biographical sketches and a relatively complete roster of the unit.

After the war, many hundreds of unit histories were written, and virtually all of them have a certain sameness of presentation and format. Conventions of style became formalized, and the outlook towards leaders, officers, specific battles and campaigns, and the enemy became standardized. Only a few unit histories published during wartime escaped this stylization. Noel's cut-and-paste account is pathetically incomplete and contradictory regarding the mission of the brigade in any of its campaigns, but his viewpoint as a Texas soldier is different from that of any subsequent narrative.

Two reprints of the book were issued in 1961. Charles Sanders' handsome and elegant facsimile edition has a perceptive introduction, but no textual annotations or index. Jack Rittenhouse's Stagecoach Press edition is entirely reset, with Martin Hall's superb introductory matter and 71 annotations, although the text has been tampered with by corrected spellings and a few deletions. It, too, has no index. The most exhaustive study of the Sibley campaign and the units involved is Martin Hardwick Hall and Sam Long, *The Confederate Army of New Mexico* (Austin: Presidial Press, 1978, 422pp.), with rosters and muster rolls.

Noel planned to revise and enlarge his book after the war, but never did so. One of the two copies at the University of Texas has the extensive manuscript notes and corrections of B. F. Frymier, one of the brigade members. Many years later, Noel wrote his *Autobiography and Reminiscences* (Chicago: T. Noel Company, 1904, 348pp.), in which he changes his attitude of support of Sibley as a commander to one of bitter antagonism. Although this autobiography adds to our knowledge of Noel's Texas years as frontier scout, it is a vastly inferior book to his war memoir.

Coulter 345. Crandall 2642. Harwell *In Tall Cotton* 134. Howes N167. Nevins I-138. Rader 2487. Wagner-Camp (1953 ed.) 420a.

155   Oberholser, Harry Church (1870-1963)

THE BIRD LIFE OF TEXAS.

Austin & London: University of Texas Press, [1974].
Edited by Edgar Kincaid, Jr., with the assistance of Suzanne Winckler and John L. Rowlett. Preface by Pat Ireland Nixon. Foreword by John W. Aldrich. Paintings by Louis Agassis Fuertes.
Two volumes: xxviii,530; [10],531-1069pp. 36 color plates. 74 illus. 2 maps. 31cm.
Cloth. Boxed.
The Carrie Herring Hooks Series Number One.
Verso of title: Composition by G & S Typesetters, Austin, Texas. Text printed by the TJM Corporation, Baton Rouge, Louisiana . . . Binding by Universal Bookbindery, Inc., San Antonio, Texas.

Other issues:

THE BIRD LIFE OF TEXAS

By Harry C. Oberholser

Edited by Edgar B. Kincaid, Jr.

Paintings by Louis Agassiz Fuertes

The Bird Life of Texas provides the first detailed history and natural history of the state's numerous and varied bird population. In the realm of state bird books it is outstanding. The thirty-six water colors and thirty-six black-and-white drawings are by the celebrated American wildlife artist Louis Agassiz Fuertes. The Species Account includes a brief description of each bird, its world range, when and where it can be seen in Texas, and an account of its haunts and habits. Distribution maps and photographs of major bird habitats are also included. The two-volume boxed set, beautifully illustrated and handsomely produced, will be a welcome addition to any fine library.

Number One in the Corrie Herring Hooks Series

$60.00

(A). Special edition of ten copies, "bound with a special added page tipped in. Jo Downs had imposed Edgar Kincaid's head on the bondy of a Cassowary," with a humorous caption noting that the "Cassowary is a rare bird indeed . . ." Same collation.

(B). *A Fuertes Portfolio of Texas Birds: the Color Plates from the First Edition of the Bird Life of Texas.* Austin & London: University of Texas Press, [1974]. 46 loose unnumbered leaves of text and 36 color plates. 31cm. Boxed. Limited to 750 numbered sets, signed by Edgar Kincaid.

This may well be the most important work ever published in Texas. Roy Bedichek called it "one of the great ornithological works of all time." John Graves states that "it is the final word on the subject, and I expect it will undoubtedly remain so for as long as English is spoken and read and birds are watched on this patch of North American soil that we call Texas. . . . It is a rich and lovely and satisfying book, and it will be of great value not only to those of us who currently interest ourselves in natural things, but to innumerable people not yet born."

In the spring of 1901 Harry Oberholser and Louis Fuertes joined Vernon Bailey on an expedition of the U.S. Biological Survey to the Big Bend region of Texas; this meeting marked the beginning of a remarkable publishing adventure that culminated a full seventy-three years later. The three men were dedicated naturalists, and the project nearly ended before it had fully begun when Fuertes got trapped halfway down a cliff 300 feet above the Rio Grande. Oberholser and Bailey executed a daring rescue (see Vol. I, p. 225) and Fuertes immediately resumed his work drawing the bird he had retrieved.

Bailey's survey of the mammals of the region was published in 1905, but Oberholser had his report on birds withheld because he felt it was not yet "reasonably comprehensive." In 1927 Fuertes' paintings and drawings were deposited in vaults by the government for safekeeping until Oberholser finished his text. By 1941, when Oberholser retired, the text was over three million words and totalled 11,754 typed pages. He was still not satisfied, however, and Edgar Kincaid joined him in improving the text.

In 1950 Frank Wardlaw came to Texas to head the new University of Texas Press. He had been in Austin less than a week when Roy Bedichek collared him and told him his first project should be the

Oberholser work. Wardlaw readily agreed, and asked Oberholser to submit the book; he later recalled: "Several weeks later Lelon Winsborough, my four-foot, eleven-inch secretary, went down to get the mail. She came back with the news that there was a manuscript . . . at the post office which she couldn't carry. It weighed 105 pounds." It took Wardlaw eleven years to persuade Oberholser to pare down the text to a mere million words. Oberholser died in 1963 with the task still not complete; Edgar Kincaid masterfully completed the paring and, in the words of John Graves, "updated it with recent material and added to it his own penetrating and often eloquent observations."

A lady named Corrie Herring Hooks, who had known and helped Oberholser, died before the project was complete. Her daughter, Mrs. Marrs McLean, gave generous aid. A National Science Foundation grant was obtained and expended. Other financial aid was received and disbursed; Kincaid agreed to continue without compensation. Wardlaw's first publishing project at Texas was actually his last; it finally appeared, twenty-four years after he came to Austin, the week after he left the University of Texas to take over the Texas A & M Press. In one of his most eloquent essays, ("The Book That Was Too Big for Texas," *Scholarly Publishing,* January, 1975), Wardlaw wrote: "Roy Bedichek once described Oberholser's work as 'a book that is too big even for Texas.' Well here it is, seventy-three years after Oberholser began it. Nothing, dear Bedi, is too big for Texas."

The long delays were worth it. The two volumes, totalling nearly a million words of text, catalogue and describe the bird life of Texas from 1535 to 1973. Fred S. Webster, Jr., states: "The study begins in 1535 and no earlier only because, with the exception of some prehistoric fossils, remembered details of bird life were interred with civilizations of our ancient Indians. It stops in 1973 simply because if it had not stopped the volumes would never have been published."

Edgar Kincaid states that Louis Agassiz Fuertes (1874-1927) "was the first American to make a life-long career of painting these wonderful creatures so that they look alive. Fuertes' skill is much appreciated by birders and ornithologists, most of whom do not care for the wooden portraits by primitive artists, the melodramatic actors-in-feathers of John James Audubon, the daubs and dribbles of abstractionists, or the tiny, fuzzy, awkward, or off-color images too often caught by the camera. . . . Nowadays, in the waning years of beautiful birds, it is soothing to contemplate these quite Fuertes plates, accurately and joyously painted at the dawning of the twentieth century.''

The Fuertes plates were stored in light-proof vaults by the U.S. Government, yet some of the originals had lightly faded. Roger Tory Peterson retouched the only badly faded plate, that of the Vermilion Flycatcher. When advance proofs were sent in 1974 to the International Ornithological Congress being held in Canberra, Australia, Dorothy Cooper Hartshorne reported that some of the world's leading ornithologists "initially expressed surprise that Fuertes had ever painted birds in Texas. However, they quickly concluded that, while Texas might be forgotten, publication of L.A.F. plates was a not-to-be-ignored major event!''

The text includes detailed scientific data and infinitely careful studies of plumages, taxonomy, habitats, and habits, as well as special sections on the history of Texas ornithology and on the ecology of Texas birds. There is much more, however, for the lengthy descriptions abound in personal observations and details of sightings by both Oberholser and Kincaid. "Here is almost everything the inquiring birder or nonbirder wants to know about the activities of the species," says Fred S. Webster. "The Specimen comes to life. . . . *The Bird Life of Texas* chronicles the excitement of discovery and the pathos of change. . . . The lens was true; the images clear.''

156 Oberste, William Herman (1899-)

TEXAS IRISH EMPRESARIOS AND THEIR COLONIES: POWER AND HEWETSON, MCMULLEN & MCGLOIN, REFUGIO-SAN PATRICIO.

Austin: Von Boeckmann-Jones Co., 1953.
xii,310,[66]-75pp. Illus. Maps (4 folding). 24cm.
Cloth.
Limited to 300 numbered, autographed copies.

Other issues:
(A). Second edition, and first trade edition. Austin: Von Boeckmann-Jones Co., 1973. Same collation. Cloth, dustjacket.

This is the best account of the early Irish settlements in Texas. Harbert Davenport called it "a magnificent work. It is a product of

twenty years of tireless research and is irreplaceable as a chapter in the overall history of the colonization of Texas. Monsignor Oberste spent many years as pastor of the Catholic Church in Refugio in the heart of the Irish colonies in Texas, and is the author of numerous other books on the history and culture of the area, including the general editorship of the latter part of the monumental Castaneda series, *Our Catholic Heritage in Texas.''*

Oberste states that ''the story of the Irish colonies in Texas is one which has long needed to be told. The purpose of this volume then is to describe the arrival in Texas of these immigrants at the invitation of the Mexican authorities, under the sponsorship of the Texas Irish empresarios, James Power, James Hewetson, John McMullen, and James McGloin.'' Just as the story of the Spanish colonies has been told by Carlos E. Castaneda, the Austin colonies by Eugene C. Barker, and the Robertson Colony by Malcolm D. McLean, the Irish colonies receive in this volume the treatment of their place in Texas history. One other significant pre-revolutionary colony, that of Green DeWitt, has been studied in Ethel Zivley Rather's scholarly *DeWitt's Colony* (Austin: University of Texas Bulletin 51, 1905) and in the subsequent work by Edward A. Lukes, *DeWitt Colony of Texas* (Austin: Jenkins Publishing Company, 1976).

In addition to his decades of research and lifetime of personal contacts, Oberste was especially fortunate in having access to the privately owned manuscripts of the James Power family and the James Hewetson family. These were made available for study to Oberste for the first time, and add immeasurably to the importance of his work. Oberste says that ''this study is based almost exclusively on primary sources. . . . Some of these documents have never been published heretofore. . . . Regrettably no accumulation of documents belonging to the Empresarios McMullen and McGloin could be discovered.'' Oberste also travelled to Ireland and Mexico City to do research.

The settlements were made as a result of colonization contracts made in the 1820's by the Mexican government. Since the colonists were to be actual rather than nominal Roman Catholics, the contracts were easier to obtain. Getting the colonies started, on the other hand, was considerably more difficult. The colonists suffered considerably from incursions, and actually helped buffer eastern settlements in

Texas. Moreover, the contracts frequently overlapped, and much effort was expended sorting out boundaries. Oberste adds to his text an account of the earlier colonizing effort of Felipe Roque de la Portilla, whose daughter married James Power.

Oberste also provides a fine narrative of the role of the Irish in the Texas Revolution and the Texas republic. The study is supplemented by a group of excellent maps and a list of the individual Power and Hewetson land grants. Because there were so few available documents on the McMullen and McGloin colonies, these of necessity receive less substantial treatment. The colonization efforts of Martin DeLeon are discussed ephemerally, but have as yet never been treated fully.

157 Olmsted, Frederick Law (1822-1903)

A JOURNEY THROUGH TEXAS; OR, A SADDLE-TRIP ON THE SOUTHWESTERN FRONTIER; WITH A STATISTICAL APPENDIX.

New York: Dix, Edwards & Co., 321 Broadway . . ., 1857.
[2],xxiv,516pp. Frontis. Folding map. 19cm.
Cloth.

Other editions:
(A). [Second printing]. New York: Mason Brothers, 108 & 110 Duane Street, 1859. Same collation.
(B). [Third printing]. New York: Mason Brothers, 5 and 7 Mercer Street, 1860. Same collation.
(C). London: Sampson Low . . ., 1859. Same collation. First English edition.
(D). *Wanderungen durch Texas und im Mexicanischen Grenzlande.* Leipzig: Verlagsbuchhandlung von Carl B. Lorck, 1857. [20],286pp. 20cm. Wrappers. First German edition.
(E). Same as (D). Leipzig: G. Senf, 1867. xix,286pp. 20cm.
(F). New edition, edited by James Howard. Austin: Von Boeckmann-Jones Press, 1962. xv,[1],299pp. Cloth. 24cm. New material: "A Note on this Edition." "Acknowledgements." "After-Word." Untrustworthy index. Portions deleted from text. Appendices deleted. Words "respelled." First edition printed in Texas, but bastardized, unscholarly, and unreliable.
(G). Facsimile edition. New York: Burt Franklin, [1969]. [2],xxxiv,516pp. Cloth. Research and Source Works Series 348. American Classics in History and Social Science 78.

(H). Facsimile edition. Austin & London: University of Texas Press, [1978]. [II],xxxiv,516pp. Cloth. The Elma Dill Russel Spencer Foundation Series. New foreword by Larry McMurtry. It is irritating that none of these modern editions has a reliable index.

(I). Facsimile edition. [New York: Time-Life Books, 1981]. Calf. 20cm. Cloth. [Also condensed version as part of Olmsted's *The Cotton Kingdom . . . N.Y.*, 1861. 2 vols. Map. Also: N.Y., 1862. London, 1861. N.Y., Modern Library, 1953.]

The most civilized of all 19th century books on Texas, this is also the most interesting and the most dependable. Olmsted's account of his travels in Texas and the South has been almost universally applauded: James Russell Lowell wrote that "no more important contributions to contemporary American history have been made," and Harriet Beecher Stowe, praising its account of slavery, called it "the most thorough expose of the economical view of this subject which has ever appeared." C. W. Raines said that there has been "no better book yet written of travels in Texas." Among recent critics, Arthur M. Schlesinger said it is "an indispensable work in the process of recapturing the American past." Rupert Richardson deemed it "the best portrayal of ante-bellum life extant." Larry McMurtry praised it as "an intelligent, lively book, packed with keen observation and lightened by a delicate strain of humor. . . . [It] remains one of the most readable of 19th century American travel books."

The book is the second volume of a trilogy on the South by Olmsted, "Our Slave States," condensed later in America as *The Cotton Kingdom* and in England as *Journeys and Explorations in the Cotton Kingdom*. The first volume was *A Journey in the Seaboard Slave States* (1856) and the third was *A Journey in the Back Country* (1860). Olmsted, whose eyesight was impaired by sumac poisoning as a child, made his travels through the South with his brother, Dr. John Hull Olmsted, to improve their health, to see the South, and to report on what they saw to the New York *Times*. Fifteen articles on Texas by Olmsted appeared in the *Times* between March 6 and June 7, 1854, signed "Yeoman." His brother then edited the articles and Olmsted's diary into a book for publication. Inexplicably, the material in the *Times* articles of May 13, May 18, and June 3 is omitted in the book. It appears, however, in C. C. McLaughlin [ed.], *The Papers of Frederick Law Olmsted*, Baltimore, 1981, vol. II, pp. 281-306. In 1861, Daniel R. Goodloe assisted in condensing and revising all three volumes of the trilogy down from 185,765 to 27,625 words for the single volume edition, which was dedicated to John Stuart Mill.

"The great extent and capacities of Texas," Olmsted wrote, "as well as its distinct position and history," encouraged him to devote a whole volume of his trilogy to the single State of Texas. The brothers left Baltimore by train on November 10, 1853, reaching Natchitoches on December 15, and arriving in San Augustine at Christmas time. Olmsted traveled for two thousand miles in Texas on "'Mr. Brown,' our mule; a stout, dun-colored, short-legged, cheerful son of a donkey, but himself very much of a gentleman. . . . He was endowed with the hereditary bigotry of his race, but while in our service was always, if not by hook then by crook, amenable to reason. When gentle persuasives failed, those of a higher potency were exhibited, and always with effect."

They rode through East Texas along the Old San Antonio Road, which "could hardly be called a road. It was only a way where people had passed along before." Each night they stopped at a nearby farm, where they slept on the cabin floor and dined on the Texas staple of pork, corn-bread, and sweet potatoes. "The meals are absolutely invariable, save that fresh pork and sweet potatoes are frequently wanting. There is always, too, the black decoction of the South called coffee, than which it is often difficult to imagine any beverage more revolting." Once they tried Gail Borden's canned meat biscuit, but threw it away after a single bite.

In Caldwell, Olmsted was treated to an ante-bellum Texas hotel, noteworthy because "the principal room had glass windows. Several panes of these were, however, broken, and the outside door could not be closed from without; and when closed, was generally pried open with a pocket-knife." This was in the midst of a strong norther, and there was no fire in the fireplace. "Supper was, however, eaten with such rapidity that nothing had time to freeze on the table." Of East Texas, Olmsted said: "Upon the whole, this is not the spot in which I should prefer to light, burn, and expire."

They stopped awhile in Austin, then went down through the German settlements to San Antonio, to Eagle Pass and across the border briefly, then through the coastal region to Houston, Liberty, and Beaumont. "The common dress" of some of the Mexican women, he wrote in that Victorian era, "was loose and slight. . . . It was frequently but a chemise, as low as possible in the neck, sometimes even lower." He was most impressed with the German pioneers, who did not leave all the work to slaves, who built strong houses and fences, and who generally exercised considerably more energy and interest in the world than the Anglo settlers, many of whom he paints as shiftless.

A German farmer told Olmsted that "here in Texas, they do not have any pleasure. When they come together sometime, what do they? They can only sit all round the fire and speet! Why, then they drink some whisky; or may be they play cards, or they make great row. They have no pleasure as in Germany." Why, then did he come to Texas? "Because here I am free."

The mixture of Anglo-Americans, Europeans, and Mexicans in Texas offered strange contrasts. "You are welcomed by a figure in blue flannel shirt and pendant beard, quoting Tacitus, having in one hand a long pipe, in the other a butcher's knife; Madonnas upon log-walls; coffee in tin cups upon Dresden saucers; barrels for seats, to hear a Beethoven's symphony on the grand piano; . . . a fowling-piece that cost $300, and a saddle that cost $5; a bookcase half filled with classics, half with sweet potatoes."

Reflecting on the early settlement of Texas, Olmsted says: "Austin was, I believe, no mischievous conspirator . . . though, doubtless not unwilling to initiate events whose course would pass beyond his responsibility and control. The colonists themselves went as individuals . . . with the single motive in most cases, of making more money and having a better time in Texas than they could have in the States. . . . The land was fertile; that was the kernel of the matter." The pioneers, Olmsted maintains, were unconcerned with legalities, saying in effect: "We saw the land lying idle; we took it. This to other nations is all that we can say. Which one of them can cast the first stone?" I have read no more astute explanation in any analysis of the American pioneer movement.

Olmsted offers many insights into economic and social life. He gives one of the earliest descriptions of the Texas cattle ranch. He describes hoe-downs, fandangoes, army posts, rattlesnakes ("He lay coiled with a huge head, a wide-open [mouth] and a forked tongue, dancing about in ecstasy of malice"), horse-shoeing, and attitudes towards Sam Houston. Of the estimated 12,000 Indians: "Nothing can be more lamentable than the condition of the wandering tribes. They are permanently on the verge of starvation. Having been forced back, step by step, from the hunting-grounds and the fertile soil of Lower Texas to the bare and arid plains, it is no wonder they are driven to violence and angry depredations.''

A Journey Through Texas is a splendid, enlightening book. Olmsted got little financial return from it, unfortunately. The publisher—can you ever trust one?—convinced him not only to put up money for publication but to buy into the publishing firm as well. The book appeared in January, 1857, and by the end of the summer the firm declared bankruptcy. It was just as well for Olmsted. He managed to get the job of designing and creating Central Park in New York that same September. When the war began, Lincoln appointed him head of the U.S. Sanitary Commission, which Olmsted utilized to begin what is now the International Red Cross. After the war, he went on to create Yosemite National Park and to design the grounds around the U.S. Capitol and at Stanford University. He designed the Biltmore Mansion in Ashville, the University of California at Berkeley, and the Chicago World's Fair grounds of 1893. For a time he also was manager-foreman of John C. Fremont's Mariposa Ranch in California. Few men of letters have led a richer life.

Basler 4365. Campbell, p.57. Clark 481. Coleman 3431. Dobie, pp.48 and 52. Graff 3097. Howes O79. Rader 2549-50. Raines, p.159. Sabin 57243.

158   Paine, Albert Bigelow (1861-1937)

CAPTAIN BILL MCDONALD, TEXAS RANGER: A STORY OF FRONTIER REFORM.

N.Y.: Made by J. J. Little & Ives Co., 1909.
448pp. 21cm. Frontis photograph. Seven tinted illus. by D. C. Hutchison.
Blue cloth, stamped in white, dustjacket.
Facsimile of Introduction Letter by Pres. Theodore Roosevelt. Dedicated to E. M. House.

Other issues:
(A). Same, bound in full morocco, gilt.
(B). Same, bound in red cloth with a portrait of McDonald pasted down on front cover.

[Note: All three of the above issues are from the same printing of the text, with "Special Subscription Edition" printed on title page. Howes, Adams, and other bibliographers have attempted to establish priority, without success. Subscribers were given a choice of three cost categories, from cheapest to most expensive being blue cloth, red cloth, morocco. A publisher's dummy of 32 pages was also issued.]

[c]. Facsimile reprint. Austin: State House Press, 1986. Cloth. New index.

This is the life of the most famous Texas Ranger of the time, the man who it was said would "charge hell with a bucket of water." It is also the origin of the most famous of all Texas Ranger stories, one that has been falsely attributed to almost every other Texas Ranger captain, living and dead: when McDonald arrived on a train to quell a riot, he was asked why he had come alone; he replied, well, there was only one mob, wasn't there? This one fight, one Ranger story has been told thousands of times with many variations, but the version recounted by Paine is the first.

Paine writes with perhaps too much adulation of his subject, and with virtually no criticism whatsoever. It was no secret that McDonald encouraged the well-known Paine to do the biography, and both E. M. House and Theodore Roosevelt supported eagerly the idea of a biography of this ideal rough-and-ready lawman. It is significant that the copyright is in the name of McDonald, not Paine. The importance of the book, however, lies not merely in the stories of McDonald's prowess, but in its bringing nationwide attention to the legend of the Texas Ranger. From Paine's book it was only a short hop to the motion picture stereotype that persists to the present day.

McDonald (1852-1918) came to Texas in 1866 from Mississippi, and attended and graduated from Soule's Commercial College in New Orleans in 1872. Incredibly, he taught penmanship in Henderson and then became a grocer. After a short time, he became a deputy sheriff of Wood County, and his reputation as a lawman began to grow. He was appointed special ranger and U.S. Marshal in Hardeman County in the 1880's, and his exploits in No Man's Land and the Cherokee Strip soon made him a Texas legend. He became a captain of the Texas Rangers in 1891, serving until 1907 with ever-increasing renown. In 1896 he was sent alone to stop the Fitzsimmons-Maher prize fight; in 1905 he escorted Pres. Theodore Roosevelt through Texas; in 1906 he was in charge of the investigation of the Brownsville Riot; in 1912 he was bodyguard to Pres. Woodrow Wilson. All but the last of these are recounted vividly by Paine, along with accounts of his fights against cattle thieves, outlaws (he stood down Bat Masterson, who seldom backed away from a fight), train and bank robbers, rioters, etc.

There are several appendices of original letters and documents totalling 49 pages, including reports of the Fitzsimmons-Maher prize fight, reports from Captain McDonald to the Adjutant-General, and documents relating to the Brownsville Affair of 1906.

Walter Prescott Webb points out accurately that McDonald was not a better Ranger than the others of his time, but was the essence of the tradition, and "perhaps unconsciously, made himself the symbol of all it had been. He was himself a frontier phrasemaker and coiner of epigrams, and was so picturesque and daring that others coined phrases about him. . . . To his other gifts Bill added a good fighting Scotch name, a fine face lined with sun, wind, and character, a pair of mild blue eyes, a soft voice, and a 'suddenness'—things that made him irresistible to friend or enemy. In every sense of the word, Bill McDonald was what athletes call a natural. The philosophy that supported him, and had supported all the great Rangers before him, Bill McDonald articulated in striking phrases: 'No man in the wrong can stand up against a fellow that's in the right and keeps on a-comin.' "

Adams Guns 1669. Adams One-Fifty 110. Campbell, p.78. Dobie, p.60. Howes P14. Rader 2570.

159 Parker, Amos Andrew (1791-1893)

TRIP TO THE WEST AND TEXAS, COMPRISING A JOURNEY OF EIGHT THOUSAND MILES, THROUGH NEW YORK, MICHIGAN, ILLINOIS, MISSOURI, LOUISIANA AND TEXAS, IN THE AUTUMN AND WINTER OF 1834-5, INTERSPERSED WITH ANECDOTES, INCIDENTS AND OBSERVATIONS.

Concord, N.H.: Printed and Published by White & Fisher, 1835.
276pp. Two plates. 19cm.
Cloth.

Other issues:

(A). *Trip to the West and Texas . . . With a Brief Sketch of the Texian War . . . Second Edition.* Concord, N.H.: Published by William White; Boston: Benjamin B. Missey, 1836. 380pp. Three plates. 18cm. Cloth. Some copies have a folding map: "Texas. Nathl. Dearborn & Son, Engraver & Printer, Boston."

(B). Facsimile reprint of (A). Austin: Pemberton Press, 1968. [14],380[16]pp. 4 illus. Map. 23cm. Cloth, dustjacket. Introduction by James M. Day. New index. Brasada Reprint Series.

(C). Facsimile reprint of the first edition. New York: Arno Press, 1973. 276pp. Illus. 22cm. The Far Western Frontier Series.

Parker, an observant chronicler, visited Texas just prior to the revolution. Ray Allen Billington states: "His descriptions of the Texan settlements and people are vivid and discerning. He also reveals the cultural conflicts with Mexico which played a part in the Texas Revolution. Because this is one of the earliest travel books written in English about Texas, it is of great value."

Parker, son of a wealthy United States Senator from New Hampshire, was a lawyer, judge, and author. He outlived three wives, dying at the age of nearly 102. James M. Day writes of him: "He was not quite forty-three years of age when he set out on a thrilling adventure into the little known western country, with Texas being the ultimate, but not only goal. Parker embarked on his trip in September, 1834, and by early February, 1835, was back in New Hampshire, having traveled some eight thousand miles. Having sufficient money, he journeyed in style. . . . Parker stayed a little over a month in Texas, visiting such places as San Augustine, Nacogdoches, Hall's Ferry on the Brazos, San Felipe, Columbia, Brazoria, and Velasco."

Five thousand copies of the first edition were printed. By the end of 1836, a new edition was required, with numerous alterations. The sections on Illinois, Missouri, and the Mississippi Valley were deleted, and a "Sketch of the Texian Revolution" of 56 pages was added. This was one of the earliest accounts of the war in a book. A table of contents and chapter divisions were also added, as well as one additional plate; some copies were issued with a folding map of Texas.

Parker is especially careful in noting the physical condition of the lands he visited. Day points out that Parker, "being impressed by the inexpensiveness and abundance of land, analyzed its productivity and the types of crops it would grow. The animals of Texas are given considerable discussion, but the 'ever active mocheto' [mosquito] seems

to get more than its share of attention. Beasts not thought of today—
alligators, panthers, bears—excited his curiosity and brought forth
comment. Parker noted so many deer that systematic hunting was not
necessary." He also describes the buffalo and mustangs.

While in Nacogdoches, Parker met some Texas land speculators; he
states: "An instance of the little value placed upon land was stated to
me while here. An American had a fine looking dog that a Spaniard
took a fancy to; he asked the price and was told a *hundred dollars*. The
Spaniard replied, he had no money, but would give him a scrip for
four leagues of land! The bargain was immediately closed . . . truly, the
old adage, 'dog cheap,' ought to be reversed." A league was 4428
acres.

Of the people, Parker comments: "In some publications the people
of Texas have been slandered. They have been called a set of robbers
and murderers, screening themselves from justice, by fleeing from
their own country and coming to this. It would be strange, indeed, if
there were not such instances; but whoever travels over the country,
will find them as pleasant, obliging and kind as any people in the
United States. In the towns, you generally find a billiard room; and
near it, a race course. At these resorts, are found the favorite
amusements of the inhabitants. I went all through the country,
unarmed and unharmed; nor did I at any time feel in jeopardy of life
or limb."

Buck 276. Clark III-82. Graff 3183-84. Howes P74. Phillips *Sporting Books* 286. Rader
2588-89. Raines, pp.161-62. Rusk II-120. Sabin 58643. Streeter 1172.

160   Pichardo, Jose Antonio (1748-1812)

PICHARDO'S TREATISE ON THE LIMITS OF LOUISIANA
AND TEXAS: AN ARGUMENTATIVE HISTORICAL TREATISE
WITH REFERENCE TO THE VERIFICATION OF THE TRUE
LIMITS OF THE PROVINCES OF LOUISIANA AND TEXAS;
WRITTEN . . . TO DISPROVE THE CLAIM OF THE UNITED
STATES THAT TEXAS WAS INCLUDED IN THE LOUISIANA
PURCHASE OF 1803.

Austin: The University of Texas Press, 1931, 1934, 1941, 1946.
Edited and translated by Charles Wilson Hackett.

Four volumes: xx,630; xv,618,xxii,623,xiii,415pp. 5 maps (4 folding). 24cm.
Cloth, dustjackets.

Other issues:
(A). Facsimile reprint. Freeport, N.Y., 1971. Four volumes. Cloth.

The Pichardo treatise is one of the first studies of Texas history by a committed scholar. The Hackett edition is its first publication in any language; it is also one of the most ably edited of all books on Texas. Herbert Gambrell deemed it "easily the most important reference work on the colonial history of Texas yet published in English." F. B. Steck called it "a work of inestimable value and a lasting credit to the high scholarship of editor and translator; a rich storehouse of bibliographical and historical data." Herbert E. Bolton called it "a work of great importance." Carlos E. Castaneda said that "if the original Treatise is a monument to the industry of the compiler, so it is also to that of the editor." Eugene C. Barker asserted: "No one who reads Pichardo's monumental brief can doubt that Spain and not France owned Texas in 1763 and thereafter."

When President Jefferson persisted in claiming that the territory included in the Louisiana Purchase extended to the Rio Grande, the Spanish government ordered that historical data be gathered to prove Spain's ownership of Texas. The result was that in 1808 Father Pichardo was named head of a historical commission to ascertain the historic boundary of Louisiana and Texas. Four years later Pichardo delivered to the viceroy in Mexico City a treatise of 3000 folio pages totalling a million words. When Secretary of State John Quincy Adams was later given the treatise to study, he was forced to agree in the Treaty of 1819 that Texas indeed belonged to Spain. Few works of history have had a more direct effect on international diplomacy and law or on the subsequent history of the area involved.

During Pichardo's research, he amassed a personal collection of over 6,000 books and manuscripts, and examined thousands more. As a linguist who knew Spanish, French, Italian, Dutch, English, Greek, Hebrew, and Latin, he was able to study the sources in the language in which they were written. Pichardo says that during the four-year study "I worked uninterruptedly night and day, without even leaving my room." The original manuscript is now in the Mexican National Archives.

Hackett states: "Father Pichardo has done a monumental work in compiling and in presenting historical data of such volume and of such prime importance to the Texas-Louisiana region. [His] utilization of documentary source materials has been enormous; in fact, it is doubtful if any important event connected with the Louisiana-Texas area in the period before 1811 was studied without reference to basic primary sources related to it. . . . On the whole Father Pichardo's conclusions are sane and correct."

The value of publishing the treatise in English is less in the light it sheds on the border question than in the enormous wealth of data it presents on the history of Texas. Pichardo examined and included in his report literally thousands of documents relating to Texas. Many of these no longer exist and many others have never before been brought to light. With the addition of Hackett's superb annotations, the treatise provides us with one of the fundamental resources on the early history of Texas.

Hackett himself worked for fifteen years translating and editing the Pichardo treatise. In the process he and assistants Charmion Clair Shelby and Mary Ruth Splawn produced 3,137 footnotes and added 486 bibliographical citations to the treatise. Hackett, as director of Latin American studies at the University of Texas, had an immense impact on the school. During his stewardship, it had more courses relating to Latin America than any other American university and it built the most comprehensive Latin American library and archives in the English-speaking world. Sadly, the writing of the treatise and the translating of it seems to have overwhelmed both men. Pichardo died of illness derived from his overwork a short time after completing his manuscript; Hackett committed suicide not too long after publication of the last volume of his translation.

Clark I-23. Rader 2664.

161   Pickrell, Annie Doom (1871-   )

PIONEER WOMEN IN TEXAS.

Austin: Published by The E. L. Steck Company, [1929].
474pp. 23cm.
Cloth.

Other issues:

(A). Reprint, omitting the original Steck imprint and substituting: Austin and New York: Jenkins Publishing Company, The Pemberton Press, 1970. 23cm. Cloth, dustjacket.

The best book on women in early Texas, this is a useful and fascinating compilation of biographies of 77 notable Texas women, compiled from recollections and memoirs of women who came to Texas prior to statehood. Including both prominent ladies and pioneer settlers, the volume is one of the best sources of authentic grass roots history of social life in frontier Texas, containing valuable material relating to the Texas Revolution, Republic of Texas, Civil War, Reconstruction, and the cattle industry.

Biographies in the volume include Margaret Lea Houston, Rebecca Fisher, Frances Van Zandt, Joanna Troutman, Julia Lee Sinks, and Mary Crownover Rabb as well as the wives of Josiah Bell, Edward Burleson, Stephen Dardin, C. C. Dyer, A. J. Hamilton, James Pickney Henderson, Reuben Hornsby, Robert Kleberg, John J. Linn, Herman Lungwitz, George W. Smyth, and Edwin Waller. Contributors included Sam Houston's daughters, Albert Sidney Burleson, Carol Hoff, Walter P. Webb, R. L. Batts, Starkey Duncan, Mrs. Frank Andrews, Mrs. R. L. Henry, and Mrs. W. P. Hobby.

The book provides a mine of material on social life and pioneer folkways in Texas, and includes many of the only surviving anecdotes relating to famous early Texans. These include such priceless accounts as when Mrs. Edward Burleson pulled shingles off the roof to cook with after her husband rode away on one of his Indian campaigns without first chopping wood for the family. It includes one of the basic accounts of the scalping of Josiah Wilbarger, and many accounts of Indian affrays and slave life unavailable elsewhere. As might be expected, there is much relating to frontier religious activities.

The volume, compiled as it is from family recollections, naturally suffers from a lack of precise historical accuracy, and must be used with caution. Many are handed-down tales, forever impossible to verify or deny. For example, Pickrell recounts the McCormick family recollection of Joseph McCormick on the evening before the Battle of San Jacinto: "The soldiers were in camp on the night of April 20, 1836, on the famous San Jacinto battle field, the small cannon in place, and all soldiers had been ordered to retire. McCormick picked a spot for his slumber hard by one cannon. He proceeded after the most approved Scotch method to make himself comfortable for the night. Part of his preparation consisted in tying the musquito bar to the cannon and then tucking it in tight around as he stretched out for slumber. Now this whole matter became ludicrous in the eyes of some soldiers close at hand, and after McCormick was well into the land of Nod, one man slipped up to the cannon and fired it . . . Excited? McCormick? Not a bit of it! He but turned about beneath his mosquito netting and inquired soberly: 'Boys, have they got here yet?' The joke turned upon the perpetrators. The ammunition had been wasted, and McCormick was as calm as a June day.''

Most of the recollections have the ring of truth, even if naturally stretched a bit. Of Mary Ashmore Smith of Milam County, Pickrell gives this account of a surprise Indian attack on the Smith cabin: ''As the Indians came within gun-shot, Smith began firing. . . . Mary observed that her husband's supply of ammunition was running low [but the lead and moulds were outside in a wagon]. Mary, with never a thought of her husband's restraining advice, dashed through the door, out across the yard, arrows whizzing by her, one or two striking her askance on the arm and the shoulder, on to the loaded wagon, to dive deep in the remembered spot for the precious molds and lead, to return, still running, to the cabin, to begin moulding bullets immediately, her husband hardly aware that she had ever left his side.''

Descendant of a veteran of San Jacinto, alumna of the University of Texas, and state historian of the Daughters of the Repubic of Texas, Pickrell devoted most of her career to accumulating data on early Texas families. The D.R.T., so active in preserving Texas historical sites, artifacts, and archives, has produced relatively little in published history. This volume is one of the exceptions. Most of the material in the book was derived from family records and recollections, much of which would have been lost but for the work of Annie Pickrell.

A recent volume adding fifty more biographies of notable 19th century women is Evelyn M. Carrington [ed.], *Women in Early Texas* (Austin: Jenkins Publishing Company, 1975, 308pp.). Two other similar works are Mary D. Farrell and Elizabeth Silverthorne, *First Ladies of Texas: The First One Hundred Years,* 1836-1936 (Belton: Stillhouse Hollow

Publishers, 1976, 427pp.) and Ann Fears Crawford and Crystal Sasse Ragsdale, *Women in Texas* (Burnet: Eakin Press, 1982, 394pp.).

162   Pike, James (1834-1867)

THE SCOUT AND RANGER: BEING THE PERSONAL ADVENTURES OF CORPORAL PIKE, OF THE FOURTH OHIO CAVALRY, AS A TEXAS RANGER, IN THE INDIAN WARS . . .

Cincinnati and New York: J. R. Hawley & Co., 1865.
xi,19-394pp. 25 plates. Errata leaf. 21cm.
Cloth with plain back. In the first issue, the frontispiece portrait is in an oval. Also, the last words at the end of the third line of page 151 are "Indian Red." The statements in some previous bibliographies that the first issue is determined by what side Pike's hair is parted on are misleading.

Other issues:
(A). Same as above, second state. No errata leaf. Frontispiece portrait is in a rectangle. Last words at the end of the third line of page 151 are "Jim Ned." Gilt pictorial spine showing a man stabbing another man.
(B). Same as (A), with 1866 on title page.
(C). *Scout and Ranger; Being the Personal Adventures of James Pike of the Texas Rangers in 1859-60.* Princeton: Princeton University Press, 1932. xxviii,164pp. 8 illus. 22cm. Addendum slip laid in. New preface and "Ranger Pike and Texas in 1859" by Carl L. Cannon. Narratives of the Trans-Mississippi Frontier Series. Contains only the Texas portion of the book.
(D). Facsimile reprint of (A). New York: Da Capo Press, 1972. Same size and collation. The American Scene: Comments and Commentators Series.

This is an interesting reminiscence of a Yankee who became a Texas Ranger and later a Union spy. J. Frank Dobie said "Pike tells a bully story to be ranked along with the personal narratives of those other two vivid ranger chroniclers, James B. Gillett and N. A. Jennings." E. Merton Coulter wrote that "this is a remarkable narrative, surprisingly true in its main discussions but undoubtedly embellished in details. It is peppered with characteristic travel incidents, local customs, and descriptions of the country traversed." Gen. W. T. Sherman became well-acquainted with Corporal Pike during the war, almost fatherly in fact, and praised his "skill, courage and zeal," but warned Pike that "for yourself, you should now cool down."

Pike seems never in his life to have cooled down. The son of a fire-eating country newspaper editor, he once had to save his father and his newspaper office from a mob with drawn six-shooters. Tired of being a printer's assistant in Ohio and Missouri, he joined a horse drover heading for Texas, learning when they arrived that he had helped drive a stolen remuda. Failing to get a printing job in Austin in early 1859, he joined John Henry Brown's Texas Ranger company at Belton. During the next two years he saw almost continual action in the vicious Indian campaigns of that period, including ranger service under J. M. Smith. His recollections of these events are among the most vivid on record and, except for an occasional exaggeration, verifiably accurate.

Corporal Pike tells the truth in his narrative, but not the naked truth. He maintains that his simple recital of the bare facts contains "more of the strange and the heroic, than could be conceived by the fertility of a Dickens or a Dumas." Carl L. Cannon, in his rather inept introduction to the Princeton reprint, credits Pike's memory as "little short of uncanny. . . . The author was guilty of very few discrepancies of fact. This is shown by checking his statements against contemporary records, the recollections of pioneers, and the findings of present-day historians," of whom Cannon names R. C. Crane, E. E. Dale, and Rupert N. Richardson. Nevertheless, Pike's account of helping in the capture of Cynthia Ann Parker is impossible, as he had already left Texas when that occurred. There are other embellishments, mostly minor exaggerations. As Dobie said, "how reliable Pike is, is hard to say. The fact that his narrative generally tallies with known facts lends authenticity to his personal remarks on those facts. But in some instances he apparently arrogated to himself the experiences of others."

When Texas voted to secede, Pike left Texas, making his way northeastward by passing himself off as the nephew of Albert Pike. He joined an Ohio cavalry unit and saw extensive service. Pike was utilized by various commanders as a scout and as a spy within Confederate lines. Some of his escapades would be hard to believe if not proved by official war records. Grant used Pike to take a secret message to Sherman in 1863, for example. A letter from Sherman praises Pike: "He got a canoe . . . and came down the Tennessee over the Muscle Shoals, all alone, for over one hundred miles of river, every mile of which was picketed by the enemy, and reached me safely." In 1864 he was captured, once again behind enemy lines, and imprisoned in Charleston. With special aid from Generals Butler, Grant, and Thomas, an attempt was made to exchange for him, but before this took place he escaped.

Upon his return he was promoted from corporal to captain, with an astonishing number of recommendations. Gen. George Crook wrote that Pike "is well known to almost every commander in this Department for the invaluable services he has rendered as a scout and on secret service . . . sometimes performing the most dangerous services." Gen. Thomas called him "an energetic, capable, and conscientious man." Gen. Grant wrote that "Corporal Pike has proved himself brave and energetic." Gen. Sherman wrote a typical one-liner: "Trust the bearer."

After the war, Pike returned to Hillsboro, Ohio, to write his book. His preface is dated June 21, 1865, so he wasted no time. He then rejoined the army as an officer and went west to San Francisco. Assigned to Indian service, he died sometime in 1867. "His end," states Cannon, "as the story drifted back . . . was that while at dinner a surprise attack was made on the post by hostile Indians. All the Whites seized their rifles and rushed from the room to repel the raid. Pike's rifle jammed and in his anger he broke the barrel over a rock, exploding the cartridge and receiving a wound from which he never recovered."

Coulter 372. Dobie, p.60. Graff 3286. Howes P369. Nevins I-146. Rader 2671. Raines, p.165. Sabin 62816.

163 Pike, Zebulon Montgomery (1779-1813)

AN ACCOUNT OF EXPEDITIONS TO THE SOURCES OF THE MISSISSIPPI, AND THROUGH THE WESTERN PARTS OF LOUISIANA, TO THE SOURCES OF THE ARKANSAW, KANS, LAPLATTE, AND PIERRE JUAN, RIVERS: PERFORMED BY ORDER OF THE GOVERNMENT OF THE UNITED STATES DURING THE YEARS 1805, 1806, AND 1807. AND A TOUR THROUGH THE INTERIOR PARTS OF NEW SPAIN, WHEN CONDUCTED THROUGH THESE PROVINCES, BY ORDER OF THE CAPTAIN-GENERAL, IN THE YEAR 1807.

PROSPECTUS OF
PIKE'S EXPEDITION

To the sources of the Mississippi, and through
the western parts of Louisiana, to the sources
of the Osage, Arkansaw, Kans, La Platte, and
—— rivers.

*Performed by orders of the government of the United
States, during the years 1805, 1806, and 1807*

ALSO,

A tour through the internal parts of

NEW SPAIN,

When conducted through those provinces by order
of the captain general, in the year 1807.

THIS work will be prepared for the press by
major Z. M PIKE. It will be divided into three
parts, but comprised in one volume, large octavo.

Philadelphia: Published by C. & A. Conrad & Co., No. 30 Chesnut Street . . . John Dinns, Printer, 1810.

5,[3],105,[11],[107]-277,[5],65,[1],53,[1],87pp.

Frontis. 3 folding tables. 6 maps (5 folding). 24cm.

Boards with printed label; also calf. A few copies are known with the maps in a separate quarto folder.

Other issues:

(A). *Exploratory Travels Through the Western Territories of North America . . . and the North-Eastern Provinces of New Spain . . .* London: Printed for Longman, Hurst, Rees, Orme, and Brown, Paternoster-Row, 1811. xx,436pp. 2 maps (1 folding). 27cm. Boards with printed label; also calf. First English edition.

(B). *Voyage au Nouveau-Mexique . . . pour Reconnotre les Sources des Rivieres . . . dans l'Interieur de la Louisiane Occidentale . . .* Paris: Chez D'Hautel, Libraire, rue de la Harpe, n. 80, pres le College de Justice, 1812. Two volumes. 20cm. 3 folding maps. Marbled wrappers with printed labels; also calf. First French edition.

(C). *Reize naar Nieuw-Mexico en de Binnenland van Louisiana . . .* Amsterdam: C. Timmer, [1812-1813]. Two volumes. 3 folding maps. 22cm. Plain wrappers; also calf. First Dutch edition.

(D). *Reise durch die Westlichen Gebiete von Nord-America . . .* Weimar: In Verlage des Landes-Industrie-Comptoirs, 1813. xvi, 556pp. Folding table. Folding map. 20cm. Calf. First German edition.

(E). *Exploratory Travels through the Western Territories of North America . . .* Denver: W. H. Lawrence & Co., 1889. xii,[xv]-xxiv,25-394pp. Illus. Maps. 28cm. Cloth. Reprint of London, 1811, edition, with introduction by William M. Maguire.

(F). *The Expeditions of Zebulon Montgomery Pike, to Headwaters of the Mississippi River, Through Louisiana Territory, and in New Spain, during the Years 1805-6-7.* New York: Francis P. Harper, 1895. Three volumes. 24cm. Edited with annotations by Elliott Coues. Limited to 1150 numbered sets, the first 150 on handmade paper. Definitively-annotated edition.

(G). *The Southwestern Expedition of Zebulon M. Pike.* Chicago: The Lakeside Press, R. R. Donnelley & Sons Company, 1925. xxii,[2],239pp. Frontis. Folding map. 17cm. Cloth. Edited, with an introduction, by Milo Milton Quaife.

(H). *Zebulon Pike's Arkansaw Journal: In Search of the Southern Louisiana Purchase Boundary Line.* [Colorado Springs:] The Stewart Commission of Colorado College; [Denver:] The Denver Public Library, [1932]. xcvi,200pp. Illus. Maps. 24cm. Edited by Stephen Harding Hart and Archer Butler Hulbert. Edited version of part of Pike's journal.

(I). *The Journals of Zebulon Montgomery Pike, with Letters and Related Documents.* Norman: University of Oklahoma Press, [1966]. Two volumes. Illus. Maps. 24cm. Cloth, boxed. Edited with annotations by Donald Jackson. American Exploration and Travel Series 48. The best edition.

(J). Facsimile reprint of the first edition. New York: Readex Microprint, [1961]. 21cm. Cloth.

(K). Facsimile reprint of (G). Freeport, N.Y.: Books for Libraries Press, [1970]. 23cm. Cloth.

(L). Facsimile reprint of (H). Westport, Conn.: Greenwood Press, [1972]. 22cm. Cloth.

Pike's narrative marks the beginning of serious American interest in Texas. Other than the few pages in the English translation of Pierre Pages' *Voyages* and the John Sibley government report on the Red River area, it is the first description of Texas in English. Milo M. Quaife called it "one of the great chronicles of American pioneering achievement. . . . No one who reads the narrative can fail to perceive the dauntless spirit which animated the fiery young leader, nor the loyalty and devotion which inspired his band of devoted followers. . . . They wrote a new chapter in the annals of human daring . . . and added a volume of abiding worth to the literature of New World exploration." Elliott Coues said of Pike's narratives that their "effect was enormous; their results proved far-reaching; and some of these are still in evidence . . . [and] will endure . . . so long as any interested in the beginnings of our Great West finds a place in the hearts of the people." C. W. Raines wrote: "We hail Pike as the first American writer at some length on Texas."

In 1800, Spain secretly ceded Louisiana to the French. In 1803, Napoleon, faced with the probability of losing Louisiana to England since he could not afford the money and troops to defend it, made virtue of necessity and sold it to the United States. The purchase was the crown of Thomas Jefferson's presidency, yet he knew almost nothing about the territory he had purchased, not even its exact boundaries. During the subsequent four years he dispatched a number of expeditions to learn about it and to assert American control over as much of it as possible. Lewis and Clark went westward from St. Louis; Sibley, Dunbar, and Freeman explored the Spanish border region in Texas; and Pike was sent to explore the southernmost border region north of New Spain.

This occurred during the era of the Burr-Wilkinson conspiracy; those two men managed to alarm both the Spanish and the American governments with their plots and to mystify scholars to the present day. Wilkinson was Pike's commander, and it was under his direct orders and instructions that Pike made his expedition. Pike was accompanied by Wilkinson's son, as well as by the mysterious Dr. John H. Robinson, whose role has never been successfully explained. Prior to and during the Pike expedition, Wilkinson was being paid by the Spanish government as their own secret agent in the United States.

Young Zebulon Pike was clearly acting as a spy as well as an explorer, but equally clearly he was performing in behalf of his country and not as a lackey for Wilkinson. Of other members of his party, this cannot be said. Pike states: "I literally performed the duties . . . of astronomer, surveyor, commanding officer, clerk, spy, guide, and hunter." Donald Jackson explains: "The geopolitical aspects of his . . . expedition take on new meaning as we sense the atmosphere of confusion, self-interest, and bad faith in which Spain and the United States approached the problems created by the Louisiana Purchase. Pike entered the Spanish borderlands at a sensitive time, when war was possible at any moment, and never thought of himself solely as an explorer. He was a spy—and proud to be one." Both nations knew the Texas border regions, and the disputed boundary, might some day be the scene of armed conflict, and one of Pike's goals was to collect military intelligence.

Pike set out from St. Louis on July 15, 1806, and traveled westward, sighting the Colorado peak now bearing his name on November 23. He then moved southward to seek the Red River for his return home. By February, 1807, he came to the upper reaches of the Rio Grande, having accidentally (or by design) missed the Red River entirely. Spanish authorities learned of his presence and sent a force to arrest him and his men. They were taken to Santa Fe and then sent on to Chihuahua. Pike's maps and papers were confiscated, but he managed to retain his diary and journals by secreting them in the gun barrels of his men. Apparently he was able to convince the Spaniards that he had entered New Spain by accident, as he was escorted by armed guard through Texas via San Antonio to the Sabine, where he was released. He arrived at Natchitoches in June, 1807, having thus had the opportunity to examine New Mexico and Texas in some detail, at the expense of the Spanish government.

After reporting directly to Secretary of War Henry Dearborn, Pike found himself embroiled in the Burr-Wilkinson scandal, but was soon able to prove his innocence in these intrigues. He visited Thomas

Jefferson in Washington, and doubtless provided both the President and the War Department an excellent intelligence report on Texas and on its civil and military leaders. There being no "top secret" classification at the time to bind him, he then began to prepare his papers for publication. He included not only his Southwestern tour, but also his earlier expedition up the headwaters of the Mississippi River.

Pike wrote from Philadelphia to a friend that in May, 1808, he had contracted "with the firm of Conrad, Lucas & Co. of this place to print and publish my Tours, for which I allow them 20 pr.Cent on all the sales, and pay besides the expenses of printing." On June 8, the publisher advertised in the Philadelphia *Aurora* that the book would be published "in three months." The publication process, however, developed into a fiasco, and the book was not issued for two more years. Coues says Pike, although "versed in the arts of war, was quite innocent of literary strategy, though capable of heading an impetuous assault upon the parts of speech. He may have acquired an impression . . . that a book is made by putting manuscript in a printing-press and stirring it about with a composing-stick, which, like a magic wand . . . will transfigure the homeliness of the pen into a thing of beauty and joy forever."

The publisher provided him with no editorial assistance whatever, and printed the text a little at a time as Pike sent it in. The result is a hodge-podge of journals, correspondence, and statistics, with no order and not even paged consecutively. The volume is full of the type of errors that any respectable publisher of the time would have been expected to correct. The Texas material is scattered throughout, in the journals, in the statistics, and in the appendices. The latter include a general description of Texas, comments on manners, customs, terrain, climate, and military forces, with interesting material on life in San Antonio.

Pike calls Texas "one of the richest, most prolific, and best watered countries in North America" with "one of the most delightful temperatures in the world," but suffering from a government "perfectly military, except as to the ecclesiastical jurisdiction." He reports on the military dispositions, but says the militia are a mere "rabble made somewhat respectable by a few American riflemen . . . amongst them." The religion was entirely "Catholic, but much relaxed." In "energy, patriotism, enterprise of character, and independence of soul" the Texans are "perhaps the most deficient" in the world.

The publisher soon went bankrupt and Pike received no recompense. Pike died valiantly at the age of 34 a few years later in the American invasion of Canada during the War of 1812; the government did not pay his widow for his services on the 1806 expedition until forty years afterwards.

In 1811 an English edition was prepared by Dr. Thomas Rees, from a manuscript copy sent to England while the American edition was being printed. This edition has a much better arrangement, with corrections of grammar. From this London edition the French, Dutch, and German translations were made. Baron von Humboldt wrote to President Jefferson claiming that Pike had stolen his map, and while it is clear that Pike made full, unacknowledged, and unauthorized use of Humboldt's map of New Spain, it is also clear that he added immensely to it in many details. Jefferson wrote an apology on Pike's behalf to Humboldt in 1813.

In 1889, an edition was published in Denver of the Southwestern journals, taken also from the London edition of Dr. Rees. William Maguire, who was familiar with the territory covered by Pike, provided new introductory material. This was followed in 1895 by the massive three-volume edition of Elliott Coues, for long the best and still a classic edition, with lengthy preliminary material, excellent though harsh critical commentary, extensive annotations, and an index. In this edition, the text is rearranged into a more consistent format. Coues enlisted the aid of F. W. Hodge, A. W. Greely, J. W. Powell, R. G. Thwaites, and even ex-President Benjamin Harrison in preparing this superb edition.

In 1907, Herbert E. Bolton discovered the original captured papers of Pike in the Mexican archives; through the efforts of Elihu Root, these were returned to the United States, where they now reside in the National Archives as Special File No. 6, along with the other materials on the expedition, which comprise the Zebulon Pike Papers, Record Group 94. Many of the recovered papers were published in July, 1908, in the *American Historical Review* (vol. xiii, no. 4). In 1949,

W. Eugene Hollon wrote a useful biography, *The Lost Pathfinder: Zebulon Montgomery Pike* (Norman: University of Oklahoma Press, 1949, 240pp.).

Finally, in 1966, Donald Jackson issued an edition that should remain the best and most useful edition for some time to come. It not only includes the full text of Pike's original journals, but over 400 pages of correspondence and reports relating to the expedition. Jackson's edition also includes 60 plates reproducing in facsimile many of Pike's maps and journal entries, six other maps, and numerous illustrations.

Field 1217. Graff 3290. Howes P373. Rader 2672. Raines, p.165. Rittenhouse 467. Sabin 62836. Shaw & Shoemaker 21089. Streeter 1047. Wagner-Camp 9.

164   Pinckney, Pauline A.

PAINTING IN TEXAS: THE NINETEENTH CENTURY.

Austin and London: Published for the Amon Carter Museum of Western Art, Fort Worth, by the University of Texas Press, [1967].
Introduction by Jerry Bywaters.
xx,232pp. 12 color plates. 117 illus. 31cm.
Cloth, dustjacket.
[Verso of title:] Type set by Service Typographers, Inc., Indianapolis.
Printed by the Steck Company, Austin, Bound by Universal Bookbindery, Inc., San Antonio.

Although it leaves much to be desired, this is by far the best work on art in early Texas. It consists of a discussion of more than sixty artists who painted in Texas during the nineteenth century, splendidly illustrated, based on extensive research into a subject about which little had been previously known or written. Elizabeth H. Walmsley called it "an important addition to the history of painting in Texas. Her research makes available much new information concerning the artists and their environment. Moreover, the volume is truly delightful reading, entertaining from start to finish."

In the Introduction, Jerry Bywaters points out how sparse is the data on art and artists in early Texas, and states: "This book contributes much toward mitigating many of these documentary shortcomings concerning the art and artists of the period to which this study limits itself. The personal diligence and 'searching' instincts of the author have brought to attention obscure pictorial examples which have remained unknown or little noted over these many years. Many 'new' and interesting artists are brought to light and life.'' This excellent essay by Bywaters is the only attempt at critical analysis in the book. It makes one wish Bywaters had written the main text and Pinckney the introduction.

Pinckney's text is primarily biographical. She provides a permanently useful guide to the artists of the period, and a beginning towards a catalogue of surviving works. Unfortunately, she too often fails to provide the present location of works she has obviously seen. She provides us with almost nothing in the way of artistic or social criticism. In this regard, she has been adequately defended by David H. Wallace, who wrote: ''Such studies [as hers], be it noted, can scarcely be anything other than chronicles, for American development was too fluid in the main to permit the rise of distinctive regional schools before the twentieth century. Texas was no exception to this rule. Her early artists were of such varied origins, and their mutual contacts, except among the German and French settlers, were so incidental that a Texas style as distinct from Texan subject matter is not to be found.''

Obviously, Pinckney's goal was to find and present the facts only, and the extensive bibliography and annotations indicate the lengths to which she carried her search. It is especially disappointing, therefore, to find so many errors of fact in the book, and sad that she was so unversed in Texas history. She tells us that Chief Bowles was ''Texas' number one enemy.'' She says that Gen. Edward Burleson was a member of the Convention of 1833, but not that he was Vice President of the Republic of Texas. The Spanish Governor's Palace in San Antonio, she says, was built in 1849. She quotes and cites William Bollaert's journal, but makes no reference to his own delightful Texas drawings. Rafael Chovel is given the name Ralph. The superb lithographs of Edward Everett in the George W. Hughes memoir of his 1846 tour through Texas (originals now at Amon Carter Museum) are not mentioned at all. Strange asides are inserted, such as a discussion of Sam Houston's attitude on Annexation.

Obviously, no one proofed the text who knew the German language, although a large percentage of the text is devoted to German artists.

This results in the embarrassing inclusion of three non-persons as artists: Eigenthum d. Verleger, Gezeicht von C. O. Bahr, and Gedr von I. Williard, which actually mean, respectively, "property of the publisher," "drawn by C. O. Bahr," and "Printed by I. Williard." The names of Charles Willson Peale, Thomas Gimbrede, Augustus Hoppin, James Smillie, and Henry Cheever Pratt are misspelled in the text. The combined resources of the sponsor and publisher should have been able to provide editorial aid to prevent these and other errors.

165 Polley, Joseph Benjamin (1840-1918)

HOOD'S TEXAS BRIGADE; ITS MARCHES, ITS BATTLES, ITS ACHIEVEMENTS.

New York and Washington: The Neale Pubishing Company, 1910.
347pp. 25 plates. 22cm.
Cloth.

Other issues:
(A). Facsimile reprint. Dayton, Ohio: Morningside Bookshop, 1976. Same collation. 23cm. Cloth.

This is an account of the military actions of one of the most battle-scarred regiments of the Civil War. John H. Reagan once said: "I would rather have been able to say that I had been a worthy member of Hood's Texas Brigade than to have enjoyed all the honors which have been conferred upon me. I doubt if there has ever been a brigade, or other military organization in the history of the world, that equalled it in the heroic valor and self-sacrificing conduct of its members, and in the brilliancy of its services." Charles W. Ramsdell, Sr., said: "It is safe to say that no single brigade on either side in the Civil War gained greater or more merited fame than Hood's Texas Brigade."

The brigade originally consisted of the 1st, 4th, and 5th Texas Regiments with about 3,500 men. During the war recruits enlarged the size to about 4,480 men. Few units suffered more casualties: at its surrender, the unit had only about 447 officers and men. During the course of its service, it was singled out for special praise by Robert E.

Lee, James Longstreet, Stonewall Jackson, and Jefferson Davis. Lee actually led the brigade in person on one charge during the Battle of the Wilderness.

Polley writes from the philosophy that "the majority of readers [are] more interested in what is done than in the how and the wherefore of it" and states flatly: "The righteousness of the cause for which it fought and suffered is taken for granted and confessed by every fair-minded and native-born American." The volume consists of a chronological narrative of the brigade's service between 1861 and 1865, interspersed with numerous official reports and with fascinating eye-witness accounts by private soldiers. The anecdotal reminiscences are especially interesting and give flavor to an otherwise straightforward narrative, although Polley contributes some episodes of his own. Ramsdell states: "The author's happy style has made the book very readable, very unlike the great bulk of regimental and brigade histories. . . . Humor and tragedy are mingled in genuine reflection of the life of the camp; but tragedy predominates. . . ."

Polley writes, for example: "One night indeed, grown tired of inaction and longing for excitement, the boys of the First took French leave of their officers, and went in a body across the Potomac, and there waked up not only General Sickles and the Union troops then under his command, but spread consternation on the streets of Washington City by the report circulated by themselves that they were the advance guard of the Confederate army. General Sickles assembled his troops in battle array and called lustily for reinforcements, and these were on the way when daylight came and revealed the absence of a single Confederate on his side of the river. In brief, the Texans went over 'on a lark,' and, having enjoyed it, returned to their quarters before daylight."

John B. Hood wrote his own reminiscences of the war in *Advance and Retreat: Personal Experiences in the United States and Confederate States Armies* (New Orleans: G. T. Beauregard, 1880, 358pp.). Polley also published another book entitled *A Soldier's Letters to Charming Nellie* (N.Y. and Washington: The Neale Publishing Company, 1908, 317pp.), but doubts have been raised as to whether these letters were actually written during the war or composed later. A number of other Texans who were members of Hood's Texas Brigade wrote memoirs. Decimus et Ultimus Barziza's *The Adventures of a Prisoner of War . . . by an Escaped Prisoner of Hood's Texas Brigade* (Houston, 1865) is one of the rarest Confederate books; it was reprinted in 1964 by the University of Texas Press. Nicholas A. Davis' *Campaign from Texas to Maryland* is entered here separately. Mary Lasswell edited *Rags and Hope: The Recollections of Val C. Giles, Four Years with Hood's Brigade* . . . (New York: Coward-McCann, 1961, 280pp.), and John C. West wrote *A Texan in Search of a Fight, Being the Diary and Letters of a Private Soldier in Hood's Texas Brigade* (Waco: J. S. Hill, 1901, 189pp.).

Col. Harold B. Simpson has written a number of recent works on Hood's Brigade, including what will likely remain the essential source set on the unit, a four-volume series with titles as follows: *Hood's Texas Brigade in Poetry and Song* (Hillsboro: Hill Junion College Press, 1968, 296pp.); *Hood's Texas Brigade: Lee's Grenadier Guard* (Waco: Texian Press, 1970, 512pp.); *Hood's Texas Brigade in Reunion and Memory* (Hillsboro: Hill Jr. College Press, 1974, 369pp.); and *Hood's Texas Brigade: A Compendium* (Hillsboro: Hill Jr. College Press, 1977, 614pp.)

Howes P465. Krick 401. Nevins I-147.

166   Ramsdell, Charles William, Sr. (1877-1942)

RECONSTRUCTION IN TEXAS.

New York: Columbia University; Longman, Green & Co., Agents; London: P. S. King & Son, 1910.
324,[12]pp. 25cm.
Cloth; also printed wrappers.
Studies in History, Economics and Public Law, Volume XXXVI, Number 1, Whole Number 95.

Other issues:
(A).   Facsimile reprint. Gloucester, Mass.: Peter Smith, 1964. 324pp. Cloth.
(B).   Facsimile reprint. Austin & London: University of Texas Press, Published in Cooperation with the Texas State Historical Association, [1970]. Texas History Paperbacks Series.

This is the best political history of the Reconstruction era in Texas. Published as a revision of his dissertation the year Ramsdell received his doctorate from Columbia, it remains today the most accurate, sober, and detached discussion of one of the most emotional periods of Texas history. E. C. Barker called it "the best study of the political and social history of Texas from 1861 to 1874."

Charles Ramsdell was known for years as the dean of Southern historians. He served as president of both the Southern Historical Association and the Mississippi Valley Historical Association. He was associated with the University of Texas for nearly forty years, served as an officer of the Texas State Historical Association for thirty-five years and as an editor of its *Quarterly* for twenty-eight years. Chapters III through VI of this work appeared in the *Quarterly* before publication in the book.

The book begins with chapters on secession, Texas' part in the war, and the political and moral collapse immediately after Appomattox. These are followed by accounts of the two reconstruction attempts, Presidential and Congressional. Ramsdell traces President Johnson's establishment of freedmen's bureaus and his attempts to expedite and ease the nation back together, then describes the Congressional over-throw of Johnson's policies, the military rule of Texas, the radical government of E. J. Davis, and the return to representative government in 1874.

The great value of Ramsdell's book is that he explains and analyzes that turbulent era neither as a partisan Southerner nor as a civil rights advocate but as an objective observer, at least as objective as possible for such an emotion-packed subject. Since he lived and wrote while participants were still alive, and since he was one of the best researchers Texas has produced, Ramsdell was able to do for Reconstruction what has never adequately been done for the Texas Revolution or the Texas Republic. Without espousing or intruding his personal politics, what-ever they may have been, Ramsdell unfolds his narrative from each side's point of view. His conclusion that Reconstruction as practiced in Texas was unwise is a masterpiece of understatement.

Ramsdell emphasizes political events and personalities, and treats many facets of Reconstruction—such as the plight of the Negro, frontier troubles, labor and the farmer, and daily life of the people—somewhat superficially. His treatment of the Negro question suffers from paternalism. But his portrayals of the main characters of the period are well-documented and fascinating. Generals Reynolds and

Sheridan, for example, are shown to be the self-serving scoundrels that they really were. The account of Reynolds' abortive attempt to weasel his way into the U.S. Senate is delightful, but fair; and the incompetence of Sheridan in non-military affairs is shown to be even more glaringly evident in Texas than in Louisiana. Governor Throckmorton, on the other hand, is justly praised and Governor Pease is treated objectively. The extraordinary conflict between Governor A. J. Hamilton and his brother, Senator M. C. Hamilton, is one of many interesting threads that run through the narrative.

His sympathetic but damning appraisal of Governor E. J. Davis, who engineered the atrocious semi-colon court scandal and who attempted armed resistance when his successor tried to take office, is a high spot of Texas historical literature. Praising Davis for his personal integrity and honesty in fiscal matters (during an era unsurpassed for corruption), Ramsdell concludes:

"The administration of Davis was responsible for more of the bitterness with which the people of Texas have remembered the reconstruction era than all that happened from the close of the war to 1870. In fact the word reconstruction recalls to most people first of all the arbitrary rule of this radical governor; and certainly the name of no Texan has gone down to posterity so hated as his. But after all, Davis has not been fairly judged. He was self-willed, obstinate, pig-headed almost beyond belief; a most intense and narrow partisan, who could see nothing good in an opponent and nothing evil in a friend. Surrounded by a group of the most unprincipled adventurers that ever disgraced a government, he suffered from their advice and their acts. Yet his administration was his own and he guided it with the iron hand of a martinet; he had no regard for the popular will, he consulted no desires but his own, and he was absolutely devoid of tact. But, apparently without scruples in matters purely political, Davis was personally honest. . . . In many respects he was the best of the faction that nominated him for governor in 1869; but no man could have been worse fitted by temperament for the delicate task before the local Republicans at that time. When circumstances demanded the most painstaking moderation in order to overcome the effect of the Congressional policy, E. J. Davis and his radical associates succeeded only in plunging the Republican party in Texas into irretrievable ruin.''

Many other studies of Reconstruction have been written since Ramsdell's book, one of the best of which is Carl H. Moneyhon's *Republicanism in Reconstruction Texas* (Austin: University of Texas Press, 1980), in which Moneyhon writes: "While I do not agree with their conclusions regarding Texas Republicanism, Charles W. Ramsdell, *Reconstruction in Texas* and William C. Nunn, *Texas under the Carpetbaggers* provide the groundwork from which every study of reconstruction in the state must proceed. Throughout my work I was impressed with the solid scholarship and insights of Ramsdell. . . .'' Both Nunn and Moneyhon have built upon Ramsdell's base and added new perspectives to our understanding of one of the most difficult periods of Texas history.

Howes R42. Rader 2758.

167   Raymond, Dora (Neill) (1889-   )

CAPTAIN LEE HALL OF TEXAS.

Norman: University of Oklahoma Press, 1940.
xiii,[1],350,[2]pp. Illus. by Louis Lundean and Frederic Remington.
Folding map. 23cm.
Cloth, dustjacket.

Other issues:
(A). Facsimile reprint. Norman: University of Oklahoma Press, [1982]. Same collation. Cloth, dustjacket.

This is a charming, carefully researched biography of one of the most enigmatical Texas peace officers. Allan Nevins said of it: "As an adventure story this is a remarkably full and interesting book, replete with Lee Hall's battles against outlaws, ruffians, hostile savages, greasers, and murdering feudists. But it is something better than an adventure story; it is a well-rounded character study of one of the most impressive figures the Texas border ever produced, wrought with sublety and skill.'' Claude Elliott called it ''a grand story, brilliantly told, of a colossal, though magnificent failure,'' and Stanley Walker said it "represents one of the most conscientious and thorough bits of research ever to come out of the Southwest."

Dora Raymond's previous books were on the Franco-Prussian War and on Byron and Milton. "Neither poet," she writes, "has cost me more arduous days than my present subject, a Texas Ranger who lived through the 'smoking seventies' and on into the hectic century we call our own. His trail has led me through the length of Texas and into Mexico, to the Kiowa-Comanche Reservation, to New Orleans, and across the Pacific to the Philippines."

Jesse Lee Hall was born in 1849 and came to Texas in 1869. During the next ten years, in rapid succession, he served as school teacher, deputy sheriff, city marshal, legislative assistant, lieutenant in the Texas Rangers under L. H. McNelly, and captain of rangers. He helped break up the Taylor-Sutton feud, assisted in arresting King Fisher, and was present at the killing of Sam Bass. In the 1880's he served as Indian agent and ranch manager, and in the 1890's served in the Spanish-American War in the Philippines as head of the Macabebe Scouts. Hall's family life, portrayed a bit too sentimentally by the author, was a fiasco. His bride hated the ranger service, the only type of work for which Hall was suited. His numerous business ventures were for the most part dismal failures. Unable to cope with the change of the 20th century, he took to drink and died in 1911.

As a fighting ranger and lawman, few if any surpassed Lee Hall. William S. Porter lived for awhile on Hall's ranch in La Salle County, and O. Henry's *Heart of the West* owes much of its content to Porter's experiences with Hall. Frederic Remington came to Texas to interview him, became a friend, and wrote and illustrated Hall's exploits for *Harper's Magazine*. Remington frequently urged Hall to write his own life story, but Hall never did. Al Jennings wrote that Hall's rangers once captured 479 outlaws in one year, an exaggeration possibly but indicative of Hall's reputation among those who knew him.

Henry Nash Smith wrote of Dora Raymond's biography: "Mrs. Raymond, who holds a chair of history at Sweet Briar, has made painstaking use of every relevant bit of evidence concerning her subject—not only a store of manuscripts and clippings in the possession of Hall's daughter, Mrs. Isham Keith, but contemporary Texas newspapers, the reminiscences of Frederic Remington, N.A. Jennings and others . . . and the official files of the Indian Bureau and the War Department. . . . The book is a good one, but [her] style seems to me sometimes overwrought.'' Nevins summed up the book's strengths and weaknesses when he said ''Raymond is gentle in dealing with some of Hall's deficiencies. . . . We might see the man more clearly had she been franker. But she has given us a vivacious and spirited study of a remarkable frontier leader.'' I would only add that she also shows better than any other ranger biographer the enormous psychological pressures felt by the frontier lawmen. Most of these men, like Hall, were never able to comprehend or come to terms with modern Texas, and few entered the 20th century gracefully.

Adams Guns 1827. Dobie, p.60. Howes R83.

168   Reagan, John Henninger (1818-1905)

MEMOIRS, WITH SPECIAL REFERENCE TO SECESSION AND THE CIVIL WAR.

New York and Washington: The Neale Publishing Company, 1906.
Edited by Walter Flavius McCaleb. Introduction by George P. Garrison.
351pp. 22cm.
Cloth, dustjacket.

Other issues:
(A).   Facsimile reprint. Austin and New York: The Pemberton Press, 1968. 351,[11]pp. 22cm. Cloth, dustjacket. Volume VIII in Brasada Reprint Series. Introduction by John H. Jenkins. New index.

One of the most important volumes of personal recollections relating to the Confederacy, Reagan's *Memoirs* also cover the period of the Republic of Texas, the Cherokee Wars, Congress in the 1850's, Reconstruction, and politics of the 1870's and 1880's. They are a classic of 19th century American political autobiography.

John H. Reagan immigrated to Texas from Tennessee in 1839, at age 21, in time to serve in the Texas army in the campaign against Chief Bowles and the Cherokees and as a Texas Ranger in other campaigns. He became the first county judge of Henderson County, and after some years entered Congress in 1857. In 1861 he served in the Secession Convention of Texas and as Texas' first Confederate congressman. He was soon appointed to Jefferson Davis's cabinet as Postmaster-General and for a time as Secretary of the Treasury. Throughout the war he was privy to the highest councils of the Confederate government.

After the war he was imprisoned with Davis and held in solitary confinement for nearly a year, as were two other authors of basic Texas books, Francis R. Lubbock and William Preston Johnston. Upon his release, he helped write the Texas Constitution of 1866 and was offered the governorship of Texas by the Reconstruction authorities, but refused on grounds of principle. Reagan became U.S. Senator in 1887, and was the author of the Interstate Commerce Commission Act. He was married three times and had eleven children.

Reagan's memoirs are intimate and readable, and a fundamental document for understanding the leadership of the Confederacy, as well as for Texas political activities during the entire latter half of the 19th century. The last hundred pages of the work consist of appendices containing Reagan's major state papers. Chief among these are his 1865 Fort Warren letters, of which *Handbook of Texas* states:

"After the war Reagan was imprisoned for several months at Fort Warren in Boston harbor. On May 18, 1865, he addressed a letter to President Andrew Johnson, urging the wisdom and justice of a more lenient attitude toward the people of the South and warning the President against the evil consequences of the policies being urged by Northern partisans. A second Fort Warren letter, dated August 11, 1865, advised the people of Texas to accept the results of the war, acknowledge the extinction of slavery, admit the Negro to civil rights, and permit him to vote with educational and property qualifications. This policy was urged as a means of avoiding the evils of military government and unqualified Negro suffrage, but Reagan's motives were not understood, and he lost standing among his Texas constituents."

The misunderstanding was forgotten, however, as Reagan's talents and deep concern for the welfare of Texas became evident in the ensuing forty years. In 1903 he retired to write his memoirs, finishing them a few days before his death. Walter F. McCaleb edited them into final form, and Neale released the completed book in 1906. Reagan's private papers, totaling over five thousand documents and imprints, became one of the basic collections of the Texas State Archives. The best biography of Reagan is *Not Without Honor: the Life of John H. Reagan* (Austin: University of Texas Press, 1962) by Ben H. Procter, one of Texas' most prominent historians.

Agatha, p.71. Graff 3434. Howes R100. Krick 412.

169   Reed, St. Clair Griffin (1867-1948)

A HISTORY OF THE TEXAS RAILROADS, AND OF TRANS-PORTATION CONDITIONS UNDER SPAIN AND MEXICO AND THE REPUBLIC AND THE STATE.

Houston: The St. Clair Publishing Co., 3702 Mt. Vernon St., [1941].
x,822pp. 24cm.
Cloth.
[Verso of title:] An Autographed Advance Subscription Limited Edition. Typography, Printing, and Binding in the U.S.A. by Kingsport Press, Inc., Kingsport, Tennessee. Printed label pasted inside front cover: "Each copy of this limited edition . . . is numbered and autographed by the author."

Other issues:
(A).   Same as above, with "Second Edition" on copyright page.
(B).   *A History of the Land Grants and Other Aids to the Texas Railroads by the State of Texas.* Houston: The St. Clair Publishing Co., [1942]. [51]pp. Printed wrappers. Reprint of chapter XXIV.
(C).   Facsimile reprint. Salem, N.H.: Ayer Publishing Co., [ca. 1978]. Cloth.
(D).   Facsimile reprint. New York: Arno Press, 1981. Buckram.

One of the most comprehensive studies of the railroading history of any state, this is by far the best on Texas railroads. Eugene C. Barker called it a "truly remarkable book . . . no less than an encyclopedia—a readable encyclopedia for the most part—of the railroad transportation history of Texas. . . . The author reveals comprehensive knowledge of the problems of federal and state legislation regulating rail transportation and a sympathetic understanding of social, economic, and political conditions back of such legislation. He does not exculpate early management from common charges of disregarding public interest, but he does defend [Texas] railroads against more or less conventional general charges of public exploitation. For example, the long chapter on 'Land Grants and Other Aids' ought to be required reading for economists and historians who persist in interpreting the past in terms of the present, often partisan terms of the present.''

Reed was certainly qualified for the task. He entered Colgate as a teenager, had to return home when his father was drowned in the storm that destroyed Indianola, and later returned to finish school. Immediately upon graduation in 1888, he went to work as a freight clerk for the New York, Texas, and Mexican Railway, later absorbed by Southern Pacific. He worked under William J. Craig, who had at the time been working for Texas railroads for 18 years, starting when Texas had only 711 miles of railroad. When Reed began, the Interstate Commerce Commission had been in existence less than a year, and the Railroad Commission of Texas had not yet been formed. Reed worked for Southern Pacific for 49 years, reaching the position of general freight manager for the entire system and serving as editor of the *Southern Pacific Bulletin*. At his retirement in 1937, he had been a railroad man for almost exactly half of the hundred years since railroad history had begun in Texas (with the 1836 formation of the Texas Railroad, Navigation, and Banking Company), and almost two-thirds of the time that there had actually been railroads in Texas.

Reed began writing his book at the age of seventy, and published it at the age of seventy-four. The original manuscript is now in the University of Houston Library. Before his death at the age of eighty-one, Reed also wrote virtually every article on the myriad of Texas railroads for the *Handbook of Texas*. In my copy of his *History of Texas Railroads*, he wrote an inscription to Elizabeth Cullen of the Library of Transportation History of the Bureau of Railway Economics, ''as an expression of my thanks for your help in gathering facts for this book.'' It also contains a tipped-in letter from Reed to Cullen dated Houston, February 1, 1943, which states in part: ''You will be glad to know that I have made a little money on this my first venture as an author and publisher. I am still selling and have only about 400 out of 2500 left. . . .'' These apparently sold out soon afterwards, for a second edition was published about 1942.

The volume contains 58 chapters that include transportation by water and wagon, pioneer railroad efforts during the republic, government ownership plans, and the building of the first railroad in Texas in 1853. There are also sections on rate-making, rate cases, pools, agreements, mergers, land grants, railroad stocks and bonds, taxation, and one chapter on each Texas railway, short or long, small or powerful. There are chapters on the free pass controversies, on the methods of obtaining business "within the law," on tram roads, on logging roads, on electric railways, on the intracoastal canal, on mileages and classes of roads, on ports and steamship lines, on important legal cases relating to railroads, on federal controls, and on the relationship between railroads and the shipping of various commodities. Reed makes use of C. S. Potts, *Railroad Transportation in Texas* (Austin: University of Texas Bulletin 119, 1909), an early scholarly study that is still of value.

Reed states that in doing his research, "every effort has been made to verify every statement made; to deal fully and fairly with all persons, places and issues. Accuracy and authenticity have been further sought by submitting each chapter to an official of the railroad to which it relates or to a recognized authority on the subject treated. But no railroad official or other person has influenced . . . any opinion expressed." That he was able to achieve this goal in a field so fraught with bias and prejudice is quite an accomplishment. That so much of the book is fascinating reading, despite the technical nature of the subject, is truly remarkable.

In this regard, I cannot help quoting Dr. Barker's comment that "every professional historian with a modicum of modesty has suffered at times a feeling of envy in reading books written by non-professional historians. Mr. Reed's . . . book may well cause a professional historian to ask himself embarrassing questions. Why do we, who ostensibly give our whole time to history, accomplish so little while lawyers, geologists, and business men, who make their livings otherwise, write such good history? I excuse myself from answering that question publicly."

170 Reid, Samuel Chester, Jr. (1818-1897)

THE SCOUTING EXPEDITIONS OF MC CULLOCH'S TEXAS RANGERS; OR, THE SUMMER AND FALL CAMPAIGN OF THE ARMY OF THE UNITED STATES IN MEXICO—1846; INCLUD-ING SKIRMISHES WITH THE MEXICANS, AND AN ACCU-

RATE DETAIL OF THE STORMING OF MONTEREY; ALSO,
THE DARING SCOUTS AT BUENA VISTA; TOGETHER WITH
ANECDOTES, INNCIDENTS, DESCRIPTIONS OF COUNTRY,
AND SKETCHES OF THE LIVES OF THE CELEBRATED PAR-
TISAN CHIEFS, HAYS, MC CULLOCH, AND WALKER.

Philadelphia: G. B. Zieber and Co., 1847.
251pp. 12 illus. Map. 17cm.
Cloth.
[Verso of title:] Stereotyped by L. Johnson and Co., Philadelphia. Printed by King
and Baird.

Other issues:
(A). Same, dated 1848.
(B). Philadelphia: J. W. Bradley, 1859. Same collation.
(C). Philadelphia: J. E. Potter and Company, [1859]. Same collation.
(D). Philadelphia: J. W. Bradley, 1860. Same collation.
(E). Philadelphia: J. E. Potter and Company, [1885]. [2],251pp. 20cm. Cloth. Includes
     a printed presentation leaf.
(F). Facsimile reprint of first edition. Austin: The Steck Company, 1935. [4],251pp.
     21cm. Cloth. Original Narratives of History and Adventure Series. 2000 copies
     printed.
(G). Facsimile reprint of first edition. Freeport, N.Y.: Books for Libraries Press,
     [1970]. 23cm. Cloth.

This is the best contemporary account of the Texas Rangers in the
northern campaigns of the Mexican War. Written by a Louisiana
lawyer who served with the rangers under Jack Hays and Ben
McCulloch, it is an excellent account of one of the most rambunctious
military forces ever assembled out of Texas. Jeff Dykes called it "a
highly entertaining eyewitness account, based on Reid's field diary, of
the activities of Gen. Taylor's army. McCulloch's Texas Rangers were
the eyes and ears of Taylor and the intelligence they provided had
much to do with his success." Of this group of Rangers, W. P. Webb
said: "Their part was to be the first in action, the last out; to fight,
not to parley."

Samuel C. Reid, Jr., was the son of a noted naval captain of the
War of 1812, a man who had suffered capture by pirates and who had
seen plenty of action—and also the man who is credited by *Dictionary
of American Biography* with the design of the present form of the

American flag. Young Reid became a lawyer in Louisiana but yearned for action of his own. In the Mexican War he got his chance.

Reid's account covers the period June-October, 1846, during which Reid's regiment, the 6th Louisiana Volunteers, served under Zachary Taylor in Northern Mexico. Reid says that, "feeling confident that his regiment would be kept in the rear to garrison the different posts, he resigned his rank, and proceeded to Matamoros, where he joined the company of Texas Rangers . . . kept for scouting service by General Taylor." It was a fortunate decision, for it put Reid in the forefront of the action, particularly in the operations during the capture of Monterrey, during which Reid's group, states one later historian, "shrieking like Comanches, captured almost single-handed the Bishop's Palace. Reid was back in Louisiana at the time of the Battle of Buena Vista, but he includes a brief account of the Texas Rangers in that battle based on second-hand information.

The Texas Rangers with whom Reid served were an incredibly mixed bag of men. One observer called them "gifted with the intelligence and courage of back-woods hunters," but W. P. Webb has pointed out that the unit included lawyers, doctors, poets, surveyors, and legislators. Gen. Hitchcock wrote when they appeared in camp: "Hays' Rangers have come, their appearance never to be forgotten. Not any sort of uniform, but well mounted and doubly well armed. . . . The Mexicans are terribly afraid of them."

Stephen B. Oates wrote about McCulloch's Rangers: "The Texas Rangers were veteran Indian fighters, known for their extraordinary courage and endurance. As individual fighters they were virtually incomparable. . . . But as soldiers who had to respect rank and order, these Rangers were beyond hope; they soon proved themselves so wild and tempestuous and utterly uncontrollable that even Taylor, as spirited and independent as any man, came to regard them as barbarians, as 'licentious vandals.' For no sooner had they arrived in Mexico than they began to commit shocking atrocities. They raided villages and pillaged farms, they shot or hanged unarmed Mexican civilians. On one occasion Taylor lost his temper altogether and threatened to jail the lot of them. The occasion was a Fourth of July celebration at Reynosa in which the Texans stole two horse buckets of whiskey to wash down a meal of Mexican pigs and chickens which they had killed 'accidentally' while firing salutes to honor the day.''

Reid called the Fourth of July celebration a mere ''jollification.'' He justifies the Reynosa atrocities by saying its ''inhabitants are a set of the most irreclaimable scoundrels that are to be found anywhere in the valley of the Rio Grande—a race of brigands whose avowed occupation is rapine and murder.'' The Texans remembered well the savage treatment of the Mier prisoners in that region, and Reid said the Texans were upset because the Mexicans would walk down the streets ''with the most consummate impudence.'' When many of them ''were found shot, or hung up in the chapparal during our visit'' it was because ''during some fit of remorse and desperation, tortured by conscience for the many evil deeds they had committed, they had recklessly laid violent hands upon their own lives! Quien sabe!''

After Monterrey, Taylor grudgingly commended them for gallant action, and watched them ride off with unmitigated relief. Publicly, Taylor announced: ''The general feels assured that every individual in the command unites with him in admiration of the distinguished gallantry and conduct of Col. Hays, and his noble band of Texian volunteers—hereafter we are brothers.'' Privately, he wrote home that ''the mounted men from Texas have scarcely made one expedition without unwarrantably killing a Mexican'' and indulging in ''every other form of crime.'' Luther Giddings wrote of this event: ''The commanding general took occasion to thank them for the efficient service they had rendered, and we saw them turn their faces toward the blood-bought State they represented, with many good wishes and the hope that all honest Mexicans were at a safe distance from their path.''

Reid understood and sympathized with the attitude of the rangers. He does not hide their violence but neither does he condemn it. His chief complaints are against the restraints imposed by higher command; they had come, in his and the rangers' opinion, to kill Mexicans. In every contest they did just that, until none were left or until commanded to stop.

Reid's book is best at the anecdotal level, giving one of the clearest surviving accounts of life in camp, scouts, forays, skirmishes, sprees, and practical jokes. The Texans were out for vengeance, without doubt, but they were also in this first American foreign war for fun, and of vengeance and fun Reid gives us aplenty. For biographies of McCulloch and Hays, see Victor M. Rose, *The Life and Servcies of Gen. Ben McCulloch* (Philadelphia: The Press, 1888,260pp.) and James K. Greer, *Colonel Jack Hays: Texas Frontier Leader and California Builder* (New York: E. P. Dutton, 1952, 428pp.).

Agatha, p.34. Campbell, p.175. Clark III-390. Dobie, p.60. Field 1271. Graff 3451. Haferkorn, p.49. Howes R175. Raines, p.172. Sabin 69088.

171 Richardson, Rupert Norval (1891-)

TEXAS, THE LONE STAR STATE.

New York: Prentice-Hall, Inc. 1943.
xix,[3],590pp. Illus. Maps. 23cm.
Cloth, dustjacket.
[Published January, 1943].

Other issues:
(A). Second printing, November, 1947.
(B). Third printing, July, 1950.
(C). Fourth printing, May, 1953.
(D). Fifth printing, June, 1955.
(E). Sixth printing, June, 1956.
(F). Second edition. Englewood Cliffs, N.J.: Prentice-Hall, Inc., 1958. 460pp. Illus. Maps. 24cm. Cloth, dustjacket.
(G). Third edition. Englewood Cliffs, N.J.: Prentice-Hall, Inc., 1970. xi,448pp. Illus. Maps. 24cm. Cloth dustjacket. With Ernest Wallace and Adrian N. Anderson as co-authors.

This is the standard single-volume history of Texas, more reliable than all previous and all subsequent histories of the state except that written by Seymour V. Connor. Elizabeth Gatlin summed it up as "a concise, well-written general history of Texas." Seymour Connor said it "is not only one of the best textbooks on any subject, it is also the foremost single volume available on the history of Texas." Claude Elliott wrote that its publication ended "the quest for a dependable, comprehensive, and readable book on Texas."

Richardson's parents came as pioneers to West Texas by covered wagon, and Richardson was born in a log cabin on their ranch in 1891. He graduated from the University of Chicago in 1914 and served as an officer in World War I. He received his doctorate at the University of Texas in 1928. Except for some time spent teaching at the University of Texas, Richardson worked at Hardin-Simmons University in Abilene for over sixty years; he was president of the university from 1943 to 1953. For many years he was active in the state historical marker program, and is responsible for some 5,000 historical markers planted throughout the state. He authored several other significant books, notably *The Comanche Barrier to the South Plains Settlement* (Glendale: A. H. Clark Co., 1933, 424pp.), *The Greater Southwest* (Glendale: A. H. Clark Co., 1934, 506pp., with Carl Coke Rister), and *The Frontier of Northwest Texas, 1846 to 1876* (Glendale: A. H. Clark Co., 1963, 332pp.). There is a short volume on Richardson by Katharyn Duff, et al., *Rupert N. Richardson: The Man and His Works* (Abilene: Hardin-Simmons University, 1971).

Dr. Richardson inscribed a copy of this book to me as follows: "Inscribed to John H. Jenkins with high appreciation of your service to history through your writings and publications. [I have several times tried to force myself to delete this first sentence, but have not succeeded—J.H.J.]. This book was conceived while I was a graduate student in the classes of Eugene C. Barker during the 1920's. He is truly 'the old master.' It was made possible because he and other members of the history faculty, Walter P. Webb especially, permitted me to teach there in summers and some semesters during the lean depression years. Notwithstanding a heavy teaching load, I could do some research in the university library and public records in Austin. Prentice-Hall, Inc., invited me to write the book for their state history series. Designed for the general reader, it came to be used more as a college text. I do not know how many copies were sold, my estimate is not more than two thousand. Later editions, the last shared by Professors Ernest Wallace and Adrian Anderson, have been in much greater demand as a college text."

The second edition (1958) is a complete revision, "with practically every paragraph rewritten," containing some fifty pages of new material. The third edition, with Ernest Wallace and Adrian N. Anderson as co-authors, brings the text further up to date. Further textual revisions are introduced, and much new illustrative material added, as well as more extensive bibliographical citations. A few minor errors still persist, as is inevitable, such as C. A. Gulich for C. A. Gulick and James Harper Star for James Harper Starr.

Of the earlier school histories of Texas, the most famous is Mrs. Percy V. Pennybacker's *A New History of Texas for Schools* (Tyler, 1888). It went through several editions between 1888 and 1938, and I own a copy which she has extensively revised and enlarged in her hand for still another edition. The Pennybacker history is significant because it introduced many tales, some false and some true—such as Travis drawing the line—into the mainstream of public conscience and which no amount of revisionism has been able to alter.

No school history of Texas since Richardson's is of any significance at all, except Seymour V. Connor's *Texas, A History* (New York: Thomas Y. Crowell, 1971, 481pp.), which I recommend as a well-written, balanced history. In a number of respects, such as general anaylsis and bibliography, Connor's book is better than Richardson's. The other school histories, however, are for the most part poorly written and weighted to preposterous lengths with attempts to appease minority pressure groups by introducing insignificant and sometimes even nonexistent black and Mexican heroes into the picture and by downplaying the bitter racial rivalries which made up so much of Texas history. Moreover, state and local textbook committees have gained so great a throat-hold over writers and publishers that by the time a manuscript has been approved, all of its spark and much of its integrity has vanished. Battered by the attempts of liberal extremists to rewrite history, by the pigheadedness of right-wing vigilantes on the textbook committees, and by the pseudo-psychology of social scientists, modern school textbooks on Texas catch little of the spirit and almost none of the flavor of Texas history. What J. Frank Dobie said in 1952 is still true in 1982: "It would require a blacksnake whip to make most juveniles, or adults either, read these productions, as devoid of picturesqueness, life-blood, and intellectual content as so many concrete slabs. No genuinely humanistic history of the Southwest has ever been printed."

172 Richardson, Willard (1802-1875), and David Richardson (1815-1871)

THE TEXAS ALMANAC, FOR 1857, WITH STATISTICS, HISTORICAL AND BIOGRAPHICAL SKETCHES, ETC., RELATING TO TEXAS.

Galveston: Prepared, Printed and Published by Richardson and Co., at the New Office, 1856.

[6],7-159,[1]pp., plus 48pp. of adv. 22cm.

Printed wrappers.

10,000 copies printed.

Other issues:

(A). *The Texas Almanac, for* 1858 . . . Galveston: Prepared, Printed and published by Richardson & Co., at the "News" Office, 1857. [6],7-192pp., plus 84pp. of adv. 5 plates. 21cm. Printed wrappers. A few copies are known with a folding map of Texas by J. H. Young. 25,000 copies printed.

(B). *The Texas Almanac for* 1859 . . . Galveston: The Galveston News . . . by W. & D. Richardson & Co., at the "News" Office, 1857. [6],7-194pp., plus 84pp. of adv. 22cm. Printed wrappers. This issue contains defamatory remarks on Col. John Forbes in the article by N. D. Labadie on the San Jacinto campaign, pages 54 and 55.

(C). Same as (B), second issue. Col. John Forbes is not attacked by name, and a preliminary leaf is inserted, headed "Notice to the Public," stating that no defamation of Forbes was intended.

(D). *The Texas Almanac for* 1860 . . . Galveston: The Galveston News . . . by W. & D. Richardson, [1859]. 228pp., plus 92pp. of adv. 21cm. Printed wrappers.

(E). *The Texas Almanac for* 1861 . . . Galveston: The Galveston News . . . by W. & D. Richardson, [1860]. [2],336pp. Folding map in some copies. 20cm. Printed wrappers. 30,000 copies printed. Preface undated. Pages 246-252 contain U.S. statistics.

(F). Second issue of (E). Preface dated November 1860. Pages 246-252 contain a list of county officials, and other Texas material.

(G). *The Texas Almanac for* 1862 . . . [Houston:] The Galveston News . . . by D. Richardson, [1862]. 56,[6]pp. 21cm. Printed wrappers.

(H). *The Texas Almanac for* 1863 . . . [Austin:] D. Richardson, [1862]. 64pp. 20cm. Printed wrappers.

(I). *The Texas Almanac for* 1864 . . . Austin: The State Gazette . . . by D. Richardson, [1864]. [10],11-48pp. 22cm. Printed wrappers.

(J). *The Texas Almanac for* 1865 . . . Austin: The State Gazette . . . by D. Richardson & Co., [1864]. [10],11-64pp. Printed wrappers.

(K). *The Texas Almanac for* 1867 . . . Galveston: The Galveston News . . . by W. Richardson & Co., [1866]. 360pp. [adv. on pp.285-360]. 20cm. Printed wrappers. No almanac was issued for 1866.

(L). *The Texas Almanac for* 1868 . . . Galveston: The Galveston News . . . by W. Richardson & Co., [1867]. 312pp. [adv. on pp.251-312]. Also three unnumbered leaves of adv. placed at random between signatures within the volume. 20cm. Printed wrappers.

(M). *The Texas Almanac for* 1869, *and Emigrant's Guide to Texas* . . . Galveston: Published by W. & D. Richardson & Co., [1868]. 288pp. 19cm. Printed wrappers.

(N). *The Texas Almanac for 1870, and Emigrant's Guide to Texas* . . . Galveston: Prepared, Printed and Published by Richardson & Co., at the "News" Office, 1869. 288pp. 19cm. Printed wrappers.

(O). Variant of (N). Preface dated January 1, 1870.

(P). *The Texas Almanac for 1871, and Emigrant's Guide to Texas* . . . Galveston: Richardson & Co., [1871]. 290pp. 19cm. Printed wrappers.

(Q). *The Texas Almanac for 1872, and Emigrant's Guide to Texas* . . . Galveston: Published by Richardson & Co., [1871]. xiv,242pp. 19cm. Printed wrappers.

(R). *The Texas Almanac for 1873, and Emigrant's Guide to Texas* . . . Galveston: Published by Richardson, Belo & Co., [1872]. 240pp. 18cm. Printed wrappers.

(S). *The Texas Almanac, 1857-1873: A Compendium of Texas History*. Waco: Texian Press, 1967. xvi,792pp. Illus. 24cm. Cloth. Introduction by Walter Moore. Compiled by James M. Day. Contains a selection of articles from the original almanacs.

The Richardson almanacs comprise one of the finest research sources for virtually every aspect of 19th century Texas history. Particularly in the pre-war issues, there are literally dozens of memoirs, biographies, and historical essays of great value. Most of these articles were written from interviews with participants, or by the participants themselves. Much of our surviving eyewitness information on the Texas Revolution and Republic of Texas appears in the Richardson almanacs, as well as a vast amount of economic and statistical data. Every volume, excepting only the war issues, is a separate mine for the researcher.

Willard Richardson became editor of the Galveston *News* in 1843 and majority owner in 1845. David Richardson joined the firm in 1852 and acquired a small interest in the firm. Willard was a native of Marblehead, Massachusetts, and David a native of the Isle of Man; they were not kin. Some time in 1855 or 1856 David and the plant foreman came up with the idea for an almanac and, according to David, inserted a notice in the *News* announcing that one was forthcoming without notifying Willard in advance. Willard, though upset, agreed to test the project, which became an immediate success. David became supervising editor of almost all of the subsequent almanacs.

The chaos of the Civil War, particularly the blockade and occupation of Galveston Island, forced the newspaper to move inland to Houston. Remarkably, scaled-down versions of the almanacs were nevertheless issued during every year of the war. During this period, however, David and Willard parted company temporarily, Willard publishing the *Galveston Weekly News* in Houston and David publishing the *State Gazette and Texas Almanac Extra* in Austin. They quarrelled publicly over ownership of the almanac, but finally settled their differences. No almanac was issued in 1866, but beginning in 1867 the series was resumed, emphasizing immigration. The Panic of 1873 so distressed the firm that the almanac was discontinued.

Col. Alfred H. Belo bought into the firm in 1866 and after the deaths of the Richardsons bought control in 1875. In 1885 he established the Dallas *Morning News*, which with the Galveston *News* gave rise to the Belo newspaper dynasty. George B. Dealey, who had started as an office boy in 1874 on the Galveston *News*, became general manager of the Belo interests after Alfred Belo's death in 1901. Dealey began to issue Texas almanacs sporadically, publishing almanacs in 1904, 1910, 1911, 1912, and 1914. In the mid-1920's, Dealey bought out the Belo interests and began regular publication of annual almanacs in 1925, under the editorship of Stuart McGregor. Issues were published annually through 1929, then biennially thereafter. The 20th century issues are valuable primarily for economic and statistical data.

The Richardson almanacs were both influential and controversial, apparently intentionally. The general anti-Houston tone of many of the published eyewitness memoirs of early Texas history infuriated Sam Houston. In 1859, on the floor of the U.S. Senate, Houston blasted the "production purporting to be a Texas almanac" for the slanders it contained against him: "The *author* of this almanac, Willard Richardson—I must immortalize him—if reports be true, and I have no reason to doubt them, had he been assigned to his proper place, would have been dignified by a penitentiary residence before this time, owing to the pecadilloes with which he was charged. . . . He still goes on from sin to sin, from abuse to slander."

In addition to the wealth of material on early Texas history, the Richardson almanacs, particularly the post-war issues, are rich in articles on cattle and sheep ranching, railroads, commerce, and annual statistical data. By 1869, *The Texas Almanac* was, according to its editors, "the largest secular publication of the kind in the United States." In 1967, publisher Robert E. Davis of Texian Press and Dr. James M. Day compiled the most significant articles into a single well-indexed volume. Day states, however, that "the aim has been to include those articles of significance to the general sweep of Texas history and with this in mind many specialized articles'' were omitted.

Other almanacs for Texas were issued during both the 19th and 20th centuries but most of these, such as those issued by James Burke, Jr., were intended for farmers and contain little of value except statistical data. Two exceptions are C. W. Raines' *Year Book for Texas,* 1901 (Austin: Gammel Book Company, 1902, 436pp.) and *Year Book for Texas . . . Vol. II* (Austin: Gammel-Statesman Publishing Company, 1903, 483pp.). These are every bit as valuable as the early Richardson almanacs, and full of articles, biographies, reports, and statistics unavailable else-where, including special articles by Isaac Joslin Cox, Mrs. Percy B. Pennybacker, George P. Garrison, John A. Lomax, and Adina de Zavala.

Howes T138. Rader 3070. Raines, p.174.

173 Rickett, Harold William (1896-)

WILD FLOWERS OF THE UNITED STATES: TEXAS.

New York: McGraw-Hill Book Company, [1969]. Publication of New York Botanical Garden. General Editor: William C. Steere. Assistants: Wesley Everett Niles and Virginia June Beasley. Collaborators: Donovan S. Correll, Cyrus Lundell, Howard Irwin, Lloyd H. Shinners.
Volume Three in a series of six, comprising two separately bound parts: Part I: xi,[1],274pp. Part II: [6],275-553,[3]pp. 157 plates (some in color). 33cm.
Cloth, boxed.
[At end of second part:] This first edition of the third volume of six volumes . . . has been published in 1969. The illustrations and text have been printed by offset lithography by W. S. Cowell Ltd. at their press in the Butler Market, Ipswich, England. The Typographical design is by Lewis F. White. The typeface is English Monotype Caslon Old Face. The Paper has been specially made by John Dickinson, Croxley, Hertfordshire, England.

This is the most comprehensive guide to the wild flowers of Texas. It is a monumental publication as yet so unheralded that it has not even been mentioned in most review columns, and is little known outside botanical circles. William C. Steere said it is ''the first comprehensive treatment of the more conspicuous herbaceous plants of an enormous yet distinctive area'' with a ''very considerable body of new information about plants appearing for the first time." Fred S. Webster, Jr. called it "a definitive treatment of Texas wild flowers."

It is chauvinistically pleasing to note that the *Wild Flowers of the United States* series is divided into six sections: northeastern states, southeastern states, southwestern states, northwestern states, the Rocky Mountain region—and Texas. Rickett explains why Texas is given this entirely separate distinction: "Texas is not only one of the largest states of the Union, but also, to the botanist, one of the most floristically interesting. The third volume of this series was originally planned to include . . . the entire southwestern area, from Texas to the Pacific." But it was found that the area included too much variety, and "as we might perhaps have foreseen . . . Texas was largely responsible for this impossible bulk, and, at the same time, presented within its own borders a floristic picture of exceptional interest. The present volume [*Texas*] is the result."

Steere points out that there had long been a "lack of any dependable means by which to identify the numerous and beautiful wild flowers that, at certain seasons, ornament the mountains and prairies of Texas. . . . The great state of Texas has so far no comprehensive scientific floristic treatment." Rickett adds that "no one scientific work includes all the plants of Texas, though one is in preparation." He further states that "in all, over four thousand species of flowering plants have been recognized in Texas," which have been divided in this work into fourteen general groups for description, explanation, and illustration. Grasses, sedges, rushes and flowering trees and shrubs have been deliberately omitted. The main desert plants such as the cacti are treated only minimally.

The work centers around approximately eleven hundred excellent color photographs taken by ninety different named photographers, with hundreds of line drawings by Rachel Speiser. The project is the result of grants from David and Peggy Rockefeller (to whom the work is dedicated), James A. Elkins, Nina Cullinan, the National Geographic Society, and others.

Special recognition is given to the previous publication of one of the collaborators, Howard S. Irwin, whose *Roadside Flowers of Texas* (Austin: University of Texas Press, 1961, 295pp.), with sixty-four pages of color drawings by Mary Motz Wills, has for two decades been the basic guide for thousands of Texas flower lovers. Other standard botanical works include Robert A. Vines, *Trees, Shrubs, and Woody Vines of the Southwest* (Austin, 1960); W. A. Silvius, *Texas Grasses* (San Antonio, 1933); B. C. Tharp, *Texas Range Grases* (Austin, 1952); Frank W. Gould, *The Grasses of Texas* (College Station, 1975); Del Weniger, *Cacti of the Southwest* (Austin, 1969); and Billie Lee Turner, *The Legumes of Texas* (Austin, 1959). A pioneering work still of value is John M. Coulter, *Botany of Western Texas* (Wash., 1891-1894). Cyrus Lundell began in 1942 a monumental scientific identification project *Flora of Texas,* terminated with volume three in 1969 and encompassed in Donovan S. Correll and Marshall C. Johnson, *Manual of the Vascular Plants of Texas* (Renner: Texas Research Foundation, 1970, 1881pp.).

174   Rister, Carl Coke (1889-1955)

BORDER CAPTIVES: THE TRAFFIC IN PRISONERS BY SOUTHERN PLAINS INDIANS, 1835-1875.

Norman: University of Oklahoma Press, 1940.
xi,[1],220,[2]pp. Illus. 2 folding maps. 22cm.
Cloth, dustjacket.

This is the best analytical account of Texas Indian captivities. Ohland Morton called it ''a compelling account of the captive traffic in the Great Plains country. . . . Professor Rister, in his calm, scholarly manner tells the stories of raids in which women and children were taken and sold into slavery or forced to live among the Indians. . . . The result is an account of significance in providing a helpful background for a comprehensive view of Indian-settler relations.'' Rupert N. Richardson called it ''a genuinely interesting book. He has not forgotten the high standards of the historian, with the result that his study is quite authoritative.''

In most of their raids, the Comanche, Kiowa, Cheyenne, Apache, and Arapaho made a concerted effort not only to capture horses and valuables, but to capture women and children as well. The women were used for pleasure and as slaves; the children, if pliable, were trained as warriors. When the Plains Indians learned that ransoms would be paid, traffic in captives became a significant source of revenue for many bands of Indians. Rister's work is a study of the known captivities, about which there is a surprising amount of surviving literature.

The work is more than a series of cruel episodes; it is a sociological study of the effects of this traffic on Indian life as well as on the captives themselves. The Comanches, for example, early learned that Texans would pay the highest prices to get their captured relatives back (the going rate ranged between two hundred and two thousand dollars in trade goods) but that they were also much more tenacious, ruthless, and formidable in chasing and chastizing the captors. Mexicans across the border in Coahuila, Chihuahua, and Sonora were easier plucking, but brought much smaller, if any, ransom.

Rister also studies individual captive cases. Some, like Herman Lehmann and Cynthia Ann Parker, became almost completely Indianized; others, like Nelson Lee, were able to escape. For any woman or child captured by a nomadic tribe, the experience had predictable psychological results and lasting effects. In his study of these, Rister provides valuable insights. The captives also tended in many cases to cause domestic problems within the Indian camps. Not all captors were glad they brought a light-haired beauty back to the teepee. Many of the most vicious acts of cruelty against the captives were performed by squaws and other Indian children.

Rister's *Comanche Bondage* (Glendale: Arthur H. Clark, 1955) relates to the outpost of Beales Colony and to the more specific captivity of Sarah Ann Horn, including a complete annotated reprint of *A Narrative of the Captivity of Mrs. Horn, and Her Two Children, with Mrs. Harris, by the Comanche Indians* (St. Louis: C. Keenle, 1839). This is not to be confused with the 1838 pamphlets on the fictitious captivities of Caroline Harris and Clarrissa Plummer. Another excellent captivity account is *Rachael Plummer's Narrative of Twenty-One Months Servitude as a Prisoner Among the Comanchee Indians* (Houston: Telegraph Power Press, 1838). This Rachel Plummer narrative was my most exciting find as a bookhunter. It was known to have been printed but no copy had ever been found until mine, which is now at Yale University. With introductory material by Archibald Hanna and William S. Reese, it was reprinted by us in facsimile in 1977.

Rister wrote a number of other significant books on the western Texas border region, the best of which are *The Southwestern Frontier* (Cleveland: Arthur H. Clark, 1928); *Southern Plainsmen* (Norman: University of Oklahoma Press, 1938); *Fort Griffin on the Texas Frontier* (Norman: University of Oklahoma Press, 1956); and, with Rupert N. Richardson, *The Greater Southwest* (Glendale: Arthur H. Clark, 1934). Richardson's *The Comanche Barrier to South Plains Settlement* (Glendale: Arthur H. Clark, 1933) and *The Frontier of Northwest Texas, 1846 to 1876* (Glendale: Arthur H. Clark, 1963) are also useful.

175 Rister, Carl Coke (1889-1955)

OIL! TITAN OF THE SOUTHWEST.

Norman: University of Oklahoma Press, 1949.
Foreword by Everett DeGolyer.
xxiii,467,[1]pp. Illus. Folding chart. Maps (1 folding). 24cm.
Cloth, dustjacket.

This volume is the best general history of the Texas oil industry that has so far been written. Whereas C. A. Warner's *Texas Oil and Gas Since 1543* is primarily statistical, Rister delves more (but not enough) into the social history of the industry and into the lives of the oilmen. His narrative is well-annotated and includes an extensive bibliography and lengthy but inadequate index. In doing research for the book, Rister visited 27 libraries and archives and travelled more than 35,000 miles interviewing "indulgent oilmen, from roustabouts to company executives." John S. Spratt called it "the most comprehensive volume on the petroleum industry of the region . . . a fine piece of work."

Everett DeGolyer in his introduction praises Rister for his "unbiased and unprejudiced" work, and points out the need for oil history that "recounts not only men's deeds but the thinking which compelled their actions. Deeds are material and can be dated, measured, and otherwise specifically described. The thinking which impels action, however, is less tangible." Rister manages to present a good deal of the background of the oil discoveries, but not enough to give his narrative much spark.

Walter Rundell, in an excellent article in *Southwestern Historical Quarterly*, October, 1963 (volume 67, number 2) entitled "Texas Petroleum History: A Selective Annotated Bibliography," states: "Rister's volume is the most comprehensive and scholarly study yet made. . . . It becomes a bit repetitious as one oil field after another is brought in. The author misses much of the excitement inherent in the oil field. Slight attention is given to transporting, refining, or marketing functions. . . . The author's attitude is one of complete impartiality."

Rister attempts to interpret the significance, influence, and impact of the industry, and includes an excellent chapter on "the impacts of petroleum." He also points out the puzzling lack of other analyses of the industry: "Without prejudice . . . it can be said that the significance of petroleum, its constant, pervasive influence, is so thoroughly neglected as to constitute a major flaw in historical writing. It is as if the Industrial Revolution . . . could be estimated without reference to steam or steel." Rister's own analysis neglects or ignores the enormous influence of the oil industry on Texas politics and government, and tells little about the scams and crooked deals that were rampant during the wildcatting days. He makes a few factual errors, such as saying the Dad Joiner discovery (Daisy Bradford Number 3) came in on October 3, 1930, and that the Dallas *Morning News* "relegated the news of it to the Sports Section." Actually, it came in a month earlier and was front page news. The folding map listed for page 408 is actually opposite page 88.

Although much of Rister's text is devoted to a rather monotonous recounting of facts, he does include a wealth of social history. Rister quotes a letter, giving no exact date but apparently written in 1866, from George W. O'Brien telling of the oil fever and foretelling what would happen 35 years later: "The great excitement of this age is oil. It promises to lay in the shade the great 'South Sea Bubble' or any other bubble of any age. This region of Texas will be wild upon the subject within a few months. A company has been organized . . . and a man and the money has already gone north to buy the necessary machinery to search the bowels of the earth for *oil*. . . . None doubt but what oil will be found and . . . we will make our fortune."

176 Rivera, Pedro de

DIARIO Y DERROTERO DE LO CAMINADO, VISTO, Y
OBCERVADO EN EL DISCURSO DE LA VISITA GENERAL DE
PRECIDIOS, SITUADOS EN LAS PROVINCIAS YNTERNAS DE
NUEVA ESPANA.

Guathemala: Por Sebastian de Arebalo, 1736. [78]pp. 28cm. Vellum.

Other issues:
(A). Paraphrase translation by Retta Murphy in "The Journey of Pedro de Rivera,
1724-1728," *Southwestern Historical Quarterly*, vol. XLI, no. 2, October, 1937,
pp.125-141.
(B). Reprint of the first edition. Mexico: [B. Costa],1945. 170,[5]pp. Plate. Folding
table. Map. 21cm. Printed wrappers. Introduction and extensive annotations by
Guillermo Porras Munoz. Limited to 1000 numbered copies.

This is one of the best and earliest eyewitness accounts of colonial
Texas. Henry R. Wagner maintains that it is "the most important
printed document extant relating to the frontier provinces." Rivera
describes day-by-day what he saw on his landmark journey, including
comments on the people, villages, terrain, resources, customs, and
products. He gives summaries of the Indian tribes and customs, as
well as much topographical and geographical data. He discusses the
missions and their problems, and makes recommendations which
ultimately were accepted and resulted in the closing of the East Texas
missions and their removal to San Antonio in 1731.

We know little of the early life of Rivera, except that he was serving
as governor of Tlascala in 1724 when the Viceroy ordered him to
Mexico City to receive instructions for a *revista*, or inspection tour, of
the northern presidios. He left on November 21, 1724, toured Nueva
Vizcaya, and reached Parral in January, 1726. During 1726 he toured
New Mexico, Sonora, Sinaloa, and Chihuahua. In the summer of 1727
he toured Texas, returning to Mexico City in June, 1728. He was
accompanied by a topographer, Francisco Alvarez y Barreyro, who
produced color maps of the regions traversed, some of which are still
extant, as are Rivera's official reports, in the national archives of
Mexico and Spain.

Rivera's instructions included the power to order changes in the
presidios. He reduced the garrisons at Adaes, Bahia, and San Antonio
and completely closed the garrison on the Neches River. He ordered
the correction of abuses that he found, including the practice whereby

the officers sold goods to their soldiers at exorbitant prices. His most important discovery was that there were virtually no civilized nor Christianized Indians at the missions, and his reports on the failure of the missionaries at conversion led to drastic changes in Spanish colonial policy.

Clark I-25. Howes R322. Palau 270267. Sabin 19955. Wagner *Spanish Southwest* 98.

177   Rives, George Lockhart (1849-1917)

THE UNITED STATES AND MEXICO, 1821-1848: A HISTORY OF THE RELATIONS BETWEEN THE TWO COUNTRIES FROM THE INDEPENDENCE OF MEXICO TO THE CLOSE OF THE WAR WITH THE UNITED STATES.

New York: Charles Scribner's Sons, 1913.
Two volumes: viii,[2],720; vi,[2],726pp. 15 maps (2 folding). 24cm. Cloth.

Other issues:
(A). Facsimile reprint. New York: Kraus Reprint Co., 1969.

This remains one of the fundamental studies of the Texas question and its effect on Mexican-American relations. Eugene C. Barker praised it for its "excellent judgment and singularly lucid historical style," pointing out that not only did Rives make extensive use of Mexican, British, and Amerian archives, but also that "no important printed material has escaped his survey." William R. Shepherd called the work "the first comprehensive account of the subject, revealing its author as a scholar capable of applying the erudition acquired in other realms of thought to the narration and interpretation of historical events. It won for him admission to the American Academy of Arts and Letters." Norman Tutorow in 1981 said that "despite its age, this is still one of the best studies of the diplomacy of the period."

Rives graduated from Columbia College in New York in 1868 and Trinity College at Cambridge in 1872, then received his law degree at Columbia in 1874. He was one of the men responsible for converting Columbia to a university, and for the creation of the New York Public Library. From 1887 to 1889 he was Assistant Secretary of State of the United States. His extensive writings ranging from Shakespearean studies to historical monographs prepared him for the final achievement realized in his *United States and Mexico.*

Rives examines his subject predominantly from the standpoint of diplomacy. The fifty-one chapters (of which eighteen are exclusively, and most of the rest at least partially, devoted to Texas) analyze the actions of the governments in the contest for control of Texas and the Southwest. Rives states: "The events which led up to the war between the United States and Mexico, with all its momentous consequences to both nations, have been very generally misapprehended. On the American side the war has been treated in histories of the United States as a mere episode in an all-embracing struggle over slavery, which it was not. Mexican historians have treated it as the unescapable result of American aggression in Texas, which it was not."

The conclusions reached by Rives are that Jackson, while far from being an impartial spectator regarding Texas, was determined to observe the proper neutral obligations incumbent in treaties with Mexico; that Texas was the real issue in the election of 1844 and proved the popular demand for westward expansion; and that American leaders did not intend to force a war with Mexico and felt it could be averted. Although he slips into occasional minor factual errors, his account of the settlement of Texas, the Texas Revolution, and the Texas Republic is especially valuable, as it gives a picture of those events as viewed from outside Texas—in both Mexico and the United States. It also comprises an excellent study of how events in Texas were influenced by, and became an influence upon, historical developments in North America as a whole. Seymour V. Connor has pointed out that Rives "surveys the principal events in the diplomatic relations of the two nations but fails to examine Mexican actions in terms of the constant political flux. Nor does he thoroughly consider American diplomacy in Whig-Democratic differences."

178 Roberts, Daniel Webster (1841-1935)

RANGERS AND SOVEREIGNTY.

San Antonio: Wood Printing & Engraving Co., 1914.
[6],[11]-190pp. Illus. 20cm.
Cloth.

Other issues:
(A). Lackey, B. Roberts. *Stories of the Texas Rangers*. San Antonio: The Naylor Co., [1955]. ix,105pp. 22cm. Cloth, dustjacket. Almost a word-for-word plagiarism of *Rangers and Sovereignty*.

(B). Facsimile reprint. Austin: State House Books, 1987. Cloth. Also includes his wife's memoirs. New index. New introduction by Robert Wooster.

This account of the Frontier Battalion of Texas Rangers was written by one of its field captains. This group of rangers, wrote Walter Prescott Webb, "left behind a tradition of courage and heroic individual action which is unsurpassed by any organization in any country in the world." The book is poorly written (J. Frank Dobie said Roberts "was better as a ranger than as writer"), but the volume gives a remarkable, concise account of the service of one of the most active of all Texas Ranger units.

Roberts' narrative begins with a chapter on the Deer Creek Indian fight of 1873, during which he was wounded and came under the observation of the veteran Indian fighter, C. Rufus Perry. When Perry became captain of the newly formed Company D, Texas Rangers, in 1874, he chose Roberts as one of his lieutenants. When Perry resigned, he recommended Roberts for company commander. "This was done over our First Lieutenant, W. W. Ledbetter, who was a splendid gentleman. Mr. Ledbetter feeling the sting a little quit the service."

The next year Roberts married, and took his young wife along with him in the field. With the exception of one short period during 1878, he served as ranger captain in the field continuously until 1882. His narrative recounts the astonishing string of battles with Indians, outlaws, rustlers, murderers, and feuding families during those years when the small ranger force was virtually the only law enforcement entity in western and southern Texas. "We had to meet a condition, not a law, of savage atrocity," he said. For the United States forces in Texas, except for those under Mackenzie and Bullis, he had little respect: "We will not quarrel with as big an 'hombre' as 'Uncle Sam' but his striped breeches did sag on us, when we needed help."

The Roberts account is accurate, in the main, when dealing with events in which Roberts participated personally. Ramon Adams, in his *Burs Under the Saddle* (pp. 435-36), outlines the factual errors in Roberts' account of the Sam Bass gang. But Roberts received this material second hand, and his personal experiences are written with few errors. It is in these episodes that the courage of the rangers stands out.

One time, for example, he rode up behind four stagecoach robbers fleeing towards Mexico: "I bore in slightly towards them. I saw them fixing their guns for business, but I made no demonstration to show

them that I saw it. I got up in talking distance of them, and . . .
'jollied' them a little, but kept gaining on them. I saw they had their
guns across their saddles, in front of them. I tried to engage them in
. . . conversation. A man named Jackson was riding on the left,
thumb on the hammer of his gun, and I knew he was a bad hombre.
I rode up nearly to his side . . . and almost as quick as lightning, I
jerked my pistol and shoved it against him, telling him to turn that
gun loose, or I would kill him. . . . Jackson was stubborn, and held
to his gun until he could almost feel my bullet, when his hands
limbered and his courage likewise."

An essential companion work to *Rangers and Sovereignty* is the small
book by his wife, Lucvenia (Conway) Roberts, *A Woman's Reminiscences
of Six Years in Camp with the Texas Rangers* (Austin: Press of Von
Boeckmann-Jones Co., 1928). Known as the "Assistant Commander"
of Company D, she was in the field with her husband during most of
his time of service. Her memoirs are full of incidents of tent life in
West Texas, and include some excellent photographs of the Rangers
in the field and in camp. Mrs. Roberts, said Dobie, "was a sensible
and charming woman with a seeing eye."

One of the many oddities of the Naylor Publishing Company of
San Antonio, which for several decades was the largest vanity press in
Texas, was their 1955 book by B. Roberts Lackey, *Stories of the Texas
Rangers*. This book is virtually a verbatim reprint of *Rangers and
Sovereignty,* with only a few changes from first to third person. After
being challenged with this fact, the publishers inserted a curious
printed slip in each copy reading: "Through error, the publishers of
Stories of the Texas Rangers failed to insert, in this book, a statement to
the effect that *Stories of the Texas Rangers* is, to a large extent, a
reprinting of *Rangers and Sovereignty.*" I have been unable to learn how
Lackey became the "author" or to hold the copyright; perhaps his
middle name indicates some family connection.

Adams Guns 1870. Dobie, p.60. Howes R339.

179   Roemer, Ferdinand von (1818-1891)

TEXAS, MIT BESONDERER RUCKSICHT AUF DEUTSCHE
AUSWANDERUNG UND DIE PHYSICHEN VERHAELTNISSE
DES LANDES NACH EIGENER BEOBACHTUNG GESCHILD-

ANNOUNCING . . . . . .

The Translation and Publication of Ferdinand von Roemer's Interesting Historical and Scientific Book

"TEXAS"

by

OSWALD MUELLER

THE CENTENNIAL has brought to light much of the colorful and interesting history of Texas. Among the early writings, perhaps no account surpasses ROEMER'S "TEXAS," written in 1847 by Dr. Ferdinand von Roemer, the eminent German scientist, well-known to geologists and botanists, but perhaps not to the average Texan.

The translation of this book was stimulated by an excellent biographical sketch of Dr. Roemer, as well as a brief review of the book itself, which appeared in the Southwest Review, and which was written by Dr. S. W. Geiser of Southern Methodist University.

For the benefit of such who have not read the article by Dr. Geiser, the following may be of interest:

Dr. Roemer was sent to Texas in 1845 to make investigations, as many Germans had the intention of leaving their native land and settling in Texas. Most of his traveling was done on a mule, dubbed the "scientific mule" by friends, and this mode of travel afforded the time and leisure of making intimate observations. These observations are recorded in his "TEXAS" in his inimitable way. The topography of the country, the colonists and their hardships, the Indians and their depredations, the flora and the fauna, the rangers, the missions, the Alamo — all are described to hold the attention of the reader from beginning to end.

Dr. Roemer's travels led him from Galveston to the fort on the San Saba. His journey from Houston to New Braunfels, which consumed seventeen days, portrays vividly the hardships endured by the early settlers, traveling over indistinct trails in wagons drawn by oxen or horses. His excursions while at New Braunfels extended in all directions, enabling him to give a detailed description of San Antonio, Austin, Bastrop, Caldwell, LaGrange, and other hamlets and settlements. Nothing seemed to escape his notice, and everything was recorded with German minuteness and exactness. The dress worn by the colonist, the food he ate, the price of beef, temperature recordings, the inns and hotels, elections, celebrations, botanical names, and a host of things are mentioned, which make this book a veritable mine of information.

His descriptions of the various Indian tribes, such as the Lepans, Comanches, Caddos, and Wacos are masterful and of inestimable value to anyone interested in the Indians living here a century ago. Dr. Roemer went among them and gained his information through personal contact.

In short, this book will not only have a tremendous appeal to the lover of early Texas history, it will prove indispensable to the student of early Texas history, since the introduction, the twenty-four chapters, and a map, contain information which no other book can supply.

ERT ... MIT EINEM NATURWISSENSCHAFTLICHEN ANLANGE UND EINER TOPOGRAPHISCH-GEOGNOS-TISCHEN KARTE VON TEXAS.

Bonn: Bei Adolph Marcus, 1849.
xiv,[2],464pp. Folding map. 22cm.
Cloth. Also wrappers.
Errata on p.[xv]. On p.464: Bonn: Gebrudt bei Carl Georgi.

Other issues:

(A). *Texas, with Particular Reference to German Immigration and the Physical Appearance of the Country, Described through Personal Observation.* San Antonio: Standard Printing Company, 1935. xii,301pp. Folding map. 24cm. Cloth. Translated from the German by Oswald Mueller. Preface by Donald C. Barton, dated Houston, July 12, 1935. First edition in English.

(B). Facsimile reprint of (A). Waco: Texian Press, [1967]. 24cm. Cloth, dustjacket.

(C). Reprint of (B), 1983. New prefaces by Dona B. Reeves and O. T. Haywood. New index.

This is one of the first scientific investigations of Texas made by someone qualified to do so. More than that, as Rupert N. Richardson said, it is "the best account available of the Texas frontier at that time." J. Frank Dobie states that "Roemer saw more and told about it in a livelier and more diverting way than any brace of other travelers between Cabeza de Vaca and Frederick Law Olmsted." Samuel W. Geiser said: "It is intensely interesting because of the light it throws on the country, the life, and the men of early Texas. The narrative has a vivacity and at the same time an honesty and solidity that make it an invaluable source for the social history of that day in Texas." Ever since the first publication of his book, Roemer has been known as "the father of Texas geology," a title which does not give him broad enough credit.

Roemer came to Texas at the instigation of Prince Carl of Solms-Braunfels to investigate the mineral resources of Texas and to produce a competent map of the country. With financial assistance from Alexander von Humboldt and the Berlin Academy, Roemer arrived in Texas in 1845, at the age of 28. Humboldt sent with him a letter of recommendation stating: "Dr. Roemer, like a book, needs only to be opened to yield good answers to all questions." During the ensuing year and a half, Roemer explored most of the settled areas except deep East Texas, going as far north as Dallas and as far west as the ruins of the Mission San Saba. Part of his tours were in the company of Ashbel Smith and Matilda Houstoun; the latter in her sprightly book describes Roemer as a young man who neglected his toilet, ate voraciously, loved his cognac, rode horseback poorly, had no teeth, always had a cigar in his mouth, and was forever poking about in the mud of Texas rivers, to the "amusement of us all, and especially to the negroes, who take intense delight in watching his proceedings." He was, she said, "gentlemanlike and well-informed, and indefatigable in his endeavors."

When he returned to Germany in late 1847, Roemer worked at the Royal Academy of Science in Berlin, with its financial assistance, to produce his book. He states that he is particularly indebted to Baron von Meusebach for assistance. He finished his manuscript at Poppels-dorf-at-Bonn in August, 1849. He confesses that he found it impossible to present the scientific report without including his observations on Texas and Texans. These are the observations that delight and inform us today. Roemer tells us that the whiskey punch is the national drink of Texas, and that when the legislature adjourns in Austin "the numerous grog shops are deserted as they depended chiefly upon these people for patronage."

At the Tremont House in Galveston, he reports on the last Christmas celebration of the Texas Republic: "A large company, intent on [revelry] was already assembled when we arrived. Among them were several generals, colonels, majors and a number of captains. A stranger just arrived from Europe would conclude that Texas possessed a large standing army upon hearing these high military titles. I myself knew . . . not to take these titles too seriously, since they were often only honorary ones. . . . A friend informed me that Texas boasted of at least forty persons who carried the title of general."

At Torrey's Trading Post near Waco, he watched "an Indian whose duty it was to beat the pelts [traded in by Indians for dry goods] in order to rid them of insects. To watch this one at work always furnished me entertaining amusement, for his face betrayed with each lick how the performing of such menial work for the pale faces was repulsive to his national inclination for laziness—and his consciousness of Indian dignity." He also accompanied Baron von Meusebach and Robert S. Neighbors on their expedition to make their famous treaty with the Comanche Indians, thus leaving us a splendid account of one of the most interesting events in the history of Texas Indian relations.

To Roemer, however, the most important aspect of his tour was his scientific investigation. The map he produced is the first geological map of Texas, and one of the most accurate of its time. His fossil discoveries instigated a whole series of subsequent investigations. Donald C. Barton has stated that "much of his geological observation and reasoning is just as good now and always will be as good as it was when he made them." What Audubon's short trip to Texas caused in ornithological circles, Roemer's report caused in a dozen other areas of natural history, in such diverse areas as botany, ethnology, agriculture, and climatology. His study of the German settlements and recommendations regarding the future prospects of German colonization—not all favorable, by any means—came to be regarded as the most dependable analysis of its time.

Incredibly, the book was not published in English for nearly a century. Oswald Mueller, after reading an early version of Samuel Wood Geiser's essay on Roemer in *Southwest Review,* translated the Roemer volume in 1934. It is a competent, though literal, translation that preserves Roemer's errors in spelling proper names and "insofar as clarity permits, the flavor of Roemer's style." Dobie thought it a bit long on literal and short on flavor, but I disagree. My only complaint is that neither Mueller's edition of 1935 nor the reprint of 1967 contains an index.

Dobie, p.52. Graff 3549. Howes R407. Raines, p.177. Sabin 72593.

180 Santa Anna, Antonio Lopez de (1795-1876)

MANIFIESTO QUE SUS OPERACIONES EN LA COMPANA DE TEJAS Y EN SU CAUTIVERIO DIRIGE A SUS CONCUIDADANOS DE GENERAL ANTONIO LOPEZ DE SANTA-ANNA.

Veracruz: Imprenta Liberal a Cargo de Antonio Maria Valdes, 1837.
108pp. 20cm.
Printed wrappers.

Other issues:
(A). *Manifesto of General Santa Anna.* Translation of the bulk of the text and some of the documents, in *United States Magazine and Democratic Review,* vol. III, no. 12, December, 1838, pp.305-320.

(B). Garcia, Genero [ed.]. *Las Guerras de Mexico con Tejas y los Estados Unidos.* Mexico: Vda. de C. Bouret, 1910. 344. 21cm. Documentos Ineditos o Muy Raros para la Historia de Mexico, volume XXIX. Contains the full text of Santa Anna's work, but with the documents arranged in a different order.

(C). Castaneda, Carlos E. *The Mexican Side of the Texas Revolution, by the Chief Mexican Participants* . . . Dallas: P.L. Turner Company, Publishers, [1928]. vii,391pp. 24cm. Cloth. Contains Santa Anna's account on pages [2]-89, but does not include the 25 documents following Document Number 9.

(D). Facsimile reprint of (C). Dallas: P. L. Turner Company, Publishers, [1956]. Same collation. 23cm. Cloth.

(E). New edition of (C). Austin and Dallas: Graphic Ideas Incorporated, publishers, 1970. xi,402pp. 22cm. Pictorial cloth. "This edition changes the original only by minor corrections, a new index, and the addition of new illustrations." The Santa Anna text is on pages [2]-91.

(F). *Documentos Ineditos o Muy Raros para la Historia de Mexico: Antonio Lopez de Santa Anna.* Mexico: Editorial Porrua, 1974. 894pp. Cloth. Limited to 1000 numbered copies. Contains the full text and documents, pp.[119]-206.

Written by the Mexican commander-in-chief shortly after being released by the Texans, this is one of the most important sources on the Texas Revolution. It contains Santa Anna's own account of the Texas campaign, the capture of the Alamo, the Goliad Massacre, the Battle of San Jacinto, his capture and imprisonment, the details of the making of the treaties of Velasco, and his meetings with Andrew Jackson after his liberation by the Texans. It is especially important because it differs greatly from those of all other participants, both Texan and Mexican, as well as differing from his own subsequent writings on the subject.

The first part of the text is dated at Santa Anna's home at Mango de Clavo, May 10, 1837. This is followed by a series of nine letters and documents written during the Texas campaign, including the full text of his lengthy defense of his actions in the campaign written to Secretary of War Tornel on March 11, 1837, two weeks after his return to Mexico. These are followed by twenty-five numbered and two unnumbered documents further relating to the war in Texas.

The *Manifiesto* was issued to counter charges levelled against Santa Anna after his return to Mexico. During his captivity, the Mexican nation was in sincere mourning and in justified apprehension for his safety. Black mourning bands were officially decreed in his honor. But when news was released of his having signed the treaties of Velasco agreeing to Texas independence and of his journey to Washington ostensibly to verify these to the American government, as well as rumors of his cowardice and incompetence at San Jacinto, the Mexican nation turned against him with a vengeance. On March 1, only a week after his return, he was defeated in the election in Congress for the presidency by a vote of 68 to 2.

On March 11, therefore, he wrote his first attempt to exculpate himself. Learning that Ramon Martinez Caro, Vicente Filisola, Jose Urrea, and others were denouncing various of his Texas actions, and unable to squelch the rampaging rumors, he prepared the *Manifesto* and had it published in Vera Cruz sometime shortly after May 10. Fearful of what his secretary, Martinez Caro, was going to say about him, Santa Anna apparently arranged for his arrest and the ransacking of his papers on May 21.

Santa Anna claims in the *Manifiesto* that the "great victory" at the Alamo cost him only 70 dead and 300 wounded, and that he was forced to execute the Fannin prisoners because the national government had ordered that all Texans be treated as pirates. He maintains that his capture was due to his subordinates' incompetence and that he did not run from the field but rode "through the enemy's ranks" in order to reach Filisola and get aid. He says, regarding his orders to Filisola and the 4000 Mexicans to retreat from Texas, that he never meant the orders to be obeyed. He asserts that the treaties granting Texas independence were a ploy to obtain his release.

It is a fascinating study to compare the accounts of these Mexican generals after the San Jacinto fiasco. Although all of them contain a certain number of lies, distortions, alterations of documents, and denials of responsibility (as do the Texan accounts), they comprise an invaluable and essential resource for any understanding of the Texas Revolution. Santa Anna's *Manifiesto,* possibly the most distorted of all, is interesting even in its distortions.

Howes S98. Rader 2880. Raines, p.181. Sabin 76739. Streeter 930.

181 Santleben, August (1845-1911)

A TEXAS PIONEER: EARLY STAGING AND OVERLAND FREIGHTING DAYS ON THE FRONTIERS OF TEXAS AND MEXICO.

New York and Washington: The Neale Publishing Company, 1910.
Edited by I. D. Affleck.
321pp. 21cm.
Cloth, dustjacket.

Other issues:
(A). Facsimile reprint. Waco: From the Press of W. M. Morrison, 1967. 21cm. Cloth.

Santleben's memoirs contain the most important account of stage coach and freight service in Texas. Walter Campbell said that "there is nothing better in its field," and Robert Krick called Santleben's book "a Texas classic of considerable scarcity." Charles Ramsdell, Sr., said it "presents an interesting picture of the ante-railroad days on both sides of the Rio Grande, and especially of the methods and difficulties of transportation between Texas and Mexico when it was dependent upon the slow, squeaking, clumsy Mexican oxcarts or even the trains of huge freight wagons drawn by mule-teams. . . . Here is presented considerable data, both social and economic, that may be of service to the future historian of the Texas frontier."

Santleben came to Texas in 1845 from Germany as an infant in arms. Upon arrival in Galveston Bay, the ship he was on struck a bar and sank, drowning all but a handful of the passengers. He and his parents survived, but landed in Texas penniless. The family settled in Castro's colony, but it was years before they recovered from the loss. Santleben was put to work full-time at twelve, and at fourteen became the youngest pony express carrier in the United States. He drifted to Mexico for a few years as a teenager, then served as a scout in the 3rd Texas Calvary (Union) along the border and in Louisiana. In 1867, he formed the first stage-coach line between Mexico and Texas, a truly extraordinary feat because of the traditional ill-will between Mexico and Texas, not to mention the Indian and bandit problem that was then at its height.

For nearly thirty years, Santleben ran this remarkable stage and freight line against all odds. He remarks that he personally conducted journeys in South and West Texas totalling over 126,000 miles—more than most of the ranger and explorer expeditions travelled combined. In those trips he transported millions of dollars of bullion and thousands of people. "I will also state," he said, "that I hauled more money from Mexico during that period, on stages and wagons, than any other person.'' In one section of his book he lists by names and dates 392 people killed by Indians in that region—listing only those he knew of and could remember.

Santleben seems to have been immune—at least, he certainly speaks as though he felt immune—from the dangers. Half a dozen times, in his narrative he states that he never had any problem with Indians or outlaws, and then proceeds to give the details of an Indian scrape or outlaw encounter in which he participated. His review of his trips, of the cargoes he hauled and the people he escorted, leaves us a unique record of one of the most dangerous, tedious, and important occupations on the frontier. From Santleben we learn in great detail every aspect of the stage business. Sadly, the coming of the railroad put Santleben & Company out of business and the old man spent his last years as a San Antonio ward politician in charge of city sanitation.

He also includes many social and biographical recollections of his section of Texas, including tales about his friend Big-foot Wallace and his employer Henri Castro. He gives details of life in the Castro colony and in post-war San Antonio. His account of childhood in German Texas brings to mind the stories about Herman Lehmann before his capture. Santleben tells of going out after the family oxen when he was nine years old: ''Generally I found it prosy business wandering through the mesquite bushes in search of my oxen, but one foggy morning I had an exciting experience when I saw a panther in my path feasting on a calf he had killed. He was only a few feet in front of me, but he was so intent on satisfying his hunger that he only looked at me without rising. I, on the contrary, was very much startled . . . and I slowly backed away . . . and then I ran towards home at the top of my speed. I was bare-footed, as was usual with country boys in those days . . . and my toes clawed the ground and helped me along. I was making pretty good time when I stepped on a large rattlesnake that was coiled in my path . . . but before he could strike I made a frantic leap in the air and landed beyond his reach. . . . But these adventures did not make me abandon my search, which I continued. . . .''

Campbell, p.99. Dobie, p.79. Graff 3676. Howes S104. Krick 441.

182 Schmitz, Joseph William (1905-1966)

TEXAN STATECRAFT, 1836-1845.

San Antonio: The Naylor Company, 1941.
viii,[2],266pp. 23cm.
Cloth, dustjacket.

Other issues:
(A). Special numbered, autographed edition, with inserted leaf reading: "This de luxe edition of *Texan Statecraft, 1836-1845* is limited to two hundred numbered copies signed by the author."

This monograph provides the best analysis of the diplomatic activities of the Republic of Texas. Eugene C. Barker called it "a complete survey of the diplomatic history of the Republic . . . the first comprehensive study that has been made. It is based upon a careful study of the sources and is authoritative." R. Earl McClendon said it is an "authoritative . . . contribution to the existing literature in the field of Texas history." Isaac Joslin Cox called it a "useful, clear-cut narrative" that is "both useful and timely . . . as the first comprehensive study in the field." Rupert N. Richardson said it comprises "a good treatment of the entire subject of [Texan] foreign relations."

Numerous volumes have been published on the diplomacy of the Texan republic and on the annexation issue, but most of these have been from the viewpoint of other nations dealing with Texas. The Schmitz work is devoted to the Texan diplomatic activities and Texan efforts to establish itself with the outside world as a recognized independent nation. The twelve chapters consist of an explanatory essay on how the nation was established, on the efforts to gain official recognition from the United States, on initial annexation negotiation, on obtaining British and French recognition, on the Lamar foreign policy, on James Treat's Mexico submission, on the alliance with Yucatan, on James Hamilton's European diplomacy, on Houston's foreign policy, and on the final negotiations concerning annexation.

One aspect of the work that has generally been overlooked is the excellent study Schmitz makes of economics in the Republic of Texas. In each section, he shows how economic necessities influenced Texan foreign policy and limited the freedom of her diplomats in every avenue of their endeavors. Schmitz also shows clearly that in such men as Sam Houston, Anson Jones, Ashbel Smith, James Hamilton, and others, Texas possessed some of the most intelligent and capable diplomats in the world during that era.

Schmitz's 21-page bibliography is imposing, but not all works cited in his annotations are included in the bibliography. A few spelling and date errors occur in the 600-odd footnotes, but on the whole these are extremely useful. The style of the main narrative lacks grace, and Schmitz occasionally becomes confused in the use of terms such as bill, resolution, treaty, ratification, and confirmation.

Schmitz wrote another useful but tentative work entitled *Thus They Lived: Social Life in the Republic of Texas* (San Antonio: The Naylor Company, 1935, 141pp.). Stanley Siegel's *A Political History of the Texas Republic, 1836-1845* (Austin: University of Texas Press, 1956, 281pp.) is an excellent study of the Texan domestic politics of the era, and William R. Hogan's *The Texas Republic: A Social and Economic History,* entered here separately, is a splendid study. The two Schmitz books, Siegel, and Hogan comprise the basic secondary monographs on the Republic of Texas.

183   Sheffy, Lester Fields (1887-1967)

THE FRANCKLYN LAND & CATTLE COMPANY, A PANHANDLE ENTERPRISE, 1882-1957.

Austin: University of Texas Press, [1963].
xvi,402pp. Illus. Maps. 24cm.
Cloth, dustjacket.
The M. K. Brown Range Life Series, No. 8.

This is one of the best accounts of international corporate development of Texas lands. Joe B. Frantz called it "the fullest book on ranching." Margaret Hartley said that "the material [Sheffy] has chosen, with his imaginative use of it, has made the story of the White Deer Lands live." William T. Field stated: "Written by an acknowledged master in the field . . . the book is at once informative, readable, and entertaining . . . a narrative of men of heroic stature representing British and American interests, wresting a mighty empire from a land permeated with seemingly overwhelming difficulties. Lester

Fields Sheffy with almost flawless execution has produced a magnificent chronicle of frontier America . . . a ranching masterpiece.''

The Francklyn Land and Cattle Company was organized in New York in 1882, and began operations with the purchase of a little over a half million acres of Texas land. The owners represented some of the wealthiest men on two continents, including the Cunards and the inimitable Lord Rosebery, of whom Sheffy writes: ''It is said that Lord Rosebery had three ambitions: he wanted to become Prime Minister of England, to marry the wealthiest woman in Britain, and to win the English Derby—all three of which he accomplished.'' Major Ira H. Evans became president of the company and Col. B. B. Groom was chosen general manager of the ranch. The operations in Texas during the subsequent decades brought into the picture such men as Charles Goodnight, Murdo McKenzie, I. F. Ikard, George Tyng, Dan Waggoner, Temple Houston, and T. D. Hobart.

The operation was notable for its foresight in such areas as development of water and grass resources, range management, and elaborate use of credit. The company pioneered in scientific stock breeding and diversification of ranch economy. The ranch lands at one time shared a hundred miles of border with the Kiowa-Comanche reserves, prompting complicated and unending troubles. The discovery of oil prompted an entirely new series of operations. Sheffy states that ''the story of the Francklyn Land and Cattle Company abounds in drama, intrigue, and adventure. In that respect it is a typical story of the land where its history was unfolded.''

Through the aid of M. K. Brown, Sheffy was enabled to use the vast collection of company files, ledgers, range reports, and correspondence now deposited in the Panhandle-Plains Museum in Canyon, Texas. Sheffy had also written a related biography, *The Life and Times of Timothy Dwight Hobart, 1855-1935* (Canyon: Panhandle-Plains Historical Society, 1950, 322pp.). Sheffy spent his entire career in the Panhandle, serving as founding president of the Panhandle-Plains Historical Society and editor of its review for eighteen years.

An interesting comparison volume to this work is W. M. Pearce, *The Matador Land and Cattle Company* (Norman: University of Oklahoma Press, 1964, 244pp.), published almost simultaneously with the Sheffy book and about a ranch created the same year as the Francklyn. The

Matador operation, with Scottish backers, had operations throughout the American West but with the Texas Panhandle as its home range. The Matador was liquidated in 1951 and the Francklyn in 1957. Other books for comparison are William Curry Holden's *The Espuela Land and Cattle Company: A Study of a Foreign-Owned Ranch in Texas* (Austin: Texas State Historical Association, 1970), which is an enlargement and expansion of the same author's *The Spur Ranch: A Study of the Inclosed Ranch Phase of the Cattle Industry in Texas* (Boston: Christopher Publishing House, 1934); Virginia H. Taylor's *The Franco-Texan Land Company* (Austin: University of Texas Press, 1969); and an exceptionally fine work by A. Ray Stephens, *The Taft Ranch: A Texas Principality* (Austin: University of Texas Press, 1964).

184 Shipman, Alice Jack (Dolan) (1889-)

TAMING THE BIG BEND: A HISTORY OF THE EXTREME WESTERN PORTION OF TEXAS FROM FORT CLARK TO EL PASO, BY MRS. O. L. SHIPMAN.

[Austin:] Von Boeckmann-Jones Co., 1926.).
viii,215pp. Illus. Folding map. 24cm.
Cloth.

This worthwhile account of the Big Bend region during the 19th century is especially valuable because one of Shipman's major sources was her pioneer father, of whom she writes: "To my father, Captain Pat Dolan, I am especially indebted. He has lived on the Texas frontier for seventy-five years and with remarkable clearness of mind recalls the stirring events of the days gone by." She also quotes extensively from other pioneers and transients in the region, such as John L. Bullis, commander of Indian scouts under Mackenzie; A. J. Fairmore and P. Bougad on the El Paso Salt War; Mexican outlaw Victor Ochoa; and Texas Ranger T. T. Cook.

The work contains chapters on the early mail routes, the boundary commission, the camel experiment and transportation, the military posts, freighting, civil affairs, Indian campaigns, the El Paso Salt War, Texas Ranger campaigns, ranching, outlaws, mining, and Mexican revolutionary activities after the turn of the century. This is followed by a section of sketches of early pioneer and ranching families.

The narrative is straightforward and for the most part without flavor; the text is cut-and-paste throughout. The wealth of information she provides, however, makes up for the general flatness of the text, and some of the first-hand accounts she quotes are fascinating. Her father, Pat Dolan, was both a sheriff and a Texas Ranger in the region, and his influence on the narrative is readily apparent. He provided much of the material on John Selman, John Wesley Hardin, Pat Garrett, and the outlaw years.

Regarding her own life in this desolate region, Mrs. Shipman states: "If a newcomer was the son of a titled father, he did not parade the fact. . . . If a man's past had been a bit too colorful, that was overlooked. But the path of his women folk was far narrower and stricter. So long as a woman remained in what the westerner called her 'place,' she was the object of the greatest respect and the tenderest consideration, but let her wander from its limitations and her path was not pleasant. If she was masculine in thought or actions she was severaly criticised; the westerner wanted his women folk domestically inclined."

Mrs. Shipman's extensive papers and correspondence are at the El Paso Public Library. She was also the author of *Letters, Past and Present* . . . (No place, no date, 137pp.), containing letters to her nieces and nephews relating to life in West Texas.

Adams Guns 2006. Adams Herd 2063. Howes S422.

185 Siringo, Charles Angelo (1855-1928)

A TEXAS COW BOY, OR, FIFTEEN YEARS ON THE HURRI-CANE DECK OF A SPANISH PONY. TAKEN FROM REAL LIFE BY . . . AN OLD STOVE UP "COW PUNCHER," WHO HAS SPENT NEARLY TWENTY YEARS ON THE GREAT WESTERN CATTLE RANGES.

Chicago: M. Umbdenstock & Co., Publishers, 1885.
xii,[13]-316pp. 2 illus. 20cm.
Pictorial wrappers, the front wrapper containing the title in full and the back wrapper a scene, "Representation of Life in a Cow Camp."
1000 copies printed.
Other issues:

(A). Same as above, cloth edition. In this issue the front and back wrappers, both printed in color, are inserted with the back wrapper used as a frontispiece and the front wrapper used as an additional title page. 20cm. 1000 copies printed.

ꞌ (B). Second edition, enlarged. Chicago: Siringo & Dobson, Publishers, 1886. xii,[13]-347pp. 19cm. Cloth. Verso of title: "Copyrighted by Charles A. Siringo, 1886." In this new edition, "Representation of Life in a Cow Camp" is used as frontispiece and the pictorial title page is omitted. The added material consists of a dedication, an Index to Addenda, and a 31-page Addenda, of which Dobie states: "The Addenda tells how to get rich and go broke in the cattle business and gives an unvarnished account of how brutish cowboys treat their horses."

(C). Variant of (B). Chicago and New York: Rand, McNally & Co., Publishers, [1886]. xii,[13]-347pp. plus 5pp. of adv. 19cm. Same color frontis. as (B). Red pictorial cloth. Some copies have no adv.

(D). Facsimile reprint of (B). Chicago: The Eagle Publishing Co., 1890. 347pp. plus 3pp. of adv. Frontis. No color title page. Pictorial wrappers, with adv. on back wrapper and on inside front and back wrapper.

(E). Facsimile reprint of (C). Chicago and New York: Rand, McNally & Co., no date. 347pp. plus 4pp. adv. No color title page. Cloth.

(F). Facsimile reprint of (D). Dated 1892 on title page.

(G). Same as (F), dated 1893 on title page.

(H). Facsimile reprint of (E). No. 56 in Globe Library Series. In this form the book was reprinted in pictorial wrappers, without title page date, more or less continuously until 1912. B. B. Harvey, editor of Rand, McNally, reported in 1935: "Our records date back only to 1901. Between that year and 1912, when our publication of the book was discontinued, we printed 98,000 copies."

(I). New York: J. S. Ogilvie Publishing Company, 57 Rose Street, no date. 251pp., including a 6pp. "Publisher's Note" and varying pages of adv. Pictorial wrappers. This edition is entirely reset, issued initially about 1914 on cheap pulp paper. In this form, the work was reissued frequently until 1926. The publishers reported they printed a total of 58,000 copies. Some of these bear a copyright dated 1914. Some appear as Railroad Series No. 97.

(J). New York: William Sloane Associates, [1950]. xl,198pp. Illus. 22cm. Cloth, dustjacket. [Verso of title]: "Published simultaneously in Canada by George J. McLeod, Ltd." Best edition, with lengthy introduction by J. Frank Dobie and other added material, drawings by Tom Lea, and typography by Carl Hertzog.

(K). Reprint of (J). Lincoln: University of Nebraska Press, [1966]. 21cm. Bison Book No. 341.

(L). Reprint of (K). Verso of title: Second printing: February, 1969. 19cm.

(M). Reprint of (K), 1979. Paperback.

This is the most authentic book on the Texas cowboy. William Reese called it "the first autobiography of a cowboy, and unquestionably one of the most important range books." J. Frank Dobie said that "no record of cowboy life has supplanted this rollicky, reckless, realistic chronicle," and that it is "the most-real, non-fiction book on cowboy life." Will Rogers commented: "Why, that was the Cowboy's Bible when I was growing up." J. Evetts Haley said that "no single writer typified the achievement of cowboy literature, from the plane of the dime novel to one of character and distinction, so well as Charlie Siringo."

In his partly facetious preface, Siringo states that his sole purpose in writing the book was to make money, to "bring me in 'shekels' enough to capsize Paris." He says he first dreamed of writing a lurid dialect love story, but "finally hit upon the idea of writing a history of my own short, but rugged life." Siringo, born near Matagorda Bay in 1855, describes his childhood on the Texas coast during the Civil War, including a number of anecdotes of interest to Texas-Confederate studies, especially relating to the battle fought in the Matagorda Bay region. He went to St. Louis with his family after the war, only to run away. He describes in fascinating detail his life along the Mississippi, including being a participant in the race between the "Natchez" and the "Robert E. Lee." Returning to Texas, he became a full-time cowboy at sixteen, working for Shanghai Pierce. By the 1870's he was a regular trail driver on the Chisholm Trail.

In 1880 he rode with a posse of Texas cowboys to New Mexico to track down Billy the Kid. Siringo, who knew Billy the Kid personally, devotes several chapters to the escapades of the Kid, which he later expanded into a full-length biography. Some of Siringo's statements about Billy the Kid are rather harshly dealt with by Ramon Adams in *Burs Under the Saddle*, #360, and Jeff Dykes writes that much of the Billy the Kid material in Siringo "is now known to be highly exaggerated (to be as kind as possible)." In general, Siringo is accurate concerning Billy the Kid activities of which he had direct knowledge; he runs into trouble by depending too much on the Billy the Kid tales of Ash Upson, who attempted to fill in the blanks for Siringo.

In the narrative, Siringo relates all these cattle drives, outlaw chases, and cowboy adventures frankly and with obvious glee—he was not yet thirty when he wrote his book. He writes, for example: "We went back to the ranch and found that it had changed hands in our absence. 'Shanghai' Pierce and his brother Jonathan had sold out their interests to Allen, Pool & Co. for the snug little sum of one hundred and ten thousand dollars. That shows what could be done in those days, with no capital, but lots of cheek and a branding iron. The two Pierces had come out there from Yankeedom a few years before poorer than skimmed milk.'' Siringo also admits to having branded mavericks with his own brand while rounding them up for another outfit.

The best description of Siringo that I have seen is in *Silver Strike* (Boston, 1932) by William A. Stoll, who wrote: "He was deadly with a Colt's 45, a weapon he carried at all times . . . yet he had never, so far as anyone knows, taken a human life. He was shrewdly intelligent, infallible in his judgment of human nature, and courageous to the point of recklessness; he was quick and nervous normally, but in a critical moment, or an emergency, cold and steady as a rock. He was relentless on a scent. He was a rattler who never struck—a personality as interesting as any I have met along the frontier.'' In *A Texas Cowboy,* Siringo makes vague hints about gunfighting, but little that is concrete. At the end of Chapter Sixteen, he states: ''I will now drop the curtain for awhile. Just suffice it to say I had a tough time of it during the rest of the winter and came out carrying two bullet wounds. But I had some gay times as well as tough. . . .'' Later writers about Siringo have shown conclusively that Siringo not only killed men, but was several times shot himself.

After publication of *A Texas Cowboy,* Siringo worked for the Pinkerton Detective Agency for 22 years, then retired to write more books on cowboys and outlaws. *A Cowboy Detective* and *Riata and Spurs* relate mainly to his outlaw-chasing days as a Pinkerton man, while *A Lone Star Cowboy,* published in 1919, is something of a rehash of his first book. In this last work, he states: ''This volume is to take the place of 'A Texas Cowboy,' the copyright of which has expired. Since its first publication, in 1885, nearly a million copies have been sold.'' It is more likely that something like one-fourth of that number have actually been printed in all editions combined.

Adams Burs 360. Adams Guns 2032. Adams Herd 2077. Agatha, p.57. Dobie, p.119. Graff 3804. Howes S518. Merrill *Aristocrat.* Reese *Six Score* 99.

186 Smith, Ashbel (1805-1886)

REMINISCENCES OF THE TEXAS REPUBLIC; ANNUAL ADDRESS DELIVERED BEFORE THE HISTORICAL SOCIETY

OF GALVESTON, DECEMBER 15, 1875 . . . WITH A PRELIMI-
NARY NOTICE OF THE HISTORICAL SOCIETY OF GALVES-
TON.

Galveston: Published by the Society, 1876.
xvi,[17]-82pp. 23cm.
Printed wrappers. 100 copies printed.

Other issues:
(A). Same as above. Issued about 1920, this edition is textually identical to the
    original but is not a facsimile. It does not have the signature numbers on
    pages [17], 33, 49, 57, 65, 73, and [81], and it has a small circle in the center
    of the rules on pages 28, 43, 58, 64, and 79. Has "No. 1" on half-title page.
(B). Same as (A), except has "No. 1" on half-title page, and slightly different type
    fonts on title page.
(C). Facsimile edition. Austin: The Pemberton Press, 1967. XIV,[iii]-xvi,[17]-86,[9]pp.
    22cm. Cloth. Brasada Reprint Series. Contains a new introduction by John H.
    Jenkins, a bibliography of Ashbel Smith, index, and illustrations.

Written by one of the wisest men of early Texas, this is the most
astute first-hand account of the diplomatic activities leading to annexation. No one, with the exception of Sam Houston and Anson Jones,
was more intimately involved in the process of acquiring international
recognition of the Republic of Texas and bringing about annexation
than Dr. Ashbel Smith.

Smith was born in Hartford, Connecticut, and graduated Phi Beta
Kappa from Yale at the age of nineteen. He taught school in North
Carolina, returned to Yale and took a degree in medicine in 1828. In
1831 he did advanced medical study in France, joining the social circle
of Marquis de Lafayette, James Fenimore Cooper, and Samuel F. B.
Morse.

In 1837, Smith moved to Texas, accepting the position of Surgeon
General of the Army. In 1839 he was the hero of the yellow fever
epidemic in Galveston, and wrote a treatise on the epidemic, now
famous in medical circles, entitled *An Account of the Yellow Fever Which
Appeared in the City of Galveston, Republic of Texas, In the Autumn of* 1839
(Galveston, 1839).

In 1842 he was appointed Charge d'Affaires to England and France
by President Sam Houston. After his return in 1844, he served as
Secretary of State under Anson Jones. Smith was a Confederate

brigadier general in the Civil War, and frequent member of the Texas Legislature. He served as President of Texas Medical College, helped found Prairie View University, and was a founder and President of the Board of Regents of the University of Texas.

On December 15, 1875, Smith delivered the annual address to the Galveston Historical Society. Its importance was recognized by the society, which immediately voted to publish the address in full. Smith added an Introduction, dated Evergreen, Harris Co., Texas, January, 1876, in which he states:

"It has not been my purpose to set forth a full history of annexation; but only to present portions of the inside history of that great measure and of the men and parties connected with it which fell within my own knowledge and personal observation—to relate facts, opinions and purposes which were better known to me than to any [other] man now living. The work I have undertaken, whether I have succeeded in it or not, is not useless nor unimportant. Gentlemen called by the confidence of their fellow citizens to fill the highest offices in the late republic of Texas, were charged with crimes, machinations and conspiracies, which if true would destroy for their good name all claim to be esteemed honest men or patriotic citizens. The time has come for their authoritative refutation, and for an authoritative clearing away of the mist with which interest, suspicion, passion, prejudice and ignorance have clouded the history of a measure which brought on a mighty war in its train, made presidents of the United States, baffled aspirants to the presidency, and added a million of square miles to the territories of the mighty American union."

The text is personal but objective, a blended narrative of anecdote and analysis. Smith reviews the Texas border question, the various votes and movements for recognition and annexation in Texas and the United States, his activities in France and England, and the treaties which he negotiated. He carefully treats the slavery issue and corrects the "grave" errors in the "incomplete and otherwise not wholly reliable history of Texas by Yoakum."

The personal recollections give an insight into the lives of many of the leaders in 19th century Texas, and fascinating accounts of how Texas was viewed by leaders in France, England, the United States, and Mexico. It is a loss to history that Smith never prepared a full autobiography of his active life. There is one inadequate biography of Smith by Elizabeth Silverthorne, *Ashbel Smith of Texas: Pioneer, Patriot, Statesman,* 1805-1806 (College Station: Texas A & M University Press, 1982).

Howes S574. Rader 2934. Raines, p.190.

187   Smith, Edward (1818?-1874)

ACCOUNT OF A JOURNEY THROUGH NORTH-EASTERN TEXAS, UNDERTAKEN IN 1849, FOR THE PURPOSE OF EMIGRATION. EMBODIED IN A REPORT: TO WHICH ARE APPENDED LETTERS AND VERBAL COMMUNICATIONS, FROM EMINENT INDIVIDUALS . . .

London: Hamilton, Adams & Co., Paternoster Row; Birmingham: B. Hudson, Bull Street, 1849.
vi,[5]-188pp. 2 folding maps. 19cm.
Cloth.

Prepared by an educated and perceptive observer, this is an excellent eyewitness account of northeastern Texas. William W. Webb said Smith "possessed a rare faculty of systematising his knowledge and great facility as a writer." Thomas Clark said "the report is filled with interesting description and statistical information for prospective emigrants to Texas," and Marilyn Sibley called it "especially valuable for its objective description of the economy of the region."

Dr. Edward Smith was educated at Queen's College, Birmingham, and graduated from London University in 1848, the year before accepting the commission to examine Texas. Upon his return to England, he was elected a fellow of the Royal College of Surgeons and the Royal College of Physicians. He became a researcher and inventor in chemistry and medicine, and became recognized as a leading world authority on dietetics. He wrote a number of books on these fields.

In March of 1849 a British colonizing venture headed by Henry Frearson commissioned Dr. Smith and a young civil engineer named John Barrow to examine northeastern Texas to estimate its merits for prospective emigrants from England. Smith and Barrow sailed from

Liverpool on April 10, 1849, arriving at Shreveport via New York on May 21. They then travelled overland into Texas as far as Dallas, studying the area in considerable detail and returning to Shreveport in June. They sailed back to England, impressed with the quality of the climate, soil, and prospects of the region. Both began to write books on the subject. John Barrow issued his exceedingly rare *Facts Relating to North-Eastern Texas Condensed from Notes Made during a Tour Through That Portion of the United States of America for the Purpose of Examining the Country as a Field for Emigration* (London: Simpkin, Marshall & Co., 1848. 68pp.).

Smith spent the early fall of that year at Fall House, near Heanor, Derbyshire, preparing his more extensive book, completing the text in October. Smith's account is nearly unique among Texas immigrant guides in that he "in no instance" consulted any other of "the works written on Texas, but are content to lay before you the results of our own inspection and inquiry only." His volume is therefore spontaneous and fresh, and contains an exceptional view of this region of Texas just at the time that active settlement was starting. He includes two very fine maps, one of Texas as a whole and the other the best representation of the Marshall-Dallas region up to that time.

The volume itself consists of description, extensive statistical information, and discussion of the soil, communications, resources, travel routes, climate, and products of the area, which he says encompass "everything the heart could wish." He also includes a detailed section of "Directions to Emigrants," and a pragmatic essay on slavery. Especially interesting are the lengthy reports on Texas lands prepared for him by Jacob DeCordova and the section of "Verbal Communications" in which he quotes from settlers in the region whom he personally interviewed. Smith also includes the full text of the Texas Constitution of 1845, the first printing of that document in England.

As a result of the reports of Smith and Barrow, a consolidated group of colonizing companies was formed in 1850 as the United States Land Company, with artist George Catlin as superintendent of the Texas department. Catlin, due to personal financial troubles, soon resigned. Groups began to ship out for Texas, with Jacob DeCordova as receiving agent in Texas, Sir Edward Belcher as British agent and Lt. C. F. Mackenzie in charge. The largest group wound up about fifty miles north of Waco on 27,000 acres of the lands of Richard B. Kimball, in present Bosque County. W. S. Shepperson states that "the colony quickly proved a catastrophic failure. Its almost immediate trend of *de mal en pis* was accentuated by Mackenzie's well-meaning, but naive, military discipline, the insistence by some to maintain cultivated, but often leisurely habits, the crop failures of 1851, and finally the Comanche Indian raids. Because of these factors, the City of Kent [as the settlement was called] was turned into a desolate outpost less than twelve months after its founding. . . . As the public became familiar with the disaster surrounding the first experiment, interest waned, and [the British Company] slipped into the lengthening column of ill-fated attempts to transport Britons to Texas. And so it was that Texas, true to her robust historical tradition, stimulated in Britain as in America some of the most valiant hopes, valueless schemes, and violent feelings registered during the mid-nineteenth century."

Bradford 5018. Clark III-411. Graff 3843. Howes S589. Paullin 2781. Rader 2939. Raines, p.190. Sabin 82444.

188   Smith, Justin Harvey (1857-1930)

THE ANNEXATION OF TEXAS.

New York: The Baker and Taylor Co., 1911.
ix,[1],496,[1]pp. 23cm.
Cloth.
Verso of title: Press of the New Era Printing Company, Lancaster, Pa.
Note: The Jenkins Garrett copy has a tipped in letter from the author dated 127 Newbury St., Boston, Oct. 19, 1911, in which Smith states the work "came from the press a few days ago."

Other issues:
(A). New York: The Macmillan Company, 1912. Same collation.
(B). New York: The Macmillan Company, 1919. Same collation.
(C). Corrected edition. New York: Barnes and Noble, Inc., 1941. ix,496pp. 23cm. Cloth.
(D). Facsimile reprint of the 1911 edition. New York: AMS Press, [1971]. Same collation. 23cm. Cloth.

This is the most comprehensive study of the movement to bring Texas into the Union. The *American Historical Review* said of it: "Few books of history have more decisively settled controversy on their subject." St. George Sioussat said it "evidenced the author's characteristics as a scholar: a tireless searching for all possible sources, consultation of the originals themselves, knowledge through travel of the regions described, critical discernment, and a cumulative presentation of voluminous footnotes." Eugene C. Barker called it "a solid and comprehensive history of the annexation of Texas, based on a minute study of practically all the sources. Every phase of the subject is painstakingly, and, in most cases, it seems, conclusively covered. . . . On most points, it probably says the final word." Thomas Maitland Marshall said it is "the only adequate treatment of the subject."

Smith summarizes the significance of the annexation movement: "The annexation of Texas, it can be justly said, was a very interesting, important, complicated and critical affair. In involved issues and consequences of no little moment in our domestic politics. It gave us an area greater than England and France together . . . and paved the way for the acquisition of [California]. . . . It extinguished a nation that might have become a strong and unfriendly rival and might have caused the disruption of the Union. It removed an excellent opportunity for certain leading European powers to interpose in the affairs of this continent. It presented a field of battle on which our diplomats and those of England, France, Mexico and Texas waged a long an intricate struggle . . . and it brought these five nations to the verge of war."

Smith's overriding themes are that annexation was a desirable and legitimate part of American expansion and that it was not the result of a slavery plot. His conclusions are basically that the Texas Revolution was a necessary response to Mexican despotism, that American aid to the revolution was spontaneous and not government-inspired, that it was in American interest to recognize Texas as a nation, that annexation sentiment was largely non-partisan, that the election of 1844 was not a plebiscite on the annexation question, that British interests in maintaining Texas as an independent nation were adverse to American interests, and that Tyler's efforts to achieve annexation were sound statesmanship and not merely political.

This revision upset the prevalent theme, particularly among northern writers, that the movement to bring Texas into the Union was a deliberate conspiracy of the slave interests to extend slavery westward and upset the precarious political balance between slave and free states established by the Missouri Compromise. Smith's viewpoint stood almost unchallenged for sixty years until the appearance of Frederick Merk's *Slavery and the Annexation of Texas,* which effectively presented the case for the validity of the slave conspiracy thesis. Thus Barker appears to be in error in thinking the Smith analysis is probably the final word. As my entry for the Merk volume points out, the controversy still rages, and neither Smith nor Merk has presented a totally convincing case for either of their viewpoints.

The volume is the result of an astounding amount of research. Smith states that his work "is based almost exclusively on first-hand sources, though all previous works of any importance on the subject have been fully examined. Use has been made of substantially all the diplomatic papers—American, British, French, Mexican and Texan." There are, nevertheless, some irritating errors of fact and inexplicable lapses of judgment, such as his claim that the defeat of the Mier Expedition (with a loss of 261 men) "considerably impaired . . . the fighting strength of the [Texas] nation." On one page, England "could not afford to fight" the United States over the Texas question; two pages later, England is prepared "to undertake a war in order to establish the Sabine [as] a perpetual barrier against us." Barker justly complains that Smith's "unexplained references to 'a well known historian,' 'the author of this passage,' etc., are at the present day inexcusable." Some of the errors were corrected in the 1941 edition.

The Price Daniel Library at Liberty has a letter about the book from Charles Francis Adams to Smith dated November 16, 1911, in which he states: "I am one of the not very large number of those who remember the election of 1844 and the issue then supposed to be decided. . . . My grandfather [John Quincy Adams] bitterly opposed the annexation of Texas, and yet you show (p.329n) that he recognized the fact that he was resisting the inevitable. . . . You do not distinctly set forth in your narrative the character Texas then bore, and which as a matter of fact, it subsequently introduced into the Union. Texas, it must be remembered, was . . . filled with speculators, adventurers,

fugitives from debt and the law, and ruffians generally. . . . The New England element was, therefore, wholly justified in exerting its every effort to prevent such a community association and moral partnership. . . . Judging by your narrative, one would suppose that when we introduced Texas into the Union we introduced a community at least respectable. Such was not the fact. It was immoral, lawless, pro-slavery, uneducated, grasping, and generally brutal—in a word, half-civilized. A whole chapter would be necessary to make your narrative complete in all its aspects. Nevertheless, you are, in my judgment, perfectly right in your general conclusion. . . . Wholly unaware of the fact, my grandfather, and those who exerted themselves so strenuously against the annexation of Texas, were fighting the stars in their courses.''

Smith dedicates the volume to George P. Garrison, who had recently died while editing *Texas Diplomatic Correspondence,* and acknowledges the special assistance given him by Theodore Roosevelt, Porfirio Diaz, Elihu Root, Henry Cabot Lodge, J. Franklin Jameson, and Worthington C. Ford. He makes particular mention of Ephraim Douglass Adams, author of *British Interests and Activities in Texas* (Baltimore, 1909). Smith and Adams conducted their research at the same time, occasionally at the same place. Since their viewpoints sometimes coincided and sometimes collided, something of a conflict developed between the two.

The Annexation of Texas was instigated by Smith as a preliminary study to his monumental two-volume history, *The War with Mexico* (New York: The Macmillan Company, 1919), which won the Pulitzer Prize in 1920 and the first Loubat Prize in 1923. This work, for which Smith said he utilized over 100,000 manuscripts, 1200 books, and 200 periodicals, remains both the most comprehensive and most controversial study of the Mexican War of 1846-48, and contains a great deal relating to Texas.

Griffin 4215. Howes S634. Rader 2945. Trask 5721.

189 Smithwick, Noah (1808-1899)

THE EVOLUTION OF A STATE: OR, RECOLLECTIONS OF OLD TEXAS DAYS.

Austin: Gammel Book Company, [1900].
Compiled by Nanna Smithwick Donaldson.
[10],9-354pp. 8 illus. 19cm.
Cloth.

Other issues:

(A). Same as above, with special tipped-in title page. Limited to 10 copies, bound
    in full morocco, gilt. Copy No. 1, which is in my personal collection, was
    issued to Nanna Smithwick Donaldson.
(B). Facsimile reprint. Austin: The Steck Company, no date (circa 1935). [xii],9-
    354pp. 4 illus. 21cm. Cloth. 2500 copies printed initially, and reprinted several
    times without alteration.
(C). Same as (B). Austin: Steck-Vaughn Company, [1968]. New introduction by
    James M. Day. Best edition.
(D). Reprint. Austin: University of Texas Press, [1983]. xiii,[3],264pp. Illustrations
    by Charles Shaw. Foreword by L. Tuffly Ellis. Cloth, dustjacket.
(E). Paperback edition of (D).

Of all Texas memoirs, this is the most fun to read. J. Frank Dobie
called it the "best of all books dealing with life in early Texas."
Rupert N. Richardson praised it as "rich in detail and bears evidence
of a high degree of accuracy." James M. Day said that "Smithwick
was unschooled, but wise in the ways of the world, and he set down
his thoughts with such zest that the reader is mentally swept into the
stream of his story."

Smithwick's work is one of the most anecdotal of all early Texas
memoirs. It is full of insights into the major and minor events of his
time, and he gives us a fascinating depiction of social life in Texas
when it was a colony and a republic. Smithwick served with the Texas
Rangers and lived for awhile with the Comanches, learning their
language and representing them in making a treaty with the Texans
in 1838. He gives us anecdotes available nowhere else on men he knew
such as James Bowie, Sam Houston, Stephen F. Austin, David G.
Burnet, Gail Borden, Padre Michael Muldoon, R. M. Williamson,
and others. He tells of smuggling, counterfeiting, gambling, drinking,
and dancing with a frankness lacking in most other Texas autobiographies.

Smithwick came to Texas in 1827 at the age of 19 and became a
blacksmith in San Felipe. He was run out of town by vigilantes in 1831
and lived along the Sabine until 1835, when he joined the army and

fought in the Texas Revolution. He lived in the Bastrop region until 1860, when he moved to California. During the last two years of his life, while almost totally blind, he dictated his memoirs to his daughter, Nanna Smithwick Donaldson. Portions had been printed in the late 1890's in the Galveston *News* and the Dallas *Morning News* under the title, "Half Century Reader."

Smithwick offers some perceptive commentary on the reasons why people came to Texas before the revolution. He freely admits that "many hard things have been said and written of the early settlers in Texas, much of which is unfortunately true. Historians, however, fail to disciminate between . . . those who went there to make homes . . . and the outlaws and adventurers who flocked into the towns. . . . Faulty [civil and criminal] statutes in the United States sent many a man to Texas. . . . It was the regular thing to ask a stranger what he had done, and if he disclaimed having been guilty of any offense, he was regarded with suspicion." He tells of one man, Bob Stewart, "whose capacity for contracting debts was only limited by his credit. [He] had an original way of disposing of duns. When a creditor presented a bill, Bob would dismiss him with the rebuke, 'Go and pay your own debts and don't come bothering me about mine.' "

In the 1830's Smithwick floated in and out of the Redlands of East Texas, and he tells numerous tales of "the many hard characters there. . . . The only semblance of government was the office of alcalde, presided over by old Bill Lindsey, a well-meaning old fellow, as ignorant of the law as of grammar." Smithwick gives intimate, eyewitness details of the counterfeiting of Mexican coins and land titles. The coins (made of copper from a melted whiskey still) were accepted even when recognized as fakes because there was no other hard currency to be had, and they "passed current in the community until the plating began to wear off, when he gathered them in, and, treating them to a fresh coat, sent them out again." The land titles were forged grants of Juan A. Padilla; Smithwick says "any good plug of a pony would buy an eleven-league grant. [They were] the foundation for all the land litigation that has vexed the souls of settlers ever since."

Bradford 5116. Clark III-105. Dobie, p.52. Graff 3872. Howes S726. Rader 2948. Sabin 85099.

190   Solms-Braunfels, Prince Carl of (1812-1875)

TEXAS: GESCHILDERT IN BEZIEHUNG AUF SEINE GEOGRA-
PHISCHEN, SOCIALEN, UND UBRIGEN, VERHALTNISSE,
MIT BESONDERER RUECKSICHT AUF DIE DEUTSCHE
COLONISATION EIN HANDBUCH FUER AUSWANDERER
NACH TEXAS.

Frankfurt am Main: Johann David Sauerlander's Verlag, 1846.
x,134pp. 2 folding maps. 20cm. Boards.

Other issues:

(A). Second state of above. Same sheets, with new printed wrappers added bearing
the notice: "Zweite Ausflage." Also adds plans of Fredericksburg and Neu-Braun-
fels.

(B). *Texas*, 1844-1845. Houston: The Anson Jones Press, 1936. [12],141,[3]pp. 4 illus.
4 plates and endpaper maps. 28cm. Brown cloth. Verso of title: "Of this first
edition in English seven hundred and fifty copies have been printed, of which
this is_____." Most copies I have seen have no number written in.

(C). Remainder binding of (A), with white end sheets with two maps pasted down
inside front and back covers, or loosely inserted. Blue cloth.

    Written by a forthright observer, this is one of the most practical
guidebooks for European immigrants to Texas. Sister Agatha said that
"for an expression of stocky, practical German observation of early
Texas, Braunfels' account is to the point. There is no 'flowery'
phrasing nor embellished style in the immigration guide of the founder
of New Braunfels. He calls a spade by its name and offers no
modifying apologies. . . . It is certainly different from any other
immigration guide."

    It is, in fact, the most candid book about Texas immigration ever
written. Prince Carl's extensive tours through Texas in the last years
of its independence led him to view the Texans with great skepticism,
and he warns repeatedly against trusting them. The Texan, he says,
will "because of his own or another's interest, pervert the truth in
ninety-nine cases out of a hundred." "In Texas the majority of men
die either on account of the lack of reliable doctors or through their
own ignorance and quack remedies." "When a drunken American
mistreats or kills an Indian, not even a rooster would bother to crow."
"In the early times almost all the individuals who immigrated into
Texas from the United States had been convicted of murder or theft."

"The law has no force and the lawyers and judges, who as a rule are good-for-nothing, can, nevertheless, protect that party lying closest to their heart." The Texas Rangers "choose their own officers, but do not obey them."

Prince Carl offers interesting commentary on the geography of Texas. His maps are generally accurate, and were prepared with the assistance of John C. Hays. Carl's comments on the terrain are frequently wry: "The hilly region is termed mountainous by the American, but this does not correspond to our idea of mountains." "The accuracy of most surveyors' maps depends on the human eye alone. A few tracts have been surveyed with the aid of a chain. Neither a surveyor's table, a sight-vane, a sextant, nor any other surveying instrument has yet been used in Texas. Much less has anyone thought of applying trigonometry in measuring the area of the state."

He also offers some perceptive comments on the future of agriculture, and is perhaps the first to recommend the planting of oranges as a commercial enterprise. "The soil of Texas," he admits, "undoubtedly is one of the most fertile on the earth," and "the pastures in Texas are as extensive as the sky." The Texan, however, "is usually too lazy to prepare a garden. Rather than go to such trouble he prefers to live on salted meat, bacon, corn and coffee and to deny himself any greenery either for nourishment or for beautifying the home." He claims the rattlesnake bite "is never fatal," and states: "The alligator ranks first among the dangerous animals. . . . We have shot some as long as fourteen feet near New Braunfels on Comal Creek."

He gives most Texas towns a poor rating. "Liberty on Trinity River is of no importance." Of San Felipe: "Besides an interesting collection of fossils which were dug out of the bank of the Brazos, there is nothing of interest." "Nacogdoches . . . cannot be recommended." "Houston has more houses than citizens. [The Buffalo Bayou dock] affords the town some life. Otherwise it would only be a gathering place for loafers . . . who go there mainly to gamble and to trade horses with the hope of defrauding someone." "The chief justice of the San Antonio district has among his peculiar habits a set rule to be already in an intoxicated trance by 9 o'clock in the morning." The Texans in almost all towns "are self-opinionated and boastful, unpleasing in their social dealings, and very dirty in their manners and habits.''

In being so outspoken, Prince Carl states that ''I am striving to protect the immigrant, as well as to aid and accommodate him, through the publication of this book.'' ''Since almost every American is more or less crafty,'' the European immigrants should deal only with other immigrants. Unfortunately, some of them have learned Texan ways too well: ''Those whose whole ambition is to imitate the American in his habits are as a rule ten times as bad. I admonish my countrymen to be doubly cautious with them.''

Prince Carl and his book are a study in paradoxes. He loathes the Texans, but recommends William Kennedy's extreme pro-Texas book as the best guide. He offers every possible drawback to European immigration, but urges them to come. He was a devout Catholic, but founded a Protestant settlement. Herbert Fletcher said of him: ''Prince, snob, and cousin to Queen Victoria, he led a group who were willing to face the hazards of a new world to escape royalty and snobbery.'' A dashing, romantic officer (knighted for gallantry), he was the epitome of a character from Walter Scott, yet he wrote like H. L. Mencken. A prince among princes, he came to Texas and worked side by side with indigent laborers to build a colony in the wilderness. Of his own contribution to the colony, he says only that he hopes ''that the little I have contributed will have a favorable influence.''

Agatha, p.3. Clark III-241. Graff 3889. Howes S751. Raines, p.42. Sabin 86505.

191   Sonnichsen, Charles Leland (1901-)

PASS OF THE NORTH: FOUR CENTURIES ON THE RIO GRANDE.

El Paso: Texas Western Press, The University of Texas at El Paso, 1968-1980.
Designed by Carl Hertzog.
Two volumes: xii,467; ix,[3],140pp. Illus. Maps. 25cm.
Cloth, dustjackets.
[Verso of title of volume I:] S. D. Myres, Editor. Map and Chapter Initials by Jose Cisneros. [Verso of title of volume II:] E. H. Antone, Editor. Dustjacket and Chapter Drawings by Jose Cisneros. Maps Drawn by Don Bufkin. Picture Selections by Millard G. McKinney.

Other issues:
(A). Second printing of volume I, 1968, with slight revisions.
(B). Third printing of volume I, 1975.
(C). Fourth printing of volume I, 1980.

This is a splendid history of the area centering around El Paso and
Juarez. William C. Pool called it "a remarkable and readable history
of the community of El Paso and the adjacent valley of the Rio
Grande. . . . It is no easy task to record four centuries of local history
and maintain a balanced narrative, but, in this regard, Professor
Sonnichsen has succeeded admirably. . . . *Pass of the North* is a
significant contribution to Texas and Western American history." The
Pacific Historical Review said that "Sonnichsen is fascinated by people
and his book teems with biographical sketches. He has the knack of
uncovering anecdotes from half-forgotten manuscripts and bringing
individuals to life. Not surprisingly, he is at his best in detailing the
lives of hidalgos, padres, colonial adventurers, frontier bandits, confidence men, and prostitutes."

The narrative encompasses a broad sweep of Southwestern history,
from Cabeza de Vaca, Juan de Onate, and Zuniga though Zebulon
Pike, Josiah Gregg, James Magoffin, George W. Kendall, George
Ruxton, Jack Hays, R. S. Neighbors, W. H. Emory, John S. Ford,
and Joseph E. Johnston, all of whom visited and had something to
say about the Pass of the North. As El Paso and Juarez grew each to
be the largest town along either side of the border (eventually achieving
a combined population of over a million), the area witnessed the
activities of John Selman, John Wesley Hardin, Jim Gillett, Jeff
Milton, Bill McDonald, Pancho Villa, and other lawmen and outlaws.

The Pass of the North was also a critical place in passing events of
importance: as the northern gateway for New Spain, as the refuge of
the 1680's New Mexico Indian rebellion, as the command post of the
western exploration surveys, in the transcontinental railway projects,
in the Salt War of 1877, and in the Mexican revolutionary activities of
the early 20th century. Sonnichsen says "it adds up to a remarkable
story—a story that should be told—a reminder in a rootless age of the
deep roots of one community. It must be a tale of two cities, for El
Paso is part Mexican, and Juarez is more American than it sometimes
likes to admit. The river brought them both to life. They could not

do without each other. This is the story of how they came to be, how they grew, and how they changed from the old days to the new.''

Sonnichsen did research on the work for over thirty-five years. It was completed and submitted to his publishers, Devin-Adair, in 1966, but the size of the manuscript intimidated that house and eventually it fell to Texas Western Press during the golden years of Carl Hertzog's tenure. The publication of the first volume, with its beautiful maps and illustrations and its 1,583 footnotes, occurred in March, 1968, in spite of a harrowing experience during the publication process. Carl Hertzog, writing in *Password* (Winter, 1971), tells what happened:

''We had corrected the page proofs and made up about a hundred pages which had been sent to Leland [Sonnichsen] for final checking. . . . He finished the proofs and started for our office. A terrific March wind was stirring up the worst sandstorm I ever saw. Our new plant at the south end of the [University of Texas at El Paso] campus was surrounded with bulldozers which helped the dust considerably. I wouldn't go out. I was sitting in my office when I heard a scream. My wife was in the outer office looking out the window when Leland drove up. He disembarked with a roll of galley proofs under one arm and the bunch of page proofs in the other hand. Just as he reached the sidewalk, a gust of wind blew his hat off. As he grabbed for his hat, another gust blew the loosened proofs from under his arm. . . . All the proofs went flying down the street with Leland in hot pursuit. I jumped out of the door and ran after him picking up proofs as we went along. These proofs were important, the only copy of the corrections and final alterations. At the end of the block we had to descend into an arroyo as proofs were still flying through the air. It was rocky and steep. I picked several pages from thorns on mesquite bushes (the first time I knew what mesquites were good for). Surprisingly, we recovered almost all the proofs, enough to guide us in reconstructing missing pages. When some of the [unrecovered] proofs were blown across the Rio Grande, south of Hart's Mall, I said, 'Leland, this book of yours is an instant success. It already has international distribution.' ''

Sonnichsen's text is brilliant regarding the individuals who played a role in the area's history during its four centuries, but lacking in other areas, such as economic, political, diplomatic, and scientific history.

Pass of the North is social history, but it is social history at its best. It is far more scholarly than his two feud books; excellent though they are, they were written for a general audience and are too surfeited with imaginary conversations. These two works are *I'll Die Before I'll Run: The Story of the Great Feuds of Texas* (New York: Harper & Brothers, 1951) and *Ten Texas Feuds* (Albuquerque: University of New Mexico Press, 1957). In the same vein is his *Roy Bean: Law West of the Pecos* (New York: The Macmillan Company, 1943).

192   Sowell, Andrew Jackson (1848-1921)

RANGERS AND PIONEERS OF TEXAS, WITH A CONCISE ACCOUNT OF THE EARLY SETTLEMENTS, HARDSHIPS, MASSACRES, BATTLES, AND WARS BY WHICH TEXAS WAS RESCUED FROM THE RULE OF THE SAVAGE AND CONSECRATED TO THE EMPIRE OF CIVILIZATION.

San Antonio: Shepard Bros. & Co., Printers and Publishers, 1884.
[2],411pp. Illus. 19cm.
Cloth.

Other issues:
(A). *Selected Chapters from "Early Pioneers and Texas Rangers" Published in the Seguin Enterprise.* Seguin: The Seguin Enterprise, 1936. 24pp. 21cm. Printed wrappers. Excerpts from the first edition, with bowdlerized text, of portions relating to the Guadalupe County area.
(B). Facsimile reprint. New York: Argosy-Antiquarian, Ltd., [1964]. Same collation. 22cm. Cloth. Verso of title: "Edition Limited to 750 copies. . . . Printed in the United States of America by Sentry Press, New York, N.Y."

One of the basic sources on the vicissitudes of the pioneer settlers in Texas, this work contains numerous accounts gathered from participants, as well as one of the best of all first-person ranger campaign narratives. Edward Eberstadt dubbed it "one of the most important and authentic accounts of the Indian Wars in Texas."

Sowell states that "the incidents . . . have been gathered from sources most reliable," mostly from men and women "whose names have as yet found no place in history. . . . They bore the heat and the burden of the day, and their deeds should live." These deeds, "worthy of the pen of our best historians," relate to "the Indian troubles mostly.'' In this regard, Sowell acknowledges that his book necessarily suffers the same problem of all gathered recollections. ''One thing,'' he admits, ''which greatly bothers me in collecting these incidents, is being deficient in dates, which is very necessary . . . but I will try to give the facts as near as I can, as they were related to me by the old pioneers. For instance, one will be relating some incident . . . and you will ask, 'When did that occur?' 'Well,' he will say, 'I do not recollect exactly, but I think it was in the fall or winter or spring or so and so;' and, of course, there are likely to be some errors of this kind.''

Sowell's book was written some years earlier than Wilbarger, Brown, and other Indian depredation lore of Texas, and while he was still a young man in his mid-thirties. This gives many of his accounts an immediacy not available elsewhere. For example, he tells of how he himself had recently come upon a fine double-long cabin in West Texas, unoccupied but with ''chairs, tables, bedding, clothes and various other things scattered about in the passageway and rooms.'' He soon learned that the entire family had been killed: ''Some of the children were found dead and scalped at the milk-house, as if they had sought refuge there when the savages made the attack on the house. As these people had no relations in this country, everything remained as it was the day of the massacre, except that the bodies had been removed.''

The volume is divided into three sections. The first section consists primarily of Indian affrays as related to Sowell by participants. The last of these is dated January 25, 1883, and relates to the release from captivity of a blind woman previously thought to have been killed by Indians. Sowell visited her and her rancher husband: ''He was reading a newspaper to his blind wife, while in her hand she held a boquet [sic] of fragrant cape jessamines [in] absolute happiness.'' The second section includes the adventures of members of the Sowell family in Texas in the 1830's and 1840's, and material relating to the Texas Revolution and republic. Notable in this section are some eyewitness accounts, such as Dillard Cooper's ''Remembrances of the Fannin Massacre'' and R. N. Brown's eyewitness account of the Johnson and Grant Expedition of 1835.

The last section, comprising almost half the book, is Sowell's own narrative of his experiences in the Wichita Campaign of 1870-1871, entitled "Campaign of the Texas Rangers to the Wichita Mountains in 1871." It is evident that he either intended from the beginning of the campaign to write about it or at least had determined to do so before the campaign ended, for he quotes a letter from one of his comrades (whom he had not seen since the campaign) in which the man comments: "I presume you are still at work on your book." In this section, Sowell writes his best prose, and leaves us a vivid account.

He tells of his first real fight, without pulling any punches: "Said I, George, there they are; we are in for it now. . . . 'Boys,' said Sergeant Cobb, suddenly looking around, 'what do you say to a charge?' 'All right Ed,' came from the rangers . . . I will admit that I felt weak about the knees, and something like a chill would creep up my back every time I cast my eyes towards [them]. . . . As wicked as I was, I asked God to shield me in the battle. . . . We were about to play a desperate game; eleven ranger boys against forty-one picked warriors. . . . Our boys were good shots, but an Indian is hard to hit. . . . We done but little damage. . . . Some of the boys advised [Larkin] Cleveland to get down and shelter himself [but] he said he guessed not, and again raised his gun to fire. About this time a large Kiowa ran up on his horse, about seventy yards off, and shot an arrow at Cleveland, cutting the brim of his hat. He concluded then to dismount. . . . [At last] the Indians were repulsed and ran, carrying their shields on their backs, to receive our fire as they went off."

Dobie, pp.58 and 60. Graff 3909. Howes S801. Raines, p.193.

193 Sowell, Andrew Jackson (1848-1921)

EARLY SETTLERS AND INDIAN FIGHTERS OF SOUTHWEST TEXAS . . . FACTS GATHERED FROM SURVIVORS OF FRONTIER DAYS.

Austin: Ben C. Jones & Co., Printers, 1900.
viii,844pp. 12 plates; also illustration in the text. 24cm.
Cloth.

Other issues:

(A). Same, except no copyright notice on verso of title. Also, the letters in the title are all the same size; in the first printing the initial letters in the words of the title are slightly larger than the rest of the letters. The remainder of the text is apparently from the same printing as the first issue.

(B). Facsimile reprint. New York: Argosy Antiquarian, Ltd., [1964]. Two volumes: [iv],vi,[3],vi-viii,[2],351; [vi],353-844pp. 23cm. Cloth, boxed. New introduction by Joe B. Frantz. Verso of title: "Edition limited to 750 copies."

(C). Facsimile reprint. Austin: State House Books, 1986. New index.

Not an expansion of *Rangers and Pioneers,* this is an entirely different work containing hundreds of accounts of incidents in pioneer Texas. Dobie called it "meaty with the character of ready-to-fight but peace-seeking Texas pioneers. Sowell will some day be recognized as an extraordinary chronicler." Joe B. Frantz said that "Sowell had a feature writer's eye for a good story and his sensitivity for change of pace and mood. He was aware of one necessity so often forgotten by chroniclers of the past—to make his story interesting and readable."

The work contains 132 accounts of early pioneers, mostly as told by them directly to Sowell. "They were the men who cut the brush and blazed the way for immigration, and drove the wild beast and wilder men from the path of civilization." Notable among these are lengthy recollections received first-hand from Bigfoot Wallace and Benjamin F. Highsmith. Sowell had published a short biography of Wallace in 1899, to which this adds new material received from the famous old ranger. The Highsmith memoir provides a wealth of valuable information on the battle of Velasco in 1832, on the Texas Revolution, on the battles of Plum Creek (1840) and Salado (1842), and on the early battles of the Mexican War in South Texas. The volume also includes three chapters devoted to the diary of Henri Castro, founder of Castroville.

Most of the work, however, relates to Indian fights and Texas Rangers. This material is fresh and for the most part does not appear in Brown, Wilbarger, or other works. Sowell, from a family of rangers and himself a former ranger, describes the ranger as a man who "will stand by a friend and comrade in the hour of danger, and divide anything he has got, from a blanket to his last crumb of tobacco."

The book was printed by the Austin firm of Ben C. Jones, and most copies of the original edition were destroyed in that firm's disastrous fire a few years after publication. Apparently some unbound sheets were saved, however, for a small number were bound up later with a new title page added. I have in my collection a letter from W. H. Lowdermilk & Co. dated December 22, 1961, stating that "we have three more copies of the Sowell at the binders," indicating that they had come into possession of a group of the original unbound sheets.

Dobie, p.58. Graff 3907. Howes S797. Rader 2957.

194 Spaight, Ashley W. (1821-1911)

THE RESOURCES, SOIL, AND CLIMATE OF TEXAS: REPORT OF COMMISSIONER OF INSURANCE, STATISTICS, AND HISTORY.

Galveston: A. H. Belo & Co., Printers, 1882.
x,360pp. Folding map. 23cm.
Cloth.

This is the first reliable statistical account of Texas. Preceded only by the works of private writers and by the excellent Richardson *Texas Almanacs,* it presents for the first time the tabulated statewide data received by Commissioner Spaight from official inquiries. Previous compilations were all more or less erratic in the accuracy of their data, necessarily derived privately and all too frequently presented with ulterior promotional motives. Spaight's volume is the first official attempt to accurately describe the state.

The work is arranged alphabetically by counties. Of the 170 organized counties, Spaight was able to elicit and verify returns from 167. "Of the three organized counties from which no returns have been received, I have gleaned sufficient information from reliable outside sources to enable me to include them in this report." A section at the end discusses the unorganized counties, mostly in the Panhandle and Southwest Texas. In this section he quotes from Texas Ranger Captain G. W. Arrington, G. W. Singer, H. C. Smith, Dr. William Hunt, William S. Mabry, Col. N. L. Norton, and others.

For each county, Spaight gives essential data such as population (in 1870 and in 1880), colored population, property values, physical description in great detail, current land prices, geology and minerals, railroads, county organization, agriculture, schools, manufactures, religious institutions, and climate. Full details on cattle and stock raising are presented, providing the most reliable statistics on the Texas cattle industry during this key period. The large folding map may be considered the first modern and truly accurate map of Texas.

Ashley W. Spaight was an 1852 graduate of the University of North Carolina and a member of the Alabama legislature during the Mexican War. He moved to Liberty County, Texas, in 1860, and became captain of the "Moss Bluff Rebels" from that area in the Confederacy. He was soon promoted to colonel and led the famous "Spaight's Regiment" during the remainder of the war. He was a member of the Constitutional Convention of 1866. In 1881, Gov. O. M. Roberts appointed Spaight as Commissioner of Insurance Statistics, and History to replace V. O. King, who had first organized the department. Spaight had charge of the state library, which burned to the ground in the great fire of November 9, 1881, that destroyed the capitol. Fortunately, Spaight's work on his book was under way in another location.

Spaight worked for nearly two years on the project, from April, 1880, until December 1, 1882, when he submitted the final manuscript to Governor Roberts. He states in his letter of transmittal that "there is not a paragraph in this report that was not prepared by myself" and that no part of it was "inspired by self-interest of local attachment." He also acknowledges the assistance of Norman G. Kittrell, "who for a period of four months, with unflagging industry, brought his rare aptitude for statistical research to my aid in the compilation of this work."

Adams Herd 2126. Raines, p.193.

195 Spell, Lota Mae (Harrigan) (1885-1972)

MUSIC IN TEXAS: A SURVEY OF ONE ASPECT OF CULTURAL PROGRESS.

Austin, 1936. [No publisher or printer is named].
[12],157pp. Illus. 23cm.
Printed wrappers.

Other issues:
(A). Facsimile reprint. New York: AMS Press, 1973. Same collation.

This privately printed volume has never been supplanted as the basic guide to the music history of Texas. It consists of sections on

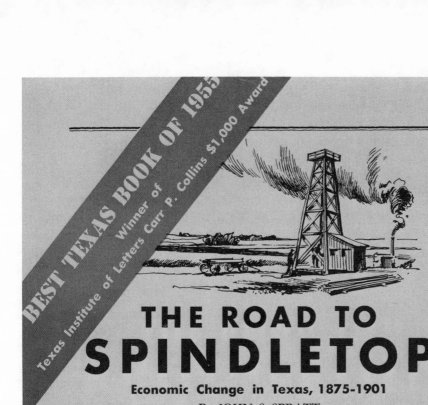

Indian music, Spanish mission music, Mexican folk music, German-Texas music and musicians, Mexican War music, Southern music, music publications in Texas, World War I music in Texas, Texas singing societies, opera in Texas, music education in Texas, symphony orchestras in Texas, Texas folk music, and musical compositions by Texans. The volume is carefully annotated and amply illustrated.

Lota Spell was the daughter of William H. Harrigan, superintendent of Mexican railroads. Born in Big Spring, she was educated in Texas and Mexico, studying music under August Schemmel in San Antonio and at the Grand Ducal Conservatory in Germany. From 1905 to 1910 she was a professional pianist in Europe and Mexico. She also later studied at Virginia Institute, Columbia University, University of Chicago, and received her Ph.D. at the University of Texas. She then became director of the Latin American Library at the University of Texas and editor of three music journals.

Nettie Lee Benson wrote of her: "Lota Spell's linguistic ability in German, French, Italian, Latin, and Spanish, along with her interest in music, led her into research in musical development throughout the western hemisphere, especially in the Southwest and Mexico, and this brought her wide recognition. Her articles appeared regularly in many important quarterlies and reviews, both musical and historical, and she was generous with her time and energy to encourage and assist others who were interested in these fields." Her research papers, manuscripts, and extensive library are now in the University of Texas Archives.

One subsequent work is also useful: Ernest Clyde Whitlock and Richard Drake Saunders, *Music and Dance in Texas, Oklahoma, and the Southwest* (Hollywood: Bureau of Musical Research, 1950). This volume includes about a hundred pages of biographical sketches. There are a number of good books on the cowboy songs, folk songs, and ballads of Texas, especially John A. Lomax, *Cowboy Songs and Other Frontier Ballads* (New York: The Macmillan Co., 1938) and W. A. Owens, *Texas Folk Songs* (Dallas: Southern Methodist University Press, 1950).

196 Spratt, John Stricklin (1902-)

THE ROAD TO SPINDLETOP: ECONOMIC CHANGE IN TEXAS, 1875-1901.

Dallas: Southern Methodist University Press, [1955].
xxix,337pp. Drawings by Ed Bearden. 24cm.
Cloth, dustjacket.

Other issues:
(A). Paperback edition. Austin: University of Texas Press, [1970]. Same collation.
Texas History Paperbacks TH-5.

This is a scholarly study of farming, ranching, and industry in Texas after recovery from the devastating reconstruction years and before the discovery of oil at Spindletop. Robert S. Maxwell called it "a valuable addition to the literature of the recent history of Texas . . . that should become a standard reference." Stuart McGregor deemed it "a permanent contribution" and Wayne Gard called it "an able book that fills a real need." David B. Trimble said "the author has a readable style and has been scholarly in his development of ideas and choice of material; his conclusions and disagreements with other authorities are logically supported, and his approach to his subject is completely dispassionate."

"The purpose of this book," Spratt writes, "is to detect and explore discernible economic trends in the development of Texas during the last quarter of the nineteenth century, and to determine the long-range significance of these long-range indicators. The trends reveal a large degree of metamorphosis in the economic system of the state. . . . This volume does not by any means represent an attempt at a definitive history of the economic growth of Texas during the period considered—or an anecdotal one."

Spratt's work begins with an excellent bibliographical essay (eccentrically entitled "Foreword") of the previous economic writings of the period. He then summarizes the economic conditions in Texas at the end of Reconstruction, and discusses various special subjects in succeeding chapters, including cotton farming, the Grange, the Farmers' Alliance, the railroad commission, labor unions, ranching, and nascent industries. Railroads are given only minor treatment, although he points out that mileage grew from 500 to 10,000 during the period. The important lumber industry and the beginnings of petroleum production are barely treated at all. Seventeen charts in the appendices add to the value of his research.

Spratt concludes: "In 1870, less than half of the State of Texas had been settled, and that by self-contained farmers, while the other half remained a wilderness. By 1900 the entire state had been transformed into an empire with commercial agriculture the prevailing industry." While West Texas could hardly be called a wilderness and while Texas was probably not yet an economic empire in 1900, Spratt is closer to the truth in stating that on "the morning of January 10, 1901, Texas veered sharply toward an industrial economy. The doom of agricultural leadership was sealed at Spindletop."

Stuart McGregor also called the volume "a framework for future historical thinking and writing in a neglected field." While the Spratt work has yet to be superseded, a number of excellent studies of special aspects of the period have been written in recent years, such as Alwyn Barr's *Reconstruction to Reform: Texas Politics, 1876-1906* (Austin: University of Texas Press, 1971) and Billy M. Jones *The Search for Maturity* (Austin: Steck-Vaughn Company, 1965). Notable studies of the economics of large ranching and land development operations have appeared in the M. K. Brown Range Life Series of the University of Texas Press. A number of leading Texas historians have adopted the period for special study and it is likely that many new monographs will be forthcoming.

Adams Herd 2138.

197   Stapp, William Preston (1809-   )

THE PRISONERS OF PEROTE: CONTAINING A JOURNAL KEPT BY THE AUTHOR, WHO WAS CAPTURED BY THE MEXICANS, AT MIER, DECEMBER 25, 1842, AND RELEASED FROM PEROTE, MAY 16, 1844.

Philadelphia: G. B. Zieber and Company, 1845.
164,[4]pp. 19cm.
Printed wrappers; also cloth.

Other issues:

(A). Serialized in full in *Texas Siftings* in 1882.
(B). *The Prisoners of Perote: Story of the Mier Expedition.* [La Grange: La Grange
      Journal, 1933]. 108pp. 20cm. Printed wrappers. A reprint from the 1887-1888 La
      Grange *Journal* newspaper reprint. Textually unreliable.
(C). Exact facsimile of original with additional preliminary title. Austin: The Steck
      Company, 1935. [2],164,[4]pp. 21cm. Original Narratives of Texas History and
      Adventure Series. James M. Day states that 3000 copies were printed, quoting
      Steck editor R. H. Porter verbally, but in a letter to me dated October 28,
      1970, Porter states that 2000 copies were printed.
(D). Reprint. Austin: University of Texas Press, [1977]. xxiv,226pp. Cloth. Foreword
      by Joe B. Frantz.

This was the first book to appear on the Mier Expedition; it is still
one of the best. Stapp was a highly literate private soldier, observant
and interested in what went on around him. His account, written with
no other axe to grind besides the normal contemporary Texas animus
for all things Mexican, contrasts sharply with the other major account,
Gen. Thomas J. Green's *Journal of the Texian Expedition Against Mier.*
Wayne Gard called it "a lively account, with understandable expres-
sions of outrage."

Stapp was born in Kentucky in 1809, migrated with his family to
Texas in 1830. He settled in De Witt's Colony in Gonzales, and served
in the Texas Revolution in the Lavaca Volunteers and in Jacob Eberly's
company. He was well-educated; the book abounds in classical references, as well as literary and musical allusions. He was, however, a
poor speller of contemporary names, such as Bascus for Vasquez,
Loredo for Laredo, Fanning for Fannin, Guerero for Guerrero, and
McCullough for McCulloch.

Stapp begins with a summary of events in Texas from 1836 to 1842,
the Vasquez and Woll expeditions, and the Dawson Massacre. He
joined the Texas forces under Alexander Somervell in October, 1842,
and his first-hand account begins at that point, commencing: "Near
eight hundred of the most gallant spirits of western Texas responded
to the requisition, with whom the author found himself associated in
an enterprise which, however disastrously it afterwards terminated,
wore at its outset the most attractive hues of daring chivalry and high
adventure."

The account continues with vivid but wordy descriptions of the
march to the Rio Grande, the Battle of Mier, the surrender of the
Texans, their imprisonment and attempts to escape, the drawing of

the black beans, the removal to Mexico City, and imprisonment in Perote Prison. Stapp was released on May 16, 1844, at the instigation of his uncle, Gen. Milton Stapp of Indiana, to whom the book is dedicated. Stapp then recounts his stay in Mexico after his release. Much of this latter is paraphrased material from Brantz Mayer's *Mexico as It Was and as It Is,* and lacks the vitality of the rest of the narrative.

Immediately after his return, Stapp began writing his book, primarily during the month of October, 1844. It was published in April, 1845. In addition to the separate reprints, the book was reprinted serially in the LaGrange *Journal* in 1887-1888. An excellent analysis of the book, as well as biographical information on Stapp, appears as a chapter of Dr. James M. Day's fine book, *Black Beans and Goose Quills: Literature of the Texas Mier Expedition.* (Waco: Texian Press, 1970).

Stapp, steeped in romanticism, turns some flowing phrases, as the following eulogy to the greatness of Texas indicates: "The story of her romantic devotion to liberty; the promptness with which she entered upon her seemingly hopeless resistance to oppression; her unshrinking courage and unyielding firmness through the most imminent perils and overwhelming disasters; her romantic generosity in the intoxication of victory, and the glory and lustre of her unaided emancipation from the thraldom of the tyrant, had collectively so dignified and adorned her struggle in the eyes of the world, as to excite an intense and universal solicitude for her welfare. Scarcely had the wisdom of her civil councils perfected the symmetry and order of her institutions, ere the door of the halls of nations was flung open for her admission; and her youthful hands clasped in the glaived embrace of the most august and powerful governments of the earth."

Stapp found little to praise about the Mexicans, and nothing to praise about Santa Anna. In the first paragraph of the book he writes of Santa Anna: "This infuriate Attila brought [the whole Mexican army] to exterminate the gallant opponents of his usurpation and despotism." Another tirade against Santa Anna is a 73-line paragraph of 785 words. He remarks on Negroes in Mexico: "Amongst these swarthy, ill-visaged beggars, we not infrequently noted the ebony visages of runaway slaves from Texas, who find refuge and protection from the philo-negrists of this place."

About Texas and Texans, Stapp states: "To a climate and soil whose salubrity and fertility suffers from any attempt at embellishment. . . . Texas unites a government matchless for the wisdom and liberality of its provisions, reciprocally blessing and sustained by a people, the most chivalrous and generous amongst families of men." On the Alamo: "The heroic Travis and his gallant band of patriot spirits beat back the Mexican dictator with his swarming thousands, until, literally spent with carnage, they piled their immortal forms upon one gory hecatomb, and sunk to sleep in everlasting fame."

Agatha, p.32. Dobie, p.58. *Fifty Texas Rarities* 27. Graff 3949. Howes S891. Raines, p.194. Sabin 90483. Streeter 1610.

198   Sterne, Adolphus (1801-1852)

HURRAH FOR TEXAS! THE DIARY OF ADOLPHUS STERNE, 1838-1851.

Waco: Texian Press, 1969.
Edited by Archie P. McDonald.
xii,[2],169pp. Frontispiece and 4pp. of illus. 23cm.
Cloth, dustjacket.

This diary is one of the most informative and complete that has survived for the period of the Republic of Texas. William Seale called it "the most engaging one of its kind available on the subject of the Texas Republic." Its able editor, Archie McDonald, praised it for "its richness of material, its vividness of description, and its many incisive and human comments. . . . Any modern biographer or historian dealing with its period cannot afford to overlook it."

Adolphus Sterne was one of the most intelligent men in Texas. Born to Jewish parents in Germany, he settled in Texas in the mid-1820's as a merchant. He spoke English, German, French, Spanish, Yiddish, Portuguese, and Latin, and soon was a leader in the Nacogdoches community, acquiring some 16,000 acres of land during the next decade. He supported the Fredonian Rebellion and was captured, tried for treason, sentenced to be shot, imprisoned in chains, and finally reprieved. He was a leader of the revolutionary movement, and as Texas Agent sent several companies of troops to Texas in 1836 at his own expense, including the New Orleans Greys. Sam Houston lived for awhile in his home, and was baptized there. Sterne was serving in the Texas Senate at the time of his death in 1852.

His diaries cover the period from September 28, 1840, through April 4, 1844, and from February 2, 1851, through November 18, 1851. Preserved by the family, they were donated to the Texas State Archives in 1925 by his son, who was at that time the oldest living native Texan. The diaries were first published in the *Southwestern Historical Quarterly* (volumes XXX-XXXVIII) from October, 1926, through January, 1935, edited by Harriet Smither. McDonald states that "Eugene C. Barker is reported to have observed that when they ran out of copy they threw in a little more of the Sterne material. An examination of the installments would seem to indicate that this was not necessarily said with tongue-in-cheek. They vary in length greatly, and there is little coherence of thought in the various installments. Perhaps the most serious defect of the edition was the deliberate elimination of any material considered 'personal' . . . and the accidental deletion of many lines, even entire entries. Not infrequently entries were run under incorrect dates."

Moreover, the diary of James Ogilvy, former partner of printer Samuel Bangs, was initially published in the quarterly as having been written by Sterne. Thus all of the diary attributed to Sterne between November 26, 1838, and January 20, 1840 (*Southwestern Historical Quarterly*, volume XXX, pp.139-155, 219-230, 305-324), is actually the diary of James Ogilvy. Sterne had obtained and retained Ogilvy's diary, and the first entry in Sterne's own diary reads: "Having sometime ago . . . seen my descd Friends Jas Ogilvys Diary & seen, and learnt its usfullness I come to the determination to Keep one. . . ." This error, although caught later and mentioned in a footnote by Smither, has caused embarrassment and grief to historians in the decades since.

Sterne's entries in his diaries are frequently mundane, but as frequently pungent. Writing from Austin on December 10, 1840, he says: "On this Evening Gel [Gen.] Houston was attacked by Col [S. W.] Jordon of the late Federal army and had it not been for my interference Jordon would have killed him with an axe." On July 28, 1841, he writes: "Learnt for the first time to day that old Jimmy gaines Senator Gaines from Sabine County [who ran the famous Gaines

Ferry] has two living wives now in Texas—oh! dear!—he is the man who preaches morality, yes, and he is the man who made a Prisoner of me in february 1827 [Gaines was against the Fredonian Rebellion] . . . and now he is a Senator of the Republic of Texas—the greatest *Traitor* in that Body, the Correspondent of Almonte & Santave, in 1834 & 1835 a Spy upon Texas!—& now—god save the mark—a grave Senator.''

Sterne tells us a great deal not only about people and politics, but about daily life and business as well. On November 8, 1840, he says: ''[A. C.] Dodd paid him in Pear River worthless shinplasters, Dodd obligating himself to [James S.]. Mayfield that said worthless paper was good as Silver . . . all of which has turned out to be a Humbug.'' We only wish he had started his diary earlier. On Christmas Eve, 1840, for example, he tells of ''a Ball this Evening, went off tolerable well, but [not like] our *Old Balls* like we had in 1833, 4 & 5.''

Archie McDonald did an excellent job of editing the diaries for the first book edition. Many errors in the original transcription of the difficult-to-read diaries were corrected, and the text is published exactly as Sterne wrote it with one exception: ''Periods, a punctuation mark apparently unknown to Sterne,'' McDonald states, ''have been included to establish cohesiveness of thought.'' The volume is enhanced by the inclusion of detailed footnotes, but the index is poor. There are a few minor factual errors in the annotations, and a major one in the title, which inexplicably implies that the diaries begin in 1838.

199 Stiff, Edward

THE TEXAN EMIGRANT: BEING A NARRATION OF THE ADVENTURES OF THE AUTHOR IN TEXAS, AND A DESCRIPTION OF THE SOIL, CLIMATE, PRODUCTIONS, MINERALS, TOWNS, BAYS, HARBOURS, RIVERS, INSTITUTIONS, AND MANNERS AND CUSTOMS OF THE INHABITANTS OF THAT COUNTRY; TOGETHER WITH THE PRINCIPAL INCIDENTS OF FIFTEEN YEARS REVOLUTION IN MEXICO: AND EMBRACING A CONDENSED STATEMENT OF INTERESTING EVENTS IN TEXAS, FROM THE FIRST EUROPEAN SETTLEMENT IN 1692, DOWN TO THE YEAR 1840.

Cincinnati: Published by George Conclin, 1840.

[Verso of title:] Cincinnati. Stereotyped by Glezen & Shepard. West Third Street.

367,[1]pp. Folding map. Two plates. 20cm.

Cloth.

Other issues:

(A). *A New History of Texas . . . Down to the Present Time: and a History of the Mexican War, including Accounts of the Battles of Palo Alto, Resaca de la Palma, and the Taking of Monterey.* Cincinnati: G. Conclin, 1847. [6],9-336,[8]pp. 20cm. Cloth. Front cover dated 1846.

(B). Cincinnati: G. Conclin, 1847. 320,[16]pp. 20cm. Cloth.

(C). *. . . Taking of Monterey, the Battle of Buena Vista, with a List of the Killed and Wounded, the Capture of Vera Cruz, and the Battle of Cerro Gordo.* Cincinnati: G. Conclin, [1847]. 244,[74],17pp. 21cm. Cloth.

(D). Cincinnati: G. Conclin, 1847. 246,[74],15pp. 20cm. Cloth.

(E). Cincinnati: G. Conclin, 1848. 254pp.

(F). Cincinnati: G. Conclin, 1849.

(G). *. . . Battle of Cerro Gordo, with an Account of the Late Battles in and Near the City of Mexico: to which is Added the Treaty of Peace with Mexico.* Cincinnati: H. M. Rulison, Queen City Publishing House, 1857. 254pp. 19cm. Cloth.

(H). Facsimile reprint of the first edition. Waco: Texian Press, 1968. [18],367,[1]pp. 21cm. Cloth. Dustjacket. 21cm. Excellent new introduction by Tony E. Duty.

Stiff's work is one of the most controversial guide books written by a visitor to early Texas. C. W. Raines called it "one of the best books on Texas issued during the Republic." Wright Howes called it "one of the objective accounts of Texas affairs issued in the days of the Republic." Thomas W. Streeter commended its "gossipy comments on various named individuals and on life in Texas in general, making it quite an entertaining book." Thomas D. Clark, on the other hand, said it "has little merit." The fairest appraisal is by Tony E. Duty in the introduction to the Texian Press edition of the book:

"Stiff's *The Texan Emigrant* is a well-written, comprehensive guide to Texas which fairly outlined the hardships and privations facing the immigrant to Texas in 1839, as well as his prospects for gaining fame and fortune. It contains errors which are understandable because of the author's necessary reliance upon second-hand-accounts with their misrepresentations and omissions and the reader must also keep in mind that the entire book is heavily slanted toward the Mexican government. . . ."

Little is known about Colonel Stiff except that his title was self-appointed, that he was born in Bedford County, Virginia, and that he was prior to his Texas tour a hatter in Baltimore. He spent what he called his "long sojourn in Texas" in the warmer months of 1839, although Francis Moore, Jr., claimed he was in Texas for sixty days at most. Marilyn Sibley stated in a letter to me that she had learned that "sometime after leaving Texas, Stiff published a newspaper at Cedar Bluff, Cherokee County, Alabama. He shot and killed a man, and ended up in jail in Ashville, Alabama, where he committed suicide by an overdose of laudanum. Along the way, he wrote a pamphlet entitled 'The Assassin of Coosa,' the only [known] copy of which is in the State Department Archives at Montgomery, Alabama. He was buried in an unmarked grave in the Cardon family cemetery near Centre, Alabama."

Stiff's guide is most useful for the light it sheds on such Texas settlements as Houston, which he states consisted of 382 houses and a population of three thousand, of which only about forty were women. He deprecates the moral character of the citizens, pointing out that there were 65 places of business, 47 of which were saloons or gambling houses. Part of his displeasure at the citizenry of Houston may be explained by the fact that he served as Deputy Constable of the town while he was in Texas, and was twice discharged. A review in the *Telegraph and Register,* March 2, 1842, states: "He . . . was discharged from office for drunkenness. He was afterwards (owing to the intercession of a few friends and his own promise to do better) reinstated in office; but a few days afterwards was found drunk and quarrelling in the market, and was promptly discharged from office again by the Mayor."

This also explains why Stiff speaks so disparagingly about Francis Moore, Jr., who was Mayor of Houston at the time, and also explains why the *Telegraph's* review of Stiff's book was so severe, since Moore was also editor of the paper. The review states: "To those Texian emigrants who like *Col.* Stiff emigrated *from* the Republic [of Texas] because they were too vicious and too shiftless to conduct any honest business there, and who derived no other benefit in visiting the country than a *stolen title,* the book may be useful; but to all persons desiring to acquire accurate information relative to the country or its inhabitants it is . . . useless. . . . Indeed, the copy now before us was handed to us by an emigrant, who said he 'bought it at an auction for a bit, and got *bit* at that.' "

Stiff's viewpoint throughout the book is decidedly pro-Mexican. He castigates the Texas Revolution as having been fought by opportunists who "rebel first and find out the reason afterwards." He gives a totally biased account of the revolution, generally praising Santa Anna except for the Goliad Massacre. He recounts an interview with a female survivor of the Alamo, as well as an account of the Goliad affair related by an escapee. He devotes considerable space to the life and land activities of Gen. Moseley Baker, a minor Texas Revolution figure.

The first edition includes a rather detailed folding map of Texas by George Conklin of Cincinnati and two crude but interesting woodcut plates. These plates, overlooked by Streeter in his bibliography, are of Galveston Bay, with a Texas flag flying, and of the Battle of San Jacinto. Later editions of the book were expanded to include material on the Mexican War.

Bradford 5210. Clark III-244. Graff 3989. Howes S998. Rader 2983. Raines, pp.195-96. Sabin 91727. Streeter 1367.

200 Sullivan, W. John L. (1851-1911)

TWELVE YEARS IN THE SADDLE FOR LAW AND ORDER ON THE FRONTIERS OF TEXAS.

Austin: Von Boeckmann-Jones Co., Printers, 1909.
[8],[3]-284pp. Illus. 21cm.
Cloth.

Other issues:
(A). Facsimile reprint. New York: Buffalo-Head Press, 1966. Verso of title: "Michael Ginsberg, General Editor . . . Buffalo Head Press Books are published by J Bar M Inc. and distributed by James F. Carr, 41 Fifth Avenue, New York." 22cm. Cloth.

These memoirs were written by a sergeant in Company B, Frontier Battalion, Texas Rangers. The author served under Bill McDonald and others between 1888 and 1900, a period for which there are few surviving ranger recollections. The original edition is very rare, and until its reissue in 1966 it was little known to scholars.

Sullivan was born in New York and orphaned at eight years old. His stepfather moved to Arkansas and soon afterwards joined the Confederacy, leaving Sullivan and his brother in the hands of a man who turned out to be a child-beater and thief. Nearby Confederate troops threatened to hang the man, and Sullivan, though still a child, joined their unit. In 1871 he became a Texas cowboy and began moving herds up the Chisholm Trail. Gradually, he fell into law enforcement work, as deputy sheriff and as agent for the Pinkertons. In 1888 he joined Bill McDonald's company of Texas Rangers, serving until about 1900, when he retired to his ranch in West Texas. Shortly afterwards, he accidentally shot himself in the leg, leaving him a semi-invalid. He became doorkeeper at the Texas Legislature and during his later years wrote his autobiography.

His memoirs lack flavor, the wording obviously being provided by a person of more education than Sullivan. Nevertheless, the book provides us with a first-hand account of Texas Ranger activities in West Texas during the 1890's, particularly at Amarillo, Quanah, and El Paso. For some reason, the chapters are not arranged in chronological order, but the dates are accurate enough to suffice. Sullivan chased and captured bank robbers, cattle thieves, murderers, and train robbers, and had his share of gunfights. As ranger sergeant, he was in charge in a number of episodes, although he does not overplay his own role. He was present at the hanging of Bill Longley and at the Fitzsimmons-Maher Fight in El Paso, and did duty with John Selman during the period just after Selman killed John Wesley Hardin. His memoirs include some excellent photographs of the rangers on duty and of various outlaws.

Sullivan's own personality was low-keyed, but he was quite proud of being a Texas Ranger. While arresting a one-armed outlaw who hesitated before surrendering his weapon, he told the man "that I would not hurt a hair on his head for the world if he did not make a play; 'but if you do make a bad break,' I added, 'I will cut you off at your pockets.' " After considering the implications, the man surrendered. In 1896, Sullivan was invited to be marshal and honoree at the cowboy's reunion at San Saba. Quanah Parker was in charge of the Indians. Although "thirty saloons were open day and night" and although one night "about two thousand cowboys bunched up together and commenced firing their sixshooters off in the air," Sullivan says, "I served them four days and nights as an officer and never jailed a single person. The whole town was turned loose to the cowboys and other visitors [including Quanah and his Comanches]. There never was better behavior known in such a large crowd before."

He relates that Quanah Parker had brought his new favorite wife: "Quanah stole this squaw from another Comanche, and his men got mad and deserted him and he went to New Mexico, where he stayed for several months. The Comanche, whose wife was stolen from him, finally wrote to the Chief and told him if he would give him eleven hundred dollars he could keep her and could come back and take charge of his tribe. Quanah at once paid the money, and again became chief of the Comanches. I found Quanah and his men to be easily controlled, and they gave me no trouble whatever."

Adams Guns 2165. Adams Herd 2201. Graff 4027. Howes S1129. Rader 3007.

201 Sweet, Alexander Edwin (1841-1901), and John Armory Knox (1850-1906)

ON A MEXICAN MUSTANG, THROUGH TEXAS, FROM THE GULF TO THE RIO GRANDE.

Hartford, Conn.: S. S. Scranton & Company, 1883.
[Verso of title:] Franklin Press: Rand, Avery, and Company, Boston.
672pp. 23cm. 265 illus. by Armand Welcker.
Pictorial gilt cloth. Also full calf, gilt.
The first state of the first edition contains no page numbers in the Contents section after Chapter XXIII, only "ooo" after each subsequent chapter heading. The 1883 edition is also known with the following imprints on the title page: (1) Houston and St. Louis: T. N. James & Co. (2) Syracuse: Watson Gill. (3) Cleveland: C. C. Wick & Co. (4) Cincinnati: The Cincinnati Book and Bible House. (5) Chicago: C. B. Beach & Co. (6) Philadelphia: Thayer, Merriam & Co. (7) San Francisco: A. L. Bancroft & Co. (8) New York: J. S. Ogilvie Publishing Company.

Other issues:

(A). *Humoristische Reise durch Texas von Galveston bis zum Rio Grande, aus dem Englischen, von Reinhold Teuscher.* Jena: H. Costenoble, 1884. xii,475,[1]pp. 167 illus. 23cm. Cloth.

(B). *On a Mexican Mustang, through Texas, from the Gulf to the Rio Grande.* London: Chatto and Windus, 1884. [2],5-672,1-32pp. 265 illus. 20cm. Cloth.

(C). Chicago and New York: Rand, McNally & Company, Publishers, 1891. 514,[4]pp. 23cm. Cloth.

(D). Same as (C), dated 1892.

(E). Chicago and New York: Rand, McNally & Company, Publishers, no date. (ca. 1901). [6],15-290,[6]pp. 18cm. Pictorial wrappers.

(F). London: Chatto and Windus, 1905. 672pp. "A New Impression, with Two Hundred Sixty-Five Illustrations." On page 672: "Spottiswoode & Co., Ltd., Printers, Newstreet Square, London." 21cm. Cloth.

(G). New York: Ogilvie, 1917. 672pp. Cloth.

This delightful book is the best volume of 19th century Texas humor. Sister Agatha said that "for honest fun and a really good picture of the simple, straightforward cowboy, Sweet and Knox were among our best interpreters. . . . For Texas background and for an introduction into the spirit of early Texas life, the book must be read entire. There is none like it. . . ."

Alex Sweet was born in New Brunswick, and moved in 1849 to San Antonio, where his father became mayor. He studied in New York and Germany, returning in time to serve in the Texas-Confederate cavalry. J. Armory Knox was born in Ireland in 1850 and came to Texas as an itinerant sewing machine salesman. Somehow the two men met and began in 1881 to publish a weekly humor magazine, *Texas Siftings*. Their magazine became world famous, expanding from Austin to New York in 1884 and London in 1887. Contributors included Joaquin Miller, Bill Nye, and Opie Read.

In 1882 they published *Sketches from Texas Siftings,* a book made up of pieces from their magazine. That same year they began serializing in the magazine the stories that would make up *On a Mexican Mustang through Texas.* The book was deliberately intended to offer, in the words of dour C. W. Raines, a "view of the manners and customs in Texas . . . not presented in the orthodox way."

Sweet and Knox, in *Texas Siftings* and in *On a Mexican Mustang* probably did more than any other source towards creating the image of the "typical" Texan. Rather than denying the image of the Texan as a special breed, they did all they could to expand it. For example, they wrote:

"The typical Texan is a large-sized Jabberwock, a hairy kind of gorilla, who is supposed to reside on a horse. He is half alligator, half human, who eats raw buffalo, and sleeps out on a prairie. He is expected to carry four or five revolvers at his belt, as if he were a sort of perambulating gunrack. He also carries a large assortment of cutlery in his boot. It is believed that a failure to invite him to drink is more dangerous than to kick a can of dynamite. The only time the typical Texan is supposed to be peaceable is after he has killed all his friends, and can find no fresh material to practice on. It is also the belief in the North that all the Texans are typical Texans. . . ."

In spite of the irreverence and exaggerations, or perhaps because of them, the work is valuable today for the light it sheds on life in Texas after the Civil War, especially in San Antonio, Houston, Galveston, and Austin. There is also material on cowboys, Indians, outlaws (John Wesley Hardin, the Sutton-Taylor Feud), Mexicans, German settlers, gambling, and politics, as well as a substantial amount of anecdotal Texas history.

One unforgettable section in the book dercribes being given a tour through the Alamo by an "aged gentleman" who gives a graphic but confusing account of the battle. After the tour, Sweet and Knox's traveler comments:

"There are a great many different and conflicting accounts of the battle; so many, in fact, that I, who have heard all of them, or nearly all, am harrassed with doubts about any battle ever having been fought there at all. If what the old residents and the historians say be true, then there is not a spot within a quarter of a mile of the Alamo where Travis did not yield up his life rather than submit to the hireling foe, who would have shot him, anyhow. There is not a hole or corner in the whole building where Crockett . . . did not offer up, with the butt of his rifle, from eleven to seventy-five Mexicans, most of them of high rank. Adding up all the Mexicans the historians have killed, it aggregates a number that is fearful to even think of. I have read every thing that has been invented on the subject, including some very poor poetry I made myself; I have had strangers from the North tell me all about it; and I have come to the conclusion, that, after all, I know very little about the battle of the Alamo.''

Adams Guns 2174. Adams Herd 2217. Agatha, p.52-55. Dobie, p.53. Rader 3024. Raines, p.198. Wright III-5337.

202 Taylor, Nathaniel Alston (1835-1913)

THE COMING EMPIRE; OR, TWO THOUSAND MILES IN TEXAS ON HORSEBACK.

New York, Chicago, New Orleans: A. S. Barnes & Company, [1877].
389pp. plus 2 leaves of adv. Pages 4-5 are incorrectly numbered 6-7. Pages 9-10 are duplicated. 19cm.
Cloth.
The first edition has ''H. F. McDanield and N. A. Taylor'' listed as co-authors.

Other issues:
(A). Reprint, [1878]. Same collation. Contains a few revisions.
(B). New edition, with Taylor as sole author. Dallas: Turner Company, [1936]. xi,[2],383pp. Illus. 20cm. Cloth. Contains six additional essays, pp.364-379, a few textual corrections, an index, and a new preface by Natalie Taylor Carlisle.
(C). Same as (B). Title page imprint covered by a label reading: ''Houston, Texas, M. T. Carlisle.''

This is one of the most pleasant accounts of a traveller through Texas. Frank Dobie said in 1924: ''In addition to being the most delightful of all Texas books of travel, his book contains the most information on the social conditions of pioneer Texans.'' C. W. Raines called it ''quite readable; instructive as well as entertaining.''

There has been a great deal of confusion regarding the authorship of this book. The original edition carried the names of H. F. McDanield and N. A. Taylor as joint authors, and the last paragraph of the introduction reads: ''This little volume is the joint work of two hands, but we have generally used the single pronoun, as one is less cumbersome than two.'' Most bibliographies, then and now, list both as authors and a few have attributed the trip and journal to McDanield. The 1936 edition, however, omits McDanield altogether and deletes the last paragraph of the introduction.

Actually, McDanield had nothing to do whatsoever with the trip or the writing of the book. Taylor needed financial help to publish the book and McDanield agreed to underwrite publication only upon the condition that his name should appear as joint author—and before Taylor's at that. Taylor made the trip and wrote the book. His journals and manuscript in the possession of his descendants offer conclusive proof.

Taylor was born in Wake Forest, North Carolina, and grew up in a prominent family. His daughter states that "it was his lot to be often in the presence of some of America's greatest men," among whom were Lewis Cass and Thomas Hart Benton. He attended Wake Forest, the University of Virginia, the University of North Carolina, the University of Pennsylvania (where his uncle was president), and the New York College of Law, receiving five degrees including doctorates in philosophy and law. During his subsequent literary career he wrote for five New York dailies and for *Scribner's, North American Review,* and *Southern Literary Messenger,* mostly under the initials "N.A.T." He moved to Texas in 1859, settling near Boerne. His daughter says he "served also as Texas Ranger and Indian fighter; his body bore arrow scars from wounds received in conflicts." During the Civil War he served in Hawpt's Cavalry Regiment, later known as the 21st Texas Dismounted Cavalry under Polignac, rising to the rank of colonel and adjutant-general. After the war he worked for various Texas newspapers, including the Dallas *News,* Houston *Post,* and Galveston *News.*

In 1875, Taylor became a stockholder in Texas Western Railway, projected to connect with the southern route to the Pacific. At the company's instigation, he made a tour to study the proposed route from Houston to Presidio del Norte. He left Houston on January 2, 1876, on horseback. "My paraphernalia," he says, "consisted of one extra blouse, a haversack, a pocket map and compass and spy-glass; my arms of a pocket-knife." He travelled through San Felipe, Lockhart, New Braunfels, San Antonio, Boerne, Mason, Fort McKavett, Fort Concho, Presidio del Norte, and across the Rio Grande, covering almost a thousand meandering miles by horseback, then by stage to Fort Davis and Austin, and by railroad back to Houston.

The value of Taylor's narrative is in his observations on the people and places he visited. Intensely curious, he had a knack of getting strangers to open up to him. On a creek near La Grange he got a young man to tell him the legends of Strap Buckner (Aylett C.

Buckner). He got close-mouthed German farmers to talk endlessly of life on the frontier. Soldiers, both white and black, at the outposts accepted him into their confidence. Taylor reflects on the geology, geography, agriculture, industry, botany, and society of each place visited. Almost every day of his trip westward he regales us with something humorous he saw or heard.

Throughout the book, Taylor makes glowing predictions for the future of Texas, of which some are prescient and some far-fetched. Of the former, his predictions regarding oil in Texas were later remarked upon when the Corsicana and Spindletop fields came in. Taylor also had pet prejudices. Ralph Steen commented on one of these: "His most pronounced prejudice is directed at the cattleman. In his opinion the cattleman, through long association, assumes the qualities and characteristics of a Texas steer. The sheepman, on the other hand, copies the lamb and lives a life that is 'chaste, beautiful, and refined.' There are many people in Texas who will challenge this theory."

A fascinating volume for comparison is Ellen Bowie Holland's *Gay as a Grig: Memories of a North Texas Girlhood* (Austin: University of Texas Press, 1963, 161pp.), which includes a section containing letters written home to Britain by her uncle, William Bowie, who makes perceptive comments on life in Texas in the 1870's.

Clark I-140. Dobie, p.52. Howes M81. Raines, p.143.

203 Texas Folklore Society Publications

    I. Thompson, Stith [ed.]. *Publications of the Folk-Lore Society of Texas: Number I.* Austin, 1916. 111pp. 25cm. Printed wrappers. On back wrapper: "Press of Morgan Printing Co., Austin, Texas. Reprint edition under title of *Round the Levee,* Austin, 1935. [6],111pp. with new preface by J. Frank Dobie.

    II. Dobie, J. Frank [ed.]. *Publications of the Texas Folk-Lore Society, Number II.* Austin, 1923. 110pp. 23cm. Printed wrappers. Reprint edition under title of *Coffee in the Gourd,* Austin, 1935. [6],110pp., with new preface by Dobie.

    III. Dobie, J. Frank [ed.]. *Legends of Texas.* Austin, 1924. x,[2],279pp. 24cm. Printed wrappers; also cloth. Verso of title: "University of Texas Press, Austin."

    IV. Dobie, J. Frank [ed.]. *Publications of the Texas Folk-Lore Society, Number IV.* Austin, 1925. 133pp. 23cm. Printed wrappers; also cloth.

V. Dobie, J. Frank [ed.]. *Publications of the Texas Folk-Lore Society, Number V.* Austin, 1926. 190pp. 23cm. Printed wrappers.

VI. Dobie, J. Frank [ed.]. *Texas and Southwestern Lore.* Austin, 1927. 259pp. 23cm. Cloth. Verso of title: "University of Texas Press, Austin."

VII. Dobie, J. Frank [ed.]. *Follow de Drinkin' Gou'd.* Austin, 1928. 201pp. 23cm. Cloth. Verso of title: "University of Texas Press, July, 1928."

VIII. Dobie, J. Frank [ed.]. *Man, Bird, and Beast.* Austin, 1930. 185pp. 23cm. Printed wrappers; also cloth. Verso of title: "University of Texas Press, Austin."

IX. Dobie, J. Frank [ed.]. *Southwestern Lore.* Dallas: Published . . . by the Southwest Press, [1931]. v,[1],199pp. 23cm. Printed wrappers; also cloth.

X. Dobie, J. Frank [ed.]. *Tone the Bell Easy.* Austin, 1932. 199,[1]pp. 23cm. Printed wrappers; also cloth. Verso of title: "Printed by the University of Texas Press, Austin."

XI. Dobie, J. Frank [ed.]. *Spur-of-the-Cock.* Austin, 1933. 112,[1]pp. 22cm. Printed wrappers; also cloth. Verso of title: "Printed by the Capital Printing Company, Inc., Austin."

XII. Dobie, J. Frank [ed.]. *Puro Mexicano.* Austin, 1935. [6],v-x,261pp. 23cm. Cloth.

XIII. Dobie, J. Frank, and Mody C. Boatright [eds.]. *Straight Texas.* Austin, 1937. [10],348pp. 23cm. Cloth. Verso of title: "Published by the Steck Company, Austin."

XIV. Dobie, J. Frank, Mody C. Boatright, and Harry H. Ransom [eds.]. *Coyote Wisdom.* Austin, 1938. [6],5-300pp. 23cm. Cloth, dustjacket.

XV. Dobie, J. Frank, Mody C. Boatright, and Harry H. Ransom [eds.]. *In the Shadow of History.* Austin, 1939. iv,[2],187pp. 23cm. Cloth.

XVI. Dobie, J. Frank, Mody C. Boatright, and Harry H. Ransom [eds.]. *Mustangs and Cow Horses.* Austin, 1940. xi,429pp. 23cm. Cloth, dustjacket.

XVII. Dobie, J. Frank, Mody C. Boatright, and Harry H. Ransom [eds.]. *Texian Stomping Grounds.* Austin, 1941. [8],162,[1]pp. 23cm. Cloth.

XVIII. Boatright, Mody C., and Donald Day [eds.]. *Backwoods to Border.* Austin and Dallas, 1943. [4],vii-xv,[1],235pp. 23cm. Cloth. J. Frank Dobie, General Editor. Verso of title: "Printed in the U.S.A. by The Steck Company, Austin."

XIX. Boatright, Mody C., and Donald Day [eds.]. *From Hell to Breakfast.* Austin and Dallas, 1944. [4],vii-x,215pp. 23cm. Cloth. J. Frank Dobie, General Editor.

XX. Boatright, Mody C. *Gib Morgan: Minstrel of the Oil Fields.* [El Paso], 1945. [6],ix-xi,[1],104pp. 23cm. Cloth. J. Frank Dobie, General Editor. Verso of title: Printed at El Paso by Carl Hertzog.

XXI. Boatright, Mody C. [ed.]. *Mexican Border Ballads, and Other Lore.* Austin, 1946. vii,[1],140pp. 23cm. Cloth. Verso of title: "Printed by Capital Printing Company, Inc., Austin."

XXII. Boatright, Mody C. *The Sky Is My Tipi*. Dallas: Southern Methodist University Press, 1949. [4],vii-ix, [1],243pp. 24cm. Cloth, dustjacket.

XXIII. Owens, William A. *Texas Folk Songs*. Austin and Dallas, 1950. [4],8-302pp. 28cm. Cloth, dustjacket. Mody C. Boatright, General Editor. Musical Arrangements by Willa Mae Kelly Koehn. Verso of title: "Printed . . . by Mid-State Printing Co., Jefferson City, Missouri."

XXIV. Hudson, Wilson M. [ed.]. *The Healer of Los Olmos and Other Mexican Lore*. Austin and Dallas, 1951. ix,[1],139pp. 24cm. Cloth, dustjacket. Mody C. Boatright, General Editor. Preface by J. Frank Dobie. Verso of title: "Printed . . . by Von Boeckmann-Jones Company, Austin."

XXV. Boatright, Mody C., Wilson M. Hudson, and Allen Maxwell [eds.]. *Folk Travelers: Ballads, Tales, and Talk*. Austin and Dallas, 1953. vi,[2],261pp. 24cm. Cloth, dustjacket. Verso of title: "Printed . . . by Wilkinson Printing Company: Dallas, Texas."

XXVI. Boatright, Mody C., Wilson M. Hudson, and Allen Maxwell [eds.]. *Texas Folk and Folklore*. Dallas: Southern Methodist University Press, 1954. xv, [1],356pp. 24cm. Cloth, dustjacket. Verso of title: "Printed . . . by Wilkinson Printing Company, Dallas."

XXVII. Boatright, Mody C., Wilson M. Hudson, and Allen Maxwell [eds.]. *Mesquite and Willow*. Dallas: Southern Methodist University Press, [1957]. viii,203pp. 24cm. Cloth, dustjacket. Verso of title: "Wilkinson Printing Company, Dallas, Texas."

XXVIII. Boatright, Mody C., Wilson M. Hudson, and Allen Maxwell [eds.]. *Madstones and Twisters*. Dallas: Southern Methodist University Press, [1958]. x,169pp. 24cm. Cloth, dustjacket. Verso of title: Printed . . . by Wilkinson Printing Company, Dallas."

XXIX. Boatright, Mody C., Wilson M. Hudson, and Allen Maxwell [eds.]. *And Horns on the Toads*. Dallas: Southern Methodist University Press, [1959]. x,237pp. 24cm. Cloth, dustjacket. Verso of title: "Printed . . . by Wilkinson Printing Co., Dallas."

XXX. Boatright, Mody C., Wilson M. Hudson, and Allen Maxwell [eds.]. *Singers and Storytellers*. Dallas: Southern Methodist University Press, 1961. [6],298pp. 24cm. Cloth, dustjacket. Verso of title: "Printed by Wilkinson Printing Company, Dallas."

XXXI. Boatright, Mody C., Wilson M. Hudson, and Allen Maxwell [eds.]. *The Golden Log*. Dallas: Southern Methodist University Press, [1962]. vi,168pp. 24cm. Cloth, dustjacket. Verso of title: "Printed . . . by Wilkinson Printing Company, Dallas."

XXXII. Boatright, Mody C., Wilson M. Hudson, and Allen Maxwell [eds.]. *A Good Tale and a Bonnie Tune*. Dallas: Southern Methodist University Press, [1964]. vi,274pp. 24cm. Cloth, dustjacket.

XXXIII. Hudson, Wilson M., and Allen Maxwell [eds.]. *The Sunny Slopes of Long Ago*. Dallas: Southern Methodist University Press, [1966]. viii,[12],[3]-204pp. 24cm. Cloth, dustjacket.

XXXIV. Hudson, Wilson M. [ed.]. *Tire Shrinker to Dragster.* Austin: The Encino Press, 1968. vi, [2],248pp. 24cm. Cloth, dustjacket. Verso of title: "Designed by William D. Wittliff."

XXXV. Hudson, Wilson M. [ed.]. *Hunters & Healers: Folklore Types & Topics.* Austin: The Encino Press, 1971. ix,[3],171,[1]pp. 24cm. Cloth, dustjacket. At end: "Printed by Capital Printing Company."

XXXVI. Hudson, Wilson M. [ed.]. *Diamond Bessie & The Shepherds.* Austin: The Encino Press, 1972. vii,[3],158pp. 24cm. Cloth, dustjacket. Verso of title: "Design: William D. Wittliff."

XXXVII. Abernethy, Francis Edward [ed.]. *Observations & Reflections on Texas Folklore.* Austin: The Encino Press, 1972. viii,[2],151,[2]pp. 24cm. Cloth, dustjacket. At end: "Printing: Capital Printing Company."

XXXVIII. Abernethy, Francis Edward [ed.]. *The Folklore of Texan Cultures.* Austin: The Encino Press, 1974. xxxi,[1],366pp. 24cm. Cloth, dustjacket.

XXXIX. Abernethy, Francis Edward [ed.]. *Some Still Do: Essays on Texas Customs.* Austin: The Encino Press, 1975. xx,153,[3]pp. 24cm. Cloth, dustjacket. At end: "Capitol [sic] Printing Company."

XL. Abernethy, Francis Edward [ed.]. *What's Going On? (In Modern Texas Folklore).* Austin: The Encino Press, 1976. xi,[3],309pp. 24cm. Cloth, dustjacket.

XLI. Abernethy, Francis Edward [ed.]. *Paisanos: A Folklore Miscellany.* Austin: The Encino Press, [1978]. ix,[3],180pp. 24cm. Cloth, dustjacket.

XLII. Abernethy, Francis Edward [ed.]. *Built in Texas.* Dallas: E-Heart Press, [1980]. 276pp. Cloth, dustjacket.

XLIII. Abernethy, Francis Edward [ed.]. *Legendary Ladies of Texas.* Dallas: E-Heart Press, 1981. xii,224pp. 27cm. Cloth; also wrappers.

XLIV. Abernethy, Francis Edward [ed.]. *T for Texas: A State of Folklore.* Dallas: SMU Press, 1982. xiii,277pp. Cloth.

XLV. Abernethy, Francis Edward [ed.]. *Folk Art in Texas.* Dallas: SMU Press, 1985. 203pp. Cloth.

XLVI. Abernethy, Francis Edward [ed.]. *Sonofagun Stew.* Dallas: SMU Press, 1985. 171pp. Cloth.

XLVII. Abernethy, Francis Edward [ed.]. *Hoein' the Short Rows.* Dallas: SMU Press, 1987, 184pp. Cloth.

The most comprehensive assemblage of folklore relating to Texas, this is also one of the longest running series of books published in Texas. In 1907, George Lyman Kittredge of Harvard urged John A. Lomax to found a branch of the American Folklore Society in Texas. In 1909, at the instigation of Lomax and L. W. Payne, Jr., the society was formally created, with Payne as first president and Lomax as secretary. There were sixty-six charter members. In 1910 a circular was published announcing the aims of the society, and in 1912 a pamphlet by W. H. Thomas was issued entitled *Some Current Folk-Songs of the Negro.* Except for the American Folklore Society itself, the Texas Folklore Society ranks as the oldest folklore organization in the United States.

The first volume of the series appeared in 1916, after which World War I intervened. With the addition of J. Frank Dobie to the society's ranks, publications were resumed in 1923 and continued annually, with a few exceptions. Membership included a copy of the annual publication. In 1937, Mody Boatright joined Dobie as editor of the series, and Harry H. Ransom was added a year later; in 1943, Dobie resigned and left the general editorship to Boatright, who guided the series for the next two decades. In 1953, Wilson M. Hudson and Allen Maxwell joined Boatright as editors. In 1963, Boatright resigned and Hudson became editor until 1971, when Francis Abernethy took over. The headquarters of the society seems to have followed its editors from Austin to Dallas to Austin to Nacogdoches to Waco.

During the years when no annual publication was issued, the society sent its members some other noteworthy book with a printed "in lieu of" notice inserted. These included J. Frank Dobie's *Coronado's Children;* Mody C. Boatright's *Tall Tales from Texas* (Dallas: Southwest Press, 1934); William A. Owens' *Swing and Turn: Texas Play-Party Games* (Dallas: Tardy Publishing Co., 1936); Solomon A. Wright's *My Rambles as East Texas Cowboy, Hunter, Fisherman, Tie Cutter* (Austin: Texas Folklore Society, 1942); Roy Bedichek's *Adventures with a Texas Naturalist;* Americo Paredes' *With His Pistol in His Hand* (Austin: University of Texas Press, 1958); Mody Boatright's *Folklore of the Oil Industry* (Dallas: SMU Press, 1963); Jack and Anna Kilpatrick's *Friends of Thunder* (Dallas: SMU Press, 1964); Francis Abernethy's *Tales from the Big Thicket* (Austin: University of Texas Press, 1966); and Martha Emmons' *Deep Like the Rivers* (Austin: The Encino Press, 1969).

The folklore volumes contain not only folklore and folk tales, but contributions on Texas and Southwestern history, ethnology, linguistics, biography, music, and dance. The volumes contain articles by several hundred leading Texas authors, and as a rule are both interesting to read and scholarly contributions as well. Some of J. Frank Dobie's best writings appear in these volumes. Almost all of the volumes have gone through repeated printings, and most of the early volumes were issued in both cloth and in printed wrappers. In 1973, James T. Bratcher published *Analytical Index to Publications of the Texas Folklore Society* (Dallas: Southern Methodist University Press, 1973,

322pp.), one of the most comprehensive indices ever published in Texas, covering the first thirty-six volumes of the series. In addition to the annual publications and substitute volumes, the society published two separate series: the Range Life Series under Dobie's direction and Paisano Books under Hudson's direction. The society also issued a few pamphlets on special subjects.

204 [Texas. General Land Office]

AN ABSTRACT OF THE ORIGINAL TITLES OF RECORD IN THE GENERAL LAND OFFICE.

Houston: National Banner Office—Niles & Co., Printers, 1838.
182pp. (page 90 is skipped in the numbering). 32cm.
Self-wrappers.
1000 copies printed.

Other issues:
(A). *Abstract of Land Certificates, Reported as Genuine and Legal, by the Travelling Commissioners Appointed under the "Act to Detect Fraudulent Land Certificates,"* Passed January, 1840. Austin: Cruger & Wing, Printers, 1841. 356pp. 29cm. Plain wrappers.

(B). *Abstract of Land Claims, Compiled from Records of the General Land Office of the State of Texas* . . . Galveston: Printed at the Civilian Book Office, 1852. 610,[2],16,[2]pp. 22cm. 200 copies printed.

(C). Burlage, John, and J. P. Hollingsworth [comps.]. *Abstract of Land Claims, Compiled from the Records of the General Land Office and Court of Claims of the State of Texas.* Austin: Printed by John Marshall & Co., at the State Gazette Office, 1859. vi,[1],670pp. 25cm. Half calf.

(D). *Abstract of Titled and Patented Lands, Compiled from the Records of the General Land Office, of the State of Texas: Arranged by Counties, Embracing All the Lands in the State, Titled and Patented Prior to the First Day of December,* 1859. Austin: Printed by John Marshall & Co., State Printers, 1860. [2],1600pp. 21cm. Two volumes, paged continuously.

(E). *Abstract . . . Supplement . . .* Austin: Printed by William B. Harkness, 1862. 348pp. 18cm. Supplement to (D), covering December 1, 1859, to January 1, 1862.

(F). *Abstract . . . [Supplement] . . .* Austin: State Gazette Office, by Jo. Walker, State Printer, 1867. 234 [actually 243]pp. 27cm. Boards. Supplement to (D), covering January 1, 1862, to December 31, 1866.

(G). *Abstract . . . [Supplement] . . .* Austin: Printed by J. G. Tracy, State Printer, 1871. 513pp. 20cm. Supplement to (D), covering January 1, 1867, to August 31, 1871.

(H).   *Abstract of Land Titles of Texas, Comprising the Titles, Patented, and Located Lands in the State* . . . Galveston and Austin, 1878-1902. 25 volumes.

(I).   *Abstract of All Original Texas Land Titles Comprising Grants and Locations to August 31, 1941.* Austin: General Land Office, Bascom Giles, Commissioner, 1941-1942. 8 volumes. Also *Supplements A-H,* 1945-1979.

(J).   Facsimile reprint of first edition. Austin: The Pemberton Press, 1964. 182pp. Preface by Mary Lewis Ulmer.

A virtual Domesday Book for Texas, this is one of the essential research tools on Texas lands and their settlement. It comprises a listing of all persons granted title to land in Texas, with date of grant, location, amount of land, and other details. Thomas W. Streeter called it "one of the fundamental sources of information on the settlement of Texas." Mary Lewis Ulmer said of it: "While collectors of Texana, landsmen and historians will value this book, all Texas genealogists . . . will find it especially desirable. It should be the first source checked in the search for Texas ancestors."

The original edition of 1838 was the first attempt to gather together the valid land titles of Texas. It includes data on the various Mexican empresario grants, up to the Texas Revolution in 1836, when all land grants were frozen. The grantees are grouped under the empresario responsible, with separate sections, each with its own title page, on the grants of Stephen F. Austin; Talbot Chambers for Milam's Colony; Jose Antonio Navarro for Green DeWitt's Colony; George W. Smyth for the Provisional Government of Texas in 1835; grants by the Commissioners at Nacogdoches, 1791-1835; Charles S. Taylor for the Provisional Government of Texas, 1835-1836; George A. Nixon for the colonies of Burnet, Vehlein, and Zavala; William H. Steele for Robertson's Colony; Jose Antonio Navarro special grants in DeWitt's Colony and Bexar district; and titles issued by Samuel May Williams, Francis W. Johnson, and Robert Peebles under Coahuila y Texas grants. The earliest grant is dated October 18, 1791, to an Indian trader named Edward Murphy, and the latest is dated February 27, 1836, to William Fairfax Gray. Only eight complete copies are known out of the original edition.

The 1841 edition records over twenty thousand Texas landowners, listed by counties, with many details. This is probably the nearest to a census of the Republic of Texas that exists. Gifford White compiled, from the 1840 tax rolls in the Texas State Archives, an interesting comparison volume with the slightly misleading title *The 1840 Census of*

the Republic of Texas (Austin: The Pemberton Press, 1966), listing the
land holdings and personal property of nearly eleven thousand Texans.

Later editions were published as more and more of the Texas public
lands were put up for sale or granted for service. Most of these
editions list grantees by county. The Burlage and Hollingsworth edition
of 1859 is especially useful because it is arranged alphabetically by
grantee.

Victoria H. Newsom, a research specialist at the General Land
Office, compiled *Imprints on Texas History: An Annotated Bibliography of
General Land Office Publications, 1836-1975* (Austin: General Land Office
1976), which is useful for the various publications concerning Texas
lands and land titles. The best guide to using all the various Texas
legal resources is Marian Boner, *A Reference Guide to Texas Law and
Legal History: Sources and Documentation* (Austin: University of Texas
Press, 1976). Benjamin F. Pauls *Republic of Texas Second Class Headrights,
March 2, 1836-October 1, 1837* (Houston: Privately Printed, 1974) is an
alphabetical guide to land office records covering over 5000 grants
made during that period. For earlier land records, an excellent study
is Virginia H. Taylor, *The Spanish Archives of the General Land Office of
Texas* (Austin: The Lone Star Press, 1955), with a 107-page appendix
listing 4200 names of original grantees. Thomas Lloyd Miller's *Bounty
and Donation Land Grants of Texas, 1835-1888* is entered here separately.

205   Thorpe, Thomas Bangs (1815-1878)

OUR ARMY ON THE RIO GRANDE, BEING A SHORT
ACCOUNT OF THE IMPORTANT EVENTS TRANSPIRING
FROM THE TIME OF THE REMOVAL OF THE "ARMY OF
OCCUPATION" FROM CORPUS CHRISTI, TO THE SURREN-
DER OF MATAMOROS; WITH DESCRIPTIONS OF THE BAT-
TLES OF PALO ALTO AND RESACA DE LA PALMA, THE
BOMBARDMENT OF FORT BROWN, AND THE CEREMONIES
OF THE SURRENDER OF MATAMOROS: WITH DESCRIP-
TIONS OF THE CITY, ETC.

Philadelphia: Carey and Hart, 1846.
[Verso of title:] Stereotyped by Jos. C. D. Christman. T. K. & P. G. Collins,
Printers.

[2],ix,[10]-300pp. Illus. 18cm.
Printed wrappers; also cloth.

Other issues:
(A). Variant issue, ending with page 196, omitting the official reports.

This book, although hastily prepared, contains a wealth of eyewitness material relating to the Mexican War along the South Texas border. Most of the illustrations are from drawings made by Thorpe himself. As a supporter and political ally of Gen. Zachary Taylor, many official doors were opened to him. Through this and two other books by Thorpe, Taylor received the national prominence that led to his election as President. Milton Rickels states of the book: "The writing itself shows signs of haste in composition, both in language and structure, but the narrative generally moves easily and is lively and colorful."

Thorpe writes: "In the spring of 1844, pending the negotiation for the annexation of Texas, two regiments of infantry, and one of dragoons, constituting *a corps of observation,* were concentrated near the Sabine, by order of President Tyler. The command of this corps was entrusted to Gen. Taylor, who was instructed, in general terms, to protect Texas from Mexican invasion during 'the negotiation.' In the midsummer of 1845 the army of observation was augmented . . . and denominated the 'Army of Occupation'. . . . On the 3d of August the whole . . . had landed at St. Joseph's island, in Corpus Christi bay, near the mouth of the Nueces. About the middle of August a document was found among some wrecked goods on the shores of Aransas bay, which proved to be a war proclamation of the Mexican government. . . . On the 13th of January, 1846, Secretary [of War] Marcy, for the president, ordered Gen. Taylor to move his force toward the Rio Grande." Marching overland, Taylor arrived north of the Rio Grande late in March. General Mariano Arista moved northward with a Mexican Army.

In May, Thomas Bangs Thorpe left his editorial offices in New Orleans and sailed for the Rio Grande, bearing dispatches for General Taylor. After arriving at Taylor's camp, Thorpe remained as a war correspondent for the New Orleans *Daily Tropic,* of which he was part owner. George W. Kendall, editor of the New Orleans *Picayune,* also came to report on the ensuing campaign. Hostilities began on the Texas side of the Rio Grande with the battles of Palo Alto and Resaca de la Palma on May 8 and 9, resulting in the precipitous retreat of the Mexican army.

Thorpe states: "The author was among those who were deeply excited by the stirring incidents connected with our little army on the Rio Grande, in the months of April and May, 1846, and he was on the battle fields, and among the heroes, almost immediately after the occurrences that have rendered them immortal in the history of the country. The idea of writing the following little volume, was suggested by the accumulation of materials, collected for the transient purpose of varying the columns of a daily paper." Thorpe acknowledges the aid and assistance of Gen. E. P. Gaines and Gen. William J. Worth.

In June Thorpe returned to New Orleans to write his book on the campaign. He began sending Carey and Hart parts of the manuscript as early as June 16, and on June 25 wrote to them: "I believe I shall give you one of the most readable books of the season. . . . I have been over the whole ground . . . kept a voluminous journal etc. . . . I shall have the only descriptions of the battles and subsequent scenes ever published." His friends in the military continued to provide him with official reports. In early October, 1846, the book was released.

The volume is marred by Thorpe's conventional attitude towards the war and his blind acceptance of American manifest destiny. The Americans meet battle "with eyes flashing with enthusiasm, and a proud consciousness of coming victory," and are "children of destiny . . . the passive instruments in the hands of an overruling power to carry out its great designs." Palo Alto is a "scene singularly thrilling and sublime." Nevertheless, Thorpe gives us the best picture of the Texas arena of the Mexican War even though coming through the eyes of a fervent believer in its validity. The first 196 pages are Thorpe's narrative in 23 chapters, interspersed with quotations from participants, followed on pages 197-240 with a wealth of "official reports" and on pages 241-293 with "despatches of Gen. Taylor, previous to actual hostilities," the latter covering the period July 20, 1845-April 22, 1846.

Thorpe subsequently published *Our Army at Monterey* . . . (Philadelphia: Carey and Hart, 1847), a sequel covering that siege, and including material on Texas troops, and a campaign work, *The Taylor Anecdote*

Book: Anecdotes and Letters of Zachary Taylor (New York: D. Appleton, 1848). All three works were heavily plagiarized by other writers on the Mexican War. This fact, combined with Thorpe's nationwide repute as a humorist, short story writer, and artist, gave his works perhaps a more influential role than has previously been recognized. There is a very good biography of Thorpe by Milton Rickels, *Thomas Bangs Thorpe: Humorist of the Old Southwest* (Baton Rouge: Louisiana State University Press, 1962, 275pp.).

Haferkorn, p.53. Howes T236. Rader 3121. Raines, p.204. Sabin 95665.

206   Tyler, Ronnie Curtis (1941-   )

BIG BEND: A HISTORY OF THE LAST TEXAS FRONTIER.

Washington: Office of Publications, National Park Service, U.S. Department of the Interior, 1975.
xi,[1],288pp. Illus. Maps. 24cm. Pictorial wrappers.
Other issues:
(A).   Reprint, 1984. Same collation. National Park Service Handbook 128.

This is the best account of the history of the *despoblado,* the uninhabited land. John R. Jameson called it "a thoroughly researched and well-written history of the Big Bend region. It should satisfy both the specialist and the layman for the author knows his complex subject, one which has frustrated some of the historians of the Southwest." Mitchell Wilder said it "is in the best traditions of Western history. His narrative combines an understanding of the region's physical setting with a clear description of its exploration and settlement. . . . [It] brings us a new vision of the Mexican boundary and the startling world of the Big Bend."

The volume was prepared in cooperation with the National Park Service and the Amon Carter Museum of Western Art. This collaboration made available a wealth of early maps and photographs which greatly enhance the book. The photographs of Ansel Adams, W. D. Smithers, and Robert T. Hill and maps and lithographs from the various government boundary surveys are supplemented by the stunning modern photography of Bank Langmore. Many of these are reproduced in full color.

For a barren region deemed uninhabitable, the Big Bend has nevertheless had an extraordinarily exciting history. Tyler's lambent narrative recounts the numerous explorations of the region, beginning with the Spanish *entradas* in the 16th century, and tells the manner in which the Pueblo tribes and the Plains Indians adapted to the region, the Comanches making a virtual highway through it. This Comanche War Trail, wrote Col. Emilio Langberg during the 1850's, was "wider than any 'royal road'" and "so well beaten that it appears that suitable engineers had constructed it." After the Spanish had failed to tame the region, various Texans and American military men tried. These included expeditions by Jack Hays, Samuel Maverick, William H. Emory, Joseph E. Johnston, and many others. The boundary survey teams found the great gorges of the Rio Grande both beautiful and treacherous.

Finally, when the Southern Pacific reached Alpine in 1882, the region was opened for mining and ranching. Even then, permanent settlements were few. Well into the 20th century, the area was subjected to repeated depredations by Mexican bandidos, such as Pancho Villa. Texas Rangers and Federal cavalry had to establish semi-permanent stations to protect the scattered populace. In the 1930's, Amon Carter and others led the movement to create a national park out of the region. The Big Bend National Park, roughly the size of Rhode Island, remains today "the last of the Texas frontier."

Two other books of value have been written on the Big Bend: Mrs. O. L. Shipman's *Taming the Big Bend*, entered here separately, and Carlysle G. Raht, *The Romance of Davis Mountains and Big Bend Country* (El Paso: The Raht Books Company, 1919, 381pp.). The other major national park in Texas is described in Pete Gunter, *The Big Thicket: A Challenge for Conservation* (Austin: Jenkins Publishing Company, 1971, 172pp.).

207   Urrea, Jose (1779-1849)

DIARIO DE LAS OPERACIONES MILITARES DE LA DIVISION QUE AL MANDO DEL GENERAL JOSE URREA HIZO LA CAMPANA DE TEJAS.

MEXICO AND TEXAS.*

THE publications at the bottom of this page, relative to the
campaign in Texas, are from three of the most influential of the
Mexican leaders on that memorable occasion, and appeared almost simultaneously. They are all calculated to throw a light
upon the transactions of the period in question, and important on
account of the various official documents by which they are illustrated; but there are circumstances that give to the first of these
pamphlets a peculiar interest. This contains a plain, unvarnished,
and soldier-like exposition of the events of the campaign, and,
among others, of the massacre of Fanning and his unhappy companions in Goliad, the whole odium of which dark affair is shown
to attach solely to Santa Anna. This aroused the hero of Tampico
in his quiet retreat of Manga de Clavo, near Vera Cruz, which he
characterizes in his pamphlet as "el termino di mi carrera publica"
(the termination of his public career.) Some, however, there were,
sceptic enough to doubt the sincerity of this declaration, and the
appearance of General Urrea's Diary has shown the reasonableness
of such a surmise. Had General Santa Anna really considered
his public career as terminated, and been as philosophically indifferent to the future, as he has professed to be, Urrea's pamphlet
would have raised no emotion in his bosom. Such, however, was
not the case. No sooner did the publication make its appearance,
than Santa Anna and his partisans make every effort to suppress it,
and so effectually have they succeeded in doing it, that the copy
before us was obtained only by a happy manœuvre. This fact will
lead the reader to conclude that, in spite of all Santa Anna's pro-
testations to the contrary, he is not so indifferent to public opinion,
as he would fain have the world believe, and that, consequently, he
may, as yet, be induced to recal the assertion, "that his public
career is closed."

* Diario Militar del General Jose Urrea, durante la Primera Campana de Tejas.—
Victoria de Durango, 1838.

(Military Diary of General Jos. Urrea, during the first Texas Campaign.)

Manifesto que de sus Operaciones en la Campana de Tejas, y en su Cautiverio
dirige a sus conciudadanos, el General Antonio Lopez de Santa Anna—*Vera
Cruz*, 1837.

(Manifesto of operations in the Campaign in Texas, and of his captivity, addressed to his fellow-citizens by General Antonio Lopez de Santa Anna.)

Esposician de los operaciones en la Campana de Tejas, del General D. Vicente
Filisola.—*Mejico*, 1837.

(Exposition of operations in the Campaign of Texas, by General D. Vincent
Filisola.)

Victoria de Durango: Imprenta del Govierno a Cargo de Manuel Gonzales, 1838.
136pp. 20cm.
Printed wrappers; also full morocco.

Other issues:

(A). Castaneda, Carlos E. *The Mexican Side of the Texas Revolution by the Chief Mexican Participants* . . . Dallas: P. L. Turner Company, Publishers, [1928]. vii,391pp. 24cm. Cloth. Contains a translation by Castaneda of the *Diario* on pages [204]-283 but omits the lengthy note on page 23 of the original, all of the 55 original documents occupying pages 53-127 of the original, and the postscript on pages 128-135 of the original. First edition in English.

(B). *Documentos para la Historia de la Guerra de Tejas.* Mexico: Editorial Nacional, 1952. Printed wrappers. Limited to 500 numbered copies. Includes a complete facsimile reprint of the original edition.

(C). Facsimile reprint of (A). Dallas: P. L. Turner Company, Publishers, [1956]. Same collation. 23cm. Cloth.

(D). New edition of (A). Austin and Dallas: Graphic Ideas Incorporated, Publishers, 1970. xi,402pp. 22cm. Pictorial cloth. "This edition changes the original only by minor corrections, a new index, and the addition of new illustrations." The Urrea text occupies pages [210]-291.

Written by the perpetrator of the Goliad Massacre, this is a fundamental work on the Texas Revolution. Edward Eberstadt called it "a rare and important diary of the military operations conducted by Gen. Urrea after he took over Filisola's command, and a prime source for the massacre of Fannin's men." Urrea makes a blistering attack on his arch-enemy, Vicente Filisola, and places the blame for the Goliad Massacre squarely on Santa Anna, who he claims ordered the massacre.

The work begins with an attack on Filisola and the "animosity, undisguised petulance, and baseness" of his *Representacion,* followed by Urrea's diary from January 9, 1836, through June 1, 1836, and a further defence of his actions, dated Durango, August 19, 1837, against the charges levelled by Filisola. Urrea then presents 55 official letters of the campaign dated from November 25, 1835, through August 26, 1836, and a postscript quoting from Martinez Caro's *Verdadera Idea.* The narrative is so vituperative as to be obviously usable only with caution. The documents include a number of important letters unavailable elsewhere, as well as some that have frequently been reprinted. Some of the latter differ greatly from Urrea's version, leading to the conclusion that he altered the texts whenever it was in his interest to do so. On the other hand, Urrea charges Santa Anna with the same crime, claiming he misquoted orders to Urrea in his *Manifesto que de Sus Operaciones* in order to make it appear that Urrea ordered the massacre of Fannin's men on his own volition. On the whole, Urrea's account is about as reliable as Filisola's in most respects, except where the two are charging each other with crimes, and more reliable than Santa Anna's or Martinez Caro's.

General Urrea claims that Santa Anna's orders "with regard to the fate decreed for the Fannin prisoners were very emphatic" and states that "I wished to elude these orders as far as possible." He quotes from a junior officer, Nicolas de la Portilla, who states that Urrea ordered the men to be saved but Santa Anna overruled him. To get any clear picture of this My Lai-type controversy, it is necessary to compare the accounts of Santa Anna, Filisola, Martinez Caro, Urrea, and others—and even then, there is room for doubt.

Urrea was appointed general-in-chief of the Mexican forces on June 8, 1836, shortly after retreating across the Rio Grande, and removed from command in early September. By this time, Filisola had been able to convince the war department of his innocence in ordering the general retreat from Texas. In 1838, Filisola published *Analisis del Diario Militar del General D. Jose Urrea* (Matamoros, 1838, 180pp.), which is far more extensive than the work he is attacking. It has never been translated in spite of being one of the most important sources on the Texas campaign. Urrea and Filsola remained bitter enemies throughout the rest of their lives. Urrea died about the time Filisola's *Memorias* were published, so Filisola had the last word.

In the *United States Magazine and Democratic Review* (volume III, no. X, October, 1838, pp. 132-145) there is a fascinating article entitled "Mexico and Texas" which compares and quotes extensively from the accounts of Urrea, Filisola, and Santa Anna. The editors state that "there are circumstances that give to the [Urrea] pamphlet a particular interest. This contains a plain, unvarnished, and soldier-like exposition of the events of the campaign. . . . No sooner did the publication make its appearance, than Santa Anna and his partisans make every effort to suppress it, and so effectually have they succeeded in doing it, that the copy before us was obtained only by a happy manoeuvre."

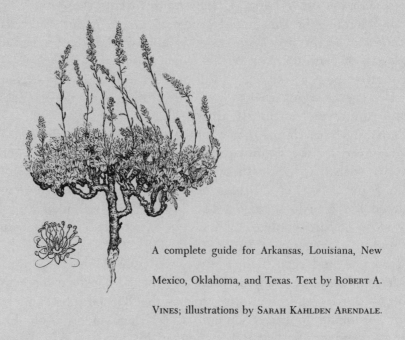

A complete guide for Arkansas, Louisiana, New Mexico, Oklahoma, and Texas. Text by ROBERT A. VINES; illustrations by SARAH KAHLDEN ARENDALE.

TREES, SHRUBS, AND WOODY VINES OF THE SOUTHWEST

Accurately describes and superbly illustrates more than 1200 species of native and naturalized woody plants. Twenty-five years of labor went into this monumental work.

1116 pages   1240 drawings $25.00

University of Texas Press 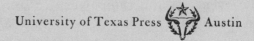 Austin

It is true that only a handful of copies of Urrea's *Diario* have survived, and apparently none got to Texas at an early date. If any had, it is likely that it would have been translated and published at the same time that the Bordens issued their translation of Filisola's *Representacion*.

Clark III-251. Graff 4448. Howes U31. Rader 3516; Raines, p.208. Sabin 98152. Streeter 940.

208   Vines, Robert A. (1907-   )

TREES, SHRUBS, AND WOODY VINES OF THE SOUTHWEST.

Austin: University of Texas Press, 1960.
xii,1104pp. 29cm.
Cloth, dustjacket.
Drawings by Sarah Kahlden Arendole.

Other issues:
(A). Second printing, 1969. Same collation.
(B). Third printing, [1972]. Same collation.
(C). Fourth printing, 1976. Same collation.
(D). Fifth printing, [1981]. Same collation.
(E). Sixth printing, [1986]. Same collation.

This is one of the outstanding contributions to the botany of Texas. A review in *American Forests* states: "This monumental work, describing 1231 species of woody plants, with 1240 illustrations, is an incredible achievement in the history of natural science publishing. It is an immense production, indispensable to naturalists of the region."

Vines states in regard to his twenty-five year project: "Some of the problems encountered in the preparation of the book may be of interest to the reader. In order to gain a firsthand knowledge of the plants in the field, the author has traveled more than 250,000 miles by auto- mobile. Areas inaccessible by automobile were reached by foot and on horseback. Collecting plants in the dry regions of the Southwest is not always an easy matter, for much of the area is desert-like and mountainous. Owing to the failure of some plants to produce flowers and fruit in especially dry years, collecting trips to certain areas had to be deferred for as long as several years, until rainfall restored the depleted ground moisture."

The book was initially intended to cover only Texas. B. C. Tharp explains that Vines ultimately discovered that "a great majority of

Texas plants crossed the state line into adjacent states whose climate was similar. Further investigation revealed that the number of species found in adjoining states, but not in Texas, was comparatively few. It thus became evident that they might be included without unduly increasing the length of the book, and without materially altering the original emphasis on Texas.'' For this reason, the work was expanded to include Louisiana, Arkansas, Oklahoma, and New Mexico. Howard S. Irwin, author of *Roadside Flowers of Texas,* spent a year reworking the text.

The volume is divided into 102 chapters, each chapter representing a different plant family. Both native and naturalized plants are included, naturalized plants being ''those which, after being introduced into an alien region, have escaped cultivation and have continued to reproduce themselves.'' One of the outstanding features of the book is the inclusion of heterogeneous data concerning the uses to which the plants, and combination of the plants, can be put. These include uses as building materials, food, condiments, cosmetics, medicines, fibers, oils, and waxes. Suggestions are also given as to methods of aiding propagation.

B. C. Tharp unwisely attacked the book when it was published on the grounds that Vines made a ''deliberate and intentional failure to use devices long cherished by professional taxonomists as essential to plant identification'' and that he ''provides an abundance of material detail meriting professional dissent and adverse criticism.'' He claimed its best use would be by ''average intelligent laymen . . . to browse interestedly through its pages of an evening.'' The work, however, has been since widely accepted by professionals and laymen alike, and has been regularly reprinted, an almost unheard-of event for a thousand-page scientific text.

The University of Texas Press has issued two of a series of field guides by Vines, each ''drawn from Robert A. Vines' monumental *Trees, Shrubs, and Woody Vines of the Southwest* which contain new and updated information with full descriptions of every tree in the area.'' These are *Trees of East Texas* and *Trees of North Texas.* Until this series is complete, the accepted popular guide remains *Forest Trees of Texas,* 8th edition, 1963, published for the Texas Forest Service by Texas A & M.

**209 A VISIT TO TEXAS, BEING THE JOURNAL OF A TRAV-
ELLER THROUGH THOSE PARTS MOST INTERESTING TO
AMERICAN SETTLERS, WITH DESCRIPTIONS OF THE
SCENERY, &C. &C.**

New York: Goodrich & Wiley, 124 Broadway, 1834.
[Verso of title:] Mahlon Day, Printer, 374 Pearl-Street.
iv,[9]-264,[4]pp. 4 plates. Folding map in color by W. Hooker. 19cm.
Cloth.

Other issues:
(A). Same title as above, continuing: *Second Edition. With an Appendix, Containing a
Sketch of the Late War.* New York: Van Nostrand and Dwight; Mobil: Woodruff,
Fiske, and M'Guire, 1836. xi,[1],262pp. 14cm. Cloth. No map or plates. Verso
of title: "Scatcherd and Adams, Printers, 38 Gold Street."
(B). Facsimile reprint of first edition. Austin: The Steck Company, [1952]. 19cm.
Cloth, boxed.
(C). Facsimile reprint of first edition. [New York:] Readex Microprint, [1966]. 19cm.
Cloth. With a new unsigned 3-page Foreword.
(D). Facsimile reprint of first edition. Ann Arbor: University Microfilms, [1966].
19cm. Cloth. March of America Facsimile Series No. 70.
(E). *A Visit to Texas in 1831: Being the Journal of a Traveller Through Those Parts Most
Interesting to American Settlers, with Descriptions of Scenery, Habits, etc.* Houston:
Cordovan Press, 1975. xv,184pp. Illus. Folding map. 23cm. Edited by Robert
S. Gray. Limited to 1000 numbered copies, signed by Gray.

This anonymous work is one of the most important accounts of
Texas during a critical period in its history. Homer S. Thrall called it
"a vivid picture of the country and its resources." C. W. Raines
called it "a very rare book, containing a readable sketch of Texas."
Thomas W. Streeter said it "gives a fresh and interesting picture of
life in Texas at that time." Thomas Clark said it has "fine descriptions
of natural scenery, prairies, some natural history, and an account of
political conditions."

The unknown author of this valuable book arrived in Brazoria,
Texas, in March, 1831, to inspect the country and check on the title to
the lands he had purchased from the Galveston Bay and Texas Land
Company. He made a leisurely journey from Brazoria to Harrisburg,
Anahuac, Galveston Island, and San Felipe. His visit was made just
prior to the trip made by Mary Austin Holley, providing an interesting
comparison to her glowing text. In general, he is considerably more

objective, even caustic, than Mrs. Holley, although he left with a generally high opinion of the prospects for the settlement of Texas. The map by Hooker is a revision of the map in Holley, and the four plates are said to be the earliest sporting scenes of the American West, one being the first to show the art of capturing mustangs. Material from *A Visit to Texas* was stolen without credit by David B. Edward and other writers, and was plagiarized at length by Charles Sealsfield in *The Cabin Book; or Sketches of Life in Texas* (New York, 1844).

The author came to Texas with certificates to 20,000 acres of land. "I had doubtless made a judicious purchase; and in what a country! How nobly would twenty thousand acres look, wherever I might determine to locate my estate! . . . Twenty thousand acres! Twenty thousand acres! What an estate! How many cattle and human inhabitants would it be able to support!" But he found no agent of the company, and no surveyors. He soon came to doubt the validity of his Galveston Bay Company scrip. John Austin, alcalde of Brazoria, told him that he "regarded the certificate I held, and the scrip which it represented, as of no value whatever. He was confident that the government would never recognise the right claimed by the company." The author then vents a considerable amount of spleen against the company, so much so that David Woodman's *Guide to Texas Emigrants* (Boston: M. Howes, 1835) was possibly published to counter the attack; it devotes much space to a refutation.

No one knows who wrote *A Visit to Texas*. Frederick Law Olmsted in *Journey Through Texas* attributes it to one "Fiske." Wright Howes said it may have been written by a Col. Morris or a Dr. M. Fiske. No satisfactory reason for either of these attributions has ever been given. There is an excellent book written by Asahel Langworthy, who came to Texas about the same time as the unknown author, and he has been suggested as a possibility. Langworthy's book is entitled *The Constitution of the Republic of Mexico . . . with Sundry Other Laws . . . Relating to Coahuila and Texas . . . with a Description of . . . That Interesting Country* (New York: Ludwig & Tolefree, 1832). This is a rare and useful compilation of documents relating to Texas colonization.

Marilyn Sibley in her splendid study, *Travelers in Texas, 1761-1860,* writes: "A similarity of content between this book [*A Visit to Texas*] and the pamphlet attributed to Asahel Langworthy suggests that the same person wrote both. Both, for example, include at the end a detailed meteorological chart covering the period from March 1 to September 20, 1831, and kept at Anahuac . . . [Langworthy's] seven pages of subjective description touch many subjects considered in *A Visit to Texas*. The visits of both writers centered about Galveston Bay and Texas Land Company operations at Anahuac; both mention John Davis Bradburn and David Gouverneur Burnet; both link Jean Lafitte with Galveston Island; and both comment on a steam mill at Harrisburg, where the owner was selling lumber at forty dollars per thousand feet. Furthermore, both writers were Northerners who hated cold weather and were enchanted by the Texas climate."

Unfortunately, this attribution is unlikely, although possible. Certainly, both men were in Texas at the same time, and saw many of the same things and many of the same people, but there the similarity stops. Their writing styles differ considerably, as does their spelling. Langworthy has "Camanches" and the other has "Comanches." Langworthy uses "prairie" and the other uniformly uses "Prairie." Langworthy hyphenates New-Orleans, the other does not. Langworthy has Brassoria, Guadalope, St. Felipe, Arrasansas, and Rio-del Norte; the other has Brazoria, Guadaloupe, San Felipe, Aransaso, and Rio Bravo. Langworthy capitalizes Mustang; the other has mustang. Langworthy invariably leaves out the "c" in "Mc", spelling names as M'Gloin and M'Mullin; the other has McNeil, etc. It is, of course, possible that these differences were due to two different editors, except that neither work appears to have had the benefit of an editor.

Langworthy speaks of Stephen F. Austin, Esquire, and simply of "Austin"; the other uniformly refers to him as "Col. Austin." More importantly, Langworthy refers repeatedly to "Major David G. Burnet" and "Major Burnet"; the anonymous author calls him David S. Burnet and Mr. Burnet throughout, and calls him "a new settler from New Jersey." Langworthy says Major Burnet has travelled extensively through Texas, and quotes a lengthy letter from Burnet written in 1830 which begins: "Having spent two years in Texas . . ."

Both authors print a weather chart giving the daily weather at Anahuac from March through September, 1831. This is indeed striking coincidence, although the later author could merely have cribbed it from Langworthy's pamphlet. Not even this is possible, however,

because upon examination one finds that the two charts differ substantially. On March 5, Langworthy has the weather as "rain" and
the other has "pleasant." On March 29, Langworthy has it "clear"
and the other has it "cloudy & high wind." On April 17, Langworthy
has "showers" and the other has "pleasant and calm." Their temperature readings differ almost every day: for March 16, Langworthy has
morning-noon-evening readings as 52-56-59 and the other has 48-63-
62. Langworthy left Texas for the United States on May 16, so he
could not have kept the chart included in his book.

Langworthy wrote to Stephen F. Austin from New York on January
5, 1831 (*The Austin Papers*, II, 575) that he owned 100,000 acres of Texas
land. The anonymous author states he owned 20,000 acres. On March
7, 1831, Langworthy was on the schooner *Angelia* anchored off Galveston
Bay, about to sail for Matamoros (*Ibid.*, 607). The anonymous author
sailed directly from New Orleans to Brazoria on the sloop *Majesty* and
first sighted Galveston Island on March 12, sailing past without
stopping. There is still another problem with the attribution to
Langworthy: in late 1834 or early 1835, Langworthy died. Samuel
Swartwout wrote to Sam Houston on May 18, 1835, that Mrs.
Langworthy had begun to "administer upon her late Husband's
estates." Swartwout's description of Langworthy's land dealings in
Texas, as well as the Langworthy pamphlet itself, make it clear that
Langworthy had nothing against the Galveston Bay Company, and
that his own holdings in Texas were purchased from Jose M. Carbajal
and not from the land company. He may actually have become an
agent for the company. The other author, on the other hand, is
downright libelous in his antagonistic remarks about the Galveston
Bay Company, and a lawsuit was threatened by the company against
a reviewer who supported the denunciation, forcing a retraction. It
might be added that Burnet was deeply involved with the company,
and that he and Langworthy were obviously close friends. Finally, if
Langworthy wrote the book and then died early in 1835, who wrote
the 1836 edition, which is enlarged and includes an account of the
Texas Revolution?

Consequently, we must reluctantly conclude that, enticing as are
the coincidences, unless further evidence appears we must look for
someone other than Asahel Langworthy as author of *A Visit to Texas*.

I doubt very much that it was anyone named Fiske, but I have no hint as to who actually wrote it.

Bradford 5374. Clark III-114. Graff 1336. Howes T145. Jones 962. Rader 357. Raines, pp.83 and 210. Sabin 95133. Streeter 1155.

210   Walton, William Martin (1832-1915)

LIFE AND ADVENTURES OF BEN THOMPSON, THE FAMOUS TEXAN, INCLUDING A DETAILED AND AUTHENTIC STATE-MENT OF HIS BIRTH, HISTORY AND ADVENTURES, BY ONE WHO HAS KNOWN HIM SINCE A CHILD.

Austin: Published by the Author, 1884.
Printed by Edwards and Church, Newsdealers.
[8],[5]-229pp. 15 woodcut plates by J. F. Eaton. 17cm.
Pictorial wrappers.

Other issues:
(A).   Bandera: Frontier Times, 1926. 104pp. 27cm. Printed wrappers.
(B).   Houston: Frontier Press of Texas, 1954. [2],5-232pp. Illus. 22cm. Cloth. Verso of title: "1000 copies of this book were printed August, 1954, by Scardino Printing Company, at Houston, Texas." Omits Walton's preface and the original illustrations but includes a five-page section of new illustrations at the end of the book.
(C).   Facsimile reprint of first edition. Austin: The Steck Company, 1956. 229,[1]pp. 21cm. Boards, boxed. The original illustrations appear in color, of which an inserted leaflet states: "Carol Rogers, a talented Austin artist, added the color, using an 1884 style." 2500 copies printed, of which 2100 were given away and 400 offered for sale.

This is the life story, taken from his own lips, of one of the most notorious lawmen and gunmen who ever lived. William F. Kelleher said that "probably no man, before or since, crowded more excitement into forty-three years of life than did Ben Thompson." Floyd Streeter, mentioning Hickok, Earp, Masterson, Hardin, and Billy the Kid, stated: "While every one of these men was brave beyond question and made an excellent record, Ben Thompson was the most dangerous in deadly combat with a pistol . . . He engaged in more deadly encounters with a pistol than any other gunman then living and won every battle but the last. This record made him the most feared fighter of his day.'' Bat Masterson, in 1907, stated: "It is doubtful if in his time there was another man living who equalled him with a pistol in a life-and-death struggle.''

W. M. Walton was a prominent attorney in Texas before and after the Civil War, being partner at one time with Gov. A. J. Hamilton and briefly with Gov. E. M. Pease. He was a colonel in the Confederate army, and attorney general of Texas in 1866. In his short book of Civil War reminiscences, *An Epitome of My Life* (Austin: Waterloo Press, 1965), he says: "I suppose no lawyer in Texas or in the South has defended more men charged with murder than I have . . . Success usually attended me. I do not say this as a vain glory—but state it because it is the simple truth.'' He had known Ben Thompson since Thompson's first trial for murder, at the age of thirteen, in Austin in 1856. Walton (along with Dudley G. Wooten and others) also defended Thompson at his 1882-1883 murder trial in San Antonio.

In 1882, while Thompson was city marshal of Austin and Walton a leading criminal lawyer, the two men began working on the story of Thompson's life. When Thompson was gunned down in San Antonio two years later, Walton completed the text and had it printed. In the preface, he states: "Some two years ago the life of Thompson was written. Much of what was written was taken from his own lips, and the foregoing preface prepared. Thompson never had the mss. published, but let it rest. His life from that time has been hurriedly, but, in the main, correctly sketched, and the whole is now given to the public. His wife and children will receive largely of all sales that are made.''

Very few copies were printed and even fewer sold. For some reason the book, unlike many other gunmen paperbacks, did not go through the process of dozens of cheap pulp reprints. Ramon Adams states: "I can remember when a copy of the original paperback could be bought for ten cents from a bushel basket that sat in front of an Austin, Texas, bookstore [Gammel's]. Now this book is exceedingly rare.''

Ben Thompson's life was a continuous string of shoot-outs that left more men dead than Billy the Kid would have been able to count. Pardoned by Governor Runnels after going to prison for his teenage killing, he became a printer in New Orleans. There he had his most celebrated fight, voluntarily locking himself in an unlighted icehouse to fight a man to the death with Bowie knives. He became a professional gambler back in Austin. When the Civil War broke out he joined John R. Baylor's command, killed another man at Fort Clark, escaped, joined another command, fought in the Battle of Galveston, served in the Louisiana campaign, was furloughed, joined Rip Ford's command in South Texas, killed some more men, and escaped.

After the war he was arrested and imprisoned, escaped, joined Emperor Maximilian's forces in Mexico, returned, stood trial, and was acquitted. He moved to Kansas and opened a gambling house, became a lawman for a railroad, engaged in numerous gunfights, returned once more to Austin, and became city marshal. So great was the fear of him that during his term not one single murder occurred in the town. Never able to keep out of trouble, he killed a man in San Antonio, resigned his office, stood trial, and was once again acquitted. A little over a year later, he and King Fisher went back to San Antonio and were both killed in what is generally assumed to be a hired killing, although the argument still rages over what actually happened.

The amazing feature of his career is that he always had prominent supporters. On the first page of the text, obviously written before Thompson's death, Walton gives a defence lawyer's view of Thompson: "The subject of this sketch is now in his thirty-seventh year . . . modest and retiring in demeanor, speaks gently, is a handsome, generous man . . . and although it has been his fate or fortune to repeatedly take human life, it has ever been done in self-defence." Andy Adams, who knew him well, said: "Ben Thompson was a chivalrous gentleman, game to the core and well-liked." James B. Gillett said he always "seemed to be the friend of the underdog in a fight." The editor of his hometown newspaper, even after Thompson had shot up his printing room and ruined much of his type, said "he had a heart which beat in kindly sympathy." When he was finally killed, the whole town turned out for his funeral, not to gawk but to do him honor.

Walton's narrative, which in effect is Thompson's autobiography, is therefore the most important record of this contradictory man. It is naturally sympathetic, but it presents the case for Thompson with factual accuracy even though its conclusions are biased in his favor. It is perhaps the most important contemporary account of any Western gunman.

There is a modern biography by Floyd Benjamin Streeter: *Ben Thompson, Man with a Gun* (New York: Frederick Fell, 1957, 217pp.). It contains many additional facts on Thompson's career, but is marred by misspelled names, incorrect dates, and other minor errors.

Adams Guns 2302. Adams One-Fifty 142. Dobie, p.121. *Fifty Texas Rarities* 47. Graff 4527. Howes W82. Rader 3584. Raines, p.212.

211   Warner, Charles Albert (1894-   )

TEXAS OIL AND GAS SINCE 1543.

Houston: Published by the Gulf Publishing Company, [1939].
vii,487pp. Illus. 23cm.
Cloth, dustjacket.

Other issues:
(A). Facsimile reprint. [Austin: R. W. Byram & Company, 1966]. Same collation. "Limited edition reprinted from the first edition, for the centennial celebration of the first Texas oil well."

The most extensive and detailed statistical treatment of the oil industry in Texas, this monograph was written by a prominent petroleum engineer and geologist who had worked in the oil industry in Texas since 1917. Ernest O. Thompson states in the Foreword: "It is high time that we had a dependable text on Texas oil and gas. C. A. Warner has now supplied that need in a most thorough and dependable work. He has performed the task in a painstaking manner, and this book will be a valuable addition to the literature of Texas." Walter Rundell called it "the classic history of Texas oil."

The work consists of a 77-page general history of oil in Texas; a 53-page analysis of the economic aspects of the Texas oil industry; a chapter on the geology of oil in Texas; six chapters on the various oil regions of Texas; a section of historical documents; and 104 pages of statistical charts. This is followed by a bibliography of 138 sources, and an index.

Warner spent over a decade gathering the material for his book, which has become the cornerstone of all subsequent research into the Texas oil industry. His approach is basically statistical, and is a work for use in research and study rather than general reading. There are production charts for all oil-producing counties and for the larger oil fields, and a number of geological maps. Between pages 112 and 131 Warner gives a condensed chronology of Texas petroleum history.

The general history in the first section is scholarly and remains the best summary of the subject. Warner attributes the first reference to Texas oil to Cabeza de Vaca, who two days after being wrecked in Texas, "utilized a pitch-like substance found there for repairing the bottoms of the vessels." He recounts at length the gradual realization in the 19th century that oil existed in Texas, through the Spindletop discovery in Beaumont in 1901, "where oil became an industry." He then traces the history of oil and gas development through 1938.

For the social history of the development of the oil industry, Carl Coke Rister's *Oil! Titan of the Southwest* is more anecdotal and more fleshed out than Warner's book. For the Spindletop era, Clark and Halbouty's *Spindletop* is the most interesting. For the West Texas discoveries, the comprehensive study is Samuel D. Myers, *The Permian Basin: Petroleum Empire of the Southwest* (El Paso: Permian Press, 1973, 708pp.). Warner also extended his own narrative in two articles in the *Southwestern Historical Quarterly* in July, 1946, and January, 1958.

212 Webb, Walter Prescott (1888-1963)

THE TEXAS RANGERS; A CENTURY OF FRONTIER DEFENSE.

Boston and New York: Houghton Mifflin Company, The Riverside Press, Cambridge, 1935.
xiv,[2],583,[1]pp. Illus. by Lonnie Rees. Photographs. 24cm.
Cloth, dustjacket.
The photograph on page 565 mistakingly identifies Ray and Arch Miller as being the two men on the right.

Other issues:
(A). Special edition, in half calf and slipcased, with notice: "Two Hundred and Five copies of This First Edition, of Which Two Hundred are for Sale, Are Autographed by the Author and Numbered."
(B). Later printing of first trade edition, "1935" dropped from title page. The photograph on page 565 is corrected to identify Ray and Arch Miller as the second and fourth men in the picture.

The Texas Rangers

by WALTER PRESCOTT WEBB
Foreword by LYNDON B. JOHNSON

First published in 1935, *The Texas Rangers* has been out of print and in continuous demand for many years. Now it is again available in a new edition, with an Introduction by Dr. Webb's friend Lyndon Johnson, and in a handsome dust jacket that reproduces in full color Tom Lea's painting *Ranger Escort West of the Pecos.*

The text remains the same as in Dr. Webb's original edition—just as the psychological makeup of today's Texas Ranger remains unchanged. Reviewing the new edition, Colonel Homer Garrison, Director of the Texas Department of Public Safety and chief of the Texas Rangers, has commented, "Whether they are 5 feet 8 inches tall or 6–5, [today's Rangers] sit tall in the saddle and cast a long shadow. And true to the tradition established by one old Ranger as it is recounted in Dr. Webb's book, they still believe, 'No man in the wrong can stand up against a fellow in the right who keeps on a-comin'.' "

Here, again, is the definitive account of this colorful law-enforcement organization. $10.00*

*Texas residents must add 2-per-cent sales tax to total amount of order.

UNIVERSITY OF TEXAS PRESS   AUSTIN & LONDON

(C). *The Story of the Texas Rangers*. New York: Grosset & Dunlap, [1957]. 152pp. Illus. by Nick Eggenhofer. 29cm. Cloth, dustjacket. First juvenile edition. Abridged.

(D). Reprint of (C), 1963.

(E). Reprint of first edition. Austin: University of Texas Press, [1965]. xx,583pp. 23cm. Cloth, dustjacket. Foreword by Lyndon B. Johnson. Illus. by Tom Lea. Publisher's note states that two poems (objected to by Chicano organizations) have been deleted.

(F). Reprint of (C). Austin: Encino Press, [1971]. 152pp. Illus. 24cm. Cloth. New preface by Terrell Webb.

(G). Reprint of (D). Verso of title: "Eighth Printing of the University of Texas Press Edition, 1980."

This is the most important work on the Texas Rangers. Stanley Walker called it "far and away the best work of its sort ever to come out of Texas." Rupert Richardson said: "Wisely conceived, profusely illustrated, and beautifully written, the book is a fitting monument to a great institution." Henry Steele Commager said that "like all really important books, it transcends its title." William C. Binkley wrote: "From the point of view of the historian the study is important not only for the light which it throws on a particular institution, but also for new clues on various phases of American history in general . . . Patient, painstaking research, a discerning application of the principles of historical criticism, an unusual ability to analyze men and events, and a vigorous, pungent style have been combined to produce an entertaining and scholarly book."

During World War I, Webb was assigned the subject of a history of the Texas Land Office for his master's thesis. Dreading the prospect, Webb one day became aware of the headlines the Texas Rangers were making along the Mexican border, then a hotbed of international intrigue. He went to E. C. Barker and suggested he write about the Rangers instead of the land office; Barker agreed. For the rest of Webb's career, the Texas Rangers were a topic about which he centered much of his study and writings—over fifty titles in the bibliography of his writings relate to the Rangers. In 1920, he submitted his thesis under the title, "The Texas Rangers in the Mexican War," and began working on a complete history of the organization. He later said: "I was off on the first lap of the great adventure, to write the history of the oldest institution of its kind in the world. The story led west, to the frontier, to vicarious adventure of the body, and to real adventure of the mind. Though I was not aware of it then, I had found my field.

"Trailing the Texas Rangers, who had in turn trailed the ancestors of some of the best people in Texas, was a combination of drudgery and fun. It was my first work with sources . . . though the records were abundant, I did not stop with the records. Like Parkman I went to all the places where things had happened. I sought out the old men, still living then, who had fought Comanches and Apaches, killed Sam Bass at Round Rock, and broken up deadly feuds inherited from the more deadly reconstruction. With a captain and a private I visited every Ranger camp on the Mexican border where there were still elements of danger; I carried a commission and had the exhilarating experience of wearing a Colt revolver in places where it might have been useful. At night by the campfires I listened to the tales told by men who could talk without notes."

Webb began to write articles on the Rangers, and then, he recalled, "I stumbled on one of the few original ideas I ever had. As a matter of fact up until that time I never had one. . . . By this time I knew a great deal about the Texas Rangers, their dependence on horses, and their love for the Colt revolver. . . . I was ready for that moment of synthesis which comes after long hours of aimless research to give understanding and animation to inert knowledge." He realized for the first time that in leaving the southern woodlands and entering the plains, the settlers had come upon an entirely new environment requiring adaptations different from all their previous experience. Initially the idea came to him through his realization that the gradual development of the Colt revolver was a response to the new style of horseback warfare of the plains. Excited as never before, he began to chase down other adaptations. "One question I asked over and over, of myself and others: What else happened? What other changes took place? . . . In this chase the Texas Rangers, formerly so exciting, became dull and prosaic fellows, and I cast them aside. . . ."

The chase led to Webb's masterpiece, *The Great Plains* (Boston: Ginn and Company, 1931). An essential book in any Texas or Western collection, it is not included as a separate entry here because its scope is too large to fit the arbitrary criteria established to keep this bibliography in reasonable bounds. It is the most brilliant book ever written by a Texan, and with *The Great Frontier* (Boston: Houghton Mifflin, 1952) made Webb the most influential of all Texas authors. From the moment of realization of the premises of *The Great Plains* until the end of his life, Webb was a scholar, historian, and philosopher of world standing. Nevertheless, in the early 1960's when I got to know him at the Barker Center, in Dobie's back yard, in his course at the university, and over an occasional poker hand, he never stopped asking the questions and never stopped enlarging his perspective.

The Great Plains won the Loubat Prize for the most important contribution in the social sciences over a five-year period. Webb recounted how he learned of the award in 1932: "The editor of our local paper called by phone late at night and our conversation went like this: 'Are you the man that wrote a book called *The Great Plains?*' 'Yes, I wrote it.' 'We have a wire from New York saying that it has been awarded the Loubat Prize.' 'The Loubat Prize? I never heard of the Loubat Prize.' 'Well, don't feel bad about that. I never heard of the book.' "

Eventually, Webb had time to return to the Texas Rangers project. He completed it in 1935, seventeen years after he had started it. My copy of the book has a tipped in letter written by Webb on February 13, 1935, to T. R. Havins in which he states: "You may be interested to learn that I finished the Ranger book this afternoon at 3:15 and that I am pretty tired." Webb took the final manuscript to Boston, where he met Ferris Greenslet, who immediately accepted the work and paid a hefty advance. When the publisher told Webb it would be necessary to issue it in two volumes, Webb refused and shortened the text. Webb later said: "Since *The Texas Rangers* was the only book about Texas that appeared in 1935, Paramount bought it for the Texas Centennial picture of 1936. Paramount made full use of the title, and little else. The picture was quite successful. I am not going to tell you what I got for it in the midst of the depression, but I will say this: what I got made the depresssion more tolerable." The amount he received was eighty percent of $11,000, a hefty sum in 1935.

The book itself aroused some controversy on both sides of the fence. The Houston family threatened a lawsuit over what Webb had said about Sam Houston, and Ferris Greenslet wrote Webb that "a libel suit accompanied by an injunction against the sale of the book would prove a pretty serious business." Nothing came of this threat; however, minority groups objected for decades about Webb's treatment of Mexican-Americans, negroes, and Indians. Edward Everett Dale, reflecting the sentiments of a number of other reviewers, wrote that Webb "shows scant confidence in the people dwelling along the right bank of the Rio Grande and rather less than that in the good faith of their border officials." Even Jack Hays' grandson wrote that Webb had been too harsh on Mexicans. Larry McMurtry said "the flaw in the book is a flaw of attitude. Webb admired the Rangers inordinately, and as a consequence the book mixes homage with history in a manner one can only think sloppy." Webb himself came to agree in part, and for years worked on and planned a revision, chapters of which are in his papers at the University of Texas Archives.

Webb's own opinion of the book may be found in a letter he wrote to Fred Gipson on August 14, 1952, offering to collaborate on a history of the Rangers for young people. Webb told Gipson that *The Texas Rangers* "was quite successful despite its pedestrian documentation. It is straight history, peppered with an abundance of facts, and I think it dependably accurate. Certainly it is not interesting and was not intended to be primarily." Gipson showed some interest, although he had apparently never read the book, for on September 8, Webb sent him a copy at his request, along with a revealing commentary on the book: "What I soon saw in writing, or after research, was that *men* were the keys to the success of the organization. In every generation, almost, some natural leader showed up and it was he who must be credited with the success of the force. Interestingly enough, there are not many of these men. I have been hard pressed to find ten in the century which the book covers. The book is actually organized around these men." Although Gipson never joined the project, Webb rewrote the text into a popular juvenile entitled *The Story of the Texas Rangers,* with illustrations by Nick Eggenhofer.

Llerena Friend wrote an interesting article entitled "W. P. Webb's Texas Rangers" in the January, 1971, issue of *Southwestern Historical Quarterly* (vol. 74, no. 3) and Necah S. Furman recounts much about the writing of the book in *Walter Prescott Webb: His Life and Impact* (Albuquerque: University of New Mexico Press, 1976. 222pp.). Other material may be found in Walter Prescott Webb, *History as High*

Adventure (Austin: Jenkins Garrett Foundation and The Pemberton Press, 1969, 206pp.). A valuable work on the activities of the ranger service that supplements Webb is Dan E. Kilgore, *A Ranger Legacy: 150 Years of Service in Texas* (Austin: Madrona Press, 1973).

Adams Guns 2333. Adams One-Fifty 145. Agatha, p.65. Dobie, p.60. Howes W194.

**213   Webb, Walter Prescott (1888-1963)
and H. Bailey Carroll (1903-1966) [eds.]**

THE HANDBOOK OF TEXAS.

Austin: The Texas State Historical Association, 1952.
Llerena B. Friend, Mary Joe Carroll, and Louise Nolen, Editorial assistants.
Two volumes: xv,[3],977; ix,[3],953pp. 25cm.
Cloth, dustjackets.

[also:]

Branda, Eldon Stephen [ed.].

THE HANDBOOK OF TEXAS, A SUPPLEMENT: VOLUME III.
Austin: The Texas State Historical Association, 1976.
xiv,[2],1145pp.
Cloth, dustjacket.

This is the most important research source on Texas, the one work that is essential for any Texas library. The editors state that "the objective in the compilation of the *Handbook of Texas* was to assemble into one useable, practical, ready-reference work the most significant information about the widest possible range of Texas topics . . . a serviceable and efficient tool which would bring together pertinent facts on a multitude of subjects, many of which, prior to this publication, could be found only in definitive works, great libraries, [etc.]." Walter Muir Whitehill in the London *Times* called it "the best systematic reference work on any of the fifty United States . . . an invaluable tool for the scholar, the journalist, or anyone else." William R. Hogan said it is "the most valuable reference work on Texas and very probably the most complete single compilation of information about any state." Frank Wardlaw said simply, "No other state has anything which is remotely comparable to it. . . . One would have to

buy a thousand books and study them for a lifetime to place at his disposal a comparable amount of information on Texas.''

The project of producing the handbook took twelve years, with more than a thousand people contributing to it. The original set has 15,896 topics; with the supplement, there are over 25,000 topics in over 3000 double-column pages. Virtually every major and minor Texas writer and historian contributed one or more articles to the work. Walter P. Webb predicted that the work ''would be indispensable to every editor, reporter, library, scholar, and teacher in Texas . . . and furnish the starting point for every investigation of things pertaining to Texas history.'' Years later, Joe B. Frantz said: ''Indeed it would, and it has, and it does.''

In the *Southwestern Historical Quarterly* for January, 1933, the executive council of the Texas State Historial Association published a proposal for a ''biographical dictionary'' of Texas to be prepared for the Texas Centennial, but the suggestion was not accepted. In 1939, Webb reviewed the idea and put his prestige and efforts behind a movement to promote the project. The state legislature agreed to help the funding, as did the Rockefeller Foundation. H. Bailey Carroll took over the slow and tedious task of overseeing the compilation of the material and the setting of standards. In 1945, Webb and Carroll issued *A Tentative List of Subjects for the Handbook of Texas,* a 101-page list of 12,605 topics which continued to grow until publication. Webb appeared as editor-in-chief and Carroll as managing editor.

Carlos Castaneda and C. W. Hackett oversaw the articles on the Spanish period, Barker the Mexican period, and others on the areas of their expertise. The advisory council included Herbert Gambrell, L. W. Kemp, Rupert Richardson, Ralph Steen, Ernest Winkler, and other prominent historians. Llerena Friend and Dorman Winfrey carried much of the responsibility. In 1963, the project of a supplement was begun, under the guidance of Joe B. Frantz and Tuffly Ellis, and under the editorship of Eldon Branda. The supplement became a project of the American Bicentennial Commission, and was published in 1976. At the time of this writing, Tuffly Ellis has just issued a call for a decade-long project of a complete revision, to be issued sometime in the 1990's. Until then, the *Handbook of Texas* will remain the bible of research on Texas.

214 Weber, David Joseph (1940-   )

THE MEXICAN FRONTIER, 1821-1846: THE AMERICAN
SOUTHWEST UNDER MEXICO.

Albuquerque: University of New Mexico Press, [1982].
Histories of the American Frontier Series, Ray Allen Billington and Howard R.
Lamar, editors. Foreword by Ray Allen Billington.
xxiv,416pp. Illus. 24cm.
Cloth, dustjacket. 1200 copies printed.
[Verso of title:] First edition.

This is the best interpretation from the Mexican perspective of the
Anglo-American acquisition of Texas and the Southwest. Ray Allen
Billington, who read the manuscript and wrote a foreword for it prior
to his death in 1981, praised the text as "meticulously prepared,
sparklingly written, and brilliantly interpreted. Its perspective will
affect all writing on western history for a generation to come."
Margaret S. Henson wrote: "Not only is there a judicious utilization
of previous studies, but Weber has also amplified earlier findings by
mining archival material to further illuminate certain areas."

The volume is the culmination of Weber's extensive studies of the
Southwest, derived from his previous nine books and numerous articles
on the subject. Grounded in unsurpassed research, it is an interpretation which advances our understanding of Texas during its most
crucial years more than any other work of modern scholarship.
Previous interpretations have mostly been either jingoist apologies or
discussions of manifest destiny. Weber, on the other hand, focuses on
the internal problems within Mexico that created the northern vacuum
in Texas which inevitably led to its loss. Texas and the Southwest, he
maintains, were lost through a neglect that was inextricably interrelated
to events and situations in Mexico itself.

Weber states that "through annexation, conquest, and purchase, the
United States acquired half of Mexico between 1845 and 1854. Within
a few moments in history, Mexico's far northern frontier thus became
a portion of the American West. . . . In general, neither Mexican nor
American historians have sharply illuminated the era. Mexican historians have slighted the history of their nation as a whole during the
first decades after independence . . . [and have] ignored almost entirely

internal developments in the Far North between 1821 and 1846, perhaps because the region no longer belongs to Mexico. This has left United States historians with an open field and they have occupied it with alacrity. United States historians, in general, however, have ethno-centrically shoved their own countrymen to the front of the stage in the events of 1821 to 1846, leaving Mexico and Mexicans, to whom the stage still belonged, to serve as the back drop."

Without question, events in the United States created the westward expansion that burst over the borders of Texas and these events are an essential part of Texas history. They are also the focal point around which the vast majority of interpretations have previously centered— such as in Rives, Smith, Merk, and Pletcher. Weber shifts the center of attention to Mexico. Other writers have treated this aspect, but none have done so with as much perception or synthesis as Weber.

Nearly a third of the volume is devoted to annotations and a bibliographical essay. The latter is especially useful in its careful analysis of both traditional and recent secondary sources, and in its discussion of the wealth of still-virtually-untapped primary materials in Spanish.

215 Weddle, Robert Samuel (1921-)

THE SAN SABA MISSION: SPANISH PIVOT IN TEXAS.

Austin: University of Texas Press, [1964].
Drawings by Mary Nabors Prewit.
xiii,238pp. Illus. 4 maps. Errata leaf inserted. 24cm.
Cloth, dustjacket.

Other issues:
(A). Paperback edition. Texas History Paperbacks TH-12.

This volume clarifies the role played by the Santa Cruz de San Saba mission and the San Luis de las Amarillas presidio in the development of Spanish Texas. David M. Vigness states that this outpost "has fascinated writers for years. Perhaps its attraction lies in this effort by Spaniards to approach the Great Plains using techniques and institutions evolved elsewhere on the northern frontier. More likely, the interest stems from the dramatic and disastrous end to the dream of converting the Plains Indians to Christianity as a means of pacifying and controlling them. Possibly the lure of silver in the hills known as Los Almagres has kept alive the interest, such as the tales told by J. Frank Dobie in his *Coronado's Children*. For whatever reason, there is a growing literature on the Spanish efforts to mount their defenses against the Plains Indians, and the San Saba affair was a highlight in that effort.''

The Spanish established the mission and presidio in 1757, along the San Saba River near present Menard. The next year the mission was attacked by Comanches, who destroyed the mission and massacred ten of its occupants. A few years later the presidio itself was moved to the Nueces River, and in 1772 moved back to the Rio Grande. Although the project failed utterly, its significance as a Plains outpost and the efforts to connect it with silver mines in Texas make it a fascinating study. It was to this site that James Bowie led a silver-seeking expedition, and throughout the subsequent decades up to the present it has been the subject of conjecture and debate.

Weddle has successfully debunked the mythology concerning the silver mines. More importantly, he recounts the history of the project in the context of Spanish objectives in the New World, showing it to be a pivot of Spanish interest in Texas.

George P. Hammond wrote that Weddle, ''a talented writer, found himself in the historic swivel point on the Spanish frontier of Texas where the line of missionary penetration of Central Texas ran up against the wily, resourceful, and numerous foe—the Plains Indians. . . . [The San Saba Mission] marked not only the most distant advance of the Spanish frontier, but it came at the very end of its existence when the king could least afford the new expenditures involved. This is the author's theme. . . . This study is well organized . . . and gives a coherent tale of one spot in the Southwest, a key in an international struggle for mastery of the continent.

Fortunately, there are a sufficiency of original letters, documents, and reports in Mexican and Texan archives to provide a full story of the founding of the mission, life in the outpost, and the final devastation of the project. Some of the best of these were published in a beautiful Lawton Kennedy book, *The San Saba Papers: A Documentary Account of the Founding and Destruction of San Saba Mission* (San Francisco:

Published by John Howell Books, 1959, 157pp.), edited by Lesley Byrd
Simpson and translated by Paul D. Nathan. Weddle himself wrote a
superb account of another Spanish mission: *San Juan Bautista: Gateway
to Spanish Texas* (Austin: University of Texas Press, 1968, 469pp.), which
is an even more important book than his *The San Saba Mission* but is
not included separately here because it deals with a mission located
on the south side of the Rio Grande. It has much Texas interest,
however, especially in its explanation of how the Spanish exploration
and settlement of Texas fit into the general scheme of Spanish military
and ecclesiastical expansion.

216   Wheeler, Kenneth W. (1929-   )

TO WEAR A CITY'S CROWN: THE BEGINNINGS OF URBAN
GROWTH IN TEXAS, 1836-1865.

Cambridge: Harvard University Press, 1968.
[14],222pp. Illus. Map. 22cm.
Cloth, dustjacket.

This fine interpretive monograph analyzes the development of urban
centers in Texas. Robert Cotner said that "this study has resulted
from wide reading in the sources, especially travel accounts and
newspapers, and a judicious use of recent research. . . . The work is
a timely synthesis." Joe B. Frantz wrote: "This book takes a view of
Texas which has not hitherto been followed. William Ransom Hogan's
Republic of Texas made excellent overtures in this direction, but did not
come far enough forward. John Spratt's *Road to Spindletop* hit the
economic beginnings, but was written before urban history became a
fad, as well as overdue. Here in remarkably economic prose, which
moves despite its spareness, the author has broken new ground."

While many Texas historians have concentrated on rural aspects of
early Texas, few have sought to evaluate the development of cities as
such. Using San Antonio, Galveston, Houston, and Austin as examples, Wheeler studies the beginnings of urban history in Texas. When
Texas became a republic, only San Antonio could lay claim to being
called urban. The other villages then in the new republic for the most
part remain villages today. Wheeler shows how the influx of immi-

grants demanded urban centers, and how the four cities in his study developed to fill this need.

It is easy to perceive how the post-war railroads influenced the development of certain cities over others, but Wheeler's study ends just as the railroad era was beginning. His work is therefore especially enlightening in showing the pre-railroad factors that created urban areas that continued to thrive. Not all immigrants to early Texas were Southern farmers, by any means, and many of those from the northern states and from overseas were merchants and skilled craftsmen. Commercial activities developed quickly in the new republic, despite its financial destitution, and urban areas were the result. Houston, Galveston, and Austin were deliberately planned to become great cities, with more foresight and imagination than has generally been acknowledged, and San Antonio set its own special pattern for growth.

Wheeler explains the unique feature of each of the four cities and how these were already markedly evident by the time of the Civil War. "The pattern for early urban development in Texas," he writes, "was formed by the end of the Civil War. Cities would rise on the upper Texas plains [Dallas, Fort Worth, Lubbock, Amarillo], but in the older section of the state none would seriously rival those already established. Galveston, Houston, San Antonio, and Austin had each developed its own particular characteristics and had shaped the design of its future growth. Moreover, by 1865 the permanent relationship between the four was cemented."

A recent book that treats of the rise of economic power in Texas is Randolph B. Campbell and Richard G. Lowe, *Wealth and Power in Antebellum Texas* (College Station: Texas A & M University Press, 1977, 183pp.).

217 White, Charley C., with Ada Morehead Holland.

NO QUITTIN' SENSE.

Austin: University of Texas Press, [1969].
Foreword by Ada Morehead Holland.
xi,[3],216pp. Illus. 23cm.
Cloth, dustjacket.

(A). Same, paperback edition.

There has been only one good book written from the black viewpoint in Texas, and this is it. There is no better book on the life of the rural black in late 19th and early 20th century Texas. Alwyn Barr wrote of it: "The history of black Texans remains largely unresearched or buried in seldom-seen theses and dissertations. The lack of written sources for the history of people who faced enforced illiteracy under slavery and limited education over a lengthy period thereafter has proved a continued problem. Thus a volume of reminiscences such as *No Quittin' Sense* is especially welcome." Wayne Gard said "the narrative embraces, besides a personal triumph, the attaining of harmonious and fair race relations without resort to violence." White's autobiography is a social document unique in Texas literature, yet in many respects universal in the story it relates.

Ada Morehead Holland, a Houston newspaper writer, first heard of the Rev. White in 1964 when she read a short notice of his efforts to distribute food "to needy people of all races." She travelled deep into the Piney Woods of East Texas to find White's church and the smokehouse he called "God's Storehouse," from which he dispensed his congregation's donations to those in need. After meeting him, she realized she had met a man of exceptional intelligence and character, and a man whose story cried to be told. "I bought a tape recorder," she says, "and my husband and I took it to Jacksonville on weekends. At such times we secluded ourselves with the Reverend White in a back room of his house and—while Mrs. White cooked lunch and dinner for us and intercepted all visitors and telephone calls—he told us of the people, places, and conditions he encountered during his childhood, and later during his adult life." She compiled his story into a manuscript, keeping it entirely in his own words and vernacular, and read it through to him several times to get his story exactly the way he wanted it told.

White was born about 1885 in East Texas into a family of poor blacks who scratched out a living so bare that his birthday present one year was "a big fat drumstick, and hadn't nobody eat even one bite off it." Growing up in Possum Trot, near Shelbyville, White had about four years of grade school and then left to become a sharecropper.

Throughout his childhood the most important element in the life of his community was church. He found he had two useful qualities, he could preach and he could trade. As a young married adult, he sharecropped, swapped, preached, and saved. Carefully, slowly, the Whites saved enough to buy their own home. Freed from debt, he decided to devote the rest of his life to helping poor people in need, a calling he followed for the next fifty years.

The white people in White's life, at least as he relates it, seem to have been for the most part kindly and helpful, although it is excrutiatingly clear that blacks in his community were expected to keep to their place. Nevertheless, he writes, "in 1920 a whole bunch of people was running for governor, and Pat Neff and a man named Joe Bailey got in a run-off. . . . They said we all had a right to vote. So I decided to try it. . . . Anyhow, I voted, and I din't have not trouble. And I been voting ever since." By force of character, the Reverend White seems to have established such an abundance of respect in the white community that he made many genuine friendships that lasted throughout his career.

White's story is important in two respects. First, it shows with great clarity and in simple, down-to-earth language what life in Texas was like for millions of blacks after Reconstruction. It records the transition of the children of Freedmen from poverty and neglect through the long decades until the Civil Rights movement of modern times. It is definitely White's story, not Ada Holland's dramatization of it. Second, it records the life of one individual black who succeeded beyond all reasonable expectation in building a rewarding and useful life in an atmosphere not so much of hostility or prejudice as of neglect.

218 Wilbarger, John Wesley (1806-1892)

INDIAN DEPREDATIONS IN TEXAS: RELIABLE ACCOUNTS OF BATTLES, WARS, ADVENTURES, FORAYS, MURDERS, MASSACRES, ETC., ETC., TOGETHER WITH BIOGRAPHICAL SKETCHES OF MANY OF THE MOST NOTED INDIAN FIGHTERS AND FRONTIERSMEN OF TEXAS.

Austin: Hutchings Printing House, 1889.
xii,[2],672pp. 37 woodcuts attributed to William S. Porter. 23cm.
Cloth.

Other issues:

(A). Second edition, 1890. Same collation. [Verso of title:] Illustrated by Owen Engraving Co., Austin.

(B). Facsimile reprint: Austin: The Steck Company, 1935. [4],xii,[2],672pp. Cloth. 2500 copies printed.

(C). Same as (B). Issued in a special slipcase in 1952 with Yoakum's *History of Texas,* of which publisher R. H. Porter states: "Concerning the special combined edition of Yoakum and Wilbarger used as gifts at the governor's conference, there was nothing distinctive except the box. The committee working on the conference wanted to give the visiting governors and dignitaries some books about early Texas. I suggested that a special package be prepared. . . . They were grouped and boxed with a special label." 48 sets issued.

(D). Facsimile reprint. Austin: The Pemberton Press, [1967]. 10,[2],iv,672,[19]pp. Illus. 22cm. Cloth. Volume One in the Brasada Reprint Series, John H. Jenkins, General Editor. New introduction by Dorman H. Winfrey. New index. 600 copies printed.

(E). Facsimile reprint. Austin: Eakin Press and Statehouse Books, 1985. 691pp. New index. Cloth.

This volume is the most thorough compilation of accounts of Indian warfare in Texas in the 19th century. J. Frank Dobie says it "stands unique among pioneer chronicles," and that its narratives "have for generations been a household heritage among Texas families who fought for their land."

John Wilbarger came to Texas from Kentucky in 1837 at the behest of his brother Josiah, who had lived near Bastrop since 1828. He served as a Methodist minister in the Bastrop area and assisted Josiah in surveying activitie. In 1858 Wilbarger County was named for this pioneer family. About 1870 John began actively collecting material for his book.

Wilbarger states that "many of the articles contained in the book were written by others, who were either cognizant of the facts themselves or had obtained their data from reliable sources." Some of the narratives came almost verbatim from articles written by John Holland Jenkins for the *Bastrop Advertiser.* The Bigfoot Wallace material came from John C. Duval. The account of the Parker Massacre is reprinted directly from James T. DeShields. The account of Sherman's 1871 tour came from Smythe's history of Parker County. Other segments were written by Capt. R. B. Barry, Mrs. A. E. Shearer, and Judge J. P. Simpson. But by far the largest part of the text came from Wilbarger's own hand: "During some twenty years I have carefully obtained from the lips of those who knew most of the facts stated in this volume. For their general correctness I can vouch, for I knew personally most of the early settlers of Texas, and have relied on those only whom I believed to be trustworthy."

Perhaps the most fascinating narrative in the book is the story of the scalping of John Wilbarger's brother Josiah in 1833. Josiah was ambushed and scalped, but remained alive under a tree near Walnut Creek just outside present-day Austin. Mrs. Reuben Hornsby, who lived about fifteen miles away on the Colorado River, dreamed not only that Wilbarger was alive but also exactly where he was lying. A search party, dubious but determined, was sent out and found him where she said he would be. Josiah lived for a number of years, although his hair never grew back. The story first appeared in 1840 in a newspaper, and was verified by all the participants. John W. Wilbarger's verison differs from that in John Henry Brown and John Holland Jenkins, but only in details.

One remarkable feature in the book is that the thirty-four woodcuts in the text signed T. J. Owen were actually done by William Sydney Porter, better known as O. Henry. Dobie recounts the story: "When the book was coming out he was a young man in Austin given to drawing as well as to writing, and from one or two men who were helping to enterprise the book affidavits have been secured proving conclusively that O. Henry was paid to illustrate it. Certainly the illustrations . . . have remarkable character even though they are at times absurd. They have a freshness, a sense of humor, and an originality that mark them as having come from no common hand."

Agatha, p.58. Dobie, pp.36,58. Howes W407. Raines, p.219.

219 Winfrey, Dorman Hayward (1924-), and James Milton Day (1931-) [eds.]

TEXAS INDIAN PAPERS, EDITED FROM THE ORIGINAL MS. COPIES IN THE TEXAS STATE ARCHIVES.

Austin: Texas State Library, 1959-1961.
Introductions by Joe B. Frantz and H. Bailey Carroll.
4 volumes. Illus. maps. 24cm.
Cloth.

The Indian Papers of Texas and the Southwest
1825-1916

Edited by

DORMAN H. WINFREY, Texas State Librarian

JAMES M. DAY, Texas State Archivist

Over ten years ago the Texas State Archives began the vital research project of locating and publishing its files of Indian papers. During the next seven years four volumes were published, each going out of print soon after its appearance. These first four volumes now fetch as high as $175.00 on the rare book market.

Now the project has finally been completed, with a fifth volume of over 300 pages, containing among other documents the rare and important Indian letters from the Texas Governors Collections of the state archives. The entire set is now available for the first time in a limited edition of five slipcased volumes.

Starting with the period when Texas included virtually all of the present Southwest (claiming most of the area west of the Mississippi and south of the Oregon Territory) and ending with World War I, these papers represent the basic source of information on the nineteenth-century Southwestern Indian. Carefully edited by State Librarian Dorman H. Winfrey and State Archivist James M. Day, the project has consumed the energy of a decade of painstaking search, organization, research, and indexing.

The work contains over 2000 pages and over 1400 letters, treaties, reports, messages, and documents. There are letters from such personalities as Sam Houston, R. B. Marcy, Kit Carson, Henry Schoolcraft, and R. S. Neighbors. The minute and detailed indexing runs over 100 pages. Each volume is profusely illustrated with contemporary works on the Indian by such artists as Seth Eastman and Frederic Remington, with numerous plates and maps, and introductions by Dr. H. Bailey Carroll and Dr. Joe B. Frantz.

The five-volume set, in slipcase: $37.50

THE PEMBERTON PRESS
1 Pemberton Parkway
Austin, Texas

Other issues:

(A). *The Indian Papers of Texas and the Southwest,* 1825-1916. Austin: The Pemberton Press, 1966. 5 volumes. Illus. maps. 24cm. Cloth, boxed. Best edition, with a supplemental volume of 412 pages containing 276 additional letters from the period 1846-1859.

This extensive collection provides original source materials on Texas Indians. W. W. Newcomb, the dean of students of Texas Indian history, wrote: "They are so valuable to the researcher, save him so much time, and are generally so well edited that [I] almost wept with joy when I first heard they were to be published." Kenneth F. Neighbours called the set "a documentary account of a facet of Texas history which will forever have significance. . . . Only those who have waded through the difficult manuscripts can truly appreciate the excellent manner of editing performed by Winfrey. . . . The assistance to scholarship is incalculable."

The set comprises official letters, documents, reports, and treaties relating to Texas Indian tribes, as follows: vol. I, 1825-1843; vol. II, 1844-1845; vol. III, 1846-1859; vol. IV, 1860-1916; and vol. V, 1846-1859. The fifth volume comprises letters from the Executive Department. In all, there are 1614 documents in 2,031 pages. There are letters from Sam Houston, Randolph B. Marcy, Kit Carson, Henry R. Schoolcraft, Jack Hays, Rip Ford, and others. Each volume is indexed separately and thoroughly, but as might be expected, Indian names and spellings cause confusion at times.

The documents are rich in first hand reports on encounters, friendly and hostile, with Indians, and many are rich in detail. Needless to say, they present the Indians through the eyes of the Texans, usually in either a hostile or paternalistic fashion. As the noted Texas ethnologist, T. N. Campbell, said: "These documents tell us far more about Texans than about Indians. What the Indians thought, said, and did is recorded indirectly, incompletely, and with expectable distortion. . . . These documents cover the declining years of the Indians in Texas and thus represent a period of social and political disorganization, rapid acculturation, and physical removal or extinction. This period is also marked by the appearance of numerous refugee Indian groups from various parts of the eastern United States."

220   Winkler, Ernest William (1875-1960)

PLATFORMS OF POLITICAL PARTIES IN TEXAS.

Austin: Bulletin of the University of Texas no. 53, 1916.
700pp. 23cm.
Printed wrappers.

This is the prime source for basic political party data in Texas, 1846-1916. C. S. Potts wrote of the work: "Not only are the materials it contains absolutely essential to anyone who would write the history of the political parties, but they are almost equally valuable to the man who would prepare himself thoroughly for participation in the public affairs of the state. The volume is a great mine of information concerning the problems of state and nation with which our fathers had to deal, and it will undoubtedly prove a most useful handbook alike for future platform makers and for students of the state's political history."

The volume consists of three parts. The first contains an excellent account by Winkler of the gradual polarization of political activity in the Republic of Texas into factions that later became political parties, and a summary of political organization during the early years of statehood. This is one of Winkler's best and most careful essays. The second part, comprising the bulk of the work, prints the official and semi-official texts of platforms themselves. It also includes nominees for office, convention officers, and committee members. The third part contains various election statistics and results. There is a thorough 47-page proper name index.

During the period Winkler was working on this project, James Ferguson became governor. Winkler was serving as state librarian. Ferguson began his outrageous process of replacing appointed state officials with political cronies, and managed to have Winkler fired and replaced with a totally incompetent preacher from Temple who gave his qualifications as follows: "It is true that I have never been a professor of history, but I remember that I served as a substitute to the teacher of history during my college course [in a Kentucky seminary]. It is true also that I have no training in library work, but I have in my own library a 1000 volumes which are catalogued." In the controversy, which drew in many of the major figures among

American historians at the time, E. C. Barker resigned as chairman of the library commission and managed to get Winkler a job as reference librarian at the University of Texas, in which position Winkler was enabled to get his book published as a university bulletin. Even this position caused a controversy; one regent of the university voted against Winkler's appointment because, he said "If you elect Mr. Winkler to this position, you are going to incur the further displeasure of the governor, and will never hear the last of it."

It is therefore somewhat amazing that Winkler was able to do such outstanding work in the book. It is not merely a cut and paste job, because many of the convention records were never or only partially published. It took tedious detective work to reconstruct the full record of party activity in Texas. As Winkler states: "This collection of platforms of the political parties of Texas aims at completeness," but "the opportunities for error are so great that doubtless many escaped correction." The years subsequent to publication have proved the general trustworthiness of Winkler's work, and it remains a basic research source and a monument to a great Texas librarian, historian, and bibliographer.

221 Wooten, Dudley Goodall (1860-1928) [ed.]

A COMPREHENSIVE HISTORY OF TEXAS, 1685 TO 1897.

Dallas: Published by William G. Scarff, 1898.
Two volumes: xxiii,[3],890; vii,[1],5-851pp. Illus. Maps. 26cm.
Cloth. Also full morocco.

Other issues:
(A). *A Complete History of Texas for Schools, Colleges, and General Use.* Dallas: The Texas History Company, [1899]. xxii,498pp. Illus. Maps. 21cm. A condensation of little value.
(B). Facsimile reprint. Austin: Texas State Historical Association, [1986]. Two volumes. Cloth. Limited to 500 sets.

This is one of the most all-inclusive compilations on Texas history through the 19th century, with contributions by leading participants in many of the events described. C. W. Raines commented on "its immense size—two royal octavo volumes of nearly 1800 pages. Reduced to a 12mo in size of page, it would contain thirty volumes. . . . The size of the work is no disparagement, but rather a guaranty of extraordinary scope and comprehensiveness. The monographs, however seemingly diverse, are all germane to the text. This plan has its merits and demerits. It throws greater labor upon the editor to have proper harmony, while it tends to secure better work on any special topic; and the rule, as I take it, holds good as to the excellence of the monographs in these volumes. Certainly it would be hard to find a more respectable array of well-known Texas writers. . . . If a man were to be restricted to one book on Texas, I would advise him to get [this one], as it makes in itself a good library on Texas." Price Daniel, Jr., writing sixty-five years later, said the work is the "most comprehensive and thorough single history for the period; a cornerstone of any Texana library."

Dudley Wooten's family settled in Texas during the Civil War. He was educated at Johns Hopkins and the University of Virginia, and returned to Texas to open his law practice. He became city attorney of Austin in 1884, the year city marshal Ben Thompson was killed. Wooten was instrumental in the chartering of the University of Texas and was county judge of Dallas County in the early 1890's. He was a founder and second president of the Texas State Historical Association, a member of Congress from 1901 to 1903, and professor of law at Notre Dame from 1924 to 1928.

In 1897 Robert E. McCleary sold *Texas Magazine* to William G. Scarff of Dallas, who induced Wooten to become its editorial supervisor. Scarff had been collecting material for a general history of Texas since 1893, and Wooten took over the general editorship of that project as well. Wooten announced in the magazine issue for November, 1897, that the work would be "the most satisfying, the most comprehensive, the most authentic chronicle of the greatest State in the American Union, that has ever been conceived or executed."

The work begins with a reprint of Henderson Yoakum's *History of Texas*. An idea of the scope of the set may be gleaned from the fact that the 926-page Yoakum text takes up less than a fourth of the Wooten set, and only 434 pages of its text. The Yoakum reprint is enhanced by the addition of annotations by Moses Austin Bryan, Frank W. Johnson, Guy M. Bryan, and Wooten himself, adding what Raines calls "the other side" to many of Yoakum's pro-Houston tendencies. Yoakum's own notes are omitted, as are his appendices.

The remainder of the text of the work is in the form of chronologically arranged articles on Texas history from Austin's colony to 1897.
In these are to be found a wealth of essays and memoirs that are
unsurpassed and still of immense value and interest. Guy M. Bryan-
contributes a book-length series of nine chapters on the Austin Colony,
the Fredonian War, and the beginning of the Texas Revolution. Dr. J.
H. Barnard's journal of the Fannin Massacre is given in full. Samuel
Bell Maxey writes on annexation and the Mexican War. Wooten
himself provides superlative essays on the Texas land system and Texan
contributions to land law. George P. Garrison called these chapters
"especially rich in documents previously unpublished."

Former Governor O. M. Roberts provides another book-length text
of 325 pages entitled "The Political, Legislative, and Judicial History
of Texas for Its Fifty Years of Statehood, 1845-1895." Of this section,
Raines said: "He has given the public the most impartial history of
Texas for the period covered that has ever been written." Gen. W. H.
King, who had been in charge of the Ranger force for many years,
contributes a "History of the Texas Rangers." Editor A. C. Gray
writes on the history of printing in Texas. The eminent E. T. Dumble
provides a monograph on Texas geography, geology, and natural
resources.

The Civil War as it affected Texas and as Texans affected it is
covered by contributions from John S. Ford, K. M. VanZandt, Charles
I. Evans, and others, including separate chapters by Mrs. S. V.
Winkler on Hood's Texas Brigade and Kate Scurry Terrell on Terry's
Texas Rangers. The work is concluded by a lengthy summary of the
significance of the last fifty years of the century in Texas, with 36 full-
page statistical tables.

Other comprehensive histories have subsequently been attempted.
Louis J. Wortham's *A History of Texas from Wilderness to Commonwealth*
(Ft. Worth, 1924) in five volumes has little present value. Competent
and lucid is *The Saga of Texas, 1519-1965* (Austin, 1965) in six volumes
edited by Seymour V. Connor, with volumes by Odie B. Faulk, David
M. Vigness, Seymour V. Connor, Ernest Wallace, Billy M. Jones, and
S. S. McKay.

Howes W673. Larned 3342. Rader 3737.

222 Yanaguana Society Publications

 I. Castaneda, Carlos Eduardo.
  A Report on the Spanish Archives in San Antonio, Texas.
  San Antonio: Yanaguana Society, 1937.
  167pp. 23cm. Cloth. Limited to 500 copies. [Verso] Artes Graficas, San
  Antonio, Texas.

 II. Menchaca, Antonio.
  Memoirs.
  San Antonio: Yanaguana Society, 1937.
  31pp. 24cm. Cloth. Limited to 500 copies.

 III. Dohmen, Franz J. [Trans.].
  Life and Memoirs of Emil Frederic Wurzbach, to which Is Appended Some Papers of
  John Meusebach.
  San Antonio: Yanaguana Society, 1937.
  39pp. 24cm. Cloth. Limited to 500 copies.

 IV. Chabot, Frederick C.
  With the Makers of San Antonio: Genealogies of the Early Latin, Anglo-American,
  and German Families, with Occasional Biographies, Each Group Being Prefaced with
  a Brief Historical Sketch and Illustrations.
  San Antonio: Privately Published, Printing by Artes Graficas,
  [1937] [8],412pp. 24cm. Cloth. No limitation notice.
  [This is also a special edition of 25 numbered, autographed copies]. Reprinted
  about 1970 by Graphic Arts.

 V. Chabot, Frederick C. [ed.].
  Texas Letters.
  San Antonio: Yanaguana Society, 1940.
  188pp. 23cm. Cloth. Limited to 250 copies.

 VI. Chabot, Frederick C. [ed.].
  Texas in 1811: The Las Casas and Sambrano Revolutions.
  San Antonio: Yanaguana Society, 1941.
  162pp. 24cm. Limited to 250 copies.

 VII. Chabot, Frederick C. [ed.].
  McFarland Journal.
  San Antonio: Yanaguana Society, 1942.
  94pp. 24cm. Cloth. Limited to 250 copies. Foreword by Louis Lenz.
  Misnumbered VIII on p. [v]. Reprinted in 1981 by Eakin Press.

This is a valuable assembly of original Texas source materials, published in seven volumes between 1937 and 1942. The Yanaguana Society was organized in San Antonio in 1933 by Frederick C. Chabot and others with the purpose "to secure historical research [materials] . . . and to encourage the publication of authentic and documented records" pertaining to Texas. Other members included M. L. Crimmins, Louis Lenz, Rena Maverick Green, Carlos E. Castaneda, Charles W. Hackett, Eugene C. Barker, Herbert E. Bolton, Chris Emmett, Hobart Huson, and other Texas historians. Unfortunately, World War II put an end to the publication series, and the society dissolved in 1947.

The first volume is an indexed listing of over two thousand Spanish records in the San Antonio county clerk's office. Since San Antonio de Bexar acted for a century as the capital of the province of Texas, many of these records relate to the whole of settled Texas. Castaneda, who prepared this text in 1923 as his master's thesis for the University of Texas, tells what happened to the large collection now known as the Bexar Archives: "In 1836 after the defeat of Santa Anna . . . the entire Archive of San Antonio de Bexar . . . fell into the hands of the Texans. At that time the collection was practically complete, but for some reasons, in 1841 certain papers from the Bexar Archives were sent to the office of the Secretary of State at Austin, and there in the course of time became badly mixed with the Nacogdoches Archives. . . . In 1896 the County of Bexar turned over to the University of Texas what was thought to be the entire collection of the Bexar Archives, retaining, as it claimed, only such documents . . . which had a legal value. The present investigation has disclosed that there were retained in the County Clerk's office over two thousand manuscripts . . . half of which are not in any sense legal papers," including correspondence and reports of immense historical value. Castaneda's volume summarizes the content of each of these documents. The Nacogdoches Archives, with the mixed-in parts of the Bexar Archives, are now in the Texas State Library. The Bexar Archives proper are at the University of Texas and are now available on microfilm.

The second and third volumes are memoirs of Antonio Menchaca, Emil Wurzbach, and John O. Meusebach, the latter two being prominent early German settlers in Texas. All of these documents were in private hands, making their publication particularly useful to scholars. John O. Meusebach's *Answer to Interrogatories* (Austin: Pemberton Press, 1964) contains further Meusebach memoirs, prepared for an 1894 legal case.

The fourth volume in the series is Chabot's noteworthy source book on early families and prominent Texans of the San Antonio region, with extensive quotations of original documents. The volume has a research value in many areas beyond the area of San Antonio. The fifth volume is a mixed bag of original hitherto unpublished letters relating to early Texas, including the Thomas Newcomb correspondence, 1839-1850, and letters relating to the fall of the Alamo and the Texas Revolution. Regrettably, the volume is unindexed and the letters are not in chronological order. The sixth volume is a goldmine of original letters and source materials relating to the Hidalgo Revolution events in Texas. The last volume is Thomas S. McFarland's Texas diary, 1837-1840, well-annotated by Chabot.

223   Yeary, Mamie (1876-   )

REMINISCENCES OF THE BOYS IN GRAY, 1861-1865.

Dallas: Published for the Author by Smith & Lamar. Publishing House M. E. Church, South. Press of Wilkinson Printing Company, [1912].
[viii],904pp. Illus. 25cm.
Cloth; also three-quarter morocco.

Other issues:
(A). Robert H. Krick, *Neale Books: An Annotated Bibliography* lists a three-volume edition of this work as appearing in the 1912 *Publisher's Trade List Annual* to be issued by the Neale Publishing Company, but no set of this work has been located, and it is improbable that it was ever published.

This compilation of original memoirs and biographies of Confederate soldiers, predominantly Texans, is for the Texas-Confederate era what Hunter's *Trail Drivers of Texas* is for the era of cattle drivers. Most of the memoirs are unpublished elsewhere; most are by ordinary soldiers.

The volume contains a whopping 2,006 entries, arranged in alphabetical order. Yeary's goal, she states, was to "place in permanent form, and in the very words of the participants . . . the personal experiences of the 'men behind the guns,' the 'boys in the line.' " She wisely points out the value to the historian of these common soldier recollections: "Where a battle line was several miles in length no one man could see it all, and the different descriptions, seemingly at variance when taken together make up the whole battle." Yeary's task took several years: some of the memoirs are dated as early as

1909; her foreword is dated McGregor, Texas, November 1, 1912. Appendices include the Confederate Constitution, a chart of members of the Confederate congresses, and an excellent 49-page "Chronological List of Engagements by States."

The entries contain some delightful insights into the life of the soldier, and some important accounts of various aspects of the war. Some are lengthy; some cryptic. John Savage of Terrell states simply: "Was promoted from Fourth Corporal to Fourth Sergeant and did more guard duty than any man in war." L. F. Garner of Del Rio maintains that he "never fired a gun at a Yankee, although I was at all the fights from Pleasant Hill to Yellow Bayou. I was horse holder, so did not carry a gun." A. B. Foster of Comanche reports that frequently "our rations were so short that we stole corn from the officers' horses and the ambulance teams until we starved the horses almost to death." W. L. Owens of Blooming Grove, on the other hand, was in numerous battles, wounded, taken prisoner, and fought hard throughout the war. He comments: "Was at Gettysburg, had a hard time, and oh, what a bad fight—saw so many good men lose their lives."

More significant accounts include those such as J. M. Polk of Austin, who writes: "Capt. Winkler, Tom Morris, and I were sent back to Texas for recruits. I recall meeting Gen. Sam Houston in the barber shop of the Fannin House in Houston. It was in April, 1862. He was on crutches, dressed in a long, loose sack coat, broad brimmed hat, coonskin vest and wore the largest gold ring I ever saw on a man's finger. He looked at me a few minutes and said: 'Well, young man, I suppose you are off for the war?' 'Yes, sir,' I answered. 'Well,' said he, 'I am too old now to be of any service to my country. Texas people refused to take my counsel. I can do them no good, and God knows that I do not wish to do them any harm. But I do not think our cause will justify the loss of so much life and property. It's American against American. But if I was young and able to do anything, and they refused to go my way, I might go with them.' "

H. S. Halbert of Waco tells of the seven Texas pickets who captured some Yankee whiskey: "The Texans soon came upon a large force of Federal pickets, and, with their heads full of whiskey, no doubt, they thought they were a match for any body of Yankees they might meet. . . . They fired a volley and charged them from all sides . . . A severe hand-to-hand struggle took place." Ultimately, seven Yankees were killed and thirty-two surrendered to the seven Texans. In the fight, a Texan and a Yankee fought for a long time with sabers. Tiring of the duel, the Texan "drew a revolver and shot him dead." The same group of Texans attacked the Federal escort of Gen. McPherson, killing the general in the melee. Halbert concludes: "Gen. McPherson was a brave and honorable enemy who fought the South with his sword and not with a box of matches like Gen. Sherman."

F. M. Martin of Oglesby tells of one of his compatriots who was surrounded by Yankees and refused to surrender, struggling with his captors and finally biting the finger off the major who grappled with him. "It was hard to keep the [Federal] soldiers from killing Joe. They took him to Gen. Osterhaus and told him that here was the man who bit the Major's finger off, and asked what must be done with him. Gen. Osterhaus looked the prisoner over from head to foot and, turning to the guard, said: 'I want you to accord him every respect due a prisoner, and I want every one of you to fight just like he did.'"

Ben Martin of Waxahachie tells of Second Bull Run: "We farmer boys raised the old rebel yell and went at them, and they ran like turkeys. This ended the second battle of Manassas." On the other hand, John H. Lewis of Mabank tells of being attacked by a large force of Yankees: "Soon about 500 cavalry charged us. It was about fifty yards to a canebrake, and I ran for dear life, and they shot at me at every jump . . . and was soon out of sight. You have heard of the 'small dog in high rye.' Well, that is nothing to a man in a canebrake trying to fight the Yankees and get away at the same time."

Perhaps all the memoirs of these ex-Confederates are best summed up by the statement of R. W. Hyder of Frost, who writes: "If I could see the reader I could tell him many things about the hardships of the soldier. I could talk to you for forty-eight hours and then not be through. My youngest child is 24 years old, and I haven't finished telling him yet."

Dornbusch III-60. Krick 576. Nevins II-248.

224   Yoakum, Henderson King (1810-1856)

HISTORY OF TEXAS FROM ITS FIRST SETTLEMENT IN 1685
TO ITS ANNEXATION TO THE UNITED STATES IN 1846.

New York: Redfield, 34 Beekman Street, 1855.
[Verso of title:] Stereotyped by C. C. Savage, 13 Chambers St., N.Y.
Two volumes: 482,11;576pp. 3 maps (2 folding). Folding facsimile. 4 plates. 23cm.
Cloth. Also calf.
Most copies of this printing were destroyed by fire soon after publication.

Other issues:
(A).   Same as above, dated 1856 on title pages.
(B).   Wooten, Dudley G. [ed.]. *A Comprehensive History of Texas, 1685 to 1897*. Dallas:
       Published by William G. Scarff, 1898. Two volumes. Illus. Maps. 26cm. Cloth.
       Contains a reprint of Yoakum on the first 434 pages. Omits Yoakum's notes
       and appendices, but adds footnotes by Moses Austin Bryan, Frank W. Johnson,
       Guy M. Bryan, and Dudley G. Wooten.
(C).   Facsimile of the first edition. Austin: The Steck Company, [1935]. Two volumes.
       22cm. Cloth. 2000 copies printed.
(D).   Same as (C). Issued in a special slipcase in 1952 with J. W. Wilbarger's *Indian
       Depredations in Texas,* of which publisher R. H. Porter states: "Concerning the
       special combined edition of Yoakum and Wilbarger used as gifts at the
       governor's conference, there was nothing distinctive except the box. The
       committee working on the conference wanted to give the visiting governors
       and dignitaries some books about early Texas. I suggested that a special
       package be prepared. . . . They were grouped and boxed with a special label."
       48 sets issued.
(E).   Same as (C). Two volumes in one. 22cm. Cloth.

This was the first scholarly history of Texas written after annexation,
and remains one of the most important sources on Texas colonization,
revolution, and republic. Although severely censured by its critics,
most historians agree as to its merits. George P. Garrison praised its
"high degree of scholarship and research . . . still recognized as one
of the prime authorities." Hubert H. Bancroft thought it "one of the
best, if not the best, history of Texas." C. W. Raines, after a review
of its faults, called it "the accepted standard of authority of today."
Herbert Gambrell called Yoakum "the first Texas historian to take his
task seriously."

Henderson Yoakum graduated from West Point in 1832 and later
became a lawyer in Tennessee. In 1845 he moved to Texas, settling

close to the home of Sam Houston, who became a lifelong friend. He served as an officer under Jack Hays in the Mexican War. Some time about 1850, he began writing his history of Texas. Herbert H. Lang states that "Yoakum was a man without superior intellectual faculties, with only ordinary literary abilities, and with no personal acquaintance with Texas prior to 1845. He never wrote a word for publication before or after he wrote his *History of Texas*. He did his writing in hurried snatches of time stolen from other pressing interests. Nevertheless, he gave to Texas one of the outstanding state histories of the nineteenth century."

On June 2, 1853, Yoakum wrote to Thomas J. Rusk: "I have been for two or three years engaged in collecting materials, and preparing a history of Texas. I have studied the subject so much, that I have become enthusiastic on it." He completed the first volume on July 3, 1854, and the second on February 26, 1855.

On September 22, 1854, he wrote to Sam Houston asking him to have "Mrs. Houston to select from your daguerreotypes the one she would prefer to have engraved and send it to me by mail. . . . Redfield I presume will have out my first volume before long. It treats somewhat of your first movements in Texas." The set was printed by Redfield in mid-1855 and issued at five dollars per set, but a fire destroyed much of the first issue and only a few sets survive with the publication date of 1855. My copy of the first issue of the work is Redfield's copy, with his publisher's stamp.

The first volume, covering Texas history through 1835, is very weak on the period prior to the establishment of Austin's colony. Yoakum acknowledges that he was unable to examine many archival collections, and even lists those which he did not use. In early 1854 he wrote to Joseph Henry at the Smithsonian asking for materials on early Texas on loan (especially the Berlandier Papers) and listing in some detail those meager sources which he had at hand. With so few resources, his account of early Texas is ill-proportioned, incomplete, and generally unsatisfactory. In the appendices to this volume, however, he includes the very valuable "Memoir of Colonel Ellis P. Bean," which is one of the most important resources on Texas history during the early part of the 19th century. It has been reprinted as *Memoir of Col. Ellis P.*

Bean, Written by Himself about the Year 1816 (Dallas, 1930) by the Book Club of Texas, incorrectly stating it was edited by *W. P.* Yoakum.

In the second volume, covering the period of the revolution and republic, Yoakum faced the opposite problem: "In the compilation of this volume, the materials were so abundant, that the great difficulty was, to select the most prominent and connected facts, so as not to make the volume too ponderous, nor to break the unity of the story." This volume must be used with care. Its value lies not in Yoakum's own judgments, which are uncritically pro-Houston, but in those areas where he is relying upon primary source materials. Yoakum had the use of materials, many no longer extant, provided to him by Sam Houston, Thomas J. Rusk, Haden Edwards, Jesse Grimes, John Forbes, John Henry Brown, Charles Gayarre, and numerous others. The 113-page appendix section contains numerous letters of Sam Houston never before published, and of the 1,266 footnotes in the main text, 739 are to original manuscripts, letters, or primary sources.

Yoakum's relationship with Sam Houston is the root of the controversy regarding the relative accuracy of Yoakum's text. Clearly, Yoakum and Houston were the most intimate of friends and shared basically the same political views. Houston employed Yoakum to buy and sell real estate, and to represent Mrs. Houston when she was charged with assaulting a ward. The Yoakum Papers (now at the University of Texas Archives) and the various collections of Houston Papers contain many evidences that Houston aided Yoakum in every way possible, even making available to him his private papers, to which no one else except the hack C. E. Lester ever had access. Yet Houston on the floor of the Senate in 1859 declared that Yoakum's book "is a work with which [I] had no connection, never having seen a page of it in manuscript." Yoakum family tradition, on the other hand, insists that Houston even accompanied Yoakum on a tour of the San Jacinto battleground to show him the Houston side of the story.

Whatever Houston's actual influence, the work has been attacked frequently for bias. David G. Burnet charged flatly that "there are, in that book, letters, dispatches, and documents which were concocted *for* the book, and long posterior to the events they refer to." Ashbel Smith, a Houston admirer, called it "hasty, prejudiced, and ignorant."

Even Judge Peter W. Gray, to whom the book is dedicated, wrote to Yoakum that he "cannot but regret" the "occasional inaccuracies." The reprint in Wooten's *Comprehensive History* contains footnotes by prominent early Texans pointing out specific errors and misjudgments, and early pioneer J. H. Kuykendall wrote out a list of errors for an article in the *Quarterly of the Texas State Historical Association* (vol. VII, no. 1) in July, 1903.

In spite of its detractors, Yoakum's history remains a necessary source. Modern historians rally to its support, with reservations. Gambrell said Yoakum managed to achieve "a degree of objectivity unusual for the amateur historian, and literary style not often equalled by the professional." Eugene C. Barker called the work "the first history of Texas to meet the standards of professional historians. . . . His book is still indispensable to a study of the period it covers."

Agatha, p.42. Howes Y10. Larned 2077. Rader 3773. Raines, p.223.

APPENDIX
A CHECKLIST OF BIBLIOGRAPHIES
RELATING TO TEXAS
(Excluding Articles in Periodicals)

B1.   Adams, Ramon F. THE ADAMS ONE-FIFTY: A CHECK-LIST OF THE 150 MOST IMPORTANT BOOKS ON WESTERN OUTLAWS AND LAWMEN. Austin: Jenkins Publishing Company, 1976. 91pp. An annotated guide to Adams' selections for a basic research collection in this field.

B2.   Adams, Ramon F. THE RAMPAGING HERD: A BIBLIOGRAPHY OF BOOKS AND PAMPHLETS ON MEN AND EVENTS IN THE CATTLE INDUSTRY. Norman: University of Oklahoma Press, [1959]. 463pp. A comprehensive checklist of 2651 works on the cattle industry, with some critical commentary.

B3.   Adams, Ramon F. SIX-GUNS AND SADDLE LEATHER: A BIBLIOGRAPHY OF BOOKS AND PAMPHLETS ON WESTERN OUTLAWS AND GUNMEN. [Norman: University of Oklahoma Press, 1969]. 808pp. New Edition, Revised and Greatly Enlarged. The revised edition contains 2491 entries; well-annotated.

B4.   Adams, Ramon F. BURS UNDER THE SADDLE: A SECOND LOOK AT BOOKS AND HISTORIES OF THE WEST. Norman: University of Oklahoma Press, [1964]. 610pp. Highly critical comments on 424 western books.

B5.   Adams, Ramon F. MORE BURS UNDER THE SADDLE: BOOKS AND HISTORIES OF THE WEST. Norman: University of Oklahoma Press, [1979]. 182pp. Critical comments on 233 additional western books.

B6.   Agatha, Sister M. TEXAS PROSE WRITINGS: A READER'S DIGEST. Dallas: Banks Upshaw, [1936]. 168pp. An intriguing and perceptive guide to Texas prose, both fiction and non-fiction. The copy in my collection contains numerous corrections and additions in Sister Agatha's hand, apparently intended for a revised edition.

B7.   Alessio Robles, Vito. LA PRIMERA IMPRENTA EN LAS PROVINCIAS INTERNAS DE ORIENTE: TEXAS, TAMAULIPAS, NUEVO LEON Y COAHUILA. Mexico: Antigua Libreria Robredo, de Jose Porrua e Hijos, 1939. 79pp. One of the first studies of early printing in Northern Mexico.

B8.   Alessio Robles, Vito. LA PRIMERA IMPRENTA EN COAHUILA. Mexico: Universidad Nacional, 1932. 43pp. The earliest study of printing in Coahuila y Texas. My copy has the author's handwritten annotations and revisions.

B9.   Andrade, Jose Maria. CATALOGUE DE LA RICHE BIBLIOTHEQUE DE ...
        LIVRES, MANUSCRITS, ET IMPRIMES, LITERATURE FRANCAISE ET ESPAGNOLE.
        Leipzig, 1869. The exceedingly valuable library of a Mexican bookseller.
        Andrade sold it to Emperor Maximilian, after whose death it wound up on
        the auction block. Hubert H. Bancroft bought most of the collection, with
        which he formed the nucleus of what has since become the Bancroft
        Library.

B10.   Arrillaga, Basilio Jose [comp.]. RECOPILACION DE LEYES, DECRETOS, BAN-
        DOS, REGLAMENTOS, CIRCULARES Y PROVIDENCIAS DE LOS SUPREMOS POD-
        ERES Y OTRAS AUTORIDADES DE LA REPUBLICA MEXICANA. Mexico: Fernan-
        dez de Lara, 1834–1866. 20 volumes. This amounts to a virtual checklist of
        official Mexican government imprints for the period.

B11.   Baillio, Ferdinand B. A HISTORY OF THE TEXAS PRESS ASSOCIATION. Dallas:
        Southwestern Printing Company, 1916. 402pp. Includes material on early
        Texas newspapers and publishers.

B12.   Baird, Violet M. TEXAS MEDICAL HISTORY IN THE LIBRARY OF THE UNI-
        VERSITY OF TEXAS SOUTHWESTERN MEDICAL SCHOOL. Dallas: Friends of the
        Medical Library, 1972. 91pp. An annotated bibliography of 246 works.

B13.   Baker, R. C., and J. B. Brown. ANNOTATED BIBLIOGRAPHY OF GROUND-
        WATER PUBLICATIONS AND OPEN FILE REPORTS OF THE TEXAS WATER COM-
        MISSION AND THE U.S. GEOLOGICAL SURVEY FOR TEXAS. Austin: Texas
        Water Development Board, 1964. 89pp.

B14.   THE BANCROFT LIBRARY, UNIVERSITY OF CALIFORNIA BERKELEY: CATALOG
        OF PRINTED BOOKS. Boston: G. K. Hall & Co., 1964. 22 volumes. 6
        supplemental volumes issued in 1969. Contains much Texana among the
        400,000 titles in this collection.

B15.   Barns, Florence Elberta. TEXAS WRITERS OF TODAY. Dallas: Tardy Publish-
        ing Company, 1935. 513pp. Short biographies of 1180 Texas authors and
        scholars, with brief quotations from their work. Includes a theme index.

B16.   Basler, Roy P. A GUIDE TO THE STUDY OF THE UNITED STATES OF AMERICA:
        REPRESENTATIVE BOOKS REFLECTING THE DEVELOPMENT OF AMERICAN LIFE
        AND THOUGHT. Washington: Library of Congress, 1960. 1193pp. Includes
        some basic works on Texas and the Southwest, but underemphasizes the
        region.

B17.   Baughman, J. L. AN ANNOTATED BIBLIOGRAPHY FOR THE STUDENT OF
        TEXAS FISHES AND FISHERIES. N.p., 1948. 240 leaves.

B18.   Bebout, Louis [ed.]. TEXAS REFERENCE SOURCES: A SELECTIVE GUIDE.
        [Austin:] Texas Library Association, 1975. 134pp. Includes annotations; a
        useful guide, particularly for the library sciences.

B19.   Bebout, Louis. UNION LIST OF MAJOR MICROFORM SETS IN TEXAS LIBRAR-
        IES. Austin: University of Texas, 1974. 108pp.

B20.   Beers, Henry Putney. SPANISH AND MEXICAN RECORDS OF THE AMERICAN
        SOUTHWEST: A BIBLIOGRAPHICAL GUIDE TO ARCHIVE AND MANUSCRIPT
        SOURCES. Tucson: University of Arizona Press, [1979]. 493pp.

B21. Beristain de Souza, Jose Mariano. BIBLIOTECA HISPANAMERICANA SETEN-TRIONAL. Mexico, 1816–1821. 3 volumes. Still valuable for the author's commentaries, based on manuscripts and archival sources no longer extant.

B22. BIBLIOGRAPHY OF PERMIAN BASIN GEOLOGY: WEST TEXAS AND SOUTHWEST-ERN NEW MEXICO. Midland: West Texas Geological Society, 1967. 163pp.

B23. BIBLIOGRAPHY OF TEXAS GOVERNMENT. Austin: University of Texas Institute of Public Affairs, 1964. 194pp.

B24. Bieciuk, Hank, and H. G. Corbin. TEXAS CONFEDERATE COUNTY NOTES AND PRIVATE SCRIPT. Tyler, [1961]. 112pp. Largely superceded by Medlar, but useful as it is arranged by counties of issue.

B25. Black, Carl, Richard Ducote, and Isabel McMahon. A SELECTED BIBLIOGRAPHY OF TEXANA: A LIST OF TITLES FROM THE TEXAS COLLECTION OF THE HOUSTON PUBLIC LIBRARY. Houston: Houston Public Library, 1958. 18pp.

B26. Bolton, Herbert E. GUIDE TO MATERIALS FOR THE HISTORY OF THE UNITED STATES IN THE PRINCIPAL ARCHIVES OF MEXICO. Washington: Carnegie Institute, 1913. 553pp. One of the most influential archival studies ever produced; still of great value.

B27. Boner, Marian. A REFERENCE GUIDE TO TEXAS LAW AND LEGAL HISTORY: SOURCES AND DOCUMENTATION. Austin: University of Texas Press, [1976]. 108pp. The best guide to the complicated field of Texas legal publications.

B28. BOOKS ON TEXAS, HER PEOPLE AND HISTORY, FROM THE RED RIVER TO THE RIO GRANDE. Dallas: Dallas Public Library, 1965. 27pp.

B29. Bradford, Thomas L. THE BIBLIOGRAPHER'S MANUAL OF AMERICAN HISTORY. Philadelphia, 1907–1910. 5 volumes. Largely outdated.

B30. Branch, E. Douglas. THE COWBOY AND HIS INTERPRETERS. New York and London: D. Appleton and Co., 1926. 277pp. Early critical study of range literature; perceptive but outdated.

B31. Bratcher, James T. ANALYTICAL INDEX TO PUBLICATIONS OF THE TEXAS FOLKLORE SOCIETY, VOLUMES 1-36. Dallas: Southern Methodist University Press, 1973. 322pp. Designed more for the researcher in folklore than for the historian, but useful to both; includes extensive indices to folk tale types, motifs, ballads, etc., and excellent folk tale synopses.

B32. Braunstein, Jules [ed.]. BIBLIOGRAPHY OF GULF COAST GEOLOGY. New Orleans: Gulf Coast Association of Geological Societies, 1970. 2 volumes (1045pp.). Includes over 12,000 entries covering the period through 1965.

B33. Brees, Mina A. TEXAS STATE AGENCY PERIODICALS IN THE LEGISLATIVE REFERENCE LIBRARY. Austin: Legislative Reference Library, 1974. 43pp.

B34. Campbell, T. N. A BIBLIOGRAPHIC GUIDE TO THE ARCHAEOLOGY OF TEXAS. Austin: Archaeology Series I, Department of Anthropology, The University of Texas, 1952. 64pp. 689 entries.

B35. Campbell, T. N. PUBLICATIONS OF THE TEXAS ACADEMY OF SCIENCE, 1892-1957. Austin: Texas Journal of Science, 1958. 40pp.

B36.   Campbell, Walter S. THE BOOK LOVER'S SOUTHWEST: A GUIDE TO GOOD READING. Norman: University of Oklahoma Press, [1955]. 287pp. Campbell, who also wrote under the name Stanley Vestal, was a Rhodes Scholar and author of numerous western books. His commentaries on Texas books tend to be superficial.

B37.   Carroll, H. Bailey. TEXAS COUNTY HISTORIES, A BIBLIOGRAPHY. Austin: Texas State Historical Association, 1943. 200pp. The first checklist on the subject; with an introduction by Walter Prescott Webb.

B38.   Carroll, H. Bailey, and Milton R. Gutsch. TEXAS HISTORY THESES: A CHECK LIST OF THE THESES AND DISSERTATIONS RELATING TO TEXAS HISTORY ACCEPTED AT THE UNIVERSITY OF TEXAS, 1893–1951. Austin: The Texas State Historical Association, 1955. 208pp. A useful, indexed guide with content summaries to 470 theses and dissertations; updated periodically in issues of the *Southwestern Historical Quarterly*.

B39.   CATALOG OF THE EDWARD E. AYER COLLECTION OF AMERICANA AND AMERICAN INDIANS, NEWBERRY LIBRARY, CHICAGO. Boston: G. K. Hall & Co., 1961. 8 volumes. Reproduces the Ayer dictionary catalogue of over 90,000 works, many of Texas interest.

B40.   CATALOG OF THE TEXAS COLLECTION IN THE BARKER TEXAS HISTORY CENTER, THE UNIVERSITY OF TEXAS AT AUSTIN. Boston: G. K. Hall & Co., 1979. 14 volumes. An outstanding publication, containing reproductions of the Library of Congress catalogue cards on the 110,000 works in the Texas Collection, which is the largest repository of Texas books.

B41.   CATALOG OF THE YALE COLLECTION OF WESTERN AMERICANA. Boston: G. K. Hall & Co., [n.d.]. 4 volumes. Now largely outdated; contains only a small portion of Yale's extensive Texas and Western holdings.

B42.   Cebrain, Juan C. [comp.]. SPAIN AND SPANISH AMERICA IN THE LIBRARIES OF THE UNIVERSITY OF CALIFORNIA: A CATALOGUE OF BOOKS. Berkeley, 1928–1930. 2 volumes. Excellent for its time; now superceded by the G. K. Hall catalogue of the Bancroft Library.

B43.   Clark, Thomas D. TRAVELS IN THE OLD SOUTH: A BIBLIOGRAPHY. Norman: University of Oklahoma Press, [1956–1959]. Three volumes. The first volume includes 331 works published 1527–1783; the second includes 239 works between 1750 and 1825; and the third 506 works between 1825 and 1860. Contains perceptive annotations.

B44.   Clark, Thomas D. TRAVELS IN THE NEW SOUTH: A BIBLIOGRAPHY. Norman: University of Oklahoma Press, [1962]. Two volumes. The first volume encompasses 508 works published 1865-1900 and the second 627 works, 1900–1955, all excellently annotated.

B45.   Clark, Thomas D., Pamela J. Bennett, and F. J. Krauskopf. FIFTY-YEAR INDEX: MISSISSIPPI VALLEY HISTORICAL REVIEW, 1914–1964. Bloomington, Indiana: Organization of American Historians, 1973. 442pp. This journal published numerous articles on Texas; E. C. Barker was a primary force in its early years.

B46.   Cochran, Mary A. [comp.]. A LIST OF BOOKS AND RELATED MATERIALS ABOUT TEXAS FOR USE IN SCHOOLS. Austin: Austin Public Schools, 1952. [98]pp. Revised, 1957. Not of much use.

B47.   Cole, Garold. AMERICAN TRAVELERS TO MEXICO, 1821–1972: A Descriptive Bibliography. Troy, N.Y., 1978. Some entries relate to Texas.

B48.   Connor, Seymour V. A GUIDE TO THE XIT PAPERS IN THE PANHANDLE-PLAINS HISTORICAL MUSEUM. Canyon, 1953. 44pp.

B49.   Connor, Seymour V. A PRELIMINARY GUIDE TO THE ARCHIVES OF TEXAS. Austin: Texas Library and Historical Commission, 1956. 91pp. Still useful, although many of the collections have been reorganized.

B50.   Connor, Seymour V. TEXAS, A HISTORY. New York: Thomas Y. Crowell, 1971. 481pp. Contains a 59-page selective bibliography, with comments on over a thousand books and articles about Texas.

B51.   Connor, Seymour V., and Odie B. Faulk. NORTH AMERICA DIVIDED: THE MEXICAN WAR, 1846–1848. New York: Oxford University Press, 1971. 300pp. Pages 185 through 276 contain an excellent analytical bibliography.

B52.   Conrad, James H. TEXAS EDUCATIONAL HISTORY, A BIBLIOGRAPHY. [Greenville, Texas: Juris Co., 1979]. 109pp. Includes 1086 books and articles.

B53.   Cook, Spruill. J. FRANK DOBIE BIBLIOGRAPHY. Waco: Texian Press, 1968. 64pp. Superceded by the McVicker bibliography.

B54.   Corbin, John B. CATALOG OF GENEALOGICAL MATERIALS IN TEXAS LIBRARIES. Austin: Texas State Library, 1965–1966. 2 volumes.

B55.   Coulter, E. Merton. TRAVELS IN THE CONFEDERATE STATES: A BIBLIOGRAPHY. Norman: University of Oklahoma Press, 1948. 289pp. Well-annotated analyses of 492 works, many of Texas interest.

B56.   Crandall, Marjorie L. CONFEDERATE IMPRINTS: A CHECK LIST BASED PRINCIPALLY ON THE COLLECTION OF THE BOSTON ATHENAEUM. Boston: Boston Athenaeum, 1955. 2 volumes. Includes over 5300 titles; supplemented in 1957 by Richard Harwell. Now being extended and revised by Michael Parrish and Robert Willingham.

B57.   Criswell, Grover and Clarence. CRISWELL'S CURRENCY SERIES: CONFEDERATE AND SOUTHERN STATE CURRENCY AND BONDS. St. Petersburg, Florida, 1957–1961. 2 volumes. Revised edition, 1976. A useful guide to Texas currency and bonds, along with Medlar's work.

B58.   Cruz, Gilberto Rafael, and James Arthur Irby. TEXAS BIBLIOGRAPHY: A MANUAL ON HISTORY RESEARCH MATERIALS. Austin: Eakin Press, 1982. [copyright 1983]. 337pp. Includes a mishmash of 5300 entries arranged topically; obviously prepared with enthusiasm, but not even equal to Rader in competence. The errors number literally in the hundreds.

B59.   Cumberland, Charles C. THE UNITED STATES-MEXICAN BORDER: A SELECTIVE GUIDE TO THE LITERATURE OF THE REGION. New York: Rural Sociology Society, 1960. 236pp.

B60. CUMULATIVE INDEX OF THE SOUTHWESTERN HISTORICAL QUARTERLY. Austin: The Texas State Historical Association, 1950, 1960, 1980. Three volumes. Detailed indices of the first seventy volumes of this essential quarterly.

B61. Daniel, Price, Jr. AN ANALYSIS OF C. W. RAINES' BIBLIOGRAPHY OF TEXAS. Waco: Daniel Catalogue 15, 1962. 52pp. Includes some commentary by Daniel; continued in his Catalogue 16.

B62. Daniel, Price, Jr. TEXAS AND THE WEST, FEATURING THE WRITINGS OF J. FRANK DOBIE: A CONTRIBUTION TOWARDS A BIBLIOGRAPHY. Waco: Daniel Catalogue 24, 1964. 32pp. One of the earliest attempts at a Dobie checklist.

B63. Daniel, Price, Jr. TEXAS AND THE WEST, FEATURING BOOKS PRINTED AND/OR DESIGNED BY CARL HERTZOG. Waco: Daniel Catalogue 19, 1963. 32pp.

B64. Daniel, Price, Jr. TEXAS AND THE WEST, FEATURING BOOKS PRINTED AND DESIGNED BY JACK D. RITTENHOUSE OF THE STAGECOACH PRESS. Waco: Daniel Catalogue 32, 1964. 16pp. Produced with warmth and affection.

B65. David, C. Dorman. SALE OF RARE TEXAS HISTORICAL MANUSCRIPTS AND AUTOGRAPH MATERIALS, BEING LETTERS, DOCUMENTS, AND BROADSIDES FROM THE COLLECTION OF C. DORMAN DAVID. Houston, 1971. 35pp. A memorable sale, in more ways than one, of spectacular Texana.

B66. David, C. Dorman. TEXAS: BOOKS, MANUSCRIPTS, AND DOCUMENTS DEALING WITH THE HISTORY OF TEXAS. Houston: The Bookman, Catalogue 6, 1964. 114pp. Includes 130 of the rarest of Texas books.

B67. Day, James M. BLACK BEANS & GOOSE QUILLS: LITERATURE OF THE TEXAS MIER EXPEDITION. Waco: Texian Press, 1970. 160pp.

B68. Day, James M., and Ann B. Dunlap. THE MAP COLLECTION OF THE TEXAS STATE ARCHIVES, 1527–1900. Austin: Texas State Library, 1962. 156pp. Reprinted Austin: The Pemberton Press, 1964. The best guide so far to Texas cartography.

B69. Decker, Peter. AMERICANA . . . A RENOWNED COLLECTION. New York: Decker Catalogues 17-21, n.d. These four catalogues and separate index include the 4989 items in the collection of George W. Soliday; many of Texas and Western interest.

B70. Decker, Peter. PETER DECKER'S CATALOGUES OF AMERICANA. Austin: Jenkins Publishing Company, 1979. 3 volumes. Includes reprints of Decker's rare book catalogues 22-50, 1944–1963, well-indexed.

B71. Dickey, Imogene Bentley. EARLY LITERARY MAGAZINES OF TEXAS. Austin: Steck-Vaughn Company, [1970]. 108pp. Primarily analytical rather than bibliographical.

B72. Dobie, J. Frank, and Jeff Dykes. 44 RANGE COUNTRY BOOKS TOPPED OUT BY J. FRANK DOBIE IN 1941, & 44 MORE RANGE COUNTRY BOOKS TOPPED OUT BY JEFF DYKES IN 1971. A reprint of Dobie's mimeographed reading list for students, with his clear and caustic comments, and a supplemental list by Dykes, with additional comments.

B73. Dobie, J. Frank. GUIDE TO LIFE AND LITERATURE OF THE SOUTHWEST. Dallas: Southern Methodist University Press, 1952. 222pp. A delightful, intensely subjective guide to Dobie's favorite books. As such, it will always be an essential volume in any Texas library. It is, however, a guide to good reading; regarding works of scholarship, it is more witty than perceptive.

B74. Dornbusch, Charles E. MILITARY BIBLIOGRAPHY OF THE CIVIL WAR. New York: New York Public Library, 1962. The second volume contains works relating to Texas.

B75. Dublan, Manuel, and Jose Maria Lozano [comp.]. LEGISLACION MEXICANA; O, COLECCION COMPLETA DE LAS DISPOSICIONES LEGISLATIVAS EXPEDIDAS DESDE LA INDEPENDENCIA DE LA REPUBLICA. Mexico, 1876. 5 volumes. Series continued in 1904 in 34 volumes. Similar to the Arrillaga series, but with significant additions. Virtually all of the decrees reprinted here were initially issued as separate imprints; 29 appear as separate entries in Streeter's bibliography.

B76. Duke, Escal F. CUMULATIVE INDEX OF THE WEST TEXAS HISTORICAL ASSOCIATION YEARBOOK, VOLUMES I-XLV, June, 1925–October, 1969. Abilene: The West Texas Historical Association, 1972. 196pp.

B77. Dykes, Jeff. MY DOBIE COLLECTION. [College Station:] Friends of Texas A & M University Library, [1971]. 43pp. Description and discussion of Dobie highlights.

B78. Dykes, Jeff C. WESTERN HIGH SPOTS: READING AND COLLECTING GUIDES. N.p.: Northland Press, [1977]. 192pp. A collection of articles on bibliographical subjects by this notable bookman.

B79. Eberstadt & Sons. THE ANNOTATED EBERSTADT CATALOGS OF AMERICANA. New York: Argosy-Antiquarian, 1965. 4 volumes. Includes reprints of the Eberstadt rare book catalogues 103-138, 1935–1956, with index. Includes hundreds of Texas books, with comments on each.

B80. Eberstadt & Sons. TEXAS, BEING A COLLECTION OF RARE & IMPORTANT BOOKS & MANUSCRIPTS RELATING TO THE LONE STAR STATE. New York: Eberstadt Catalogue 162, [1963]. 220pp. Introduction by Archibald Hanna. Contains 950 of the rarest Texas books, pamphlets, and imprints, with detailed commentaries.

B81. Eby, Frederick. EDUCATION IN TEXAS: SOURCE MATERIALS. Austin: University of Texas Bulletin 1824, 1921. 963pp.

B82. Elliott, Claude. THESES ON TEXAS HISTORY: A CHECKLIST OF THESES AND DISSERTATIONS IN TEXAS HISTORY PRODUCED IN THE DEPARTMENTS OF HISTORY OF EIGHTEEN TEXAS GRADUATE SCHOOLS AND THIRTY-THREE GRADUATE SCHOOLS OUTSIDE OF TEXAS, 1907–1952. Austin: The Texas State Historical Association, 1955. 280pp. Similar to the Carroll and Gutsch volume, with summaries of 652 theses and dissertations; updated periodically in the *Southwestern Historical Quarterly*.

B83. THE FERGUSON COLLECTION OF THE BRIDWELL LIBRARY. Dallas: Southern Methodist University, 1960. 154pp.

B84. Garibay, Angel Maria [ed.]. DICCIONARIO PORRUA DE HISTORIA, BIOGRAFIA Y GEOGRAFIA DE MEXICO. Mexico: Editorial Porrua, 1964. Two volumes. Revised and enlarged edition, 1970. The Mexican counterpart of the *Handbook of Texas*.

B85. Gaston, Edwin W., Jr. THE EARLY NOVEL OF THE SOUTHWEST. [Albuquerque:] The University of New Mexico Press, [1961]. 318pp. Discusses 40 Texas and Western novels, from *L'Heroine du Texas* of 1819 to E. M. Rhodes' *Desire of the Moth* of 1916, with plot outlines and analyses. Includes a chapter on Southwestern fiction since 1918.

B86. Gilliam, Franklin. A CATALOGUE OF A PORTION OF THE LIBRARY OF TEXANA FORMED BY E. W. WINKLER. Austin: Brick Row Book Shop Catalogue 49, n.d. 30pp. Includes 359 books from Winkler's library, and a bibliography of Winkler's writings by Llerena Friend.

B87. Gilliam, Franklin. WEBB: A CATALOGUE OF BOOKS FROM THE LIBRARY OF WALTER PRESCOTT WEBB. Austin: Brick Row Book Shop Catalogue 50, 1964. [57]pp. Includes 742 books from Webb's library, as well as many obscure editions of Webb's own writings.

B88. Girard, Roselle M. BIBLIOGRAPHY AND INDEX OF TEXAS GEOLOGY, 1933–1950. Austin: University of Texas Bureau of Economic Geology Publication 5910, 1959. 238pp. Supplements the Sellards work.

B89. Goddard, J. M., and Charles Kritzler. A CATALOGUE OF THE FREDERICK W. & CARRIE S. BEINECKE COLLECTION OF WESTERN AMERICANA. New Haven: Yale University Press, 1965. 114pp.

B90. Gonzalez de Cossio, Francisco. LA IMPRENTA EN MEXICO, 1594–1820. Mexico, 1947. 205pp. Supplement, 1952, 354pp. These supplement Medina's work of the same title.

B91. Graff, Harvey J., et al. DALLAS, TEXAS: A BIBLIOGRAPHICAL GUIDE TO THE SOURCES OF ITS SOCIAL HISTORY TO 1930. Dallas: University of Texas at Dallas, [1979]. 54pp.

B92. Greene, A. C. THE FIFTY BEST BOOKS ON TEXAS. Dallas: Pressworks Publishing, 1982. 91pp. Intelligent commentary on Texas literature.

B93. Greenleaf, Richard E., and Michael C. Meyer. RESEARCH IN MEXICAN HISTORY: TOPICS, METHODOLOGY, SOURCES, AND A PRACTICAL GUIDE TO FIELD RESEARCH. Lincoln: University of Nebraska Press, 1973. 226pp.

B94. Greer, Hilton R. AN INTRODUCTION TO TEXAS LITERATURE. Dallas, 1941. 20pp. Succinct but perceptive.

B95. Griffin, Charles C. LATIN AMERICA: A GUIDE TO HISTORICAL LITERATURE. Austin: University of Texas Press, [1971]. 700pp. This is the best guide in English to Latin Americana, with bibliographical details and commentary on 7087 works, with 39-page index.

B96. GUIDE TO GENEALOGICAL RESOURCES IN THE TEXAS STATE ARCHIVES. Austin: Texas State Library, n.d. 34pp.

B97. Gunn, Clare A. ANNOTATED BIBLIOGRAPHY OF RESOURCE USE, TEXAS GULF COAST. College Station: Texas A & M University, Sea Grant Program, 1969. 387pp.

B98. Gunn, Drewery Wayne. MEXICO IN AMERICAN AND BRITISH LETTERS: A BIBLIOGRAPHY OF FICTION AND TRAVEL BOOKS. Metuchen, N.J.: Scarecrow Press, 1974. 150pp. 1156 entries; well-indexed.

B99. Haferkorn, Henry E. THE WAR WITH MEXICO, 1846–1848: A SELECT BIBLIOGRAPHY ON CAUSES, CONDUCT, AND THE POLITICAL ASPECTS OF THE WAR. Washington, 1914. 93pp.

B100. Haley, J. Evetts. EARL VANDALE ON THE TRAIL OF TEXAS BOOKS. Canyon: Palo Duro Press, 1965. 44pp. Delightful account of a book collector and his search for rare Texana.

B101. Hargrett, Lester, and G. P. Edwards. THE GILCREASE-HARGRETT CATALOGUE OF IMPRINTS. Norman: University of Oklahoma Press, [1972]. 400pp. Much on Texas and Texas Indians.

B102. Harper, Lathrop C. TEXAS, MEXICO, AND THE SOUTHWEST, THE REPUBLIC OF TEXAS, THE MEXICAN WAR. New York: Lathrop C. Harper, Inc., Catalogue 12, n.d. 88pp. A major catalogue of 423 near-unique imprints.

B103. Harwell, Richard B. IN TALL COTTON: THE 200 MOST IMPORTANT CONFEDERATE BOOKS FOR THE READER, RESEARCHER AND COLLECTOR. Austin: Jenkins Publishing Company, 1978. 82pp.

B104. Harwell, Richard B. MORE CONFEDERATE IMPRINTS. Richmond: Virginia State Library, 1957. 2 volumes. Contains 1773 additional imprints to the Crandall bibliography.

B105. Herrera Gomez, M. C. N., and S. M. Gonzalez. APUNTES PARA UNA BIBLIOGRAFIA MILITAR DE MEXICO, 1536–1936. Mexico: Comision de Estudios Militares, 1937. 469pp. Includes nearly 2000 titles, most of which relate to the 19th and early 20th centuries; much of Texas interest.

B106. Hill, Roscoe R. DESCRIPTIVE CATALOGUE OF THE DOCUMENTS RELATING TO THE HISTORY OF THE UNITED STATES IN THE PAPELES PROCEDENTES DE CUBA, DEPOSITED IN THE ARCHIVO GENERAL DE INDIAS AT SEVILLE. Washington: Carnegie Institution, 1916. 594pp. Describes a virtually untapped source that includes much Texana.

B107. Hinshaw, Glennis, and Lisabeth Lovelace. A BIBLIOGRAPHY OF WRITINGS AND ILLUSTRATIONS BY TOM LEA. El Paso: El Paso Public Library, 1971. 54pp.

B108. Holley, Edward G., and Donald D. Hendricks. RESOURCES OF TEXAS LIBRARIES. Austin: Texas State Library, 1968. 352pp. A valuable overview.

B109. Howes, Wright. U.S. IANA (1650–1950): A SELECTIVE BIBLIOGRAPHY IN WHICH ARE DESCRIBED 11,620 UNCOMMON AND SIGNIFICANT BOOKS RELATING TO THE CONTINENTAL PORTION OF THE UNITED STATES. New York: R. R. Bowker Company, 1962. 652pp. Still the best guide to bibliographical aspects and editions.

B110. Jacobs, Wilbur R., John W. Caughey, and Joe B. Frantz. TURNER, BOLTON, AND WEBB: THREE HISTORIANS OF THE AMERICAN FRONTIER. Seattle: University of Washington Press, [1965]. 113pp. Includes checklists.

B111. Jenkins, John H. AUDUBON AND OTHER CAPERS: CONFESSIONS OF A TEXAS BOOKMAKER. Austin: The Pemberton Press, 1976. 120pp. Anecdotes and incidents of working with Texas books.

B112. Jenkins, John H. CRACKER BARREL CHRONICLES: A BIBLIOGRAPHY OF TEXAS TOWN AND COUNTY HISTORIES. Austin: The Pemberton Press, 1965. 509pp. Although it includes 5040 entries, this work needs to be enlarged and revised. The town-county cross-indexes are useful.

B113. Jenkins, John H. PRINTER IN THREE REPUBLICS: A BIBLIOGRAPHY OF SAMUEL BANGS, FIRST PRINTER IN TEXAS, AND FIRST PRINTER WEST OF THE LOUISIANA PURCHASE. Austin: Jenkins Publishing Company, 1981. 190pp. Includes 573 annotated entries.

B114. Jenkins, John H. TEXAS HISTORY: ONE THOUSAND RARE BOOKS, WITH ADDITIONAL SECTIONS ON TEXAS MAPS, PHOTOGRAPHS, AND MANUSCRIPTS, AND A SELECTION ON THE MEXICAN WAR. Austin: The Jenkins Company, Catalogue 127, 1980. 306pp. An annotated catalogue of 1198 items.

B115. Jenkins, John H. A CATALOGUE OF THE WRITINGS OF J. FRANK DOBIE, COMPRISING THE LARGEST SELECTION EVER OFFERED FOR SALE, AND FURTHER CONTRIBUTING TO A BIBLIOGRAPHY. Austin: Jenkins Company Catalogue 5, [1965]. 36pp. The 317 entries include Dobie writings missed by McVicker.

B116. Jenkins, John H. WESTERN TRAVEL BOOKS FROM WAGNER-CAMP. Austin: Jenkins Company Catalogue 55, 1974. 136pp. Includes 378 annotated entries.

B117. Ker, A. M. MEXICAN GOVERNMENT PUBLICATIONS: A GUIDE TO THE MORE IMPORTANT PUBLICATIONS OF THE NATIONAL GOVERNMENT OF MEXICO, 1821–1936. Washington: Government Printing Office, 1940. 333pp. Still quite useful.

B118. Kielman, Chester V. GUIDE TO THE MICROFILM EDITION OF THE BEXAR ARCHIVES. Austin, 1967-1971. 3 volumes. Covers the period from 1717 through 1836.

B119. Kielman, Chester V. THE UNIVERSITY OF TEXAS ARCHIVES: A GUIDE TO THE HISTORICAL MANUSCRIPTS COLLECTIONS OF THE UNIVERSITY OF TEXAS LIBRARY. Austin: University of Texas Press, [1967]. 594pp. This is probably the best guide ever compiled to an archival collection; it is a reliable and thorough descriptive catalogue of 2430 collections of Texas manuscripts, with a 173-page index.

B120. King, Valentine Overton. VALENTINE OVERTON KING'S INDEX TO BOOKS ABOUT TEXAS BEFORE 1889. Austin: Texas State Library, 1976. Facsimile of librarian King's manuscript cross-index to Texas books.

B121. Kinney, John M. INDEX TO APPLICATIONS FOR TEXAS CONFEDERATE PENSIONS. Austin, 1977. 357pp. Revised edition by Peggy Oakley.

B122. Klose, Nelson. A CONCISE STUDY GUIDE TO THE AMERICAN FRONTIER. Lincoln: University of Nebraska Press, 1964. 269pp. Of minimal value, except to the beginning student; includes material on Texas.

B123. Krick, Robert K. NEALE BOOKS: AN ANNOTATED BIBLIOGRAPHY. N.p., Morningside Bookshop, 1977. 234pp. Annotated bibliography of a noted publisher of many Texas and Civil War books.

B124. Kurtz, Kenneth. LITERATURE OF THE AMERICAN SOUTHWEST: A SELECTIVE BIBLIOGRAPHY. Los Angeles: Occidental College, 1956. 61pp. A reading list of 1000 books, mostly relating to the area west of Texas.

B125. Lamar, Howard R. THE READER'S ENCYCLOPEDIA OF THE AMERICAN WEST. New York: Thomas Y. Crowell Company, [1977]. 1306pp. A dependable guide, with contributions by leading scholars.

B126. Lane, Sister M. Claude. CATHOLIC ARCHIVES OF TEXAS: HISTORY AND PRELIMINARY INVENTORY. Houston: Sacred Heart Dominican College, 1961. 114 leaves.

B127. LATIN AMERICAN RESEARCH AND PUBLICATIONS AT THE UNIVERSITY OF TEXAS AT AUSTIN, 1893–1969. Austin: Institute of Latin American Studies, 1971. 187pp. Contains 1051 entries.

B128. Learned, Marion Dexter. GUIDE TO THE MANUSCRIPT MATERIALS RELATING TO AMERICAN HISTORY IN THE GERMAN STATE ARCHIVES. Washington: Carnegie Institution, 1912. 352pp. Includes much material relating to Texas; a virtually untapped resource.

B129. Lowman, Al. PRINTER AT THE PASS: THE WORK OF CARL HERTZOG. San Antonio: Institute of Texan Cultures, 1972. 123pp. Excellent, well-annotated bibliography of Texas' premier book designer.

B130. Lowman, Al. PRINTING ARTS IN TEXAS. [Austin:] Roger Beacham, [1975]. 107,[2]pp. Trade edition: Austin: Jenkins Publishing Company, [1981].

B131. McMurtrie, Douglas C. PIONEER PRINTING IN TEXAS. Austin: 1932. 28pp. One of the pioneer studies of early Texas printing, expanded from a *Southwestern Historical Quarterly* article.

B132. McVicker, Mary Louise. THE WRITINGS OF J. FRANK DOBIE: A BIBLIOGRAPHY. Lawton: Museum of the Great Plains, 1968. 258pp. The best bibliography so far, but one that overlooks dozens of Dobie items.

B133. Major, Mabel, Rebecca W. Smith, and T. M. Pearce. SOUTHWEST HERITAGE: A LITERARY HISTORY WITH BIBLIOGRAPHY. Albuquerque: The University of New Mexico Press, 1938. 164pp. Revised edition, 1948, 199pp. Revised edition, 1972, 378pp. A narrative, analytical study of over 600 titles, including fiction, poetry, and drama.

B134. Medina, Jose Toribio. LA IMPRENTA EN MEXICO, 1539–1821. Santiago de Chile, 1907–1912. 8 volumes. Chronological checklist of over 12,000 imprints, many relating to Texas. Supplemented by the Gonzalez de Cossio works.

B135. Medina, Jose Toribio. BIBLIOTECA HISPANO AMERICANA, 1493–1810. Santiago de Chile, 1898–1907. 7 volumes. Reprinted by Nico Israel, Amsterdam, 1968. Contains a considerable amount of material on Texas.

B136.   Medlar, Bob. TEXAS OBSOLETE NOTES AND SCRIPT. San Antonio: Society of Paper Money Collectors, [1968]. 204pp. The best guide to Texas paper money, arranged by place printed, whereas Criswell is basically chronological.

B137.   Merrill, Louis P. ARISTOCRATS OF THE COW COUNTRY. Eagle Pass: Pack-Saddle Press, 1973. 27pp. One of the classic guides to range cattle books, originally printed in *The Cattleman,* November, 1946.

B138.   Monaghan, Frank. FRENCH TRAVELLERS IN THE UNITED STATES, 1765-1932. New York: The New York Public Library, 1933. 114pp. Reprinted with supplement by Samuel J. Morino, 1961. 1583 entries, mostly with annotations; much on Texas.

B139.   Moore, E. T., and M. D. Brown. BIBLIOGRAPHY AND INDEX OF TEXAS GEOLOGY, 1941-1960. Austin: University of Texas Bureau of Economic Geology, 1972. 575pp. Supplements the works of Sellards and of Girard.

B140.   Morrison, William M. TEXAS BOOK PRICES ($1.50 to $4,000): A LIST OF 4,000 ITEMS OF TEXIANA & TEXANA, INCLUDING BOOKS, MAPS, AUTOGRAPH MATERIAL, PAMPHLETS, NEWSPAPERS, PAPER MONEY, MAGAZINES & JOURNALS. Waco, 1963. 208pp. Revised edition, 1972. Supplement by Richard Morrison, 1979. The first Texas book price guide; useful but dated.

B141.   Munnerlyn, Tom. TEXAS LOCAL HISTORY: A SOURCE BOOK FOR AVAILABLE TOWN AND COUNTY HISTORIES, LOCAL MEMOIRS AND GENEALOGICAL RECORDS. Austin: Eakin Press, 1983. 112pp. A guide to local histories in print at the time of publication.

B142.   Murphy, Virginia B., et al. NEWSPAPER RESOURCES OF SOUTHEAST TEXAS. Houston: University of Houston, 1971. 63pp.

B143.   THE NATIONAL UNION CATALOG, PRE-1965 IMPRINTS. Washington: Mansell, 1968-1980. 685 volumes and supplements. The starting point for all American bibliographical studies.

B144.   Nevins, Allan, James I. Robertson, and Bell I. Wiley. CIVIL WAR BOOKS: A CRITICAL BIBLIOGRAPHY. Baton Rouge: Louisiana State University Press, [1967]. Two volumes. The annotations make this bibliography interesting and useful; contains hundreds of Texas books.

B145.   Northouse, Cameron, and David Grossblatt. FIRST PRINTINGS OF TEXAS AUTHORS. Dallas: Pressworks Publishing, Inc. 1982. 95pp. A guide to first editions of a mixed assortment of Texas writers.

B146.   Palau y Dulcet, Antonio. MANUAL DEL LIBRERO HISPANO-AMERICANO. Barcelona and Oxford, 1948-1977. 28 volumes. This bibliography of 381,897 works contains hundreds of imprints relating to Texas.

B147.   Parke-Bernet Galleries. THE DISTINGUISHED COLLECTION OF AMERICANA FORMED BY C. G. LITTELL. New York: Parke-Bernet Sale 631, 1945. 276pp. Auction catalogue of 1141 rare books, many of Texas and western interest.

B148.   Parke-Bernet Galleries. WESTERN AMERICANA . . . THE DISTINGUISHED PRIVATE COLLECTION FORMED BY THE LATE HERBERT S. AUERBACH. New York: Parke-Bernet Sales 893 and 997, 1947-1948. 2 volumes. One of the great auction sales of Texas and western books, with 2382 items.

B149. Parke-Bernet Galleries. WESTERN AMERICANA, MANY OF GREAT RARITY: THE DISTINGUISHED COLLECTION FORMED BY W. J. HOLLIDAY. New York: Parke-Bernet Sale 1513, 1954. 266pp. Another valuable collection; 1233 entries.

B150. Parke-Bernet Galleries. RARE AND DESIRABLE WESTERN AMERICANA: COLLECTION OF DR. LESTER E. BAUER. New York: Parke-Bernet Sale 1860, 1958. 137pp. Includes 525 very rare books and pamphlets.

B151. Parke-Bernet Galleries. WESTERN AMERICANA: THE EXTENSIVE AND NOTABLE COLLECTION FORMED BY DR. HENRY W. PLATH. New York: Parke-Bernet Sale 1917, 1959. 219pp. Includes a number of Texas rarities in the 1175 entries.

B152. Parke-Bernet Galleries. THE CELEBRATED COLLECTION OF AMERICANA FORMED BY THE LATE THOMAS WINTHROP STREETER. New York: Parke-Bernet Galleries, 1966–1970. 8 volumes (7 sales and separate price index). The greatest Americana auction of the 20th century; many of the 4421 entries are Texas items.

B153. Parke-Bernet Galleries. TEXAS MANUSCRIPTS AND BOOKS, FROM THE COLLECTION OF ROBERT E. DAVIS. New York: Parke-Bernet Sale 2620, 1967. 33pp. Choice Texas items of a noted Texana collector and publisher.

B154. Parker, Lois Williams. BIG THICKET BIBLIOGRAPHY. Saratoga, Texas: Big Thicket Museum, 1970. 54pp.

B155. Paul, Rodman W., and Richard W. Etulain. THE FRONTIER AND THE AMERICAN WEST. Arlington Heights, Ill.: AHM Pub. Corp., 1977. xviii,174pp. Goldentree Bibliographies in American History Series. Topically arranged.

B156. Payne, L. W. A SURVEY OF TEXAS LITERATURE. New York: Rand McNally & Company, [1928]. 76pp. Relatively superficial.

B157. Powell, Lawrence Clark. A SOUTHWESTERN CENTURY: A BIBLIOGRAPHY OF ONE HUNDRED BOOKS OF NON FICTION ABOUT THE SOUTHWEST. Van Nuys, California: J. E. Reynolds, [1958]. 29pp. Includes some Texas books; as Powell does not consider Texas part of the Southwest, most of his bibliographical writings cover only the area west of Texas.

B158. PRE-CIVIL WAR TEXAS: A HANDLIST OF HOLDINGS IN THE LIBRARY OF THE UNIVERSITY OF TEXAS AT ARLINGTON. Arlington, 1972. 60pp.

B159. PUBLICATIONS OF THE UNIVERSITY OF TEXAS, 1882–1914. Austin: Bulletin of the University of Texas 379, 1914. 103pp. Updated periodically.

B160. Rader, Jesse L. SOUTH OF FORTY, FROM THE MISSISSIPPI TO THE RIO GRANDE: A BIBLIOGRAPHY. Norman: University of Oklahoma Press, 1947. 336pp. A poor and shallow work.

B161. Radin, P. [ed.]. CATALOGUE OF MEXICAN PAMPHLETS IN THE SUTRO COLLECTION, 1623–1888, WITH SUPPLEMENTS, 1605–1887. New York, 1971. 963;290;65pp. Useful for Texana researchers.

B162. Raines, C. W. A BIBLIOGRAPHY OF TEXAS: BEING A DESCRIPTIVE LIST OF BOOKS, PAMPHLETS, AND DOCUMENTS RELATING TO TEXAS IN PRINT AND MANUSCRIPT SINCE 1536. Austin: Gammel Book Co., 1896. 268pp. The pioneer work of Texas bibliography; still useful for its perceptive annotations. Few annotated bibliographies have withstood the passing years so well as this.

B163. Raun, Gerald G. A BIBLIOGRAPHY OF THE RECENT MAMMALS OF TEXAS. Austin: Texas Memorial Museum, Bulletin 3, 1962. 85pp.

B164. Reese, William S. SIX SCORE: THE 120 BEST BOOKS ON THE RANGE CATTLE INDUSTRY. Austin: Jenkins Publishing Company, 1976. 85pp. The annotations, as well as the selections, are excellent; a fine work by a fine bibliographer and bookman.

B165. Rittenhouse, Jack D. THE SANTA FE TRAIL: A HISTORICAL BIBLIOGRAPHY. Albuquerque: The University of New Mexico Press, [1971]. 271pp. Interesting annotations; the 718 entries include numerous Texas works.

B166. Robinson, Chandler. J. EVETTS HALEY AND THE PASSING OF THE OLD WEST: A BIBLIOGRAPHY OF HIS WRITINGS . . . Austin: Jenkins Publishing Company, 1978. A comprehensive bibliography with annotations, as well as essays on Haley and his writings.

B167. Rogers, John William. FINDING LITERATURE ON THE TEXAS PLAINS . . . WITH A REPRESENTATIVE BIBLIOGRAPHY OF BOOKS ON THE SOUTHWEST. Dallas: The Southwest Press, [1931]. 57pp. Virtually useless.

B168. Roller, David C., and Robert W. Twyman [ed.]. THE ENCYCLOPEDIA OF SOUTHERN HISTORY. Baton Rouge: Louisiana State University Press, [1979]. 1421pp. In addition to accurate articles by competent scholars, this work includes useful bibliographical references, maps, and tables.

B169. Rose, Noah H. A CATALOG OF THE WORLD FAMOUS N. H. ROSE COLLECTION OF OLD TIME PHOTOGRAPHS OF THE FRONTIER. Houston: Frontier Pix, 1952. 64pp. Describes 2402 photographs.

B170. Sabin, Joseph. A DICTIONARY OF BOOKS RELATING TO AMERICA. New York, 1868-1936. 29 volumes. An essential source for any bibliographical study of Americana, although its collations are frequently incorrect.

B171. Sellards, E. H. BIBLIOGRAPHY AND SUBJECT INDEX OF TEXAS GEOLOGY. Austin: University of Texas Bureau of Economic Geology Publication 3232, 1933. [177]pp. Supplemented by the works of Girard and of Moore and Brown.

B172. Shettles, Elijah L. RECOLLECTIONS OF A LONG LIFE. [Nashville:] Blue & Gray Press, Inc., [1973]. 186pp. Autobiography of a Texas bibliophile.

B173. Sibley, Marilyn McAdams. LONE STARS AND STATE GAZETTES: TEXAS NEWSPAPERS BEFORE THE CIVIL WAR. College Station: Texas A&M University Press, 1983. 405pp. Pages 301-377 comprise a checklist of 374 Texas newspapers published prior to 1861.

B174. Sibley, Marilyn McAdams. TRAVELERS IN TEXAS, 1761–1860. Austin: University of Texas Press, [1967]. 236pp. The most intelligent and cogent study of the literature produced by travelers to Texas; a better critical guide for the period covered than Dobie, Wagner, or Streeter.

B175. Smedley, Betty. A CARL HERTZOG HOPE CHEST. Austin: Smedley Catalogue 6, 1972. 23pp. Includes 166 rare Hertzog imprints and an introduction by Alfred Knopf.

B176. Smeins, Fred E., and Robert B. Shaw. NATURAL VEGETATION OF TEXAS AND ADJACENT AREAS, 1675-1975: A BIBLIOGRAPHY. College Station, 1978. 36pp. 458 entries.

B177. Smith, Myron J. THE AMERICAN NAVY, 1789–1860: A BIBLIOGRAPHY. Metuchen, N.J.: The Scarecrow Press, 1974. 489pp. Contains a bibliography of the Republic of Texas Navy as an appendix.

B178. Smith, Goldie Capers. THE CREATIVE ARTS IN TEXAS: A HANDBOOK OF BIOGRAPHY. Nashville and Dallas: Cokesbury Press, 1926. 178pp. Short sketches of Texas writers; of marginal value except on obscure authors.

B179. SOUTHWEST WRITERS SERIES. Austin: Steck-Vaughn Company, 1967–1969. Series of 38 pamphlets on various Texas authors, including biographical and bibliographical information.

B180. THE SOUTHWESTERN UNION LIST OF SERIALS: A REGIONAL UNION LIST OF SERIAL HOLDINGS. [Albuquerque:] Rio Grande Chapter, Special Libraries Association, 1965. 588pp. Holdings of 24 libraries.

B181. Spell, Lota M. PIONEER PRINTER: SAMUEL BANGS IN MEXICO AND TEXAS. Austin: University of Texas Press, [1963]. 230pp. The appendices to this fine biography include a preliminary checklist of 359 Bangs imprints.

B182. Steck, Francis Borgia. A TENTATIVE GUIDE TO HISTORICAL MATERIALS ON THE SPANISH BORDERLANDS. Philadelphia: The Catholic Historical Society of Philadelphia, 1943. 106pp. Contains some perceptive annotations.

B183. Stone, Marvin. THE SPANISH SOUTHWEST, AN EXHIBIT AT THE DALLAS PUBLIC LIBRARY. Austin: Encino Press, 1971. [vi],[26]pp. Preface by Tom Lea.

B184. Storm, Colton [comp.] A CATALOGUE OF THE EVERETT D. GRAFF COLLECTION OF WESTERN AMERICANA. Chicago: The Newberry Library, 1968. 854pp. A superb catalogue of 4801 of the rarest books on Texas and the West, with by far the best and most detailed bibliographical descriptions, as well as annotations; contains a 123-page index.

B185. Storm, Colton. FIFTY TEXAS RARITIES, SELECTED FROM THE LIBRARY OF MR. EVERETT D. GRAFF. Ann Arbor: The William L. Clements Library, 1946. 40pp. Graff's selection of the rarest Texas items from his personal collection; some of the selections are overrated.

B186. Streeter, Thomas W. BIBLIOGRAPHY OF TEXAS, 1795–1845. Cambridge: Harvard University Press, 1955–1960. Five volumes. The best bibliography on any section of the United States; an absolutely unparalleled achievement.

B187. Streeter, Thomas W. THE ONLY LOCATED COPIES OF ONE HUNDRED FORTY TEXAS PAMPHLETS AND BROADSIDES. New Haven: Yale University, 1957. Despite being given the opportunity to obtain it, the State of Texas let Streeter's unsurpassed collection go to Yale; the Yale-Streeter duplicates went to the Eberstadts, and in 1976 the Eberstadt Texana went to the University of Texas, partially making up for the loss of the Streeter collection. This exhibit catalogue describes 140 unique Texas imprints available only at Yale.

B188. Swanson, E. B. A CENTURY OF OIL AND GAS IN BOOKS: A DESCRIPTIVE BIBLIOGRAPHY. New York: Appleton-Century-Crofts, [1960]. 214pp. A fine annotated check-list that includes many Texas works.

B189. Tanselle, G. Thomas. GUIDE TO THE STUDY OF UNITED STATES IMPRINTS. Cambridge: The Belknap Press of Harvard University Press, 1971. Two volumes. Useful guide to publications regarding Texas, particularly in periodicals.

B190. Taylor, Virginia H. THE SPANISH ARCHIVES OF THE GENERAL LAND OFFICE OF TEXAS. Austin: The Lone Star Press, 1955. 258pp. A valuable guide to an important research source.

B191. ter Braake, Alex L. TEXAS: THE DRAMA OF ITS POSTAL PAST. [Federalsburg, Md.:] American Philatelic Society, [1970]. 298pp. Comprehensive guide to Texas postal imprints and markings.

B192. TEXANA AT THE UNIVERSITY OF TEXAS. Austin: Humanities Research Center, 1962. 44pp. Basically an exhibit catalogue.

B193. TEXANA CHECK LIST. San Antonio: Daughters of the Republic of Texas Library, 1957. 62pp.

B194. TEXAS CENTENNIAL EXHIBITION. Washington: Library of Congress, 1946. 54pp. A spectacular exhibit of 371 items of Texana gathered for the centennial of Texas statehood.

B195. THE TEXAS COASTAL MANAGEMENT PROGRAM: AN ANNOTATED BIBLIOGRAPHY OF RESEARCH ACTIVITIES IN THE COASTAL ZONE. Austin: General Land Office, Coastal Management Program, 1974. 211 leaves.

B196. TEXAS NEWSPAPERS, 1813–1939: A UNION LIST OF NEWSPAPER FILES AVAILABLE IN OFFICES OF PUBLISHERS, LIBRARIES, AND A NUMBER OF PRIVATE COLLECTIONS. Houston: San Jacinto Museum of History and Works Progress Administration, 1941. 293pp.

B197. THESES AND DISSERTATIONS ACCEPTED BY TEXAS CHRISTIAN UNIVERSITY: THE GRADUATE SCHOOL AND BRITE DIVINITY SCHOOL, 1909–1972. Fort Worth: Texas Christian University, 1973. 168pp.

B198. Trask, David F., et al. A BIBLIOGRAPHY OF UNITED STATES-LATIN AMERICAN RELATIONS SINCE 1810: A SELECTED LIST OF ELEVEN THOUSAND PUBLISHED REFERENCES. Lincoln: University of Nebraska Press, [1968]. 441pp. Many of the 11,000 items relate to Texas.

B199. Tucker, Mary. BOOKS OF THE SOUTHWEST: A GENERAL BIBLIOGRAPHY. New York: Augustin, 1938. 105pp. Early but still of some use.

B200. Tuterow, Norman E. THE MEXICAN-AMERICAN WAR: AN ANNOTATED BIBLIOGRAPHY. Westport, Conn.: Greenwood Press, [1981]. 427pp. Although this bibliography contains 4537 entries, it shows signs of both haste and ineptitude, such as calling the 1934 reprint of Raines a revised edition. The author lists the Jenkins Garrett Library but does not say what school, town, or state it is located in. Useful for research until the Garrett bibliography appears; worthless for bibliography: the Rader of the Mexican War.

B201. Vann, William H. THE TEXAS INSTITUTE OF LETTERS, 1936–1966. Austin: Encino Press, [1967]. 101pp. Mostly an account of awards presented by the institute, but includes a checklist of award-winning books.

B202. Wagner, Henry R. THE SPANISH SOUTHWEST, 1542–1794: AN ANNOTATED BIBLIOGRAPHY. Albuquerque: The Quivera Society, 1937. Two volumes (552pp.). Needs revision, but still the essential starting point for any study of Spanish Texas.

ᴪ B203. Wagner, Henry R., and Charles L. Camp. THE PLAINS & THE ROCKIES: A CRITICAL BIBLIOGRAPHY OF EXPLORATION, ADVENTURE AND TRAVEL IN THE AMERICAN WEST, 1800–1865. San Francisco: John Howell Books, 1982. 745pp. Fourth Edition, Revised, Enlarged and Edited by Robert H. Becker. Includes a smattering of Texana; unfortunately omits many of the useful commentaries that appeared in the third edition.

B204. Wallace, John Melton. GACETA TO GAZETTE: A CHECK LIST OF TEXAS NEWSPAPERS, 1813–1846. Austin: The University of Texas, 1966. 89pp. Contains information and details not in Streeter's bibliography.

B205. Walpole Galleries. RARE AMERICANA, INCLUDING THE TEXAS LIBRARY OF THE LATE J. E. BOYNTON, WACO, TEXAS. New York, Sale 355, 1925. 91pp. An early sale of 629 rare items.

B206. Walton, Ray S. CONTEMPORARY TEXAS AND SOUTHWESTERN LITERATURE. Austin: Walton Catalogue 3, 1980. 76pp. Valuable annotated catalogue of 687 works, with an introduction by Terry Halladay.

B207. Webb, Walter Prescott. TALKS ON TEXAS BOOKS: A COLLECTION OF BOOK REVIEWS. Austin: Texas State Historical Association, 1970. 94pp. Edited by Llerena B. Friend. A compilation of Webb's perceptive reviews of Texas books.

B208. WEST TEXAS IN THE SOUTHWEST: DESCRIPTIONS OF 100 SELECTED MANUSCRIPT COLLECTIONS IN THE SOUTHWEST COLLECTION, TEXAS TECHNOLOGICAL COLLEGE. Lubbock, 1967. 12pp.

B209. Wheat, Carl I. MAPPING THE TRANS-MISSISSIPPI WEST, 1540–1876. San Francisco: Institute of Historical Cartography, 1957–1963. 6 volumes. To Western maps what Streeter's bibliography is to Texas books; superb bibliographical descriptions.

B210. Whisenhunt, Donald W. CHRONOLOGY OF TEXAS HISTORY. Burnet: Eakin Press, [1982]. 174pp. Occasionally useful year-by-year summary of major events in Texas history.

B211. White, Fred, Jr. WESTERN AMERICANA, FEATURING COWBOYS, OUTLAWS, CATTLE INDUSTRY. Bryan: Fred White Catalogue 221, n.d. 302pp. A valuable catalogue of 954 items emphasizing the Texas cattle industry.

B212. THE WILLIAM B. BATES COLLECTION OF TEXANA AND WESTERN AMERICANA. Houston: M. D. Anderson Library, 1971. [28]pp.

B213. Winegarten, Ruthe, and Mary Beth Rogers. TEXAS WOMEN'S HISTORY PROJECT BIBLIOGRAPHY. Austin: Texas Foundation for Women's Resources, 1980. 349pp. Comprehensive; well-indexed.

The Texas State Historical Association
proudly announces
A valuable Texana item

A Check List of Texas Imprints, 1846-1860

Edited by E. W. WINKLER
Bibliographer, University of Texas Library

First of the check list
volumes of Texas imprints—
newspapers, books, broadsides,
pamphlets—indispensable
to the collector of Texana.
A compilation from libraries
throughout the United States.

$12.50

Box 2131 University Station, Austin 12, Texas

B214. Winkler, Ernest W. CHECK LIST OF TEXAS IMPRINTS, 1846–1860. Austin: The Texas State Historical Association, 1949. 352pp. Detailed, precise bibliographical descriptions of 1466 Texas imprints, comprising every known item printed in Texas during the period.

B215. Winkler, Ernest W., and Llerena B. Friend. CHECK LIST OF TEXAS IMPRINTS, 1861–1876. Austin: The Texas State Historical Association, 1963. 734pp. An extension of the 1846–1860 volume, with 3961 items. Streeter, Winkler, and Winkler-Friend encompass every known work printed in Texas between 1795 and 1876.

B216. Winther, Oscar O. A CLASSIFIED BIBLIOGRAPHY OF THE PERIODICAL LITERATURE OF THE TRANS-MISSISSIPPI WEST, 1811–1957. Bloomington: Indiana University Press, 1961. 626pp. Supplement, 1970. 340pp. A subject-classified checklist of 9244 items. The supplement adds nearly 5000 additional entries.

B217. Withington, Mary C. A CATALOGUE OF MANUSCRIPTS IN THE COLLECTION OF WESTERN AMERICANA FOUNDED BY WILLIAM ROBERTSON COE, YALE UNIVERSITY LIBRARY. New Haven: Yale University Press, 1952. 398pp. One of Yale's many collections containing valuable Texas research materials.

B218. Wood, A. C., and C. V. Brand. THESES AND DISSERTATIONS ACCEPTED BY TEXAS TECH UNIVERSITY. Lubbock: Texas Tech University, 1975. 204pp.

B219. Wright, Rita J., et al. TEXAS SOURCES: A BIBLIOGRAPHY. Austin: Bureau of Business Research, University of Texas, 1976. 67pp. Arranged by subject.

INDEX

(By entry number)